# READY TO TEACH
# MACBETH
## A COMPENDIUM OF SUBJECT KNOWLEDGE, RESOURCES AND PEDAGOGY

### STUART PRYKE & AMY STANIFORTH

**First published 2020**

by John Catt Educational Ltd,
15 Riduna Park, Station Road,
Melton, Woodbridge IP12 1QT

Tel: +44 (0) 1394 389850
Fax: +44 (0) 1394 386893
Email: enquiries@johncatt.com
Website: www.johncatt.com

**ISBN: 978 1 912906 91 8**

Set and designed by John Catt Educational Limited

# Reviews for
# *Ready to Teach: Macbeth*

Equipping teachers is the most important thing we can do, but this book not only equips, it also inspires, motivates, challenges, guides and supports. It asks questions and gives answers, it gives theory and shows you how, it takes what we may already know, and deepens it until you find yourself in territory you have not been in before. You leave this book not only knowing more, but also thinking more and feeling more. The result? You will be full of energy, enthusiasm and confidence and countless young people will hugely benefit.

For those of you who have taught *Macbeth* so many times you have lost count, this book will help you find a whole new lease of life and if you are new to the play, it will leave you wide-eyed and raring to go. It is a wonderful mix of the why of teaching Shakespeare as well as the what and the how. It takes what we know and develops it in new ways and all the time focuses on how we can communicate these things to young people. It is a perfect blend of academic research, challenging questions around pedagogy and practical approaches in the classroom. It is, quite simply, the book I wish I had had when I was teaching *Macbeth*. What a gift to the English teaching community and to our young people who are the ones who will perhaps benefit the most.

**Rachel Johnson, CEO PiXL**

*Ready to Teach: Macbeth* is a decadent delight for English teachers everywhere. With a play like *Macbeth*, the well of knowledge may sometimes feel unfamiliar and uncertain, but Pryke and Staniforth speak to the reader with such confidence and conviction that it becomes eminently clear that this book intends to change not only my experience of *Macbeth* itself, but the way in which I impart this to students, for the better.

Offering a calm, composed balance of both deep, powerful knowledge and the practical strategies we need within the classroom, the authors take the reader by the hand and guide them through the most meticulous representation of the text: lingering over academic interpretation and weaving it back through to a succinct depiction of the way in which we can present this academia to students. Subsequently, and rightly so, it demands that we seek to move their experience beyond the superficial to one that's steeped in the magic of the language itself.

*Ready to Teach: Macbeth* is thoughtful, established and scholarly, and I'm not sure how I managed to teach this text without it. Knowing that teachers will be using this book to deliver *Macbeth* in a way that is true, faithful and with complete authenticity to Shakespeare's heritage fills me with joy. I cannot wait to add this to my collection of go-to texts for teaching literature.

**Kat Howard, author of *Stop Talking About Wellbeing* and founder of Litdrive UK**

Over the past few years discussions around the importance of subject knowledge and how we develop this have increased. What Stuart and Amy offer in this absolutely invaluable guide is a synthesis of the reading and research they have conducted into *Macbeth*. The depth of understanding about this text is nothing short of inspirational and will be of benefit to all teachers. And yet they then give us more! Stuart and Amy also provide us with a range of practical strategies to support us in embedding that knowledge into any scheme or lesson with absolute ease.

This is the edubook gold standard – it is enriching and practical and in my mind an essential purchase if you are teaching *Macbeth*. I can't wait for this book to turn into a series!

**Freya Odell**

*Ready to Teach: Macbeth* marks a paradigm shift in the books related to the teaching of English. Often, books aimed to help English teachers focus solely on 'how to teach' an aspect so they neglect the far more important 'what to teach'. Don't get me wrong. They are useful books that focus on lots of nice, little activities related to a text or they give you some ready prepared lessons, saving you time and the opportunity to think. *Decide on the Macbeths' first song at their wedding. Decide on what Banquo's favourite animal is and why.* Sadly, no amount of sugared paper, silly hats or wackiness will make a lesson great. Instead, a knowledgeable teacher makes a lesson great.

*Ready to Teach: Macbeth* is the equivalent of the London taxi drivers' 'The Knowledge' for English teachers. *It's abaht the different routes into the play, governor.* The different ideas, thoughts, interpretations and readings. There are a hundred ways to get to a destination but Stuart Pryke and Amy Staniforth help you get to the best route. They've painstakingly worked on building an exhaustive compendium on William Shakespeare's *Macbeth* that provides you with 'The *Macbeth* Knowledge'. They've saved you time, effort and resource making with this book. I'd say that this is the book you need to read before you teach *Macbeth*. Amy and Stuart are helping you get there quicker and with less miles on the meter.

*Read this and you do not have to rely on your local Wyrd Sisters, your forthright partner or a floating dagger to guide you on what to teach, or what not to teach in* Macbeth. *Don't leave things up to some supernatural force! We all know what happens when you do that.*

**Chris Curtis, author of *How to Teach English* and Head of English**

# To our parents:

Cathy and Paul
*You always asked me to 'work hard and make [you] proud.'*
*Thank you for helping me achieve my dream.*

Julia and Alan
*Thank you for always believing in me – and thank you*
*for teaching me the power of storytelling.*

(We will be testing to see whether you have read this!)

# Acknowledgements

There are four teachers who have influenced our practice more than they will ever know, as you will see by the number of times we have referenced them in this book! Our utmost thanks goes to Chris Curtis (@Xris32), Kat Howard (@SaysMiss), Kate Jones (@87History) and Jennifer Webb (@FunkyPedagogy) for continually pushing us to be better. This book is really a product of everything we have learnt from you as English practitioners. You are all inspiring! Thank you, Jenny, for also writing the Foreword to this book. We've aimed to follow your mantra of being 'unapologetically ambitious' and 'unashamedly academic' and we hope we've done you proud!

A huge thanks must also go to Alex Sharratt, Jonathan Barnes, Gráinne Treanor and the whole team at John Catt, who have been superb and so supportive of our vision throughout this process.

Whilst this book contains our original ideas, we have also drawn heavily on the genius of others. We would like to thank the following people for allowing us to share their ideas and resources which make this book a real guide by teachers, for teachers. They include: Simon Beale (@SPBeale), Sondos Bowker (@MrsB_NE), Patrick Cragg (@GCSE_Macbeth), Heidi Drake (@mrs_denglish), Emma Illiffe, Matt Lynch (@Matthew_Lynch44), Lia Martin (@liaesthermartin), Fiona Ritson (@AlwaysLearnWeb), Caroline Spalding (@MrsSpalding), Alice Visser-Furay (@AVisserFuray) and Becky Wood (@shadylady222). We would also like to thank everyone at Team English (@Team_English1) and the Litdrive Regional Advocates (@LitdriveUK) as well as Rosie's Plaques – women of The Common Lot Theatre Company (@rosiesplaques) for the use of their photography and work in Norwich.

## Stuart's acknowledgements

Firstly, I would like to thank my mum and dad, Cathy and Paul, for the unwavering support they have shown me, not only through the writing of this book but in everything I do. You have always been there for me and although I don't say it enough, I appreciate everything you have done to help me get to where I am today. Emma, you are not only my sister but one of my best friends too. Thank you for all the laughs we have that keep me sane.

A HUGE thanks must go to the wonderful English department I am so lucky enough to work in. James Day, Pete Etchingham, Rebecca Taylor, Andrew Toon and Victoria Wright, you are the most supportive people anyone could hope to work with and I am so happy that I get to work in a department where I can truly call my colleagues my friends. I wish I could say that now this thing is published you won't have to listen to me going on about it all the time, but unfortunately I can't. Sorry!

Thanks must also go to Ashley Betts, Tracey Sibley, Nicola Shingleton, Mike Quinn and James Whatling, who have not only encouraged and supported me through this process but have listened to me talk things through when they weren't going the way I had hoped. You have all been fantastic.

I also promised an acknowledgement to my 2019/2020 year 10 class (who will be year 11 by the time this is in print) who gave me their honest opinions on which front cover to choose. I know you didn't believe I'd put this acknowledgement in, but look, here it is!

Last but by no means least, a huge thanks to Amy. How can I sum up seven years of friendship in a couple of sentences? It seems like only yesterday we were completing our PGCE at the University of East Anglia and now here we are, writing a book together! You will never know how much I have valued your friendship, support and guidance. There aren't many people who can say they've written a book with their best friend. How wonderful it is that I can!

## Amy's acknowledgements

There are many people who have helped me reach this point and write this book, and I am infinitely grateful to each and every one of them. Firstly, I would like to thank my mum, Julia, who has always championed me, supported me and believed in me. I hope I've made you proud! Likewise my dad, Alan, who has always believed in me and always knew I would end up as either a teacher or a journalist – does it count for both if I'm a teacher with a book?! My brother, Ben, is a wonderful man and I am very grateful he is my 'big' little brother. My granny, Geraldine, never stopped believing in me and encouraged me to be whatever it was I wanted in life. I will always remember fondly hazy days of orange squash and chocolate biscuits, the best, silliest games possible and her unwavering love of the terrible poems I wrote when I was five. Thank you.

I am very fortunate to have Eliot J. Fallows, Joe Levell and Davina Kesby in my life. Thank you for being my pals – you are the absolute best. Additionally, to have friends like Yasemin Kemal, Anna Fenton, Tom and Claire Dolton (and many more besides!) who have supported me throughout this writing process makes me feel very fortunate indeed.

I would like to thank everyone I work with at Iceni Academy, past and present, for their support and challenge and shared excitement about this book, and especially Stephen Plume, Duncan Carmichael, Sarah Turner and the whole English team.

I would like to thank all the students I have had the absolute privilege to work with in my career so far – I always joked with my very first class of year 10s that I was going to write a book about Macbeth – and here it is!

I would not be a teacher today if it weren't for the influence of the teachers I had at school. They shaped me and my practice, often without knowing. In particular, I carry the lessons (both academic and otherwise) Vicki Cracknell and Carole Moss (Mrs G!) taught me every day of my life.

Finally, I would like to thank Stuart, without whom none of this would have been possible. It has been an absolute joy to go on this journey with you and I couldn't be happier to have written our 'little project' with my best friend. I can't believe we've actually done it! Thank you for everything.

# Contents

**ACT V**

# Foreword by Jennifer Webb

'Confusion hath now made his masterpiece'
– *Macbeth*, Act 2, Scene 3

Shakespeare is a wielder of storms. Mists, thunder claps, crashing waves and unnatural rains act variously as warnings, laments, punishments and foils. There isn't a single Shakespeare play which is not disturbed in some way by a storm. Obvious are the great raging events: the storm which opens *Julius Caesar*; Lear's tragedy on the heath; the apocalyptic upheaval after the murder of Duncan. These great, dramatic tempests echo the potency of kingship: overt grandeur. More subtle, though, are Shakespeare's fogs. They literally muddle plot and characters, whilst introducing symbolic and textual confusion. Oberon aims for literal muddling when he asks Puck to 'cover [the wood] with drooping fog as black as Acheron' in order to confuse the mortal lovers. Fog, though, is more often a euphemism for mystery and a veil for magic. In *Cymbeline*, Imogen uses fog as a metaphor for something which clouds her vision of the future, 'a fog... that I cannot look through.' Lear curses his own daughter with 'fen-sucked fogs' which will 'infect' or cover her beauty. Most famous and fully realised of these Shakespearean fogs is undoubtedly in *Macbeth*. 'Fog and filthy air' provide a dissembling haze through which we view the action, and this lack of certainty pervades the entire piece, leaving us to question almost everything from the identity and intention of the Wyrd Sisters to the motive and ultimate responsibility for the murder of Duncan. This play is shrouded in secrecy, and we are left with questions for which we can never have definitive answers.

Teaching this play, then, requires us to cut through this fog. We must somehow lift the veil. Effective teachers find ways to break down the abstract and ambiguous: selecting what's necessary; categorising and creating schemas; highlighting what's powerful; revealing what's beautiful, and sequencing content so that learning can take place. Teaching a full Shakespeare play is like taking a group of (sometimes) reluctant teenagers on a hike across a moor and being enveloped in a heavy mist. You must have a map if you are to avoid disaster.

But where to start? The enormity of Shakespeare is, for many, a daunting prospect. Many newly qualified teachers see teaching their first Shakespeare play as a rite of passage and, though most English teachers have a subject degree, there is a real difference between studying a play as an undergraduate and navigating one with other people in mind. Compound this with the time and curricular constraints we face: not only must the play be taught, but it must be done in a series of arbitrary chunks of time over the span of a term or half term. This might also need to be interspersed with work on other topics, preparation for assessments and a whole host of other 'stuff' which we must consider in our day-to-day life at the chalkface. The challenge for teachers, then, is two-fold: we must *know* the play incredibly well, but we must also know *how* to go about teaching it – we need to have a strategy.

There are thousands of books which can help with subject knowledge for Shakespeare, but the beauty of the work carried out by Amy and Stuart is that it is tailored to the everyday needs of English teachers. Our double need is met by a book which uses 'big questions' to cut through the fog, subject knowledge essays for deepening our understanding, and a whole host of practical ideas which form the basis of sound pedagogy.

Amy and Stuart have taken their considerable knowledge, skill and experience, and poured them generously into this triumph of a book. They demonstrate enormous ambition for students by covering highly challenging academic content in a way which is manageable and motivating for teachers at any stage of their career. I am delighted to see this book come to fruition and am confident that this will provide the perfect platform from which teachers and students might truly meet the Bard.

*Macbeth* is timeless: broad in scope, rich in symbolism, and ambitious in its exploration of the human condition. It deserves the best kind of teaching. *Ready to Teach: Macbeth* is the best kind of book.

**Jennifer Webb (@FunkyPedagogy) is an English teacher and author of *How to Teach English Literature: Overcoming Cultural Poverty* (2019) and *Teach Like a Writer* (2020).**

# Introduction

It is a dull, Thursday afternoon when the question, asked with regularity and time-honoured tradition, is uttered by a student. It could be any student, at any school anywhere in the country, or, indeed, across the globe.

'What's the point in studying Shakespeare?'

What could be misconstrued as an attempt to disengage with these texts before students have even begun to get to grips with them is, in fact, a valid question. Why *should* we study the works of a man who, at first glance, appears to have no real relevance in modern society? The answer to why Shakespeare's work has endured is more straightforward than some might have you believe.

Shakespeare was born in April 1564. In his extant works he wrote about life: its simple joys and complex nuances, human wisdom, sense and judgement as well as our follies and the flaws that condemn us. Shakespeare's work is both visceral and intellectually challenging, forcing us to reflect on ourselves as members of a broader society. One would be forgiven for thinking it is remarkable that we study his work after all this time, yet the fact is, Shakespeare's stories have survived because they are still relevant over 450 years later. Time is relative in relation to the human condition. Put simply, what makes us human never changes, and it is for this reason that we recognise ourselves in characters first conceived centuries ago. Through Shakespeare, we learn our place in life.

## Macbeth

Written in 1606, *Macbeth* is one of Shakespeare's most instantly recognisable and abiding plays. 'The Scottish Play' has appeared countless times on stage and screen, with 82 professional productions in Stratford and London between 1960 and 2000. This is equal to the number of professional productions of *Hamlet* in the same period, and more than any other Shakespeare play.[1] In 2018 alone, there were 19 professional productions of the play in the UK.

But why are we still reading and performing it in schools across the world today? Whether it is because *Macbeth* can be read as a parable for our precarious global political position, because as a society we are continuing to explore the roles of gender, or because we are preoccupied with ideas around class and our place in society, it is undeniable that Shakespeare, and *Macbeth* in particular, is ubiquitous.

The themes of *Macbeth* are universal, rooted in our intrinsic sense of humanity and morality. This, in turn, shapes our scorn for the characters, whether it's directed at Macbeth, Lady Macbeth, Hecate or even the three weïrd sisters.

It is always a joy, then, to find *Macbeth* on the syllabus for GCSE study. In fact, the study of Shakespeare can be traced back to the very beginnings of compulsory secondary education, with even Victorian educationalists putting great emphasis on that 'modern' educational buzzword: cultural capital. 'The Victorians believed that exposure to high culture like Shakespeare made you a better person',[2] and so it continues to do so. When the National Curriculum was first launched in 1997, Shakespeare was the only author named for compulsory study: testament, then, to his consideration as the most important writer in the Western canon.

From *Macbeth* we learn about the fragility of the human condition, we learn about the consequences of lying and duplicity, and we are able to develop an understanding of relationships and motivation as well as an appreciation of language. This fundamental comprehension of our growth, our emotions, our aspirations and our mortality can help us understand ourselves and those around us better – and what more could we possibly want from a GCSE text?

## Purpose of *Ready to Teach*

This book is intended to be a compendium of useful knowledge, resources and pedagogy to help you plan and teach well-sequenced lessons and impart the powerful subject knowledge needed for your students to be successful Shakespearean scholars. Not only that, but we hope the resources here will also help your students to love *Macbeth* and Shakespeare, and be outspoken advocates for the works of the Bard for years to come. In order to achieve this, our knowledge-rich approaches are specifically designed to reduce the cognitive load on our students so they can enjoy the rich language, fascinating plots and brilliant characters Shakespeare creates without being overwhelmed. Our

---

1.   Jack Rear, 'Year of Macbeth', *Verdict*, <https://www.verdict.co.uk/year-of-macbeth-why-are-there-so-many-2018-macbeth-facts/>.

2.   Tracy Irish, *Teaching Shakespeare – A history of the teaching of Shakespeare in England*, (London, RSC: 2008), p. 2.

activities are designed to help students learn, retain and retrieve the powerful knowledge they need to be successful.

## How *Ready to Teach* works

Each chapter presents one or two Big Questions which can be used as the foundation of a lesson. Therefore, it is possible to teach with these resources in the sequence in which they are presented here, or, otherwise, to 'dip in' and teach with those that are most pertinent to you, your setting and your class. You can find a complete list of Big Questions further on in this Introduction, and an index at the back of the book where you can look for specific topics, characters, themes or contextual points to meet your own emerging needs as a practitioner.

Each chapter is divided into two key sections:

- **What?** – What powerful subject knowledge do you need to know, and be able to teach, in order to answer the Big Question with your students? Through essays, annotated extracts and accompanying commentaries, we hope you will feel more empowered to teach key aspects of *Macbeth* confidently and successfully.
- **How?** – What resources will you need to successfully convey your knowledge to your students, helping them to develop the key knowledge and skills they will need? Fully resourced lessons will help you save time when planning, alongside exemplar completed resources as a model for classroom practitioners. This section also considers how knowledge is sequenced to become embedded in long-term memory, ensuring students are able to develop the necessary schema for success.

Finally, you will find the **Why?** section detailing why a selection of the teaching methods explored throughout the book are effective. How do they help students embed and retrieve the knowledge they need? This section will explore the pedagogy underpinning select activities, with clear explanations as to why these resources work.

You can use these sections discretely to enhance either your subject knowledge, your resourcing or your pedagogical knowledge, or use each chapter holistically to deliver lessons with power and impact.

## The Big Questions

Any Shakespeare text can be a challenge for students to access, and this is no different for *Macbeth*. Students are frightened by Shakespeare's language and the challenges posed by having to decode it. In a desire to understand the material we present to students, translation to modern English seems to become a priority, when in actual fact this is not always the best approach in helping them to fathom what Shakespeare is saying. 'Literature is hard,' says Jennifer Webb in *How to Teach English Literature*. 'It is a complex web of symbolism, analogy, plot, character, journey, language, experience, context and writers' angst.'[3] And that is just in the text itself. If we add assessment objectives, how to write an introduction, how to embed quotations and other technicalities related to GCSE study into the mix, then students experience significant cognitive overload. Webb, quite rightly, deduces that 'readers must have a key to unlock all of this.' Big Questions are part of that key, helping teachers to sequence what they teach in a clear and coherent format, prioritising what we need students to know rather than throwing everything at them at once.

The following is an example of how the beginning of *Macbeth* could be taught. This approach is potentially recognisable to many teachers, although, as you will see, it raises significant issues with the learning process and the development of powerful knowledge. The start of a scheme of learning may look like this:

**Lesson One:** A brief overview of the social and historical context, including the role of women, the Great Chain of Being and Jacobean beliefs surrounding the supernatural.

**Lesson Two:** Read through Act I, Scene i as a class. Discuss Shakespeare's use of pathetic fallacy and clarify any tricky vocabulary before writing an analytical response to the following question: 'How does Shakespeare use language to present the witches in Act I, Scene i?'

**Lessons Three–Five:** Continue reading through Act I, completing activities for engagement and understanding. Analyse Lady Macbeth's soliloquy in Act I, Scene v before writing a response to the following question: 'How does Shakespeare use language to present Lady Macbeth as an ambitious character?'

Whilst this seems a perfectly respectable way of approaching the text, the repetitive format of teaching a section, analysing it and then moving on to the next part is limiting. It sacrifices the core knowledge students need to understand the text holistically, for honing and crafting essay skills before they are ready to do so. Having students write a GCSE mock answer on Lady Macbeth's speech after Act I, Scene v, for example, is not useful. If anything, it will only tell us they do not know the text well enough and prioritises exam skill over deep subject knowledge.

So why do we do it? Perhaps we feel as if passages of analysis written neatly in exercise books are proof that learning has taken place. Maybe it is because of our desire for students to do well in their exams and so replicating the types of

---

3.   Jennifer Webb, *How to Teach English Literature: Overcoming Cultural Poverty*, (Woodbridge: John Catt Educational Ltd., 2019), p. 11.

questions they will sit from day one *seems* like a good idea. However, we must be mindful of *what* we are teaching, *how* we are teaching it, and *why* we are teaching it.

When sequencing our schemes of work, we should be building subject knowledge carefully and clearly without muddying the waters by trying to teach essay skills parallel to this. This is where Big Questions come in. They help us to prioritise and sequence what we *need* students to know. What we want them to be able to *do* comes later. As such, you will find subject knowledge has been sequenced as and when it is needed.

Here is a suggested list of Big Questions for *Macbeth* and the ones which this book will be following:

**CHAPTER 1:**
- Who are the three 'weïrd sisters'?

**CHAPTER 2:**
- How are we initially introduced to Macbeth's character?

**CHAPTER 3:**
- What do the witches tell Macbeth and Banquo?
- What do we learn about the characters of Macbeth and Banquo from their reactions to the witches?

**CHAPTER 4:**
- What is ambition?
- Who is Malcolm?

**CHAPTER 5:**
- Who is Lady Macbeth?
- What is the relationship like between Macbeth and Lady Macbeth?

**CHAPTER 6:**
- What reasons does Macbeth give for not going ahead with Duncan's murder?
- How does Lady Macbeth persuade Macbeth to go through with the murder?

**CHAPTER 7:**
- What is the relationship like between Banquo and Fleance?
- What does Macbeth say in his famous 'Is this a dagger I see before me?' soliloquy?

**CHAPTER 8:**
- What do Macbeth and Lady Macbeth do after the murder?

**CHAPTER 9:**
- Who is the Porter?

**CHAPTER 10:**
- Who is Macduff?
- What is the reaction to Duncan's murder, and how does his death affect the Great Chain of Being?

**CHAPTER 11:**
- What is the relationship like between Macbeth and Banquo once Macbeth becomes king?
- How has Macbeth and Lady Macbeth's relationship changed?

**CHAPTER 12:**
- Why does Banquo's ghost appear to Macbeth?

**CHAPTER 13:**
- Who is Hecate?
- What are the perceptions of Macbeth amongst the Scottish nobility?

**CHAPTER 14:**
- What do the apparitions tell Macbeth?

**CHAPTER 15:**
- Who is Lady Macduff and what happens to her and her son?

**CHAPTER 16:**
- What is the relationship like between Malcolm and Macduff?
- What qualities make a good king?

**CHAPTER 17:**
- What becomes of Lady Macbeth?

**CHAPTER 18:**
- What becomes of Macbeth?

**CHAPTER 19:**
- How does the play end?

These questions look simple and they are designed to be just that. There are lots of examples of convoluted Big Questions to be found, but it is the simplicity reflected in the set above, and the process of stripping everything back, which allows us to combat the complexities of what students need to know and remember. If we preface each lesson with one or two Big Questions, we have expressed our aims to students with clarity and precision. These questions allow us to teach the core concepts whilst diagnosing whether students have learnt those concepts. Students can either answer the question or they cannot, and how well they can articulate their answers indicates whether they have grasped the key knowledge they need for success. This is not to say that students cannot be challenged. Behind every simple question lies a wealth of knowledge waiting to be discovered, and sub-questions can easily be used to stretch classes further.

Finally, Big Questions are designed to aid with retrieval practice. At various intervals throughout the scheme, students could be presented with every Big Question they have come across so far to see what they have retained. This also aids with future planning. For example, if a student struggles to answer the question 'What is ambition?', we must ask ourselves whether there is any point moving forward with the scheme before they have grasped this key theme. They must understand ambition if they are to understand the play's bloody and tragic climax.

## Lessons and resources

Obviously, each lesson needs to be adapted for the context in which you teach. It may be pertinent to pick and choose which ideas, resources or knowledge you feel are necessary to teach and use. We do hope, however, that if you cannot use the resources here, they at least spark an idea for something you *could* do. The beauty of teaching, we think, is in the almost infinite possibilities available to us as teachers to inspire, motivate and help students succeed in all they do: we hope that if this book does not provide the answer, it at least provides a seed for transformational teaching in your own classroom.

Whilst many of the activities detailed in these chapters encourage students to approach the text analytically, we are also very aware that we are not teachers of an exam; we are teachers of English. It is all too easy to delve into deep analysis of the book, poem or play we are discussing and destroy any enjoyment one could elicit from the text. Sometimes, we can be too wrapped up in finding the effect of an adjective or simile to ask the simple questions:

- What do you like about the scene?
- What do you not like?
- Has anything we have read today surprised you?
- Did what you think would happen, happen?
- What do you think will happen next and why?

The primary purpose of Shakespeare's plays was to entertain. Yes, we want our students to learn, but we want them to be entertained by the texts we teach too. Therefore, have a collection of these questions at your disposal. They are not mentioned again through the book, as they are something we would ask periodically throughout the reading of the entire play. They are simple, yes, but powerful. Never underestimate the power of asking students what they like.

## A note on vocabulary

At the end of each chapter, we have included 'Key vocabulary' one could teach to aid student understanding of core concepts in lessons. Whilst you will find some activities where vocabulary is explicitly taught in this book, these key words have been added to teach at your leisure at any point in your lesson where you feel it would be appropriate. There is no one way to teach vocabulary, but we both admire and regularly refer to the work of Alex Quigley if you would like some further guidance on this.

## A final note

We must be experts if we are to teach successfully. To learn successfully, knowledge must be foregrounded, and so our book is written to be deliberately knowledge rich. We must also understand how teaching and learning work, and our book aims to develop these three things in a concise and useful way.

We hope that our book will give you the confidence, knowledge and skills to help your students excel with their study of Shakespeare, whilst, very importantly, cutting down on your workload in the classroom.

As an aside:
We have written this book together. However, from this point forward you will see that we switch our pronoun choice to 'I' purely for your ease as the reader.

Stuart Pryke and Amy Staniforth

July 2020

## Resources included in *Ready to Teach: Macbeth* can be found here:

*https://tinyurl.com/y2bykoc2*

We have made every effort to credit original ideas, resources and strategies. Thank you to everyone who has kindly given us permission to share their work.

## The plot of *Macbeth*

### ACT I

*Macbeth* takes place in Scotland and opens with the appearance of three witches. They express their intentions to meet with Macbeth, a soldier who, as part of King Duncan's army, is fighting two invading forces from Norway and Ireland. Following their success in battle, Macbeth and his fellow general, Banquo, encounter the witches on a heath. The witches prophesy that Macbeth will be given the title of Thane of Cawdor and that eventually he will be crowned king. Banquo, in asking what the future holds in store for him, is informed that while he will never be king himself, he will beget a line of kings. Confused by what he has been told, Macbeth demands to hear more, but the witches vanish. Macbeth and Banquo are sceptical of what they have heard, but news soon reaches Macbeth that he has been made Thane of Cawdor. The previous holder of the title is found to have been a traitor, aligning himself with the invading Norwegians. As a result, he is sentenced to death and Macbeth awarded with his position. This, of course, seemingly proves the first part of the witches' prophecies as true.

With this in mind, Macbeth begins to entertain the idea that what the witches have said will come true. When Malcolm, King Duncan's son, is proclaimed the Prince of Cumberland, meaning he is now heir to the throne, Macbeth recognises that he does indeed desire to see himself take the crown. However, he is uncertain as to whether he should act or let fate run its course without his intervention. Duncan and Macbeth make plans to dine at Macbeth's castle at Inverness. Macbeth writes ahead to his wife to inform her of the impending visit and his communion with the witches.

Upon hearing his news, Lady Macbeth is adamant as to what should happen next. She desires to see her husband become King of Scotland and believes the pair should murder Duncan in order to obtain the crown, refusing to listen or consider Macbeth's protestations when he comes to the conclusion that they should not proceed with their plans. Whilst she plays the humble host and servant to Duncan, she convinces Macbeth to go through with the deed. Act I ends with Macbeth and Lady Macbeth set in their plans. They will murder Duncan and take the throne for themselves.

### ACT II

Macbeth sees an image of a floating dagger beckoning him towards Duncan's chambers. While Duncan is sleeping, Macbeth commits regicide by stabbing Duncan. Aghast at what he has done, he returns to Lady Macbeth, who could not carry out the murder herself because of the physical similarities between Duncan and her father. Macbeth's guilt threatens to derail their scheme; he brings the murder weapons back with him, something which was not part of the plan. Lady Macbeth returns the daggers, bloodying her hands in the process. The two wash their hands of blood as a knocking is heard at the gates. Macbeth and Lady Macbeth return to their chambers, ready to feign ignorance as to the events that have taken place.

A drunken porter answers the knocking at the gates. Macduff, the Thane of Fife, has arrived at the castle to call on Duncan. Upon discovery of Duncan's body, Macduff screams for everyone to awake. Macbeth and Lady Macbeth, adopting a façade of innocence, emerge with the other inhabitants of the castle, appearing appalled at the news that Duncan is dead. Macbeth, in an attempt to divert suspicion from himself, kills Duncan's guards, placing the suspicion on them as perpetrators of the act. He claims to have done this in a fit of rage in response to their supposed crime. Malcolm and Donalbain, fearing for their lives, decide to flee Scotland. Donalbain travels to Ireland and Malcolm to England, leaving Macbeth free to take the throne.

### ACT III

With Macbeth now king, Banquo voices his suspicions to himself that Macbeth has gained the crown through foul means. Macbeth, meanwhile, is not secure in his kingship. He is haunted by the prophecy given to Banquo that said he would beget kings. He sees Banquo as a threat and hires a group of murderers to kill not only Banquo but Banquo's son Fleance as well. Banquo is brutally murdered, although Fleance escapes, leaving Macbeth incredibly fearful. Whilst Fleance lives, Macbeth's kingship is vulnerable.

At the feast, surrounded by his guests, Macbeth is haunted by the appearance of Banquo's ghost. Somewhat inconsolable, Macbeth rants and raves at the ghost, begging it to stop tormenting him. Lady Macbeth tries to gain control of the situation, but the damage is already done and suspicions against Macbeth begin to mount.

## ACT IV

Having become increasingly more unstable, Macbeth seeks out the witches so they can tell him more of his future. They summon a series of apparitions, the first being an armed head which tells Macbeth to beware Macduff, the Thane of Fife. The second apparition, a bloody child, tells Macbeth that 'none of woman born' will be able to harm him. The third, a child with a tree in its hand, tells Macbeth he will never be defeated until Birnam Wood moves to Dunsinane Hill.

Macbeth, in hearing this, feels secure, knowing that the things the apparitions have spoken of are an impossibility. All men are born of women and forests cannot move. Upon hearing Macduff has gone to England to meet with Malcolm, Macbeth calls for Macduff's castle to be seized and orders for anyone found there to be killed. Lady Macduff and Young Macduff are savagely slaughtered as Macbeth's violent acts intensify.

Macduff, meanwhile, learns that Malcolm has secured an army in England. Malcolm is initially wary of Macduff's motives, but the two soon align themselves against Macbeth, whose tyranny has brought Scotland to her knees. News of Macduff's family's murder reaches England; Macduff is devastated and vows to get revenge.

## ACT V

Lady Macbeth, overcome with guilt, has taken to sleepwalking, in which she unwittingly reveals her complicity in the events that have taken place throughout the play. She becomes increasingly agitated when trying to remove what she believes to be a spot of blood on her hand. She is slowly driven to the point of absolute despair and ends her life. Macbeth is told the news of his wife's death and muses on the futility of life and the choices he has made. With the threat of invasion building, Macbeth prepares for battle, although he is still convinced that he cannot be harmed because of what the apparitions have told him.

Meanwhile, whilst marching towards Macbeth's castle, Malcolm, Macduff and the invading forces reach Birnam Wood. Malcolm instructs his soldiers to cut down the boughs of trees to hold in front of them and disguise their numbers. The soldiers continue their march, and from a distance it looks as if the forest itself is moving. Macbeth begins to understand that the impossible is coming true. Birnam Wood, as he was warned, has indeed moved to Dunsinane.

Macbeth's forces clash with Malcolm's. Macbeth is greeted by Macduff on the battlefield. Macduff declares he was, 'from his mother's womb / Untimely ripped' (born by caesarean section). Another impossible prophecy has come true and Macbeth realises he is not the invincible figure he has been led to believe he is. He continues to fight, but Macduff beheads him, ending his reign of terror and deceit.

As the play draws to a close, Malcolm is proclaimed king, restoring order to society and promising to bring home those who have left Scotland under Macbeth's tyranny. The play ends with Malcolm inviting all to see him crowned at Scone.

# ACT ONE

# CHAPTER 1
## Act I, Scene i

*Who are the three 'weïrd sisters'?*

**What?**

There are few plays with a more arresting opening than William Shakespeare's *Macbeth*. The supernatural and nightmarish appearance of the witches would have been a terrifying sight for a contemporary audience, and their appearance sets the tone for the rest of the play. They are the first characters we hear from, and their words speed the audience through to *Macbeth*'s inevitable conclusion: their actions and influence thread through almost every decision the eponymous tragic hero makes, and the audience can be under no illusion but that their power is terrifying and vast.

It is often tempting, when teaching a text with such rich historical, social and cultural context as *Macbeth*, to frontload teaching with a lesson – or more – focusing on the important facts that will aid students' later understanding of the play. Planning a lesson that covers the role of women, the role of kingship, the Divine Right of Kings and more can *feel* like good sense. In actual fact, however, this is not what students need to know in the first moments of studying this play. Often, these things are better saved for the moment at which they become most relevant. For example, whilst work on the role of women in Jacobean society is fundamental in understanding the role of Lady Macbeth, it will be more applicable and relevant to students to study this when they first meet her.

If students already think that Shakespeare might not be relevant to their own lives, starting by teaching them about what life was like and how different it was to modern society (without the context of, and interest in, the plot and characters of the play) can be more isolating than comforting.

Good and timely knowledge of context can truly help to enrich students' understanding of a text. It can open up new perspectives. Additionally, approaching the teaching of context in a more bespoke way can also help students weave it into their answers without creating a 'historical knowledge dump' at the start of an essay. It is undeniable that the increase in importance of AO3 in GCSE English Literature means that students must be able to demonstrate a better grasp of the social, historical and cultural context of the texts they are writing about. However, the very best answers, as illustrated in many examiners' reports, are those where context is used judiciously to support the students' thesis or analysis. Ruth Johnson, Qualifications Developer for AQA GCSE English, says, 'Above all, teaching of context should be rooted in the text. It shouldn't need or lead to history lessons but should use the text itself as a window into the context of the text.'[1]

## Scene analysis: Act I, Scene i

Act I, Scene i is the joint shortest scene in *Macbeth*, yet there is a great deal of joy in its analysis. It is linguistically rich and is a move of brilliance on Shakespeare's part with regard to 'setting the scene' for the remainder of the play. It also sets up the characters of the witches, with Shakespeare including many supernatural stereotypes. With minimal costume, and with a need for the audience to recognise characters immediately, the use of stereotypes here quickly confirms to the audience that they are seeing supernatural creatures on the stage – a terrifying prospect for a Jacobean spectator.

*Macbeth* opens with a stage direction that portends the tumultuous journey the characters – and audience – will embark on in the following hours. 'Thunder and lightning. Enter three witches' is the stage direction we read in the First Folio, and the pathetic fallacy used here creates a clear sense of the unsettled atmosphere to come.

Shakespeare uses a large number of interrogatives in this scene, with the dialogue opening with a question: 'When shall we three meet again? / In thunder, lightning, or in rain?' The witches, though, have the answers to these questions and begin to make their earliest prophecies in the play. However, each of the three witches differs in the knowledge they hold:

> *Shakespeare reveals the Weïrd Sisters' degrees of foreknowledge...*
> *The First Witch asks questions... which indicates the least amount*
> *of prescience. The Second Witch has more definitive knowledge...*
> *but the Third Witch reveals the most detailed information.*[2]

---

1.  Ruth Johnson, 'GCSE English Literature – how we are assessing context', https://www.aqa.org.uk/subjects/english/gcse/gcse-english-literature-how-we-are-assessing-context-transcript, (2019).

2.  David Worster, 'Performance Options and Pedagogy: "Macbeth"', *Shakespeare Quarterly*, Vol. 53, No. 3 (Autumn 2002), https://www.jstor.org/stable/3844345, pp. 362–378.

Despite appearing always as one group, they have their own strengths and skills: their relationship is not an entirely equal one and they must work together to influence Macbeth's life. It is true to say that there is strength in numbers, and especially in the number three.

> *Not only is three a magic number for witches... but the number is part of the scenic patterning: the Witches speak singly in turn three times each before chanting the final couplet in unison.*[3]

The witches know that the 'hurly-burly' will be finished 'ere the set of sun' – a fact which sets the audience's expectations for their later actions and would have solidified, for a contemporary viewer, the power and terror these three characters hold. This ability to control destiny and fortune foreshadows the remainder of the play and gives the audience expectations that the witches are able to accurately predict the future.

An audience might also infer that the fact the witches and Macbeth will meet 'ere the set of sun' is, in itself, foreshadowing. Their meeting is due to take place before the sun sets, and so with the coming of darkness also comes the metaphorical darkness of the first set of prophecies and the destruction they spark. The sunset could also represent the end of the old regime – King Duncan's reign – and the beginning of Macbeth's journey. Later in the play, Shakespeare repeatedly refers to King Duncan as being associated with light – the sun is regularly metaphorically associated with him – and thus the sunset here is the first indication that his reign is drawing to a close.

A contemporary audience may also have expected the witches to speak in riddles, and the oxymorons Shakespeare uses in Act I, Scene i reflect this. The witches describe that they will meet Macbeth when 'the battle's lost, and won.' This sets up for the audience, at this early stage, the paradoxical thread that runs throughout the play and becomes a central pillar in Macbeth's later downfall. This phrase in particular hints at the problems that will befall the characters of the play: 'The witches may refer to the battle which Duncan's forces have won against his enemies, although Macbeth's triumph here will eventually have disastrous consequences for Duncan.'[4] Many of the decisions Macbeth has to make throughout the play are not between two clear-cut options, and his ability to separate truth and fiction becomes less effective as the play goes on. Appearance is not always the same as reality, and here Shakespeare reminds us of this.

---

3.    Ed. Sandra Clark and Pamela Mason, *The Arden Shakespeare: Macbeth*, (London: Bloomsbury, 2015), p. 128.

4.    Ibid., p. 129.

The witches' speech is deliberately equivocal, not only in this scene but elsewhere in the play, and this motif of subterfuge is a fascinating early addition. The audience hears no more than a handful of lines before they are asked to question and puzzle over what the characters are saying, placing them in a not dissimilar position to Macbeth himself.

Similarly, the witches comment that 'fair is foul, and foul is fair' and this in itself is paradoxical. It also demonstrates to the audience the lengths the witches will go to: everything that happens that is awful to others is exactly what the witches delight in. The audience sees them as a genuine threat. Similarly, Shakespeare here is suggesting that the things that might at first appear nice may not necessarily be so. Whilst Macbeth and Lady Macbeth are tempted by the allure of kingship, the reality of the situation is far darker and more 'foul' than their initial expectations. Shakespeare is reminding us, even at this early stage, to be watchful for the things that seem too good to be true. Even the opening of the play 'render[s] all of reality unstable.'[5] Nothing is as it seems.

This stereotypically supernatural behaviour continues as the witches refer to their familiars, Gray-Malkin and Paddock. At the time, it was believed that the Devil would bestow evil spirits in the form of animals, known as 'familiars', on witches. These familiars were believed to assist witches in carrying out their evil deeds, and often took the form of a range of animals. It is often interpreted that Gray-Malkin and Paddock are a cat and a toad respectively, and it is thought that Shakespeare took this from a text which provided some inspiration for *Macbeth*. In *Discoverie of Witchcraft*, Reginald Scot writes that: 'Some say [witches] can keepe divels and spirits in the likenesse of todes and cats',[6] which gives some credence to the interpretation of these animals in this way. The name Gray-Malkin refers to the colour of the cat (grey). The 'Malkin' portion of the name was used as a diminutive of Matilda or Maud, which came to be used in dialect to name a cat.[7] The name 'Paddock' comes from the Middle English word for a frog or a toad: 'Paddok'.[8] By specifically mentioning their familiars, Shakespeare here is really driving home to the audience the powerful role these characters hold.

5.    Susan E. Schreiner, 'Appearances and Reality in Luther, Montaigne, and Shakespeare', *The Journal of Religion*, Vol. 83, No. 3 (July 2003), pp. 345–380, https://www.jstor.org/stable/1205708.

6.    Reginald Scot, *Discoverie of Witchcraft*, (Book I, Chapter IV), p. 10, [accessed via https://www.bl.uk/collection-items/the-discovery-of-witchcraft-by-reginald-scot-1584].

7.    Merriam-Webster, 'Grimaulkin', https://www.merriam-webster.com/dictionary/grimalkin.

8.    Dictionary.com, 'Paddock', https://www.dictionary.com/browse/paddock.

Finally, the witches state they will 'hover through the fog and filthy air', and this murky atmosphere is metaphorical: the witches bring ambiguity and darkness, and this is reflected clearly in the words that Shakespeare chooses. The witches excel at subterfuge, and even here, at this early moment, not everything is clear.

Not only this, but the implication of 'filthy air' is also suggestive of infestation and pollution. There is, already, a lack of purity in the play: the witches bring with them darkness and dark deeds. They are filled with evil and are not pure. Their words here, and the sense of infestation and pollution, are reflected in Lady Macbeth's later words: 'pall thee in the dunnest smoke of hell'. Macbeth and Lady Macbeth repeatedly call for darkness throughout the play: the witches already have it.

## A history of witchcraft

Shakespeare lived and wrote in a society that was, in all respects, deeply suspicious of, and paranoid about, witchcraft. Witches posed a real and perceptible threat. During Shakespeare's life, the fear of witchcraft was almost deafening in public discourse, with King James I himself preoccupied with the perceived power witchcraft had over his reign.

Accusations of witchcraft were rife throughout the early modern period, with estimates suggesting that, in the 16th and 17th centuries alone, some 40,000 people were executed for their apparent links to witchcraft.[9] The time period is characterised as having been driven by mass hysteria: panic bred panic, and this in turn drove up the number of women tried and killed.

Witches pervade modern consciousness, and many modern interpretations of witches can be linked back to Shakespeare's presentation of them. Even today, the phrase 'witch hunt' is often used metaphorically to denote a campaign, usually a very public one, deliberately intended to discredit or cast aspersions on a person. It is sometimes used as a tactic to intimidate political opponents,[10] and this concept of a 'witch hunt' – metaphorical or otherwise – is an interesting one. If women acted beyond the given gender conventions for their time, they would often be considered witches. Could it be argued, therefore, that the accusation of witchcraft was used to suppress independent thought and confidence?

---

9.  Peter Leeson, 'THE "WITCH CRAZE" OF 16th & 17th CENTURY EUROPE: Economists uncover religious competition as driving force of witch hunts', https://ehsthelongrun.net/2018/06/26/the-witch-craze-of-16th-17th-century-europe-economists-uncover-religious-competition-as-driving-force-of-witch-hunts, (2018).

10. Merriam-Webster Dictionary, 'Witch-hunt', https://www.merriam-webster.com/dictionary/witch%20hunt.

There are, of course, some commonly held beliefs about witchcraft which appear prominently in *Macbeth*. It was believed that witches could cause shipwrecks and storms, force crops to fail and kill babies. Almost anything that went wrong in a community or in society writ large could, and often was, blamed on witches, with innocent women scapegoated and punished for their supposed crimes.

However, the reality of contemporary thought on witches was far more complex than this. Witches were thought to have been women who had made pacts with the Devil. Some evidence suggests that women were thought to be more susceptible to making such pacts because they were not thought to be as intelligent as men. In Kramer & Sprenger's *Malleus Maleficarum*, the authors write:

> *Just as through the first defect in [women's] intelligence that are more prone to abjure the faith; so... they inflict various vengeances by witchcraft. Wherefore it is no wonder that so great a number of witches exist in this sex.*[11]

Despite this Middle Ages stance, which would be described today as misogyny, Shakespeare's witches are presented as being innately intelligent. They are able to manipulate Macbeth to act in the way he does through just four short appearances in the play (and only two where they communicate directly with the doomed Thane). Whilst his many crimes might be partially attributable to the fact that Macbeth demonstrates a deep-rooted sense of ambition and desire for power, it is the manipulation by the witches (as well as by his wife, Lady Macbeth, who is also demonstrably shrewd and calculating) that drives Macbeth to ensure the prophecies he is given come to fruition. Without the catalyst caused by the intelligent manipulation by the witches, arguably the plot of *Macbeth* would be very different. He himself says he has 'no spur / To prick the sides of [his] intent': it is their prophecies and promises that spur him on.

But where did this Jacobean obsession with witchcraft come from?

The roots of witchcraft stem from long before Shakespeare's time, though the fear appeared to have reached a fever pitch by the time he was writing, with witch trials prevalent in the centuries either side of Shakespeare's writing.

Whilst it is difficult to pin down a worldwide history of witches and witchcraft, it is important that, in almost all cultures, 'magic, sorcery, religion,

---

11. Heinrich Kramer and James Sprenger, translated by Rev. Montague Summers, *Malleus Maleficarum*, (New York: Dover Publications Ltd, 1971), p. 112.

folklore, theology, technology, and diabolism'[12] mark the fundamentals which underpin the actions of witches. These features appear across world folklore and mythology as well as many world religions, bringing together, across time and space, a common assumption for huge swathes of humankind: witchcraft exists.

Etymologically speaking, the word we use today – 'witch' – comes from the Old English word 'wicca',[13] but the concept of, and belief in, witchcraft extends throughout recorded history.

Greek mythology was rich with witchcraft, though the characters whom we would today consider supernatural were not always named as such. The most infamous of these were the Fates – or Moirai. The role of the Fates in mythology was to assign individual destinies to mortals at the moment of their birth. Their power was believed to be so great that their decisions could not even be overruled by Zeus, the king of all gods and men.[14] The witches in *Macbeth*, of course, have a similar impact on Shakespeare's tragic hero, using their power to heavily influence him into causing his own destruction.

The witches are the only true group of characters in *Macbeth*, and thus often gain comparison to the Greek chorus. There is an important difference, though. Merriam-Webster holds two definitions for the role of the Greek chorus:

'1: a chorus in a classical Greek play typically serving to formulate, express, and comment on the moral issue that is raised by the dramatic action or to express an emotion appropriate to each stage of the dramatic conflict

2: a group of people who with persistence express especially similar views or feelings about a particular action or series of actions.'[15]

The first definition is not entirely applicable to Shakespeare's witches. The Greek role of the chorus was to be the speakers who are removed from the action and comment on it from a separate, almost disinterested perspective. This cannot be true for the witches, who are embroiled in the heart of the action, manipulating Macbeth and the decisions he makes. However, the second definition is more relevant. At no point do the witches divert from their sole purpose: their vision is fixed on Macbeth and on, as Hecate describes in Act IV, Scene i, 'draw[ing] him on to his confusion.'

---

12. Jeffrey Burton Russell, 'Witchcraft', https://www.britannica.com/topic/witchcraft, (2020).

13. Etymonline.com, 'Witch', https://www.etymonline.com/word/witch, (2020).

14. Encyclopedia Britannica, 'Fate', https://www.britannica.com/topic/Fate-Greek-and-Roman-mythology, (2020).

15. Merriam-Webster Dictionary, 'Greek Chorus', https://www.merriam-webster.com/dictionary/Greek%20chorus, (2019).

Greek mythology also features, similar to the Fates, the Graeae ('grey witches'): three sisters. They were believed to be the daughters of two sea-deities, Phorcys and Ceto,[16] and thus there is a link, even spanning 2000 years, between these figures and their Jacobean counterparts who were so intrinsically believed to be linked with shipwrecks and storms.

Despite a clear influence from ancient texts, in the West beliefs around witchcraft largely stemmed from the Bible and, in particular, the teachings of the Old Testament. In Exodus 22:18 it is written: 'Thou shalt not suffer a witch to live', and it is believed that this verse gave rise to the fear, and persecution, of women accused of witchcraft. In the early modern period this view was given further credence when witchcraft was officially recognised by the church and belief in witchcraft became doctrine.[17] It became officially recognised by the church that people had every right to be fearful of any person (mostly a woman, but sometimes a man) who was in some way 'other'. The confirmation of witchcraft being officially recognised by the church led to the beginning of systematic witch hunting.

Most women suspected of witchcraft were killed because they were old, poor or in other ways economically vulnerable (for example, widows or unmarried women) and were often living with mental illnesses. It was a persecution of the poorest in a bid to find an explanation for many issues in society – a case of scapegoating those who needed support the most.

Following official sanctioning of the belief in witches by the church, it did not take long for laws concerning the supernatural to come into place in England. The 1542 Witchcraft Act, in particular, brought about a sea change in attitudes. Until this point, witchcraft was not considered a crime. After the legislation was enforced, many more women were persecuted as a result. It is believed that witchcraft was made a crime as a result of the 'general tendency to remove offenses from ecclesiastical jurisdictions',[18] and was the first of numerous laws passed against witchcraft. This Act was renewed in 1562, demonstrating a long-term commitment to dismantling apparent supernatural acts and a clear, ongoing fear of witches. Not only this, but by removing the responsibility of punishing witchcraft from the church, harsher punishments could be meted out to those 'proven' to be witches.

---

16. Greek Mythology, 'Graeae', https://www.greekmythology.com/Myths/Monsters/Graeae/graeae.html, (2020).

17. Parliament UK, 'Religion and Belief: Witchcraft', https://www.parliament.uk/about/living-heritage/transformingsociety/private-lives/religion/overview/witchcraft/.

18. Dries Vanysacker, 'Reviewed Work: Witchcraft and the Act of 1604 [Studies in Medieval and Reformation Traditions 131] by John Newton, Jo Bath', *Church History and Religious Culture*, Vol. 90, No. 4 (2010), pp. 697–699, https://www.jstor.org/stable/23922534.

There were lulls in England's panic about witchcraft, however. When Edward VII came to power, he repealed a number of Acts, including the 1542 Witchcraft Act, and many were not reinstated until early in the reign of Elizabeth I. The new law during her reign 'imposed the death penalty for killing humans by witchcraft, but allowed those who were convinced of harming humans or killing animals the lesser punishment of a year's imprisonment and four sessions on the pillory for the first offence, a second offence of this type being punishable by death.'[19]

By 1602, Lord Chief Justice Anderson wrote that 'the land is full of witches... they abound in all places... the Devil sucks their blood; for they have forsaken God, renounced their baptism, and vowed their service to the Devil.'[20] This is far removed from the previous scepticism, and is demonstrative of an even wider belief in, and fear of, witches, and really demonstrates the feeling in the country at the moment of James I's coronation, and his own beliefs about the supernatural.

### KING JAMES I: *DAEMONOLOGIE*

One can only imagine, in a society on the brink of supernatural hysteria, the thrill and terror of seeing the witches on stage. This frenzy in society was encouraged by James I's own obsession with witchcraft. The roots for this lay in the mysterious and dark events of his own personal circumstances.

James I's future wife, Anne of Denmark, was very nearly shipwrecked on her way to meet her future husband. The weather was so terribly destructive that the ship had to turn around and return to port. James I decided to sail to Denmark to collect her himself and yet, on their return journey, his fleet was caught in such a violent storm that one of the ships sank. James I blamed witches for this, claiming that they must have put a curse on him and his ships.[21]

This event sparked something of an infatuation with witchcraft for James I. Throughout his reign, he became a renowned witch hunter, and between 1590 and 1591 conducted Scotland's first large-scale witch hunt.[22] Indeed, such was his obsession with witches that in 1597 he wrote a book on them: *Daemonologie*.

19. Dries Vanysacker, 'Reviewed Work: Witchcraft and the Act of 1604 [Studies in Medieval and Reformation Traditions 131] by John Newton, Jo Bath', *Church History and Religious Culture*, Vol. 90, No. 4 (2010), pp. 697–699, https://www.jstor.org/stable/23922534.

20. R. Trevor Davies, *Four Centuries of Witch Beliefs*, (London: Routledge, 2011), p. 39.

21. The History Jar, 'Anne of Denmark and the witches of Copenhagen', https://thehistoryjar.com/2018/10/18/anne-of-denmark-and-the-witches-of-copenhagen, (2018).

22. James Sharpe, *Witchcraft in Early Modern England*, (Routledge: Oxon, 2001), p. 7.

His works are often attributed as having been a key influence on Shakespeare when writing *Macbeth*. Many of the rituals and practices James I described in *Daemonlogie* are recognisable in Shakespeare's play.

In particular, throughout *Daemonologie* James I is preoccupied with the ability of witches to conjure storms: 'They can rayse storms and tempestes in the air, either upon Sea or land'.[23] These references are mirrored throughout the play: the opening stage direction even alludes to the power of the witches as they appear following 'Thunder and lightning,' and in Act I, Scene iii the witches describe a pilot of a ship 'Wrecked as homeward he did come.'

Playwrights often included elements which would either flatter the reigning monarch or appeal to their interests. By presenting witches who reflect so closely James I's own 'studies' of them, Shakespeare may well have courted favour with the King: important when we consider that James I himself was sponsoring Shakespeare's company who, by 1604, had renamed themselves for him, becoming 'the King's Men'.

### WITCHES OR FAIRIES?

Regardless of our knowledge of witches, the incidence of calling these three creatures 'witches' appears to be something of a modern misnomer. Shakespeare's only reference to these characters as 'witches' comes in a piece of reported speech, when the woman who refused to give the witch her chestnuts in Act I, Scene iii declares 'Aroynt thee, witch'. It is odd that Shakespeare only uses this word once and, even then, not as a direct piece of on-stage dialogue. In the First Folio published in 1623 (following Shakespeare's death in 1616) the opening scene does not attribute the name 'witch' to the lines, merely providing their character names as '1', '2' and '3'. There is a stage direction that does mention witches ('Thunder and lightning. Enter three witches'), but there is evidence to suggest that many stage directions in his plays may not have been from Shakespeare himself but filled in, later, by editors and actors after the fact.[24] One could argue that this means Shakespeare perhaps never intended us to know these characters specifically as 'witches'.

Instead of referring to them as 'witches', we hear characters refer to them directly, if at all, as 'weïrd sisters'. In the unpublished diaries of Simon Forman, a contemporary of Shakespeare's who wrote often about his trips to the theatre, he similarly does not mention the word 'witch', but instead

23. King James I, *Daemonologie*, (Project Gutenberg EBook), (accessed via http://www.gutenberg.org/files/25929/25929-pdf.pdf), Chapter 5, p. 37.

24. Alexis Soloski, 'Beware of the bear – the dilemma of stage directions', *the Guardian*, (2009), https://www.theguardian.com/stage/theatreblog/2009/mar/04/stage-direction-shakespeare-stoppard.

describes the characters as 'three women fairies or nymphs',[25] which supports this view.

The fact that Forman's diary describes them as 'fairies' is also supported by the way Shakespeare writes for the witches. They speak in trochaic tetrameter. The only other Shakespearean characters who speak in this way (as opposed to blank verse or prose) are the fairies in *A Midsummer Night's Dream*.[26] It could be interpreted, then, that Shakespeare's witches were intended to be more closely aligned with the concept of fairies.

Generally speaking, Shakespearean fairies are drawn from two different traditions. The fairies of *A Midsummer Night's Dream* are drawn from courtly narratives of sixteenth century writing and are characterised by their benevolence and lightness of spirit. However, medieval sensibilities presented fairies as 'dangerously mischievous, demonic or evil'.[27] This presentation of fairies can be traced back to Chaucer, perhaps indicating the literary canon to which Shakespeare wished to belong, but it also aligns the characters of the witches with a rich tradition of otherworldly, supernatural creatures with which the audience would have been familiar as symbolic of the 'other': mysterious and potentially very dangerous.

That Shakespeare has his characters refer to the witches as the 'weïrd sisters' is interesting, as the etymology of 'weïrd' gives us another interpretation as to their purpose. Originating in the Old English word 'wyrd', the original meaning was that someone who was 'wyrd' had the ability to control destiny and fortune; Shakespeare's witches are able to control Macbeth's destiny through their prophecies and manipulation.[28]

By looking at the broader history of their naming conventions – from 'fairies' through 'weïrd sisters' to 'witches' – we are able to establish a range of interpretations and lenses through which we can examine their presentation and actions. Just as their impact in *Macbeth* is complex, so is our contextual understanding of their roles.

### THE WITCHES: *HOLINSHED'S CHRONICLES*

The roots of *Macbeth* lay in *Holinshed's Chronicles of England, Scotland and Ireland*, published between 1577 and 1587. In the two volumes, there are

---

25. Judith Cook, *Dr Simon Forman*, (New York: Vintage, 2002), p. 188.

26. Amanda Mabillard, 'Trochaic Tetrameter in Shakespeare', *Shakespeare Online*, (2000), http://www.shakespeare-online.com/plays/macbeth/macbethfaq/witchmetre.html.

27. https://www.bl.uk/shakespeare/articles/fairies-re-fashioned-in-a-midsummer-nights-dream.

28. Etymonline.com, 'Weïrd', <https://www.etymonline.com/word/weïrd>, (2020).

storylines familiar to any Shakespeare fan, with evidence of links to his extant plays – in particular, *King Lear, Macbeth* and *Cymbeline*. The writers describe, in some detail, the characters we have come to know as the three witches. However, their presentation in Holinshed is remarkably different from that which we encounter in *Macbeth*, and in some respects reflects more closely the concept of 'fairies' mentioned in Forman's diaries. Whereas Shakespeare's witches are 'so wither'd and so wild in their attire, / that [they] look not like th' inhabitants o' th' earth', Holinshed's equivalent are 'the goddesses of destinie, or else some nymphs or feiries, indued with knowledge of prophesie by their necromanticall science'.[29] 'Goddesses', of course, conjure a different tone entirely to that of these 'wither'd' creatures, but it is a difference borne out in the dictionary when we examine the etymology of the word 'witch'.

The Merriam-Webster dictionary currently holds five definitions for the noun 'witch', of which the first three are:

1. One that is credited with usually malignant supernatural powers; especially: a woman [practising] usually black witchcraft often with the aid of a devil or familiar: sorceress – compare 'warlock'
2. An ugly old woman: hag
3. A charming or alluring girl or woman.[30]

Certainly, in *Macbeth* the first two definitions are immediately applicable to Shakespeare's witches. In Act I, Scene i they discuss their familiars, appear in the midst of 'thunder and lightning' and are described by Banquo in Act I, Scene iii as 'wither'd'.

However, as unlikely as it may seem at first glance, it could also be argued that the third definition is applicable. Macbeth in particular is entranced by the witches and the prophecies they give him: arguably they are the core catalyst for the events of the rest of the play. Whilst Banquo in Act I, Scene iii is less certain of their gender, their allure for someone who craves power as much as Macbeth does is entirely nonpareil.

---

29. Raphael Holinshed, *Holinshed's Chronicles of England, Scotland and Ireland*, (1577), Vol. II: The historie of Scotland, pp. 170–171, (accessed via http://www.cems.ox.ac.uk/holinshed/extracts2.shtml).

30. Merriam-Webster Dictionary, 'Witch', https://www.merriam-webster.com/dictionary/witch.

## Act I, Scene i at a glance

## RESOURCE 1.1

Pathetic fallacy – sets tone and begins to explore themes of darkness and evil. Recognisable to a contemporary audience as a signifier of witches and witchcraft.

They are never referred to as witches in dialogue, but Shakespeare creates a group of undeniable witches through their speech and actions which play in to contemporary stereotypes.

*Thunder and lightning. Enter three Witches.*

**First Witch**
When shall we three meet again?
In thunder, lightning, or in rain?

**Second Witch**
When the hurly-burly's done,
When the battle's lost, and won.

**Third Witch**
That will be ere the set of sun.

**First Witch**
Where the place?

**Second Witch**
Upon the heath.

**Third Witch**
There to meet with Macbeth.

**First Witch**
I come, Gray-Malkin!

**Second Witch**
Paddock calls.

**Third Witch**
Anon.

**All**
Fair is foul, and foul is fair,
Hover through the fog and filthy air.
*Exeunt.*

This is almost *in media res*: this is a question often used at the end of a conversation.

Paradoxical statement – could foreshadow how Macbeth believes he's won when he becomes king but his ultimate downfall is a loss.

Paradoxical statement emphasising the witches' delight in bad things and their hatred of things going right or well. Foreshadows Macbeth's first line in Act I, Scene iii which links him to them at this early stage and hints at the harmful effects they will have on him.

Emphasises the darkness and moral ambiguity the witches bring to the play and to Macbeth's life.

Further pathetic fallacy emphasises the negative connotations of the witches, even at this early stage.

In answering the question, the witches show their skills in paradoxical prophecy.

Heaths are part of Scotland's wilderness, signifying that the witches will meet Macbeth beyond civilised society.

Witches' familiars – a cat and a toad. This reaffirms to a contemporary audience they are witnessing the actions of witches. The name 'Gray-Malkin' refers to the colour grey and the diminutive of the name Matilda or Maud (frequently used for a cat). 'Paddock' comes from the Middle English word for a frog or toad; 'Paddok.'

## How?

As previously mentioned, frontloading the teaching of *Macbeth* with context might feel logical, but can in fact prove fruitless. It can be cold and alienating to students who may already feel that Shakespeare's writing is inaccessible to them. This lesson therefore begins with an immediate immersion into the world of *Macbeth*. You may find it useful to drip-feed some context around witches where it is relevant to the students' knowledge and understanding of the scene, especially where their cultural capital regarding modern interpretations of witches and witchcraft may need further development.

## Pre-reading activities

### CONNOTATIONS

As the scene opens with 'thunder and lightning', you may like to start the lesson by having students consider the connotations of these words. In doing so, you may find that they are able at this point to draw out some key themes of the play, including darkness and evil. They may also be able to draw on their knowledge of pathetic fallacy to suggest something about the atmosphere of the play. This activity need not be long, as diving into the text is crucial to foster engagement.

It could be done simply as two mind maps, or you could use images to help students consider the prompts.

### BIG QUESTION

The next stage of the lesson would be to introduce students to the Big Question:

*Who are the three 'weïrd sisters'?*

This, again, opens itself up to some good paired and class discussion considering the word 'weïrd'. Particularly where students have existing contextual knowledge of *Macbeth*, you may find they are able to link this to the witches, but otherwise discussions around the word 'weïrd' are bound to be fruitful. They may consider the meaning of the word to be 'odd' or in some way unsettling. Students may also notice that 'weïrd sisters' is presented in speech marks in the Big Question and therefore may make some consideration of this in its context as a quotation: who says this? Who is being described?

There are many ways to help students engage with challenging linguistic concepts and ideas, and this is just one such resource. Students' understanding of the word 'weïrd' deepens when one considers the etymology of the word itself. This also helps students understand more about the witches before meeting them: an important moment where they can start to understand the wider history of the characters they will soon meet.

Resource 1.2 itself is very simple, guiding students from their own knowledge of the word 'weïrd', the etymology, a chance to couch this in their own terms and, finally, an opportunity to create an image that will remind students of the root and meaning of the word. Their understanding of the word 'weïrd' in this broader sense can be revisited later, and the image they draw can help them later recall the nuances of this.

## RESOURCE 1.2

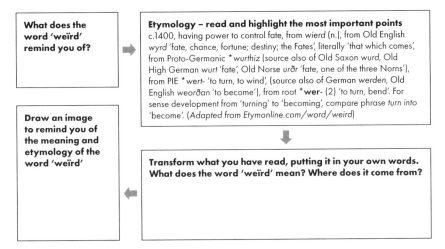

| What does the word 'weïrd' remind you of? | Etymology – read and highlight the most important points |
| --- | --- |

c.1400, having power to control fate, from *wierd* (n.), from Old English *wyrd* 'fate, chance, fortune; destiny; the Fates', literally 'that which comes', from Proto-Germanic *\*wurthiz* (source also of Old Saxon *wurd*, Old High German *wurt* 'fate', Old Norse *urðr* 'fate, one of the three Norns'), from PIE *\*wert-* 'to turn, to wind', (source also of German *werden*, Old English *weorðan* 'to become'), from root *\*wer-* (2) 'to turn, bend'. For sense development from 'turning' to 'becoming', compare phrase *turn into* 'become'. (*Adapted from Etymonline.com/word/weird*)

**Draw an image to remind you of the meaning and etymology of the word 'weïrd'**

**Transform what you have read, putting it in your own words. What does the word 'weïrd' mean? Where does it come from?**

## Reading the scene

Introducing your students to the scene at this point is effective, as the discussions in the lesson so far mean they will hopefully feel ready to tackle some of the Bard and will have had their interest sufficiently piqued to explore the witches. I believe the best way to do this is to present them with the scene without talking about how some students find Shakespearean language difficult. Making comments like this, in an often well-intentioned attempt to allay fears so that students know other people might feel like them, can often be counterproductive. Rather than soothe them, it can instead create additional worry about the language they are about to encounter, creating barriers which will later need to be dismantled.

In each chapter, I will suggest some key questions you might ask to help students discover the main points in the scene. These are not comprehensive, but are intended to be the starting point for discussions. They could be asked during or after reading, depending on your students.

1. What does 'hurly-burly' mean?
2. What is confusing about lines like 'lost, and won'? Why might Shakespeare have used this obfuscatory language?
3. What predictions do the witches make in this scene?
4. Who are Gray-Malkin and Paddock? Why is this relevant?
5. What might the line 'fair is foul, and foul is fair' mean? Why is it confusing? What might Shakespeare be trying to do here?

Having read the scene, perhaps with volunteer readers, it is important to get every student reading Shakespeare themselves. This scene is remarkably short and the language unthreatening; students often enjoy creating mini-performances of it to present to their peers. This activity also enables you to emphasise the fact that this is a living text intended to be performed and is not just something we now see written down on the page.

Have students, in groups of three, create short presentations of the scene, acting these out for the rest of the class. It could be interesting to then show students different cinematic and theatrical interpretations, many of which are available online. This helps emphasise, again, *Macbeth*'s status as a play to be performed.

## Crunching: Judicious appraisal of a scene

The language in Act I, Scene i is rich, and almost every word could be unpicked and explored in more detail. However, one really important skill when studying literature, as we know, is the ability to be judicious regarding the selections we make when analysing. If we were to ask students to analyse every word that they found interesting or that they felt to be significant in this scene, it would be very overwhelming. I suggest that the next activity you try with them is to 'crunch' the scene.

'Crunching' scenes is an easy and effective way of helping students to retain the most important things to remember, whilst also encouraging them to make independent decisions as to what they deem to be important. Neil Bowen, in *The Art of Poetry: Power and Conflict*,[31] introduces the crunch method to aid understanding of the main messages in the poem being reduced. Act I, Scene i of *Macbeth* lends itself well to 'crunching' because of its short length and sparse dialogue.

'Crunching' the scene involves students picking out what they think is the most important word in each line. Prewarn them that they will have to justify their choices to ensure they think carefully about the words they choose. You can see what this could look like in Resource 1.3.

---

31.  Neil Bowen, Karen Elson, Neil Jones and Kathrine Mortimore, *The Art of Poetry: Power and Conflict*, (Bristol: Peripeteia Press, 2017), p. 20.

## RESOURCE 1.3

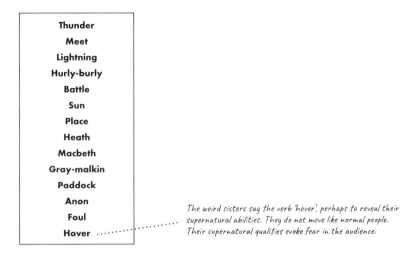

Thunder
Meet
Lightning
Hurly-burly
Battle
Sun
Place
Heath
Macbeth
Gray-malkin
Paddock
Anon
Foul
Hover

*The weird sisters say the verb 'hover', perhaps to reveal their supernatural abilities. They do not move like normal people. Their supernatural qualities evoke fear in the audience.*

It is highly likely students will pick out the majority of the words listed in Resource 1.3. They are the most distinguishable in the short lines of dialogue Shakespeare has the witches speak. At this point, you can ask students to justify their choice of words, checking their knowledge of each through their explanations, as in Resource 1.3.

It is likely that some of the choices students will make will be words linked to sound. By examining these words in more detail, we get a sense of what is to come in Act I, Scene ii, where the Captain describes Macbeth's actions in battle. By examining words such as 'battle' and 'hurly-burly', which are loaded with the suggestion of sound, we allow students to get a head start on understanding the witches' influence over Macbeth: students already get a sense of the witches' abilities of prophecy.

### Quotation explosions

There are many ways to help students access and consider Shakespeare's authorial choices, and one such way is through quotation explosions. You could provide students with a sheet like Resource 1.4. The prompt questions allow students to feel supported in exploring quotations and provide a starting point which can be reassuring to students who panic when presented with a blank page.

This is, at first glance, a very simplified approach to unpicking quotations. However, by teaching students these three steps – and having students feel confident in this approach – we are teaching them the skills they need to analyse any text they are faced with: whether this is *Macbeth*, unseen poetry or texts they encounter in adult life.

There are three steps to this method – a method I was first introduced to by Lia Martin – which allows students to focus on the key knowledge needed to unlock a quotation. The core three questions are as follows:

1. Who says the line/whom or what is it about?
2. Explain what the line means.
3. Explain what the line suggests.

When modelled, it might look something like Resource 1.4.

## RESOURCE 1.4

**'There to meet with Macbeth'**

Who says the line/whom or what is it about?
*The witches.*

Explain what the line means.
*The witches want to meet with Macbeth.*

Explain what the line suggests.
*The line suggests Macbeth is being targeted by the witches; they clearly have something planned, implying they will change his life in some way.*

In following this method, students are guided from the surface detail, through understanding and comprehension and down into the matter of inference: a vital skill for being a successful reader.

It could be that you select several quotations for the students to explore using this 'quotation explosion' method, but it is also a good challenge to have students pick out, either whilst reading or soon afterwards, the moments they believe are worthy of further exploration. This also opens up opportunities for students to consider justification of their choices: if they are to sift through their extensive knowledge of a book or play in an exam, we want to ensure the textual references they make are suitably judicious ones.

In completing an activity such as this, students move from deduction to inference in three steps and are supported throughout. Students could then move on to further inference work using guided questions.

## Guided questions

Guided questioning is also about encouraging detailed exploration of the language a writer uses and aims to teach students the ability to unpick a quotation. There are many ways to set out guided questions, but this one uses small prompts to support students in unpicking the phrase. This could be edited and differentiated to add additional support or challenge as needed.

## RESOURCE 1.5

| | |
|---|---|
| Highlight any words that suggest noise | What kind of noises do those words suggest? What impression of the situation do these words give you? |

**When the hurly-burly's done,**
**When the battle's lost, and won.**

| | |
|---|---|
| Where has Shakespeare used a paradox? How does this make you feel? Why? | Is there anything else you find interesting about this quotation? What? Why? |

## Answering the Big Question

Understanding and being able to recall key knowledge is vital to success in English alongside all subjects. We should teach our students what they need to know if we are then going to teach them the skills to analyse and explore their knowledge in the context of an exam. Whilst students will not, as of yet, have committed any knowledge to their long-term memory from their study of *Macbeth*, the more times a student is asked to consolidate and recall key knowledge, the more likely they are to remember it long term.

To finish the lesson, it is important to give students the chance to capture in writing their understanding of the Big Question. This is useful if it is done in students' books, as they can then refer back to this knowledge when needed and, importantly, see how much their knowledge has moved on as they progress in their study of *Macbeth*. Where time is available at the very end of a lesson, sharing some of their answers to the Big Question can help students consolidate their knowledge further and add anything to their own answers that they may have missed.

## Suggested 'Extra Challenge' activities

- Witches or fairies? Discuss.
- 'The Witches. An unholy trinity?' Write an extended response expressing your thoughts on this question. (N.B. This activity requires further understanding of the play.)
- 'Why is it that ev'ry noise appalls me?' What is the significance of sound in Act I, Scene i? (N.B. This activity requires further understanding of the play.)

## Key vocabulary:
Weïrd, supernatural

# CHAPTER 2
## Act I, Scene ii

*How are we initially introduced to Macbeth's character?*

## What?

### Scene analysis: Act I, Scene ii

It does not take Shakespeare long to introduce his audiences to the frenzied, furious and fierce world of eleventh century Scotland, a country standing on the precipice of catastrophe. As Robert Wilson observes:

> *A rebellion has broken out; a foreign predator has invaded in order to exploit this internal conflict and drawn the opportunistic support of a noble who had formerly been the close and loyal support of the King.*[1]

Audiences will see as they progress through *Macbeth* that Shakespeare is sympathetic to Duncan and his rule compared to the tyrannical anarchy of Macbeth's kingship, yet there is no denying an indication of Duncan's apparent negligence. This insurgency underscores a weakening grip on his rule and the fragility of the forces he has sent to quell the uprising. Indeed, the first word of the Captain's speech, 'doubtful', implies that Scottish forces do not have the upper hand; the two warring factions are both described in the report as being 'two spent swimmers'.

It is important to note here that Shakespeare's play is a work of fiction, yet the conflict between Scotland and Norway anchors itself in history with elements that are inevitably fabricated. Through study of the *Anglo-Saxon Chronicles*, it is evident that Shakespeare could be referencing real invasions. They state that 'Cnut [King of Norway from 1028 to 1035] led an army into Scotland on his return from

---

1. Robert Wilson, 'The Sense of Society in Macbeth', in *Critical Essays on Macbeth*, edited by Linda Cookson and Bryan Loughrey (Essex: Longman, 1988), p. 39.

pilgrimage to Rome'[2] in 1031. Historical records show us that Scotland was the victim of many skirmishes from Scandinavian forces across the eleventh century, so even if the invasion of 1031 is not the exact battle Shakespeare is referencing, it is not unrealistic to believe that the fictional Duncan would be fighting a 'Norweyan lord'. Indeed, it is never stated explicitly in the play why the Norwegians are invading Scotland or why Macdonald is rebelling against his king with Irish forces in tow, yet there is plenty of eleventh century evidence to suggest the real Duncan was weak and ineffective, something which carries over to the play.[3]

Graham Bradshaw observes that:

> *Apart from Henry VI, Duncan is the only Shakespearean monarch who does not lead his army into battle. He is hors de combat: we first see him as an elderly non-combatant, waiting anxiously on the edge of the battlefield for news of what Banquo and above all Macbeth – the real saviour of Scotland – have accomplished.*[4]

Duncan is far removed from the battle occurring on his territory. The fact he has to arbitrarily stop and interrogate a Captain who has been a part of the battle shows us he has no real clue as to what is happening to the men who are defending his kingship and country: he is not a witness to the fight. This in turn causes us to question how tactical Duncan has been, or whether he has resorted to relying completely on the strength of his soldiers to win the war. Either way, Shakespeare's presentation of Duncan is far from favourable at this point.

One could argue that through this criticism of Duncan and his inability to maintain control, Shakespeare is in fact praising King James I, alluding to his ability to unify England and Scotland. Many have commented on *Macbeth* and its role as a piece of royalist propaganda. (Shakespeare is said to have used the play to cement his family's position as supporters of the king after his father was found to have ties to those involved in the Gunpowder Plot.) Shakespeare is highlighting the unforgivable qualities of a weak king, to a king who has brought two countries together, celebrating the coalescence of Scotland and England in the process.

The Captain's brutal descriptions of the battle he has survived are enough to convey to us the savagery that humans are capable of, and the lengths

---

2.   'The Anglo Saxon Chronicles', *The Avalon Project: Documents in Law, History and Diplomacy*, (2008), https://avalon.law.yale.edu/medieval/ang11.asp.

3.   G.W.S. Barrow, *Kingship and Unity: Scotland 1000–1306*, (Edinburgh: Edinburgh University Press, 2015).

4.   Graham Bradshaw, *The Connell Guide to Shakespeare's Macbeth*, (Wiltshire: Connell Guides, 2012), p. 52.

Duncan must go to in trying to maintain peace. Whilst many leap on the Captain's speech as evidence of Macbeth's nobility and reverence to his king, the report itself contains an insinuation of something much more sinister. We are told Macbeth's blade 'smoked with bloody execution', implying he slaughtered enemy soldiers with relentless speed and defied his fate. The Captain acknowledges that 'Fortune' favoured Macdonald and yet Macbeth was still capable of emerging victorious, presenting Macbeth as someone who, even at this early point in the play, will let nothing and no one stand in his way.

What is particularly evident here is the apparent ease with which Macbeth 'carved out his passage' to reach Macdonald and the simplicity with which he carries out the subsequent evisceration of his enemy. Shakespeare makes it known that Macbeth is already desensitised to violence before he even makes an appearance on stage. This is mirrored later when Macbeth is faced with the moral quandary of killing his king: his private battle to go through with Duncan's murder is not one which is concerned with violence or gore. It is instead an internal conflict, one where he wrestles with the morality of his actions rather than the physicality of them.

Death is a central theme of Act I, Scene ii. When asked for Macbeth and Banquo's response to this fresh attack from their Norwegian enemies, the Captain reports that 'they doubly redoubled', surmising the pair were taking delight in the 'reeking wounds' of their enemy. This in itself is ominous. Shakespeare is hinting that Macbeth takes sadistic pleasure in the agony he inflicts upon these invaders, causing us to question what other terrifying and appalling deeds Macbeth is capable of.

In fact, the Captain goes further, describing how Macbeth kills: 'he unseamed him from the nave to th'chops / And fixed his head upon our battlements.' Here, it is almost as if Macbeth is flaunting his innate savagery and brutality, warning others not to cross him unless they wish to meet a similar fate. This is foreshadowing. Ironically, Shakespeare shows us Macbeth's own final moment as Macduff reappears on stage 'with Macbeth's head': he has met the same fate as those he has slain. This final image of Macbeth's decapitated head delivers Shakespeare's key message in a visceral manner: it is foolish to try to usurp a king, as Macbeth did to Duncan. Fate will always mete out a just punishment for those who do.

This ominous subtext is even greater as Act I, Scene ii links to the witches' paradoxical statement that 'fair is foul, and foul is fair' in ways which are not always obvious; the witches have already warned audiences that appearance is very different from reality and their message pervades the Captain's speech. Whilst Duncan may be credulous in response to the eye-witness accounts which tell of Macbeth's bravery and loyalty, Shakespeare ensures that audiences are more sceptical in their trust. This link between the Captain and the witches could be explored further still.

One could argue that Shakespeare, through the Captain, references the *abilities* of witches. Following the defeat of the rebel Macdonald and the 'kerns' (Irish forces), the Scottish army would be forgiven for thinking their problems were over. However, the Norwegian invaders begin a fresh assault which brings yet more bloodshed, an issue presented by the Captain as being like 'shipwrecking storms and direful thunders' arriving just as spring appears, a clear metaphor for the anarchy and tumult of battle that ensues even though they were on the brink of victory. Yet attributing the similarities of 'shipwrecking storms' to the fight must be anything but coincidental. Shakespeare continues to connect the witches with shipwrecks throughout the play, and so it would be wrong to dismiss the Captain's words as some sort of fanciful description. This line is wonderfully ambiguous, and the Captain's metaphor for the battle alludes to the havoc wreaked by witches, their ability to control the weather and the promise of impending death to anyone who dares cross them.

This reference to death is further explored when the Captain makes reference to Golgotha, an allusion to Christ's crucifixion. The gospels of Matthew and Mark translate the term to mean 'the place of [the] skull', a vivid image of rotting and decay. Perhaps Lew Wallace offers one of the most striking descriptions of the place of Christ's death. In his novel *Ben Hur: A Tale of the Christ*, Wallace describes Golgotha as 'a space upon the top of a low knoll rounded like a skull, and dry, dusty, without vegetation except some scrubby hyssop.'[5] The Captain ponders on whether Macbeth and Banquo's renewed efforts to fight and kill were to 'memorise another Golgotha', meaning their aim was to make that battlefield as infamous a location.

But what does Golgotha really represent? In one sense, it is the place of suffering and sacrifice; the end of life. Conversely, it is the beginning of hope and belief. Christ's physical self may no longer exist, but his message endures. This idea of endings and beginnings can also be applied to this moment in Shakespeare's play, with the promise of a new dawn for Scotland and Macbeth himself. It is this battlefield and the atrocities committed on it which force Duncan to strip the Thane of Cawdor of his title and bestow it upon Macbeth. We see an end to the Norwegian rebellion and get a glimpse of hope and a brighter future for Scotland. However, this future will not come to fruition, for Scotland will ultimately be led to ruin by Macbeth.

Shakespeare's reference to Golgotha cannot be coincidental. This religious place which saw the sacrifice of God's only son may foreshadow Macbeth's actions at the beginning of Act II. As king, Duncan would have been seen as God's spokesperson on Earth. By committing regicide, Macbeth will, essentially, commit the same acts as those who saw Christ murdered.

---

5.  Lew Wallace, *Ben Hur: A Tale of the Christ*, (London: Pan Books, 1959), p. 303.

To conclude, students will, quite rightly, grasp on to the fact that Macbeth is presented as a victor and a man who would lay down his life for king and country. His downfall later in the play is made all the more shocking because of the verbal accolades bestowed on him by the Captain. Yet, when this scene is read in hindsight, there is more we can discuss and evaluate. It is necessary to ask ourselves whether Shakespeare wants his audiences to view Macbeth as a hero at all. By allowing audiences to be sceptical, we always remain at a distance from him: we become critical observers of his rapid ascent to eminence and subsequent fall into madness.

### Duncan in *Holinshed's Chronicles*

Comparing Shakespeare's Duncan to the Duncan found in *Holinshed's Chronicles* is incredibly revealing. Duncan, in Act I, Scene ii, is an ineffective king. As discussed, he relies heavily on the Captain to relay news of the invasion Scotland suffers, seemingly keeping his distance from the battle and, as such, calling into question his ability as a strong leader. He is kingly in that he carries himself regally, but the battles others are fighting for him are evidence of his weakening grip on law, order and loyalty. This is mirrored, one could argue, in Macbeth's own kingship at the end of the play.

This weakening grip is alluded to in Holinshed, where Duncan is described as 'softe and gentle of nature'. Holinshed even goes on:

> To hold Duncan accountable for the continual insurgences he suffers (because of his kind, merciful demeanour): 'it was perceyued how negligent he was in punishing offenders, many misruled persons tooke occasion thereof to trouble the peace and quiet state of the common wealth.'[6]

At first glance, then, the difference between the Duncan in *Macbeth* and the Duncan in Holinshed does not appear to be too striking. Shakespeare, however, departs from overtly criticising Duncan; his comments on Duncan's weaknesses are far more subtle, whereas Holinshed's language to describe the King is far more inflammatory.

Indeed, Shakespeare goes so far as to emphasise Duncan's qualities as a man. Even Macbeth, Duncan's murderer, recognises Duncan as someone who:

---

6.  Arthur F. Kinney, 'Scottish History, the Union of the Crowns and the Issue of Right Rule: The Case of Shakespeare's *Macbeth*', in *Renaissance Culture in Context: Theory and Practice*, ed. Jean R. Brink, William F. Gerntrup, (Abingdon: Routledge, 2017), pp.40–41.

*Hath borne his faculties so meek, hath been*
*So clear in his great office, that his virtues*
*Will plead like angels, trumpet-tongued, against*
*The deep damnation of his taking off.*

It is clear 'the evident purpose of [Shakespeare's] departure from Holinshed's account is to deepen the pity of Duncan's end and heinousness of a crime which lacks the poor palliation of its victim's incompetence. "Vaulting ambition" is shown to be the usurper's sole motive, as [he] himself recognises.'[7]

## The Captain's speech at a glance

## RESOURCE 2.1

Here, the Captain says that fortune favoured Macdonald before he was defeated. The same will happen to Macbeth. Fortune favours him when he carries out his plans to kill the King, yet it will soon turn against him and he will suffer the consequences.

Macbeth is described as 'valour's minion'. The Captain is saying he is the follower of great courage in the face of danger. Nothing will stop him in his goal to kill Macdonald.

Macdonald's head is paraded to the world as a warning to all who would seek to overthrow the King. Shakespeare's message is clear – if one tries to disrupt the Great Chain of Being, the consequences will be severe.

The battle has clearly been raging for a long time. The 'spent swimmers', representing the two opposing sides, are exhausted by their fight, meaning who would be victorious remained unclear for a long time.

> **Captain**
> Doubtful it stood,
> As two spent swimmers, that do cling together,
> And choke their art. The merciless Macdonald
> (Worthy to be a rebel, for to that
> The multiplying villainies of nature
> Do swarm upon him) from the Western Isles
> Of kerns and galloglasses is supplied,
> And Fortune, on his damned quarry smiling,
> Showed like a rebel's whore. But all's too weak:
> For brave Macbeth (well he deserves that name),
> Disdaining Fortune, with his brandished steel,
> Which smoked with bloody execution,
> Like Valour's minion, carved out his passage,
> Till he faced the slave,
> Which ne'er shook hands, nor bade farewell to him,
> Till he unseamed him from the nave to th' chops,
> And fixed his head upon our battlements.

Macdonald's fate potentially foreshadows that of Macbeth's, whose own head is brought onto stage by Macduff in the final scene.

Macbeth's blade 'smoked', an indication of the speed with which he kills his enemies. He is presented as a brave, noble warrior, someone who is desensitised to violence.

Macdonald is described as 'merciless'. He is ruthless and unforgiving. Interestingly, he is an image of what Macbeth will become later in the play. Although Macbeth is fighting against Macdonald at this point in the play, he will soon adopt the barbaric and callous ways of this traitor.

Macdonald is supported by forces from the 'western isles' and, as a result, fortune begins to favour him. This could reflect the invasion from neighbouring countries that Macbeth will experience as king.

---

7.    Ed. A.W. Verity, *Shakespeare: Macbeth*, (Cambridge: Cambridge University Press, 1952), p. xviii.

# How?

## Retrieval

One of the analogies presented to me at a continuing professional development (CPD) session to help understand the processes of retrieval practice was that of driving a car. When we first learn to drive, there are multiple factors we have to be aware of: accelerating and braking, using the clutch to change gear, and potential hazards. There is a lot to consider. We start off slowly and pick up more as our confidence increases. And why does our confidence increase? Practice. Each new driving lesson allows us to revisit the processes of driving and the knowledge we need to operate the vehicle safely. Eventually we become capable of more and the act of driving becomes natural to us; we no longer really think about the need to change gears, to brake, to check our blind spots. We just do it. This, in essence, is what retrieval practice is doing for our students. It allows them to revisit past learning until it becomes a part of their procedural memory, memory which 'does not require conscious recall'.[8]

Starters should be designed to help students recall information from memory, consolidating knowledge and plugging any gaps that need filling. This does not necessarily have to be complicated; there are plenty of recall strategies one can use and you will come across several as you read this book. Information retrieval is extremely important, and whilst English teaching should not just be distilled to recall and instruction, it certainly helps in assisting students with understanding the basics, which in turn can lead to greater understanding of higher-level concepts.

As students begin to build their knowledge of a text, it can be difficult to decide which ideas should be selected for recall. With this in mind, I look at what prior information students have learnt that will help them in their current lesson. As we are only on Act I, Scene ii here, this is not much of an issue, but you will see from Resource 2.2 that I have carefully considered which aspects of Act I, Scene i I want students to remember.

## RESOURCE 2.2

These recall questions are simple to plan and an effective way of helping teachers see who has retained knowledge from previous lessons. Whilst they may not necessarily be the most challenging questions one could ask of students, they cover areas of extreme importance.

---

8.    Kate Jones, *Retrieval Practice: Research and resources for every classroom*, (Woodbridge: John Catt Educational Ltd, 2019), p. 19.

---

**Chunked Revision**

**Act I, Scene i**

*Complete the following questions in full sentences. Each answer should be no more than three sentences.*

1. What happens in this scene?

4. Why do the witches speak in paradoxical couplets? ('Fair is foul, and foul is fair')

2. How is pathetic fallacy used to establish a dark, sinister atmosphere?

5. What is the purpose of the witches? How is Shakespeare trying to make his audience feel?

3. What is the significance of Gray-Malkin and Paddock?

6. Finish the quotation: 'Hover through the...'

---

## Pre-reading activities

### BIG QUESTION

Once students have completed the questions and discussed the answers as a class, introduce the Big Question for the lesson:

*How are we initially introduced to Macbeth's character?*

This is the question students must be able to answer by the end of the lesson. Whilst the primary function of Big Questions is to test whether students have successfully learnt the required knowledge to be successful, they can be used in other ways too. Instead of just reading the question to students and moving on, Big Questions can be the basis for their own activity.

Draw students' attention to the wording of the question. The word 'initially', for example, would suggest that our perception of Macbeth will eventually change. With this in mind, students can study the Captain's speech from a critical perspective. Whilst the Captain is commending the bravery of Macbeth and lavishing praise on his skill and prowess as a warrior, students will understand this is only a snapshot of his character and not one which will last.

## Reading the scene

### STRATEGIES FOR READING SHAKESPEARE

Students can become so preoccupied with trying to decode what they are reading that quite often they do not focus on how they should be reading it. Sometimes it is not necessary to understand every single word printed on the page when so much of the understanding is rooted in the delivery of the words. Reiterate to students that they should read from punctuation mark to punctuation mark instead of pausing at the end of a line as many are prone to do (even if there is nothing there which dictates they should do so). It may be useful to model this for them. The Captain's speech is the first extended piece of dialogue students will come across. I usually read a small section of the speech out loud to make explicitly clear that I am using the punctuation to control the fluidity of my delivery rather than line breaks. Students will later get the chance to read the same section of the speech to each other, allowing them to experiment, examine and scrutinise their own delivery. Above all, I want students to savour the words and realise that Shakespeare is not something to fear.

Once students have established how to read Shakespeare's speech on a technical level, you should think about reading the entire scene for meaning and to contextualise what has just been read. Key questions you could ask include:

1. What is currently happening in Scotland?
2. How have Macbeth and Banquo fought in the battle?
3. What news does Ross bring with him?
4. What does King Duncan decide to do as a result of this news?
5. Do you think Duncan is a strong or weak king?

Once the scene has been read and understood, revisit the Captain's speech. If students are struggling to understand it, draw their attention to more manageable areas of his report. Starting your discussion of the speech with the line, 'brave Macbeth (well he deserves that name)', for example, is one that students will be able to grasp easily, a spark for further discussion. Couple this with 'merciless Macdonald' and students will begin to make the connections needed to decode Shakespeare's language; they will begin to understand the Captain speaks in favour of Macbeth and against Macdonald. As teachers, I believe we have a tendency to jump straight into the complexities of Shakespeare without always establishing core knowledge first. Ensuring students have a firm understanding of what is being said on a basic level first will help them with the analysis that will come later.

## Find it, highlight it, annotate it

The Captain describes Macbeth before we even have the chance to meet him, and so his dialogue is crucial in helping our students form their first impressions. Whilst the first scene of the play is short, and therefore relatively 'low threat', Scene ii is slightly more challenging. It may be a good idea to direct them to where they need to look with a quick 'Find it, highlight it, annotate it' task. This was first introduced to me by Emma Illiffe and requires students to identify particular words or lines in the text before answering a question on them. It looks something like this:

## RESOURCE 2.3

**Captain**
Doubtful it stood,
As two spent swimmers, that do cling together,
And choke their art. The merciless Macdonald
(Worthy to be a rebel, for to that
The multiplying villainies of nature
Do swarm upon him) from the Western Isles
Of kerns and galloglasses is supplied,
And Fortune, on his damned quarry smiling,
Showed like a rebel's whore. But all's too weak:
For brave Macbeth (well he deserves that name),
Disdaining Fortune, with his brandished steel,
Which smoked with bloody execution,
Like Valour's minion, carved out his passage,
Till he faced the slave,
Which ne'er shook hands, nor bade farewell to him,
Till he unseamed him from the nave to th' chops,
And fixed his head upon our battlements.

1. Find a line which shows the Captain was not sure which side would win. What does he compare the situation to? Why do you think he makes this comparison?

2. Find a word the Captain uses to describe the rebel, Macdonald. What impression do we get of Macdonald's character?

3. Find one word the Captain uses to describe Macbeth. Now find two words Duncan uses to describe Macbeth. What impression are we given of Macbeth's character?

4. Find a line which shows Macbeth's actions were particularly bloody. Why do you think Macbeth is associated with violence so early on in the play?

5. Find two lines that describe what Macbeth does to Macdonald. What is the effect of this graphic description?

Look at question two as an example. Students are asked to find a word the Captain uses to describe Macdonald. This, of course, is 'merciless'. Students would highlight this word and answer the question that follows. In this instance, you could expect a response that reads something like this:

> *'Merciless' implies that Macdonald is inhumane when he fights. He is strong and determined and spares no one in his efforts to win the battle. He sounds like a formidable enemy.*

It might be worth completing one of these questions as a class before allowing students to complete the rest independently. Discuss the task with students and allow them to share their ideas. Checking their understanding is vital. There is no point moving on to the next part of the play if students cannot explain what the Captain is saying or clarify the trickier aspects of the speech.

## Repetitions

Having looked at the language in greater depth, I always feel it is a good idea to revisit the speech verbally at this point. Now that students understand what the Captain is saying and the technicalities of how to read Shakespeare, pairing them up and giving them a small section of the speech to deliver to one another can be a really effective way of consolidating the meaning behind the words. The following activity is similar to the acting exercise of 'repetitions' in its most basic form. Students repeat the same set of lines in different ways based on the cues provided by the teacher. For example, you might flash the following instructions up on the board:

Read the following section of the speech as if the Captain:

* is full of **admiration** for Macbeth and his achievements on the battlefield.
* is **angry** because of what he has had to endure.
* is **eager** to tell Duncan of everything he has seen.

Activities such as the one above are extremely important. Not only do they build confidence in dealing with language, but they remind students that this is a living, breathing text. Shakespeare's works should never be condemned to stay on the page in our classrooms.

## Answering the Big Question

There are numerous ways for students to engage with the Big Question at the end of a lesson. One simple method is to get students to practise extended responses by getting them to write an answer to the question.

The key to helping students with a written response is not to overcomplicate things. Notice how the Big Question is not reminiscent of the type of task students are required to complete at GCSE. It is always tempting to get students to produce a GCSE style response, perhaps because of the demands of specifications, yet I would argue that planning for this at this stage in the scheme can be detrimental. Students should not have to grapple with the requirements of the exam at the same time they are building knowledge of a text, particularly at this point in their studies; to do so would put students in danger of cognitive overload. This task is not designed to improve exam skills. It is part of the lesson as a way of helping you assess whether students have understood the Captain's speech. It allows them to discuss their ideas in a deeper, more meaningful sense than a recall of pure facts as seen earlier in the lesson.

## What? How? Why?

However, this does not mean we cannot use the same approach as a GCSE response. I find one of the most effective ways of helping students write an extended answer is to break down the main question into three sub-questions that follow the same principles of this book: 'What? How? Why?' Becky Wood (@shadylady222 on Twitter) has written extensively on the benefits of using these sub-questions.[9] Often, teachers are tempted to try to 'support' students with rigid structures such as PEE, PEEL or PETER. In fact, these acronyms can lead to placing unnecessary restrictions on students, or inadvertently encouraging an over reliance on scaffolding when students approach extended writing. If students can answer the 'what', the 'how' and the 'why' of each Big Question, they will naturally incorporate the elements we expect to find in a typical literature response. The three sub-questions you could give to your students for this task may be:

- What is the Captain saying about Macbeth?
- How is the Captain saying these things about Macbeth?
- Why is the Captain saying these things about Macbeth?

This helps direct students' thoughts and is a way to help them draw out deeper knowledge and understanding of the extract instead of simply regurgitating a quotation with no further exploration or inference.

## Because/but/so

As an alternative to writing a paragraph, you could use the 'because/but/so' method to help students respond to the Big Question. Taken from *The Writing Revolution* by Judith C. Hochman and Natalie Wexler, this increasingly popular activity is a simple and effective way of forcing students to think deeply about their responses and manipulate their knowledge in order to complete the same sentence starter three different ways using the conjunctions 'because', 'but' and 'so'.[10] It is not as easy as it may first appear! In this lesson, the following sentence

9.    Becky Wood, 'Why I no longer PEE', https://justateacherstandinginfrontofaclass. wordpress.com/2018/10/28/why-i-no-longer-pee/.

10.   Judith C. Hochman and Natalie Wexler, *The Writing Revolution*, (San Francisco: Jossey-Bass, 2017) p. 40.

stems will help students think about what is said about Macbeth and how this influences our preconceptions of him:

1. In his report, the Captain presents Macbeth as a brave and loyal fighter **because**
2. In his report, the Captain presents Macbeth as a brave and loyal fighter **but**
3. In his report, the Captain presents Macbeth as a brave and loyal fighter **so**

Students should be made aware of the purpose of each conjunction in order to understand which areas of their knowledge they should draw from. For example:

- **Because** is used to show you are about to offer an explanation or reason for your argument.
- **But** is used to introduce a statement that contrasts with what you have just said.
- **So** is used as another way of saying 'and for this reason' or 'therefore'. It allows the writer of the sentences to explain the consequence of the statement they have made.

With this in mind, your students may finish the sentence stems like this:

1. In his report, the Captain presents Macbeth as a brave and loyal fighter **because** he has managed to kill Macdonald and put an end to the rebellion that threatened Duncan's reign.
2. In his report, the Captain presents Macbeth as a brave and loyal fighter **but** also as someone who is capable of extreme brutality and violence.
3. In his report, the Captain presents Macbeth as a brave and loyal fighter **so** audiences understand his strength and ability to fight against the odds to get what he wants.

This method, of course, works for any text and context, but it is advisable to have a go at completing the sentence stems yourself before giving them to your students, to ensure they are doable.[11]

---

11. Judith C. Hochman and Natalie Wexler, *The Writing Revolution*, (San Francisco: Jossey-Bass, 2017) p. 42.

## Suggested 'Extra Challenge' activities

- Once the crowd realised Jesus was dead, 'one of the soldiers pierced Jesus' side with a spear, bringing a sudden flow of blood and water' (John 19:34). How does Shakespeare align Macbeth to the brutality of a Roman soldier through the Captain's allusion to Golgotha?
- 'Scotland *becomes* Golgotha in Shakespeare's *Macbeth*.' Discuss.
- To what extent is the Captain a reliable witness?

## Key vocabulary:

Valour, merciless

# CHAPTER 3
## Act I, Scene iii

*What do the witches tell Macbeth and Banquo?*
*What do we learn about the characters of Macbeth*
*and Banquo from their reactions to the witches?*

## What?

### Scene analysis: Act I, Scene iii

Act I, Scene iii can be divided into three clear moments. Firstly, we have the witches preparing for the arrival of Macbeth and Banquo. Then, we have the prophecies given to the two men. Finally, the audience witnesses the aftermath of the witches' actions as Macbeth begins to have his first regicidal thoughts. It is a vitally important scene which acts as the catalyst for so many later events in the play.

The scene opens with the witches recounting to one another their actions since their last meeting, and these are all heavily rooted in contemporary expectations and understanding of witches. 'They are capricious and vindictive… and like a metaphysical mafia they terrorise people who refuse to subsidise them.'[1] The terrible actions Shakespeare describes here demonstrate the evil deeds of which the witches are capable, and highlight the dangerous predicament Macbeth will put himself in by consorting with them. The second witch has been 'killing swine'. It was believed that if a pig was found dead it was the work of witches, so again Shakespeare is reaffirming for the audience their own beliefs surrounding witchcraft.[2]

---

1. Lars Kaaber, *Murdering Ministers: A Close Look at Shakespeare in Text, Context and Performance*, (Newcastle-upon-Tyne: Cambridge Scholars Publishing, 2016), p. 17.

2. Diane Purkiss, *The Witch in History: Early Modern and Twentieth-Century Representations*, (London: Routledge, 1996), p. 209.

The first witch has focused on meting out punishment on the husband of a woman who had upset her. The actions of the witches here are very stereotypical. He is a sailor, and her plan is to shipwreck him to try to bring about his death. However, there are further details that really illustrate the supernatural skills of these witches. In order to reach his ship, she will 'in a sieve... thither sail'. This is too specific an image to be accidental. In his 1591 pamphlet *Newes from Scotland*, James Carmichael explores the trial of a woman accused of trying to shipwreck King James I. It is reported in the text that 200 witches 'all they together went by Sea each one in a Riddle or Ciue'[3] in order to cause the shipwreck. King James I was obsessed with this event and it would have been well known and feared in contemporary society. There is strength in numbers. The other witches tell her they will conjure winds to speed her on her way, so her mission is successful and he will be 'tempest-tossed'.

Whilst they are unable to completely destroy the sailor, they *are* able to push him to the point of destruction. The witches describe how 'though his bark cannot be lost / it shall be tempest-tossed'. In other words, while they cannot entirely silence him, they do have a degree of influence over the events in his life, though they are not able to amend the bigger picture of the sailor's fate. The same is true for Macbeth. Whilst the witches are able to give him prophecies, it is their manipulation of him rather than their intrinsic actions that allows Macbeth to destroy himself. Whilst the witches influence them, it is partially the actions of these men which bring about their ultimate downfall.

It is almost as if the witches truly relish their ability to push these men to the point of destruction; revelling in the fact that it is ultimately the men who bring about their own ruin. It is tantamount to a kind of perverse entertainment for them, an opportunity to show their skills, talents and powers. Each time they meet, they share their accomplishments with one another, an almost witch-like one-upmanship.

The drum which sounds to denote the approach of Macbeth and Banquo is possibly used to build the tension of their approach: Shakespeare deliberately heralds the arrival of his tragic hero. Whilst drums would have been ordinarily associated with the entrance of an army, the two men arrive alone.[4] Perhaps, as well as making a clear moment of ceremony as the protagonist makes his first entrance, Shakespeare also hints at Macbeth's status as a fierce soldier and warrior.

---

3.　James Carmichael, *Newes from Scotland*, (1591), https://www.sacred-texts.com/pag/kjd/kjd11.htm.

4.　Ed. Sandra Clark and Pamela Mason, *The Arden Shakespeare: Macbeth*, (London: Bloomsbury, 2015), p. 139.

The witches, in the moment of Macbeth's arrival, refer to themselves as the 'weïrd sisters'. The etymology of 'weïrd' has strong links to the ability to control fate and destiny. Shakespeare's use of the word here is likely intended to be a clear reminder to the audience that their true manipulation of Macbeth starts now.

### THE ARRIVAL OF MACBETH AND BANQUO

The first line of the tragic hero echoes (and almost mimics) the witches' own words, emphasising the already close link between the two and the witches' ability to prophesise: it is almost as if they know what he is likely to say or are able to influence his words. It calls into question Macbeth's ability for autonomous thought or decision-making in the remainder of the play. 'So foul and fair a day I have not seen' demonstrates not only that he is already confused and unable to see clarity in his environment but also that he already cannot see the 'clear, rational certainty which is in the natural order of the good.'[5] Their duplicity and equivocation appears to have impacted him even before he meets them in person. What hope can Macbeth truly have to avoid his fate if this is the extent to which they are already able to manipulate and influence him?

This line also extends and amplifies the motif of paradox in the play. Macbeth's day has been both 'foul and fair': whilst he has been in a bloody and terrifying battle, his actions have secured victory for Scotland. Similarly, it is the day that both makes him (he is about to be named the new Thane of Cawdor) and breaks him (by the end of the scene, Macbeth will have his first regicidal thought towards King Duncan).

The fact that Macbeth is also commenting on the weather as being particularly 'foul' shows that he perceives it as unusual. Shakespeare often uses unusual weather to signify approaching underlying disturbances in social order.[6] Macbeth's thoughts of regicide do a great deal to disturb the natural order and disrupt society's strong beliefs in the Great Chain of Being.

The introduction of Banquo, however, shows him to be more pragmatic than his counterpart. His initial line is preoccupied with the journey that they are on, and even when he first catches sight of the witches themselves, he looks immediately for a rational explanation as to their appearance. Whilst he admits they 'look not like th'inhabitants o'th'earth', he recognises that they are there, before him, and thus must *really* be there. His statement that they 'should be

---

5.    Irving Ribner, 'Macbeth: The Pattern of Idea and Action', *Shakespeare Quarterly*, Vol. 10, No. 2, (Spring 1959), pp. 147–159, https://www.jstor.org/stable/2866920.

6.    Sophie Chiari, *Shakespeare's Representation of Weather, Clime and the Environment: The Early Modern 'Fated Sky'*, (Edinburgh: Edinburgh University Press, 2019).

women, / And yet [their] beards forbid [him] to interpret / That [they] are so'
demonstrates that he is unable to reconcile what he sees with what he wants to be
true: he 'is presented with "incompatible" or "discordant" parts.'[7] These witches
have power and sway which would have been more commonly associated with
men, and it appears that they might carry these beards as representative of their
more masculine qualities.

### 'ALL HAIL, MACBETH, THAT SHALT BE KING HEREAFTER'

The witches lavish Macbeth with praise: 'All hail', repeated three times, is a
sign of respect and the lofty position they want Macbeth to believe he is in.
The prophecies the witches give Macbeth are clear and decisive: he will be
Thane of Glamis (a title he already has following the death of his father, Sinel),
Thane of Cawdor (a title the audience knows will imminently be bestowed
upon him following the execution of the existing Thane of Cawdor), and, later,
King of Scotland.

Macbeth, therefore, has a clear and immediate understanding of what the
witches are telling him. However, there is no level of detail in the prophecies
and they are vague enough that Macbeth almost immediately begins to second-
guess when, and under what circumstances, these things will come true: '[His]
thought, whose murder yet is but fantastical.' Consequently, it would seem that
these are self-fulfilling prophecies: in hearing them uttered by the witches,
Macbeth puts a plan in motion to ensure they come to pass.

The witches do not actually tell Macbeth to murder King Duncan, but their
lack of timescale coupled with the sense of temptation Macbeth feels when
presented with this tantalising prophecy mean that, in effect, they are guiding
him towards his future actions and therefore his own destruction. In the
sixteenth century the Devil was believed to be an internal thought: 'an interior
power that compelled the human mind'.[8] In other words, if a person had bad
thoughts, and especially if they acted upon them, they were dealing with the
Devil. A person, upon having an evil thought, could either accept it or reject it.
In Macbeth's case, he indulges in the fantasy of being king and thus later acts
on his thoughts, having been tempted by the Devil. Banquo, conversely, upon
hearing his prophecies, rejects them and thus rejects the Devil.

---

7.    Will Fisher, 'The Renaissance Beard: Masculinity in Early Modern England',
      *Renaissance Quarterly*, Vol. 54, No. 1 (Spring 2001), pp. 157–187, https://www.jstor.
      org/stable/1262223.

8.    Ed. Susan Doran and Norman Jones, *The Elizabethan World*, Darren Oldridge,
      'Witchcraft and the Devil', (London: Routledge, 2004), p. 484.

## 'THOU SHALT GET KINGS, THOUGH THOU BE NONE'

The first two of the witches' prophecies for Banquo are confusing, yet Shakespeare does not have his characters dwell on any prophecy but the third. The first prophecy ('Lesser than Macbeth, and greater') could hint at the fact that, whilst Banquo will not himself rise as far up the hierarchy as Macbeth in his role as king, he will never see his reputation sink as low as his, either. Despite his bloody murder, Banquo dies as an upstanding soldier. Similarly, the witches' second prophecy for him ('Not so happy, yet much happier') also suggests that whilst Banquo will not be happy, he does not experience the same psychological torment as Macbeth does. Banquo does not succumb to the temptation of paying heed to the witches and thus dies with a moral purity Macbeth could only wish to achieve.

The last of Banquo's prophecies is perhaps the one which could be conceded as possessing the most clarity: 'thou shalt get kings, though thou be none.' But is this a deliberate choice on the part of the witches? Whilst Shakespeare does not give us a stage direction or line for Macbeth to directly respond to this prophecy, it is rare to see any production of *Macbeth* where the actor is not directed to have a visible and visceral reaction to hearing it.

It is interesting that the witches do not reveal Banquo's prophecies until he asks them to do so. In showing an interest in what the witches foretell, it could perhaps be argued that Banquo, too, has a darker side to his character. Certainly, he seems to be as brave a soldier and as ruthless a fighter as Macbeth when we hear the two men described in the Captain's speech in Act I, Scene ii. Could it also be argued that Banquo too has the stirrings of ambition within him, like his companion?

Regardless of whether Banquo is ambitious, it is clear that he does not appear to do anything to speed along his prophecies. He is able to contain his potential ambition and desires, unlike Macbeth and his 'vaulting ambition', and thus is able to avoid entertaining the Devil. Banquo was thought, in Jacobean society, to be a direct ancestor of King James I. By presenting him as a character who takes the moral high ground and ignores the will of the witches, Shakespeare is pandering to James I. By showing Macbeth as fallible and as a character whose downfall comes from listening to the witches' prophecies, Shakespeare is suggesting that there is honour in the noble bloodline that stemmed from Banquo. Despite Banquo's bloody end, he makes the right choices.

Whilst this might be suggested as evidence of Shakespeare deliberately appealing to James I's obsession with witches, it could be argued that something altogether more subversive might be going on.

Macbeth places too much trust in the witches and their ultimately duplicitous prophecies. In doing so, Shakespeare appears to lay the blame for Duncan's murder at the feet of Macbeth rather than blaming the witches. This perhaps suggests that Shakespeare is subverting and challenging James I's assertions that witches and witchcraft can be blamed for the ills in the world as they go about their business manipulating the destiny of others. Shakespeare presents Macbeth as naïve and foolish in listening to the witches: his undoing is in the combination of his own innate ambition and their predictions. It is his own 'vaulting ambition... o'er-leap[ing] itself' which ultimately causes his downfall, perhaps prompted or encouraged by his interactions with the witches and their prophecies. Their prophecies cannot solely be to blame.

### 'WITHER ARE THEY VANISHED?'

No sooner have the two men been given their prophecies than the witches depart. Banquo once again is further focused on finding rational explanation in what he has seen and heard. He suggests that they have perhaps 'eaten on the insane root / That takes the reason prisoner' – thought to be hemlock, which was believed to make those who ate it go insane.[9]

Macbeth, however, is entirely preoccupied with the nature of their prophecies. He immediately focuses on Banquo's final prophecy: 'Your children shall be kings.' This is important to note, as it is the driving force behind many of Macbeth's later decisions, and his obsession with children and ridding Scotland of the children he perceives to be particular threats – Malcolm (who flees because of his father's murder), Fleance and Young Macduff.

Just as he did at the start of the scene, Shakespeare has Macbeth's words echo those of the witches. In repeating both Banquo's prophecies and his own – 'and Thane of Cawdor too: went it not so?' – Shakespeare re-emphasises this early obsession with the witches, tying Macbeth's fate closely to their manipulative actions. This link does not go unnoticed by the perceptive Banquo, who comments that the witches did indeed say Macbeth would be Thane of Cawdor 'to th' self-same tune and words.' Banquo's use of 'self-same' here is telling: it means that something is exactly the same as before, perhaps suggesting that Banquo has noticed the power the witches hold over Macbeth. Already, he is almost repeating their prophecies verbatim, foreshadowing the power and sway the witches will hold over him for the remainder of the play in his pursuit of their promises coming true.

Banquo's first moment of clarity as to the power of the witches comes once Ross and Angus have arrived and told Macbeth that the king 'bade [him]... call thee Thane of Cawdor'. His shock is almost palpable: 'What, can the devil speak

---

9.   Ed. Susan Doran and Norman Jones, *The Elizabethan World*, Darren Oldridge, 'Witchcraft and the Devil', (London: Routledge, 2004), p. 143.

true?' It seems to be at this moment that his anxieties about Macbeth come to fruition: his prophecies are coming true. It may be that his *own* prophecies come true, and Banquo is clearly aware already of Macbeth's obsession with the fact that Banquo's children 'shall be kings.' Banquo therefore is slightly more guarded – and could this therefore be at least partially why we see him teaching his son, Fleance, swordsmanship in Act II, Scene i?

Towards the end of the scene, Banquo's observations continue to uncover the truth of Macbeth's actions. Despite Macbeth not voicing his thoughts in anything other than asides, to those who know him well he is already acting suspiciously. Banquo describes how 'New honours come upon him, / Like our strange garments, cleave not to their mould, / But with the aid of use.' Here, Banquo compares Macbeth's new titles to ill-fitting clothes – yet these are clothes which will come to fit him the more he wears them. However, these titles do not really come to 'fit' Macbeth: his rapid actions towards regicide prevent this from being the case. He holds none of the noble qualities a king should hold.

Earlier in this scene, as well as later in the play, the imagery of clothing is repeated. When Ross and Angus arrive to name him Thane of Cawdor, Macbeth states: 'Why do you dress me / In borrowed robes?' Arguably, both Macbeth and Banquo recognise that Macbeth has been elevated above his station: a status not suited to him with his early thoughts of regicide.

**'THIS SUPERNATURAL SOLICITING CANNOT BE ILL; CANNOT BE GOOD'**

Macbeth's aside marks the audience's first true glimpse as to his inner feelings. We know he has already become quite obsessed with the prophecies of the witches, but it is in this moment that we hear his true machinations. It is clear already that he is torn by the nature of the witches' news. He knows it '[c]annot be ill' and, simultaneously, '[c]annot be good.' He 'faces a civil war within, affecting his understanding of both himself and time.'[10] He cannot hope to know precisely when these prophecies will come to pass, but he desperately craves that they will. The second prophecy has come true so fast that Macbeth's thoughts naturally turn to their prediction that he will be king.

The suggestion to which he 'yields' is the idea of murdering the king in order to usurp his position. He entertains the idea of committing the most serious crime in order to elevate his status and hasten the speed with which he can fulfil his ambition. However, we still see a moral thread running through Macbeth here.

---

10. Marina Favila, '"Mortal Thoughts" and Magical Thinking in "Macbeth"', *Modern Philology*, Vol. 99, No. 1 (August 2001), pp. 1–25, https://www.jstor.org/stable/439153.

At the thought of regicide, Macbeth finds that the image 'doth unfix [his] hair, / And make [his] seated heart knock at [his] ribs, / Against the use of nature'. It is, to him, a 'horrid image'. Etymologically speaking, 'horrid' had much stronger connotations when Shakespeare used it than it might have in modern society. Not only does it mean 'causing horror or aversion... terrible, dreadful',[11] but also perhaps has additional roots in the Latin term *horreo*, which meant to 'bristle, or have one's hair stand on end.'[12] This latter definition certainly correlates with his hair having been unfixed. It is certainly clear here that his thoughts are against 'the use of nature', and his aside sets up the dichotomy of thought that haunts him throughout the play. Whilst he will eventually go through with the murder, his understanding of God's reaction is clear.

At this point, though, he is almost paralysed by the thoughts he is having. The regicide 'yet is but fantastical' and his 'function is smothered in surmise'. In other words, his ability to act in any way at all is suppressed by his rampant imagination. He knows that to even think these thoughts is deeply dangerous. He decides, despite the regicidal thoughts, that 'chance' can put him on the throne if that is his destiny without his 'stir'. At this point, there is a clear duality to Macbeth's character, but he appears to still have a sense of hope that later leaves him as he discovers Malcolm is to be named the next king of Scotland. He is instead faced with a terrible sense of anticipation. He sees that he has good fortune coming, yet knows the crime he must commit to achieve it cannot be voiced without bringing on him the wrath of God. By the same token, he knows that if he does not act, then his 'immense chance may go glimmering.'[13]

As Act I, Scene iii closes, Shakespeare has Macbeth make promises to Banquo that he never keeps. He tells Banquo that, later, they will 'speak [their] free hearts each to other', but in reality, Macbeth never shares his true feelings with his supposed best friend. This duplicity is borne out throughout the play when, through subterfuge and concealing the truth, Macbeth does much to prevent Banquo from discovering his true plans. Macbeth only shares his true feelings with his wife and, through various asides, the audience. At this early stage, a wedge is already being driven between the two friends which will not conclude well for either of them.

---

11. Ed. Sandra Clark and Pamela Mason, *The Arden Shakespeare: Macbeth*, (London: Bloomsbury, 2015), p. 147.

12. Ibid.

13. August Goll and Julius Moritzen, 'Criminal Types in Shakespeare', *Journal of Criminal Law and Criminology*, Vol. 29, No. 5 (January–February 1939), pp. 645–667, https://www.jstor.org/stable/1136854.

## Act I, Scene iii at a glance

### RESOURCE 3.1

That he has become Thane of Glamis and Thane of Cawdor.

Perhaps he sees his life like a play – he is 'pretending' to be suited to these roles.

Perhaps this suggests that Macbeth imagines his path to kingship to be happy and easy.

Regardless of the fact that the first prophecies came true, he here hints at his fears over what he imagines he will do next.

Whilst Macbeth is not yet actively planning to murder King Duncan, the very thought of it still upsets him.

Rationalising his behaviour – Macbeth here hopes that fate will take care of things for him and he himself will not have to act to make it come true.

**MACBETH**
[Aside] Two truths are told
As happy prologues to the swelling act
Of the imperial theme. – I thank you, gentlemen. –

*Aside*

This supernatural soliciting
Cannot be ill; cannot be good. If ill,
Why hath it given me earnest of success,
Commencing in a truth? I am Thane of Cawdor.
If good, why do I yield to that suggestion
Whose horrid image doth unfix my hair,
And make my seated heart knock at my ribs,
Against the use of nature? Present fears
Are less than horrible imaginings.
My thought, whose murder yet is but fantastical,
Shakes so my single state of man
That function is smothered in surmise,
And nothing is, but what is not.

**BANQUO**
Look, how our partner's rapt.

**MACBETH**
[Aside] If chance will have me king, why chance may crown me,
Without my stir.

In other words, these roles are leading to the main job: King of Scotland.

From now on, Macbeth's speech is loaded with self-doubt and questioning. This is the first example.

An ambiguous line. It may suggest Macbeth does not know what is truth and what is not with regard to the witches' prophecies, or indeed what is good or evil about them, but could also suggest that his own understanding of good and evil is skewed.

'May', however, suggests that Macbeth acknowledges that fate may not ensure he does become king. Here, Macbeth is suggesting that he himself 'may' need to act.

## How?

### Retrieval

In Act I, Scene ii the audience is invited to understand a specific narrative surrounding Macbeth and come to a particular conclusion as to what kind of man and warrior he is. As Tom Sherrington writes in his blog 'TeacherHead', by considering 'a series of events, a process, cause and effect',[14] students can rehearse key events and key knowledge with others and therefore become more secure in retelling the 'story' of their knowledge in more detail.

---

14. Tom Sherrington, '10 Techniques for Retrieval Practice', www.teacherhead.com, <https://teacherhead.com/2019/03/03/10-techniques-for-retrieval-practice/> (accessed 4 December 2019).

A prompt, like in Resource 3.2, can help students to anchor their knowledge retrieval, and gives their peers something to 'measure' them against. It could be that the students are just given the images and asked to retell their knowledge of Macbeth from Act I, Scene ii, or they could also be given the accompanying key words to help them frame their answers.

## RESOURCE 3.2

Retell the story of Act I, Scene ii to your partner, using the following prompts to help you judge how detailed your story is.

- King Duncan

- Captain

- Macbeth

- Banquo

- Thane of Cawdor

- 'Unseamed him from the nave to th'chops'

- '[D]oubly redoubled strokes upon the foe'

- Golgotha

- 'What he hath lost, noble Macbeth hath won.'

Icons by Adrien Coquet, Ben Davis, Ben Avery, Laymik

Students can be tasked with retelling the story to the class, and this activity could even be adapted into a 'Just A Minute' style game to help really reinforce how the key beats of the scene can be retold succinctly yet in detail, whilst avoiding repetition, deviation or hesitation.

### Pre-reading activities

This scene brings with it students' first meeting with Macbeth. We have heard about him from the Captain, and we understand how King Duncan feels towards him, but we are yet to meet the character himself.

Before reading, some prediction-making can be very useful, as it helps secure students' understanding and expectations of Macbeth, Banquo and the witches before we see what truly happens. The following grid – which could be used as an oral activity instead – might help with students' ability to make predictions. The final column can be filled in after reading for students to reflect on the accuracy of their predictions and, importantly, why their predictions were similar or different from what truly happened.

## RESOURCE 3.3

|  | What do I know about these characters already? | What do I think these characters will do in Act I, Scene iii? | What do these characters actually do in Act I, Scene iii? |
|---|---|---|---|
| **Macbeth** |  |  |  |
| **Banquo** |  |  |  |
| **The Witches** |  |  |  |

### BIG QUESTIONS

It is important that students see the Big Questions before reading in this lesson so that they can assimilate what they read in relation to them. The introduction of these, and especially the second one, can tie into the discussion of Resource 3.3, too.

> *What do the witches tell Macbeth and Banquo?*
> *What do we learn about the characters of Macbeth and Banquo*
> *from their reactions to the witches?*

## Reading the scene

This scene, given its length, intricacy and importance to driving the plot, is often best read in sections, securing knowledge with each step. The first section deals with the prophecies, before dealing with Macbeth's and Banquo's reactions following the disappearance of the witches and the arrival of Ross and Angus.

### THE PROPHECIES

Read the scene up until the witches' disappearance. It is important to establish a secure baseline understanding of what happens up until this point. Cold-reading questions could include:

1. What have the witches been doing?
2. Why do you think Shakespeare includes the witches causing a shipwreck?
3. What are Banquo's initial reactions to the witches' appearance?
4. What are the three prophecies the witches give Macbeth?
5. What are the three prophecies the witches give Banquo?

## Redacting the scene

As we know, the exam asks students not only to write about language but to write about structure, too, and in Act I, Scene iii Shakespeare uses repetition throughout the scene. By using a resource like Resource 3.4, where the witches' lines to Macbeth and Banquo have been redacted to only show repeated words and phrases, we can quite quickly see their strategies and motivations for using the language – and structure – they do.

Invite students to look at the text that is left behind. What do they notice about it? They could discuss, annotate and make inferences from the redacted scene. They are likely to pick out the fact that 'hail' is repeated throughout the exchange, and this could present a lovely opportunity to explore some key Tier 2 vocabulary.

## RESOURCE 3.4

**First Witch**
All hail, Macbeth, hail to thee,

**Second Witch**
All hail, Macbeth, hail to thee,

**Third Witch**
All hail, Macbeth,

**BANQUO**

**First Witch**
Hail.

**Second Witch**
Hail.

**Third Witch**
Hail.

**First Witch**

**Second Witch**

**Third Witch**

So all hail, Macbeth, and Banquo.

**First Witch**
Banquo, and Macbeth, all hail.

There is some key information that students would benefit from drawing out here. The word 'hail', in this context, is an acclamation, and its repetition is arguably designed to flatter Macbeth. Their repetition would appeal to Macbeth's ego greatly, and it could be argued that the witches do this by design to encourage him to listen to their prophecies. The audience already knows that Macbeth is a powerful man; for Macbeth to have this idea of himself reinforced only makes him more inclined to listen to what other compliments the witches will give him. Students may also suggest that 'hail' is repeated because the witches genuinely respect Macbeth, but we know – from their manipulation and their later statement that '[s]omething wicked this way comes' in relation to Macbeth – that they do not feel this way.

Banquo, too, is 'hailed' as part of a pair – 'so all hail Macbeth, and Banquo' – but the witches do not direct this adulatory language specifically to him. Students might identify that the witches know Banquo is less likely to be drawn in by their obsequious language and so do not 'hail' him in the same way because of this.

## The prophecies in more detail

In order to be able to answer the first Big Question of the lesson, students need to secure their knowledge of the prophecies. A simple resource, as below, can be adapted to add or remove a requisite amount of information to allow your students to be challenged to complete the remainder:

## RESOURCE 3.5

| Prophecy for Macbeth | What does this mean? | What questions am I left with? |
|---|---|---|
| Hail to thee, Thane of Glamis | Macbeth is given the title 'Thane of Glamis' | Macbeth already has this title – why do the witches tell him something he already knows? |
|  |  |  |
|  |  |  |

| Prophecy for Banquo | What does this mean? | What questions am I left with? |
|---|---|---|
| Lesser than Macbeth, and greater | Seems paradoxical. Banquo will not be as powerful as Macbeth, but he will be greater – is this because his children will be kings? | How can he be 'lesser' and 'greater' at the same time? Why are the witches giving Banquo paradoxical prophecies where Macbeth's were clearer? |
|  |  |  |
|  |  |  |

## Reading the scene (Part 2)

At this point, the students can read the rest of the scene, focusing particularly on Macbeth's use of asides. Cold-reading questions might include:

1. What news do Ross and Angus bring?
2. How does Banquo react? How does Macbeth react?
3. What does Macbeth think about doing?
4. How does he react to having this thought?

## Internal thoughts v external speech

The next area of focus is to explore how Macbeth perceives himself through Shakespeare's use of asides. This will aid students in developing the knowledge they need to answer the second Big Question.

At this point, it is a good idea to invite students to consider Macbeth's internal and external thoughts. What would he want the witches to know? What would he want Ross and Angus to know? What might he share with his best friend, Banquo? Are there ideas and thoughts he would want to keep entirely to himself?

You could use Resource 3.6 to help students consider these key questions.

The sheet contains a range of quotations from Macbeth's dialogue in the scene. For each, students should put either a speech bubble (for thoughts Macbeth would be happy for others to hear) or a thought bubble (for those thoughts Macbeth would want to keep to himself).

Then, students should consider why they have made these decisions based on what they know of the character of Macbeth so far by annotating the quotations justifying their response. Why would Macbeth want people to hear, or not hear, each of these thoughts?

By doing this, students are able to better establish Macbeth's thoughts and therefore understand how he responds and reacts to the witches' prophecies. By the same token, Banquo delivers no asides. Throughout the play Shakespeare preserves the use of asides for his titular character, yet it is also pertinent that Banquo speaks all of his thoughts freely to other characters. It perhaps speaks to his openness as a character, and further highlights Macbeth's duplicitous nature.

## RESOURCE 3.6

This activity, and the scene more broadly, leads in to a good opportunity to discuss dramatic irony, which is prevalent throughout the play and is a cornerstone of any future study of Shakespeare that the students may undertake. Macbeth's asides make it clear to us that his underlying motives are being deliberately hidden from those around him. Having a clear understanding of this is vital in understanding how he reacts to the witches' prophecies.

For each of the quotations below, decide whether it is a thought Macbeth would want other people to hear or whether it is a thought he'd like to keep to himself. For public thoughts, draw a speech bubble around the quotation. For private thoughts, draw a thought bubble around the quotation. Justify the choices you make by annotating the quotations.

If chance will have me king, why,
chance may crown me,
Without my stir.

I thank you, gentlemen.

Think upon what hath chanced, and, at more time,
The interim having weighed it, let us speak
Our free hearts each to other.

Glamis, and Thane of Cawdor:
The greatest is behind.

Thanks for your pains.

[W]hy do I yield to that suggestion
Whose horrid image doth unfix my hair
And make my seated heart knock at my ribs,
Against the use of nature?

Following the exploration of a definition of dramatic irony, ask students to consider what, throughout their reading of *Macbeth* so far, could be considered as such. Their consideration should then be on the impact of Shakespeare's language here. What do the audience know that some of the other characters do not? To what extent does this change the experience of the play for the audience?

## Emotion wheel

Finally, to help students explore how Macbeth and Banquo react to the witches' prophecies, you could use an emotion wheel. This is a great resource to help students branch out from considering basic words to describe the different characters. It is easy to fall into the trap of being quite one-dimensional when describing characters' emotions, but this activity helps students both expand their vocabulary and be very specific about what the characters feel and why they might feel this way.

## RESOURCE 3.7

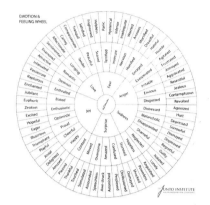

Starting on the inside of the circle, select an emotion for Macbeth and an emotion for Banquo after having heard their prophecies.

Why have you chosen this emotion?

Now, move to the middle of the circle. Which word here best explains how you think Macbeth and Banquo have reacted to their prophecies?

Finally, look at the outside of the wheel. What specific emotion do the two men feel?

Ensure you have a quotation and an explanation to show how you know they feel this way.

There are many versions of this resource largely framed around Plutchik's wheel of emotions. This activity could be further expanded to test students' knowledge of the play so far: can they identify the emotions of King Duncan, the Captain, the witches, Ross or Angus?

This activity also invites a good class discussion: what different emotions did the students select, and why? Have the same quotations led students to different conclusions as to the characters' emotions? Here students can discuss and explore authorial intent and the differing responses of audience members.

Of course, it is vital that the lesson ends with students having the opportunity to explore the Big Questions and answer them in as extended a way as they are able.

### Suggested 'Extra Challenge' activities

- In Shakespeare's time, the Devil was believed to be 'an interior power that compelled the human mind'.[15] How far are Macbeth's decisions his own?
- Act I, Scene iii sees Macbeth's first thoughts of regicide. How powerful is a thought?
- Temptation. Discuss.

### Key vocabulary:
Hail, prophecy

---

15. Ed. Susan Doran and Norman Jones, *The Elizabethan World*, Darren Oldridge, 'Witchcraft and the Devil', (London: Routledge, 2004), p. 484.

# CHAPTER 4
## Act I, Scene iv

*What is ambition?*
*Who is Malcolm?*

## What?

## Scene analysis: Act I, Scene iv

### 'HE CONFESSED HIS TREASONS'

Act I, Scene iv opens with Duncan's enquiry as to whether the traitorous Thane of Cawdor has been executed as per his command. The Thane of Cawdor's death is used to highlight Shakespeare's warning to audiences of the play: one cannot attempt to overthrow a king, disrupt the Great Chain of Being and tarnish the sanctity of the Divine Right of Kings without suffering the consequences. Malcolm delivers the news to Duncan that 'one that saw him die... did report, / That very frankly he confessed his treasons, / Implored your highness' pardon, and set forth / A deep repentance.'

The mention of Cawdor's confession is significant. Why would Cawdor admit to his treason? Surely he knows a proclamation of guilt will not spare him, particularly after his betrayal of the King? What is more, Cawdor begs for Duncan's forgiveness and shows remorse for what he has done. These are lines of surrender where the conspirators finally acknowledge that Duncan's power is too great to dismantle and overthrow, just as Shakespeare is suggesting is the case for King James I. It may be too late for the Thane of Cawdor, but it is not too late for future plotters. One way or another, they will feel the full force and aggression of the power of the very kingship they sought to destroy. Their confessions and appeals for forgiveness make them seem weak and vulnerable when juxtaposed with the superiority of authority and primacy.

Duncan seems to reflect on Cawdor and his betrayal, saying 'There's no art / To find the mind's construction in the face: / He was a gentleman on whom I built / An absolute trust.' Duncan seems to acknowledge the limits of his power that not even kingship can overcome, and rebukes himself for being unable to see Cawdor's deception. At this point, Shakespeare introduces us to what will become a major idea explored in the play: appearance versus reality. Duncan speaks of how the links between face and heart are severed. The reality of what one's heart holds is not always reflected in one's facial expression.

Duncan admits Cawdor was 'a gentleman on whom I built / an absolute trust.' It is challenging to pinpoint exactly how the King is feeling when he delivers this line. There is a hint of sorrow that Cawdor could do such a thing. 'Absolute trust' would tell us the two had what appeared to be a closer relationship, and one could certainly argue there is an element of wistfulness in Duncan's words, a longing to be able to fix the mistakes he has made in not recognising Cawdor's treachery. Perhaps his lines are propelled by the anger he feels at having been betrayed. Either way, Shakespeare cleverly foreshadows the trust Duncan will place in Macbeth, a friend and ally who will also take advantage of the close relationship he shares with the King.

The very mention of 'trust' triggers Macbeth's entrance, where Duncan bestows accolades upon him to the point of extravagance. Whilst one would expect Duncan to thank Macbeth and praise him for the duties he has completed with faith and fealty, the way he does so is somewhat strange. He freely admits he is in Macbeth's debt and exalts Macbeth in doing so. Macbeth has become the gentleman on whom he is building a trust, just like the previous Thane of Cawdor.

Duncan acknowledges how he owes Macbeth more than he will ever be able to repay, an ironic thought as, ultimately, Duncan will repay Macbeth's apparent loyalty with his life. His death will grant Macbeth unlimited power and control with an authority and influence he could only dream of before the witches shared their prophecies.

## DUNCAN'S BLIND TRUST

Here, though, Macbeth plays the part of the humble soldier, portraying a version of himself that attaches little importance to the verbal honours Duncan voices. He says, 'the service and the loyalty I owe, / In doing it, pays itself', claiming he is happy to serve his king, as it is a reward in itself, and purely his duty to do so. Like a child who follows the order of their father, and the servant who is obliged to follow the command of their master, it is Macbeth's moral obligation to uphold Duncan's reign. Yet Macbeth's words are already hollow and meaningless. He is merely playing the part of the dutiful subject whilst thoughts of kingship swell in his mind. It seems Duncan is blind to treachery as long as those who would seek to harm him profess their undying allegiance.

Banquo too is afforded his fair share of rewards. Duncan refers to him as 'noble Banquo', a quality identified to please James I (who was thought, in Jacobean society, to be a descendant of the real Banquo) and to further consolidate Banquo's status as the antithesis of Macbeth.

## 'THE PRINCE OF CUMBERLAND'

With the jubilation of victory still fresh in their minds, Duncan calls his thanes and noblemen around him to witness the naming of his eldest son, Malcolm, as the 'Prince of Cumberland', a title which identifies Scotland's heir apparent. The Scottish crown was not hereditary at this time. Heirs were chosen, meaning succession by primogeniture (the state of being the firstborn child) was not recognised.[1] This is what makes Duncan's actions here so significant. He is making a statement, and it is one which shows he can be cunning – a far cry from the feeble, negligent king we were introduced to in Act I, Scene ii.

Scotland's traditional succession laws, known as 'tanistry', meant 'a ruler's successor was elected from a parallel family line, so that for example, nephew (and not necessarily eldest nephew) succeeded uncle.'[2] What is even more interesting to note is that it was not the king's place to elect his successor, but that of the thanes.[3] Duncan's election of his son, then, is surprisingly authoritarian; he is willing to break with historic tradition in order to get what he wants. One could even argue he is inviting the others present at the announcement to challenge him and the decision he has made. Of course, they will not; news of the execution of the traitorous Thane of Cawdor rings in their ears and serves as a stark reminder of the power a king can wield.

This part of the play could be seen as an example of how *Macbeth* is royalist propaganda. James I believed strongly in the Divine Right of Kings, the idea that the monarch was subject to no earthly authority, derived his right to rule directly from God, and answered only to God. With this, James I also believed in succession by primogeniture.[4] It is easy to see how James's views are infused within the action of the play. Duncan has pointedly named his son the next King of Scotland, a hint that dynastic succession, meaning the

1. Kristin M.S. Bezio, *Staging Power in Tudor and Stuart English History Plays: History, Political Thought, and the Redefinition of Sovereignty*, (London: Routledge, 2016), p. 174.

2. A.R. Braunmuller, *The New Cambridge Shakespeare: Macbeth*, (Cambridge: Cambridge University Press, 2012), p. 16.

3. Graham Bradshaw, *The Connell Guide to Shakespeare's Macbeth*, (Chippenham: Connell Guides, 2012), p. 55.

4. Ed. Sandra Clark and Pamela Mason, *The Arden Shakespeare: Macbeth*, (London: Bloomsbury, 2015), p. 35.

transfer of the crown from father to son, will be the way forward. James I's views are everywhere.

### 'STARS, HIDE YOUR FIRES'

Duncan makes it clear that Malcolm will not be the only one with plaudits bestowed upon him; he promises others will receive honours and proclaims 'signs of nobleness, like stars, shall shine / On all deservers.' It is Duncan's reference to stars which makes this scene particularly significant; Shakespeare has introduced what will become a recurring motif throughout the rest of the play: light and darkness. With this in mind, Shakespeare is clearly associating light with values of honesty, virtue and integrity, values which Macbeth strips himself of as his terrible deeds begin to mount.

However, only nine lines later, Macbeth utters the words, 'Stars, hide your fires, / Let not light see my black and deep desires.' It is the first time Macbeth calls for darkness to assist him in concealing his ambitious thoughts from prying eyes. Macbeth is already entertaining thoughts of murder, and we know when watching the play that his ambition, which has only manifested itself as 'desires' at this point, will lead him down a dangerous route. By asking the stars to hide themselves, he is shunning the light they emit, consequently implying he is not deserving or worthy of the 'signs of nobleness' that Duncan has promised. Shakespeare begins to allude to Macbeth's hamartia (a fatal flaw in one's character)[5] here; his dark ambition is the flaw in his character which will ultimately prove fatal. The Cambridge Dictionary states that 'true Aristotelian hamartia arises when mistakes or errors cause the plot or direction of action to change in a tragic way.' Whilst what we see in *Macbeth* may not be labelled as this true Aristotelian hamartia, it could be argued that it is Macbeth's ambition that causes him to make mistakes and errors which will change the direction of the plot, spurring him on to his tragic climax.[6]

Macbeth's ambition is the cause of the tumultuous internal conflict he begins to experience, mirrored here by the juxtaposition of light and dark imagery. It would be safe to argue that Macbeth's ambition has always been a part of him: it has, however, taken the witches' prophecies and a potential obstacle to his rise to power to draw his ambition from his subconscious into his awareness. He acknowledges his desires are 'deep', an indication of their intensity and strength over him. If something is deep, it extends far down beyond the surface, and for Macbeth, that is where his desires must stay. It is important to mask

---

5. Cambridge Dictionary, 'Hamartia', https://dictionary.cambridge.org/dictionary/english/hamartia.

6. Ibid.

his ambitions if he is to succeed in achieving them, particularly as he describes them as 'black'. Whilst students tend to recognise 'black' as indicative of evil, Macbeth's reference to this colour is a direct link to what he hopes to gain. Not only is black relevant to ideas of death and evil, but it is also often present at the start of things: 'Black's potential for creation is there in the opening passages of Genesis – it is, after all, out of the darkness that God conjures light.'[7] Macbeth's 'black… desires', in a metaphorical sense, then, demonstrate his wish to create his own reign.

This brings us to an interesting piece of criticism from Charles Moseley, who argues that:

> *Macbeth is a fundamentally religious play: that is, its main area of interest is in the struggle of a man's soul between good and evil courses, where the choice of good leads to his developing his full potential, and the choice of evil to his utter and complete loss of being and identity.*[8]

It is at this moment that the audience can see that Macbeth is likely to choose evil. His 'desires' are already causing him some form of internal conflict; he believes he can distance himself from what he does by refusing to look at or acknowledge the actions carried out by his hand. ('The eye wink at the hand; yet let that be / Which the eye fears, when it is done, to see.') Macbeth hints that there is a lack of correspondence between the hands and the eyes. Maybe if he cannot see what he is doing, he can somehow hide away from himself and feign innocence. Yet just in thinking he can do this, he tells us he knows what he is doing is wrong.

Links made between eyes and evil acts are not new. Whilst Shakespeare may not have had these biblical verses in mind when writing *Macbeth*, the similarities regarding the presentation of eyes and the imagery of good and evil are undeniable. The following is found in Matthew 6:22–24. Read with Macbeth's character in mind:

> *The light of the body is the eye: if therefore thine eye be single, thy whole body shall be full of light. But if thine eye be evil, thy whole body shall be full of darkness. If therefore the light that is in thee be darkness, how great is that darkness! No man can*

---

7.  Kassia St. Clair, *The Secret Lives of Colour*, (London: John Murray, 2018), p. 262.

8.  Charles Mosley, 'Macbeth's Free Fall,' *Critical Essays on Macbeth*, ed. Linda Cookson and Brian Loughrey, (Harlow: Longman Group, 1988), p. 24.

*serve two masters: for either he will hate the one, and love the
other; or else he will hold to the one, and despise the other.*[9]

We are familiar with the phrase 'the eyes are the windows to the soul', which reflects these verses. When writing *Macbeth*, Shakespeare appears to have been influenced by the symbolic significance of eyes in the Bible to explore the links between sight and the perception of good and evil. Macbeth refuses to look at his hands, which are capable of such cruelty. His eyes must be 'unhealthy' in a metaphorical sense and his body full of darkness as a result. The biblical verses go on to discuss how no one can serve two masters. Macbeth finds himself in a similar situation. He cannot serve Duncan (his master) whilst harbouring the desires within him that would see him end his king's life. Macbeth will come to hate Duncan's kingship if not the man, and devote himself to seeing his ambitions manifest themselves in his own coronation. At this point in time, however, Macbeth tries to avoid the darkness by ignoring the acts that ambition is forcing his hands to complete.

Now that the audience recognises Macbeth's deeply rooted ambitious traits, Shakespeare immediately contrasts his tragic-hero with his counterpart, Banquo, whom he has Duncan describe as 'true' and 'worthy'. These are qualities Macbeth *should* possess, and yet the darkness within him will completely eradicate them. Whilst one may see this as simply highlighting the differences emerging between these two characters, they have been included for another reason which once again highlights the pro-royalist rhetoric Shakespeare cleverly includes to please James I. James I is also 'true' and 'worthy' and, as a result, he is presented as the rightful leader.

Duncan's dialogue ends the scene. Agreeing with Banquo that Macbeth is 'valiant', he instructs those present to follow Macbeth to his castle, where he will, unknowingly, be received by a husband who is driven by ambition and a wife whose duplicitous scheming and devious manoeuvres will drive the plot forward all the way to its devastating climax.

## Ambition

*Macbeth*, when all is said and done, is a play about ambition and the devastating ramifications it inflicts on those who pursue it. Shakespeare highlights the consequences of allowing it to proceed unchecked. Those who are ambitious are powerful, and the authority which comes with such power is used to scare those in a weaker, submissive position. Ambition isn't necessarily a bad thing, yet Macbeth's ambition to become something greater, something more powerful and dominant,

---

9. *The Holy Bible Containing the Old and New Testaments*, Authorised King James Version, www.kingjamesbibleonline.org, Matthew 6:22–24.

turns into an obsession. He is propelled by greed, and his desires are propagated by his wife, who becomes almost lustful in her determination to see her husband succeed.

In Act I, Scene iv, we see Macbeth's ambitions begin to manifest themselves as a series of choices. He deliberates between the idea of stepping back and letting fate run its course, or actively pursuing what the witches have promised him. He subtly hints he would be prepared to harm Malcolm, Duncan's son and heir, should the occasion call for it, when he describes the Prince of Cumberland as an issue to 'o'er-leap'. It is not overtly stated that Macbeth's ambition is his hamartia, but an underlying ominous threat emerges suggesting it could be, especially when, towards the end of the scene, Macbeth calls for darkness to hide his 'desires'. Shakespeare sows the seeds of Macbeth's self-destructive tendencies: his ambition will be his downfall because of these unabashed 'desires'.

Once Macbeth has been given his prophecies, it is his own innate ambition that drives the play. From the moment he has made the fatal choice to pursue power, nothing else matters to him. Eventually his ambition will crush, destroy and obliterate anything that stands in his way, from his best friend to the innocent family of his perceived enemies and, finally, his own wife. Macbeth's thirst for power drives him: he craves kingship, yet, when he achieves this goal, his aspirations instead turn to securing absolute control of Scotland. They carve a path of destruction as he tries to precariously hold on to his new role by his fingertips. He has committed the ultimate sin, regicide, in order to steal the crown for himself, but this spiralling ambition becomes irrevocably entwined with his fear of losing everything he has until he ruins himself.

To be ambitious, then, is dangerous, and those who are too ambitious will find what they seek unattainable, as Macbeth finds out. Power and authority are simply not enough to sate his appetite. Corrupt ambitions are replaced by yet more nefarious desires; greed becomes Macbeth's undoing as he is led blindly into further sin, pursuing blood-soaked fantasies which will never become a reality, for they have been tainted by the brutality he has had to commit in order to achieve them.

Shakespeare is sending a clear warning to his audiences: if one pursues their ambition, dire consequences are sure to follow. Shakespeare does not hesitate to delve into Macbeth's psyche, revealed to us through soliloquies that pause the action of the play at various intervals. We hear of the internal anguish he is forced to endure, the doubts and uncertainties that plague his mind, and the scepticism and suspicions which dominate his thoughts, causing him to shed yet more blood in an attempt to ease the conflict within him. But why does Shakespeare spend so long emphasising the dangerous qualities of ambition and the obsession it can develop into? The answer to that lies in our own history, and the Gunpowder Plot of 1605.

The ultimate sin in Jacobean England was regicide, as a perpetrator would not only be destroying the monarch, but also dismantling the Great Chain of Being and committing sacrilege against the Divine Right of Kings. The Gunpowder Plot tried to do just this in 1605, and *Macbeth* is, in part, a cautionary tale written in response. Shakespeare's own father is alleged to have had links with those who attempted to assassinate King James I. In telling a tale in which a supposed hero falls because of his desire to remove the king from the throne, Shakespeare is ingratiating himself with the monarch, proving that he is worthy of the King's patronage, whilst diverting suspicion of any involvement in the attempt on James I's life away from his father and himself. Whilst there are links between Shakespeare, his father and the Gunpowder Plot, our understanding of the intricacies of these connections are not the be all and end all of our understanding of the play. However, this knowledge adds an additional dimension to our appreciation of the complexities of Shakespeare's writing.

## The Gunpowder Plot

> *Remember, remember the fifth of November, gunpowder, treason and plot.*

So goes the old rhyme that worms its way back into public consciousness every year. Robert Catesby's infamous, failed attempt to assassinate James I with a group of English Catholics is a tale of duplicity and collusion, of clandestine networks and illicit manoeuvering, driven by the machinations of ambition. The story is one which would not look out of place in a modern-day thriller, made all the more exciting for us as English teachers through Shakespeare's alleged links with the plotters themselves and the subsequent influence this had on the choices he made when writing *Macbeth*.

Guy Fawkes, one of the plotters, has become so synonymous with the attempted assassination that he has, since his death, become a figurehead for the movement. One may be forgiven then, for forgetting it was actually Robert Catesby who was the initial mastermind behind the attack. Fawkes was recruited by Catesby who, after devising a plan to blow up the House of Lords and kill James I, was forced to share his intentions in order to turn his ambitions of reintroducing Catholicism as the state religion into a realistic plan. Perhaps Fawkes is the one everyone remembers, as he was the one discovered to be guarding 36 barrels of gunpowder deep in a cellar under the Palace of Westminster. Fawkes may be the face of the rebellion now, yet to understand the plot properly, we must begin with Catesby himself.

Catesby came from a family of recusant Catholics. Recusancy was the absolute refusal to attend Anglican services, beginning on a small scale in the late 1560s. Early recusancy 'was partly a response to the government's growing success in imposing Protestant conformity upon the parochial clergy [as well as] instructions from Rome that Catholics should not attend Protestant services.'[10]

Perhaps influenced by the firm beliefs of his parents and his experiences in the past, Catesby would involve himself in insurgency on both a small and a large scale throughout his life, with the aim of upholding the rights of the Catholic faith. His experiences would radicalise him after a series of subtle rejections of Protestantism. For example, Catesby did not attend university, most likely because those who did were required to swear the Oath of Supremacy.[11] This was an oath required by those taking public office to pledge their allegiance to, and recognise the monarch as, the Supreme Governor of the Church of England, something which would jeopardise his Catholic faith.

It is clear, then, that Catesby would have looked to James I to ease the repression imposed upon Catholics by Elizabeth. James had inherited an England that had successfully protected and defended its Protestant existence through repression and severe persecution of the Catholic administration. He gave assurances to Henry Percy, Earl of Northumberland, that he would not persecute Catholics who would 'be quiet and give but an outward obedience to the law.'[12] One cannot help but wonder how Catesby would have felt at James's promises. On the one hand, the promise of tolerating Catholics must have been encouraging, yet tolerance was not the same as acceptance.

James encouraged Catholics to practise their religion discreetly, yet this did not allow them to keep their faith in the way they desired to. As a result, observers of the time noted, 'he did more against us than Elizabeth had done in many years.'[13] Years of persecution and oppression were sure to strengthen and intensify the anger felt by the Catholic population; in Robert Catesby's case, it propelled him to action. Help was not forthcoming, however, and the misery of Catholics was compounded by 'the fact that the government had successfully convinced foreign powers, including the papacy, that the situation for Catholics had improved.'[14]

---

10. Susan Doran and Christopher Durston, *Princes, Pastors, and People: The Church and Religion in England, 1500–1700*, (London: Routledge, 2003), p. 122.

11. John Matusiak, *James I: Scotland's King of England*, (Brimscombe Port Stroud: The History Press, 2015).

12. John Watkins, *Representing Elizabeth in Stuart England: Literature, History, Sovereignty*, (Cambridge: Cambridge University Press, 2002), p. 20.

13. Michael L. Carrafiello, *Robert Parsons and English Catholicism, 1580–1610*, (London: Associated University Presses, 1998), p. 104.

14. Ibid.

Jenny Wormald explores the motives and ambitions of Catesby and his men: what did the plotters actually want? It is an interesting question and one which tends to point us in the direction of the loss of Catholic hope that James I would ameliorate the maltreatment and repression inflicted upon them by Queen Elizabeth I. James I's proclamation 'commanding priests to abjure the realm'[15] and fines imposed because of recusancy are also often cited as reasons for Catesby's plot. Interestingly, Wormald argues, 'the men who had planned the Gunpowder Plot never had "hopes" of James. Their hope was for a Catholic England, not an England containing tolerated Catholics.'[16]

In an attempt to fight for this Catholic England, Catesby ensured he recruited people that would be of use to him. Guy Fawkes (also known as Guido Fawkes) may have been recruited by Catesby because of his past experience of siege warfare. Having fought for Catholic Spain in the Eighty Years' War, Fawkes was a soldier who possessed knowledge of clear value to the cause. His allegiance to Catholic Spain meant he had not been in England for some time and so would be a valuable asset to these English crusaders fighting against a monarchy and government they deemed heretical. As Mark Nicholls states in *Strategy and Motivation in the Gunpowder Plot*, 'Anonymity is a great asset. The unidentified conspirator is able to go about his business unremarked, and any alias that he adopts, however unimaginative, is likely to withstand scrutiny'.[17]

Anonymity, however, can only last so long; Catesby's recruitment of Francis Tresham was allegedly the beginning of the plot's unravelling. The discovery of the plot can be traced back to a letter sent to Tresham's brother-in-law, the Catholic peer Lord Monteagle. Tresham, it seems, was afraid and anxious of the consequences of the plot, expressing his concerns that two of his brothers-in-law would be killed if they were successful. Alluding to the plot, Tresham warned Monteagle not to attend parliament on 5 November, and so when Monteagle 'passed on the letter to members of the privy council, [the] disclosure… led, more or less directly, to the discovery of the plot.'[18] Guy Fawkes was found guarding 36 barrels of gunpowder, which were to be used to blow up the House of Lords during the State Opening of Parliament. Whilst suffering torture, Fawkes revealed the identities of his co-conspirators, and the plotters were killed or captured and executed. The plot was a failure.

---

15. Jenny Wormald. 'Gunpowder, Treason, and Scots', *Journal of British Studies*, Vol. 24, No. 2 (1985), pp. 141–168, www.jstor.org/stable/175701.

16. Ibid.

17. Mark Nicholls. 'Strategy and Motivation in the Gunpowder Plot', *The Historical Journal*, Vol. 50, No. 4 (2007), pp. 787–807, https://www.jstor.org/stable/20175128.

18. Ibid.

So where does Shakespeare come into this? Shakespeare's associations with the plotters lie with his father, John Shakespeare. John Shakespeare's religious stance has been something of fierce debate. He was a man who, 'in outward performance... adhered to the state church of the day.'[19] However, documents once thought lost and later rediscovered – 'found hidden in the walls of the Shakespeare house'[20] – indicate John was a secret Catholic. Others argue John Shakespeare was devoutly Protestant, using his position on the Stratford Council to hire conservative clergyman whilst painting over Catholic murals in the Guild Chapel.

Regardless of his religious convictions, it is important to note that the Shakespeares were living in an area harbouring many secret Catholics. Robert Catesby's family owned the manor in Bishopton in Stratford and would frequently meet with the conspirators of the Gunpowder Plot[21] at Clopton House, as well as at the Mermaid Tavern where Shakespeare could also be found.[22] What becomes evident is that there is a real possibility Shakespeare would have known of these men, and anyone who was deemed to sympathise with Catholic notions was a menace that needed to be dealt with.

It would not be completely preposterous to argue that John Shakespeare and William Catesby (Robert Catesby's father) knew each other.[23] Could Shakespeare therefore have been concerned that assumptions would be made that his family were involved with the plot itself in some way? Perhaps his writing was a deliberate distraction from this fear; *Macbeth*, after all, would certainly divert any suspicions that could be levelled at the Shakespeares, for what happens in the play mirrors real life events. Macbeth and Lady Macbeth conspire to kill the king, just like the gunpowder plotters devised their plans to do so. Catesby and his men failed, but Macbeth and his wife succeed. Yet that success is soon followed by failure. Macbeth becomes a king whose rule remains unstable and his fear of losing what he has just stolen acts as a catalyst for his downfall; as a result he falls from grace and is violently killed just like the plotters, who took their last stand at Holbeche House. The history presented in this section has, of course, been severely truncated, yet its inclusion is necessary

---

19. Kate Emery Pogue, *Shakespeare's Friends*, (Westport: Praeger, 2006), p. 19.

20. Ibid.

21. The Manor House, Ashby St Ledgers: Home of the Gunpowder Plot, http://www. ashbymanorhouse.com/.

22. Robert Poole, *The Lancashire Witches: Histories and Stories*, (Manchester: Manchester University Press, 2002), p. 135.

23. Joseph Pearce, *The Quest for Shakespeare: The Bard of Avon and the Church of Rome*, (San Francisco: Ignatius Press, 2008).

to help us understand what Shakespeare wants to say. His message is clear: one cannot seek to kill a monarch, as it will always end in failure. Ambition is no match for the power and control bestowed upon a King or Queen because of their Divine Right. By presenting this message to audiences, Shakespeare essentially validates James I's position on the throne and, by doing this, he diverts suspicion away from himself and his family.

Shakespeare begins to sow the seeds of this message in Act I, Scene iv, where Macbeth's ambition continues to reveal itself in the form of his 'asides', suggesting they are dangerous and that Macbeth (like the conspirators) is not to be trusted.

## Macbeth's ambition at a glance

## RESOURCE 4.1

The 'aside' here means the other characters present in this scene cannot hear Macbeth. This would imply ambition is something to be kept secret. Macbeth does not want to reveal his treacherous thoughts because he knows it would be dangerous for him to do so.

Macbeth considers doing nothing and letting his ambitions remain unfulfilled. Yet the allure of power is too strong and he alternatively contemplates whether he should attempt to overcome the boundaries that Malcolm, in being named the Prince of Cumberland, now represents.

Macbeth knows his ambitions are corrupt. His hands will commit terrible deeds to help him achieve these ambitions and yet he will refuse to look at that which he knows will horrify him.

> **MACBETH**
> [*Aside*] The Prince of Cumberland: that is a step
> On which I must fall down, or else o'er-leap,
> For in my way it lies. Stars, hide your fires,
> Let not light see my black and deep desires.
> The eye wink at the hand; yet let that be
> Which the eye fears, when it is done, to see.

Macbeth describes his desires as 'black' and 'deep'. Black can connote evil, but is also the colour of authority, suggesting Macbeth wants superiority and power. The fact his desires are 'deep' would imply they are already rooted within him and it has taken the witches' prophecies for him to realise this.

Macbeth commands stars, sources of light, to 'hide [their] fires' in order to hide the ambitions that begin to fester within him. As a result, ambition becomes associated with darkness.

## How?

## Retrieval

A retrieval relay race, an idea shared by Kate Jones in her book *Retrieval Practice*, is one effective way to help students recall what has been covered in previous lessons.[24] Place students in groups of four and give every student in the group a relay race resource as seen in Resource 4.2. As you can see, the resource contains four boxes, representing each member of the group. You may wish to dedicate your relay race to a particular theme, character or topic from *Macbeth*,

---

24. Kate Jones, *Retrieval Practice: Research and resources for every classroom*, (Woodbridge: John Catt Educational Ltd., 2019), p. 84.

or you could treat this more as a 'knowledge dump' exercise and have students write down everything they know about the play in general.

For the purpose of this explanation, let's give the focus of this relay race to the presentation of Macbeth's character. Give students two minutes to write down everything they know and remember about the presentation of Macbeth's character in Act I, Scenes i to iii in the first box. Students may initially question the inclusion of Scene i, as Macbeth does not appear here, but they will have to reference it in order to recall the fact that Macbeth's first words mirror the witches' words during the play's opening scene. Students should complete this independently, focusing on their own sheet. Once two minutes are up, ask them to swap their sheet with someone else in their group. Give them one minute to read, digest and clarify the information already on the sheet before giving them another two minutes to continue recalling knowledge, this time in the second box. However, the information in the second box must not repeat what is in the first. This increases the challenge each time the sheet is swapped, and by the time students get to the fourth, they will really have to think hard about what new knowledge they can add which has not been included in the preceding three boxes. I like this activity because it allows students to share and review knowledge at each stage and, in order to avoid repetition, they have to decide what information is important and what is not.

## RESOURCE 4.2

**RETRIEVAL RELAY RACE**
For this task you will be working in groups of four. Each of you will have a retrieval relay sheet. Fill in the first box independently with as much information as you can about our topic. Swap your sheets with someone else in your group. Continue writing as much as you can about the topic BUT do not repeat anything that has already been written in the first box. Do the same for the third and fourth boxes ensuring you never repeat any information that the others in your group have already added to the sheet.

Topic:

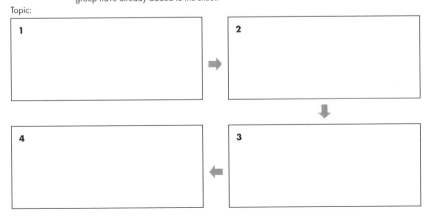

Once students have completed the relay race, ensure their recall is reviewed. This is a vital step and one which is easy to overlook. If we do not build time into the lesson to inspect and audit the knowledge recalled, we could be allowing students to develop and embed big misconceptions as they progress through our lessons. Rectifying this later on would be extremely difficult, especially if that error becomes a part of a student's long-term memory. To tackle this and to help students review their recall, I like to bring up a prepared list of bullet points which clearly details the 'non-negotiable' knowledge I want my class to have remembered over any other. That way, students can check whether they have recalled it in the first place and whether they have recalled it correctly. A bullet point list of 'non-negotiable' knowledge might look something like this:

- The witches say that 'Fair is foul, and foul is fair', telling the audience that all is not as it seems.
- Macbeth's bloody actions are reported, showing us that he is already desensitised to, and capable of, committing violent actions.
- His first words reflect those of the witches with the repetition of 'foul' and 'fair'.

This will also open up discussion, allowing students to expand on the knowledge they have included in their relay race whilst also giving them the opportunity to place it in some kind of order – something they may not have done at first.

## Pre-reading activities

### BIG QUESTIONS
Now we can introduce the Big Questions for the lesson:

*What is ambition?*
*Who is Malcolm?*

Act I, Scene iv is a relatively short scene, but an important one nevertheless. I would begin by asking students to define the term 'ambition' with a partner before asking them to share their ideas as a class. It may be an idea to steer the conversation so students reflect on their own ambitions to make the purpose of the scene applicable to their own lives. I do think it is important to discuss ambition before reading, as it allows students to anchor unfamiliar language and an unfamiliar scene on something of which they have knowledge. It will help them understand Macbeth's ambitions and how he reveals these.

## Reading the scene

Read the scene in its entirety, stopping every so often to check for understanding. Questions for this scene could include:

1. What does Malcolm reveal the traitorous Thane of Cawdor said before his death?
2. What is the relationship like between Malcolm and his father, Duncan?
3. What was the relationship between Duncan and the Thane of Cawdor like before the Thane's betrayal?
4. How does Duncan treat Macbeth upon seeing him?
5. How does Duncan treat Banquo upon seeing him?
6. Who does Duncan name heir to the throne?
7. How does Macbeth react to this?

Gaining knowledge of what happens in a scene is vital before delving into the language to explore the finer details. This is also a good opportunity to answer one of the lesson's Big Questions verbally. Discussing Malcolm and his relationship with his father is an obvious way of helping students understand who Malcolm is and the positive connection he has with Duncan because of the fact he is proclaimed heir to the throne.

## The internal and external self

Once students have the core knowledge needed to understand the scene, they can start exploring how Shakespeare uses language to craft Macbeth's character into the malicious, conniving man he becomes. Just like in Act I, Scene iii, Shakespeare focuses his audiences on the internal and external self of Macbeth. In Act I, Scene iv, the difference between these internal and external selves is very much rooted in the language Macbeth uses. Resource 4.3 will be useful in helping students see the difference between how Macbeth acts in front of Duncan and what he is truly thinking.

## RESOURCE 4.3

**MACBETH'S EXTERNAL SELF**
*The term 'external self' means...*

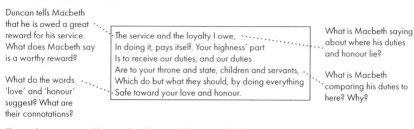

Duncan tells Macbeth that he is owed a great reward for his service. What does Macbeth say is a worthy reward?

What do the words 'love' and 'honour' suggest? What are their connotations?

> The service and the loyalty I owe,
> In doing it, pays itself. Your highness' part
> Is to receive our duties; and our duties
> Are to your throne and state, children and servants,
> Which do but what they should, by doing everything
> Safe toward your love and honour.

What is Macbeth saying about where his duties and honour lie?

What is Macbeth comparing his duties to here? Why?

*Three adjectives we could use to describe Macbeth's external self are...*
*It is important Macbeth acts in this way around Duncan because...*

**MACBETH'S INTERNAL SELF**
*The term 'internal self' means...*

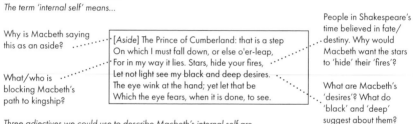

Why is Macbeth saying this as an aside?

What/who is blocking Macbeth's path to kingship?

> [*Aside*] The Prince of Cumberland: that is a step
> On which I must fall down, or else o'er-leap,
> For in my way it lies. Stars, hide your fires,
> Let not light see my black and deep desires.
> The eye wink at the hand; yet let that be
> Which the eye fears, when it is done, to see.

People in Shakespeare's time believed in fate/ destiny. Why would Macbeth want the stars to 'hide' their 'fires'?

What are Macbeth's 'desires'? What do 'black' and 'deep' suggest about them?

*Three adjectives we could use to describe Macbeth's internal self are...*
*Macbeth must keep these thoughts to himself because...*

It is important to note that the purpose of this exercise is to help students recognise the appearance Macbeth adopts and the reality behind that appearance. Students should pick up on the fact that Macbeth's ambitions, his 'black and deep desires', are heretical, and that is why he needs to keep them secret. Macbeth is conforming to expectations. He plays a part (and plays it well), saying exactly what he thinks Duncan wants to hear. Macbeth's external self, then, is one of flattery. He becomes almost fulsome in his aim to disguise his appalling ideas, hoping Duncan will have no reason to doubt his loyalty.

## Light and dark imagery

We began the lesson by looking at the overall meaning of the scene, establishing core knowledge. Now, having looked at two important sections of Macbeth's dialogue, it is essential we 'zoom in' even further and look at specific elements of language which highlight Macbeth's ambitions to an even greater extent. Focus on the last part of Act I, Scene iv from Duncan's 'My plenteous joys' line to the end of the scene.

It is important students grasp the concept of light and dark imagery and how Shakespeare creates it to mirror Macbeth's ambitions. Duncan mentions that 'signs of nobleness, like stars, shall shine / On all deservers', yet Macbeth, only several lines later, calls on those stars to 'hide' their 'fires' so they do not illuminate his heinous desires that are materialising because of his ambition. This is the first of multiple instances where characters call on darkness to shroud their offences. Ask students to highlight references to light and dark before asking them to articulate who is associated with light, who is associated with darkness, and why.

This information could then be filtered into a tracker like the one seen in Resource 4.4. If students continue to fill this out as they progress through the play, they will have a complete record of how many times light and darkness have been mentioned and by whom. They will be able to see whether light or darkness dominates in the play and *how* it dominates. Students can colour code the rows in relation to the character who refers to light or dark and see which characters are associated with which the most. Do any characters move from light or darkness, or vice versa? The idea is that students will begin to see that ambition is associated with darkness and therefore is a negative trait.

## RESOURCE 4.4

| TRACKING LIGHT AND DARK IMAGERY IN *MACBETH* | | | | |
|---|---|---|---|---|
| Act/Scene Number | Light | Dark | Quotation/Character | Significance |
| *Act I, Scene iv* | ✓ | | 'signs of nobleness, like stars, shall shine / On all deservers' – King Duncan | *Duncan says stars will shine on all those who deserve recognition for their loyalty. This makes light symbolic of hope, nobility and faithfulness. Duncan promises that others apart from Malcolm will be rewarded. It is safe to assume he is talking about Macbeth and Banquo here.* |
| *Act I, Scene iv* | | ✓ | 'Stars, hide your fires! / Let not light see my black and deep desires' – Macbeth | *By asking for the stars to 'hide' their 'fires', Macbeth is asking for light to extinguish itself. He does not want anyone to see what he is thinking about and, as a result, needs darkness to aid him in his plans. Darkness becomes associated with malice, and evil is the truth behind a fake appearance.* |
| | | | | |
| | | | | |
| | | | | |

Having looked at the idea of light and dark, students will have established that Macbeth's ambitions are manifesting themselves as immoral and damnable thoughts. At this point, I would introduce the term 'hamartia' to the class. I think it is important to introduce the idea of a fatal flaw early on in the play. I want my class to begin evaluating the choices Macbeth makes through the rest of the play, identifying those which push him closer to the brink of madness and those which are driven by ambition, greed and fear.

## Key vocabulary and 'Thinking Hard' strategies

As an NQT, I would often introduce a new word by writing it on the board and verbally explaining what it meant before asking students to record it in their books. This, of course, is not a practical way of helping students to learn it. After seeing Alex Quigley speak passionately about Tier 2 and 3 words (you can read more about these in *Closing the Vocabulary Gap*), I felt a stronger approach to vocabulary instruction was needed. This is why I have started using the 'Thinking Hard' strategies[25] in lessons when introducing new ideas and concepts. As you can see from Resource 4.5, 'Thinking Hard' allows students to learn in an effectual, valid and powerful way. What I love about these strategies is that they require low preparation but have a high impact.

## RESOURCE 4.5

**Key Vocabulary Check:** Revise the key vocabulary by completing the tasks.
**hamartia (noun):** a fatal flaw leading to the downfall of a tragic hero or heroine

| TASK ONE: READ IT | TASK TWO: TRANSFORM IT |
|---|---|
| Read about the etymology (where a word originates from) of 'hamartia'. | Transform the noun 'hamartia' into an image to help you remember it. |
| 'tragic flaw', Greek, literally 'fault, failure, guilt, sin' from *hamartanein* 'to fail of one's purpose; to err, sin', originally 'to miss the mark' | |

| TASK THREE: DEBATE IT |
|---|
| 'At what point does ambition and greed become an example of hamartia?' Answer in full sentences. |
| |

| TASK FOUR: USE IT | TASK FIVE: LINK IT |
|---|---|
| Can you use the following word in a sentence? *hamartia* | Explain in full sentences how the noun 'hamartia' links to *Macbeth*. Discuss characters and events in your explanation. |
| 1. | |

---

25. Kat Howard, *Stop Talking about Wellbeing*, (Woodbridge: John Catt Educational Ltd., 2020), p. 178.

Begin by introducing the word and explaining what it means. Discuss the etymology of the word. In this case, 'hamartia' derives from the Greek, 'fault, failure, guilt, sin'. This in itself can kindle a discussion of its own. When completing this activity with my own class, we focus particularly on how Macbeth is at fault and how he is failing his duties by asking the stars to hide their fires. We discuss what Macbeth's purpose was, what it now is and how he will fail in it.

Next, students should transform the word 'hamartia' into an image before talking through their sketch with another person in the class, explaining what they have sketched and justifying their decision, choices and interpretations. Students can then debate the word. If you ever adapt this resource for another text, I would strongly recommend removing the vocabulary from the context in which it is being taught. In this case, I would not ask students to debate 'hamartia' in relation to *Macbeth*, because I do not want them to think of the word purely in relation to the play. Instead, it is a powerful word, not exclusive to this text in particular; it is a word which has wider ramifications and is relevant in many contexts. As you can see, the opportunity for linking the word to the text comes at the very end with the 'Link It' box.

## A rich tapestry of cultural capital

Students will discover in their study of *Macbeth* that ambition is a folly. Whilst I do not think it is necessary for students to think about the Gunpowder Plot in the depth and detail explored in the 'What?' section, teachers could certainly give students enough detail for them to work out the lessons we can learn about ambition from the event itself.

I have found that the best way to address this is through expert instruction. The Gunpowder Plot is a part of the rich tapestry of cultural capital, and whilst some students will have awareness of the plot through their knowledge of bonfire night, for many others the plot might feel abstract and irrelevant. Jennifer Webb writes in her *Funky Pedagogy* blog post 'Storming the Citadel: a quest for cultural capital' that 'Students with poor cultural literacy do better when receiving direct instruction from an expert. There is nothing wrong with teacher talk that is well judged, high quality and ambitious.'[26] By giving a mini-lecture, students are able to learn from you, the expert. Students could be encouraged to take notes during the lecture or to complete an immediate retrieval activity after the lecture by writing down everything they remember.

---

26.  Jennifer Webb, *Storming the Citadel: a quest for cultural capital*, https://funkypedagogy.com/2019/06/25/storming-the-citadel-a-quest-for-cultural-capital/#more-2135.

Regardless, I would always follow this up by some low-stakes testing to ensure students have captured the key information.

## Answering the Big Questions

And so to finish, students should review the Big Questions introduced at the beginning of the lesson. This can be done verbally or written as extended writing practice, but students should be encouraged to consider the key ideas that have been introduced to them. A review task could look like this:

**WHAT IS AMBITION?**
*Ambition is...*
Consider the following in your answer:

- Your definition of 'ambition'
- What Macbeth's ambition is
- Hamartia
- Shakespeare's warning about ambition
- The Gunpowder Plot

**WHO IS MALCOLM?**
*In Act I, Scene iv, audiences learn that Malcolm is...*
Consider the following in your answer:

- Malcolm's relationship to Duncan
- Malcolm's personality
- Macbeth's views of Malcolm

## Suggested 'Extra Challenge' activities

- To what extent do you think Shakespeare was trying to curry favour with the King and absolve his family of any association with the Gunpowder Plot through *Macbeth*?
- In Act I, Scene v of *Hamlet*, the eponymous tragic-hero exclaims, 'one may smile, and smile, and be a villain.' Discuss this concept in relation to *Macbeth*.
- 'Ambition is not hamartia, it is a driving force.' Discuss.

## Key vocabulary:

Hamartia, internal, external

# CHAPTER 5
## Act I, Scene v

*Who is Lady Macbeth?*
*What is the relationship like between Macbeth and Lady Macbeth?*

## What?

As we know, the GCSE course places no emphasis on the concept of literary criticism, but it can be argued that framing characters and themes through the lens of good quality literary criticism can add a great deal to students' answers – and not just those aiming for the highest grades.

For example, by examining *Macbeth* through a feminist lens, we are afforded the opportunity to critically analyse not only the female characters, but also the broader gender roles presented by Shakespeare. That, in turn, allows us to examine how these roles have shifted over time – how a contemporary audience would view these characters and their actions compared to a modern audience. Before long, we reach a point where not only do we have students writing with compelling, embedded references to AO3, but we also have students who are able to answer an exam question with a cogent 'thesis' which, when handled well, can help them access the highest marks available in the mark scheme.

Considering a feminist reading of *Macbeth* is important, because students tend to come to one very specific reading of Lady Macbeth: that she is power hungry and/or 'mad'. Equally, though, I sometimes think I am guilty of not always stopping with students to explore how she can be read differently.

## Shakespeare the feminist?

The key question, really, is whether Shakespeare can be considered a feminist at all. Whilst 'feminism' as a term was not coined until the 1890s, and Shakespeare was writing in a time when it was illegal for women to even perform the roles of female characters on stage, it can be argued that we can call Shakespeare a staunch proto-feminist. Whilst he cannot, by dint of when he was writing, be a feminist in the way we use the term today, he was writing women who have complicated inner lives, with fears and desires and senses of humour. Arguably, that is radical for his time. In a world that viewed women as the 'weaker sex', Shakespeare wrote some of the strongest female characters in literature. He is by no means an ideal feminist, but he is a proto-feminist in that many of his female characters have true agency and drive, separate from the desires of their husbands, fathers or brothers.

## Medieval women

If we take a step right back to the eleventh century, the time period in which *Macbeth* is set, we find that most people in medieval Europe lived in small, rural communities. Peasant women were responsible for caring for the family, preparing food and tending livestock. But, during the busiest times of the year, women were expected to join their husbands and bring crops in at harvest time. Women often took large roles in cottage industries such as brewing, baking and manufacturing textiles. Women, therefore, were integral in running and operating their households and were expected, in many circumstances, to carry out manual labour.[1] Subsequently, whilst women were considered the property of their husbands or fathers, they were not seen as meek or weak. They were robust leaders of their own environments and were relied upon to maintain the household. This would have involved decision-making and, for women living in larger, richer households, managing staff and giving commands.

It is therefore not beyond the realms of imagination that a woman of the status of Lady Macbeth would be expected to fulfil a similar role in her own castle.

Whilst this gives the impression that women were quite free in medieval Europe, the role of women in this time was often dictated by biblical texts, and particularly those of the apostle Paul. In his writings, he emphasised men's authority over women, forbidding them from trying to teach or manage their husbands. In Timothy 2:12 we read: 'But I suffer not a woman to teach, nor to usurp authority over the man, but to be in silence',[2] and in 1 Corinthians 14:34 we read the instruction: 'Let your women keep silence in the churches: for it is not permitted unto them to speak; but they are commanded to be under obedience, as also saith the law.'[3] This, therefore, suggests that women's sense of power and control was very much limited to the domestic sphere and could not be exercised more broadly.

1.   British Library, 'Women in medieval society', https://www.bl.uk/the-middle-ages/articles/women-in-medieval-society.

2.   *The Holy Bible Containing the Old and New Testaments*, Authorised King James Version, www.kingjamesbibleonline.org, 1st letter to Timothy.

3.   Ibid., 1st letter to Corinthians

There were, however, women who *did* exhibit power, providing a real challenge to the stereotypical image of women as subservient and oppressed. In the church, women could hold positions of genuine responsibility. In double monasteries which housed communities of men and women, for example, it was the abbess who outranked the monks – regardless of the writings of St Paul.[4]

Outside of religion, women did have some political power, especially as queens and regents who were able to exercise authority in place of their husbands. There are several powerful queens in medieval European history, but they are the exception to the rule with regard to the everyday lives of women of the time. Most women were married off, usually as teenagers, and were then placed in charge of managing the household.

However, we do not have many extant historical sources about the lives of ordinary women in this time period – though we have more than one might suppose. Those that do exist show medieval women as resilient, resourceful and skilled. Moreover, in exceptional circumstances they were able to exhibit power, like those queens and regents described previously.

*Rosie's Plaques – women of the Common Lot Theatre Company, @rosiesplaques*

These women are, today, more frequently remembered and celebrated than they have been in the past, and this provides a good opportunity to help

---

4.   British Library, 'Women in medieval society', https://www.bl.uk/the-middle-ages/articles/women-in-medieval-society.

students understand the changing view of feminism and the role of women between the time of the real Macbeth, Shakespeare's time and our own time. For example, in Norwich in March 2019, unofficial blue plaques[5] were placed around the city by a group of real women marking historic 'rebel women' (upon their realisation that only 25 out of c.300 blue plaques in Norwich were dedicated to women). This provides compelling evidence that there were others, possibly not dissimilar to Lady Macbeth, who were ambitious and strong and brave at the time at which the play is set, but whom history has largely forgotten. For example, one of the plaques in Norwich was dedicated to 16-year-old Emma de Gauder. In 1075, a time period not dissimilar to the one in which *Macbeth* is set, she held Norwich castle against an attack from William the Conqueror.[6]

## Elizabethan women

Yet, by the sixteenth century, gender roles had not really moved on: nothing, markedly, had changed. Whilst England had a woman on the throne for the first time, remarkably her motto was 'video et tacio'.[7] Roughly translated, we can read this as 'I see, but say nothing' or 'I see, but stay silent.' This still has echoes of St Paul and his emphasis on the silence of women: despite being the Queen of England, Elizabeth was still keeping counsel.

Despite the expanse of time between the setting of *Macbeth* and the writing of the play, in the five centuries between the 11th and 16th centuries, women were still considered property. They were still expected to marry, bear children and keep a home. There are examples of powerful women, of course, but broadly, for most women, most of the time, their fundamental roles had not moved on. It is in this world we meet, and read, Lady Macbeth.

## Feminism and The Great Chain of Being

We often talk about, and teach, the Divine Right of Kings, and this part of a prominent fifteenth century philosophy focused on the 'Chain of Being'. Natural order set God at the top, followed by angels, followed by the king and so on and so forth. Even plants and animals were considered part of the chain, and the philosophy extended into familial relationships, too. The man was the head of the household, and his wife was his subordinate: a microcosm of the larger chain.

---

5.   Blue plaques are used nationwide to denote the homes and workplaces of significant people. See, for example, https://www.english-heritage.org.uk/visit/blue-plaques/about-blue-plaques/.

6.   Rosie's Plaques – women of the Common Lot Theatre Company, @rosiesplaques.

7.   Mary Thomas Crane, '"Video et Tacio": Elizabeth I and the Rhetoric of Counsel', *Studies in English Literature, 1500–1900*, Vol. 28, No. 1 (Winter 1988), pp. 1–15, https://www.jstor.org/stable/450712.

When considering gender, as we are here, Lady Macbeth subtly subverts the Chain of Being – she demonstrates throughout the play less of the typical restraint exhibited by women, and instead demonstrates more 'masculine' qualities when she pushes her husband to commit regicide. Her violation of the natural order is punished, just like her husband's, through her descent into madness and ultimate death by suicide.

### The 'Real' Lady Macbeth

*Holinshed's Chronicles* includes many influences on Shakespeare's writing. Precursors to Lady Macbeth include a woman who was 'burning in the unquenchable desire to beare the name of Queene'.[8] This suggests that she perhaps had an 'unnatural' desire for power.

However, in Holinshed's 'Description of Scotlande', men and woman are described as being equal in 'labour and painefulnesse',[9] and he describes women going to war alongside their husbands with equal courage and ferocity, saying of the women that: 'They slew the first living creature that they found, in whose bloud they not onely bathed their swordes, but also tasted therof with their mouthes.'[10]

This begs the question: is our understanding of women out of kilter with reality, or is Holinshed writing with specific women in mind? Either way, in *Chronicles* we appear to see a precursor for characters such as Lady Macbeth, and can begin to recognise her as something not so 'other', but like women who had gone before her.

### Lady Macbeth and feminism

So is Lady Macbeth evil and malicious? Is she a victim of her devotion to her husband? Is she a trailblazer, making history?

These views are, of course, ripe for dissection. Her actions are often portrayed as calculated and evil, driven by her own greed and desire for power. But by the same token, are we able to attribute her actions to her devotion to her husband? She wants to see him exalted and in what she perceives to be his 'rightful' place as King of Scotland. Should we view her as a monster because she takes it upon herself to adopt a traditionally 'masculine' role filled with ambition and power, or should she be viewed as an exemplar for female agency by taking her, and her husband's, destiny into her own hands?

---

8.   Raphael Holinshed, *Holinshed's Chronicles of England, Scotland and Ireland, (1577)*, Vol. II: The historie of Scotland, http://www.cems.ox.ac.uk/holinshed/extracts2.shtml.

9.   Ibid.

10.   Ibid.

Materialist feminism, in which gender is perceived as a social construct, with society forcing particular roles on people as part of a wider patriarchy, might argue that Lady Macbeth's eventual weakness is as a result of a patriarchal portrayal of her gender. She cannot be 'successful' in her plan because of the way that society views her, not because of what she is like intrinsically as a character. She is not trusted by the men around her, has little true economic sway of her own and lives in a society where she would be continually overruled.

The patriarchy also defines Lady Macbeth's intelligence as a flaw and as an indicator that she is 'unnatural' as a woman – which leads to those key quotations we all internalise that link so clearly to her being 'other', such as her desire for Macbeth to 'look like the innocent flower, / But be the serpent under't', a concept of duplicity which flies in the face of society's expectations of her as a subservient woman. The description of her desire to dash her own child's brains out, for example, also plays into this idea of her being in some way abnormal.

Lois Tyson argues that 'Women's allegiance to men from their own [background] always supersedes their allegiance to women from different classes.'[11] Women remain isolated from each other because of this: they are prevented from making significant changes because of their allegiance to their husbands, fathers and brothers. They have no strength in numbers. Lady Macbeth has no real way to enact her arguably feminist plans by herself because she is kept isolated from other women during the course of the play. There is evidence she knows, and exists in a similar sphere to, other women, but their relationships are not as close as those she has with men – epitomised in the line 'the Thane of Fife had a wife. Where is she now?' When the only other named female character disappears (Lady Macduff), Lady Macbeth's knowledge and understanding of the other women in her sphere is so limited that she is not aware of what her husband has done. The only way she is able to enact her plans is to manipulate her husband, Macbeth, to commit regicide and thus claim the crown.

In the nineteenth century, Sarah Siddons, who played Lady Macbeth in a theatre production, wrote of the character that she was 'a woman in whose bosom the passion of ambition has almost obliterated all the characteristics of human nature.'[12] This is fascinating. It is not her femininity that has vanished, but her entire human nature. It arguably makes Lady Macbeth's downfall less about her as a woman, per se, but more about her as a human with 'vaulting

---

11.  Lois Tyson, *Critical Theory Today: A User-Friendly Guide*, (New York: Taylor & Francis Group, 2006).

12.  Sarah Siddons and Sandra M. Gilbert, 'Unsex Me Here': Lady Macbeth's 'Hell Broth', https://www.bl.uk/shakespeare/articles/unsex-me-here-lady-macbeths-hell-broth.

ambition'. This in itself is interesting when read through a feminist lens, as Lady Macbeth's actions here are not driven by the fact that she is a woman, or that it is her acting against her role as a woman, but instead that she has agency, ambition and drive as a human first and foremost, and it is this innate human drive that leads to the destruction of her human nature, extra to her status as a woman.

Lady Macbeth, in asking to be 'unsex[ed]', is a woman trying to break free of her prescribed gender roles. In doing so, Shakespeare is arguably opening up a discussion of what women and, ultimately, people, are capable of. Is Shakespeare using Lady Macbeth's words and actions here to demonstrate the result of her frustrations with her supposed natural limits? The fact that we ask ourselves these questions demonstrates the skill of Shakespeare as a writer. He has not, in Lady Macbeth, written a stock villain. In fact, there are many points in the play where an audience feels genuine sympathy for her, particularly in her most vulnerable moment – the sleepwalking scene – and when she attempts in vain to quell the anxieties of her husband after the appearance of Banquo's ghost.

However, at this point in the play we see a much more driven and cold Lady Macbeth who asks the spirits to fill her 'from the crown to the toe, top-full / Of direst cruelty.' In this quotation the word 'direst' perhaps suggests that her ambition is at odds with her gender – or, indeed, society's perception of her gender. In order to become the superlative, she must reject her gender role – and this rejection of gender roles is seen as 'other'. Her rejection of society's expectations of her is done in a bid to gain power – and will ultimately become her downfall.

Caroline Cakebread argues that 'Lady Macbeth's singular "raison d'être" is to overcome "the scruples of her ambitious yet tender-minded husband… she is ready to sacrifice even her womanliness to her murderous intention".[13] Lady Macbeth will stop at nothing, regardless of her gender, to achieve her goals, and this summarises Shakespeare's presentation of Lady Macbeth: she is absolutely focused on the outcome of becoming queen to Macbeth's king and will leave no stone unturned.

However, a feminist interpretation of *Macbeth* also allows us to examine the male characters through a feminist lens. This is explored further in Chapter 16.

### Scene analysis: Act I, Scene v

The scene opens with Lady Macbeth reading a letter she has received from Macbeth, detailing his escapades and endeavours in battle and his subsequent fateful meeting with the witches. This allows Shakespeare to let the audience dip into the relationship between these two characters, and also frames Lady

---

13.  Caroline Cakebread, 'Macbeth and Feminism', https://studylib.net/doc/8008889/macbeth-and-feminism-dr.-caroline-cakebread-shakespeare-s.

Macbeth in the context of her relationship with her husband before we find out anything about her as an individual.

Shakespeare makes a very clear statement in Macbeth's letter about the nature of the relationship between the Thane and his wife. Macbeth writes that he wanted to tell her the news as soon as he could because she is his 'dearest partner of greatness'. She is his ally; he can confide in her and treats her as his equal. This is vital to understand, because Macbeth's later actions are carried out following Lady Macbeth's command and his belief and trust in her. Shakespeare is perhaps hinting at the fact that the relationship between the two characters is not necessarily typical of prescribed societal gender roles: Lady Macbeth is treated as more of an equal to her husband, rather than expected to be subservient and submissive.

### 'SHALT BE WHAT THOU ART PROMISED'

Macbeth, in his letter, is already assuming that he will become king because the witches' prophecy that he will become Thane of Cawdor has already come to pass. This perhaps plants the seed in Lady Macbeth's mind that the crown of Scotland should rightfully pass to her husband – a sentiment echoed in her own first line of the play where she decrees that Macbeth 'shalt be / What thou art promised.' The fact that Shakespeare has Lady Macbeth make such a firm and concrete statement introduces the audience immediately to her drive, ambition and thirst to get what she wants in life. Put simply, Shakespeare has summarised Lady Macbeth's core purpose: to push her husband on to the role she believes he deserves.

### 'TOO FULL O'TH' MILK OF HUMAN KINDNESS'

However, in the next line Shakespeare demonstrates that Lady Macbeth is devoid of belief in her husband's own drive to become king, and it is this lack of confidence that later causes Lady Macbeth to plan the murder of King Duncan. By using the metaphor that Macbeth is 'too full o'th' milk of human kindness', Lady Macbeth is suggesting that Macbeth's compassionate nature might dull his ambition and drive. It is interesting to note Shakespeare's use of 'milk' here. The role of the woman in a household would have been to nurture and feed the children. By suggesting that Macbeth is 'too full' of this symbol of femininity, Lady Macbeth might feel she already has more masculine qualities than Macbeth, but also that he is more feminine and therefore, perhaps, weaker.

Lady Macbeth's sense of control over her husband is already clear in the opening of the scene, when she encourages her husband to return home soon so that she can 'pour [her] spirits in [his] ear'. Almost immediately on hearing about the witches' prophecies, Lady Macbeth has already resolved to help her husband get what she thinks is rightfully his – and wants to waste no time in elevating him to the position of king.

### 'THE RAVEN HIMSELF IS HOARSE'

Upon discovering that both Macbeth and King Duncan are on their way back to the castle, Lady Macbeth declares that 'the raven himself is hoarse'. The raven is a harbinger of death[14] – in other words, Shakespeare is foreshadowing the forthcoming death of King Duncan. Ravens are, traditionally, carrion birds and as a result are often associated with loss and bad omens. They are associated with the dead and with lost souls. Not only that, but in world folklore they not only portend death but also more specifically unpleasant deaths. In Swedish folklore, ravens represent the ghosts of murdered people. In German stories, ravens represent lost and damned souls.[15] Additionally, as a talking bird, ravens have come to symbolise prophecy and insight. By specifically selecting a raven out of all the carrion birds he might have chosen, Shakespeare may be linking Lady Macbeth's plans specifically to the actions of the witches: already, Macbeth's and Lady Macbeth's fates are being inextricably linked to the prophecies of the witches.

Much of Lady Macbeth's soliloquy here is focused upon her desire to shed her feminine qualities and become more masculinised. It is pertinent that, at the start of this section of her speech, Lady Macbeth calls on 'spirits'. This is, arguably, an allusion to witches and witchcraft, and shows that Lady Macbeth is willing to transcend nature in order to get what she wants. The ease with which Lady Macbeth immediately invites the subversion of the natural order is symptomatic of the reason why, later, her plans fall apart: those who seek to disrupt the natural order of the Great Chain of Being will be punished for doing so.

### 'UNSEX ME HERE'

The phrase 'unsex me here' often meets with interpretations by students that can hamper their broader understanding of Lady Macbeth's and Shakespeare's presentation of gender. The most common misunderstandings heard in the classroom are either around the idea that perhaps Lady Macbeth is transgender and wishes to transition to live as a man, or, perhaps, that she is rejecting her gender altogether. Neither of these interpretations is true.

Women were typically believed to be gentle, soft and subservient. Because Lady Macbeth feels her husband has too many of these feminine qualities already, she is asking to be given more of the qualities thought to be masculine and tough. Any aspect of her character that she feels will stand in the way of her plan to kill King Duncan and have Macbeth take the crown in his place must

---

14. Ed. Sandra Clark and Pamela Mason, *The Arden Shakespeare: Macbeth*, (London: Bloomsbury, 2015), p. 156.

15. Linda Ursin, 'Raven Myths and Folklore', https://lindaursin.net/raven-myths-folklore-and-spirit-animal-info/.

be shed. For example, where she fears that she might feel guilt for her actions, she asks the spirits to 'Stop up th'access and passage to remorse' so that she can pursue her plan without distractions.

Shakespeare revisits the image of milk – Lady Macbeth asks the spirits to 'take [her] milk for gall'. This request to have her milk replaced with poison is another indicator that Lady Macbeth does not believe she is capable of conducting her plans whilst having feminine qualities. It is also suggestive of the lengths Lady Macbeth will go to, and shows her determination to see her husband on the throne. By suggesting that she would replace the way she can feed potential children with something so poisonous, she shows she will stop at nothing to get her own way for herself and her husband: she places their own success above all else.

### 'PALL THEE IN THE DUNNEST SMOKE OF HELL'
Shakespeare also continues to explore the theme, and symbolism, of darkness. Lady Macbeth asks for 'thick night' to 'Pall thee in the dunnest smoke of hell'. She is asking for her forthcoming actions to be hidden away from sight, but the darkness also metaphorically represents the evil deeds she and Macbeth are about to enact.

Additionally, this invitation of darkness alongside being hidden from view (she asks for the heavens not to 'peep through the blanket of the dark') does hint at Lady Macbeth's consideration of how she will be viewed for her plans, especially by God. This perhaps suggests that Lady Macbeth has not completely lost her sense of morality, and feeds in, subtly at this point, to her later unravelling and overwhelming guilt at her actions; these smaller, less obvious moments of subtext show us how multi-faceted she really is.

### 'GREAT GLAMIS, WORTHY CAWDOR'
Next, as we know, Macbeth enters, and Lady Macbeth is immediately obsequious in her assumed servitude. She welcomes him as 'Great Glamis, worthy Cawdor, / Greater than both, by the all-hail hereafter'. This flattery is manipulative and shrewd on her part: she is encouraging her husband to be more susceptible to her plans and manipulation by charming him first.

This is not a dissimilar tactic to the one taken by the witches, and further solidifies the link between Lady Macbeth and the three weïrd sisters. By 'hailing' her husband here, Shakespeare has Lady Macbeth's words echo those of his first meeting with the witches. As an audience, we know Macbeth was rapt by their words and their flattery of him: his wife's similar actions have the same effect on him here.

### 'LOOK LIKE THE INNOCENT FLOWER, BUT BE THE SERPENT UNDER'T'
Much of Lady Macbeth's subsequent speech relates directly to the concept of

duplicity. When she first mentions her plan for Macbeth to murder the King, she scolds her husband when his face visibly shows his shock: 'Your face… is as a book'. Her next lines are schooling him in how she believes he ought to behave: that when King Duncan visits, Macbeth should 'bear welcome in [his] eye, [his] hand, [his] tongue'. She also calls for him to 'look like the innocent flower / But be the serpent under't.' This, of course, implies that she believes Macbeth ought to look innocent and gentle, but, beneath the surface, be serpentine and poisonous.

The idea of the serpent is an allusion to the biblical story of Adam and Eve, where Eve was tempted into committing original sin by the Devil, disguised as a snake. In the Bible, Eve commits original sin by eating the fruit from the tree of knowledge. By Eve, and then Adam, eating from the tree, they invite more wickedness to enter the world. In a similar way, Lady Macbeth, by giving into temptation and encouraging Macbeth to commit regicide, is inviting further crime. Adam and Eve are rejected from the Garden of Eden for their sin. Likewise, it could be seen that Macbeth and Lady Macbeth's downfall has its root in this first crime they commit, mirroring the same fall from grace experienced by Adam and Eve. Eve is blamed for the downfall of humanity because she incited the sin they both committed, just as it is Lady Macbeth, as Shakespeare's 'Eve' figure, who persuades her husband to commit such a heinous crime. She therefore must be similarly punished.

There is some argument that these lines have a third, and significant, foundation: one which lies with the discovery and foiling of the Gunpowder Plot. To commemorate the fact that the plot was not successful, King James I had a coin created which showed a snake hiding amongst a patch of flowers. This in itself was metaphorical; the snake represented the conspirators.[16] It is likely that a contemporary audience, watching *Macbeth* just a year after the Gunpowder Plot, would have immediately recognised the weight of Shakespeare making such an allusion.

Additionally, the coin bore the Latin inscription: 'DETECTVS. QVI. LATVIT. S.C.', which translated means 'he who concealed himself is detected. By order of the Senate.'[17] This also echoes the plot of *Macbeth*: whilst Macbeth and his wife attempt to conceal their actions by behaving in this duplicitous, serpentine way, they cannot get away with their crimes, unhindered, forever. Their attempts to conceal their actions are detected by the rightful lawmakers and rulers of the country. Shakespeare again is alluding to the fact that crimes of this magnitude cannot and will not go unpunished.

---

16. British Library, 'Gunpowder Plot medal', https://www.bl.uk/collection-items/gunpowder-plot-medal.

17. Ibid.

Macbeth's remaining morality is clear in this scene: whilst Lady Macbeth has been impressive in her persuasion and rhetoric up until this point, Macbeth's comment that 'We will speak further' shows that he is still unconvinced. However, Lady Macbeth is quick to quell his anxieties and continues to push her agenda in her closing line: 'Leave all the rest to me.'

## Lady Macbeth at a glance

## RESOURCE 5.1

Representative of death – carrion birds, but they are also symbolic of prophecy, the ghosts of murdered people, and lost souls. Specifically links to the murder of Duncan but also the witches' prophecies.

Not 'King' Duncan, just Duncan. This suggests she has already mentally stripped him of his crown and bestowed it upon Macbeth.

Lady Macbeth is calling on the spirits to make her murderous, tough and free from guilt or pity for King Duncan. It is almost as if she is asking for the characteristics she would need to murder the king herself.

**LADY MACBETH**
The raven himself is hoarse
That croaks the fatal entrance of Duncan
Under my battlements. Come, you spirits
That tend on mortal thoughts, unsex me here,
And fill me from the crown to the toe, top-full
Of direst cruelty. Make thick my blood,
Stop up th'access and passage to remorse,
That no compunctious visitings of nature
Shake my fell purpose, nor keep peace between
Th'effect and it. Come to my woman's breasts,
And take my milk for gall, you murdering ministers,
Wherever, in your sightless substances,
You wait on nature's mischief. Come thick night,
And pall thee in the dunnest smoke of hell,
That my keen knife see not the wound it makes,
Nor heaven peep through the blanket of the dark
To cry 'Hold, hold'.

The possessive pronoun reflects Lady Macbeth's position running her household, but also the fact that this is her plan.

The crown of her head, but also possibly referring to the literal crown she is determined to wear.

Not a desire to become masculine, but to have her excessively 'womanly' attributes, such as compassion, supressed, so that she is able to act without guilt.

Alliterative 'm' sound is quite threatening and snarling, demonstrating her attitude here.

Seeking her milk to be replaced with bitter poison – bringing death where she should give life. This is symptomatic of her approach in the remainder of the play.

This suggests she is less worried about the reaction of God and the Heavens, and more worried that the Heavens will try to convince her not to go through with the plan.

Does not want her deeds to be known, or seen, by anyone – and especially not heaven.

Shakespeare is again referring to literal darkness alongside metaphorically dark deeds and thoughts.

## How?

## Reviewing the Big Questions

Whilst the Big Questions are a useful snapshot of each lesson, they do not encourage students' long-term knowledge retrieval. It is therefore important to revisit the Big Questions from the unit of work so far: and this is how Lesson 5 begins.

Provide students with the Big Questions covered so far. In silence, students should capture everything they can say to answer each question. This allows you to see individual students' progress over time and check their knowledge retrieval. Then, students should be encouraged to go around the class and talk to their peers, filling in missing knowledge in a different coloured pen. Finally, as a class, talk through the Big Questions, teasing out the core knowledge for each section. This allows you to identify any gaps in knowledge that will need revisiting in future lessons as well as misconceptions that need addressing.

## Retrieval

It is advisable to follow up this activity with a short, ten-question knowledge retrieval quiz which can be self-marked and gives immediate feedback to students on their progress so far.

An example of the ten knowledge retrieval questions might be:

1. Who does King Duncan name the Prince of Cumberland in Act I, Scene iv?
2. Complete the line: 'Stars, hide your fires, / Let not light see _____.'
3. What does the quotation above tell you about Macbeth at this point in the play?
4. What is the word used to describe a male dominated society?
5. How do we know King James was interested in witches and witchcraft?
6. What three prophecies do the witches give Macbeth?
7. What three prophecies do the witches give Banquo?
8. What was the Gunpowder Plot?
9. Why is the Gunpowder Plot relevant to *Macbeth*?
10. What was the role of women like in Shakespearean times?

## Pre-reading activities

When we read Act I, Scene v, there are two key speeches that stand out as important to the audience. The first is Lady Macbeth's opening speech, having read the letter from her husband. The second is her later monologue where she first calls for the tenacity to persuade her husband to commit regicide, and then begins to unfurl her Machiavellian plan when she speaks to Macbeth.

It is interesting, though, to consider pre-reading activities before discovering more about Lady Macbeth. Often, students' initial expectations of Lady Macbeth are linked to their existing contextual knowledge about 'typical' women. However, this pre-reading discussion provides the perfect opportunity to flesh out their understanding and to consider that Lady Macbeth may be more complex and multifaceted than this. It is true to say that, where students have had previous exposure to Shakespeare's strong female characters (Beatrice in *Much Ado About Nothing* and Hermia in *A Midsummer Night's Dream* are both popular Key Stage 3 texts), they may already have a broader appreciation of who Lady Macbeth will be.

When I pre-read this scene with students, I often explain to them the narrative that Macbeth has written to Lady Macbeth detailing his victories in battle, the witches' prophecies and the fact that King Duncan has bestowed upon him the title Thane of Cawdor. We then consider, using contextual knowledge, how Lady Macbeth might react to this news. It is important that when pre-reading like this we do not, as teachers, end up asking students to play 'guess what's in my head'. By helping students, through questioning, to tie their predictions back to their contextual knowledge, there are really valuable points made here relating to how a contemporary audience would react to Lady Macbeth. They, too, would likely be expecting to see a subservient woman living in a patriarchal society, who would be looking to support her husband in his endeavours without playing an active role in securing them.

## Reading the scene

Next, it is advisable to read the scene in its entirety, clarifying vocabulary and meaning whilst reading. Having an overview of the scene before looking at Lady Macbeth's monologues in more detail is important, as students need to see and understand what Lady Macbeth's ultimate goal is in the scene: to persuade her husband to kill King Duncan.

The following cold-reading prompt questions might be useful:

1. What does Macbeth tell Lady Macbeth in his letter to her?
2. What does Lady Macbeth want to happen as a result of the letter?
3. What is it about Macbeth's nature that worries Lady Macbeth?
4. Who is arriving at the castle tonight?
5. What does Lady Macbeth plan to do to them?
6. How does Lady Macbeth want Macbeth to behave? Why?

## Guided analysis

It is time, next, to focus on Lady Macbeth's monologues to help students establish an answer to the Big Question 'Who is Lady Macbeth?' Activities such as the one you can see in Resource 5.2 can help students develop independence and resilience when dealing with Shakespeare's often complex language. This means that the analysis and close consideration of the scene is scaffolded, giving access for pupils to Shakespeare's original language: a vital skill for the exam, but also important with regard to cultural capital, giving students access to the rich and striking language used by Shakespeare.

## RESOURCE 5.2

**LADY MACBETH**

The raven himself is hoarse
That croaks the fatal entrance of Duncan
Under my battlements. Come, you spirits
That tend on mortal thoughts, unsex me here,
And fill me from the crown to the toe, top-full
Of direst cruelty. Make thick my blood,
Stop up th'access and passage to remorse,
That no compunctious visitings of nature
Shake my fell purpose, nor keep peace between
Th'effect and it. Come to my woman's breasts,
And take my milk for gall, you murdering ministers,
Wherever, in your sightless substances,
You wait on nature's mischief. Come thick night,
And pall thee in the dunnest smoke of hell,
That my keen knife see not the wound it makes,
Nor heaven peep through the blanket of the dark
To cry 'Hold, hold'.

1. What does a raven symbolise?
2. What is Lady Macbeth saying will happen to Duncan once he arrives at the castle?
3. What is Lady Macbeth calling upon and how would a Shakespearean audience react to this?
4. What is Lady Macbeth asking for and why is it necessary for her to do so? Consider the historical context.
5. Why does Lady Macbeth want to be filled with cruelty? How does this go against the conventions of the stereotypical role of women?
6. What is 'remorse'? Why is Lady Macbeth asking for this to be stopped?
7. What are the connotations of 'milk'? Why does Lady Macbeth ask for her milk to turn bitter and poisonous?
8. Lady Macbeth is asking for darkness here so that no one can see her evil deeds. How is this similar to Macbeth in Act I, Scene iv?
9. Why is it important that heaven 'cannot peep through the blanket of the dark'? How is religious imagery used here?
10. When she says 'Hold, hold', what, in particular, is Lady Macbeth afraid of?

This resource could be tackled individually, in pairs or small groups, but I believe it is important for students to build some confidence, and this activity is designed to remove the possibility of overreliance on the teacher. The earlier we can breed a sense that students can, do and will understand and engage with Shakespeare, the more enjoyable they will find the rest of their study, even if they later find that the 'going gets tough' with regard to the concepts explored in the text.

### Revisiting the light and dark tracker

Through the activities in the lesson up until this point, it will hopefully have become clear to students – or certainly will be through the next activity – that Shakespeare continues to play with the ideas of light and darkness in order to convey the evil deeds Lady Macbeth has planned. At this point, invite students to revisit the light and dark tracker introduced in Chapter 4. Ask students to select two or three quotations from Act I, Scene v which illustrate Shakespeare's use of light and, in particular in this scene, imagery focused on darkness. Students may choose the following quotations:

- 'Come thick night, / And pall thee in the dunnest smoke of hell'.
- 'That my keen knife see not the wound it makes, / Nor heaven peep through the blanket of the dark / To cry, "Hold, hold".'
- 'O never / Shall sun that morrow see.'

## Exploration through oracy

Act I, Scene v often encourages students to broaden their gaze with regard to the roles of men and women in Shakespearean society. It is therefore important to allow students the opportunity to discuss the relationship between the Macbeths. There are a number of ways this task could run. However, I have found success running it as follows.

In small groups, students should be given one character: either Lady Macbeth or Macbeth. Using evidence from the play so far, but in particular Act I, Scenes iv and v, students should prepare a range of points they could use to argue that their character is the most powerful, dangerous, deceptive and manipulative. They should also consider whether they feel their character is united with their spouse in terms of their plan going forward, or whether the two are more divided.

Once students have had some preparation time, which should include seeking out quotations that support their arguments, they should have the opportunity to debate. This could be done either in paired groups or as a whole class, with the 'Macbeth' and 'Lady Macbeth' groups working together.

Having had a chance to rehearse their ideas verbally, the writing becomes more straightforward. Therefore, the lesson should end with students answering the Big Questions, using quotations, and perhaps also using the 'What? How? Why?' model of analysis. It is not even necessary for them to present these ideas in an essay format; the key here is to capture their knowledge, ready to move forward in the next lesson.

## Suggested 'Extra Challenge' activities

- To what extent is Lady Macbeth's eventual weakness a result of a patriarchal portrayal of her gender?
- Caroline Cakebread argues 'Lady Macbeth's singular "raison d'être" is to overcome "the scruples of her ambitious yet tender-minded husband... she is ready to sacrifice even her womanliness to her murderous intention"'.[18] Write a response to this.
- To what extent has the treatment of ambitious women progressed in modern society? Refer to Shakespeare's play(s) in your answer.

## Key vocabulary:

Feminism, patriarchy, duplicity

---

18. Caroline Cakebread, 'Macbeth and Feminism', https://studylib.net/doc/8008889/macbeth-and-feminism-dr.-caroline-cakebread-shakespeare-s.

# CHAPTER 6
## Act I, Scenes vi and vii

*What reasons does Macbeth give for not going ahead with Duncan's murder?*
*How does Lady Macbeth persuade Macbeth to go through with the murder?*

## What?

### The Great Chain of Being

Whilst some elements of Jacobean society are still recognisable in the modern day, the world we live in is very different. Humanity is now in the position to provide scientific explanations for things that happen in our world, underpinning these with rational thought and philosophy. This, of course, was not the case in Shakespeare's time.

The Jacobeans were forced to search for an explanation of the unexplainable through their faith and superstitions. Their doctrines included the accepted belief in 'a divinely ordained great chain of being in which every species of life, including man, had its fixed place in a hierarchical order.'[1] At the top of this hierarchy were all things spiritual, with God placed at the very top. Humans and animals would be positioned near the middle, with rocks and precious minerals at the bottom. This hierarchy could also be seen as a connection, linking the mortal world of Earth to the spiritual world of the heavens. Although many followed Christian beliefs, principles on fate and the role of stars in *mapping* one's fate were still widely believed. The chain was a way of bridging these concepts.

The Great Chain of Being would also contain rankings within its overall hierarchy. Humans themselves, for example, would be ranked: 'a magistrate would be higher than a baker, yet lower than a duke.'[2] Elements of this social

---

1.  Arthur O. Lovejoy, *The Great Chain of Being: The Study of the History of an Idea*, (New Jersey: Transaction Publishers, 2009), p. xvi.

2.  Ed. Mark Morris, *Julius Caesar*, (Cheltenham: Nelson Thornes Ltd, 2003), p. 2.

order still exist today in the form of class systems that have strengthened and weakened over time. While change in modern society is often welcomed and celebrated, however, in Jacobean society change was discouraged; one's place in the hierarchy was set.[3] Disorder and pandemonium would ensue should anyone try to change their position in the world. What is more:

> *Many historians consider beliefs such as the Great Chain of Being as instruments of social control. In a world where immense differences existed between those at the top and those at the bottom, the inequality became more acceptable if it was accompanied by a belief that it was God's will.[4]*

This is particularly profound when applied to *Macbeth*: Duncan's death is lamented by all, and initially no one voices openly their suspicions of Macbeth. With the notable exception of Macduff, they largely see it as right that Macbeth should take the throne. He is accepted because it was natural to obey those who were deemed superior.

## The Divine Right of Kings

Of course, Macbeth should not be accepted because of his superiority. Not only will he throw the Great Chain of Being into disarray by violently changing its modus operandi, but he will also violate the Divine Right of Kings. This 'Divine Right' stemmed from the belief that the monarch's 'office derived its power from God and passed to them as their inheritance'.[5] In other words, a monarch was seen as God's spokesperson on Earth, the voice of the great 'I am'. They had been chosen to rule by God, a concept deriving from the Great Chain of Being itself. The monarch would have been the closest human to God in terms of the hierarchy they were a part of, explaining why the power they held was so accepted.

In Act I, Scene vii, Macbeth fears the consequences his actions may bring about. He knows that by killing Duncan he is robbing Earth of God's voice. His crime will not only be an act of treason, but a serious act of sin. With the promise of power and Lady Macbeth's voice in his ear, Macbeth is persuaded to commit the murder. First, however, Duncan is charmed by the Macbeths in a show of false adoration.

---

3.  Ed. Mark Morris, *Julius Caesar*, (Cheltenham: Nelson Thornes Ltd, 2003), p. 2.
4.  Ibid.
5.  Contance Jordan, *Shakespeare's Monarchies: Ruler and Subject in the Romances*, (New York, Cornell University Press, 1997), p. 20.

## Scene analysis: Act I, Scene vi

### THE 'TEMPLE-HAUNTING MARTLET'

Duncan arrives at Macbeth's castle, stating it 'hath a pleasant seat'. Shakespeare clearly shows audiences how Duncan is taken in by appearances; the location of the castle may be attractive, yet lurking behind its seemingly gracious walls is a distortion of truth which the Macbeths will fully exploit in order to pull the King further into their web of lies. Duncan is not a proficient judge of character. Macbeth has pledged his allegiance to his King, but his words of fidelity are hollow, tainted by the promise of more power. Macbeth and Lady Macbeth will say what they have to say to keep their true plans inconspicuous, as Duncan remains blissfully unaware of what they are plotting.

Banquo agrees with Duncan's view of the castle, and what is interesting to note is his comment regarding the presence of a 'temple-haunting martlet', a common house bird which has built its nests in the protrusions of Macbeth's castle walls. The air and breeze, Banquo suggests, are inviting, referred to as 'heaven's breath'. The very mention of 'heaven' conjures images of paradise and ecstasy, a far cry from the corruption and sin which secretly and silently begin to swell within Macbeth's household. This bird is a 'guest of summer', a time of nourishment and vitality, yet Lady Macbeth's proclamation that 'the raven himself is hoarse / That croaks the fatal entrance of Duncan' still rings in the ears of the audience. The raven, which connects the material world with the world of spirits, possesses none of the innocence and sweet purity of the common house bird.

As such, this dualism draws our attention to the fact that Macbeth's castle appears to be safe and secure when in actual fact it is anything but. Even Banquo is taken in by the duplicity which seems to have already embedded itself in the very foundations of the castle by confirming 'The air is delicate'. For Lady Macbeth's schemes to work, it is imperative that Duncan accepts the trust which emanates from her fakery; Banquo unwittingly contributes to the Macbeths' deception by buying into this trust, too.

But why does Shakespeare choose Banquo to confirm the castle is a safe and favourable place? Clearly, he aims to show his audience why Duncan is deceived by Macbeth. If Banquo, a man characterised by nobility and virtue, is unable to spot the mendacity of the Macbeths' actions, then others have little chance of doing the same. As a result, Banquo blinds Duncan to the threat to his life and is unwittingly complicit in lulling his king into a false sense of security. Of course, Banquo will be castigated for this lack of awareness later in the play when he is the one to fall victim to Macbeth's bloodthirsty ferocity.

At this point, Lady Macbeth enters to beguile King Duncan, charming him with an air of sycophancy when she greets him. Her exchange with the king is incredibly polite; both characters flatter the other to the point where they are excruciatingly courteous. Duncan acknowledges 'The love that follows us, sometime is our trouble, / Which still we thank as love', meaning he has been troubled by the lengths his subjects have gone to in the past out of their love for him, and yet despite that trouble, he still thanks them for that love they have shown. He follows this with 'Herein I teach you / How you shall bid God yield us for your pains, / And thank us for your trouble.' Notably, Duncan asks Lady Macbeth to accept the trouble he has caused her by arriving at the castle on a whim. He is there as an act of love and she should accept this, just as Duncan does with his subjects. It is, after all, the royal thing to do. It goes without saying that Lady Macbeth will not see Duncan's arrival as trouble. His appearance signals opportunity, and the events that follow will not happen fortuitously; Lady Macbeth knows that she must act the humble host if she is to maintain Duncan's trust and appreciation.

### 'TWICE DONE, AND THEN DONE DOUBLE'

This humility takes the form of Lady Macbeth's assumed subservience; she places herself and Macbeth in an inferior position which is almost hyperbolic in its obsequiousness. Lady Macbeth ostensibly denounces her efforts to accommodate Duncan, stating that even if they were twice doubled, they would still not match the prodigious honour he has brought to their home. Lady Macbeth's use of the word 'double' could also act as a subtle link to the evil of the witches; they repeatedly echo 'double' in the spells they cast in Act IV, Scene i. Once again, references to duality come to the forefront, reminding us that appearances can be deceiving.

This duality continues to suffuse the remainder of this scene's dialogue when Lady Macbeth informs Duncan that she and her husband will always pray for him because of the honours the King has bestowed upon them. Lady Macbeth's reference to 'hermits' means that, 'because of their tremendous feelings of gratitude, she and her husband will pray so hard for Duncan that his almsmen will be able to stop praying.'[6] Her acknowledgement of prayer makes her conspiratorial desires all the more shocking. Like her husband, who will later cower under his inability to say 'Amen' and complete the prayer of those 'who lie i'the second chamber', Lady Macbeth has revealed to the audience through her dialogue that she knows there is a God, and still she blatantly chooses to shun God's will for her own selfish purposes.

---

6.    Amanda Mabillard, 'Macbeth Glossary', Shakespeare Online, (2000), http://
      www.shakespeare-online.com/plays/macbeth/macbethglossary/macbeth1_1/
      macbethglos_hermits.html.

Duncan seems to compete with Lady Macbeth as to who can self-deprecate the most. He asks Lady Macbeth where her husband can be found, expressing his wish to have ridden ahead of Macbeth on the journey home in order to be able to greet him at his castle upon his arrival. Duncan's aim to be Macbeth's 'purveyor' ('A steward who would go ahead to organise things for royal visits'[7]) means that, like Lady Macbeth before him, he has placed himself in a position of inferiority.

Perhaps Duncan's desire to humbly lower himself is one borne out of fear regarding the fragility of his reign. He feels the need to symbolically serve Macbeth because Macbeth is the one who saved him from his own inadequacy. One could argue that Duncan is trying to buy Macbeth's continued loyalty by treating him like royalty himself. If he is to avoid further betrayal, he must secure the trust of those closest to him in order to survive, something he ultimately fails to do.

Act I, Scene vi ends with Lady Macbeth turning the tables yet again in this overwhelmingly polite exchange, saying it is her duty to serve her King and, as his servant, offer everything they own to him. These words of devotion and obedience are hollow; Lady Macbeth offers Duncan everything they have and yet they are plotting to steal the one thing they *cannot* have, as dictated by the Great Chain of Being and the Divine Right of Kings. Lady Macbeth takes Duncan to see Macbeth, the threat of impending doom and the promise of more violence hanging in the air.

## Scene analysis: Act I, Scene vii

From public scenes of adoration to the private world of sinister collusion, Shakespeare moves his focus away from Duncan to the inner conflict raging within Macbeth who enters, addled and perplexed at the ominous opportunities set out before him. Unlike the previous exchange where audiences witness Lady Macbeth's public fawning over Duncan, this scene is quieter and much more secretive as Shakespeare delves fully into the turmoil felt by a man placed in an impossible position. Shakespeare's constant switching between the Macbeths' public façade and their more authentic, delusory selves (revealed away from prying eyes) mirrors his wider exploration of appearance versus reality in the play.

The scene opens with Macbeth's first extended soliloquy; as such, it is a real chance for audiences to understand what exactly is going on in his mind, away from everyone else and, more importantly, away from Lady Macbeth, whose presence seems to make Macbeth unreliable; she seems to render him inarticulate when he tries to express how he truly feels. We do not know

---

7.  Ed. John Seeley, *Heinemann Shakespeare: Macbeth*, (Harlow: Heinemann, 2010), p. 36.

whether Macbeth truly believes what he is doing and saying or whether he has been swayed by his wife's persistence and overbearing dominance to do what she wants him to do. What is important to note before we look at the soliloquy itself is Macbeth's self-imposed segregation from Duncan. We never see the two characters together after Act I, Scene iv, a fact which exposes his inability to appear the loyal servant Lady Macbeth has made him out to be. He cannot bear to be around his King, the man he has fought for, the man he would die for. His absence from the celebrations is indicative of a man at war with himself.

### 'IF IT WERE DONE, WHEN 'TIS DONE'

The scene begins, and we find Macbeth exploring the morality and immorality of regicide. He ponders the advantages and disadvantages of killing Duncan, coming to the conclusion that 'If it were done, when 'tis done, then 'twere well / It were done quickly', as if the quick speed of such an act would somehow make it acceptable. Although Macbeth considers the possibility that everything will be over and done with if the murder is completed quickly, audiences are still aware that he is subtly attempting to separate himself from the act. Shakespeare does this by having Macbeth refuse to explicitly state what it is he is planning to do, referring to the event of Duncan's death only as 'it'.[8]

With this in mind, it is no surprise that Macbeth spends most of his soliloquy convincing himself not to go through with Duncan's murder. This is the first time he appears alone on stage; Lady Macbeth is not present to manipulate his thoughts and so we learn he is hesitant and unsure because he fears the consequences of such an act.

Macbeth freely admits that if he had the ability to kill the King with the knowledge that there would be no consequences, then he would do it, risking his soul and the afterlife in the process. Yet this in itself is bizarre. Macbeth is willing to risk an afterlife of condemnation and God's denunciation and yet is uneasy at the prospect of facing the repercussions of his actions in his current life. Macbeth is deliberating whether to kill the King, and yet he does not fear God's wrath or judgement, instead focusing on the immediacy of what would happen if he went through with Duncan's murder.

The consequences that Macbeth fears seem to manifest themselves in the form of the threat of further violence. He observes that 'we but teach / Bloody instructions, which, being taught, return / To plague th'inventor.' This is not the first time he will acknowledge that one act of violence can become an unstoppable onslaught of bloodshed and savagery. One may wonder why

---

8.   Neil Bowen, Neil Jones, Michael Meally and Katherine Mortimore, *The Art of Drama Volume 2: Macbeth GCSE & Beyond*, (Bristol, Peripeteia Press, 2019), p. 121.

this is the case, and yet the answer is deceptively simple. Violence is not a last resort; it is often the first resort because it is easy to commit. Macbeth wonders whether he will suffer what he has inflicted upon Duncan, and in doing so renders himself vulnerable before he has even done anything. Macbeth is more than capable of committing despicable acts of violence and yet in this moment he seems wary of it. In contemplating the murder of Duncan, he perhaps realises that in killing the king to become king himself he will invite potential successors to commit equally heinous crimes against the crown when he is sitting on the throne himself.

### 'HE'S HERE IN DOUBLE TRUST'

Macbeth switches his thoughts from the consequences of violent actions to seeking reasons not to go through with 'it' in the first place. This rapid transition, in a way, is indicative of the conflict which is turbulent within him. He recognises Duncan is here in 'double trust', placing himself in the roles of 'his kinsman, and his subject' as well as his 'host, / Who should against his murderer shut the door'. Macbeth's relationship with the King is one of devotion and familiarity. Firstly, he calls himself 'kinsman', a word taken from the Old English 'cynn' meaning 'family' and 'race'.[9] Of course, this could also be an allusion to Shakespeare's source material for *Macbeth*; *Holinshed's Chronicles* tell us 'Duncan and Macbeth are cousins by marriage.'[10]

Macbeth considers it his duty to serve Duncan. By calling himself his 'subject', Macbeth acknowledges he is Duncan's servant. What is compelling about this testimony is that it comes in the scene just after Lady Macbeth also professes to be his servant. The difference, of course, is that Macbeth is genuine and speaks with sincerity, whereas Lady Macbeth does not; her deferential flattery is nothing but a mask to cover her false countenance. We can trust Macbeth because he is alone when he delivers his soliloquy; he has no reason to be false, no one to trick or deceive. His allegiance to his king seems genuine at this moment.

This candour is further explored through Macbeth's exploration of his role as host and the responsibilities that come with it. He says he 'should… shut the door' against anyone who would see harm done to Duncan; it is his job to see the King is safe and secure. Again, his choice of language is telling. The modal verb 'should' tells audiences that Macbeth is well aware of his moral obligations and yet he does not end up fulfilling them for his ill-gotten gains.

9.   Etymonline.com, 'kin', https://www.etymonline.com/word/kin.

10.   Ed. John Drakakis and Dale Townshend, *Macbeth: A Critical Reader*, (London: Bloomsbury, 2013), p. 5.

### 'DUNCAN / HATH BORNE HIS FACULTIES SO MEEK'

Macbeth continues to collate reasons why he should not kill Duncan, switching from examining his internal self and considering the King's character instead. He says, 'Duncan / Hath borne his faculties so meek, hath been / So clear in his great office'. Macbeth recognises that Duncan is a humble leader free of corruption and self-indulgence. This, Macbeth feels, is a reason to celebrate Duncan's kingship, and not to relinquish him of his crown. Although Shakespeare has made it clear that Duncan has his weaknesses as king, he is clearly a dutiful, principled man who possesses no moral ambiguity when it comes to loyalty to his country. Yet Macbeth's comment could also be a subtle acknowledgement of Duncan's instability. Macbeth recognises his kingship is vulnerable; indeed, he spends the beginning of the play fighting to protect it, something he feels he should continue to do.

As Macbeth comes to the end of his soliloquy, he determines how others would react if Duncan did indeed die. The heavenly imagery Macbeth uses to describe how pity for Duncan would spread is in stark contrast to the hellish symbolism which haunts the rest of the play. References to 'heaven's cherubim' combined with the 'angels, trumpet-tongued' suggest Duncan's entrance to heaven will clearly be heralded, whereas Macbeth's would not, his descent to hell an absolute certainty if he makes the choice to go through with the murder. Duncan's death will be mourned by everyone, a clear indication that despite his misgivings he is still respected; the loudest part of the conversation after Duncan's death will be the lamentations over the loss of his good character rather than his kingship.

### 'I HAVE NO SPUR / TO PRICK THE SIDES OF MY INTENT'

The last lines of Macbeth's soliloquy should be noted for the warning he seems to pose to himself. Ambition, a quality which emerges as Macbeth's fatal flaw, is something which should be treated with great care. He freely admits the only reason he would act on his intentions is because ambition drives him to do so ('I have no spur / To prick the sides of my intent, but only / Vaulting ambition, which o'er-leaps itself'). Macbeth is fully aware that ambition breeds impetuosity which, in turn, can lead to tragedy. His 'vulnerabilities – perceptual incapacities, the possibilities for inhumane actions, uncontrollable locations, and erratic movements – all appear in this soliloquy',[11] and yet by its conclusion, he has decided enough is enough and resolves to take charge of the situation in a moment of assertiveness.

---

11. Darlene Farabee, 'A Walking Shadow: Place, Perception and Disorientation in *Macbeth*', *Macbeth: The State of Play*, ed. Ann Thompson, (London: Bloomsbury, 2014), p. 141.

The relatively slow pace of Macbeth's monologue is shattered by the entrance of Lady Macbeth, a force that sweeps into the action of the scene to obliterate any doubts and qualms felt by her husband. Their dialogue is abrupt and expeditious; Macbeth's lack of knowledge as to Duncan's whereabouts is used to create tension as the audience, having spent their time in Macbeth's company, realises that 'he doesn't appear to have a grip on events, let alone a command of them, relying on his wife to keep him informed – "what news?", "hath he asked for me?"'[12] Macbeth's questions are answered with more questions from Lady Macbeth, but whereas Macbeth's are used to gain more information, his wife's are more interrogative, pointed and demanding, designed to drill into his psyche in order to flush out any weaknesses and doubts and eradicate them. Questions such as 'why have you left the chamber?' and 'Know you not he has?' when asked by her husband whether Duncan has asked for him are fraught with accusations of instability and fragility.

### 'WE WILL PROCEED NO FURTHER IN THIS BUSINESS'

Perhaps Macbeth senses these allegations, for he comes across as decisive and determined when he announces firmly, 'we will proceed no further in this business'. His attempt to gain control of the situation is evident from his use of 'we'; he is subtly telling his wife that she will also cease her scheming and devising and respect his decision. It is meant to be a moment of authority, a moment of force, and yet it is somewhat undermined by the subsequent explanation Macbeth feels he has to offer, as if his word alone is not enough to enable Lady Macbeth to accept what he has said.

Macbeth argues that he has 'bought / Golden opinions' from others because of his actions; Duncan's subsequent love and adoration for him are clearly mirrored in others, and Macbeth believes he should bask in the glory of this rather than cast these judgements of his character aside so quickly. One may wonder if Macbeth really believes what he is saying. Yes, he needs to convince Lady Macbeth the plans they have laid out for themselves are not the path they should walk down, yet it sounds as if he is trying to convince himself. Thoughts of power, glory and greatness have already begun to steadily erode his sense of moral duty and obligation to his king, and his resistance to murder seems to have emanated from fear of punishment rather than the firm decision that what he is doing is wrong and against God's will.

With fear of consequence in mind, Macbeth knows he must protect his wife, whom he clearly loves. Earlier in the play he refers to her as his 'dearest partner

---

12. Neil Bowen et al., *The Art of Drama Volume 2: Macbeth GCSE & Beyond*, (Peripeteia Press, 2019), p. 83.

of greatness'. This in itself shows that he not only wants to protect himself, but his wife as well, a fact seemingly lost on Lady Macbeth, who scorns her husband in response to his misgivings at committing such a dreadful act. She knows him well and, as such, knows how to exploit his vulnerabilities. The questions she poses are well aimed and strike with a viciousness Lady Macbeth knows will affect Macbeth; she queries his masculinity through her interrogation, accusing him of being 'drunk' when he made his promises and labelling him a coward now he has thought about the immensity of their desires and what it will take to transform them into a reality.

Lady Macbeth knows that Macbeth cannot ignore his temptations. She alludes to his wishes to be king throughout her accosting of him, asking whether he would seek that which 'thou esteem'st the ornament of life' or 'live a coward': a barbed attack on Macbeth's machismo. Referring to the crown as 'the ornament of life' is an arresting image. It is life's decoration, which would beautify the Macbeths' lives, embellishing their status and exalting them to new heights of power. From another perspective, one could argue that this choice of words unwittingly and surreptitiously alludes to the fact that their reign would be fragile; the crown is something to be handled with care, and if it is neglected it will break.

## 'WHEN YOU DURST DO IT, THEN YOU WERE A MAN'

What follows is an interesting examination of masculinity and femininity as Macbeth and Lady Macbeth's altercation explores what it means to be a man and a woman. Macbeth counteracts Lady Macbeth's aggravations by begging her to stop, saying 'I dare do all that may become a man, / Who dares do more is none.' He sees it as his duty to protect and serve Duncan, claiming anyone who does any more than that is not really a man at all. Lady Macbeth, of course, disagrees, retorting, 'What beast was't then / That made you break this enterprise to me?', stripping Macbeth not only of his masculinity but also of his humanity. 'Beast' implies something wild, something that cannot be tamed, and perhaps Lady Macbeth wants her husband to believe that she does not know who he is any more, when in reality she clearly does and is using her knowledge of him to her advantage.

Lady Macbeth's tirade continues, the length of her diatribe compared to Macbeth's brief retaliations indicative of who dominates this scene. Her views of what makes a man are clearly different from that of her husband, and she states: 'When you durst do it, then you were a man; / And to be more than what you were, you would / Be so much more the man.' She wants him to be bold, to seize the opportunities that have been set out before him, and refuses to let the fear within Macbeth devastate what they have set their sights upon. The time is right. The stage has been set. Nevertheless, Macbeth has stumbled, and so what follows is a striking challenge to his dedication to their cause.

### 'I... KNOW HOW TENDER 'TIS TO LOVE THE BABE THAT MILKS ME'

Lady Macbeth brazenly declares she would kill a child if she had sworn to her husband that she would do so. Infanticide in itself is the epitome of evil and wickedness, yet it is the grotesque descriptions alluding to the death of innocence and purity which make Lady Macbeth's words so difficult to comprehend. The actions she describes are graphic and explicit in their frankness, and yet she cleverly spins her rhetoric here to convince Macbeth to shun his moral imperative. This scenario is made all the more distressing by the fact she imagines the baby to be smiling as she kills it. Shakespeare here is creating links for an audience between Lady Macbeth and the witches: witches were often believed to commit infanticide and, by Lady Macbeth aligning herself with the same principle, her evil and wicked deeds and visions link her almost irrevocably to the actions of the 'weïrd sisters'.

In a similar episode to her 'unsex me here' speech, Lady Macbeth makes reference to what makes her a woman, rendering her feminine characteristics as qualities that should be dismissed. By killing a child, she is willing to sacrifice her maternal instincts and purge herself of the nurturing traits one would traditionally expect of a mother protecting a child (that is, of course, if Lady Macbeth is talking about her own offspring). Her description of the act of breastfeeding is compassionate and evocative. She *knows* how 'tender' the close link between woman and child can be and yet she would still reject those qualities within her if she had promised Macbeth she would do so: 'If she can thus surrender her sense of what it is to be a woman, Macbeth can surrender his sense of what it is to be a man.'[13]

Shakespeare never reveals whether the child Lady Macbeth refers to is her own and it is never mentioned in the play again. If one looks to history for an explanation, the origin of the child could be explained by the figure of Gruoch of Scotland, wife of the real MacBeth and Lady Macbeth's historical counterpart. Although the exact dates of her life are uncertain, Gruoch was married before marrying MacBeth:

> *Gruoch, as a girl, had been married before she wed MacBeth, to one Gillacomgain, who had actually slain Finlay, MacBeth's father, and made himself Mormaor of Moray in his place. By Gillacomgain, Gruoch had a son, Lulach. Gillacomgain himself was soon killed off by Malcolm the Destroyer. Thereafter MacBeth wed the widow with the infant son.*[14]

---

13. Neil Bowen et al., *The Art of Drama Volume 2: Macbeth GCSE & Beyond*, (Peripeteia Press, 2019), p. 83.

14. Nigel Tranter, *The Story of Scotland*, (Glasgow: Neil Wilson Publishing, 2012), p. 17.

Although MacBeth had his own children by Gruoch, he recognised that Lulach, being Gruoch's eldest son, had a stronger link to the throne, making plans for his step-son to succeed him.[15]

With this in mind, perhaps one could hypothesise that Lady Macbeth's theoretical killing of a child goes deeper than just illustrating that one should keep their promises. Perhaps Lady Macbeth would kill her baby from a previous marriage so that one of their own children could take the throne should her husband request it. It would certainly go some way to explaining why the child is not referred to again, although this is purely conjecture. Other explanations explore the possibilities that the Macbeths have lost a child. There is no real reason, however, why we should expect Shakespeare to offer us an explanation. The child itself does not matter. Instead, Shakespeare wants his audiences to focus on the situation in front of them, the here and now. The child is purely indicative of the lengths Lady Macbeth is prepared to go to in order to enact her plans.

### 'SCREW YOUR COURAGE TO THE STICKING PLACE'

In asking what happens if they fail, Macbeth concedes that his wife is right. He no longer argues back, but seeks reassurance instead. Lady Macbeth is now in full control of the situation, strengthened by the fact that she has a plan to bring about Duncan's demise. By saying 'screw your courage to the sticking place', Lady Macbeth is commanding her husband to find his bravery and fearlessness, concluding they will not fail if he expunges himself of any weaknesses he is deemed to have. Ensuring Duncan's guards are drunk will render the king completely vulnerable and Macbeth and Lady Macbeth will be free to do what they want.

Macbeth is clearly impressed by his wife's fearless nature and commends her by saying 'Bring forth men-children only; / For thy undaunted mettle should compose / Nothing but males.' This in itself is evidence that Macbeth desires masculinity, which is why Lady Macbeth has had such success in persuading her husband to go through with the murder by questioning his. By aiming her vigorous rhetoric at his masculinity, Lady Macbeth is able to quash his doubts in only thirty-six lines,[16] putting to bed his vacillation and coaxing him to fulfil his wants. His new-found determination to go through with the murder is mirrored through Shakespeare's structure of the scene. He is the last person to speak, issuing his wife with instructions to 'mock the time with fairest show' and reiterating that 'False face must hide what the false heart doth know.' After being on the receiving end

---

15. Nigel Tranter, *The Story of Scotland*, (Glasgow: Neil Wilson Publishing, 2012), p. 17.

16. Christopher Mills, 'The relationship between Macbeth and Lady Macbeth', *Critical Essays on Macbeth*, ed. Linda Cookson and Bran Loughrey, (Harlow: Longman Group UK Limited, 1988), p. 52.

of Lady Macbeth's lambasting, Macbeth is keen to reassert his control. The final order given is from him and not his wife. However, whilst Macbeth here seems to reassert control as the patriarch, his words echo those of Lady Macbeth from the last few scenes: he encourages her to look one way and act another, just as she encouraged him to 'look like the innocent flower, / But be the serpent under't.' Despite appearances, Lady Macbeth's dominance is still very much in play.

It is pertinent that 'false' appears twice in the last line of the first act. In a way, this final scene mirrors the very first. Both contain promises of ambiguity and equivocation which will be fulfilled in the ensuing acts. The threat of destructive stratagems, vicious deeds and shameful falsities is no longer a threat. It is a certainty. As Act I comes to its conclusion, Shakespeare promises further chaos and disorder for Scotland and the Macbeths, all of which will be steeped in the blood of royalty.

## Macbeth's doubts at a glance

## RESOURCE 6.1

This is the first time Macbeth appears alone on stage. Lady Macbeth is not here to manipulate his thoughts and so we can trust what he is saying is what he is truly feeling. Macbeth spends the majority of this speech convincing himself not to go through with Duncan's murder.

Macbeth is capable of committing acts of violence as established in Act I, Scene ii and yet here he fears his actions will bring about more violence, but against himself. He is acknowledging that one act of violence can become an unstoppable tide of savagery.

Macbeth believes that Duncan's death would be devastating for the King's subjects. Pity for him will spread quickly and many tears will be shed.

**MACBETH**
If it were done, when 'tis done, then 'twere well
It were done quickly. If th'assassination
Could trammel up the consequence, and catch
With his surcease, success: that but this blow
Might be the be-all and the end-all, here,
But here, upon this bank and shoal of time,
We'd jump the life to come. But in these cases,
We still have judgement here, that we but teach
Bloody instructions, which being taught, return
To plague th'inventor: this even-handed justice
Commends th'ingredience of our poison'd chalice
To our own lips. He's here in double trust:
First, as I am his kinsman and his subject,
Strong both against the deed. Then, as his host,
Who should against his murderer shut the door,
Not bear the knife myself. Besides, this Duncan
Hath borne his faculties so meek, hath been
So clear in his great office, that his virtues
Will plead like angels, trumpet-tongued, against
The deep damnation of his taking off;
And pity, like a naked new-born babe,
Striding the blast, or heaven's cherubim, horsed
Upon the sightless couriers of the air,
Shall blow the horrid deed in every eye,
That tears shall drown the wind. I have no spur
To prick the sides of my intent, but only
Vaulting ambition, which o'er-leaps itself,
And falls on th'other.

Macbeth is concerned about the consequences of committing regicide, saying that he would go through with the act if he knew there would be no repercussions that would affect him.

Macbeth is willing to risk the consequences of the afterlife but is fearful of what will happen in the here and now, perhaps alluding to the chaos and confusion that he knows will ensue if he disrupts the Great Chain of Being.

Macbeth is devoted to King Duncan. As his 'subject' and his 'host', he acknowledges that he should be protecting Duncan from any danger. He should not be the danger himself.

The heavenly imagery Macbeth uses to describe what would happen to Duncan in death juxtaposes the hellish imagery that pervades the rest of the play, especially during Macbeth's reign.

Macbeth considers the dangers of ambition. He ends his soliloquies by stating there is no reason to go through with Duncan's murder except his own ambition. With this thought in mind, he acknowledges that ambition can make people jump into action without thinking, only for them to run into trouble later.

## How?

### Retrieval

'Quiz Quiz Trade' is a way of involving all students and asking them to verbalise the knowledge one requires them to retrieve. Here is how it works:

Each student is provided with a question and an answer on a piece of card or strip of paper. Students are required to visit as many people in the classroom as they possibly can and complete the process. Student A will ask Student B their question. B will try to answer. A will tell them whether they are correct or address any misconceptions B may have. This is the first quiz. B will then ask their question to A, who will do their best to answer. B will, as before, tell them they are correct or give them the right answer. This is the second quiz. A and B will then trade their cards and go and find another person in the room to repeat the process. This process should be completed as many times as possible in the time given.

Seeing as students will be covering Act I, Scenes vi and vii in this lesson, questions asked in the 'Quiz Quiz Trade' would benefit students if they were based on Macbeth's character and the relationship he has with his wife. This will allow students to consider how Shakespeare has presented them to audiences so far before discussing what else we learn about the characters in these pivotal scenes.

You can see some exemplar questions in Resource 6.2. You will need to generate enough questions to allocate one per student.

## RESOURCE 6.2

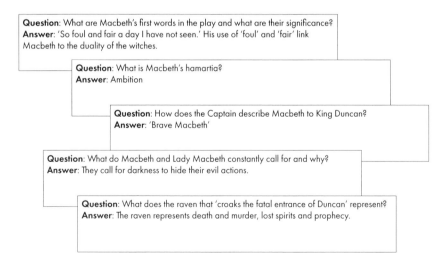

**Question**: What are Macbeth's first words in the play and what are their significance?
**Answer**: 'So foul and fair a day I have not seen.' His use of 'foul' and 'fair' link Macbeth to the duality of the witches.

**Question**: What is Macbeth's hamartia?
**Answer**: Ambition

**Question**: How does the Captain describe Macbeth to King Duncan?
**Answer**: 'Brave Macbeth'

**Question**: What do Macbeth and Lady Macbeth constantly call for and why?
**Answer**: They call for darkness to hide their evil actions.

**Question**: What does the raven that 'croaks the fatal entrance of Duncan' represent?
**Answer**: The raven represents death and murder, lost spirits and prophecy.

One may notice that the answers to these questions are very specific. Students will most likely elaborate on the answers shown here and there are always opportunities to talk about them in further detail after the task is completed. These answers are what I like to call the 'non-negotiables'. Students must know them if they are to have a chance of understanding what happens in the rest of the play. Post-task discussion is vital, particularly for retrieval tasks.

## Pre-reading activities

### BIG QUESTIONS
Once students have clarified and reviewed their answers with misconceptions addressed, introduce the Big Questions for this lesson:

> *What reasons does Macbeth give for not going ahead with Duncan's murder?*
> *How does Lady Macbeth persuade Macbeth to go through with the murder?*

### PREDICTIONS
The focus of this lesson is going to be Act I, Scene vii, but students need to read Scene vi first. It is a short scene, but no less important. Before reading Scene vi, I often ask students about how they think Lady Macbeth would act in public. Shakespeare shifts his audience from the personal and private life of Lady Macbeth to the public persona she adopts to charm and deceive her way to get what she wants. Offering students the chance to voice their predictions as to how Lady Macbeth will act in the public eye adds to their understanding of the scene, especially when they witness her intense flattery of Duncan.

## Reading the scene: Act I, Scene vi
To help guide their reading of the scene, ask the following questions:

1. How does Duncan describe Macbeth and Lady Macbeth's castle at Inverness?
2. How does Lady Macbeth behave in Duncan's presence?
3. Where does Duncan ask Lady Macbeth to take him at the end of the scene?

Drawing attention to these questions before the scene is read as a class is particularly effective for those who struggle. The questions reveal just enough about the plot of the scene to guide a reading of it without constant hands going up in the air to ask what something means. For example, having looked at the questions, students will know that Duncan will describe the Macbeths' castle in a certain way, they know there will be something particularly noteworthy about Lady Macbeth's behaviour, and they will know the scene will end with the two characters going somewhere together. Instead of reading the scene with no prior knowledge, they will already have considered, to a certain extent, what is going to happen.

For those who have a stronger understanding of Shakespeare's language, I may ask them to begin 'digging deeper' with these questions:

1. Why do you think Duncan comments on the castle's 'pleasant seat'?
2. Why is it important that Lady Macbeth behaves in this way?
3. Why do you think Shakespeare has Banquo confirm that the 'air is delicate'?

These questions are a way of kick-starting discussion. Once students have talked about the answers to these as a class, they can begin to appreciate the more subtle elements of the scene. Pinpointing Banquo's reference to the martlets building their nests in the castle walls, for example, may generate interesting comparisons to the raven Lady Macbeth mentions in Act I, Scene v.

## Character outline

Some students may find tracking certain elements of the characters quite challenging whilst trying to understand concepts such as dualism and an inner and outer self. To combat this, I always make things visual for them. For example, if my class is struggling to comprehend the idea that Lady Macbeth has a true self (an inner self that must remain a secret) and an outer self (the one which she presents to the world), I will provide them with a character outline. Jennifer Webb calls this 'a visual way to work on characterisation'[17] and it can be extremely effective. Students should locate quotations from Act I, Scene v which reveal Lady Macbeth's true personality and write them inside the character. They should then locate quotations from Act I, Scene vi which reveal how Lady Macbeth presents herself to others and write them around the outside of the character. They do not necessarily have to be said by Lady Macbeth herself, but could be other characters' observations of her. This allows students to see dualism in action and appreciate that Lady Macbeth is a character of two selves. Students could then analyse the quotations, explaining the connotations of certain words and discussing why they are of importance. A partially completed outline could look like the one in Resource 6.3.

---

17. Jennifer Webb, *How to Teach English Literature: Overcoming Cultural Poverty*, (Woodbridge: John Catt Educational Ltd., 2019), p. 67.

**RESOURCE 6.3**

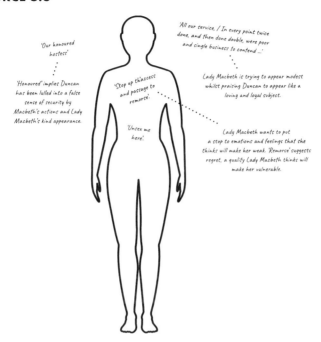

'Our honoured hostess'

'Honoured' implies Duncan has been lulled into a false sense of security by Macbeth's actions and Lady Macbeth's kind appearance.

'Stop up th'access and passage to remorse'.

'Unsex me here'.

'All our service, / In every point twice done, and then done double, were poor and single business to contend ...'

Lady Macbeth is trying to appear modest whilst praising Duncan to appear like a loving and loyal subject.

Lady Macbeth wants to put a stop to emotions and feelings that she thinks will make her weak. 'Remorse' suggests regret, a quality Lady Macbeth thinks will make her vulnerable.

An interesting character to track in this way would be Macbeth himself. Whilst Lady Macbeth is mostly determined to go through with what she deems is right, Macbeth's emotional turmoil would make for some interesting debate and ideas, particularly in terms of what he reveals to others compared to what he keeps secret. To track Macbeth in this way at this point is an optional extra, one which can easily be implemented as and when it is needed.

## Pre-reading activities and reading the scene: Act I, Scene vii

The Big Questions for this lesson revolve around Act I, Scene vii. I always start off teaching Act I, Scene vii by using prediction as a pre-reading strategy. I will ask students to use their knowledge of the play to help them infer why Macbeth would not want to kill Duncan, and as a class we think of a list of specific reasons. If students are feeling particularly creative, we will also consider how Lady Macbeth would respond to each of her husband's misgivings about committing regicide.

The first thing students will come across in Act I, Scene vii is Macbeth's soliloquy. It is tricky and complex, and I want students to appreciate its nuances without 'dumbing it down'. With this in mind, I try to remove the threat of analysing a large chunk of text by using a pre-reading activity to look at Shakespeare's choices. I have found this to be a particularly effective method, as it allows students to construct a scenario as to what is going on at that moment in the play before we read. As a result, the purpose of the scene unveils itself just enough that students can find a way into the text.

For example, by looking at the beginning of the scene, we can tell Macbeth is alone. From this, I would ask students:

- Considering what has happened in previous scenes, why is Macbeth alone?
- What can we infer about how Macbeth is feeling?
- Why is Macbeth not with Duncan, his King and guest?

To help students establish their scenarios in even greater detail, I will then ask students a broader set of questions:

- If the occupants of the castle are celebrating, what can we infer is happening offstage?
- What time of day do we think this could be?
- What impact will the time of day have on the atmosphere of the scene?

The purpose of this activity is not to get students to create an entire backstory to what is happening. After all, the answers to these questions could be (and often are) quite simple, yet it is exactly that simplicity which aids the basic understanding of the conditions of the scene. Students will mostly likely come to the conclusion that Macbeth will be serious and sombre here because of his self-imposed isolation.

Resource 6.4 allows students to read Macbeth's soliloquy without over-analysing it, something I fear we are often guilty of as English teachers. I used to be a teacher who would ask students to annotate a section of text to their heart's content, mistaking quantity for quality and confusing numerous highlighted passages as evidence of learning. Too often, however, students return to their texts and cannot understand any of their annotations. They have over-analysed to the point where nothing is meaningful any more and they cannot possibly remember it all. To avoid this from happening, I often give students Resource 6.4. In the context of this lesson, the resource allows students to condense the speech to six key areas, considering them in depth but not over-analysing to the point where notes become nonsensical.

These questions could be discussed verbally first, whilst reading, to form the basis of class discussion during the reading process.

## RESOURCE 6.4

**TASK #1**

Highlight the following words: if, were, done, but, be, here. Each word is repeated at least twice in the first few lines. What does this tell you about Macbeth's state of mind?

**TASK #2**

Look at lines 7–12. What is Macbeth saying will happen to those who commit violent deeds? What is he afraid of?

**TASK #3**

List the reasons Macbeth offers for not killing Duncan.

**MACBETH**

If it were done, when 'tis done, then 'twere well
It were done quickly. If th'assassination
Could trammel up the consequence, and catch
With his surcease, success: that but this blow
Might be the be-all and the end-all, here,
But here, upon this bank and shoal of time,
We'd jump the life to come. But in these cases,
We still have judgement here, that we but teach
Bloody instructions, which being taught, return
To plague th'inventor: this even-handed justice
Commends th'ingredience of our poison'd chalice
To our own lips. He's here in double trust:
First, as I am his kinsman and his subject,
Strong both against the deed. Then, as his host,
Who should against his murderer shut the door,
Not bear the knife myself. Besides, this Duncan
Hath borne his faculties so meek, hath been
So clear in his great office, that his virtues
Will plead like angels, trumpet-tongued, against
The deep damnation of his taking off;
And pity, like a naked new-born babe,
Striding the blast, or heaven's cherubim, horsed
Upon the sightless couriers of the air,
Shall blow the horrid deed in every eye,
That tears shall drown the wind. I have no spur
To prick the sides of my intent, but only
Vaulting ambition, which o'er-leaps itself,
And falls on th'other.

**TASK #4**

How does Macbeth believe news of Duncan's death will be received? What can we infer about how people view Duncan?

**TASK #5**

Consider the last three lines of Macbeth's monologue. What is he saying about what ambition can do to people?

**TASK #6**

'Macbeth is a weak man who is manipulated by others.' Discuss.

Students should be able to clearly explain why Macbeth does not want to kill Duncan and should identify when and why his shift in thinking takes place.

## Moral compass

This change of heart sets the scene for the return of Lady Macbeth. For this part of the lesson, I usually ask for three volunteers. Two students take the roles of Macbeth and Lady Macbeth, whilst the third acts as our 'moral compass'. As the students read their parts, the 'moral compass' should stand next to the character they think is being most persuasive at that moment, allowing the class to visualise the fluctuation of the power struggle between Macbeth and his wife. This activity can also stimulate debate. The class can ask the compass to move as long as they justify their reasons for doing so; the characters' dialogue must be at the heart of all the choices they make. Eventually, students will recognise that Lady Macbeth holds the most power in this scene. She is clearly more persuasive than her husband, whose determination to protect Duncan crumbles under her rhetoric.

## Ethos, logos and pathos

At this point, it would be useful to remind students of the three main components of rhetoric: ethos, logos and pathos (known collectively as the Aristotelian triad).

Ideally, students will have been introduced to these concepts prior to studying *Macbeth*, and they will certainly come into use here when scrutinising Lady Macbeth's methods of persuasion. In order to do this, I find Resource 6.5 particularly helpful in guiding students' thinking, allowing them to understand how Lady Macbeth manipulates her husband into committing regicide.

## RESOURCE 6.5

**LADY MACBETH**

Was the hope drunk
Wherein you dressed yourself? Hath it
slept since?
And wakes it now to look so green
and pale,
At what it did so freely? From this time
Such I account thy love. Art thou afeard
To be the same in thine own act and
valour,
As thou art in desire? Wouldst thou
have that
Which thou esteem'st the ornament
of life,
And live a coward in thine own esteem,
Letting 'I dare not' wait upon 'I would,'
Like the poor cat i'th' adage?

**LADY MACBETH**

What beast was't then
That made you break this enterprise to me?
When you durst do it, then you were a man;
And, to be more than what you were, you
would
Be so much more the man. Nor time nor place
Did then adhere, and yet you would make both:
They have made themselves, and that their
fitness now
Does unmake you. I have given suck, and know
How tender 'tis to love the babe that milks me:
I would, while it was smiling in my face,
Have plucked the nipple from his boneless
gums,
And dashed the brains out, had I so sworn
As you have done to this.

**LADY MACBETH**

We fail?
But screw your courage to the sticking
place,
And we'll not fail. When Duncan is asleep,
Whereto the rather shall his day's hard
journey
Soundly invite him, his two chamberlains
Will I with wine and wassail so convince
That memory, the warder of the brain,
Shall be a fume, and the receipt of reason
A limbeck only. When in swinish sleep
Their drenched natures lies as in a death,
What cannot you and I perform upon
Th'unguarded Duncan? What not put upon
His spongy officers, who shall bear the guilt
Of our great quell?

1. Look at Lady Macbeth's three speeches and pick the best example of logos, pathos and ethos across all three speeches. Filter the quotations into the boxes below.
2. Explain why your chosen quotation is the best example of logos, pathos and ethos you can find. How is Lady Macbeth being persuasive?

| **Logos** | **Pathos**<br>*'I would, while it was smiling in my face, have pluck'd my nipple from his boneless gums, and dash'd the brains out'. – Lady Macbeth uses pathos here by shocking Macbeth with an image of brutality and savagery. It may invoke pity for the child in Macbeth, but allow him to appreciate how serious Lady Macbeth is. She persuades him by creating a sickening image.* | **Ethos** |
| --- | --- | --- |

## Answering the Big Questions

I often like to end lessons with a quick quiz to assess what students have retained and to identify gaps in knowledge. These gaps must be addressed. After all, there is very little use in moving on to the next PowerPoint slide just because it is there, sitting waiting in a folder on a USB stick to be taught. Moving forward without acknowledging gaps in knowledge creates far more problems in the long run. As such, a simple 'exit quiz' can be a way of informing what needs to be re-taught and explained again. This scene, in particular, needs recapping for its complexity. Notice how I have filtered the Big Questions into the quiz to ensure they are revisited by students.

## RESOURCE 6.6

---

**Act I, Scene vii**

Complete the following questions in full sentences. Each answer should be no more than three sentences.

1. What reasons does Macbeth give for not going ahead with Duncan's murder?

2. What does Lady Macbeth accuse Macbeth of when he announces that they will 'proceed no further in this business'?

3. How does Lady Macbeth persuade Macbeth to go through with the murder?

4. What is Lady Macbeth's plan for killing Duncan? What does she say she will do to the guards?

5. What does Macbeth say Lady Macbeth should be rewarded with for her character? Why would this be a reward? Consider the historical context.

6. Macbeth says 'false face must hide what the false heart doth know.' What is the significance of this quotation? What is Macbeth saying?

---

## Dual coding

This next part does not necessarily need to be sequenced into lessons at this point, but I have placed it at the end of this chapter because it revolves around the end of Act I. Dual coding has seen a resurgence in popularity in our classrooms. I find it is an extremely effective way of helping students to remember the key things they need to know, which is why I use it often to revise plot points. It is not about making things look nice, nor is it about just placing a picture next to a word or chunk of text. It is about combining visuals and verbalised instruction to help students learn and retain. More can be read about this in Oliver Caviglioli's *Dual Coding With Teachers*.[18]

I begin this activity by talking through the plot, stripping it down to its core elements. I am terrible at drawing, but dual coding is not an art lesson. It is not about producing the best drawing you have ever created. Therefore, I use stick people to represent characters, with the first letter of their name in their head. I keep text to a minimum because I am verbalising what these pictures mean. Quite often I will ask students why I have drawn a certain image rather than explaining it to them outright. This, I have found, helps them to retain the information easily. Here is what a dual coded Act I of *Macbeth* might look like, a design inspired by Chris Curtis's work on pictorial mapping:[19]

---

18. Oliver Caviglioli, *Dual Coding With Teachers*, (Woodbridge, John Catt Educational Ltd., 2019).

19. Chris Curtis, 'Precision and patterns thanks to dual coding', *Learning from my mistakes: An English teacher's blog*, https://learningfrommymistakesenglish.blogspot. com/search?q=dual+coding.

## RESOURCE 6.7

I produce something like this, with my students, at the end of each act. Notice how it has broken down the plot to the main narrative. If students can retain what the dual coded plot map sets out, I am confident they can begin their study of Act II with a solid understanding of the beginning of Shakespeare's story. Students can then produce their own maps or use the one I have provided them with. Regardless, I will follow this up by asking students to talk through the map of the plot in pairs. Student A should explain the plot of *Macbeth* to their partner, following along their maps as they explain what happens. I will then ask students to switch over. Student B will describe the plot of the act in their own words. Whilst I will not be adding in a dual coding section elsewhere in this book, this is certainly an activity one could use to summarise each of the five acts.

### Suggested 'Extra Challenge' activities

- Is regicide ever forgivable?
- What influences Macbeth more? His inner morality or God's judgement? Why?
- Duality. Discuss.

### Key vocabulary:
Duality, rhetoric, spur

# ACT TWO

# CHAPTER 7
## Act II, Scene i

*What is the relationship like between Banquo and Fleance?*
*What does Macbeth say in his famous 'Is this a*
*dagger I see before me?' soliloquy?*

## What?

### Scene analysis: Act II, Scene i

In *Macbeth*, references to light are often linked directly to the concept of goodness. When King Duncan announces that Malcolm will not be the only person to gain a new title when he says 'signs of nobleness, like stars, shall shine / On all deservers', Duncan refers to Macbeth, who has been appointed Thane of Cawdor. The stars represent everything that is good, and it is for this reason that Macbeth asks for the stars to 'hide [their] fires' in Act I, Scene iv. Macbeth realises that his desires to kill the King and take the crown himself are so terrible that he does not want heaven to look on them. He does not even want to look upon them himself. His dark acts are at complete odds with the light Duncan represents.

This imagery of light is apparent in the opening of Act II, Scene i. In the First Folio, the scene opens with the entrance of Banquo and Fleance, with Fleance carrying 'a Torch before him'. This is undoubtedly metaphorical: the witches' prophecies explored the idea that Banquo's sons would be king; Fleance is literally carrying a light, symbolic of the future. He is the one leading the way, and is the one whose associations with light are most closely aligned to King Duncan and his 'golden blood'. Shakespeare, here, is promoting the idea of kingship and the role of a king – or a future king – as one who is representative of the good and the light.

The fact that at the start of Act II, Scene i the night is dark and the stars are hidden by clouds foreshadows not only the impending death of Banquo, but also Macbeth's subterfuge: Banquo continues to suspect something, but is unable to pinpoint what precisely is making him uneasy.

## BANQUO AND FLEANCE

Banquo comments that 'there's husbandry in heaven, / Their candles are all out'. At first glance, this line suggests that the sky is darkened as if the stars have been extinguished. This would be in keeping with Macbeth and Lady Macbeth's calls for darkness and for the heavens not to see the crime they are about to commit. However, it could also be symptomatic of the fact that, at this point, Banquo is similarly 'in the dark'. Whilst he may have his suspicions about his friend, he is not party to the plans his hosts are making. The lack of stars could also symbolise the impending darkness – both literally and metaphorically – as well as the forthcoming actions of Macbeth and Lady Macbeth bringing darkness on Scotland.

Aside from remarking on the almost unnatural darkness, Banquo and Fleance's initial conversation also centres around battle. Banquo asks Fleance to take at least one of his weapons: 'Hold, take my sword' and perhaps later 'Take thee that too.' This focus on weaponry and violence in the discussion between father and son is suggestive of Banquo's preoccupation with fighting and his skill as a swordsman. In showing Banquo preparing Fleance to be ready to fight with a sword, Shakespeare gives us an insight into what life might have been like in the eleventh century. It would have been the duty of a father, like Banquo, to pass on his skills to his son. This scene captures a moment of education between the two characters. Banquo has made a career out of being skilled with a sword, and now he must pass on this knowledge to his son.

However, in this scene Shakespeare presents Banquo as being somewhat distracted by bad dreams related to the witches. Before Macbeth even enters, Shakespeare explores Banquo's struggles to sleep. He has a 'heavy summons' in that he desires to sleep, but is plagued by 'cursed thoughts that nature / Gives way to in repose.' In Shakespearean England it was a commonly held belief that bad dreams were caused by demons.[1] Having recently met the witches, it is likely that a man such as Banquo would have been particularly guarded against these supernatural actions. In asking the 'merciful powers' to let him sleep peacefully, we see a character who is the polar opposite of Macbeth and Lady Macbeth. Where they have asked the spirits and heavens to either assist them in committing regicide or else cast their eyes away from their deeds, Banquo asks for salvation from his dreams. Where they have called on spirits for evil, Banquo merely wants to rest easy. When we measure Banquo against his supposed friend, Macbeth's Machiavellian schemes seem to be significantly more complex and malevolent than anything we have seen from Banquo. That Banquo will be dead in a few short scenes ought to come as no surprise, as these lines hint that he is not the same as Macbeth at all, despite them being partners in battle.

---

1.   Janine Riviere, *Dreams in Early Modern England*, (Abingdon: Routledge, 2017), p. 152.

Banquo is, however, noticeably on edge. When he hears Macbeth enter, he immediately takes his sword back from Fleance and asks 'who's there?' Despite being in the castle of his supposed ally, Banquo is uncertain and uneasy. He is able to read the broader atmosphere of the castle accurately without knowing any details of what is about to happen to the King. It could be that he feels uneasy around Macbeth, or it might be that, having considered the witches and their supernatural messages, he has set himself on edge and so is restless as a result.

### 'HE HATH BEEN IN UNUSUAL PLEASURE'

Shakespeare explores a little more of King Duncan's character next, and the audience is given further evidence that he is somewhat of an ineffective king. Despite the looming threat, Banquo comments that Duncan has been 'in unusual pleasure'. Arguably, it could be the case that, having celebrated at the feast, Duncan's 'pleasure' comes from having drunk alcohol. We know, certainly, that alcohol will go on to play a large role in Macbeth's ability to go through with the murder itself. Duncan's guard is down because he trusts his friend: in doing so he has failed to be suitably wary of Macbeth, just as the guards who will soon be drunk fail in their duty to protect him.

Above this, though, the King has also commended Macbeth, giving him 'great largess' and his wife a 'diamond'. It is clear that King Duncan sees Lady Macbeth purely as his 'kind hostess', and it is arguably therefore the case that either he does not see what is coming next or, otherwise, that Lady Macbeth's performance as the 'innocent flower' is very compelling indeed.

### 'I DREAMT LAST NIGHT OF THE THREE WEÏRD SISTERS'

Quickly, Banquo brings the conversation around to the witches. The audience would be aware that some time has passed since Macbeth's promise to 'let us speak / Our free hearts to each other.' Shakespeare has given us no indication that the two men have spoken further on what they heard. In the interim, they have seen Macbeth plot with his wife to kill King Duncan and take the crown for himself. When Banquo comments that the witches 'have showed some truth' to Macbeth, it is unclear whether Banquo merely means that the witches prophesied that he would be Thane of Cawdor or whether he truly understands the ramifications of the final prophecy and how the Macbeths plan for it to shortly come true.

Regardless, Shakespeare presents Macbeth as being entirely unwilling to engage in any detailed conversation. Not only does he claim not to have thought of the witches – another example of Shakespeare's use of dramatic irony – indeed he once again pushes back having a conversation with Banquo about the witches at all, instead stating that they could talk about what happened when they 'can entreat an hour to serve'. What Banquo does not appear to notice here, though, is that Macbeth has already assumed the royal mode of address: 'we would spend it in some words upon that business.'

Indeed, almost the entire remainder of their discussion is dripping with equivocation. Where it could be said that Macbeth is simply talking to Banquo about a future opportunity to discuss the witches, in equal terms Shakespeare seems to be alluding to the future when he hopes to be king. The words 'cleave' and 'consent' in the phrase 'if you shall cleave to my consent when 'tis' could be read in myriad ways. To 'cleave' is to be faithful, and to 'consent' is very much open to interpretation. Therefore, it could be that Macbeth is simply asking Banquo to agree to meet with him (consent to keep their appointment). It could also be that Macbeth is asking Banquo to accept his advice (consent can be read as advice). Finally, Shakespeare could be showing Macbeth asking for Banquo to continue to be faithful to him when 'it' is done – in other words, after he has murdered King Duncan. This reading seems likely when taken into consideration with the following line: 'It shall make honour for you.' In other words, Macbeth plans to reward Banquo for his allegiance.

Shakespeare presents Macbeth's lines here as being particularly heavily laden with ambiguity. Like so many other of Macbeth's actions, his deliberate duplicity covers over the dark heart of his intentions and ambitions.

Banquo, similarly, holds his cards close to his chest. His following line implies that he suspects that his friend is planning something: Banquo is happy to support Macbeth, but will only gain respect through acting honourably. He is not interested in acting dishonourably in order to get ahead: again, reminiscent of Banquo's desire to call on the spirits simply to rid him of his bad dreams. Banquo is a staunch defender of his integrity: he desires only to keep his 'bosom franchised' and his 'allegiance clear', and will not associate with corruption if it means losing either of these things. Providing that Macbeth can ensure this will be the case for Banquo, Banquo states that he will listen to his friend.

Very quickly, however, Macbeth closes down the conversation. In stating that he will do nothing to sully his good name and reputation, Macbeth realises that Banquo is no longer a viable friend or partner. It could even be this early moment that triggers Macbeth's initial thoughts to dispatch his friend. With this, Banquo and Fleance retire to bed and leave Macbeth to his final thoughts before he murders the King of Scotland.

Macbeth is left alone to wait for the bell – rung by Lady Macbeth to signify that the plans are laid and he is to go to murder the King. Whilst it is of course the case that Macbeth does not wish to reveal his plans to the servant, the way he phrases his instruction is euphemistic. 'Go bid thy mistress, when my drink is ready,' he says, 'She strike upon the bell.' Arguably, Macbeth does not wish to articulate, or even perhaps truly think about, what he is planning. Does this reveal a lasting streak of self-doubt, or second thoughts for Macbeth?

### 'IS THIS A DAGGER WHICH I SEE BEFORE ME?'

Here, we reach what is arguably one of Shakespeare's most famous speeches: the 'Is this a dagger?' soliloquy. In these few lines, the Bard explores the inner turmoil of Macbeth whilst simultaneously allowing his protagonist to explore the ongoing impact Duncan's death will have on him, even if he does not know it yet. The soliloquy also allows Shakespeare to comment on the difference between – and likelihood of – free will and predestination. The dagger that appears literally points Macbeth to his forthcoming crime and into his uncertain and unpleasant future. Does he truly have choice over whether to follow it, or has this moment been inevitable since his first meetings with the witches?

The dagger, which appears as Macbeth is left alone on stage, is most frequently explained as a figment of his imagination, or a hallucination. It is a product of Macbeth's stressed and disturbed mind; a visible marker of the hurdle Macbeth must leap in order to fulfil his ambition to become king – and possibly more noticeably a visible marker of Lady Macbeth's ambition. This moment is the final opportunity Macbeth has to withdraw from their plans, and the duality in the phrase 'Come, let me clutch thee' demonstrates this. 'Come', an imperative verb, suggests that Macbeth is commanding. However, 'let me' is more uncertain: it seems as if Macbeth is almost begging. The fact that he so soon loses his ability to be commanding and take control of the situation foreshadows his later weaknesses as king and his ultimate downfall.

Hallucinations and visions become commonplace for Macbeth from this point onwards. The first time Macbeth queried the reliability of sight came after his first meeting with the witches. Banquo questioned at the time: 'Were such things here as we do speak about?' The difference between appearance and reality is, of course, a predominant theme of *Macbeth*, and Shakespeare's use of hallucinations which Macbeth cannot tie strongly to reality emphasises that not everything is as it seems – in terms of characters' actions, but also, at this point, the things that appear in front of those characters. The dagger is a precursor for the ghost of Banquo and the visions conjured by the witches. This particular vision, then, is inextricably linked to the actions of the witches. Whether a contemporary audience might have seen the vision as conjured by the weïrd sisters or by Macbeth's own mind is unclear, though it is highly likely that these supernatural events would have evoked memories of the witches.

Macbeth recognises that what he is seeing is not real. He calls it a 'dagger of the mind, a false creation'. That he recognises the dagger as a figment of his mind, or a hallucination, is interesting in and of itself. When faced with a hallucination, most people would not recognise with such clarity the fact that what they were looking at does not exist. This suggests that Macbeth is perhaps already treading a fine line with regard to his poor mental health, which is about to be triggered fully by his committing regicide. If this is a hallucination from his mind (rather than a creation of the witches), this would suggest a level of instability in Macbeth. His recognition that the dagger is not real suggests that he maintains a level of belief in, and understanding of, reality. This dichotomy is reflective of the myriad dualities presented by Shakespeare, including notably here the conflict between guilt and ambition.

Much like Lady Macbeth has been doing since her first appearance in Act I, Scene v, the dagger 'marshall'st' Macbeth towards King Duncan's chambers and to the act of regicide. Could the dagger be a metaphor for Lady Macbeth? Both draw him on to commit the crime. The dagger encourages Macbeth towards his destination, with Shakespeare demonstrating Macbeth's ability to be manipulated and controlled. He is arguably weak in character.

An image many students pick up is that of the dagger suddenly appearing as if it has committed the act: 'and on thy blade, and dudgeon, gouts of blood'. The fact that the blood covers not only the blade but the handle, too, is proleptically foreshadowing the blood on both Macbeth's and Lady Macbeth's hands which preoccupy so many of their thoughts as the play continues. The blood on the dagger reflects Macbeth's guilt, just as the blood on his hands later both literally and metaphorically symbolises the same.

Next, however, comes the turning point of the scene. 'There's no such thing' is Macbeth's deliberate refusal to believe in the dagger as a palpable object: in doing so, Shakespeare confirms to the audience that Macbeth is of sound mind. The actions that follow cannot be blamed, in any good conscience, on Macbeth being in any way unwell. His rationalisation of the floating dagger cements his sanity: it is his thoughts and actions that finally and ultimately encourage him to commit regicide, not those of anyone, or anything, else.

Throughout this scene, Macbeth has avoided directly referencing the act of murder. Even now, alone on stage, he cannot admit to himself what he is about to do: he describes it as the 'bloody business'. From this, we can infer that Macbeth is trying to uncouple himself as far as possible from his actions in order not to be filled with the guilt he fears he will inevitably feel. He knows he must remain detached and cold: Lady Macbeth, and the witches, have convinced him that regicide is his only quick route to the crown.

Continuing with foreshadowing, Shakespeare has Macbeth consider the fact that he is about to act against nature by killing the King. To Macbeth, 'nature seems dead'. By subverting the will of God and the Divine Right of Kings, Macbeth is destroying the natural order of the world. A Jacobean audience would understand that this could not, and would not, go unpunished, and Macbeth's preoccupation with nature here suggests he, too, understands the risk he is about to take to get what he wants.

Macbeth is also concerned about the 'wicked dreams' he fears will disturb his sleep. Shakespeare, again, foreshadows Act II, Scene ii and his fears immediately following Duncan's death that he will be unable to sleep again. This lack of sleep for Lady Macbeth is what draws her on to her death. The inability to sleep is unnatural, emphasising that what he is about to do is beyond the bounds of normality.

Shakespeare's reference to the Greek goddess Hecate is interesting. The goddess of magic, witchcraft, ghosts and necromancy, Macbeth's inclusion of her in his thoughts is the start of a semantic field of evil and the supernatural. Hecate's ability to communicate with the dead – necromancy – foreshadows the appearance of Banquo's ghost, but also indicates the concept of prophecy on which the witches rely so heavily. She was often associated with crossroads, and here Macbeth is at a metaphorical crossroads. He must make the decision now to kill the King or not.

Shakespeare then has Macbeth compare himself to a wolf. In literature, wolves have several symbolic meanings. Firstly, wolves are commonly presented as loyal animals. When the audience is initially introduced to Macbeth, he appears loyal to the King. However, in this image, this particular wolf is loyal only to the spectre of death, symbolising Macbeth's betrayal of King Duncan and his allegiance to actions that will serve Macbeth alone – namely, murder: of King Duncan, of Banquo and even of Macduff's family. Wolves are often considered symbolic of destruction and death; straddling both Macbeth's previous actions in battle and those that are yet to come. Finally, wolves have come to symbolise those who have a need to trust their own instincts.[2] Macbeth, until this soliloquy, toys consistently with his own instincts, veering between wanting to, and refusing to, murder the King.

Next, we hear Macbeth describe death, personified, stalking the stage, as a wolf howls in the night. They are joined in this image by Tarquin, a rapist (immortalised in Shakespeare's tragic poem *The Rape of Lucrece*). In Roman history, it was Sextus Tarquinius's rape of Lucretia which led, ultimately, to the overthrow of the monarchy and the establishment of the Roman Republic. Not only does the story of Tarquin demonstrate the fragility of monarchy – pertinent given Macbeth's plans to kill the King – but it also ends in a way not dissimilar to Macbeth's own story. Following the rape of Lucretia, it is thought that Sextus Tarquinius fled Collatia and moved on to Gabii, where he attempted to become king of the region. His bid was unsuccessful, and he was

---

2.   Karen Elizabeth Bukowick, 'Truth and Symbolism: Mythological Perspectives of the Wolf and Crow', https://dlib.bc.edu/islandora/object/bc-ir:102331/datastream/PDF/view.

later murdered in revenge for his past crimes.[3] The subtext here suggests that Shakespeare is alluding to the fact that, even before committing the murder, his actions are doomed. His crimes can never, and will never, go unpunished.

Again, as elsewhere in the play, Macbeth asks for his actions to be hidden: where before Lady Macbeth has asked that her 'keen knife see not the wound it makes', here, Macbeth asks that the 'firm-set earth, / Hear not my steps, which way they walk'. Here, arguably, Shakespeare is making another biblical allusion. Job 20:27 states: 'The heaven shall reveal his iniquity; and the earth shall rise up against him.'[4] Macbeth is trying to hide, again from God, but this is not possible because the earth itself will give him up. Regardless of the extent to which he pleads, his actions will be found out. His later downfall is inevitable. Macbeth's later paranoia is noticeable here, too, as Shakespeare personifies the ground. Macbeth accuses the stones that 'prate of my whereabout', thereby suggesting that he is now suspicious of everyone and everything around him.

By the end of the soliloquy, Macbeth is anxious to act and to finally carry out the murder. He comments that 'words to the heat of deeds too cold breath gives.' In other words, he realises that, now he is in a position where he is determined to act, he must do so before he talks about it too much – to the extent that he no longer wants to go through with it. The juxtaposition between 'heat' and 'cold' is also interesting here, perhaps symbolising the 'heat' of the act itself and, in particular, Lady Macbeth's desire to see it done, and the 'cool' of Macbeth's own view of the murder for most of the play so far. However, Macbeth is determined, and so he is ready to kill King Duncan.

As the bell rings – the sign he has prearranged with Lady Macbeth earlier in the scene to indicate that everything is ready ('go bid thy mistress, when my drink is ready, / She strike upon the bell') – Macbeth compares the sound of the bell to a death knell for King Duncan. In Shakespeare's England (and indeed as far back as the early sixteenth century), tradition and custom dictated that three distinct bells were rung to mark a death. The first was rung when a person was dying. The second was the death 'knell', rung to mark the moment of death. The final bell, and the one which perseveres in Christian funeral services today, was the lych bell, or corpse bell, which was rung as the funeral procession reached the church.[5] That Macbeth jumps straight to describing this bell as Duncan's

3.  James M. Tolbert, 'The Argument of Shakespeare's "Lucrece": Its sources and authorship', *The University of Texas Studies in English*, Vol. 29 (1950), pp. 77–90, https://www.jstor.org/stable/20776012.

4.  *The Holy Bible Containing the Old and New Testaments*, Authorised King James Version, www.kingjamesbibleonline.org, Job 20:27.

5.  Robert Whiting, *The Reformation of the English Parish Church*, (Cambridge: Cambridge University Press, 2010), p. 171.

death knell is telling: this is not the moment before the King dies, but is instead the moment of his death: Macbeth is going to commit the murder immediately.

The very final line of Macbeth's soliloquy shows that he seemingly no longer holds his king in high regard. Macbeth knows that King Duncan is going 'to heaven or to hell', but does not pass any further comment on where he wishes Duncan to go. Tradition and belief would dictate that King Duncan's soul would pass to heaven, as the representative of God on earth. Other than being a perhaps less than effective king, there is nothing in the play to suggest Duncan would be believed to go to Hell upon death, according to Christian teachings. Is Macbeth here, then, considering his own fate once he is king? Whilst the King is God's representative on earth, Macbeth is about to take the throne in a duplicitous and sinful way. Is he really questioning the final journey of his own soul?

## The symbolism of the dagger

Even before he kills the King and takes the crown for himself, Macbeth is already plagued with the idea that he will not be able to sustain the kingship, as he has no lineage. He fears his reign will be 'barren' in that he will not produce heirs, or any heirs he does produce will not take the throne. He fears an inherent impotence.

It is difficult to consider the symbolism of the dagger without considering how much *Macbeth* relates to Freud's Oedipus theory. Thinking about Macbeth psychoanalytically, one sees his regicide has undertones of patricide. He looks up to King Duncan and craves his approval: he is fatherless and has now killed his replacement parental figure. Lady Macbeth even strengthens this fatherly link when she says she would have killed him herself had he 'not resembled [her] father as he slept'. More than this, though, is his relationship with Lady Macbeth. His action to kill the King is done at least in part to please her: she wants him to be king and she questions his masculinity when he refuses to go through with it. He is desperate for her support and deeply wishes for her to believe in him. Their relationship has Oedipal roots: he kills his 'father figure' in order to gain respect and acceptance from his 'mother figure'. It could even be argued that his 'mother figure', in this instance, is Scotland herself. Macbeth will kill Scotland's protector and use his newfound kingship to inextricably fuse himself to his country.

It is a subconsciously sexually driven act. The dagger is inherently phallic: it is the object he bears before him in order to commit his act: 'The ghostly form of that phallic apparition can be taken as the sign of an enabling disavowal.'[6] There is a deeper root to the phallic image of the dagger. Midway through the soliloquy, Macbeth references 'Tarquin's ravishing strides':

---

6. Christopher Pye, *The Regal Phantasm: Shakespeare and the Politics of Spectacle*, (Abingdon: Routledge, 1990), p. 159.

> *In unconscious elaboration, Tarquin's phallus hallucinates itself right there in the hall before him, pointing the way he should go, and Macbeth's dagger, that also hallucinates itself before him and it points the way he should go.*
>
> *In the way that Tarquin's going and Macbeth's going are assimilated one to the other, so are phallus and dagger assimilated one to the other.[7]*

Putting Tarquin to one side, the dagger therefore is not just symbolic of his guilt – it is almost a challenge to Macbeth, a taunt: Kill the King, it seems to say to him, and then try to sustain your kingship through progeny.

## Structure in the 'Is this a dagger...?' soliloquy

As with so much of Shakespeare's writing, it is not just the language that can be intrinsically analysed in this soliloquy. The structure and rhythm of Macbeth's speech reveals a great deal about his state of mind, and our first clue to this is the fact that, from the very first line of the soliloquy, Shakespeare's writing falls out of regular iambic pentameter. The first line – 'Is this a dagger which I see before me?' has an additional, unstressed syllable, giving the line a feminine ending.

> u / u / u / u/ u / u
> *Is this a dagger which I see before me?*

This is suggestive of the fact that at the speech's opening Macbeth is increasingly uncertain of what he is about to do.

However, much like Macbeth changes his mind and resolves at the end of the soliloquy to murder the King, so Shakespeare reflects this move to certainty in the structure of his writing. From the volta of the soliloquy – the turn to firm resolve – when Macbeth notices that the dagger he is hallucinating is now also covered in blood, Shakespeare's writing moves towards more masculine endings: the lines are in iambic pentameter, with each line ending on a stressed syllable.[8]

> u / u / u/ u / u /
> *That summons thee to heaven or to hell*

---

7. Ewan Fernie, *Shakespeare for Freedom: Why the plays matter,* (Cambridge: Cambridge University Press, 2017), p. 255.

8. Valerie Clayman Pye, *Unearthing Shakespeare: Embodied Performance and The Globe,* (London: Routledge, 2017), p. 56.

# 'Is This A Dagger?' at a glance

## RESOURCE 7.1

A contemporary audience might assume this is the work of the witches.

Could be a creation of his own mind – a hallucination. Indicates that he is preparing himself for the murder.

Almost an initial sense of incredulity.
*Is it a dagger?*

Imperative verb – Macbeth is still trying to take control of the situation.

But also almost asking 'permission' – shows he doesn't feel completely at ease with the situation.

Ready to be seized – presenting it to him to be used.

'A dagger of the mind' suggests he knows he has created it himself and calls into question his mental stability.

Conveys a sense that he is still not doing this by his own choice, but that the time is coming for him to act.

Still trying to rationalise the vision – he says it is his plan to kill the King which has created this dagger.

Imagery of the supernatural and evil, demonstrating the calibre of the actions he is about to take.

Asks again to be hidden/unheard as he has previously – he is still preoccupied with being found out, and knows his actions are inexcusable.

First thought of this being a hallucination, and the first mention of hallucinations and visions in the play before the regicide has even been committed.

Macbeth has a rational explanation at this point – the vision has been caused by the stress he is under.

Foreshadowing how the dagger will look shortly, reflecting Macbeth's emerging guilt before he's even acted.

Macbeth deliberately refuses to believe the dagger is real, confirming to the audience that he is thinking rationally. The murder therefore cannot be blamed on his mental health.

Macbeth has convinced himself and now knows he must act before he changes his mind again.

This bell is not the one that signifies that someone will shortly die but a 'death knell' – in other words, it signifies the moment of King Duncan's death and suggests the immediacy with which Macbeth will act once he leaves the stage.

> Is this a dagger which I see before me,
> The handle toward my hand? Come, let me clutch thee.
> I have thee not, and yet I see thee still.
> Art thou not, fatal vision, sensible
> To feeling as to sight? Or art thou but
> A dagger of the mind, a false creation,
> Proceeding from the heat-oppressed brain?
> I see thee yet, in form as palpable
> As this which now I draw.
> Thou marshall'st me the way that I was going,
> And such an instrument I was to use.
> Mine eyes are made the fools o'th' other senses,
> Or else worth all the rest. I see thee still,
> And on thy blade and dudgeon gouts of blood,
> Which was not so before. There's no such thing.
> It is the bloody business which informs
> Thus to mine eyes. Now o'er the one half-world
> Nature seems dead, and wicked dreams abuse
> The curtained sleep; Witchcraft celebrates
> Pale Hecate's offerings; and withered Murder,
> Alarumed by his sentinel, the wolf,
> Whose howl's his watch, thus with his stealthy pace,
> With Tarquin's ravishing strides, towards his design
> Moves like a ghost. Thou sure and firm-set earth,
> Hear not my steps, which way they walk, for fear
> Thy very stones prate of my whereabout,
> And take the present horror from the time,
> Which now suits with it. Whiles I threat, he lives;
> Words to the heat of deeds too cold breath gives.
> *A bell rings.*
> I go, and it is done; the bell invites me.
> Hear it not, Duncan, for it is a knell
> That summons thee to heaven, or to hell.

Other than being a perhaps less than effective king, there is nothing in the play to suggest Duncan would be believed to go to hell upon death, according to Christian teachings. Is Macbeth here, then, considering his own fate once he is king, and the ultimate fate of his own soul?

## How?

### Retrieval

Whilst we must be mindful that repeatedly revisiting and recalling moments from early in the play can be beneficial in helping our students encode the information into their long-term memory, as we move further through this scheme of learning it is important that we start to balance out the knowledge recall so that students do not focus too heavily on recalling a small number of events from the start of the play. Therefore, from this point forward, the level of detail in these knowledge recall tasks will be replicated, but relating to later moments in the play, with more occasional recall of these early moments.

There are two knowledge recall tasks included in this lesson, and whilst it could be useful to do one or the other, depending on the class you are working with there is often no harm in doing both. I would recommend starting with the cloze activity to build confidence, before moving on to asking students to recreate the dual coding activity from Chapter 6. Cloze activities reduce the cognitive load on students, allowing them to focus on their knowledge without also considering how they are going to phrase, structure or shape that knowledge.

This cloze activity is not short, but does provide a detailed summary of Act I and the key moments of the play so far. So much has happened, and it is vital that students are given every opportunity to reflect on their knowledge of this. The cloze activity could be broken down into scenes. Resource 7.2 just illustrates what the cloze activity for Act I, Scene i might look like, but it is advisable to cover the whole of Act I in this activity. It could even be completed in groups and fed back to the remainder of the class. Alternatively, students could be challenged to write their own cloze exercises for their peers to complete. This needs close monitoring to ensure that, firstly, the information they are recalling is accurate and, secondly, that students are recalling the key moments from the play and are not missing information which is already vital, or which will become vital, in future study.

## RESOURCE 7.2

---

**Act I, Scene i**

At the start of Act I, Scene i, three _____ meet on a _____. They discuss when they will meet _____, who has been fighting a battle. They are able to predict that the battle will finish before '____ ____ ____ ____ ,' emphasising to the audience that they are able to tell the _____. The witches are called away by their _____, a _____ named _____ and a _____ named _____. These animals were traditionally associated with witches. By using these _____, Shakespeare helps the audience recognise these characters.

*familiars, the set of sun, Gray-Malkin, witches, Macbeth, devices, battlefield, future, Paddock, toad, cat*

---

I always find it remarkable the detail with which students are able to recall activities where they have played an active role in dual coding a text. The alternative – or additional – knowledge recall activity at the start of this lesson relates to recreating the dual coded conceptual illustration students completed in the last lesson. There are several ways in which this can be done, and which method will work best will depend on your students.

Often, I run this activity by reintroducing the symbols or sketches I created whilst verbally walking students through the act. This can be especially effective if the images have been captured either as part of an activity on an interactive whiteboard or whilst using a visualiser. Students, in pairs, should explain the dual code to one another, seeing how much information they are able to recall from the process they went through last lesson.

Alternatively, in pairs, one student could recreate the symbols themselves (without looking back in their notes), before the other talks through the plot so far. Together, students should be able to identify any missing symbols. This activity would also work if it were broadened out at this point: once pairs have recreated the symbols and talked through what they represent, they could then join with another pair to compare their recollections. What is similar or different? Has either pair missed any crucial moments in the plot? Although this is not something we will be referring to again in the book, it is certainly an activity one could replicate in future lessons if one chooses to dual code every act.

### Big Questions

At this point, with knowledge recalled sufficiently and students now ready to develop their knowledge of the start of Act II, it is important that they are introduced to the Big Questions before they start looking at the scene:

*What is the relationship like between Banquo and Fleance?*
*What does Macbeth say in his famous 'Is this a dagger I see*

*before me?' soliloquy?*

In this lesson, the two key moments I suggest students focus on are the presentation of the relationship between Banquo and his son, Fleance, and then later on Macbeth's soliloquy being, as it is, a vital moment in the way in which the later events of the story play out.

## Pre-reading activities

It is important that students are afforded every opportunity to think carefully about characters and their relationships. You may have students who are naturally empathetic and can frame their discussion of characters around how the character might feel in any given situation. The relationship between Macbeth and Banquo is a tense friendship, and whilst students will not (thankfully!) have experienced a relationship *quite* like theirs, they will likely have had friendships which have gone through tumultuous times of lying and withholding information.

Ask students to consider the following questions:

- What did Macbeth promise to do with Banquo?
- What information has he withheld from Banquo?
- How would Banquo feel about this?

This can be a simple oracy task, but allows a point of entry into establishing the relationship between the two men in this scene.

## Reading the scene

Read the beginning of the scene up to Macbeth's soliloquy, using the following questions to ascertain what students understand:

1. What are Banquo and Fleance doing at the start of the scene?
2. Why might this be important?
3. What are Banquo and his son, Fleance, saying about the night?
4. What does this suggest? What does this remind us of?
5. What do we learn about how King Duncan is feeling?
6. What lie does Macbeth tell Banquo?
7. How is Macbeth trying to buy Banquo's loyalty?

When it comes to the 'Is this a dagger?' soliloquy, some students will have some existing cultural knowledge of this speech because of its infamy. Many more, however, may not have this vital cultural capital before they are presented with the speech, and it is the utter joy we have as English teachers to introduce our students to these vital and seminal texts, including this soliloquy.

In my early years of teaching, I would use simplified versions of *Macbeth* alongside the original source. I believed that this would help some of my students confidently access the text so their understanding of the play would be better. Even though students were presented with the original text, they tended to use the modernised versions as a crutch and, if anything, it drove a wider wedge between students' experience of the Bard and their perceived difficulties in accessing his text. Why bother, when there's an 'easier' version they could read instead? Of course, all that this gives our students is a 'diminished diet'[9] of what should be vital cultural capital to which they absolutely deserve to be exposed.

> *We shouldn't be tempted to dumb material down in a mistaken belief that our pupils can't cope. It is our job to help them to reach into the marvels and jewels which are contained within our curriculum. This is not an entitlement for the few, but the many.*[10]

Now, for me, it is all about having, and being able to convey, deep subject knowledge. Teaching this soliloquy – and teaching English literature in general – is all about how we excite, support, scaffold, nurture and challenge our students to excel: helping students access Shakespeare is part of that magical experience we all get to have as teachers, and it is a privilege we should never overlook.

## Guided analysis

Unpeeling the 'Is this a dagger?' soliloquy is a little like peeling an onion. Students can gain a good, working understanding of the text with some immediacy, but the more layers we peel, and the more times we revisit and explore specific words and phrases, the more students gain from the text. A resource such as Resource 7.3 helps students to explore this speech with guided independence. Give students a copy of Macbeth's soliloquy and present them with the questions so they are able to find, highlight and annotate the relevant sections.

Students could work on this individually, in small groups or as a whole class, using the visualiser and pooling everyone's thoughts and ideas immediately. What will work for you will depend on your students, but I would recommend finalising the ideas and annotations as a whole class so that you can ensure

---

9. I heard Mary Myatt use this brilliant phrase at ResearchED Birmingham in March 2020 and it has resonated with me since – it is the perfect summation of what using a 'simplified' version of the text does, and it is not good enough for our students.

10. Mary Myatt, *The Curriculum: Gallimaufry to Coherence*, (Woodbridge: John Catt Educational Ltd., 2018), p. 11.

students have the key knowledge they need to start encoding into their long-term memories.

The questions help guide students through independent annotation and teach them the security and confidence that will be useful elsewhere in their English GCSEs – both for Language, when reading and interrogating the source materials, and for Literature, when students need to unpick an extract or, even more importantly, guide themselves through analysing unseen poetry. The questions provide a safe scaffold, with the 'expert' providing the questions but the students seeking out the answers for themselves.

## RESOURCE 7.3

| | |
|---|---|
| 1. Highlight the rhetorical questions in this speech. Explain why there are so many. What does it tell you about Macbeth's state of mind? | 8. When does Macbeth realise the dagger isn't actually there? Why do you think it is important that Macbeth realises that it is just his mind playing tricks on him before he goes to kill King Duncan? |
| 2. Find a quotation that implies that Macbeth tries to take hold of the dagger but is unable to do so. Highlight it, and explain what it means. | 9. What do you think the dagger represents? What is it a manifestation of? Why do you think Shakespeare has Macbeth hallucinate a dagger rather than something else? |
| 3. What kind of word is 'fatal'? What are the connotations of 'fatal'? Why does Macbeth use this word? | 10. Macbeth imagines what other people are dreaming about. Highlight all the dark, twisted images. |
| 4. What is meant by 'heat-oppressed brain'? | 11. Highlight the line where Macbeth wishes for silence, so that his feet cannot be heard as he moves towards Duncan's chamber and so that he will not be discovered. How does this wish for silence create tension in the scene? How does this link to other ideas in the play so far about remaining hidden? |
| 5. Find a quotation that shows Macbeth draws his own, real dagger. Highlight it, and explain what it means. | 12. 'Whiles I threat, he lives; Words to the heat of deeds too cold breath gives.' Find and highlight this line. What does Macbeth say is happening to his courage whilst he remains here, talking and thinking? |
| 6. Find and highlight a quotation that shows Macbeth's hallucination is directing him towards King Duncan's chamber. What is the significance of the dagger leading him rather than Macbeth going under his own steam? | 13. 'I go, and it is done'. Why do you think Shakespeare has used such a short clause here? |
| 7. What appears on the blade and handle of the dagger? Why is this significant? What do you think it might represent? | 14. Why does Macbeth instruct Duncan not to listen to the bell? What does the bell signify? |

## Macbeth's character

Having completed these activities, students are well placed to begin to crystalise some of their thoughts and work more independently towards an analysis of Macbeth's character here. In *Stop Talking About Wellbeing*,[11] Kat Howard describes how Jennifer Webb encourages students to consider, and analyse, characters with regard to their emotional, physical and psychological states. By doing this, students are able to explore the character in detail: rather than looking just at, for example, Macbeth's actions in this scene, students are guided to develop a more rounded understanding of all Shakespeare has done to shape his tragic hero. Students could present their ideas as a piece of extended writing, a table or even a mind map, but the crucial thing is for them to capture these three aspects of Macbeth: his emotional, physical and psychological state.

## Light and dark tracker

There are many examples in this scene of Shakespeare exploring further the idea of light and darkness. Of course, there have been many examples of light and dark imagery in the play since Act I, Scene iv. However, Act II, Scene i brings with it some really significant moments which are worth exploring in more detail. This lesson ends, therefore, with students reviewing their light and dark tracker, adding more examples and exploring their significance to the play as a whole.

## RESOURCE 7.4

| TRACKING LIGHT AND DARK IMAGERY IN MACBETH | | | | |
|---|---|---|---|---|
| Act/Scene Number | Light | Dark | Quotation/Character | Significance |
| Act I, Scene iv | ✓ | | 'signs of nobleness, like stars, shall shine / On all deservers' – King Duncan | Duncan says stars will shine on all those who deserve recognition for their loyalty. This makes light symbolic of hope, nobility and faithfulness. Duncan promises that others apart from Malcolm will be rewarded. It is safe to assume he is talking about Macbeth and Banquo here. |
| Act I, Scene iv | | ✓ | 'Stars, hide your fires! / Let not light see my black and deep desires' – Macbeth | By asking for the stars to 'hide' their fires, Macbeth is asking for light to extinguish itself. He does not want anyone to see what he is thinking about and, as a result, needs darkness to aid him in his plans. Darkness becomes associated with malice, and evil is the truth behind a fake appearance. |
| Act II, Scene i | | ✓ | 'The moon is down; I have not heard the clock.' – Fleance | Fleance comments that whilst the sky is dark – the moon cannot even be seen – he has not yet heard the clock chime midnight. This darkness seems unnatural to Fleance, and foreshadows Macbeth's forthcoming dark deeds. |
| Act II, Scene i | | ✓ | 'There's husbandry in heaven; / Their candles are all out.' – Banquo | Banquo suggests that the sky is darkened as if the stars have been extinguished. This would be in keeping with Macbeth and Lady Macbeth's calls for darkness and for the heavens not to see the crime they are about to commit. |
| | | | | |

---

11.  Kat Howard, *Stop Talking About Wellbeing*, (Woodbridge: John Catt Educational Ltd., 2020), p. 178.

## Answering the Big Questions

To finish the lesson, students should use their knowledge to answer the two Big Questions:

> *What is the relationship like between Banquo and Fleance?*
> *What does Macbeth say in his famous 'Is this a dagger I see before me?' speech?*

## Suggested 'Extra Challenge' activities

- In the 'Is this a dagger?' soliloquy, Macbeth's uncertainty is characterised by iambic pentameter with an additional, unstressed syllable (a feminine ending). When he resolves to murder the King, the metre falls back into standard iambic pentameter with a masculine ending. How far does this construct reflect societal expectations in Elizabethan England?
- Are Macbeth's actions free will or predestination?
- In Job 20:27, it states: 'The heaven shall reveal his iniquity; and the earth shall rise up against him.' How is the idea of the exposure of guilt reflected in *Macbeth*?

## Key vocabulary:

Free will, predestination

# CHAPTER 8
## Act II, Scene ii

*What do Macbeth and Lady Macbeth do after the murder?*

## What?

### Scene analysis: Act II, Scene ii

Audiences never see the murder of Duncan on stage, a choice which is interesting to behold. Whilst one can only speculate as to why, Shakespeare transgresses his usual practice when depicting the death of a main character. After all, Banquo's brutal murder is staged in full view of the audience. Instead, Shakespeare switches the focus of the action to Lady Macbeth, who waits in the dead of night for her husband's return, the murder accomplished and the promise of royal ascension close to fruition. Perhaps Shakespeare makes this decision because the act of regicide is too loathsome to behold, being as it is both sickening and abominable. The murder of a king is too sinful to lay eyes upon; Macbeth and Lady Macbeth have kept their plans secret and so the act itself must also be hidden from the voyeuristic, prying eyes of others, audiences included. As a dramatist, the aftermath of the regicide is more interesting than the regicide itself.

Instead, our eyes scrutinise the actions of Lady Macbeth, who reveals she has taken a swig of alcohol to assist her in her plans. 'That which hath made [Duncan's guards] drunk, hath made [her] bold; / ... [and given her] fire.' Audiences are already familiar with the scheming contrivances of Lady Macbeth, and so her renewed sense of stamina and vigour would, at first glance, seem incredibly frightening. Yet behind this façade of strength and intrepid hardiness lies a weakness that threatens to reveal itself. Lady Macbeth's previous appeal to spirits and her soliciting with the supernatural has not worked as she would have hoped, and so she has had to find her own means of strength.

Lady Macbeth's qualities of boldness and 'fire' would connote fortitude, and yet her dialogue is contradictory. She presents herself as ready and prepared for the events which are about to unfold and yet she is startled at the noises which break the silence, stating 'Hark, peace; it was the owl that shrieked'. She is in a state of obvious agitation, her cool, calm exterior shattered by the screech of an owl, a bird often regarded as an omen of death.[1] In this sense then, perhaps Lady Macbeth's communion with the spirits *has* worked, and this is their way of announcing to her that the murder has taken place. After all, she continues by referring to the owl as a 'fatal bellman, which gives the stern'st good night.' A bellman would be a town crier, someone who would walk the streets to make announcements.[2] Preceded by the term 'fatal', it would imply that Lady Macbeth sees the owl as a harbinger of death.

## SOUND AND SILENCE

Shakespeare uses sound, or rather the lack of it, to render the Macbeths completely vulnerable, a rather ironic fact, seeing as they are counting on *Duncan's* vulnerability to carry out their plans.

Silence, in itself, is paradoxical. The Macbeths desire silence so they can perform their evil deeds swiftly and easily, yet, at the same time, it is tortuous and almost too much to bear. The silence, rather than providing a comfort to the Macbeths, is overwhelming, as they have no way of being able to predicate what any other characters are doing. They could be spying on them or they could be far away; whilst silence can be a comfort, here it sets the Macbeths on edge.

Lady Macbeth does her best to ignore this vulnerability by focusing on what she is able to control. She reveals the steps she has taken to enable Macbeth to put their plans into action, observing that 'the surfeited grooms do mock their charge / With snores.' There is an element of contempt here. Lady Macbeth seems to sneer at how easily she has managed to overpower Duncan's guards and relishes the uncertainty of whether they will live or die, saying 'I have drugged their possets / That death and nature do contend about them, / Whether they live, or die.' By drugging them to within an inch of their lives, we understand that death is not always a natural occurrence, just as King Duncan will find out in the final moments of his life. Lady Macbeth, by bringing the guards closer to death, is in conflict with the course of nature once more. Death is precipitated through human interference.

Macbeth enters, uttering questions and demanding to know 'Who's there?' His question mirrors Banquo's in Act II, Scene i, when Macbeth approaches him

1.   Ed. Cora Linn Daniels and C.M. Stevans, *Encyclopedia of Superstitions, Folklore, and the Occult Sciences of the World*, (Hawaii: University Press of the Pacific, 2003), p. 182.

2.   Ed. Sandra Clark and Pamela Mason, *The Arden Shakespeare: Macbeth*, (London: Bloomsbury, 2015), p. 177.

in darkness, a sign of uncertainty on both parts. Whereas Macbeth answers with 'a friend' to Banquo, Lady Macbeth does not hear or see her husband enter, too wrapped up is she in a maelstrom of panic that they will be discovered. Macbeth's question is a curious one. He must be aware that his wife is waiting for him and yet still he asks. This scene takes place in the middle of the night, and so it might be that Macbeth physically cannot see her; the darkness both the Macbeths craved in the previous act has made them somewhat erratic and insecure. On the other hand, Macbeth's questions could be a symptom of his disorientation, so perplexed is he because of the deed he has committed. Arguably, Macbeth is not in full control of himself: 'one would reasonably expect him to know it's his own wife. Whereas in the previous scene he could see things in front of him that weren't there, now he cannot see things that are in front of him: his wife.'[3]

Macbeth's wife's fear is evident; she speaks to reassure and convince herself that everything should go as planned. Again, Shakespeare employs noise here to heighten Lady Macbeth's unrest. She stops once more, saying 'Hark', but not elaborating on what she has heard. The noise, whatever it is, has passed, and she is greeted with a familiar silence which is both oppressive and accepted. She goes back to reminding herself of her past actions, revealing it was she who laid the guards' daggers out for Macbeth to find in plain view so that '[h]e could not miss 'em.' Lady Macbeth, in her desire for power, has prepared everything for her husband; all he has to do is perform the final act. This in itself is indicative of Lady Macbeth's lack of faith in her husband to go through with the deed, possibly believing that Macbeth's moral sense of right and wrong will once again act as an obstacle to getting what they want.

### 'HAD HE NOT RESEMBLED / MY FATHER AS HE SLEPT'

There is, however, a sense of irony here as Lady Macbeth encounters an obstacle of her own, one which changes our perception of her and makes us believe she is not as strong as she thinks she is. She says, 'Had he not resembled / My father as he slept, I had done't', implying Duncan bears some sort of physical parallel to her father. The cold, calculating Lady Macbeth audiences have become accustomed to have seen a rare moment of compassion from her, something she attempts to purge herself of in Act I, Scene v. This moment reveals 'a cleavage between her imaginings and her physical power to translate them into action.'[4]

---

3.  Neil Bowen et al., *The Art of Drama Volume 2: Macbeth GCSE & Beyond*, (Bristol: Peripeteia Press, 2019), p. 90.

4.  Lynn Veach Sadler, 'The Three Guides of Lady Macbeth', *CLA Journal*, Vol. 19, No. 1 (1975), pp. 10–11, www.jstor.org/stable/44325583.

This disparity is made all the more evident from Lady Macbeth's previous claims that she would dash the brains of her child out if she had sworn to Macbeth that she would do so, and yet parricide is one taboo she cannot break. One must wonder if the same protestations made by Macbeth would be as excusable to Lady Macbeth should the situation be reversed. Before, we would assume there is nothing Lady Macbeth would not do to seize power, yet finally we have an answer as to what can hinder her. Duncan must bear a striking similarity to her father if his appearance is enough to impede her murderous desires. However, 'there may be more here than the coincidental resemblance of one old man to another. Recognizing Duncan as her father, Lady Macbeth evokes the interlinked political and family structures of her society, the order the murder will violate.'[5]

Finally, Lady Macbeth acknowledges the presence of Macbeth, calling him 'husband' for the first and only time in the play. What follows is a short, pacy, disjointed series of interrogative sentences; Macbeth and Lady Macbeth are trying to make sense of their situation and the irreversible act in which they have both played a part. They are restless and apprehensive, jumpy and nervous, terrified perhaps by the possibility of discovery. Upon asking his wife whether she heard a noise, Lady Macbeth replies she 'heard the owl scream and the crickets cry'. If Lady Macbeth is aware that an owl is an omen of death, she hides its significance from Macbeth, just like she keeps her previous solicitations with the spirits from him: the supernatural is never far away.

Unsurprisingly, Lady Macbeth is the character who gains control of the situation. Macbeth laments his actions, claiming 'This is a sorry sight', only for his wife to respond, 'A foolish thought, to say a sorry sight.' She seems to scold him for his angst, determined they see their plans through to the bitter end. This is painful for Macbeth; he has committed the unthinkable and Lady Macbeth must bring him to his senses before he unwittingly reveals their plot to the rest of the castle.

### 'ONE CRIED, "MURDER"'

Yet Macbeth's agitation continues, and it seems it will take more than a brief retort to make him see the situation clearly. He becomes overwhelmingly distraught at what he has heard upon returning from Duncan's murder, fearful that he has been discovered by people in the castle who seem to have awoken. It is not entirely clear who Macbeth is talking about when he refers to the 'one [who] did laugh in's sleep' and 'one [who] cried "Murder"'. This ambiguity

---

5.  Ed. Alexander Leggatt, *William Shakespeare's Macbeth: A Sourcebook*, (Abingdon: Routledge, 2006), p. 151.

may originate from the maniacal state Macbeth has found himself in, woefully recollecting events that have only just occurred. Indeed, there is debate amongst Shakespearean critics as to whom Macbeth could be referring to, with 'some editors... [assuming] them to be Malcolm and Donalbain'.[6] Let us consider the possibility that Macbeth *is* referring to Duncan's sons here. They wake themselves; one laughs in their sleep and the other shouts 'Murder', rousing them to consciousness before saying their prayers and settling back down to sleep. Seeing as Duncan is associated with heavenly imagery earlier in the play, it stands to reason that Malcolm and Donalbain would themselves be seen to affiliate with God. After all, Malcolm has been made Duncan's heir; it is his divine right to be God's spokesperson on Earth. Macbeth mentions how they cried 'God bless us' and 'Amen', as if they had seen his bloody hands.

If the voices are *not* those of Malcolm and Donalbain, Macbeth could be talking about their servants. The identity of the voices, however, is not really the significant aspect of this tale that Macbeth recounts; the fact he cannot say 'Amen' in response to their blessings is what concerns him the most, and although Lady Macbeth dismisses his concerns, telling him to 'consider it not so deeply', for Macbeth, the situation is dire. 'Amen', usually uttered at the end of a prayer, means 'so be it'; if he could say it, Macbeth would be part of that blessing too and yet he cannot. The severity of his actions, his guilt and his realisation that he has committed the ultimate sin prevent him from articulating such a holy word; the Great Chain of Being is sacrosanct and Macbeth will fall foul of its sacred order.

It could be argued that Macbeth, in a way, is expecting this. He knows what he has done is wrong; considering his sin he seems to wittingly deplore his own actions without asking outright for forgiveness, claiming 'I had most need of blessing'. Already there is evidence he is tormented by his actions, something which will never go away. It lies dormant, it simmers, priming itself to cripple its subject when the time is right, something Macbeth will find out once he is crowned king. Lady Macbeth recognises Macbeth's suffering, advising her husband that thoughts like the ones he is having 'will make us mad', a statement that foreshadows the delirium she will be driven to by the play's bloody and tragic end. Lady Macbeth is firm in her expectations. Having been anxious and skittish during the opening of the scene, she is now blunt and practical, increasing the pace and the urgency to act. As her husband bemoans his actions, Lady Macbeth is cold and clinical, eager for Macbeth to overcome his doubts and fears.

However, he cannot.

---

6.   Ed. Sandra Clark and Pamela Mason, *The Arden Shakespeare: Macbeth*, (London: Bloomsbury, 2015), p. 180.

### 'MACBETH SHALL SLEEP NO MORE'

His fears consume him, and he ignores his wife's wishes and continues to speak, plagued by unease and trepidation. He believes he has heard another voice commanding him to 'sleep no more', and observing that 'Macbeth does murder sleep', yet the origin of these remarks remains unknown. Whereas before Macbeth seemed certain who was praying (although ambiguous to audiences), now he only mentions 'a voice', nameless and alien.

The voice appears to be hallucinatory, harking back to the 'heat-oppressed brain' Macbeth believes he could be suffering from when he sees the dagger. The extreme pressure he has created for himself means he is now in the grip of paranoia, a state he has been in since his entrance, when he asks his wife 'Didst thou not hear a noise?'

Indeed:

> *It is difficult not to invest some sympathy in Macbeth at this point, so eloquent and terrified is his emotional state, expressing an almost childlike helplessness and yearning repetition of the word 'sleep' seven times in less than ten lines.[7]*

It is interesting that Macbeth has been compared to a child in this scene, for Lady Macbeth adopts somewhat of a maternalistic role with her use of imperatives. Macbeth needs direction and, like a child who looks to their mother for guidance, finds it in Lady Macbeth.

Sleep, a soothing influence on 'hurt minds', a 'bath' that soothes aches and pains of a day's work, a source of strength and 'chief nourisher in life's feast', has been destroyed by Macbeth. His words are almost prophetic; all creatures need sleep in order to survive and yet Macbeth will become so plagued by his emotional instability that he will be denied it, condemned to experience every moment of his gradual destruction. If sleep brings peace, then no sleep is clearly linked to guilt.

The voice Macbeth claims to hear continues to cry '"Sleep no more" to all the house' as if his actions will rouse all from their slumber. Note how every noise 'cries' out. Duncan's murder has been committed silently by Macbeth and yet this silence is shattered by the noise that surrounds it. Nature and humanity are viscerally reacting to Duncan's murder: whilst Macbeth called for silence, his crimes are quickly surfacing, evidenced through these distressed sounds.

What is particularly ominous is that by stating 'Glamis hath murdered sleep, and therefore Cawdor / Shall sleep no more', the voice is an echo of the first two

---

7.   R.S White, *Ambivalent Macbeth*, (Sydney: Sydney University Press, 2018) p. 161.

greetings of the witches, excluding the third, which recognises Macbeth as king. This, then, links Macbeth's paranoia to the supernatural, and by excluding his future royal title there is a suggestion that whilst he may have a crown, he will never truly be a king.

Macbeth's preoccupation with the voice he claims to hear leaves him unable to function; once again, Lady Macbeth must gain control if their plans are to succeed. As Macbeth tries to ascertain the origins of the voice he hears and the meaning behind its sinister words, Lady Macbeth, perhaps curious, perhaps exasperated, asks 'Who was it that thus cried?' before deducing that her husband's ramblings are not to be taken so seriously. This in itself is ironic. Lady Macbeth is quick to denounce her husband's fears that he will never sleep again, and yet it is she who will cease to do so by the play's end, a state which will ultimately lead to her untimely death. In response, she tells Macbeth that he is weakening his strength by obsessively pondering over such things, not even waiting for an answer to her previous question. Speaking once more in imperatives, she tells Macbeth to 'Go, get some water / And wash this filthy witness from your hand.' She notices the daggers and once again, with ire, asks 'Why did you bring these daggers from the place? / They must lie there. Go, carry them, and smear / The sleepy grooms with blood.' A vivid image of a mother and child manifests itself in this scene. Although Lady Macbeth cannot be described as a typical maternal figure, her authoritarian and domineering behaviour, especially in the way she constantly instructs Macbeth, creates a portrait of a dysfunctional mother scolding her son.

One may ask why Lady Macbeth has not noticed the daggers until this point. Perhaps she is not thinking clearly either, although she does a good job of hiding this whilst her husband is present. Her initial ignorance of Macbeth's possession of the weapons mirrors the fact she did not see her husband when he first entered; although it is clear she has a better grip of the situation than has Macbeth, she is still feeling overwhelmed at having to take charge, a disappointing reality which only highlights her husband's struggles to complete what they have planned. He refuses to return to Duncan's chamber to dispose of the weapons, saying 'Look on't again, I dare not.' Macbeth, someone who has committed acts of brutality in the past without so much as a second thought, is suddenly sickened by them.

Macbeth, crippled by what he has done, draws shame from his wife at his weakness. 'Infirm of purpose' she seems to spit, before instructing him to give her the daggers in order to return them to their rightful place. Lady Macbeth chides him through her frustration. Time is of the essence; the longer Macbeth spends in his state of contrition, the stronger the possibility of discovery. Lady Macbeth compares the sleeping and the dead to pictures, saying only a child would fear 'a painted devil.' In her eyes, there is nothing for him to be frightened of, although this contrasts with her later appearance, when she needs a light constantly by her side, just like a child might. She must be at her wits' end by this point, for she has been left to deal with the immediate repercussions of Duncan's murder as her husband deplores what he has done.

Without waiting for him, Lady Macbeth decides quickly to 'gild the faces of the grooms withal' if Duncan 'do bleed'. By wondering if the King still bleeds, Lady Macbeth could be alluding to cruentation, in which it was believed that a corpse would bleed to signify the presence of its murderer. Indeed, 'a number of late-sixteenth and seventeenth century inquests [saw] coroners and their juries [utilise] corpse-touching to elicit cruentation as a tool of investigation',[8] and even James I refers to it in *Daemonologie*.[9] Perhaps this is why Macbeth refuses to return. Not only is he afraid to look at what he has caused, but his reappearance by Duncan's corpse would reveal him to be the murderer if it began to bleed once more.

Lady Macbeth's use of the word 'gild' is odd, as to 'gild' means to cover thinly with gold. This may be symbolic of Duncan's royalty; Macbeth refers to Duncan's blood as 'golden' in the next scene, highlighting its distinction as blood spilled from the sovereign. However, it could also be a reference to 'old gold [which] was red'.[10] If this is indeed the case, then Lady Macbeth is symbolically painting devils on the faces of the grooms.[11]

### 'EVERY NOISE APPALS ME'

As Lady Macbeth exits, a loud knocking commands the audience's attention. It acts as an intrusion into the secretive world of the Macbeths and one which promises to wake the castle, threatening discovery. Macbeth asks himself where the knocking is coming from, a sign, perhaps, of the disorientation that has ravaged him since Duncan's murder. Something that may add to Macbeth's agitation is that he seems to think that he is acting out of the ordinary. As members of the audience, we can see that Macbeth's reaction is not hyperbolic in any way; the fears, the anxieties and the apprehension are all natural reactions to the awful crime he has committed, and yet he still asks himself 'How is't with me, when every noise appals me?' He feels as if he should not be acting in the way he does, and yet he still cannot help himself.

---

8.  Sara M. Butler, *Forensic Medicine and Death Investigation in Medieval England*, (New York: Routledge, 2015), p. 140.

9.  Ed. Sandra Clark and Pamela Mason, *The Arden Shakespeare: Macbeth*, (London: Bloomsbury, 2015), p. 182.

10. Ibid.

11. Ibid.

It should come as no surprise then, that Macbeth cannot concentrate on one thing for too long and that his attention immediately turns from the sound of knocking to the state of his own hands, asking 'What hands are here?' as if the blood that dries on them has made them unrecognisable. These hands, which have translated his thoughts into action, now appear to be alien to him. It is almost as if Macbeth does not believe they are capable of committing such an act, stating 'they pluck out mine eyes.' Just looking at his hands destroys his sight.

Macbeth's refusal to look at his hands because they have performed an evil deed is reminiscent of Lady Macbeth's earlier call to the spirits to shroud her 'in the dunnest smoke of hell' so that her knife cannot see the 'wound it makes'. The two situations correlate in the sense that the perpetrators of such acts refuse to behold the consequences of their actions. They are keen to cut off their sense of sight if it means saving themselves from the guilt they will have to suffer.

This idea of sight and sightlessness is a crucial developmental phase in infancy. Children are obsessed with games such as 'peekaboo'. The reason that this is such a popular game is because of object permanence, and children learning about the things around them being concrete – and continuing to exist – regardless of whether or not they are in sight. In asking for their actions not to be seen, even by themselves, Macbeth and Lady Macbeth enter a state almost of infancy: if they cannot see what they have done, they cannot suffer the guilt or negative effect of their actions. Whilst Macbeth and Lady Macbeth do not act like children per se, it is perhaps the case that Shakespeare is making another deliberate allusion to childhood. Lady Macbeth has already commented that Macbeth's fear of Duncan's body is child-like – ''tis the eye of childhood / That fears a painted devil'. Later in the play, Lady Macbeth is in a child-like state, needing a 'light by her continually'. Perhaps they believe that they are more innocent and deserve more protection than they actually do. Or perhaps they are just incredibly naïve to the repercussions of their heinous acts.

Macbeth, however, is less naïve than his wife. He recognises guilt cannot easily be purged from oneself. His personal interrogation ends with an enquiry as to whether 'all great Neptune's ocean' will be able to wash the blood from his hands. Macbeth's reference to Neptune highlights his fear of what is to come; if the Roman god of the sea cannot cleanse Macbeth of the blood which physically dries on his hands and symbolically stains his morality, nothing can. Sensing his act is irreversible, Macbeth answers his own question: 'No'. His hands will turn the many oceans 'incarnadine', a bright crimson, 'Making the green, one red.'

This final line is worthy of further examination. Some editions of *Macbeth* do not include punctuation in 'making the green one red', meaning actors delivering this line are not obliged to place emphasis on a particular word. However, other editions, including that used here, place a comma after 'green', meaning 'one red' commands our attention; reading the line in this way means the sea has wholly taken on the appearance of blood, stressing the 'totality' of its change in colour.[12]

The transformation of the seas' colour from green to red is possibly a biblical allusion too, referencing the first of the Ten Plagues inflicted on Egypt by God in response to the Pharaoh's refusal to free the Israelites from slavery. In both *Macbeth* and the record of the Plagues from the Book of Exodus, water becoming blood is a consequence of God's wrath. Macbeth, by killing God's spokesperson on earth, has become the subject of God's fury. Washing his hands in water will not free him of his guilt, but instead taints and infects something pure and lifegiving, a subtle message that Macbeth will ruin everything he touches.

### 'A LITTLE WATER CLEARS US OF THIS DEED'

Lady Macbeth enters once more, apparently unable to excuse her husband for his cowardice, ashamed perhaps that he has not embodied the qualities she believes a man should possess. She exclaims how her hands are now red, but she shames 'to wear a heart so white.' The image of red against white is a striking one; Lady Macbeth is now stained with the blood of a king she has helped to savagely slaughter and there is no denying that both are complicit in this terrible act. Blood-covered hands form a motif Shakespeare has used in another of his plays. Just like the conspirators who murder Julius Caesar bathe their hands in his blood as a sign of responsibility for his murder, Lady Macbeth's red hands highlight the responsibility she bears and the blame she shares.

Once again, the pace of the scene increases as Lady Macbeth issues her orders like a dysfunctional mother. Believing that 'a little water clears [them] of this deed', Lady Macbeth is clearly trying to disassociate herself and her husband from the violent act they have planned and committed. Notice how dismissive she seems to be of this momentous event, calling it a 'deed' as if their acts are mundane and commonplace. They are, of course, anything but, and Shakespeare makes it very clear to audiences that one cannot run away from their actions. Whilst the blood on their hands, a visual reminder of what they have done, may easily be removed, it is their memory of such actions which will slowly erode the façade of innocence they come to adopt. Guilt, after all, cannot be controlled, cannot be contained. As the Macbeths

---

12. Ed. Sandra Clark and Pamela Mason, *The Arden Shakespeare: Macbeth*, (London: Bloomsbury, 2015), p. 183.

will discover, it slowly eats away at their sense of morality until there is nothing left but a relic of their former selves. Macbeth seems to have some semblance of the lasting effects of guilt. Wondering whether 'all great Neptune's ocean' will wash the blood from his hands is really highlighting a greater concern; Macbeth is asking if he will ever be cleansed of his guilt. Lady Macbeth, however, believes only a 'little water' is needed to restore order, highlighting how she shuns the idea of feeling guilty. She is more interested in constructing virtuous pretences so others perceive them both as innocent. Telling Macbeth to gather himself and put on his nightgown, Lady Macbeth creates this fakery with apparent ease, an ironic moment considering it is she who will end up revealing – in her confused mutterings at the play's end – what they have done.

As the knocking at the door continues, Macbeth realises he is not the man he was, lamenting 'to know my deed, 'twere best not know myself.' To acknowledge his deed is to realise that he has transformed into someone unrecognisable. In a moment of sombre reflection, perhaps even regret, Macbeth answers the knocking at the door with 'Wake Duncan with thy knocking. I would thou couldst.'

## Knocking

Macbeth and Lady Macbeth exit with the sounds of knocking continuing to reverberate through the castle. Knocking, in itself, is a motif which is noteworthy, an auditory representation of Macbeth's fear of his fate. In Act I, Scene iii, when Macbeth first has thoughts of harming Duncan to win the crown, he says the thought makes his 'seated heart knock at [his] ribs'. Macbeth fears the repercussions of this 'horrid image'; it frightens him that he could even envisage such a thing, and now that it has happened, this knocking, this intrusive action, is revisited. Instead of an internal, private knocking, the noise can be heard by all, a sign that Macbeth's private thoughts have physically manifested themselves in the real world. Macbeth's fate is knocking for him not just metaphorically but literally. Macduff, Macbeth's nemesis and foil and the man who will eventually kill him, waits to be let in. If Macbeth is sin, Macduff is morality, and it invades the castle which, thus far, has been devoid of honesty and truth.

## The motif of hands in Acts I and II

Macbeth spends most of the first two acts in deep thought, wrestling with his inner conscience and moral self. Having been presented with the alluring promise of power, Macbeth wonders whether he should commit acts of violence to get what he wants or whether he should wait for 'chance' to crown him. As we see in Act II, Scene ii, Macbeth *does* act. His thoughts may have propelled him to this moment, yet it is his hands which have metamorphosed these thoughts into reality. Hands are the tools we use to execute our will.[13] In most cases, hands are instruments that carry out deeds of good, yet they can also become weapons – dangerous and volatile.

Hands are referenced throughout most of Act II, Scene ii; at this moment in the play they are symbolic of guilt and act as a reminder of what the Macbeths have done, admonishing them for their behaviour. By Macbeth's hands, Duncan is dead. Audiences are not invited to witness the regicide itself, perhaps because of its deplorability. Shakespeare constantly reminds us just how sinful Macbeth's act is. No performance of the play could ever hope to fully present audiences with an accurate and authentic representation of the sheer horror of royal murder. In fact, the same is true for Macbeth at the end of the play, and one wonders whether this is deliberate. After all, Macduff still commits regicide even though Macbeth is a tyrant.

Hands, then, are used to allude to the abhorrence of the act, rather than showing it explicitly, something Shakespeare would not be able to do with royal viewership in mind. Indeed, James I was not the only monarch to watch the play. King Christian IV of Denmark, in visiting his sister, Queen Anne, joined James I in watching the King's Men, Shakespeare's company, perform *Macbeth*.[14] Shakespeare would not want to anger any royal viewers with a depiction of regicide. Instead, quite deliberately, Shakespeare seems more concerned with, and draws the audience's attention to, the psychological impact of the murder rather than the murder itself.

It is this psychological impact that Lady Macbeth tries to alleviate from her husband, saying 'a little water clears us of this deed.' Of course, her actions are futile. Washing their hands may rid them of Duncan's blood, but not of the guilt that will infest them later in the play. The act of handwashing is worthy of further exploration. Its origin as a symbolic act can be traced back to Pontius Pilate, the fifth governor of the Roman province of Judea and the man who is now best known as presiding over the trial of Jesus Christ, eventually ordering his death by crucifixion. Pilate, standing in front of a crowd baying for the death of Christ, washed his hands as a way of proclaiming he would not be seen as being a part of what was being asked of him. In Matthew 27:24 it is written:

---

13. The ideas explored here are heavily drawn from the work of Mathew Lynch (@Mathew_Lynch44 on Twitter), originally shared as part of the LitDrive (@LitdriveUK) Regional Advocate CPD sessions.

14. Ed. J.H. Walter, *The Player's Shakespeare: Macbeth*, (Oxford: Heinemann Educational Publishers, 1962) p. 3.

*When Pilate saw that he could prevail nothing, but that rather a tumult was made, he took water, and washed his hands before the multitude, saying, I am innocent of the blood of this just person: see ye to it.*[15]

There has always been a connection between the washing of flesh as emblematic of the cleansing of the soul. The very purpose of baptism is to purge one of sin; with this in mind, Lady Macbeth's observation that 'a little water clears us of this deed' could be alluding to her wish to purify both of them of their guilty conscience. Research, after all, suggests that 'people often feel less guilty after washing their hands. Purity is the central notion of morality.'[16]

Audiences may wonder why Macbeth is so taken aback by the appearance of his hands, especially considering his past actions. Whilst hands represent guilt and fear in Act II, in Act I they are symbolic of loyalty and disloyalty. Even Macbeth himself cannot fathom who (or what) he has become, asking 'What hands are here?' He has undergone a transformation, marked by the change in his hands' purpose. In Act I, Scene ii, audiences hear Macdonald has been killed by Macbeth's hand. The Captain, in his report about Macbeth's prowess, notes he 'ne'er shook hands, nor bade farewell to him'. This is a clear sign of loyalty to Duncan; Macdonald is a clear threat to his kingship and must be eliminated. Macbeth is not willing to offer any sign of peace or extend a hand of friendship. Instead, he meets his grisly end when Macbeth 'unseamed him from the nave to th' chops'. Macbeth's hands are capable of committing violence, yet this violence is born out of loyalty to his king rather than self-gain.

The same cannot be said for Lady Macbeth, who literally takes Duncan by the hand to lead him to Macbeth when the King first arrives at the castle. 'Give me your hand,' Duncan instructs before telling Lady Macbeth to 'Conduct me to mine host.' The dualism of 'fair' and 'foul', ever present throughout the play, is brought to the fore once more at this moment. The loyal hand of Duncan is taken by the duplicitous hand of Lady Macbeth, who leads her king towards inescapable danger.

The motif of hands in Acts III, IV and V is further explored in Chapter 17.

---

15. *The Holy Bible Containing the Old and New Testaments*, Authorised King James Version, www.kingjamesbibleonline.org, Matthew 27:24.

16. Brad J. Bushman, Laurent Bègue and Hanyi Xu, 'Washing the guilt away: effects of personal versus vicarious cleansing on guilty feelings and prosocial behavior', National Center for Biotechnology Information, (2014) https://www.ncbi.nlm.nih.gov/pmc/articles/PMC3937805/.

## Act II, Scene ii at a glance

# RESOURCE 8.1

Lady Macbeth refers to Macbeth's actions as 'deeds'. One could argue she cannot bring herself to say what they have actually done: committed the act of regicide. ⋯⋯⋯

Lady Macbeth, like a dysfunctional mother, instructs Macbeth to stop thinking about the act he has just committed. Thinking about the murder will turn them mad. Ironically, by the end of the play, Lady Macbeth is driven mad by what they have done.

Notice how Macbeth ⋯⋯ thinks he hears a voice cry. He is not certain, which perhaps mirrors the disorientation he feels after killing his King.

The voice Macbeth hears at this moment could be hallucinatory. Sleep, the 'nourisher' of life, is needed to survive. If Macbeth has 'murdered' sleep, it means he is condemned to destroy himself.

**LADY MACBETH**
These deeds must not be thought
After these ways; so, it will make us mad.

**MACBETH**
Methought I heard a voice cry, 'Sleep no more.
Macbeth does murder sleep', – the innocent sleep,
Sleep that knits up the ravelled sleave of care,
The death of each day's life, sore labour's bath,
Balm of hurt minds, great Nature's second course,
Chief nourisher in life's feast,–

**LADY MACBETH**
What do you mean? ⋯⋯⋯⋯⋯

**MACBETH**
Still it cried, 'Sleep no more' to all the house;
'Glamis hath murder'd sleep, and therefore Cawdor
Shall sleep no more. Macbeth shall sleep no more.'

**LADY MACBETH**
Who was it that thus cried? Why, worthy thane,
You do unbend your noble strength, to think
So brainsickly of things. Go get some water
And wash this filthy witness from your hand.
Why did you bring these daggers from the place?
They must lie there. Go, carry them, and smear
The sleepy grooms with blood.

**MACBETH**
I'll go no more.
I am afraid to think what I have done;
Look on't again I dare not. ⋯

Referring to the titles of Glamis and Cawdor echoes the first two greetings of the witches, perhaps insinuating the supernatural is linked to Macbeth's paranoia. The third greeting, that which refers to Macbeth as king, is missing. This omission may signify that whilst he may have the crown, he will never truly be king, for he has not been chosen by God.

Once again, Lady Macbeth takes control of the situation. She gives Macbeth a set of clear instructions he must follow if they are to make it through the night without being caught.

Lady Macbeth seems to be dismissive of Macbeth's fears. He has disappointed her through his cowardliness. Her response is blunt, as if she has no time for him.

Lady Macbeth, once more, disregards her husband's fears, saying she weakens his strength by obsessing over his actions.

Hands in this scene represent guilt and violence. Blood covers the hands of Macbeth and Lady Macbeth by the end of the scene, and even though they wash it off, both will be driven mad by the culpability and blame they share.

Macbeth may fear returning to the scene of the crime because Duncan's bleeding body could expose him as the murderer. It was believed bodies of murdered victims would begin bleeding in the presence of their murderer (a process known as cruentation).

# How?

## Retrieval

Retrieval challenge grids are a low preparation, high impact way of formatively assessing gaps in pupil knowledge. They are, put very simply, grids containing a series of questions that cover past content. Kate Jones explains: 'the… grids are designed to challenge every individual in the classroom. Each question will be worth a certain amount of points [which] increase as the level of difficulty increases.'[17] You will see in Resource 8.2 that the challenge rises, not by the style of question, but by how long ago the knowledge was initially introduced to students.

## RESOURCE 8.2

| | | | |
|---|---|---|---|
| Why does Macbeth see a dagger? | What reasons does Macbeth give for not going ahead with Duncan's murder? | How does Macbeth call for darkness in Act I, Scene iv and what is the significance of this? | What are the three prophecies the witches give Banquo? How do these differ from Macbeth's prophecies? |
| How does Shakespeare use Banquo to confirm to Duncan that Macbeth and Lady Macbeth are loyal people? | What does Lady Macbeth say she would do if she promised her husband to do so? | What does the term 'hamartia' mean? What is Macbeth's hamartia? | What is the purpose of the Captain's speech in Act I, Scene ii? |
| What were the Great Chain of Being and the Divine Right of Kings? | Why does Lady Macbeth ask to be 'unsexed'? What does this really mean? | What does the phrase 'look like the innocent flower, / But be the serpent under't' show us about Lady Macbeth? | What techniques has Shakespeare used in the phrase 'fair is foul, and foul is fair'? What does it suggest? |
| One point | Two points | Three points | Four points |

## Pre-reading activities

The following pre-reading strategies were first introduced to me by Alice Visser-Furay.[18] They have one, simple objective: to help students become confident, independent readers. Initially, I used these strategies to help students read what Visser-Furay calls 'authentic, academic'[19] texts: texts that would increase cultural capital. However, I knew these methods could help students with fictional texts too. These strategies could be used for any scene and any play. Their purpose is not to help students understand every single one of Shakespeare's words, but they give them enough help to increase their independence and become the confident readers we know they can be.

---

17. Kate Jones, *Retrieval Practice: Research and resources for every classroom*, (Woodbridge: John Catt Educational Ltd., 2019), p. 95.

18. @AVisserFuray.

19. Visser-Furay used this phrase at the 2019 New Voices Conference. It stuck with me because of her determination to help all children access texts that would increase their cultural capital whilst challenging and engaging them.

It is all too easy to jump straight into a scene without laying any sort of foundation for students to build their knowledge. I always used to be guilty of this. My class would come in, we would quickly assign parts to read and off we went, reading somewhat disjointedly and – inevitably – pausing many times whilst I briefly explained what was going on without stopping to gauge, at any point, students' understanding. It was me telling them what I knew rather than helping them discover the text themselves. This, put bluntly, made the reading process utterly pointless. Most of my students were not understanding the dialogue, and my brief explanations which tried to get everyone 'up to speed' meant Shakespeare's subtle nuances and complexities went largely ignored.

## ANTICIPATION GUIDE

To combat this, I now sometimes start by asking students to participate in an 'Anticipation Guide'. This involves showing students a series of statements, designed around the scene they are about to read. Students should stand up if they agree with the statement or sit down if they disagree, being prepared to explain their thoughts. For Act II, Scene ii, you could use the following statements:

1. Macbeth, having prepared himself to kill the King, will be unaffected by his actions once the murder is complete.
2. Lady Macbeth will continue to exert more power over Macbeth.
3. Lady Macbeth is a weak character.
4. Macbeth is more likely to expose the truth of the murder.
5. Macbeth is holding Lady Macbeth back from fulfilling her grand ambitions.

The statements require students to use their knowledge of what has happened prior to this scene to make predictions about ideas which will be explored in the scene they are about to read. When I first completed this activity, I was surprised at how many students had something to say. The discussion went on for far longer than I had intended, yet all of it was useful and produced some incredibly perceptive responses alongside some lively debate.

## REDACTED LINES

This discussion leads clearly into the next phase of prediction and inference. Provide students with a copy of Resource 8.3.

## RESOURCE 8.3

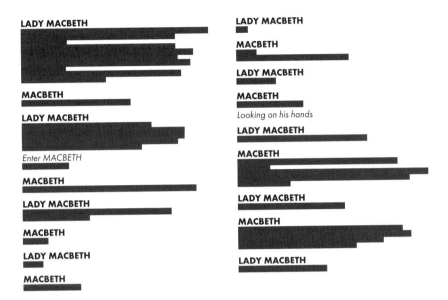

Whilst this does not cover the entire scene, it gives students enough evidence to be able to make their predictions as to what is happening at this moment between Macbeth and Lady Macbeth. Without access to the dialogue, ask students what new inferences they can make. Whilst this may initially confuse them, it is important they realise that most of what is said is in what is *not* said. Students could answer the following questions if they need direction:

- What do the lengths of the lines tell you about how each character is feeling at this point?
- Can you spot any patterns in the lengths of the lines? Who is speaking more? What does this imply?
- What do you think the pace of the scene will be like? What is happening at this moment in the play to set this pace?
- Can you link any of your ideas back to the statements in the anticipation guide? Does this new evidence prove or disprove any of your previous inferences?

Students could make notes on the actual resource, or this could be the basis for another class discussion. Either way, I think it is important to stress to students that their inferences may be incorrect. The purpose of this activity is not to find a 'right answer', but simply to help them understand what could be happening when they eventually get around to reading the scene.

## INFERENCES FROM VOCABULARY

At this point, however, students are still not going to read the scene. Instead, they are going to look at vocabulary from Macbeth and Lady Macbeth's dialogue, using it to enhance and extend their inferences and predictions further still. If using this strategy for other texts, there are no 'correct words' to choose to help students make their predictions. I like to pick words that challenge students, not just in terms of the word itself, but where it fits contextually with the rest of the scene (or whatever form of writing you are studying).

The words from Act II, Scene ii I might choose are:

| | | | | |
|---|---|---|---|---|
| bold | fatal | bellman | surfeited | grooms |
| drugged | confounds | hark | resembled | descended |
| amen | methought | balm | nourisher | noble |
| brainsickly | filthy | Neptune | multitudinous | incarnadine |
| blood | white | constancy | poorly | deed |

Give one word to each student and ask them to move around the room. Students should explain what their word means to another student, who will explain what their word means in return. To add an extra level of challenge, students could see if they can connect their words in any way and make a new inference. Students are allowed to swap should they wish, and if they do not know what their word means, they should find someone who does. If no one in the class knows, a note should be made and the word picked up when it is read in context with the rest of the scene. Take feedback at the end of the activity and gather class insights as to what the words mean, how they could connect to the scene itself and whether they prove or disprove any other inferences made in previous activities.

## MAKING PREDICTIONS

At this point, ask students to draw together their inferences made from the previous tasks. Ask them the following questions:

1. What do you think Macbeth and Lady Macbeth will be feeling in this scene?
2. How do you think the actors playing Macbeth and Lady Macbeth would deliver their lines in the scene?
3. What big ideas do you think Shakespeare will explore in this scene?

## Reading the scene

The next strategy is one shared by Simon Beale (@SPBeale) on Twitter. Originally used by Beale to aid academic reading in history, I trialled the method to help students understand Shakespeare's complex language and was very pleased with the results. To begin, give students a copy of the scene to read through. Divide the scene up into three sections. I would recommend doing this before the lesson begins, but if students have their own copies of the text, you may want them to do this themselves. Where you divide the scene up is up to you, but as a rough guide, try to make the sections as equal as possible.

Assign parts and read the scene. Ask students to give each section a title based on what has happened in it. Then ask students to summarise what happens in each section in two or three bullet points and take feedback to check their understanding. Whether you read through the entire scene first before summarising each section is up to you, but I always find reading a section and then completing the title and bullet points before reading the next section is logical, especially if students are new to this strategy. You can see an example of how this might look in Resource 8.4.

## RESOURCE 8.4

| | | |
|---|---|---|
| Enter LADY MACBETH<br><br>**LADY MACBETH**<br>That which hath made them drunk, hath made me bold;<br>What hath quench'd them hath given me fire.<br>Hark, peace; it was the owl that shrieked,<br>The fatal bellman, which gives the stern'st good night.<br>He is about it. The doors are open,<br>And the surfeited grooms do mock their charge<br>With snores. I have drugged their possets<br>That death and nature do contend about them,<br>Whether they live, or die.<br><br>**MACBETH**<br>Who's there? What ho? | **LADY MACBETH**<br>Alack, I am afraid they have awaked,<br>And 'tis not done. The attempt, and not the deed<br>Confounds us. Hark. I laid their daggers ready;<br>He could not miss 'em. Had he not resembled<br>My father as he slept, I had done't.<br>My husband?<br><br>**MACBETH**<br>I have done the deed.<br>Didst thou not hear a noise?<br><br>**LADY MACBETH**<br>I heard the owl scream and the crickets cry.<br>Did not you speak?<br><br>**MACBETH**<br>When?<br><br>**LADY MACBETH**<br>Now. | **Section title**<br>*Lady Macbeth's fear*<br><br><br><br><br><br><br>**Section summary**<br><br><br>*Lady Macbeth has set out everything ready for Macbeth to commit the murder, but is worried he won't do it.*<br><br>*She could not murder Duncan herself because he looks like her father when he sleeps.*<br><br>*Macbeth enters. The two have heard noises which unsettle them.* |

Whilst the class reads, ensure students pick up on the vocabulary they were unsure of during the previous task. Ask students what they think the word means now they can see it in context. Come up with a definition together. Reread certain lines where the word appears and dual code collaboratively to help students understand the definitions.

I would also recommend rereading the entire scene. This will allow you to ask deeper questions to push students' thinking. Questions you could ask include:

1. What are the positives and negatives of silence during the scene's opening?
2. What does Lady Macbeth's inability to kill Duncan herself suggest about her?
3. Why do you think this is the only time Lady Macbeth refers to Macbeth as her husband?
4. What do you think is stopping Macbeth from saying 'Amen'?
5. Why does Macbeth ask 'What hands are here?' What is he really asking?
6. Someone outside the castle is knocking to be let in. What could this sudden interruption symbolise?
7. What image does Shakespeare create to show Lady Macbeth is complicit in the murder?

The process of guided reading is a long one and will probably take you most of the lesson, yet try not to let that put you off. Once students have a full understanding of what happens in the scene, they can work on increasing their deeper knowledge. Is this strategy needed for every scene? Probably not. The point is, the strategy is there to be drawn upon when needed.

## Theatrical choices

Once students have an understanding of the scene, provide them with Resource 8.5, allowing them to enhance that understanding and apply deep subject knowledge to what happens. This is designed to aid students in exploring the scene, but also to share their own opinions on how they think events would play out, something I think is important not to neglect. We must remember, after all, that *Macbeth* is a play, and it is easy to lose the theatricality of the text when reading it in class behind desks. There is no right answer here, just the opportunity for exploration and creativity.

## RESOURCE 8.5

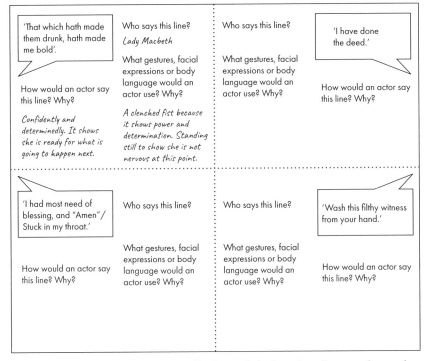

| | | | |
|---|---|---|---|
| 'That which hath made them drunk, hath made me bold'. | Who says this line?<br><br>*Lady Macbeth*<br><br>What gestures, facial expressions or body language would an actor use? Why? | Who says this line?<br><br>What gestures, facial expressions or body language would an actor use? Why? | 'I have done the deed.' |
| How would an actor say this line? Why?<br><br>*Confidently and determinedly. It shows she is ready for what is going to happen next.* | *A clenched fist because it shows power and determination. Standing still to show she is not nervous at this point.* | | How would an actor say this line? Why? |
| 'I had most need of blessing, and "Amen" / Stuck in my throat.' | Who says this line? | Who says this line? | 'Wash this filthy witness from your hand.' |
| How would an actor say this line? Why? | What gestures, facial expressions or body language would an actor use? Why? | What gestures, facial expressions or body language would an actor use? Why? | How would an actor say this line? Why? |

Not only are students asked to recall who said the line, but they are directed to consider how the line would be said and what the actors playing Macbeth and Lady Macbeth would be doing as they say them. If students are struggling to convey the characters' feelings, they could refer back to the emotion wheel used in previous lessons. It may also be an idea to watch a small snippet of this scene from a filmed production to help complete the first section of the resource, bearing in mind some of our students have never had the opportunity to step inside a theatre before and experience a live performance.

### The motif of hands

Resource 8.6 on the motif of hands in *Macbeth* is particularly useful in getting students to consider Shakespeare's purpose. The sheet provides students with a series of quotations, and whilst some of them do not reference hands explicitly, they do provide us with an indication of Macbeth and Lady Macbeth's actions. The resource then asks students what hands represent throughout the beginning of the play. I particularly like resources like these that ask students to track symbols and motifs, because they allow students to appreciate that writers *do* have plans. 'Did the writer really mean that?' is a question I get asked a lot in my classroom. Sometimes the answer may genuinely be 'no', but in many cases, I think students do not realise that writers have something to say and that they will find inventive and exciting ways to act as a conduit for the messages they wish to convey.

## RESOURCE 8.6

### MOTIF: HANDS IN ACT I AND ACT II

**Your task:**
Consider the quotations and make notes as to what hands represent in Act I and Act II of 'Macbeth'.
How does their meaning and significance change as the play progresses? Why does their meaning change?

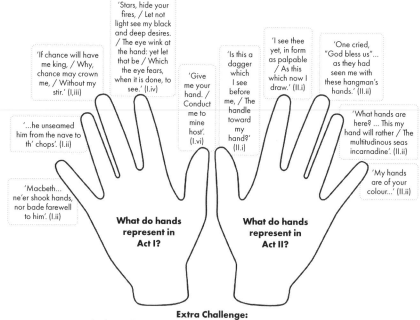

'Stars, hide your fires, / Let not light see my black and deep desires. / The eye wink at the hand: yet let that be / Which the eye fears, when it is done, to see.' (I.iv)

'If chance will have me king, / Why, chance may crown me, / Without my stir.' (I.iii)

'Is this a dagger which I see before me, / The handle toward my hand?' (II.i)

'I see thee yet, in form as palpable / As this which now I draw.' (II.i)

'One cried, "God bless us"... as they had seen me with these hangman's hands.' (II.ii)

'Give me your hand. / Conduct me to mine host'. (I.vi)

'...he unseamed him from the nave to th' chops'. (I.ii)

'What hands are here? ... This my hand will rather / The multitudinous seas incarnadine'. (II.ii)

'Macbeth... ne'er shook hands, nor bade farewell to him'. (I.ii)

'My hands are of your colour...' (II.ii)

**What do hands represent in Act I?**

**What do hands represent in Act II?**

### Extra Challenge:
Why do you think Shakespeare uses the motif of a hand to present these ideas to the audience? What is he criticising or warning the audience about?

## Answering the Big Question

To finish, ask students to complete a piece of exploratory writing:

Discuss Macbeth and Lady Macbeth's actions after the murder of King Duncan. Include:

- what Macbeth and Lady Macbeth do immediately after the murder.
- quotations which help you explain their state of mind.
- your own opinions on Macbeth and Lady Macbeth's actions.

Ensure students have an understanding of the command word in the task. To 'discuss' means to 'present key points', meaning the purpose of the task is to ascertain what students have learnt from the scene whilst providing them with the opportunity for some extended writing practice.

## Suggested 'Extra Challenge' activities

- Would the play be more or less effective if Shakespeare had portrayed the regicide on stage? Why?
- In Matthew 27:24 it is written, 'When Pilate saw that he could prevail nothing, but that rather a tumult was made, he took water, and washed his hands before the multitude, saying, I am innocent of the blood of this just person: see ye to it.' Discuss this in relation to *Macbeth*.
- 'People often feel less guilty after washing their hands. Purity is the central notion of morality.'[20] To what extent is this true for Macbeth?

## Key vocabulary:

Motif, culpable

---

20. Brad J. Bushman, Laurent Bègue and Hanyi Xu, 'Washing the guilt away: effects of personal versus vicarious cleansing on guilty feelings and prosocial behavior', National Center for Biotechnology Information, (2014), https://www.ncbi.nlm.nih.gov/pmc/articles/PMC3937805/.

# CHAPTER 9
## Act II, Scene iii

*Who is the Porter?*

### What?

The Porter is, undoubtedly, a very divisive character! The very mention of him is likely to elicit one of two responses from English teachers: those who believe his character is extremely important to Shakespeare's message and those who begrudgingly set themselves up for a challenging lesson because it is difficult to convey exactly what he adds to proceedings. I grant that this may be a sweeping generalisation, but I am of the mind that the study of the Porter is often neglected when one teaches *Macbeth*. The inclusion of his character in the extract provided for the Edexcel English Literature paper in 2019 only goes to show that no element of a text should be ignored. The Porter is an important character and one who serves a purpose, even if that purpose is not immediately clear to us at first.

### Scene analysis: Act II, Scene iii

Whilst the scene may be theatrically necessary for those playing Macbeth and Lady Macbeth to wash their hands and change their clothes, the Porter's entrance signals a shift in tone for *Macbeth*; the beginning of Act II, Scene iii is at huge odds with the events that have occurred only moments before. Such is the immensity of this change that it is almost bewildering for an audience. The high stakes and moral anguish of Act II, Scene ii, which sees Macbeth and Lady Macbeth's plans dangerously close to careening out of control, are defused by the presence of a comedian. His banterous and often lewd conversation with Macduff (revealed to be the source of the knocking) seems completely out of place. Shakespeare has brought his eponymous character to a state of such extreme distress that this change in direction does not seem fair, let alone right. However, whilst students are likely to justify the Porter's inclusion with a comment about his character serving as 'comic relief', he serves another purpose which deserves to be explored.

## 'HERE'S A KNOCKING INDEED'

The action begins with a continuation of the knocking first heard in the previous scene; the private and clandestine realm of the Macbeths is about to be invaded by the outside world, symbolic of their fate which will catch up with them. Secrets, it seems, cannot be buried for long. The Porter enters, muttering to himself. 'Here's a knocking indeed,' he proclaims before adding 'If a man were porter of hell-gate, he should have old turning the key.' The Porter may be a comedic character, but his dialogue is tinged by the ominous.

In his first line, he seemingly compared his role as Macbeth's porter to being the porter of 'hell's gate.' This, of course, is an unwitting comparison; the Porter is unaware of Macbeth's actions that have transformed the castle from a place of loyalty to a hive of deceit. Duncan is dead, and nothing holy or pure can exist there any more. The castle will always be the scene of regicide and, through the Porter's words, is just one step away from transmuting into hell itself.

Hell is alluded to even further, with the Porter calling out 'knock, knock, knock. Who's there, i'th' name of Belzebub?' This line (a possible origin of the 'knock knock' joke?) references a name given for the Devil in Christian theological sources: 'Belzebub', one of the seven princes of hell. The Porter, in imagining himself as the porter of hell, claims to ask his question in the Devil's name. In a way, the same is true for the Porter in his cold reality; he speaks in the name of Macbeth, his master now devil-like in his killing of King Duncan.

## 'HERE'S A FARMER'

Amongst his ramblings, the Porter also wonders about the type of people who would be knocking and the sins they have committed to condemn them to that place. He imagines a farmer, an equivocator and a tailor, each trooping their way to an afterlife that will punish them to everlasting suffering and misery. Arguably, these three professions are not chosen at random, but instead are metaphors for the behaviour that has led Macbeth to his unlawful ascension to power. The Porter relays to the audience the very actions that have driven the farmer, equivocator and tailor to the gates of hell, and they bear a remarkable similarity to Macbeth's own:

> *The farmer, has, through his hoarding [of the harvest], acted detrimentally to the well-being of society; private gain has prevailed over the public interest. The equivocator has committed treason; the tailor has stolen from clothing that properly belongs to another.*[1]

---

1.   John B. Harcourt, "'I Pray You, Remember the Porter'", *Shakespeare Quarterly*, Vol. 12, No. 4, 1961, pp. 393–402, www.jstor.org/stable/2867456.

John B. Harcourt observes that these three characters have been chosen 'because of their relevance to the dramatic situation'. Macbeth, a man compelled by selfish and callous ambition, thinking only of himself, has committed treason in its most extreme form – that of regicide – and lied about it. Doing so has enabled him to steal the crown, and (if we are to continue with Shakespeare's clothing metaphor) the royal robes 'which were not his by right.'[2] It could be argued that Shakespeare decides to present these three sins as manifestations of three different people to show audiences that just *one* sin would be enough to condemn one to hell. Frederic B. Tromly sums it up best when he says 'the path [to hell] is well trodden because it is not reserved for spectacular crimes like regicide.'[3] If a porter of hell 'should have old turning the key', it means human criminality is common. The fact that Macbeth has committed all three of these sins places his actions in context with society's morals. He cannot possibly redeem himself, and yet, somehow, letting the audience judge Macbeth's actions against those of the imaginary sinners makes him more human. Yes, he has committed regicide, but his sins, those of self-gain, equivocation and theft, are, according to the Porter, often seen.[4]

### 'THIS PLACE IS TOO COLD FOR HELL'

It should come as no surprise then, that the Porter eventually gives up his imaginary role as hell's gatekeeper, perhaps because of the sheer enormity of the task at hand; there are simply too many people to let into hell. He claims 'this place is too cold for hell', 'cold' obviously containing its own negative connotations. This is followed by his desire to have 'let in some of all professions that go the primrose way to the everlasting bonfire', an attractive and enticing but sinful path to hell. The Porter, in this sweeping statement, claims everyone, including the audience, has felt temptation at some point in their lives, warning a vast number will end up knocking on the gates of hell for doing so. His comment is an interesting one, for it continues to humanise Macbeth; whilst it may be too strong to claim the audience feel an affinity with him, they will certainly recognise feelings of allurement, and so perhaps are not right to judge him in the way they do. Of course, Macbeth's punishment stems from the fact that he has acted on these desires, but it provides an opportunity for self-reflection, especially for contemporary audiences who would very much

---

2.  John B. Harcourt, '"I Pray You, Remember the Porter"', *Shakespeare Quarterly*, Vol. 12, No. 4, 1961, pp. 393–402, www.jstor.org/stable/2867456.

3.  Frederic B. Tromly, 'Macbeth and His Porter', *Shakespeare Quarterly*, Vol. 26, No. 2, 1975, pp. 151–156, www.jstor.org/stable/2869244.

4.  Ibid.

have believed in hell as a punishment for sins committed in life. Shakespeare's message, told through the Porter, is almost parable-like, ironic seeing as so much of what he says contains hellish imagery.

This simple story, told to illustrate a moral lesson, is one Shakespeare wants his audiences to remember. 'Remember the porter,' the character cries before opening the gates. Whilst 'remember' is often seen as an instruction directed at Macduff and Lennox to tip him, there is something more sinister lurking in these words. They are seemingly prophetic; the Porter is a comical character, but his comments about temptation and its pathway to hell are severe. 'Remember the porter' could well be an instruction to audiences to remember what he has said, a warning that they, like the imaginary sinners, could meet the porter of hell's gates one day. Of course, the Porter *is* memorable because of the immense contrast between his comical self and the seriousness of other characters. As such, it is most unlikely that any audience would *not* 'remember the porter.'

## The equivocator

As a side note, Shakespeare cleverly links the imagined equivocator to help serve the play's greater purpose by making somewhat of an 'in-joke' to his audiences about ambiguity. In keeping with his royalist stance, Shakespeare could be alluding to Father Garnet here, a priest arrested for his complicity in the Gunpowder Plot who famously used equivocation (meaning one thing but saying another) in his testimony in an attempt to avoid execution.[5] Garnet failed and was killed on 3 May 1606. A contemporary audience 'would immediately have understood this line as a mockery of the Catholics' perceived practice of equivocation.'[6] Shakespeare, once again, is subtly warning his audience that treason will always be followed by the direst of inescapable consequences.

Shakespeare seems to persist with this mockery; the equivocator is not the only sinner who relates to Father Garnet. In an alternative interpretation of the Porter's imagined travellers to the gates of hell, it could be argued that the farmer is a subtle nod to Garnet too. 'Farmer' was one of Garnet's pseudonyms, meaning Shakespeare could be mocking his attempts to absolve himself of any wrongdoing during his trial.[7] What is more, Shakespeare could be making reference to 'relics from Garnet's execution in the talk of "napkins", another

---

5. Ed. Sandra Clark and Pamela Mason, *The Arden Shakespeare: Macbeth*, (London: Bloomsbury, 2015), p. 185.

6. Sue Fielder, *Oxford Literature Companions: Macbeth*, (Oxford University Press, Oxford, 2014), p. 31.

7. Peter Milward, 'Meta-drama in Hamlet and Macbeth', *Shakespeare's Christianity: The Protestant and Catholic Poets of Julius Caesar, Macbeth and Hamlet*, ed. Beatrice Batson, (Texas: Baylor University Press, 2006), p. 15.

word for handkerchiefs which were often used by Catholic spectators at executions to mop the blood of martyrs.'[8] The connections do not stop there. If it is the case that *Macbeth* was first performed for King James in December 1606 (rather than August),[9] the Porter's welcoming of a tailor could possibly refer to a tailor questioned in November 1606. This tailor was interrogated for being in possession of a stalk of grain on which Garnet's blood was said to have splashed, creating an image of his face and known, therefore, as 'Garnet's straw'.[10]

This is where Shakespeare's genius lies. His work has a multitude of interpretations that plumb almost infinite depths: audiences, students and scholars can all read in the character of the Porter – and indeed any Shakespearean character – the ghosts of the real men and women who informed Shakespeare's evocative verse.

## The Porter 'pre-figured'

Fredric B. Tromly argues that the Porter has already been 'pre-figured' in an earlier scene. Lady Macbeth, in Act I, Scene vii, when chastising her husband for his perceived cowardice, paints a picture bearing a striking similarity to the presentation of the Porter when he first arrives on stage:

> *Was the hope drunk*
> *Wherein you dressed yourself? Hath it slept since?*
> *And wakes it now to look so green and pale,*
> *At what it did so freely? From this time*
> *Such I account thy love. Art thou afeared*
> *To be the same in thine own act and valour,*
> *As thou art in desire?'*

'The figure of the impaired Porter literalizes the images'[11] Lady Macbeth paints of her husband once he has claimed they shall 'proceed no further in this business'. The Porter has 'been intoxicated, has overslept, and is now hungover ("green and pale")',[12] much as Macbeth has seemingly appeared to have been to his wife.

---

8.  British Library, 'The Trial of Henry Garnet, 1606', British Library, (2020), https:// www.bl.uk/ collection-items/the-trial-of-henry-garnet-1606.

9.  RSC, 'Dates and Sources', RSC.org.uk, (2020), https://www.rsc.org.uk/macbeth/ about-the-play/dates-and-sources.

10. Ibid.

11. Frederic B. Tromly, 'Macbeth and His Porter', *Shakespeare Quarterly*, Vol. 26, No. 2, 1975, pp. 151–156, www.jstor.org/stable/2869244.

12. Ibid.

Shakespeare's comparison of the two men, here, is inescapable – beat for beat, the descriptions of Macbeth and the actions of the Porter are inextricably linked. The two men both teeter on the brink of hell – Macbeth from his act of regicide, and the Porter in his fantasies as he works the gates of hell. Could the Porter's ramblings be portents of Macbeth's future?

Macbeth, considered a powerful man at the start of the play, is now more like the drunken fool. In not following his wife's every word, as far as she is concerned he is the one who has acted foolishly. Similarly, though, in acting out in support of the prophecies of the witches, it is clear that Macbeth is not all that great a man: his actions are demonstrative of the fact that he is still susceptible to human folly, much like the Porter has fallen to the follies of drunkenness. Macbeth's greed and ambition have overtaken his ability to think and plan rationally.

Lady Macbeth's consideration of Macbeth's drunken hopes soon moves on to the disparity between his 'act and valour' and his 'desire'. This is mirrored again by Shakespeare in the Porter's speech, where 'the Porter proceeds to lament that drink "provokes the desire, but … takes away the performance." Drink provokes the same pathetic impotence which Lady Macbeth throws in the teeth of her husband.'[13]

## Alcohol in *Macbeth*

Alcohol is often present in Shakespeare's plays. In fact, according to Buckner B. Trawick, each one of his plays contains at least one reference to alcohol, or at the very least some sort of thematic element that alludes to it.[14] Indeed, whenever drink appears, it is usually because of a celebration and shows we are creatures of habit for alcohol. As it is in modern society, alcohol is often used in Shakespeare's work as a source of comfort for his characters; it brings joy and is often consumed as a social activity promoting high spirits. In *Macbeth*, however, this is quite different. There are lighter moments in the play where alcohol *must* be present, although it may not be referenced explicitly: occasions such as Macbeth's celebration feast would be quite a dull affair without it. Yet when alcohol *is* referred to directly, it is in a negative sense; Shakespeare explores its dark side effects and the adverse influence it can hold.

13. Frederic B. Tromly, 'Macbeth and His Porter', *Shakespeare Quarterly*, Vol. 26, No. 2, 1975, pp. 151–156, www.jstor.org/stable/2869244.

14. Brooke Nguyen, 'Dressed in Drunk Hope: Alcoholism in Shakespeare's Macbeth', *Magnificat: A Journal of Undergraduate Non-fiction*, (2012), https://commons.marymount.edu/magnificat/dressed-in-drunk- hope-alcoholism-in-shakespeares-macbeth/.

Shakespeare would have been well versed in drink. Albert H. Tolman argues that 'in Shakespeare's day the drinking of alcoholic liquors was universal. Everybody drank, and at some time in his life even the most abstemious man was likely to be overcome by his potations.'[15] Ale or wine was a staple of a typical diet, mostly likely 'due to [a] lack of clean water', meaning 'alcohol was the primary form of liquid nourishment.'[16] Up until the Reformation, it seems society was indifferent when it came to the subject of alcohol, something which soon changed as religious tensions between Catholics and Protestants began to increase. Part of these tensions included insulting each side with accusations of drunkenness, leading to 'both sects [scrutinising] the place of drink in their version of a Christian society.'[17] Excessive drinking was frowned upon; drinking in moderation was very much encouraged.

Shakespeare subtly makes reference to society's criticisms of excessive drinking in Act II, Scene ii. Lady Macbeth drinks just enough alcohol to make her 'bold' in comparison to the guards (and perhaps Duncan?), who have consumed copious amounts, leading to an intoxication so extreme they have passed out into a drunken stupor. It is the alcohol, then, and their decision to drink heavily, that leads them to their deaths.[18]

Alcohol can also be linked to Shakespeare's characters' failures and the shame that follows such failure. Duncan's guards drink and so fail in their duty to protect their king; they are sound asleep when Macbeth creeps past them to commit regicide. Macbeth is also deemed a failure in the eyes of his wife during his momentary lapse when he refuses to press ahead with their plans to kill Duncan. In Act I, Scene vii, upon hearing Macbeth wishes to 'proceed no further in this business', Lady Macbeth hisses back: 'Was the hope drunk / Wherein you dressed yourself?' By alluding to her husband's potential use of alcohol and linking it to his inexplicable moral U-turn, Lady Macbeth is

---

15. Albert H. Tolman, 'Shakespeare Studies: Part IV. Drunkenness in Shakespeare', *Modern Language Notes*, Vol. 34, No. 2, (1919), pp. 82–88, www.jstor.org/stable/2915672.

16. Brooke Nguyen, 'Dressed in Drunk Hope: Alcoholism in Shakespeare's Macbeth', *Magnificat: A Journal of Undergraduate Non-fiction*, (2012), https://commons.marymount.edu/magnificat/dressed-in-drunk- hope-alcoholism-in-shakespeares-macbeth/.

17. Iain Gately, *Drink: A Cultural History of Alcohol*, (New York: Gotham Books, 2009), p. 106.

18. Brooke Nguyen, 'Dressed in Drunk Hope: Alcoholism in Shakespeare's Macbeth', *Magnificat: A Journal of Undergraduate Non-fiction*, (2012), https://commons.marymount.edu/magnificat/dressed-in-drunk- hope-alcoholism-in-shakespeares-macbeth/.

blaming his failure on his being drunk, accusing him of being cowardly, and attacking his masculinity.

The link between masculinity and alcohol is one the Porter himself consolidates. Swaggering on stage in his drunken state, the Porter is often seen as a comedic character, offering much-needed light relief after the horrific murder of Duncan. Indeed, his description of the physical side effects of excessive alcohol consumption are enough to cause anyone to be embarrassed. He openly states, 'drink sir, is a great provoker of three things… nose-painting, sleep and urine', when talking to Macduff when he first enters Macbeth's castle. Whilst the type of alcohol consumed may have differed from class to class, the effects of alcohol are all the same: audiences watching the Porter list these 'symptoms' of alcohol indulgence would be well aware that he speaks the truth. This jocular remark, however, is followed by something which could be interpreted as slightly more sinister. He goes on to say that alcohol 'provokes the desire, but it takes away the performance.' Of course, this crude remark is made in a sexual sense; the Porter is referring to alcohol's ability to render a man impotent.

In context with the rest of the scene, what is said seems nothing more than banter between two men, yet, when linked to previous comments made by Lady Macbeth, things become a little more serious. When Macbeth announces he does not want to proceed with Duncan's murder, Lady Macbeth questions whether drink is behind his reasons to stop their plans. It is a scathing attack on his masculinity: is it drink, she wonders, that has provoked his desire but taken away his 'performance'? He is impotent and therefore useless to her. By alluding to his virility, Lady Macbeth is issuing her husband a challenge: to go through with the murder or be shamed forever as less than a man.

## The sound of knocking

After the secretive and private nature of Duncan's murder, the quiet world of the Macbeths is shattered by the sound of knocking at the castle gates. It is persistent, an unwelcome intrusion which threatens to reveal their blatant guilt and a sound which 'appals' Macbeth. Lady Macbeth, only moments before, is startled by the sound of an owl; this relentless knocking is much more emphatic. The silence desired by the couple is no more. Whilst it is clear the knocking serves to build tension as audiences nervously await to see if it will rouse anyone from their sleep, it also serves a deeper, symbolic purpose: one which recurs at various intervals through the action. As discussed in Chapter 8, knocking is symbolic of fate arriving. Macbeth has killed the King, a moment which seals his destiny: his 'fate' is ready to invade the castle. Macduff, the man who will eventually kill Macbeth, is waiting on the other side of the castle gates.

Whilst most references to knocking occur in Act II, Scene ii, Macbeth references a different kind of knocking early on in the play. Upon hearing the witches' prophecies, which are confirmed to hold some truth, Macbeth speaks of a 'horrid image' of regicide that makes his 'heart knock at [his] ribs'. It goes without saying that murderous thoughts must be followed with preoccupations on the consequences of committing such an act. Unfortunately, Macbeth's ambition makes him blind against such physical signals of panic, even though the knocking of his heart occurs incredibly quickly after these thoughts begin to manifest themselves.

The speed at which fate is ready to catch up to these characters is demonstrated once more in Act II, Scene ii. Shortly after Macbeth commits Duncan's murder, knocking begins to occur, forcing the pair to go to bed, ready to feign their innocence. Macbeth's final words, 'wake Duncan with thy knocking. I would thou couldst', could imply a sense of regret, but are certainly indicative of the noise which reverberates around the castle. Duncan cannot be awoken and Macbeth's fate is sealed; the knocking will continue repeatedly until the castle gates (or the gates of hell if the Porter is to be believed) are open and Macbeth is dealt with by Macduff.

Like Macduff's persistent hammering on the gates of Macbeth's castle, the motif of knocking appears again and again throughout the play. In Act IV, Scene i, Macbeth goes to find the witches in order to learn more about his future. It is at this point, a scene where fate is a major theme, that the act of knocking is mentioned once again. This time it is by the second witch who announces: 'Open, locks, / Whoever knocks.' Macbeth is invited into their domain in an attempt to learn more of his future. It is interesting that knocking is referenced again here, because the person 'knocking' is Macbeth himself, yet his fate is waiting for him, hidden in the warnings the witches pose.

Finally, the motif of knocking appears one last time in the play when Lady Macbeth is sleepwalking, driven mad by the guilt which slowly erodes her mind. As she incessantly washes her hands, she alludes to past plots and machinations, saying: 'There's knocking at the gate', echoing Macduff's arrival at the end of Act II, Scene ii. It is referenced again as audiences realise this is the moment her fate has caught up with her; she simply cannot survive because of the things she has done.

## The Porter at a glance:

## RESOURCE 9.1

The Porter says that if 'Hell Gate' had a porter, they would have plenty of experience in 'turning the key', hinting at the extent to which humanity sins.

The constant knocking in this scene is symbolic of Macbeth's fate approaching. Macduff, the man who will eventually kill Macbeth, waits on the other side of the castle gates.

The knocking continues, showing how fate is persistent. It will not stop until it is fulfilled.

The third and final person the Porter lets in to hell is a tailor who has stolen from clothing that belongs to another. Macbeth has, in a sense, done the same thing; he has stolen the crown, a royal 'garment' from Duncan, to ascend to new heights of power. The three sinners, then, all represent an aspect of Macbeth's sinful actions, alluding to his condemnation to hell for what he has done.

Macbeth's murderous actions have transformed the castle into hell. Nothing good or holy can exist there any more. The Porter muses on what being the porter of the gates of hell would be like.

**Porter**
Here's a knocking indeed: if a man were porter of Hell Gate, he should have old turning the key. (Knock) Knock, knock, knock. Who's there, i'th' name of Belzebub? Here's a farmer that hanged himself on th'expectation of plenty. Come in time. Have napkins enow about you; here you'll sweat for't. (Knock) Knock, knock. Who's there, in th'other devil's name? Faith, here's an equivocator that could swear in both the scales against either scale, who committed treason enough for God's sake, yet could not equivocate to heaven. O, come in, equivocator. (Knock) Knock, knock, knock. Who's there? Faith, here's an English tailor come hither, for stealing out of a French hose. Come in, tailor; here you may roast your goose. (Knock) Knock, knock. Never at quiet. What are you? But this place is too cold for hell. I'll devil-porter it no further. I had thought to have let in some of all professions that go the primrose way to the everlasting bonfire. (Knock) Anon, anon, I pray you, remember the porter.

These words could act as a request on behalf of the Porter to remember to tip him.

The Porter imagines three sinners entering hell. The farmer has hoarded his harvest, acting detrimentally to the wellbeing of society. His selfish ways and their knock-on effects mirror Macbeth's own self-serving actions.

The second person the Porter pretends to welcome into hell is an equivocator who has committed treason. Like before, this imagined sinner shares the same qualities as Macbeth, who has, only moments before, committed treason by going through with Duncan's murder. Like the equivocator, Macbeth will not be able to talk his way into heaven after what he has done.

The Porter soon 'gives up' his role as the porter of 'Hell Gate' because of the sheer enormity of the task. There are too many people to let in.

These words are almost prophetic. The Porter, through his comments on temptation, is instructing the audience to remember his warnings. They too could one day be knocking on the gates of hell.

## How?

## Retrieval

Something which works particularly well for retrieval practice is 'flipped questioning', where a teacher provides students with an answer and they have to think of the question which goes with it. This is particularly effective because it is something that students of all abilities can access, depending on the answers you give them. For example, I might provide some in my class with the following:

| If this is the answer, what's the question? | |
| --- | --- |
| **ANSWER** | **QUESTION** |
| Lady Macbeth | |
| Duncan | |
| The Captain | |

These answers are ones I would expect the majority, if not all, of the class to access. They are so generic that a multitude of questions could be asked. This, however, does not mean they are not useful. For students who struggle to understand the relationships between the characters, using these 'wider' answers first is a way of helping them to access the text, which in turn will allow them to challenge themselves further. For example, an answer of 'Lady Macbeth' may have the question 'Who is Macbeth's wife?' For 'Duncan', one may put 'Who does Macbeth murder?'

Greater thinking occurs, however, when answers are more specific. This is why retrieval practice that does not just focus on the major points of content is particularly effective. Concentrating on what we would deem the 'most important parts' can sometimes have a negative effect on the memorisation of details. Research suggests that constant repetition of details results in them becoming more and more subsumed into other, large matters that are already known, which means they lose distinctiveness.[19] With this in mind, specific answers require specific questions, which may look like this:

| **ANSWER** | **QUESTION** |
| --- | --- |
| Lady Macbeth reveals she would kill her own child if she had sworn to do so. | *What extreme lengths does Lady Macbeth say she would go to, showing her comparable strength to her husband?* |
| So they can divorce themselves from their actions. | *Why do both Macbeth and Lady Macbeth call upon darkness in the play?* |
| He believes he should shut the door against the murderer. | |
| Equivocation | |
| Hamartia | |

Notice how vocabulary can be tested through 'flipped questioning'. If the answer, for example, is 'hamartia', I would expect a student to write a question along the lines of 'What is the correct term for a fatal flaw in one's character?'

---

19.   Pedro de Bruyckere, *The Ingredients for Great Teaching*, (London: SAGE, 2018), p. 59.

This could then lead to further questions such as 'What is meant by the term "fatal flaw"?' and 'What is Macbeth's hamartia?' to ensure students have grasped key concepts.

'Flipped questioning' challenges can be increased even further. Providing students with quotations as answers for students to frame a question around can generate some interesting responses. Here is a model of what this may look like, with some example questions mirroring what students could say:

| ANSWER | QUESTION |
|---|---|
| 'Signs of nobleness' | *What does Duncan say stars, which will shine on all deservers, are like?* |
| 'Golgotha' | *Which place does the Captain compare the battlefield to in Act I, Scene ii?* |
| 'Vaulting ambition' | *What is the only reason Macbeth can give for going through with Duncan's murder?* |

Students also enjoy making their own versions of this activity. Give them the opportunity to come up with their own answers and ask them to swap with a partner before asking them to think of questions that link to the new set they have. This can lead to an interesting 'flipped questioning' discussion which may look something like this:

> **Teacher:** *Stuart, give me one of your answers, please.*
> **Stuart:** *A raven.*
> **Teacher:** *Excellent. Amy, if that's the answer, what is the question?*
> **Amy:** *Which bird does Lady Macbeth say will croak 'the fatal entrance of Duncan'?*
> **Teacher:** *Well done. Can you remember why Shakespeare has Lady Macbeth reference a raven of all birds?*
> **Amy:** *Because a raven is seen as symbolic of death which foreshadows Duncan's murder in the following scenes.*
> **Teacher:** *Well remembered. Let's pick up on that idea of foreshadowing...*

This type of questioning can be pacy, and students enjoy the reversed aspect of it.

## Pre-reading activities

And so we come to the Porter scene. One thing I find particularly interesting is the fact that this character is a literal image of Lady Macbeth's description of Macbeth as a drunk man (in Act I, Scene vii, when she accuses him of being a coward). To help students remember this fact, I provide them with Resource 9.2, a quick language activity which acts as a pre-reading exercise to introduce the Porter's character.

## RESOURCE 9.2

> From what you can remember, briefly explain what has happened to cause Lady Macbeth to say this.

> Highlight references to intoxication in Lady Macbeth's speech and explain what image she is hoping to create of her husband.

**LADY MACBETH**
Was the hope drunk
Wherein you dressed yourself? Hath it slept since?
And wakes it now, to look so green and pale,
At what it did so freely? From this time
Such I account thy love. Art thou afeard
To be the same in thine own act and valour
As thou art in desire? Wouldst thou have that
Which thou esteem'st the ornament of life,
And live a coward in thine own esteem,
Letting 'I dare not' wait upon 'I would',
Like the poor cat i'th' adage?

> Lady Macbeth is describing the effects of alcohol here. Highlight where Lady Macbeth is exploring the effects of alcohol. How are these effects different from when she drinks alcohol as Macbeth goes to kill Duncan?

> How is 'green and pale' ambiguous? What could it mean?

This also sets the tone for the scene ahead. Whilst there is no doubt the Porter is used as light relief, his presence is also menacing and certainly has impact.

### Reading the scene

Having discussed the image of a drunken man, read the first part of the scene, up to 'I pray you, remember the porter.' Here, questioning should be used to link Lady Macbeth's image of a drunk man to the Porter. Questions to ask whilst reading could include:

1. What is the Porter doing when he first enters?
2. How is he similar to Lady Macbeth's description of Macbeth's cowardice?
3. Who does the Porter imagine himself to be?
4. Who is the first person the Porter imagines knocking on the gates and why?
5. Who is the second person the Porter imagines knocking on the gates and why?
6. Who is the third and final person to knock on the gates and why?

## Analysing the sinners

At this point, pause and review. This part of the play can be quite confusing for students because of the brief appearance of a character who never returns to the action again. To help students consider his purpose, provide them with Resource 9.3, which has been partially completed so you can think about how it could be used.

## RESOURCE 9.3

**'Knock, knock, knock. Who's there, i'th name of Belzebub?'**

| Who are they? | Farmer | Equivocator | Tailor |
|---|---|---|---|
| What have they done and why would this lead them to hell? | _____ _____ _____ _____ | _____ _____ _____ _____ | The tailor is knocking on the gates of hell because they have stolen fabric from clothing. This theft has led them to eternal suffering. |
| What are their similarities to Macbeth? | 1. Macbeth, like the farmer, is self-centred and only interested in himself<br><br>2.<br><br>3. | 1. Macbeth uses ambiguous language to make Duncan think he is loyal<br><br>2.<br><br>3. | 1. Macbeth has also stolen something which was not his<br><br>2.<br><br>3. |

This has been designed to help students reveal the reasons why the actions of the three sinners are significant. Although they may seem like the rambling creations of a drunken man, they are snapshots of Macbeth's own character. Begin by asking students to identify what the sinners are said to have done and, most importantly, what this says about them as people. Secondly, consider the reasons why this might lead them to hell. Thirdly, discuss how they have demonstrated similar qualities to Macbeth. Completing these three steps will help students consider the purpose of this scene.[20]

---

20. Icons from The Noun Project – 'Farmer' and 'Tailor' by Grégory Montigny, 'Telling Lie' by Gan Khoon and 'Flame' by kiddo, RU.

## Character mat

To consolidate knowledge of the Porter, students could complete Resource 9.4. I first came across the design for this resource from Sondos Bowker (@MrsB_NE on Twitter). It is designed to be clear and easy to use, allowing students to learn the information it contains by completing a series of mini activities to help them retain the most important points.

## RESOURCE 9.4

### THE PORTER in *Macbeth*

**Reduce**
In no more than 50 words, summarise who the Porter is and the purpose of the scene in which he appears.

**Transform**
Transform the information into two small images and label them.

**Read**
Read the information on the Porter.
The Porter is a character who is seen as light relief for audiences after the intensity of the murder of Duncan. He is there to make the audience laugh, yet his ramblings, brought on by drinking an excessive amount of alcohol, also contain a more ominous message. The Porter believes himself to be the gatekeeper of hell when he goes to answer a knocking at the castle gates. Shakespeare could be suggesting that Macbeth's castle has transformed into a hellish place after the heinous crime that has been carried out there. Imagining who could be on the other side, he thinks of a farmer who has hoarded produce, an equivocator, and a tailor who has stolen cloth. Each of these actions has set them on the path to hell, telling the audience that if Macbeth does not redeem himself, he is also destined for the 'everlasting bonfire', as they all have something in common. Macbeth has acted out of self-interest (like the farmer), he has lied (like the equivocator) and stolen the royal robes from Duncan (like the tailor who has stolen material).
The Porter comments that the constant knocking means there is never any quiet; perhaps the road to hell is well travelled. The knocking, however, symbolises Macbeth's fate, which has come for him. Macduff is on the other side of the gate, the person who will eventually murder the ultimate sinner.

**Magpie**
Select at least 3 key words from the information that you could use when writing about the Porter. Make sure you define them.

| Key word | Definition |
| --- | --- |
| | |
| | |
| | |

**Explain**
1. Why do you think Shakespeare needs to make audiences laugh at this point in the play?

2. Why do you think the Porter compares Macbeth's castle to the gates of hell? What are the connotations of hell?

3. The Porter pretends he is welcoming an 'equivocator' to the castle. Why would an equivocator be sent to hell? What examples of equivocation have we seen in the play so far?

Ask students to read the information, highlighting a maximum of three sentences that help them understand the Porter's character in more detail. Once they have finished this, they should reduce the information to no more than fifty words, transform what they have learned into a series of two images and 'magpie' vocabulary they could use when talking about the Porter themselves. Students should also have a go at engaging with the information in a critical way and should answer the questions which have been created to make them think deeply about what they have been learning across the lesson before taking feedback.

The class could refer back to Lady Macbeth's speech here, paying particular attention to her reference to alcohol and its effects, comparing her views to the Porter's rather frank commentary on the ramifications of consuming too much. Alcohol has played an important role in the events that have played out so far, and I think it would be interesting for students to see how a woman of high social rank views alcohol compared to someone of lower status; as it turns out, their opinions are quite similar. Perceptive students may pick up one major similarity that both characters identify. The Porter, when speaking to Macduff, says alcohol 'provokes the desire, but it takes away the performance.' Of course, this line leads to much hilarity when taken at face value. However, Lady Macbeth recognises the same consequence for her husband. She accuses him of being drunk when he made his promise to kill Duncan, stating the after-effects of alcohol have taken away his 'performance': his ability to commit regicide. Allowing students to connect these two moments will enable them to understand how alcohol affects us all in the same way, regardless of status, wealth and power. It is a small moment where characters stand on equal ground in the play.

## Answering the Big Question

Using the activities from today's lesson, ask students, as usual, to respond to the Big Question.

## Suggested 'Extra Challenge' activities

- 'Alcohol is inextricably linked with failure in Shakespeare's *Macbeth*.' Evaluate this statement in light of your knowledge of the play.
- 'The path [to hell] is well trodden because it is not reserved for spectacular crimes like regicide.'[21] Equivocation, self-gain and theft are often seen. With this in mind, how is Shakespeare placing Macbeth's crimes in context with society's morals?
- To what extent could the Porter's ramblings be portents of Macbeth's future?

## Key vocabulary:

Equivocation, ambiguous/ambiguity

---

21. Frederic B. Tromly, 'Macbeth and His Porter,' *Shakespeare Quarterly*, Vol. 26, No. 2, (1975), pp. 151–156. www.jstor.org/stable/2869244.

# CHAPTER 10
## Act II, Scene iii continued
## Act II, Scene iv

*Who is Macduff?*
*What is the reaction to Duncan's murder, and how does*
*his death affect the Great Chain of Being?*

## What?

### Scene analysis: Act II, Scene iii (continued)

#### 'MAKES HIM STAND TO, AND NOT STAND TO'

Macduff and Lennox enter the castle and are greeted by the Porter. As mentioned previously, the fact that it is Macduff that has been knocking and disturbing the peace of the castle is significant. Macduff brings with him questioning and judgement, and is, of course, the character who will bring about Macbeth's ultimate downfall.

It becomes immediately clear what time this scene takes place. With the murder itself having happened during the night, the Porter remarks that they have been 'carousing till the second cock' – in other words, the party continued until dawn had broken. Therefore, Macduff also brings with him the literal light of the day and, by extension, the metaphorical torch to shine on Macbeth and Lady Macbeth's dark deeds. When Macduff arrives, it becomes clear that the truth will inevitably out.

The Porter describes to Macduff how alcohol 'provokes the desire, but it takes away the performance' and that it 'sets him on, and it takes him off… makes him stand to, and not stand to'. These are all sexual innuendos, and whilst lechery and drunkenness are not Macbeth's vices, Frederic B. Tromly argues that there is a 'similarity between the state of mind created by the conjunction of drink and lechery in the Porter and the one created by the interplay of good and evil impulses in Macbeth.'[1] The Porter and Macbeth are similarly impaired, just by different things; as a result, neither is able to carry out their jobs effectively or achieve their own ambitions.

By the same token, the phallic imagery of impotence in the line 'makes him stand to, and not stand to' in particular is very relevant to the interpretation of Macbeth himself. He wishes to pass his crown on to his children, and is often preoccupied with the witches' prophecy that Banquo's sons will be king. As far as we are aware, Macbeth does not have an heir; his reign will end with no one to pass his crown to. His failure to start a dynasty of kings comes from his lack of children: it is literally his seeming impotence that will put an end to his ambition. His cruel, regicidal actions will have been for nothing.

In Shakespeare's having the Porter report these symptoms of drunkenness to Macduff, we perhaps also see something about Macduff himself. In a few, short scenes his whole family will be dead – 'all [his] pretty chickens, and their dam / At one fell swoop'. Any ambition of Macduff's to establish a successful lineage is gone at the hands of Macbeth, and so, in his desire to remove this despotic king, Macduff also falls foul of his ambition: it has rendered him impotent. Macduff, however, in murdering Macbeth, places the rightful heir back on the throne, ending Macbeth's cruel reign and in turn rendering *him* impotent. Therefore, the Porter's exploration of impotence here resonates for the audience in relation not only to Macbeth, but arguably, later, to Macduff, too.

**'IS THY MASTER STIRRING?'**

Once Macduff has entered and the Porter has departed, Shakespeare presents the audience with a tense exchange between Macbeth and Macduff. Throughout the conversation, Macbeth's comments are all polite but very brief. These short comments could be representative of the fear Macbeth feels: if he says little, he is less likely to be found out. Even when Macbeth is described by Macduff as being a 'worthy Thane', Macbeth still lies and tells him that the King has 'not yet' arisen. He goes even further than this, suggesting that anything that is genuinely a pleasure to do – like caring for the King – does not feel like work or any trouble: 'the labour we delight in physics pain'. Brian Vickers describes this as an 'insincere welcome'.[2] It is almost as if Macbeth is overstating his obsequiousness in order to try to divert attention from his crimes. It is not dissimilar to the tactic employed by Lady Macbeth when King Duncan first arrived at their castle.

1.  Frederic B. Tromly, 'Macbeth and his Porter', *Shakespeare Quarterly*, Vol. 26, No. 2 (Spring 1975), pp. 151–156, https://www.jstor.org/stable/2869244.

2.  Brian Vickers, 'Shakespeare's Hypocrites', *Daedalus*, Vol. 108, No. 3 (Summer 1979), pp. 48–83, https://www.jstor.org/stable/20024620.

## 'THE NIGHT HAS BEEN UNRULY'

Shakespeare's attention then turns towards the weather, and the difficult night experienced by those whom the Porter has welcomed. As Macduff goes to awaken the King, Lennox makes conversation with Macbeth regarding the night's events, commenting that 'The night has been unruly'. Whilst Lennox is not yet aware of the King's death, there have been many symbols that portend the news. There have been wild winds which have blown down chimneys, and this would evoke for the audience ideas about the witches who were widely believed to be able to conjure storms. This, as well as suggesting a supernatural influence on the night, is also a use of pathetic fallacy: the unsettled night at large reflects the deeply unsettled night at Macbeth's castle, although the noise that would accompany such a tempest remains unheard inside the castle walls; Lady Macbeth has only heard 'the owl scream and the crickets cry', denoting their abode is shrouded in silence. Perhaps their wishes for silence and to be hidden have been granted by their 'supernatural solicitings', but their actions have had loud and grandiose repercussions outside the castle walls. The Macbeths have disrupted nature and have therefore caused terrible storms, as witnessed by Macduff and Lennox, although they remain unaware of their relevance.

Not only are there wild winds, however. Lennox also comments that he 'heard i'th' air, strange screams of death', suggestive of the fact that the balance of nature, and natural order itself, have been upset by the murder of the King. On a personal level, Macbeth's crime is 'both ethical and political.'[3] However, 'once evil is unleashed... it corrupts all of the planes of creation... [including] the physical universe.'[4] Macbeth's crimes have literally broken nature; Scotland now faces 'the all-embracing destructive force of evil which touches every area of God's creation.'[5]

This is a trope heavily relied upon by Shakespeare, with storms also raging in *Julius Caesar*, accompanying the assassination of Caesar himself. Shakespeare draws often on this comparison of, and sympathy between, the human and natural worlds. Shakespeare again revisits the unruliness of the weather in the conversation between Ross and the Old Man in Act II, Scene iv: 'one man's crime has thrown the entire universe out of harmony.'[6]

Lennox also claims to have heard an 'obscure bird / [which] clamoured the livelong night.' This 'obscure bird' is an owl, a bird associated not only with

---

3. Irving Ribner, 'Macbeth: The Pattern of Idea and Action', *Shakespeare Quarterly*, Vol. 10, No. 2 (Spring 1959), pp. 147–159, https://www.jstor.org/stable/2866920.

4. Ibid.

5. Ibid.

6. Ibid.

darkness, but also with prophecy, linking the omen, and the event of the night, to the witches' actions.

In Greek and Roman mythology, owls also symbolised imminent death, and it was a commonly held belief in Roman society that the deaths of Agrippa, Julius Caesar, Augustus and Commodus Aurelius were all accompanied by the hooting of an owl.[7] Another Roman superstition was that witches could transform into owls.[8] Therefore, not only does this bird have associations with death, but the audience is also reminded of the three witches and the part they played in the murder of King Duncan.

Similarly, in English folklore it was believed that the screeching of owls foretold death, and that if the house of an ill person was flown past by a screeching owl, the ill person would shortly die.[9] English folklore also dictated that a screeching owl indicated a forthcoming – or existing – storm,[10] and this correlates with the weather as described by Lennox.

Arguably, Shakespeare has not just included this exploration of weather in *Macbeth* to create evidence that the natural world order has been destroyed. Weather in the spring of 1606, when *Macbeth* was most likely written, was also unusual: there were wild tempests and upward of 2000 people died in the area surrounding the Severn Estuary as a result. Huge storm surges also destroyed arable farmland and livestock in Somerset, Bristol, Barnstaple, Gwent and East Anglia.[11] Whilst these events did not take place in the Scottish setting of *Macbeth*, it can be argued that a contemporary audience would have been aware of the events elsewhere in the country.

These 'real world' references would not have gone unnoticed even by the people of London, despite the paucity and speed of news. Not only this, but by linking the events of the play (through references to the weather) to the same incidents happening in real life, Shakespeare would have brought a sense of realism and therefore fear to an audience. Less than a year earlier, King James I had narrowly escaped a plan to end his life via the Gunpowder Plot.

---

7.   Dr R. Mark Gaffney, *Where the Birds Make Their Nests: A Study of the Birds of the Bible*, (XLibris Corporation, 2010).

8.   Ibid.

9.   Barry Madden, 'Wildlife in Common: Barn Owl', Norfolk Wildlife Trust, https://www.norfolkwildlifetrust.org.uk/news-and-articles/articles/all-articles/wildlife-in-common-barn-owl.

10.  *National Geographic*, 'Delving into cultural myths, tales and beliefs about wild birds', https://blog.nationalgeographic.org/2016/11/08/delving-into-cultural-myths-tales-and-beliefs-about-wild-birds/.

11.  'Weather in History 1600 to 1649AD', https://premium.weatherweb.net/weather-in-history-1600-to-1649-ad/.

Contemporary understanding may well have tied the weather in 1606 to God's wrath for the attempt to subvert the Divine Right of Kings, just as Shakespeare presents in *Macbeth*. Similarly, with James I's preoccupation with witches, the weather of 1606 may have been considered to have been the result of witchcraft, reminding the audience of the link between the witches and the events of the previous night. In doing this, Shakespeare cleverly links the fates of King Duncan and the planned fate of James I, demonstrating through the play and the downfall of Macbeth himself that those who plan crimes such as these will never go unpunished.

### ''TWAS A ROUGH NIGHT'

The brevity of Macbeth's next comment is worth further consideration. Macbeth very deliberately downplays the appalling weather, and Lennox's long exploration of what he saw and heard is met with just four words in reply: ''Twas a rough night.' This is at odds with the fact that Lennox has commented that he cannot, in his life, remember a night of such awful weather. Despite knowing that his actions have shaken the very foundations of life in Scotland, Macbeth is desperate to attach little importance to Lennox's words for fear of giving away his heinous crimes. Of course, the night has been rough for Macbeth too. He is affected by what he has seen and what he has done. His words here are equivocal: he is acknowledging the impact of his actions on himself whilst trying to hide the truth from Lennox. Alternatively, it could be that Macbeth has reached an uneasy peace with what he has done: he has, perhaps, become fundamentally disinterested in what he has done in the knowledge that he will soon be king. His attitude here is 'laconic, even ironic.'[12] It is not an attitude that can last for long.

### 'HORROR, HORROR, HORROR'

Macduff soon returns, having made the awful discovery that the King has been murdered. His repetition of 'horror' here is visceral, Shakespeare emphasising the appalling and unimaginable sight with which Macduff has been faced. It is so horrific, in fact, that his heart and mouth cannot begin to understand, comprehend or explain what he has seen. It is interesting that Shakespeare has Macduff repeat the word 'horror' three times. As explored elsewhere, the number three is almost inextricably linked to the act of the witches: there are three of them who give Macbeth and Banquo three prophecies each. They have three key scenes (if one overlooks the Hecate scene, of dubious authenticity). Their actions are also

---

12. Thomas F. Connolly, 'Shakespeare and the Double Man', *Shakespeare Quarterly*, Vol. 1, No. 1 (January 1950), pp. 30–35, https://www.jstor.org/stable/2866204.

closely linked with the murder of the King – after all, it was their prophecy that inspired Lady Macbeth and Macbeth to concoct their evil machinations, and the audience is further reminded of this in Macduff's tricolon.

As Macbeth's words become increasingly laconic, in turn, Macduff's become increasingly hyperbolic. He cannot find the words to describe the horror of what he has seen, saying that 'Tongue nor heart cannot conceive nor name thee.' This is an example of antimetabole.[13] Antimetabole is a rhetorical device in which a speaker repeats words 'in reverse order for emphasis.'[14] Whilst Macduff does not repeat the specific words in reverse order, his matching of the body part and their function is reversed. It would be sensible to expect Macduff to match 'tongue' – the first noun – with 'name' – the verb a tongue could do. Instead, he has reversed the verbs. This could be testament to his level of panic and confusion having seen the King's dead body. He is shocked and distressed: his use of increasingly hyperbolic language is perhaps Macduff's attempt to clutch at the words he could use to describe what he has seen.

So entirely baffled is he by what he has seen that he declares that 'Confusion now hath made his masterpiece.' At this point, 'personified, disorder formally enters the action as a concept and a working dramatic construct.'[15] Disorder reigns over Scotland, and the murder of Duncan, Macduff states, is the *pièce de résistance* of anything disorder could possibly achieve. This line acknowledges that more panic and disorder will befall Scotland before the climax of the play: this is only the start.

The play is 'not just a study of regicide and tyranny but of a man who… is capable of acting in defiance of the restraints of both human nature and religion.'[16] His act against religion is of course the regicide, which was considered a crime directly against God. However, Macbeth's religious crime also extends to the murder of the *person* of King Duncan, not just the man in the position of king. His crime, as Macduff puts it, is 'sacrilegious'.

As explored elsewhere, King Duncan would have been considered holy. Therefore, Macduff's comment that the murder has 'broke ope / The Lord's anointed temple' compares King Duncan's body to an actual religious, sacred building – he imagines the body as a church which has been destroyed and

---

13. Literarydevices.com, 'Epizeuxis', http://www.literarydevices.com/epizeuxis/.

14. Collins Dictionary, 'Antimetabole', https://www.collinsdictionary.com/dictionary/english/antimetabole.

15. B.L. Reid, '"Macbeth" and the Play of Absolutes', *The Sewanee Review*, Vol. 73, No. 1 (Winter 1965), pp. 19–46, https://www.jstor.org/stable/27541080.

16. Jane H. Jack, 'MacBeth, King James and the Bible, *ELH*, Vol. 22, No. 3 (September 1955), pp. 173–193, https://www.jstor.org/stable/2871874.

desecrated. Macduff describes the sight as being so awful that those who look upon the murder scene will be met 'with a new Gorgon' – in other words, a sight so horrific it will metaphorically turn those who look on it to stone. The murder scene is horrific in two ways – 'it is terrifying in itself and terrifying for the symbolic perspectives Macduff sees in it.'[17] The concept of Duncan's body being church-like in its status naturally encourages the audience to look towards biblical allusion. In 1 Corinthians it is said:

> *Know ye not that ye are the temple of God, and that the Spirit of God dwelleth in you? If any man defile the temple of God, him shall God destroy; for the temple of God is holy, which temple ye are.*[18]

Whilst this extends to any person – every person's body is sacred and thus any murder is a crime against God – this Bible verse is also particularly evocative of the concept of the king as being sacred and of the punishment that will surely befall the perpetrator: 'him shall God destroy'.

As Lennox and Macbeth leave, Shakespeare again has Macduff repeat a word: 'Awake, Awake!' Macduff is attempting to wake the rest of the castle; however, this is sharp juxtaposition, given that he has been unable – and will forever be unable – to wake King Duncan. It is the desperate cry of a man almost at a loss: he is calling for the others in the castle to come and bear witness to the horrific scene.

### 'SHAKE OFF THIS DOWNY SLEEP, DEATH'S COUNTERFEIT'

In the following lines, Macduff has begun to understand and started to internalise the fact that King Duncan is indeed dead and not just sleeping. Through his speech, Shakespeare continues to explore the role and importance of sleep. This echoes Macbeth's panic in Act II, Scene ii, where he thinks he heard a voice cry 'Sleep no more. / Macbeth does murder sleep'. Macduff here describes sleep as being 'death's counterfeit', again emphasising the fact that King Duncan's new state is not the same as being asleep. This demonstrates that Lady Macbeth's earlier comment – that 'the sleeping and the dead are but as pictures' – was not true. There is no similarity between Duncan asleep and Duncan dead: her attempt to reassure Macbeth that sleep and death are indistinguishable was false. This is particularly pertinent when one takes into

---

17. Richard S. Ide, 'The Theatre of the Mind: An Essay on Macbeth', *ELH*, Vol. 42, No. 3 (Autumn 1975), pp. 338–361, https://www.jstor.org/stable/2872708.

18. *The Holy Bible Containing the Old and New Testaments*, Authorised King James Version, www.kingjamesbibleonline.org, 1 Corinthians 3:16–17.

account the fact that 'Glamis hath murdered sleep'. If it is truly the case that he can 'sleep no more', his only alternative form of rest is death, a fate befitting one who has murdered the king in the name of ambition.

### 'GREAT DOOM'S IMAGE'

Macduff also describes the scene of Duncan's murder as '[t]he great doom's image'. This is a reference to the Last Judgement,[19] an image of Christian iconography which was often portrayed in parish churches across the country. It would have been an image which was very familiar to the audience, who would have known that it signified the end of the world. In murdering the King, Macbeth has brought about this very event. Similarly, his actions of regicide have triggered the beginning of the end of his *own* world, though he is not yet aware of this.

This image of the Last Judgement is further expanded upon by Lady Macbeth as she enters. Whilst she refers to the 'trumpet' with specific reference to the sound of the bell, 'trumpet' is also evocative of biblical iconography. In 1 Corinthians 15:51–52 in reference to the act of Judgement, we read that 'we shall all be changed... at the last trump'.[20] Here, the last trumpet of Duncan's reign has sounded and all of Scotland will suffer as a result; Macbeth's sin is Scotland's sin and thus all will have their sense of morality tested. Therefore, for some of these characters, their efforts to redeem themselves in the eyes of Christ begins at this very moment. Macduff, for example, is at the start of a journey which will end with him returning the rightful king to the throne. His motives at this early point in the play, to seek the truth behind King Duncan's murder, are, arguably, because he desperately wants to do the morally right and just thing. He wishes to divorce himself from the sin of Scotland caused by Macbeth, and thus secure his place in heaven.

Whilst Macduff later has an unequivocal understanding of the duplicity of the Macbeths, for now, at least, he appears to be taken in by Lady Macbeth's performance. Her arrival on stage is greeted by him describing her as a 'gentle lady', and her initial reaction to the murder is not just shock ('Woe, alas') but, interestingly, demonstrates an assumed level of disbelief that such an event could take place in *her* house – as if she believes her castle to be beyond reproach. Here, she is trying to further divorce herself, and by extension her husband, from the night's crimes. Banquo, whether knowingly or unknowingly, partially discredits Lady Macbeth's words here. Whilst she wishes to draw

---

19.  A.R. Branmuller, *The New Cambridge Shakespeare: Macbeth*, (Cambridge: Cambridge University Press, 2008), p. 169.

20.  *The Holy Bible Containing the Old and New Testaments*, Authorised King James Version, www.kingjamesbibleonline.org, 1 Corinthians 15:51–52.

attention to the idea that it is particularly shocking the crime took place in her castle, Banquo's worldview is broader. He says that the crime would be 'too cruel anywhere', which is a more authentic response to the situation, and perhaps allows Macduff to begin to realise the reality of what has occurred. Macduff, from this point onwards, says little, and he becomes much more an observer than an active participant in the conversation. He is quietly biding his time, watching and waiting in the shadows to take action against the Macbeths.

Macbeth's return to the scene gives Macduff a further opportunity to try to remove himself from the situation. To those listening to his speech, he gives the impression that having seen the King's body he would rather die, as there is nothing left worth living for now the King has been murdered. However, the audience – and Lady Macbeth – both know that Macbeth's words here are more closely linked to his own guilt: for him, life has lost meaning not because the King has died but because it was his actions that caused the death: 'This is meant… to deceive, but it utters at the same time his profoundest feeling.'[21]

### 'THE FOUNTAIN OF YOUR BLOOD IS STOPPED'

When Duncan's sons, Malcolm and Donalbain, enter, the scene becomes preoccupied with discussions of, and references to, blood. Macbeth's explanation to the two sons is not, initially, to tell them their father is dead. Instead, he declares that the 'fountain of [their] blood / Is stopped' – in other words, their life source has ended. Shakespeare is using blood metaphorically here to suggest that it is life-giving. It was Duncan's blood that gave life to Malcolm and Donalbain. Now Duncan has been robbed of his own life force. There is also perhaps an intertextual reference to Thomas More's *Utopia* here.[22] In *Utopia* More writes: 'the springs both of good and evil flow from the prince over a whole nation, as from a lasting fountain.'[23] In other words, in the case of Duncan, the 'fountain' of his life and deeds flooded Scotland with good. Macbeth, in stopping this flow, has stopped the goodness, replacing it with evil. He has spilled literal blood, and will go on to flood Scotland with much more before the play's end.

Just as Macbeth metaphorically felt like he would never be able to wash his hands clean, so the groomsmen have been literally covered in blood. Lennox comments that 'Their hands and faces were all badged with blood'. To 'badge'

21. John Russell Brown, *A.C. Bradley on Shakespeare's Tragedies: A Concise Edition and Reassessment*, (Basingstoke: Palgrave Macmillan, 2007), p. 126.

22. Ibid., p. 193.

23. Thomas More, *Utopia*, (Cassell and Company, 1901), https://www.gutenberg.org/files/2130/2130-h/2130-h.htm.

means to mark or identify a person as a member of a particular tribe, or followers of a particular master.[24] Here, the grooms are identified as the King's men, but also, and crucially for Macbeth and Lady Macbeth at this point, as his murderers.

On Macbeth's admission that he has murdered the servants, the audience realises that events may not have played out as planned. He has acted beyond what was agreed between him and his wife. Whilst ostensibly he has done this so that the servants are unable to speak out against him, his violent actions arouse suspicion in Macduff. Macduff begins to question him: 'Wherefore did you so?' This not only conveys a sense of Macduff's scepticism of Macbeth's actions, but is also suggestive of the particular type of masculinity Macduff represents. Macduff, 'even in his state of grief and shock... is astonished by this new burst of violence.'[25]

Macbeth, 'in a speech that verges steadily towards hysteria',[26] attempts to clarify why he has committed this double murder, telling the assembly that he felt that 'the expedition of [his] violent love / Outran the pauser, reason.' This is an early precursor to his later, reflexive murders, where his decisions come faster and often with less than suitable reason applied to the situations. He does not stop to think, as he has not stopped to think here.

## 'HIS SILVER SKIN LACED WITH HIS GOLDEN BLOOD'

Macbeth's preoccupation in this speech is with the blood that covered both Duncan and the guards, and some of these references are used figuratively. This is noticeable when Macbeth describes the body of Duncan, and his 'silver skin laced with his golden blood'. Comparing Duncan's body to precious metals is evocative of the 'anointed temple' in Macduff's description: he was precious and sacred, much like a church, its treasures, and perhaps the holy relics it would hold. Additionally, the use of these precious metals is often ascribed to the regard with which the characters are held by one another: their reputations.[27] For example, one of Macbeth's reasons for not wishing to kill King Duncan was that he had 'bought / Golden opinions from all sorts of people'. Now, he remembers the high regard in which Duncan was held. Perhaps this is Macbeth presenting the commonly held view of Duncan to not arouse suspicion. He killed the guards

24. Collins, 'Badge', https://www.collinsdictionary.com/dictionary/english/badge.

25. Jarold Ramsey, 'The Perversion of Manliness in Macbeth', *Studies in English Literature, 1500–1900*, Vol. 13, No. 2, Elizabethan and Jacobean Drama (Spring 1973), pp. 285-300, https://www.jstor.org/stable/449740.

26. Ibid.

27. Thalia Phillis Howe, 'Color Imagery in "Macbeth" I and II and the "Aeneid" II a Pedagogic Experiment', *The Classical Journal*, Vol. 51, No. 7 (April 1956), pp. 322–327, https://www.jstor.org/stable/3293345.

*because* of the precious, sacred position Duncan held in society as the King. Alternatively, his recollection of Duncan's blood as 'gold' could also suggest his realisation of the magnitude of what he has done: he has destroyed the most precious thing in Scotland and cannot shake his thoughts of this.

The concept of lace is also an interesting one. It implies that Duncan was fragile and delicate: an image at odds with the general concept of kingship as being strong and powerful. 'Lace' is evocative of the same fragility we see from Duncan's reign in Act I, Scene ii.

### 'GASHED STABS'

This fragility and destruction of King Duncan's body continues. The sibilance in the phrase 'gashed stabs' is harsh and threatening, emphasising the 'breach in nature' caused by killing the King. Shakespeare compares it to a 'breached' shoreline, flooded by seawater. This could evoke the biblical floods which accompanied a range of sins (the most famous of which was the flood sent to wipe the Earth clean of sin, survived only by Noah, his family, and the animals he rescued). Biblically, God meted out punishments for the sins of humanity, and floods were one way in which humanity was punished. The 'breaching' of King Duncan's body, therefore, could invite similar punishment. The image of the 'breach' is also reminiscent of a besieged city or castle, broken into by marauders. The emphasis here is very much on the fact that Duncan's murder will cause widespread devastation across Scotland.[28] This is true both in the immediate sense – Macbeth's actions will lead to further murders – and in relation to the belief that God would apportion judgement on the country because of Macbeth's crimes.

The metaphors with which Shakespeare plays deepen. He describes the murderers – Macbeth here playing along with the consensus that the guards murdered the King – as being 'steeped in the colours of their trade'. However, it is the daggers which receive the focus of this image, described as being 'unmannerly breeched with gore.' Shakespeare's choice of 'breech' (rather than 'breach') is fascinating. Whilst this could be a miscommunication when transferring the Folio from handwritten notes to print, there appears to be a significant meaning to Shakespeare's use of these words. 'Unmannerly' – in this context meaning that the blood they are covered in is not befitting of the daggers (as Duncan's blood was too precious to be spilled) – is not far removed from 'unmanly'. In this instance, Shakespeare is implying that the daggers' actions were cowardly – their actions not befitting any 'man' who would use them. This ties in with the specific spelling of 'breeched'. In Elizabethan England, it was commonplace for children,

---

28.   Ed. Sandra Clark and Pamela Mason, *The Arden Shakespeare: Macbeth*, (London: Bloomsbury, 2015), p. 194.

regardless of gender, to wear long gowns. When boys grew older, and were considered men, they began to wear trousers – they were 'breeched'.[29] Combined, this image could imply that Macbeth realises that in an attempt to become more 'manly' and murder the King, he has instead – by committing regicide when Duncan was defenceless and asleep in bed – become more unmanly.

In a further manipulative action, Lady Macbeth realises that she must intervene in order to take the focus away from her husband. He has acted in haste, without discussing his plan with his wife, and looking on she knows that he runs the risk of being discovered. Whilst Shakespeare gives no stage direction for what she does, her line 'Help me hence, ho', combined with Macduff's reaction to ask the assembly to 'Look to the lady', suggests her behaviour is clearly unusual. Most directors take it as read that Lady Macbeth faints at this moment. This would be an action suited to the moment in two ways. Firstly, the men would be acting in a protective capacity over the only woman in the space. By her fainting, their attention must be drawn to her and thus away from what Macbeth is saying. Secondly, her behaviour correlates with Macduff's assumption that '[t]he repetition [of the news] in a woman's ear / Would murder as it fell.' Very few believe her fainting to be genuine. It appears to be a deliberate action designed to reduce the attention on her husband, but also perhaps to reduce any suspicion on her. She is, after all, an innocent and weak-willed woman who faints at even the thought of blood. Despite wanting to be rid of her feminine qualities, it is ultimately her femininity on which she must rely to not arouse suspicion of her implication in the crime.

Shakespeare repeats the instruction to 'Look to the lady', either side of what is most likely an aside between Malcolm and Donalbain. This emphasises the frantic nature of the scene and the panic that has befallen the castle. Shakespeare then explores Malcolm and Donalbain's immediate fears for themselves and their initial plans to flee Scotland. Their comments, too, where they question 'Why [they] hold [their] tongues', also implies that they may have early doubts as to Macbeth's innocence: there is a certain echo of Lady Macbeth's earlier comments for him to 'bear welcome in your... tongue'. It is almost as if, despite Lady Macbeth's efforts, Macbeth has still not been able to properly hide his crimes.

Malcolm and Donalbain are in a state of shock about their father's untimely death, but are also fearful for their own lives. There is the chance that if they stay where they are, 'fate... [will] rush and seize [them]'. Macbeth's castle is not a place of safety for them and they agree to leave: 'Let's away'.

---

29. Mary Ellen Lamb, 'Engendering the Narrative Act: Old Wive's Tales in "The Winter's Tale", "Macbeth" and "The Tempest", *Criticism*, Vol. 40, No. 4 (Autumn 1998), pp. 529–553.

### 'LET US MEET AND QUESTION THIS MOST BLOODY PIECE OF WORK'

Banquo's next thought is for the men to spend time working out who was behind the King's murder: 'let us meet / And question this most bloody piece of work / To know it further.' Through this line and the remainder of his speech, Banquo is positioned as 'the representative and mouthpiece of loyalty for the entire group.'[30] This is likely a nod to the contemporary belief that Banquo was an ancestor of James I: despite his close historical alignment with Macbeth, he is transformed by Shakespeare into a spokesperson for morality.

This does not just show Macbeth that Banquo already has doubts in the suggestion that it was the King's servants, but also has the potential to worry Macbeth, as he wonders who Banquo might point the finger to next. Macbeth, therefore, is quick to agree with Banquo, telling the men to 'put on manly readiness / And meet i'the hall together.' Perhaps in doing so he feels he can help influence what the others think, even if they have already discredited his statement that the guards were at fault. Macbeth means for the men to not only get dressed, but arm themselves, thereby acknowledging to the others that perhaps he, too, has moved on from thinking the servants murdered the King. Of course, the audience knows the real truth here, but Macbeth's actions are intended to emphasise the version of himself that he is portraying: someone who is as disgusted and appalled by the murder as everyone else.

Malcolm and Donalbain agree to flee, which later encourages further suspicion in their actions. Before they depart, Donalbain declares that 'There's daggers in men's smiles'. This is a continuation of the running motif of deception and duplicity: Donalbain acknowledges that it is now important to know who is trustworthy. It is evocative of Lady Macbeth's declaration that 'False face must hide what the false heart doth know.' Both brothers also acknowledge that the murder of their father puts them in a perilous position, and so the scene closes with the brothers fleeing.

## Who is Macduff?

Act II, Scene iii marks only the second appearance of Macduff (and his first lines) in the play, and, given the crucial role Macduff plays later on, Shakespeare ensures there is much in the scene to help the audience understand the extent to which he is a foil for, and the antithesis of, Macbeth. Macduff, in the play, stands for morality.

The play, in part, is so narratively 'neat' because of the various, mirrored, rise and fall actions of pairs of characters. As Macbeth rises to power, so Banquo falls. Following Banquo's murder in Act III, Scene iii, Macbeth's fall is

---

30. Olive Henneberger, 'Banquo, Loyal Subject', *College English*, Vol. 8, No. 1 (October 1946), pp. 18–22, https://www.jstor.org/stable/370443.

mirrored in Macduff's rise. Macduff stands for 'the agent of nemesis for both the private and public wrongs of Macbeth.'[31] This idea of Macduff being the cause of Macbeth's downfall can be traced back to his first speaking scene. His repetition of 'O horror, horror, horror' on discovering the body of King Duncan is juxtaposed with Macbeth's actions and emphasises how horrific Macbeth's crimes truly are. His words are those of a man who exhibits greater moral judgement and belief than Macbeth.

He also voices in this scene the first query as to Macbeth's actions, asking, having heard that Macbeth has murdered the guards: 'Wherefore did you so?' This suggests that Macduff has a strong moral compass, and a keen eye for the hidden motives of other characters. He says relatively little in the scene, but carefully spectates. It is this observation of others that helps him later develop his growing mistrust of Macbeth and ultimately his actions to seek out Malcolm and depose Macbeth from the throne.

Macduff is also clearly a deeply religious man, who can barely consider a crime as great as regicide. This is evident through his repeated descriptions of King Duncan as a sacred place, but is further displayed through the symbolism of it being Macduff who knocks at the castle door and awakens the Porter. If we turn again to the Bible, we can read in Luke 12:36 that the Lord 'cometh and knocketh'.[32] Similarly in Revelation 3:20, we read that Christ will 'stand at the door, and knock'.[33] Macduff brings with him eventual discovery of Macbeth's crimes, judgement of his actions and, finally, punishment, delivering what could be argued to be divine retribution.

Another strength of Macduff's is his decisive, commanding actions. His use of imperative verbs here – 'Approach', 'Awake', 'Ring the alarum bell' and 'Up, up, and see' all show Macduff to be more forceful than Macbeth, and yet at the same time he is able to take care of Lady Macbeth and consider the gentle tone with which the news ought to be delivered to a woman who, in appearance and societal expectations, would die at the news.

Of course, Macduff's character continues to develop as the play draws on to its inevitable conclusion: he stands for the moral good, for the will of God and as the direct opposite of the eponymous tragic hero, Macbeth. You can read more about Macduff and masculinity in Chapter 16.

---

31. Ed. John Drakakis and Dale Townshend, *Macbeth: A Critical Reader*, (London: Bloomsbury, 2013), p. 39.

32. *The Holy Bible Containing the Old and New Testaments*, Authorised King James Version, www.kingjamesbibleonline.org, Luke12:36.

33. *The Holy Bible Containing the Old and New Testaments*, Authorised King James Version, www.kingjamesbibleonline.org, Revelation 3:20.

## Macduff in history

Macduff is another character rooted in a true historical counterpart, with the belief that he is loosely based on Duff, the tenth century King of Alba. Duff appears in both *Chronica Gentis Scotorum* and *Orygynale Cronykil of Scotland*, both precursors and influencers of *Holinshed's Chronicles*, from which *Macbeth* is largely drawn. Whilst these books are not necessarily held up by modern historians as being particularly accurate in their history, their influence on Shakespeare is clear. In *Chronica Gentis Scotorum*, it is suggested that Macduff (as he is called in *Chronica*) had a reign overwhelmed by what was believed to be the influence of witchcraft – much like Shakespeare's portrayal of Macbeth himself. Indeed, in the *Orygynale Cronykil of Scotland*, it is also suggested that Macduff was murdered as a result of his reign.

It is suggested in *Chronica* that, owing to the friendship Macduff extended to Malcolm and Donald (King Duncan I's sons), he was exiled from Scotland by Macbeth. Macduff seems to have held, in reality, a similar ability to behave duplicitously as did Macbeth, though in his case it appears to have been linked more heavily to self-preservation as opposed to a bid to enact any Machiavellian plan of his own. He is described as having 'turned upon [Macbeth] the blithe and merry look of innocence' before making plans to immediately flee Scotland. In reality, Macduff's journey to England and to Malcolm's castle was a direct reaction to Macbeth's behaviour towards him. In *Chronica*, de Fordun writes that 'the King, one day, took occasion… to upbraid him, more cruelly than usual… and then added plainly that he should stoop his neck under the yoke.'[34] This could be a reference to the Roman tradition of 'passing under the yoke' to admit defeat. Upon hearing Macduff had arrived in England, Macbeth 'besieged all Macduff's castles and strongholds, took his lands and estates, commanded everything that seemed precious or desirable to be confiscated.'[35] This echoes, almost entirely, the story of Macduff in Shakespeare's *Macbeth*.

Shakespeare also appears to have drawn upon *Chronica Gentis Scotorum* to influence his presentation of Macduff as a character who brings truth and justice. Macduff is quoted as having said:

> *For, the higher the rank, the more grievous the fall. In sooth, the higher a man is raised on the ladder of honour, the more ought he to be distinguished for his virtues; and the higher he climbs*

34. Johannis de Fordun, *Chronica Gentis Scotorum*, (University of Toronto, 2011), https://archive.org/stream/johannisdefordun02ford/johannisdefordun02ford_djvu.txt.

35. Ibid.

*up the steep of virtue, the greater shame to him if he fall into the depths of vice.*[36]

It is Macduff who brings about the ultimate downfall of Macbeth, through encouraging Malcolm to return to Scotland and seize the throne, but also through his final, decisive act of defeating Macbeth in battle and returning to the stage holding aloft Macbeth's decapitated head.

### Scene analysis: Act II, Scene iv

The scene is short, but reveals a summary of the impact of Macbeth's actions so far: nature is behaving strangely because of Macbeth's subversion of the natural order.

It is interesting to note that, much like in the case of the Porter, this is the only time Shakespeare includes the character of the 'Old Man'. It is also the only occasion where Ross acts as something more significant than a messenger and begins to explore some of his own views on the dark acts that have taken place.

As the scene opens, the audience is exposed to just how unheard of nature's reaction to the events of the last night have been. The Old Man, who remembers the last seventy years (implying he is older, even, than seventy), comments that he has never seen anything as awful as what has happened that night: 'this sore night / Has trifled former knowings.' Whether this is hyperbolic or not, it is still clear that what he has witnessed has horrified him.

In remembering the past seventy years there is an implication that Shakespeare's Old Man is, in himself, acting at odds with God's will. In Elizabethan England an average lifespan would have been around 30 years of age, and lower for the urban poor.[37] The age 'threescore years and ten' is taken from Psalm 90, and suggests that living far beyond this is in itself unnatural.[38] The inclusion of this is suggestive of the fact that nature has been subverted, and this subversion of nature had been true in Scotland for some time. Historically, King Duncan was not the first king to be murdered whilst on the throne: the country's bloody and sinful past exhibits itself in the Old Man's unnatural age. Unnaturalness is ingrained in all aspects of society, reflecting a long, brutal and regicidal past in which Macbeth is only the latest incarnation of sin, cruelty and evil.

---

36. Johannis de Fordun, *Chronica Gentis Scotorum*, (University of Toronto, 2011), https://archive.org/stream/johannisdefordun02ford/johannisdefordun02ford_djvu.txt.

37. Stefan Flores, Shakespeare's World/Stage, https://www.webpages.uidaho.edu/~sflores/345world.html.

38. Ed. Sandra Clark and Pamela Mason, *The Arden Shakespeare: Macbeth*, (London: Bloomsbury, 2015), p. 197.

## 'DARK NIGHT STRANGLES THE TRAVELLING LAMP'

Despite both Macbeth and Lady Macbeth pleading to have their actions hidden from the heavens, Ross is adamant that the foul weather and unnatural behaviour of nature is precisely because God has seen the murder of the King. Ross's initial speech is laden with references to the unnatural darkness that permeates Scotland. The personification in Ross's line 'dark night strangles the travelling lamp' (the sun) also implies this sense of unnatural acts: the sun has been snuffed out, and the violent vocabulary reflects the brutal downfall of the kingdom. Macbeth and Lady Macbeth believed that in killing the King they would be freed to live out Macbeth's given prophecies. The image of the night 'strangling' the lamp is almost the opposite of freeing. The image is oppressive: 'it destroys the present in reaching ahead for the future and smothers reason.'[39] The world is closing in on them and the situation and the metaphorical darkness of what they have done is apparent.

This imagery of darkness and death is further explored in the line 'darkness does the face of earth entomb'. Lady Macbeth's call for darkness has been answered, but with it comes imagery of death. This could be emblematic of the fact that the Macbeths called for darkness in order to commit bad deeds, or that the world has now darkened *because* of those dark deeds. Most likely the darkness that has befallen Scotland is a direct result of the actions of the Macbeths: the darkness has come and actively enshrouded the earth the very day after the light of the country, King Duncan, has been extinguished. Macbeth and his wife have achieved what they perceived to be their ideal: darkness has fallen, ready for them to take the crown. However, the situation is clearly 'unnatural, / Even like the deed that's done.'

## 'A FALCON... WAS BY A MOUSING OWL HAWKED AT AND KILLED'

Ross and the Old Man go on to discuss a range of situations in which nature has acted against itself in unusual and alarming ways. The Old Man comments that, last Tuesday: 'A falcon, towering in her pride of place / Was by a mousing owl hawked at and killed.' Of course, at face value a bird as fast and powerful as a falcon being downed by an owl is indicative of the destruction and confusion of nature, but this image also reflects the recent events of the play. The falcon represents King Duncan, who has been unseated and murdered by the owl – Macbeth. Macbeth's ambition, much like the owl, has broken the natural order

---

39. Harold E. Toliver, 'Shakespeare and the Abyss of Time', *The Journal of English and Germanic Philology*, Vol. 64, No. 2 (April 1965), pp. 234–254, https://www.jstor.org/stable/27714634.

and the mechanisms of the Great Chain of Being.[40] In the Great Chain of Being, a smaller bird like an owl has its place below a falcon, just as Macbeth's place is below the King's. In subverting this in the image of the birds, Shakespeare reflects the macrocosm of Scottish society. The less powerful man, Macbeth, has uprooted the King and replaced him 'against the use of nature'.

Similarly, Ross's recall of the King's horses' behaviour shows the disruption of nature. These horses, which previously have been docile, have now '[t]urned wild in nature'. Worse than this, though, is the fact that the Old Man reports "Tis said they eat each other.' This cannibalisation pushes the dark and unnatural imagery to a new level: nature itself is not only acting unnaturally, but has now turned upon, and is destroying, itself. Even nature itself cannot escape these dark acts. The cannibalisation of the horses evokes a dark thought about the circle of life: the horses are destroying themselves just as Macbeth is destroying the lives of many people in Scotland.

This is not the first time Shakespeare has mused on the idea of cyclical horror and destruction. Macbeth is caught in his own mini cycle of violence, but Scotland is part of a longer history of violence. There have been bloody acts before and there will be bloody acts to come: Scotland does not learn from her own mistakes, and it is clear at this point, with the horses almost enacting the brutality of the humans around them, that a perfect Scotland is unobtainable.

### 'GOOD MACDUFF'

Ross and the Old Man's exploration of the weird behaviour of nature is interrupted by the arrival of Macduff, and Ross's take on the character is immediately clear from his use of the phrase 'good Macduff'. The men discuss the latest news on the brutal murder of King Duncan and, at least initially, Macduff seems clear on who committed the crime: 'Those that Macbeth hath slain.' However, it is important to note that, rather than commenting on the men themselves, he instead chooses to recall in particular the actions Macbeth took towards the men – he killed them. Shakespeare is drawing the audience's gaze to the attentiveness Macduff has paid to Macbeth's story. By making Macbeth central to this statement, Shakespeare is foreshadowing the future conflict between these characters. Simultaneously, Shakespeare is also further emphasising to the audience that killing comes naturally to Macbeth – something we know to have been true during Macbeth's time on the battlefield, but which has now become a compulsion in his bid to gain the crown.

---

40. B.L. Reid, '"Macbeth" and the Play of Absolutes', *The Sewanee Review*, Vol. 73, No. 1 (Winter 1965), pp. 19–46, https://www.jstor.org/stable/27541080.

However, Macduff is not satisfied with the assumption that it was the King's guards who committed such a savage crime. Having fled Scotland for England and Ireland respectively, it is Malcolm and Donalbain who now come under the lens of Macduff's suspicion. Malcolm and Donalbain's quick departure means that accusing them of murder is a valid assumption. By mentioning Malcolm and Donalbain to Ross and the Old Man, he is almost able to scrutinise their opinions, thereby allowing him the opportunity to perhaps seek affirmation for his own belief or test his theory out on others. Macduff must know, with Macbeth on his way to Scone to be crowned, that he will not be able to act alone against the institution of the crown if he is the only person at this point who believes Macbeth is guilty. He must have allies. However, Ross is aligned with Macbeth and so the suggestion of Malcolm and Donalbain as suspects in their father's murder must be appealing to him or, at least, more appealing than believing his comrade could be guilty of such a heinous crime. Ross judges their supposed behaviour poorly: if they have murdered their father in order to take the crown, theirs is '[t]hriftless ambition'. There is a link here to Macbeth's 'vaulting ambition' – in other words, both Macbeth's and potentially Malcolm's and Donalbain's ambition will be ultimately unprofitable and wasteful. No good can come of it.

Ross's attention turns to the resting place of King Duncan, whom Macduff says has been taken to Colmekill for burial. This was, historically, the traditional burial place for kings[41] and in being historically accurate, Shakespeare is once again showing reverence to James I and reaffirming the Divine Right of Kings. At the end of *Macbeth*, the titular character – despite having been king – is denied this burial rite, demonstrating that unseating a king leads to no reward.

Macduff's final line is really significant when considered in the light of Shakespeare's wider reference to clothing throughout the play, and the link between clothing and the role people assume. Macduff is a reluctant part of the bid to discover the truth of Duncan's murder, commenting that he wishes their 'old robes sit easier than [their] new.' He has been cast in a new role as he works to understand the root of the regicide. It is also apparent that he is reluctant to take this role *because* he feels he should never have been put in this position. The King should not have died in this way; there should be no need for any of them to wear these metaphorical new robes.

---

41. Ed. Jonathan Blake and Eric Rasmussen, *Macbeth*, (Basingstoke: Macmillan, 2009), p. 53.

## Act II, Scene iv at a glance

## RESOURCE 10.1

70 years – suggests how odd and unusual these events really are, as the Old Man cannot recall seeing such strange and awful things.

Also suggests that this man is particularly old – he has outlived the average age considerably. Could this be a hint towards nature behaving unnaturally?

Despite the Macbeths' protestations, heaven has seen, and is appalled, by Macbeth's actions.

'Kiss' juxtaposes 'entomb' and emphasises the lack of goodness and metaphorical 'light' in the world.

Horses are cannibalising one another – another example from Shakespeare of how nature is acting in an unnatural way. Horrific image. Macbeth has killed his king, a crime reflected in the behaviour of the horses.

**Old Man**
Threescore and ten I can remember well,
Within the volume of which time I have seen
Hours dreadful and things strange; but this sore night
Hath trifled former knowings.

**Ross**
Ha, good father,
Thou seest the heavens, as troubled with man's act,
Threatens his bloody stage. By th' clock 'tis day,
And yet dark night strangles the travelling lamp.
Is't night's predominance, or the day's shame,
That darkness does the face of earth entomb
When living light should kiss it?

**Old Man**
'Tis unnatural,
Even like the deed that's done. On Tuesday last,
A falcon towering in her pride of place
Was by a mousing owl hawked at and killed.

**Ross**
And Duncan's horses, a thing most strange and certain,
Beauteous and swift, the minions of their race,
Turned wild in nature, broke their stalls, flung out
Contending 'gainst obedience, as they would
Make war with mankind.

**Old Man**
'Tis said they eat each other.

**Ross**
They did so, to th' amazement of mine eyes
That look'd upon't.

*Enter Macduff*

Here comes the good Macduff.

He has never seen anything as awful as the murder of the King – emphasising how dreadful Macbeth's actions have been.

Could be talking about literal darkness – the 'travelling lamp' is the sun. The violent imagery could also refer to the murder of Duncan; the 'light' of the kingdom.

Imagery of death emphasises Macbeth's deed.

Falcon represents Duncan, unseated by the smaller, less powerful owl (Macbeth). Macbeth, like the owl, has subverted nature and the Great Chain of Being.

Owls also represent ill omens and are birds who guide souls to the underworld. Is this where Duncan's soul has gone?

## How?

## Retrieval

In this lesson, I have planned to use an oracy retrieval task. This takes the idea of the retrieval placemat and allows for the teacher to use a more specific slide of questions, helping students to quiz one another on a specific topic. In *Retrieval*

*Practice*, Kate Jones quotes Blake Harvard, who said: 'We should aim to make the classroom simpler.'[42] It is easy to create complex resources for retrieval practice, but sometimes the easiest are the best!

## RESOURCE 10.2

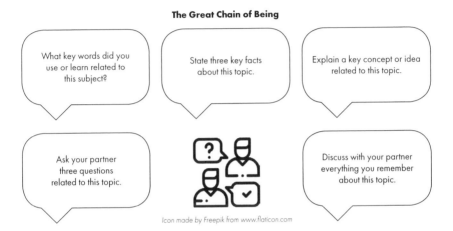

**The Great Chain of Being**

What key words did you use or learn related to this subject?

State three key facts about this topic.

Explain a key concept or idea related to this topic.

Ask your partner three questions related to this topic.

Discuss with your partner everything you remember about this topic.

*Icon made by Freepik from www.flaticon.com*

## Pre-reading activities

The remainder of Act II, Scene iii is complex; there is a lot of action and many reactions to the death of King Duncan. Before reading, it is important to encourage students to discuss what they believe will be the reaction to King Duncan's death. They should use their knowledge of social and historical context in order to do this, and could also consider how different characters will react, differently. For example, in the castle are his sons, a collection of Lords, and the Macbeths, and now Macduff has arrived, too. How will these characters' reactions be different? Why? It is the 'why' that is important here. Obviously, these characters are going to be 'shocked', but what is it specifically about the situation that would appal them? For example, Malcolm and Donalbain have lost their father. Their grief will be different from that of the lords. It is identifying these subtle differences that gets students thinking hard: instead of subsuming all the characters into one mass, they are thinking carefully about the very specific nuances of each reaction in turn.

---

42. Kate Jones, *Retrieval Practice*, (Woodbridge: John Catt Educational Ltd., 2019), p. 77.

## Reading the scene

The next step is to read the remainder of the scene with the students' predictions fresh in their minds. The scene is quite fast paced and there are few big pieces of dialogue. This means that students can often understand the scene well, and I believe it is important in this moment to allow the reading to take place organically, without, on a first pass, becoming embroiled in the minutiae of the scene.

However, it is important to know in advance what core knowledge you want students to take from the scene, and these questions, which could be posed during or after reading, might help with that.

1. Why has Macduff arrived at the castle?
2. How does Lennox describe the night's weather? Why is this significant?
3. What is Macduff's reaction to Duncan's murder?
4. This scene is filled with noise. How is this different from the previous scene, and why is this important? What impact does it have on the audience?
5. What does Macbeth admit he has done? How does Macduff react?
6. What does Lady Macbeth do in reaction to the news? How far is her reaction genuine?
7. What do Malcolm and Donalbain decide to do when they hear of their father's death?

## 'Words, Words, Words'

Just as the retrieval practice at the start of the lesson allows students to keep focused on the task in hand in a straightforward manner, so does the next building block towards understanding this scene and, in particular, the characters' view of the King's death. Chris Curtis has a fantastic resource for approaching this with students. Often one can be guilty of focusing too much on the broader techniques of writing: we talk about the metaphors, similes and structural devices employed by writers. When we think about the writing as a deliberate construct, it is sometimes too easy to rely upon these techniques. What we do not always focus on to a similar extent are individual words, something Curtis writes about in his book *How to Teach English*.[43] When we consider how important the King was, there are many individual words that are as rich for analysis as any broader 'techniques' employed by Shakespeare.

In Resource 10.3, adapted from Curtis's 'Words, Words, Words' idea, I have taken just a handful of key words that convey King Duncan's perceived value, and the reaction to his murder. For each word, students simply need to come up with three reasons as to why Shakespeare has used each of them.

---

43. Chris Curtis, *How to Teach English*, (Carmarthen: Independent Thinking Press, 2019).

## RESOURCE 10.3

| Gold | Blood |
|------|-------|
| 1. *Shows he is precious* | 1. |
| 2. *He is important* | 2. |
| 3. *He is valuable* | 3. |
| **Silver** | **Bloody** |
| 1. | 1. |
| 2. | 2. |
| 3. | 3. |
| **Laced** | |
| 1. | |
| 2. | |
| 3. | |

As Curtis writes: 'the great thing about looking at things like this is that it declutters the thought process and places emphasis on the understandable.'[44] Even more importantly than this, he comments: 'If we don't get students to think about words, then we are not getting them to explore meaning.'[45]

The words 'gold' and 'silver' are likely to evoke connotations of the King having been precious and valuable. 'Laced' might invite suggestions of delicacy. 'Blood' and 'bloody' are so at odds with the words that have gone before them that the audience is as shocked as the characters: the violent shift in vocabulary mimics the sudden and shocking regicide.

## Because/but/so

It is also really effective to then have students write analytically about these individual words. Because they have already considered multiple interpretations, they are able to layer this analysis in their writing and develop some really detailed and perceptive comments on Shakespeare's intent as a writer. They could even utilise the 'because/but/so' method here, from Judith C. Hochman and Natalie Wexler's *The Writing Revolution*, as discussed in Chapter 2. To move students from the 'Words, Words, Words' resource to more detailed analysis, this method provides a good frame to prompt students to write in detail. Hochman and Wexler explain this: 'the specificity of the prompts makes them far more powerful than an open ended question.'[46] Once completed, the resource could look something like this:

---

44. Chris Curtis, *How to Teach English*, (Carmarthen: Independent Thinking Press, 2019), p. 153.

45. Ibid.

46. Judith C. Hochman and Natalie Wexler, *The Writing Revolution*, (San Francisco: Jossey Bass, 2017), p. 14.

- Shakespeare uses the word 'golden' to describe King Duncan's blood **because** *it helps the audience interpret Duncan's body as being like a relic or some kind of decorated place of worship.*
- Shakespeare uses the word 'golden' to describe King Duncan's blood **but** *also describes his skin as 'silver', suggesting that everything about him was like the most precious of metals.*
- Shakespeare uses the word 'golden' to describe King Duncan's blood **so** *we can infer that Duncan was very precious to the characters and to the people of Scotland.*

## Tension graph

It is important to not only look at the individual reactions of the characters in this scene, but also the overarching 'shape' of it. As the murder is discovered and more people learn about it, Shakespeare's play reaches an almost fever pitch of tension. This activity helps represent this tension in a visual way.

Tension graphs are simple to set up with students, but have a remarkable impact on their understanding of the text. I have used them for moments in a variety of texts where an emotion builds – pity for Scrooge in Stave II of *A Christmas Carol* or tension in *Of Mice and Men* as Lennie's story builds to its inevitable conclusion, or to track the oscillating relationship between Benedick and Beatrice's feelings towards one another in *Much Ado About Nothing*. It also works well synoptically, looking back over a text to pick out emotions. Here, it is used to track the tension through Act II, Scene iii, and how the tension is impacted by each event of the scene.

Firstly, students need to draw a graph. Events in the scene will run along the x-axis, with a scale of tension, from 0 to 10, up the y-axis.

Students then need to plot the key events from the scene, starting with the entrance of Macduff, labelling the x-axis as they go. Part of the appeal of this activity is that students can have a say in what they feel are the most important moments of the scene, and this can provoke some really interesting classroom discussions. Alternatively, a graph with pre-selected events could be given to students. This could be beneficial where students need additional scaffolding, allowing them to focus really carefully on finding the quotations and considering their explanations as the key skills they need to develop.

When the moments from the scene have been plotted, the plot points can be joined together to create a line graph, and it is this visual representation which will help them with understanding how tension rises and falls.

Students will need to select a quotation with which to label each point, as evidence for why they feel each moment is a certain 'level' of tension. This is often most easily done as they plot the points initially. The final step of creating the tension graph is for students to explain why they have plotted each moment of tension where they have, and why the quotation shows that.

The final result might look like Resource 10.4.

## RESOURCE 10.4

1. The start of the scene is probably the least tense moment of the scene, but it certainly isn't without tension after the incessant banging at the castle gates. The fact that Macduff is looking for Macbeth, who has just killed the King, adds some tension because we know this is the beginning of Macbeth trying to avoid being found out.

2. The awful weather Lennox has experienced reflects the fact that Macbeth has acted against nature and subverted the Great Chain of Being. It also reminds the audience of the supernatural and the influence of the witches, because they could cause storms. It is more tense than the last point on the graph, because Macduff by now has gone to wake up the King, and the audience already knows he is dead, as does Macbeth. It is almost as if we are watching him squirm.

This is a good activity with which to conclude the analysis Act II, Scene iii, because it allows students to think holistically about the scene and appreciate the rise and fall of tension as well as the input Macduff has in this. Students are often really engaged by this scene, and an activity like this is almost like seeing 'behind the curtain' to the inner workings of the Bard's work. Not only does this help students' understanding and appreciation of the writer's craft, but it can also help teach students about shaping their own fiction writing.

### Reading the scene: Act II, Scene iv

There are some key moments and images in this scene which will really help students understand the conversation between Ross and the Old Man:

1. What has 'dark night' done to the 'traveling lamp'? What does this mean?
2. How does Shakespeare link the behaviour of the owl and the falcon to how Macbeth has acted towards the King?
3. What have the horses been doing? Why is this significant?
4. What does Macduff question Ross and the Old Man about? Why?
5. Where has Macbeth gone?
6. Where has King Duncan's body gone?

## Nature imagery analysis

The subversion of traditional nature imagery in this scene warrants some additional consideration. This activity asks students to consider what Shakespeare says is happening, what one would ordinarily expect to happen and the significance of why each element of nature is acting out of turn. A partially completed example of this can be seen in Resource 10.5.

## RESOURCE 10.5

| Quotation | What would be expected? | What does the subversion represent? |
|---|---|---|
| 'By th'clock 'tis day, and yet dark night strangles the travelling lamp.' | If it is daytime, the sun should be in the sky, but it is still dark. | The Macbeths' desire for darkness has been granted. The darkness has fallen across Scotland because of the terrible crimes Macbeth has committed. The sun has been snuffed out, and the violent vocabulary reflects the brutal downfall of the kingdom. |
| 'A falcon towering in her pride of place, Was by a mousing owl hawked at and killed.' | | |
| ''Tis said they eat each other.' | | |

## Answering the Big Questions

At this point in the lesson, students are well equipped to answer the Big Questions.

## Revision clock

The end of Act II marks an excellent moment for some reflection on learning, and for students to gather their thoughts, understanding and knowledge on Act II as a whole. I recommend using a resource such as Resource 10.6 – a revision clock – allowing students to capture their knowledge and you to gain a clear sense of students' understanding and progress.

Each question or mini task is designed to take five minutes. In this revision clock, each 'time' has a key word for them to 'knowledge dump' in relation to Act II. This introduces a sense of challenge to the lesson, whilst also developing students' skills of working under time constraints. When I use this resource I always do so with a timer on the board so that students really find the rhythm of writing to time in this way. It is also possible to frame this resource so that the tasks or prompts get progressively more difficult as the clock progresses. However, in this instance, the prompts are given in chronological order, encouraging students to think about the major beats of Act II as they work.

## RESOURCE 10.6

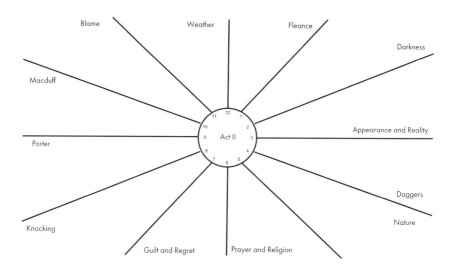

This is an idea I have often used for different texts, and it is one taken from Jennifer Webb's *How to Teach English Literature: Overcoming Cultural Poverty*.[47] I encourage students to write in two pens of different colours. In one colour, they capture everything they know about that question or topic in the time allocated. Then, after the revision clock is complete, they can fill in the gaps in their knowledge in a different colour – either through paired or grouped discussion, or as part of some whole-class feedback. This not only helps me to spot the gaps in knowledge that might need reteaching before further retrieval practice can be implemented, but also flags to students the areas on which they should focus their initial revision of the act.

## Suggested 'Extra Challenge' activities

* Frederic B. Tromly argues that there is a 'similarity between the state of mind created by the conjunction of drink and lechery in the Porter and the one created by the interplay of good and evil impulses in Macbeth.'[48]

47. Jennifer Webb, *How to Teach English Literature: Overcoming Cultural Poverty*, (Woodbridge: John Catt Educational Ltd., 2019) p. 148.

48. Frederic B. Tromly, 'Macbeth and his Porter', *Shakespeare Quarterly*, Vol. 26, No. 2 (Spring 1975), pp. 151–156, https://www.jstor.org/stable/2869244.

To what extent is this true?
- To what extent have Macbeth's crimes impacted all of Scotland?
- In 1 Corinthians it is said: 'Know ye not that ye are the temple of God, and that the Spirit of God dwelleth in you? If any man defile the temple of God, him shall God destroy; for the temple of God is holy, which temple ye are.' With this in mind, can Macbeth be redeemed?

## Key vocabulary:
Mercurial, omen, ominous

# ACT THREE

# CHAPTER 11
## Act III, Scenes i, ii and iii

*What is the relationship like between Macbeth*
*and Banquo once Macbeth becomes king?*
*How has Macbeth and Lady Macbeth's relationship changed?*

## What?

From the beginning of the play, Banquo is positioned by Shakespeare as someone who, like Macbeth, could emerge a hero. Just like Macbeth, he receives prophecies from the witches which promise to change the fortunes of his family, but while Macbeth chooses a path of betrayal, Banquo stays loyal to Duncan. Put simply, he is there to act as a foil for the traitorous Macbeth, his morality unstained by the obsession and vicious savagery which grips Shakespeare's tragic hero. Banquo is everything Macbeth is not: trustworthy instead of duplicitous, a father instead of childless, an observer of fate rather than one who actively participates in trying to change it. In Act III, Scenes i to iii, audiences witness a once devoted friendship disintegrate into suspicion, envy and malice.

## Scene analysis: Act III, Scene i

The beginning of Act III lets the dust settle after a frenetic and chaotic few scenes. Banquo's opening speech is characterised by cynicism and distrust; one can imagine him lurking in the shadows as he delivers his lines, observing events as they play out and offering his opinions on Macbeth's seemingly rapid ascent to power.

Macbeth is not present, but Banquo delivers his lines to him as if he is. He lists what his friend has gained, saying 'Thou hast it now… / As the weïrd women promised.' Shakespeare, here, suggests the suspicions dividing their friendship run deeper than they appear. The combination of 'hast' and 'now' makes it seem that Banquo has recognised that what Macbeth has gained is temporary; power is ephemeral and can be lost just as 'easily' as it is gained. Of course, Banquo *would* think this. After all, he is expecting his progeny to be crowned at some point in the future.

### 'I FEAR THOU PLAYED'ST MOST FOULLY FOR'T'

Banquo's conjecture is amplified further when he says, 'and I fear / Thou played'st most foully for't.' Banquo worries that Macbeth has done something terrible in order to obtain the crown. He entertains the possibility that something equivocal has occurred. If this is the case, it has certain ramifications for the audience's perspective of Banquo's character that are rarely explored. A vital question must be posed: should we be suspicious of Banquo, or at the very least critical of him? He doubts Macbeth and yet he does not voice his scepticism. He does not even tell anyone of their consultation with the witches. Why?

Perhaps it is because Banquo cannot actually do anything to make his prophecy come true immediately. After all, he will not become king himself, but will be 'the root and father / Of many kings.' He has already fathered Fleance, and so there is nothing for him to do but wait, unlike Macbeth, who could act whenever he wants. Regardless of speculation, the fact remains that Banquo's unvoiced qualms have given Macbeth free rein, something Macbeth has taken advantage of in order to commit unthinkable crimes.

The witches' words of dualism pervade the play, and Banquo's speech is no exception. Believing Macbeth 'played'st most foully' for the kingship is a direct reference to their 'Fair is foul, and foul is fair' incantation from Act I, Scene i. The fact that Banquo repeats these words at this point shows Macbeth is living the 'fair' life which was promised him, obtained through 'foul' means. What is more interesting, however, is Banquo's use of 'played'st'. We often associate 'play' with games, an activity one participates in for amusement or fun. Perhaps Banquo is being critical of Macbeth's perception of competition; the kingship is Macbeth's end goal and he will stop at nothing to win it.

Macbeth references the idea of 'play' too. Each time, he alludes to it in the context of acting. Banquo, it seems, has seen through the 'false face' adopted by Macbeth to get what he wants. He may see Macbeth as nothing but an actor, a 'player' who aims to deceive those around him in order to accumulate more power. This is something Macbeth himself comes to recognise as the play hurtles towards its resolution. In his 'Tomorrow, and tomorrow, and tomorrow' speech, Macbeth compares life to 'a walking shadow, a poor player', meaning he believes life to be nothing but an illusion, like a pitiful actor who worries about their time on stage before disappearing forever. If we are to link these two events, it could be argued that Banquo has seen through the illusion Macbeth has created because it is so poorly 'acted'.

### 'MYSELF SHOULD BE THE ROOT AND FATHER OF MANY KINGS'

Yet Banquo is not the ideal hero we often make him out to be. When he begins deliberating his own prophecy, audiences realise he himself is starting to succumb to the seductive nature of the supernatural, albeit briefly. He comments on his role as the 'root... of many kings', a reference to himself as the origin of a royal line which will anchor itself in Scotland's history. Through this deliberation, however, Banquo's character invites criticism. When he speaks of the 'truth' emanating from Macbeth's prophecies, he anticipates his will come true too and wonders whether they 'set [him] up in hope'. Although he fears Macbeth's success, it has also blinded him from the wisdom he voiced in Act I, Scene iii.

Banquo is cautious of the 'truths' told by 'instruments of darkness'. He believes that the supernatural, in order to lead people into danger, often tell trivial truths which consequently make people believe everything else they are told when these small, unimportant things come to fruition. Now, Banquo seems to have forgotten his own words. He has become susceptible to these 'instruments of darkness' since he has seen how favourably they look upon Macbeth.

Macbeth's entrance causes Banquo to put the thought out of his mind. A 'sennet sound[s]' when Macbeth enters, the trumpets part of a ceremonial notice of arrival which confirms he has been crowned king.[1] What follows is a conversation full of artificial plaudits which both Banquo and Macbeth bestow upon one another in an attempt to maintain a charade of friendship. Macbeth is secretly envious of Banquo's role as a father, whilst Banquo is fearful of Macbeth's actions. There are, however, subtle shifts in behaviour which reveal how the dynamic between them has moved on and developed. Macbeth, when inviting Banquo to a celebratory feast, continues to use the first person plural 'we'; he has done this before, but it is only here that he actually has a right to use such language now that he is the King of Scotland. Banquo has also changed his language, acknowledging the imbalance of power between them. Although he once stood as Macbeth's equal, he now addresses him as 'your highness' and 'my lord' throughout their conversation. Macbeth is superior and Banquo must recognise this.

### 'GOES FLEANCE WITH YOU?'

Macbeth informs Banquo that Malcolm and Donalbain have fled to England and Ireland respectively, cleverly describing them as 'bloody cousins' in order to 'remind' the other characters that they are the ones who are being accused of Duncan's murder. Referring to their crime as 'parricide' – the killing of one's close relative – further shifts the blame away from Macbeth, who swiftly changes topic and asks Banquo whether Fleance is due to join him on his ride. This causes a sense of unease; Macbeth speaks warmly to his friend, yet there is no denying he is calculating the likely success

---

1.  Ed. Sandra Clark and Pamela Mason, *The Arden Shakespeare: Macbeth*, (London: Bloomsbury, 2015) p. 201.

of his next murderous plan. He must kill Banquo to eradicate any future lineage and murder Fleance to prevent the witches' prophecy from coming true.

As Banquo leaves, there is no doubt he has been targeted because of Macbeth's jealousy and fear. Macbeth has won the crown, and yet his lust for power, and more importantly for maintaining it, remains unsated. From his first line of the scene, 'Here's our chief guest', Shakespeare is warning audiences more blood will be spilled. Bearing in mind Duncan was Macbeth's 'chief guest' only four scenes before, we are still keenly aware that to be such is a clear sign of death. These characters are not really 'chief guests' but 'chief' *targets*, and must be eliminated if only to settle Macbeth's tormented mind. This goes to show how far Macbeth has fallen; he instructs Banquo, 'Fail not our feast', knowing full well his friend will not be attending the celebrations. There is a cruel irony here, as, technically, Banquo will *not* fail to attend the feast; he will make his presence felt in other ways.

Here, then, we realise Macbeth has become just as scheming and malicious as was Lady Macbeth when we first met her. Gone are his doubts as to whether they should 'proceed… further in this business'. Macbeth has the crown and is determined to keep it, which makes him very dangerous indeed.

### 'OUR FEARS IN BANQUO STICK DEEP'

Macbeth's conviction comes at a cost, and not just a human one. Once Banquo has left, Macbeth reveals his true state of mind: he is fearful and alone, trapped in his own thoughts and unable to escape them. His desire has transformed into an obsession, and it is here that Macbeth's mental capacity to think logically dissolves. His crown may give him power, yet as audiences witness when he delivers the 'to be thus is nothing' soliloquy, he is weak, desperate and perhaps even vulnerable.

Macbeth opens with his immediate fear: he will not keep the crown, nor shall it be passed to any of his descendants. 'Our fears in Banquo stick deep,' he acknowledges, once again using 'our' to denote his newly attained royal status. Shakespeare connects Macbeth and Banquo in this speech; both characters, alone on stage, have discussed only minutes apart how they fear one another, evidence perhaps of how their relationship has completely crumbled because of the events that have taken place. Macbeth's use of 'stick deep' is an indication of both his mental and physical anguish, caused by the fear which consumes him. Clearly his worries cannot easily be removed; they are lodged in him, causing immense suffering and misery. What is interesting, however, is how these words can be interpreted in a literal sense. Macbeth's fears cause him to seek the services of those who murder for a fee; the weapons they wield will 'stick deep' in Banquo because of the fear Macbeth experiences.

These fears are elaborated even further when Macbeth, saying 'in his royalty of nature reigns that / Which would be feared', professes that the very way

Banquo carries himself is regal. This observation is a thought-provoking one, for if he has pointed out that Banquo can present himself in this way, it would imply Macbeth feels he himself cannot. If this is the case, this moment acts as a precursor to Macbeth's final thoughts on life's meaning, voiced in Act V, Scene v, where he says, 'Life's but a walking shadow, a poor player, / That struts and frets his hour upon the stage, / And then is heard no more.' This is exactly what Macbeth is afraid of in Act III, Scene i. At this moment, his anxieties tell him he is only playing the part of a king for a temporary time and he will, eventually, disappear into oblivion with no heir to take his place, leaving the crown free for Banquo's lineage to seize. Banquo is kinglike. Macbeth is not.

Macbeth believes Banquo to have a 'dauntless temper' and a 'wisdom that doth guide his valour', qualities Macbeth wishes he could have; after all, he was unable to go through with Duncan's murder at first, revealing he does not have the fearless temperament he admires so much in Banquo. It could be argued, then, that Macbeth is coming to the conclusion that Banquo would be a greater king than would Macbeth, which makes his decision to murder his former ally all the more tragic. No longer is Macbeth serving Scotland; he is serving only himself. 'There is none but he, / Whose being I do fear,' he says. He is afraid of what Banquo knows and what he could do if given the opportunity. Banquo is a threat and must be eliminated.

### 'MY GENIUS IS REBUKED'

Macbeth even goes so far as to say his 'genius is rebuked, as it is said / Mark Antony's was by Caesar.' Here, he is referring to 'the Roman tutelary spirit [a protector, guardian or patron] accompanying a person from birth, Socrates' daimon'.[2] As is often the case, his words hold deeper meaning. Shakespeare dramatises this reference to historical figures in another of his tragedies, *Antony and Cleopatra*.[3] In Act II, Scene iii of that play, the following exchange takes place between Mark Antony and a soothsayer, someone who is supposed to be able to foresee the future:

**MARK ANTONY**
Say to me,
Whose fortunes shall rise higher, Caesar's or mine?

---

2.   Jeremy Tambling, *Histories of the Devil: From Marlowe to Mann and the Manichees*, (London: Palgrave Macmillan, 2016), p. 43.

3.   Ed. John Wilders, *The Arden Shakespeare: Antony and Cleopatra*, (London: Thomson Learning, 1995), p. 144.

**SOOTHSAYER**
Caesar's.
Therefore, O Antony, stay not by his side.
Thy daemon – that's thy spirit which keeps thee – is
Noble, courageous high, unmatchable,
Where Caesar's is not. But near him, thy angel
Becomes afeard, as being o'erpower'd: therefore
Make space enough between you.
**MARK ANTONY**
Speak this no more.

. . . . . . . . . . . . . . . . . . . . . . . . . . . . . . . . . . . . . . . . . . . . . . . . . . . . . . . . . . . . . . . . . .

The two situations are almost identical. Like Macbeth, Mark Antony converses with supernatural forces and is offered a glimpse into his future. In both, one figure is presented to them as a threat to their power. The Soothsayer warns Mark Antony to avoid Caesar (Gaius Octavius) because his spirit is weakened and vulnerable when Caesar is around. Macbeth, alluding to this moment in his soliloquy, is saying that aligning himself with Banquo will scare his 'guardian angel', and all competition between the two of them will result in Banquo's favour. Macbeth fears he could be defeated by Banquo just as Mark Antony was defeated by Caesar. Macbeth believes that to avoid this he should take his fate into his own hands and challenge the witches' predictions.

To do this, Macbeth goes through how he believes events played out when he first met the witches. Listening to him do this is enlightening and shows audiences how his relationship with Banquo has broken down completely. He believes Banquo 'chid the sisters', scolding them for only focusing on Macbeth instead of sharing their auguries with him too. Although Banquo does use an imperative when he speaks to the witches ('Speak then to me'), it may be that Macbeth is deliberately misremembering the strength of Banquo's confrontation in order to give further justification for his murderous thoughts and to genuinely convince himself that what he is about to do is the right course of action. Macbeth is already consumed with guilt about Duncan's murder; constructing a clear rationale for his actions will assuage his fear of feeling further guilt.

Macbeth sees it as his duty to act, bemoaning the 'fruitless crown' and 'barren sceptre' he has been presented with. Describing these royal objects as such tells audiences Macbeth feels the objects hold little to no meaning. They have no purpose and will continue to hold no purpose until his kingship is secure. Security, of course, will be gained through lineage, something Macbeth does not have, therefore rendering it 'barren'. The importance of producing an heir, preferably male, at this time, is something Neil Bowen et al. explore in further detail:

> *In a society in which fatherhood formed a vital cornerstone of male identity and was the bedrock of male power, Macbeth's sterility, his inability to produce a son and heir, fundamentally undermines his authority and emasculates him.*[4]

This emasculation is keenly felt by Macbeth, who feels the sceptre would be 'wrenched' from him by an 'unlineal hand'. The action of wrenching, of course, suggests force, as if it is being torn away from him after some sort of struggle to keep hold of it, made all the more bitter because of who is taking it from him.

The consequences of this 'theft' are dire: 'For Banquo's issue have I filed my mind; / For them, the gracious Duncan have I murdered'. It is not difficult for an audience to see Macbeth's anger, confusion and desperation. Once more, he fully acknowledges Duncan as a 'gracious' king; Duncan did not deserve death, and yet it was a necessary loss in order for Macbeth to ascend to the throne. Murdering him, however, means Macbeth is no longer the man he was. His mind is polluted and tarnished, a point he expresses with bitter realisation as he deals with the prospect that he has sacrificed himself for the sake of Banquo's issue, something which majorly agitates him. In doing this, he has given away something even more valuable than the crown he so desperately desired: his soul, or, as he describes it, his 'eternal jewel', has been traded with the Devil for a power which will not last. Essentially, Macbeth has condemned himself to damnation, faced with the idea of playing the Devil's fool forever.

The fact this could all be for Banquo's children becomes incomprehensible to him; he speaks about them with disgust, almost in an accusatory tone as he grapples with the fact that he suffers 'To make them kings, the seed of Banquo kings.' If Macbeth is to maintain power, he cannot let this happen, and so his soliloquy ends with him directly challenging his destiny: 'come fate into the list, / And champion me to th'utterance.' Macbeth will do all he can to stop the prophecy from coming true, a terrifying prospect for someone who has already committed the unthinkable to get what he wants.

### RHETORIC: PARALLELS TO ACT I, SCENE VII

The murderers enter and Macbeth is keen to know what they have to say. His collusion with them alone shows how he has disgraced himself; there is no small

---

4.  Neil Bowen et al, *The Art of Drama Volume 2: Macbeth GCSE & Beyond*, (Bristol: Peripeteia Press, 2019), p. 122.

talk, no niceties. Macbeth asks them whether they have considered his proposal to murder Banquo, yet before they can reply, he cleverly spins a web of rhetoric in an attempt to convince them that his former friend and ally deserves the fate he will pay them to deliver.

In some editions of the text, Macbeth's speech to the murderers is relineated to be presented as prose, rather than verse. In this way, the prose he uses shows how he has lowered himself in consorting with these outliers of society.[5] However, here Shakespeare is doing more than just lowering Macbeth to the ranks of the murderers. It is true that he has murdered in cold blood and thus is socially similar to these men, but Macbeth's use of prose here highlights his true duplicity. In casting off the shackles of speaking in verse, Macbeth is deliberately attempting to ingratiate himself with the murderers. In doing so, he hopes to compel them to do his bidding: he sounds like them, and therefore they may be more likely to trust him. It is a manipulative and calculated act on Macbeth's part. In addition, Shakespeare here is demonstrating the deliberate distancing in Macbeth and Banquo's close relationship. As he persuades the murderers to kill his comrade, he deliberately speaks less like his friend. This is manipulative of the murderers and simultaneously hints, perhaps, at the fact that Macbeth feels a need to separate himself from the actions he is ordering, in order to not feel as tormented about the death of his companion as he might otherwise feel.

Macbeth is clearly impassioned when speaking to these murderers. He is:

> ... *not satisfied with mere mercenaries. He tries to inspire the murderers to a motivated slaughter – a justifiable revenge – upon Banquo, who according to Macbeth, is the one 'in the times past, / Which held you so under fortune.'*[6]

Indeed, this verbal attack which Macbeth has launched into has clearly been planned and designed to make the murderers feel as if they have a personal stake in Banquo's demise.

Macbeth's aim may also be to make the murderers despise Banquo so that the blame for his friend's death will not lie solely at his feet; the murderers, after all, would be acting in their own self-interest instead of solely carrying out Macbeth's will. Yet, having explored his true feelings only moments before, audiences know that everything Macbeth is saying to the murderers about Banquo is erroneous.

---

5.   Robert Beardwood and Kate Macdonell, *Insight to Text Guides: William Shakespeare's 'Macbeth'*, (St. Kilda, Australia: Insight Publications Ltd, 2012), p. 14.

6.   Joan Hartwig. 'Macbeth, the Murderers, and the Diminishing Parallel', *The Yearbook of English Studies*, Vol. 3, 1973, pp. 39–43, www.jstor.org/stable/3506854.

Isolated and away from the prying eyes and ears of his wife, we can trust Macbeth's soliloquy; in reality, Macbeth sees Banquo as kingly. In the presence of the others, however, Banquo is referred to only as 'he', and presented as someone who has made the lives of these murderers both strenuous and unforgiving.

This is obviously a fabrication, a yarn presenting Banquo as someone who has obstructed the murderers from elevating their social status, keeping them from reaching their proper standing in life. Macbeth alludes to what these men initially believed: he *himself* was the one who had oppressed them, but he soon shifts the blame onto Banquo. Unlike before, where Macbeth's 'face… is a book, where men / May read strange matters', Macbeth is now clearly adept at lying and has become used to the duality he must adopt in order to protect his royal status. Here, he plays off the murderers' intellect, suggesting even a mad person would be able to identify Banquo as the perpetrator of this injustice he says they have suffered.

One observation of this scene is that the murderers say very little at first; Macbeth is left to do a lot of the talking. In leaving him to speak, we begin to see how Macbeth adopts the same strategies as his wife in order to persuade the murderers to kill Banquo.[7] Shakespeare parallels this scene with Act I, Scene vii in the way he structures the action. For example, both scenes precede murders; in Act I, Scene vii, Macbeth, after his soliloquy, is interrupted by his wife, and says very little as Lady Macbeth scolds him and uses rhetoric to get what she wants. The same happens here. Once again, Macbeth voices his thoughts and is interrupted by the arrival of the murderers and Macbeth's servant. The only difference is the role Macbeth plays; whereas before he was the one being persuaded, now he is the persuader. These parallels can be seen right down to the methods both characters use to get their way, and it seems Lady Macbeth has taught her husband a thing or two.[8] Lady Macbeth, upon hearing her husband does not wish to go through with Duncan's murder, asks 'Was the hope drunk / Wherein you dressed yourself? Hath it slept since?' Macbeth, in this scene, also uses two rhetorical questions one after the other to goad the murderers into accepting his contract:

> *Do you find*
> *Your patience so predominant in your nature*
> *That you can let this go? Are you so gospelled*
> *To pray for this good man, and for his issue,*
> *Whose heavy hand hath bowed you to the grave,*
> *And beggared yours for ever?*

---

7.  @GCSE_Macbeth, 8 June 2018, https://twitter.com/GCSE_Macbeth/ status/950477320720211968.

8.  Ibid.

The similarities are too striking to be coincidental. If the major beats of the scene are parallel, it must mean they conclude in the same way too: with death.

What follows is a well-constructed piece of rhetoric and one which links again to the many references to hierarchy in the play. Macbeth at this point switches back to his formal and kingly blank verse, demonstrating his power and the fact that he is now more confident in dealing with the murderers. His rhetoric flows in blank verse in a way in which it does not in prose, and he is able to 'wow' the men with his undeniable skills of oracy. Macbeth incredulously asks the murderers if they would pray for a man who has allegedly forced them into a life of destitution. The first murderer, in reply, says 'We are men, my liege', prompting yet another stirring oration from Macbeth.

Once again, Macbeth adopts the same strategies as his wife who, in order to get what she wants earlier in the play, both criticises and mocks her husband's masculinity. Perhaps Macbeth approaches the murderers with similar methods because he knows how effective they can be: after all, Lady Macbeth's scorn at his apparent weaknesses hurt his pride, thus heightening his determination to prove he can do what he has promised.

Macbeth believes the label of 'men' is as useful as the label of 'dogs', saying there are many different types of breed that possess unique qualities, just as many men have characteristics that others may not share. These unique qualities create a natural hierarchy, with some features more desirable than others. Macbeth makes it clear that humans are the same. In referencing 'hounds, and greyhounds, mongrels, spaniels, curs, / Shoughs, water-rugs and demi-wolves', and comparing their rank and order to that of men in terms of their desirable qualities, he is stripping people of their humanity, saying they are no better than beasts. This is ironic, really, considering Macbeth is nothing more than a savage beast himself, acting animalistically and for his own ill-gotten gains, for what he has done to Duncan and what he plans to do to Banquo.

Macbeth, in ranking these breeds of dog, states it is easy to distinguish 'the swift, the slow, the subtle, / The housekeeper, [and] the hunter'; there is no secret here as to what his preferences are. Through his metaphor, he is asking the murderers what kind of men they are, clearly seeking to separate those whose qualities he can exploit away from those for whom he has no use. He addresses them with a clear proposal: 'Now, if you have a station in the file / Not i'th' worst rank of manhood, say't, / And I will put that business in your bosoms / Whose execution takes your enemy off…'. Notice the pun Shakespeare uses with his use of 'execution', which means to 'carry out' whilst also subtly alluding to how Banquo will meet his end.

Determinedly, Macbeth states, 'Both of you know Banquo was your enemy' before confirming 'So is he mine'. This is really quite clever; whilst Macbeth has lowered himself by colluding with these murderers, to them he is a source of elevation. Macbeth has made the murderers feel included, raising their standing by allowing them to converse with him. In essence, he is offering them what Banquo allegedly took from them: a voice and chance to prove themselves. Carrying out the king's instructions signals that opportunity, and Macbeth makes no secret of the fact that he is somewhat desperate and the murder should happen urgently. Macbeth needs them to do this in secret if he is to maintain the 'loves [he] may not drop' from mutual friends he shares with Banquo, masking 'the business from the common eye'. By the end of the scene, Macbeth and the murderers share a common enemy, and this makes them one, united in their hatred for Banquo.

Macbeth is quick to shut down any protestations. The first murderer tries to speak ('Though our lives –'), but the King is quick to shut him down. He clearly wants to protest something, but Macbeth showers the murderers with praise ('Your spirits shine through you') before they can say anything else. He knows exactly how he wants this murder to play out: from his questioning of Banquo's movements to the time the murder must occur, Macbeth has planned with a precision more reminiscent of his wife than himself. Nothing must be overlooked. Only then will Macbeth feel secure.

### 'IT IS CONCLUDED'

The scene ends with the murderers 'resolved'. Once again, Shakespeare's parallels between the scenes that precede the murders of major characters become evident. Moments before Macbeth goes to murder Duncan in Act II, Scene i and before the murderers leave to kill Banquo in this current scene, Macbeth 'ritualizes the business in fateful couplets':[9]

> 'Hear it not Duncan; for it is a knell
> That summons thee to heaven, or to hell.'

> 'It is concluded: Banquo, thy soul's flight,
> If it find heaven, must find it out tonight.'

This is a fascinating similarity. Macbeth talks directly to Duncan and Banquo even though they are absent from the action. It is a last moment of truth from Macbeth, the last thing he will say to them which he genuinely means. There are even links to be made in the language he uses, primarily in his reference to 'heaven', perhaps because that is where audiences believe both characters would end up. What is most interesting is that Macbeth alludes to

---

9.    Joan Hartwig, 'Macbeth, the Murderers, and the Diminishing Parallel', *The Yearbook of English Studies*, Vol. 3, 1973, pp. 39–43, www.jstor.org/stable/3506854.

the possibility of Banquo and Duncan *not* entering heaven. When one takes into account the sheer enormity of the sins Macbeth has committed compared to the others, it seems almost ludicrous that he could entertain such a possibility. The scene ends with the image of Banquo's 'soul's flight', reminiscent of a bird, and a sombre sign that he will not be alive for much longer.

## Scene analysis: Act III, Scene ii

This scene acts as a brief interlude between the planning of Banquo's murder and the act itself; it begins with Lady Macbeth asking whether Banquo has 'gone from court' and telling one of her servants to inform Macbeth she would like to 'attend his leisure'. This in itself exposes the seeds of estrangement the couple are beginning to experience; the fact that Lady Macbeth must ask a servant to reach out to her husband implies their relationship is already beginning to break apart and they are 'struggling to maintain physical proximity with each other.'[10] It cannot possibly survive the guilt which weighs them both down, however best they try to ignore it.

Having presented Lady Macbeth as a strong, confident woman thus far, Shakespeare offers audiences a glimpse into her own fears. Like Banquo and Macbeth before her, she voices these alone: to do so in front of others would denote weakness and vulnerability. Even though these feelings are rising within her, it is important for Lady Macbeth to maintain a façade of strength, especially as her husband finds it increasingly difficult. She must be resolute for them both. Lamenting that 'Naught's had, all's spent, / Where our desire is got without content', she acknowledges their 'achievements' have offered them nothing in the way of harmony.

She continues to reflect, observing ''Tis safer to be that which we destroy, / Than by destruction dwell in doubtful joy.' Surprisingly, she believes it is better to be murdered than be the murderer; the dead, after all, are at peace, whilst the murderer collapses under the weight of uncertainty and guilt even though they have what they want, highlighted through the oxymoron 'doubtful joy'. Her calm exterior is beginning to crack, foreshadowing the downfall she will later experience. Stephen Greenblatt poses a vital question here when he writes:

> But what exactly did [Lady Macbeth] expect? Tyranny comes about, as her words acknowledge, through destruction, the destruction of people and of a whole country. That she somehow thought that their personal contentment, safety, and joy could be achieved by this means is in keeping with the fatal shallowness

---

10. Neil Bowen et al., *The Art of Drama Volume 2: Macbeth GCSE & Beyond*, (Peripeteia Press, 2019), p. 99.

*she voiced when she washed the murdered king's blood off her hands: 'A little water clears us of this deed.'*[11]

This 'shallowness' is perhaps the source of their struggles. So concerned are they with seizing and keeping the crown that they have neglected to consider how the sheer enormity of their actions will affect them. It seems both Macbeth and Lady Macbeth assumed they could navigate the stormy seas of guilt with ease, yet that is far from the truth.

### 'WHAT'S DONE, IS DONE'

In reality, the couple, who have always shared intimately their feelings regarding their plans, are driving themselves apart as they begin to keep secrets from one another. Lady Macbeth, for example, decides not to share her doubts and fears with Macbeth when he enters, even though he makes no secret that he feels the same. Instead, she attempts to reassure him, saying 'what's done, is done.' On the surface, Lady Macbeth is instructing Macbeth to ignore what he cannot change. However, these lines echo Macbeth's introspection from Act I, Scene vii where he says, 'If it were done, when 'tis done, then 'twere well / It were done quickly.' The word 'done' can mean both 'ended' and 'performed'.[12] In both Lady Macbeth's and Macbeth's use of the word, there is a sense of finality and conclusion. There is a difference, though, in what precedes the word 'done'. Macbeth, in saying 'if it were', shows dubiety.[13] Murder, at this point, is still only a possibility. On the other hand, Lady Macbeth says 'is done'. It is clear she is saying the act has been 'performed' and the fallout 'ended'. There is nothing more to be said, although having seen her voice her fears just moments before, one wonders whether she truly believes what she is saying. The idea of the doing and undoing of things recurs constantly through the play and Lady Macbeth is right. 'What's done, is done', but this will be the cause of their undoing.

Macbeth rebukes his wife's claim, believing credible threats to their reign will still emerge. This is the first time we see husband and wife alone together since Act II, Scene ii, yet the dynamic between them has changed. Just by looking at who speaks the most reveals an imbalance of power, but it no longer belongs to Lady Macbeth like before. This time, it has shifted to her husband, who ignores his wife's requests to move on and forget the past.

11.  Stephen Greenblatt, *Tyrant: Shakespeare on Power*, (Vintage, London, 2019), p. 103.

12.  Ed. Sandra Clark and Pamela Mason, *The Arden Shakespeare: Macbeth*, (London: Bloomsbury, 2015), p. 163.

13.  @GCSE_Macbeth, 5 December 2017, https://twitter.com/GCSE_Macbeth/status/938141357478211584.

## 'WE HAVE SCORCHED THE SNAKE, NOT KILLED IT'

Most interpretations of the 'We have scorched the snake, not killed it' speech agree that Macbeth is referring to Duncan and his lineage. 'Scorched' means slashed or wounded;[14] Duncan may be dead, but Malcolm and Donalbain still present Macbeth, who is concerned they are biding their time before they retaliate and strike, with an issue.

As a side note, some editions of *Macbeth* adopt the term 'scotch'd' instead of 'scorched'. This is a revision made by Lewis Theobald (1688–1744), a Shakespearean editor.[15] 'Scotch'd' is a verb meaning to 'notch, slash, hack or cut',[16] so both choices suggest a form of lashing out with the intent to damage.

Snakes, of course, represent lies, vindictiveness and deceit; Macbeth echoes his wife's command to 'look like the innocent flower, / But be the serpent under't' here. Whereas before they were the serpents, Macbeth now assigns the term to his enemies; his apprehension that he himself will become the victim of deceit and malice manifests itself in these opening lines.

Macbeth seems to be berating Lady Macbeth for her incompetent observation of 'what's done, is done', believing the 'snake' to 'close, and be herself, whilst our poor malice / Remains in danger of her former tooth.' He acknowledges that further violence will be required in order to protect himself and his wife from the threats that may present themselves. This scene, then, sees Macbeth at a crossroads. He could listen to his wife and attempt to put an end to his paranoia, or engage in further violence, entering a cyclical nature of bloodthirsty existence.

He chooses, somewhat unsurprisingly, the latter option, displaying outright narcissistic and totalitarian traits, stating, 'But let the frame of things disjoint, both the worlds suffer, / Ere we will eat our meal in fear, and sleep / In the affliction of these terrible dreams'. The 'frame' Macbeth references is the universe; the Great Chain of Being, the thing holding all in place. It is clear to see he is only thinking of himself at this moment. In true tyrannical style, he is willing to cause immense destruction to get what he wants, a trait Greenblatt describes as 'vicious indifference to anyone and anything else'.[17]

---

14.  David and Ben Crystal, *Oxford Illustrated Shakespeare Dictionary*, (Oxford: Oxford University Press, 2015), p. 262.

15.  Louisa Susanna Cheves McCord, *Political and Social Essays*, (Charlottesville: The University Press of Virginia, 1995), p. 431.

16.  Harriet C. Frazier, *A Babble of Ancestral Voices: Shakespeare, Cervantes, and Theobald*, (The Hague: Mouton, 1974), p. 80.

17.  Stephen Greenblatt, *Tyrant: Shakespeare on Power*, (Vintage, London, 2019), p. 106.

Notice how Macbeth reveals that 'both the worlds suffer'. Exactly what this second world entails is subject to discussion. On a basic level, it would seem Macbeth is referring to the world he is in and the world of the afterlife, especially as he goes on to discuss Duncan's new-found peace in death. However, his lines become much more sinister if one takes 'both worlds' to mean the metaphysical and supernatural worlds, for this would imply Macbeth believes he has power to tamper with and intrude on a realm in which he has no experience. He is willing to 'take on' something transcendental as an act of self-preservation, no matter the cost.

Macbeth, without realising, agrees with his wife that it is 'Better [to] be with the dead', because the dead are at peace, rather than having to endure the 'torture' of 'restless ecstasy'. What is most pertinent here is that Macbeth refers to 'Duncan… in his grave', saying he 'sleeps well', having escaped 'life's fitful fever', just another example of imagery pertaining to sickness or disease. His words hark back to Lennox's observation that 'Some say the earth / Was feverous and did shake' in Act II, Scene iii when describing the 'unruly' night of the King's murder. Perhaps Macbeth, in thinking of life as a 'fever', is suggesting the only way to cure this sickness is through death. He may be trying to justify his murderous actions, believing he has brought Duncan true peace, or acknowledging he will only put a stop to his paranoia if he dies himself. One can recover from a fever, and perhaps this is a glimmer of hope for Scotland, but death is the thing, in Macbeth's eyes, that makes one untouchable, when he states, 'nor steel, nor poison, / Malice domestic, foreign levy, nothing, / Can touch [Duncan] further.'

### 'MAKE OUR FACES VIZARDS TO OUR HEARTS'

Lady Macbeth attempts to ease the troubled and disturbed Macbeth during the brief dialogue she is given. In this moment, audiences can fully appreciate the emerging divide between husband and wife and the role reversal that has occurred. Macbeth instructs Lady Macbeth to present Banquo with 'eminence, both with eye and tongue', a direct parallel to her instructions to him upon Duncan's arrival to their home in Act I, Scene v.

These parallels extend further. Macbeth, in instructing Lady Macbeth to use flattery as a way of securing people's allegiance, says their faces should be 'vizards to [their] hearts'. A 'vizard' is a mask; Macbeth hopes their faces will shield their true intentions and emotions just as Lady Macbeth advised her husband on the eve of Duncan's murder. These are instructions Macbeth has adopted, and adopted well. He began with a 'face… where men / May read strange matters'. He is now adept at lying. His face no longer reveals 'strange matters'. Instead, he does what he must in order to keep the crown.

## 'O, FULL OF SCORPIONS IS MY MIND, DEAR WIFE'

What follows is a repeated attempt by Lady Macbeth to calm him, although her efforts are rendered futile and Macbeth responds with what has become one of the most famous lines in the play: 'O, full of scorpions is my mind, dear wife'. It is an ugly, grotesque image, one of infestation and corruption. Scorpions are hideous creatures, a reflection of the thoughts his mind now holds. They are unseemly and repulsive, and by revealing this to his wife, he is fully aware that this is not how things should be. Scorpions are also dangerous adversaries, suggesting Macbeth cannot challenge his thoughts; he must succumb to them and let them 'win', although this will have dangerous consequences for him and, by extension, Scotland. By following his thoughts, he himself would become this dangerous adversary, a scorpion striking maliciously at anyone who lashes out at him.

Another, somewhat more sweeping interpretation, is that Macbeth could be contemplating death by suicide as a way of obtaining the peace he so desperately desires. It would certainly make sense, given his having deplored Duncan's tranquility in death only moments before. Scorpions, it was long believed, possessed a 'suicidal tendency'.[18] In moments of danger, for example 'if trapped and faced with imminent death, or even captivity, [a scorpion] would kill itself with its sting.'[19] Macbeth may not be faced with 'imminent death' at this point, but he is certainly trapped, if not by Banquo or Duncan's sons, then by his own mind. Any further actions he takes, if they have not already, will lead to his own downfall, not necessarily dying by suicide, but an end nevertheless.

## 'BE INNOCENT OF THE KNOWLEDGE, DEAREST CHUCK'

Lady Macbeth's last line in the scene ('What's to be done?) is a question, signalling how dependent she has become on her husband to know what is going on. Macbeth does not tell her what this dreadful deed will be. Instead, he tells her to 'be innocent of the knowledge, dearest chuck', but the secret he hides is further evidence of their crumbling relationship. Although Macbeth still uses terms of affection towards her such as 'chuck' and 'dear wife', they ring hollow. He may even be using them to assert his rank over his wife, as 'chuck' is 'always used by the more powerful character (in terms of gender or class) to the less powerful.'[20] Macbeth is becoming the man Lady Macbeth hoped he would be earlier in the

---

18.  Ed. Demitra Papadinis, *The Tragedie of Macbeth: A Frankly Annotated First Folio Edition*, (North Carolina: McFarland and Company, Inc., Publishers, 2012), p. 225 (quoting Chris Andrews, *Poetry and Cosmonogy*, (Atlanta, GA: Rodopi, 1999), p. 101.)

19.  Ibid.

20.  Ed. Sandra Clark and Pamela Mason, *The Arden Shakespeare: Macbeth*, (London: Bloomsbury, 2015), p. 213.

play, but in doing so, he excludes her from his plans, and it seems she is almost forced to retake her position as the submissive partner in the relationship.

The scene ends with a rather frightful speech. Macbeth is now fully invested in evil as a way of achieving his objectives, a dangerous trait which eradicates any sense of morality he may have had left. Once more, Macbeth's words reflect previous statements made earlier in the play. By asking the 'seeling night' to 'Scarf up the tender eye of pitiful day', Macbeth echoes his previous command to the stars to 'hide' their 'fires' and Lady Macbeth's request for 'thick night' to 'pall thee in the dunnest smoke of hell'. Darkness allows these characters to commit acts of violence in secret, but also allows them to disregard what they have done as if not seeing something means it did not happen. Here, Macbeth is asking the night to blind the light of the day. 'Seeling' refers to an early and cruel practice of falconers, who would seal the eyes of a hawk to prevent it from seeing its surroundings: 'A needle and thread were passed through both eyelids, so as either to shut out the whole of the light, or only a part, as the two ends of the thread were more or less closely knotted.'[21] It sounds barbaric, yet perhaps that is why it seems a particularly fitting metaphor for Macbeth to use at this point.

### 'TEAR TO PIECES THAT GREAT BOND'

He continues by instructing the night to 'tear to pieces', with a 'bloody and invisible hand', that 'great bond / Which keeps me pale'. His reference to invisibility shows how, in his mind, violent acts must be kept secret. Whilst one may argue that Macbeth is attempting to disaffiliate himself from these brutal actions, it is probably to avoid arousing suspicion rather than because he is ashamed of what he is doing, like before. He has already acknowledged a universe-changing event will have to take place before he succumbs to his fear, but violent acts must now be committed by an 'invisible hand' in order to extinguish any misgivings about his leadership which could lead to direct challenge.

The 'great bond' Macbeth references is a little more cryptic. It could be referring to Banquo's 'bond' to life and the metaphysical world. His presence certainly keeps Macbeth 'pale', or in other words, afraid. His death, right now, is the only thing which will bring calm to Macbeth's mind. But what if the bond was something inherent within Macbeth? If it was something which 'binds Macbeth to common humanity',[22] it would appear, by asking night to destroy it, that he has sold himself to the forces of darkness completely. Destroying

---

21.  Delabere P. Blaine, *An Encyclopaedia of Rural Sports*, (Edinburgh: Thomas and Archibald Constable, 1875), p. 700.

22.  Ed. Sandra Clark and Pamela Mason, *The Arden Shakespeare: Macbeth*, (London: Bloomsbury, 2015), p. 214.

the bond between himself and humanity would enable Macbeth to do what he wants without fear of consequence; he would feel no obligation to his moral self, as it simply would not exist any more.

Act III, Scene ii ends with a sense of foreboding. Macbeth observes that 'Light thickens... Whole night's black agents to their preys do rouse.' The darkness he asked for has arrived; it has accepted his invitation, and with the idea of 'night's black agents' rousing, there is a sense that true evil is beginning to wake, something which will dominate the rest of the play and drive the action to its bloody climax.

Lady Macbeth is surprised by her husband's words, but he commands her to go with him, saying evil deeds must be followed by more horrendous acts. The last time audiences saw Macbeth and Lady Macbeth exit together, just the two of them, was in Act II, Scene ii, having just dealt with the immediate aftermath of Duncan's murder. They were united in their cause but filled with uncertainties as to what would happen next. Reflecting this, Act III, Scene ii has them exit together once more, yet their relationship is fractured and crippled and they are certain that more atrocities must be committed if they are to keep a hold of the throne.

## Scene analysis: Act III, Scene iii

### THE THIRD MURDERER

Act III, Scene iii is short, but its events have an impact on everything else that follows. As Macbeth only spoke with two murderers earlier, audiences may be surprised to find a third murderer has arrived to carry out Macbeth's plans. The other two themselves question his unforeseen appearance, asking 'But who did bid thee join with us?' to which the unknown party simply replies, 'Macbeth'. They seem to trust him, however, stating he knows their orders. The question remains: who is the third murderer?

His identity has come under much scrutiny, with possibilities as to who he could be ranging from Ross and Seyton to Macbeth and even Lady Macbeth herself.[23] What we *do* know is he must be someone close to Macbeth:

> *All that is definitely known concerning the third murderer is that he was the first to hear the approaching horses, he was the first to call for silence lest Banquo hear their voices, he knew the customs of the palace, he identified Banquo, he was distressed*

23. Theodore Halbert Wilson, 'The Third Murderer', *The English Journal*, Vol. 18, No. 5, 1929, pp. 418–422, www.jstor.org/stable/803801.

*that the light had been struck out, and he noted that Fleance had escaped.*[24]

There is little evidence regarding the third murderer's appearance to narrow the list of contenders down to one person. As such, our attention must turn to why he appears in the first place. It seems Macbeth's concerns regarding Banquo force him to send someone else to ensure the murder is seen through to its end. In true authoritarian style, Macbeth is unwilling to relinquish control to the two men he has hired to kill his former ally. Everyone must be watched and scrutinised to ensure they are doing what they are told. Regardless of Macbeth's motives, the arrival of a third murderer means the odds are overwhelmingly stacked against Banquo.

Before noting the time of day, the first murderer invites the third to join them, stating, 'The west yet glimmers with some streaks of day.' Shakespeare may be alluding to the fact that there is still a glimmer of hope whilst Banquo lives; darkness does not yet reign completely. Additionally, the sun is setting and the 'glimmers' are all that light the scene. If Banquo has represented light until this point in the play, the sunset is suggestive of the fact that his life is about to be ended, much like the light of day.

### 'LET IT COME DOWN'

As Banquo enters with Fleance, who is carrying a torch, he notes the weather, saying 'It will be rain tonight', prompting the first murderer to reply 'Let it come down.' Arguably, the first murderer is making a 'grim jest'[25] at this point; rain, after all, is the least of Banquo's worries, seeing as he is about to experience a rain of blows which will end his life. It is a rallying cry for the murderers to attack.

Here, the light goes out, seemingly extinguished by the first murderer, who replies 'Was't not the way?' when the third murderer asks who put it out. It seems Macbeth's own paranoia in sending the third murderer has caused the failure of their assignment. Fleance escapes, most likely able to slip away, 'invisible' (if one refers back to Macbeth's words in Act III, Scene ii) under the cover of darkness now the light has been extinguished. The fact that the murderers question one another shows they both had different versions of the plan, leaving audiences to realise Macbeth should never have sent someone else in a moment of instability. It has only confused things, and as Banquo cries out 'Fly, good Fleance', there is no doubt his prophecy, that he will be the 'father to a line of kings', will come true.

---

24. Ibid.
25. Ed. A.R. Braunmuller, *The New Cambridge Shakespeare: Macbeth*, (Cambridge: Cambridge University Press, 2008), p. 190.

The end of the scene sees the murderers' realisation that they have failed in enacting the most important part of Macbeth's commands. The third murderer says 'There's but one down: the son is fled.' He is obviously speaking of Fleance, but in using the word 'son', Shakespeare could be alluding to the *actual* sun.[26] Fleance, as the light, has disappeared. Banquo's death means there is no hope left and Macbeth's actions have cemented his own status as a force of darkness.

## Macbeth's fear at a glance

### RESOURCE 11.1

Macbeth has fears that Banquo's lineage will take the throne from him. 'Stick deep' may imply his fears are immovable within him and ingrained in his state of mind, but also hints that they will drive Macbeth to murder Banquo. The weapons the murderers wield will literally 'stick deep' in Banquo when he is killed.

Macbeth despises Banquo's royal nature, seemingly coming to the realisation that Banquo would make a better king. Highlighting Banquo's 'dauntless temper' and 'wisdom' would suggest Macbeth believes he does not possess these qualities himself.

Macbeth is referring to a protector and guardian spirit when speaks of his 'genius'. He believes Banquo will scare away his spirit as Mark Antony's was by Caesar.

'Wrenched' implies Macbeth will put up a fight to keep his crown but that it will eventually be removed from him by force.

There is a common thread of imagery running through the play of infected and polluted minds. Macbeth believes he has destroyed any peace which was inherent within him for the sake of Banquo's children.

**MACBETH**
To be thus is nothing, but to be safely thus:
Our fears in Banquo stick deep,
And in his royalty of nature reigns that
Which would be feared. 'Tis much he dares,
And to that dauntless temper of his mind,
He hath a wisdom that doth guide his valour
To act in safety. There is none but he,
Whose being I do fear; and under him
My genius is rebuked, as it is said
Mark Antony's was by Caesar. He chid the sisters
When first they put the name of king upon me,
And bade them speak to him. Then, prophet-like,
They hailed him father to a line of kings.
Upon my head they placed a fruitless crown
And put a barren sceptre in my gripe,
Thence to be wrenched with an unlineal hand,
No son of mine succeeding. If't be so,
For Banquo's issue have I filed my mind;
For them, the gracious Duncan have I murdered;
Put rancours in the vessel of my peace
Only for them; and mine eternal jewel
Given to the common enemy of man,
To make them kings, the seeds of Banquo kings.
Rather than so, come fate into the list,
And champion me to th'utterance. Who's there?

'Fruitless' and 'barren' suggest Macbeth feels his kingship has little to no meaning if he has no children to inherit his throne. Macbeth's inability to produce an heir emasculates him and undermines his authority.

Macbeth describes Duncan as 'gracious'. He knows the former king did not deserve his fate.

Macbeth fears he has condemned himself to eternal damnation forever by selling his soul, his 'eternal jewel', to the Devil, referred to as 'the common enemy of man'.

Macbeth concludes by challenging his fate. He will do all he can to stop Banquo's prophecy from coming true, a terrifying prospect considering the heinous crimes he has already committed.

26.  Ed. A.R. Braunmuller, *The New Cambridge Shakespeare: Macbeth*, (Cambridge: Cambridge University Press, 2008), p. 190.

## How?

There is a lot of content to cover from the 'What?' section of this chapter, too much to fit into one lesson. However, I have made the decision to keep those three scenes together because of the close ties they share. As such, the process of learning described here is likely to take more than one lesson to complete, and so I have split it into three rough parts to help you with your own planning.

## PART ONE:

### Retrieval

The halfway point of the play is a good chance to revisit the 'Big Questions' which introduce each lesson. Provide students with all the Big Questions you have studied so far and ask them to answer each in as much detail as possible.

The first few questions will be duplicates of the ones you gave them last time, with the new questions students have studied since added to the end. I feel it is important to give students the opportunity to answer all of them, even those they have previously answered from the start of the scheme, because they, and you as the teacher, will begin to see past answers develop as understanding increases.

For example, the first time a student reviews the question 'What is ambition?', they may consider Macbeth's 'black and deep desires', the fact ambition is a goal and that aspirations are not always a force for good. By the time students reach *this* lesson, they will have seen just how destructive ambition can be and the fact that it causes death, develops into obsession and makes people lose sight of what is really important.

Pay particular attention to students' responses to the first few repeated questions when reviewing as a class. If students are still struggling to answer the same questions as last time, it indicates further teaching of this aspect of the text is needed.

### Pre-reading activities

Introduce the Big Question for the lesson:

> *What is the relationship like between Macbeth and Banquo once Macbeth becomes king?*

There is lots to dissect in Act III, Scene i, and so it is important students are guided through in a clear and coherent way. I think pre-reading strategies are as important here as ever, particularly considering the importance of the soliloquies this lesson will cover. A simple but effective way of helping students predict what a text will be about is through use of word clouds. They are not groundbreaking by any means, but they do help to reduce the threat of a large passage. Students can make inferences from the words they see, question words they don't know, and make simple connections between the vocabulary on the page. They are a good opportunity for us to explicitly teach vocabulary to our students, to dual code particularly challenging units of language and to discuss initial misconceptions. The word cloud example in Resource 11.2 is from Banquo's soliloquy which opens Act III, Scene i. To help students place this in context, you may want to offer the information suggested at the top of the word cloud.

## RESOURCE 11.2

This cloud is made up of words from Banquo's soliloquy at the beginning of Act III, Scene i. At this point, Macbeth has been crowned the King of Scotland. What do you think Banquo's soliloquy is about?

Give students the opportunity to debate, share their ideas and consider what Banquo could be saying. Address any queries about vocabulary. Some students may pick up on the fact that 'thou' and 'thee' are bigger than the other words, meaning they appear more often and suggesting Banquo is addressing his soliloquy to someone. If students are particularly stuck, ask them to group the words into positive and negative categories and consider what they find. For students after a little more challenge, ask them to group the words but do not tell them how. The purpose of this task, really, is to instigate discussion. The more students talk about something, the more likely it is they will engage and understand.

### Reading the scene

When reading, ask students to consider three main questions – Shakespeare's three 'big ideas' if you will:

1. Why is Banquo afraid?
2. Which word from elsewhere in the play appears once again in Banquo's speech and why?

3. What does Banquo say which suggests he could succumb to his own ambitions and what does this tell us about his character?

Using students' previous inferences, ask students to discuss these questions. For shorter soliloquies such as this one, I always find 'Think, Pair, Share' a particularly useful tool to help kindle structured student talk. Pose the questions and build in thinking time to help students consider what they want to say on an individual level before allowing them to voice their ideas to their partner. Circulate around the room to hear what students are saying to each other; intervene if necessary to address misconceptions and then invite ideas from the whole class so everyone has a chance to share.

The conversation that ensues between Macbeth and Banquo has some important elements you will want to bring to your students' attention, namely the language changes adopted by Banquo (as explained in the 'What?' section) in the way he refers to Macbeth, and Macbeth's subtle interrogation of Banquo to ascertain his movements and that of his son.

## The importance of talk

Year on year, I reflect on how I teach Shakespeare, particularly when approaching the 'most famous' parts of a particular play. Usually, when teaching Act III, Scene i, I provide students with a blank copy of Macbeth's soliloquy and a set of questions, and ask them to annotate, drawing together everyone's loose ideas at the end as part of a class discussion. I am not denouncing these types of activities; as you will already have seen, there are many examples in this book of similar ilk. However, balance is needed, and recently I have been prioritising talk over writing and seeing some outstanding results in response. Talk should be used as a tool to inform understanding rather than being the 'bolt-on' to a written activity. If we only use class discussion to sum up our ideas, we are inadvertently telling our students that talking has little value in our lessons. I think we are often scared of talk in our classrooms, of what others will think if they walk in and our students do not have a pen in their hand. It harks back to the myth that students can only learn if they are sitting in silence and writing. It goes without saying that this is not true.

The next activity is designed to generate that talk and is based on an idea originally shared by Chris Curtis as a way of helping students analyse a poem.[27] Students are given a prompt sheet full of comments they could make about the text they are studying. The teacher slowly brings up the poem line by line,

---

27. Chris Curtis, 'Teaching poetry at KS3 – Why we need more chat in the classroom', *Learning from My Mistakes*, (2019) http://learningfrommymistakesenglish.blogspot. com/2019/06/teaching-poetry -at-ks3-why-we-need-more.html.

and students have to say as much about the lines on the board as they can. Scaffolding the task in this way meant my students and I were often talking about poems for forty minutes or more, enjoying the process of analysis rather than feeling burdened by it. Resource 11.3 is adapted from Curtis's original idea to achieve similar results with one of Shakespeare's soliloquies:

## RESOURCE 11.3

| Consider the deeper meaning | Consider links you could make to other areas of the text | Consider language choices made by a writer |
|---|---|---|
| Initially, it seems the text is about _____ but deep down I think Shakespeare is saying _____.<br><br>I think Shakespeare is really saying _____. | This part reminds me of _____ because _____.<br><br>This moment is similar to _____ because _____.<br><br>Things have changed here because earlier in the play _____ but now _____. | The word '_____' makes me feel _____ because _____.<br><br>I think Shakespeare has used the word '_____' because he is alluding to _____.<br><br>The word '_____' is an interesting choice because it reminds me of _____. |
| **Consider how the writer wants to make a reader or audience to feel**<br><br>At this point, I think Shakespeare wants an audience to feel _____ because _____.<br><br>To make an audience feel _____, Shakespeare uses _____ and _____ because _____. | **How do I analyse a text?** | **Consider multiple interpretations of a text and symbolic meanings**<br><br>Shakespeare might be using _____ as a symbol because _____.<br><br>The word/phrase '_____' could mean _____ but it could also mean _____ |
| **Consider how the text has been put together**<br><br>At the beginning of the text, Shakespeare _____.<br><br>In the middle of the text, things have stayed the same/changed because _____.<br><br>By the end of the text, Shakespeare _____. | **Consider how the writer changes the tone, mood or atmosphere of the text**<br><br>Before this moment, the atmosphere was _____ but now it has changed to _____ because _____.<br><br>The tone changes from _____ to _____ when Shakespeare writes '_____' because _____.<br><br>Shakespeare establishes a _____ mood through his use of the word '_____' because _____. | **Consider authorial intent and why a writer is doing something**<br><br>Perhaps Shakespeare includes this line to criticise/teach/warn us/expose _____.<br><br>Shakespeare may be wanting to say _____.<br><br>Shakespeare could be trying to _____. |

Bring up Macbeth's soliloquy beginning 'To be thus is nothing', one or two lines at a time. Ask students to make comments about each line as they appear, using the comments on the frame to help them. Initially, talk may be stilted as students get to grips with what is required of them. Eventually, as they familiarise themselves with the comments in the frame, they will contribute more. You may need to model the type of comment you would expect them to make.

As more lines are revealed and understanding increases, students will want to make links and connections between points in the soliloquy or between the soliloquy and the wider text. They may be halfway through the speech and want to make another comment about something at the start of it. Let them. Learning is not linear. Something further down the text may have helped students understand something higher up. Regardless of where the analysis goes, students should not be required to write anything at this point. The sole focus of the task should be the class discussion; thirty minds, after all, are better than one.

## What is Macbeth's biggest fear?

Only once students have discussed the soliloquy in the depth required by this activity should any writing be introduced here, and even then, huge amounts are not needed. Think about setting the class a simple question that tests their knowledge, like: What is Macbeth's biggest fear in Act III, Scene i? This is not necessarily to get students to analyse the language, even though they will have already done this during discussion. This is more about ensuring they understand what they need to understand before moving on. As such, an example answer may look like this:

> *In Act III, Scene i, Macbeth is expressing his doubts and fears over Banquo and how much of a threat Banquo poses to his reign. Macbeth worries that Banquo would make a better king than him because he possesses wisdom and has a brave nature, qualities Macbeth feels he does not have. What concerns Macbeth more is the fact that he has no heir to pass his crown to when he dies, meaning he believes he has suffered through guilt and torment all for the sake of Banquo's sons.*

## Using analytical verbs to explore authorial intent

Having understood what Shakespeare is saying, focus should move to why he is saying it. Authorial intent is something I find a lot of students do not consider, because they fail to see texts as conscious constructs, writing about the characters as if they are real people.

To help students consider why Shakespeare has made Macbeth so fearful, the following set of analytical verbs could be used. I have found this activity, first introduced to me by Lia Martin (@liaesthermartin on Twitter), is best used once students have enough knowledge about the characters and plot to think holistically and critically. Students are given the opening to a sentence and have to finish it in different ways depending on the analytical verb they encounter. For example, you may provide students with this:

**Perhaps Shakespeare highlights Macbeth's fear of Banquo:**
- to criticise...
- to teach...
- to warn...
- to reveal the importance of...
- to challenge...
- to celebrate...

Model one for students so they know what is expected. Some may find this difficult, yet it will challenge their thinking to ensure they look beyond the obvious. Here are two examples of what could be said. Notice also the use of tentative language with the opening word 'perhaps', an important skill for students to adopt.

**Perhaps Shakespeare highlights Macbeth's fear of Banquo:**
- **to criticise** how ambition can become a dangerous and destructive obsession.
- **to teach** audiences that even powerful men have weaknesses which threaten to destroy them.

Next, ask students to extend their thoughts further. They should select two or three of their sentences and see if they can extend them with 'because', 'but' or 'so'. Once again, some may find this challenging, but adopting this scaffolded approach means they are taking the time to really think about what Shakespeare's intentions are. Model once more so students know what is expected of them. Extended sentences may look something like this. The new additions to the sentence have been placed in italics so you can see how answers are beginning to build.

**Perhaps Shakespeare highlights Macbeth's fear of Banquo:**

- **to criticise** how ambition can become a dangerous and destructive obsession *so he presents the king as anxious, nervous and tense in this soliloquy.*
- **to teach** audiences that even powerful men have weaknesses which threaten to destroy them, *but this can have dangerous consequences and lead to further tyrannical behaviour.*

As you can see, the answers are not perfect – and one would not expect them to be at this point – but through using this method, students can begin to appreciate characters as the conscious constructs they are. They have been created by Shakespeare as vessels for his message and it is a student's job to find out exactly what that message is.

Next, inform students they should extend their ideas to one of their sentences further by referencing the soliloquy both directly and indirectly. Notice how the paragraph is beginning to build by referencing language as a result of discussing authorial intent instead of just picking one random word from a quotation, assigning it a piece of subject terminology and saying something about it. Analysis should be meaningful and have purpose. Once again, the new additions are presented in italics.

**Perhaps Shakespeare highlights Macbeth's fear of Banquo** to teach audiences that even powerful men have weaknesses which threaten to destroy them, but this can have dangerous consequences and lead to further tyrannical behaviour. *When Macbeth says 'Our fears in Banquo stick deep', it implies he is finding it difficult to get rid of this weakness. 'Deep' shows he cannot remove his fear. However, it could also mean his fear will lead him to more violence. When Banquo is murdered, his wounds will 'stick deep', because of Macbeth's fear, which has driven the king to murder.*

This could be extended even further. Push your students to use their first analytical verb to lead them into a second, as so:

**Perhaps Shakespeare highlights Macbeth's fear of Banquo** to teach audiences that even powerful men have weaknesses which threaten to destroy them, but this can have dangerous consequences and lead to further tyrannical behaviour. When Macbeth says 'our fears in Banquo stick deep', it implies he is finding it difficult to get rid of this weakness. 'Deep' shows he cannot remove his fear. However, it could also mean his fear will lead him to more violence. When Banquo is murdered, his wounds will 'stick deep', because of Macbeth's fear which has driven the king to murder. *Through teaching us this, Shakespeare may also be criticising ambition, revealing how it can become a destructive obsession for some and so should be treated with great care.*

Once again, I must reiterate that the answers above are not perfect. Clarity is key, and students at first may struggle to express themselves coherently.

At this point, revisit the Big Question and ask students to consider the relationship between Macbeth and Banquo: how has it changed and why?

## PART TWO:

### Understanding rhetoric

Begin by reading Macbeth's conversation with the murderers up to the end of Act III, Scene i and ask students the following questions to ascertain their baseline understanding of the text:

1. Who, according to Macbeth, has prevented the murderers from reaching their rightful place in life?
2. What species of animal does Macbeth compare men to?
3. Why does Macbeth compare men to these animals?
4. Who, according to Macbeth, is the real enemy here?
5. What exactly does Macbeth instruct the murderers to do?

From this first read, students should pick up that Macbeth is trying to persuade the murderers to kill Banquo and that Banquo 'deserves' it because he has allegedly kept the murderers from reaching their rightful place in life.

Discuss as a class to ascertain who has understood and who has not. For those students who have a solid understanding of what has happened, ask them to reread the scene and identify the arguments and rhetorical devices Macbeth uses to persuade the murderers to go through with his plan. Ask them to collect quotations and explain what Macbeth is saying in each. For those who require more scaffolding, a low preparation, high impact 'find it activity' may help. This is where students are provided with a list of prompts which they have to look for in the text. It may look something like Resource 11.4:[28]

---

28. Icon by Adrien Coquet from the Noun Project.

## RESOURCE 11.4

**Find a line and label where:**

Macbeth reveals he has a common enemy with the murderers.

Macbeth accuses Banquo of forcing the murderers to live a life of poverty.

Macbeth suggests he has met with the murderers before.

Macbeth finds it unbelievable the murderers would pray for a man like Banquo.

Macbeth says men have different qualities that make some useful and some useless, just like different breeds of dog.

The murderers reveal the harsh conditions of their lives.

By this point, all students will have established the arguments Macbeth is using and found quotations for them. Now they should delve in further and consider why he is using these arguments: what makes them effective forms of persuasion? Remind students again of the three components of the Aristotelian Triad: ethos, logos and pathos. If you are following each lesson in this book, then students will already have come across this in Chapter 6, where they considered Lady Macbeth's use of rhetoric when persuading Macbeth to kill Duncan. If, however, you are dipping in and out of the lesson plan, some teaching as to what these components mean may be required. Drawing student attention back to Lady Macbeth's earlier use of rhetoric will be beneficial in allowing them to make connections between the two characters. They will be able to see how Macbeth is adopting his wife's earlier practices, learning and using her conniving ways to get what he wants.

### The magnifying glass

Students could review the scene independently, picking out examples of pathos, logos and ethos, or the activity could be a little more structured. An easy and effective way to do this is through the 'Magnifying Glass' method, originally shared by Jennifer Webb in her book, *How To Teach English Literature*.[29] Webb uses this method to gradually expose students to a challenging text. Here it is used a little differently. The class will already have seen the text, but this allows them to consider important quotations in isolation before rereading them in their context. Choose quotations that demonstrate pathos, logos and ethos like the example in Resource 11.5. Students can review each other's work before sharing as a class. Once students have completed this activity, reread the section in which the quotations appear, in order to develop understanding further.

---

29.  Jennifer Webb, *How to Teach English Literature: Overcoming Cultural Poverty*, (Woodbridge: John Catt Educational Ltd., 2019), p. 70.

## RESOURCE 11.5

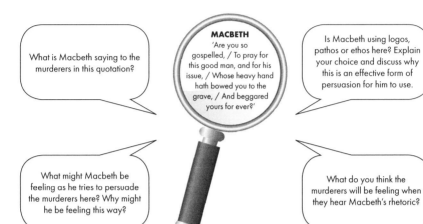

### The final couplet

The end of the scene is the perfect place to explore the parallels Shakespeare weaves into the play. Whilst there is no harm in exploring these similarities in both scenes as a whole, as described in the 'What?' section of this chapter, it is certainly worth looking at the final two couplets of Act II, Scene i and Act III, Scene i if nothing else.

Provide students with the following couplets and ask them to identify any similarities they can in terms of language and structure:

> 'Hear it [the bell] not Duncan; for it is a knell
> That summons thee to heaven, or to hell.'

> 'It is concluded: Banquo, thy soul's flight,
> If it find heaven, must find it out tonight.'

There are obvious connections between these two couplets which most students should be able to pick up on. Macbeth's repetition of the word 'heaven', for example, will most likely generate the beginning of your discussion. However, there are less transparent correlations that could be made. For example, the 'knell' in the first couplet is a bell rung at a death or funeral. Students could pick up on the idea of a funeral being an end, a finality, linking to the idea that matters are 'concluded' in the second couplet. They may also pick up on Macbeth's element of uncertainty as to where Duncan's and Banquo's souls would go. The 'knell... summons' Duncan 'to heaven, *or* to hell', and Macbeth's choice of phrase in '*if* it find heaven' suggests there is a chance Banquo's may not. If students are struggling to make these specific comparisons, put them on the board and circle the connections you would like them to make without telling them what those connections are, like so:

> '*Hear it [the bell] not Duncan; for it is a knell*
> *That summons thee to heaven, or to hell.*'

> '*It is concluded, Banquo, thy soul's flight,*
> *If it find heaven, must find it out tonight.*'

This way, students are prompted without being told the answers, and teachers do not feel as if they have to upgrade an answer themselves. Link the final couplet of Act III, Scene i, back to the Big Question.

## PART THREE:

### The relationship between Macbeth and Lady Macbeth

The third part of this series of lessons introduces a second Big Question: *How has Macbeth and Lady Macbeth's relationship changed?* Before reading the scene as a class, employ the same strategies used to predict what the relationship was like between Macbeth and Lady Macbeth in Act II, Scene ii. Just as the scene contains parallels, so does the lesson! Give students a redacted copy of Act II, Scene ii, side by side with a redacted copy of Act III, Scene ii.

## RESOURCE 11.6

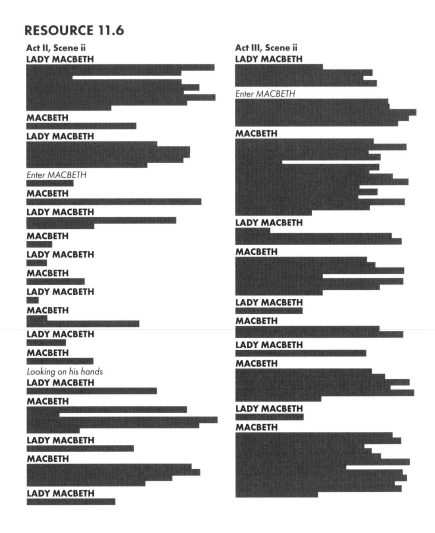

Like before, this activity gets students to look at the situation as it stands in the play through what is not said rather than what is. Ask students the following questions:

1. What are the differences between the two scenes?
2. What do these differences suggest about what has happened to Macbeth and Lady Macbeth?
3. Why do you think these things have happened?

As a pre-reading strategy, redacted lines are extremely useful. Students should, before reading the scene, be able to ascertain exactly what Macbeth is like if they recall their knowledge of how Lady Macbeth acted earlier. Take feedback and explore the ideas students come up with by using answers offered as stimulus for a debate. I quite often follow up responses volunteered with other questions such as 'Who agrees?' or 'Who disagrees?' or even 'How sure are you about that?' Small strategies like this challenge student perception that their first answer is the best one they could possibly come up with.

### Reading the scene
Read the scene, asking clarifying questions to ensure no one is left behind:

1. Why does Lady Macbeth now have to reach out to her husband through a servant?
2. Has getting what they wanted made the Macbeths happy?
3. What does Macbeth mean when he says 'We have scorched the snake, not killed it'?
4. What is the significance of the recurring imagery of a snake?
5. What is Macbeth saying about Duncan?
6. What does Lady Macbeth keep trying to do throughout this scene?
7. How does Macbeth instruct Lady Macbeth to act around Banquo and why is this significant?
8. What is Macbeth's mind like?
9. Why do you think Macbeth refuses to tell Lady Macbeth what his plans are?
10. How does Macbeth refer to Lady Macbeth throughout this scene and why do you think this is?

Now students should consider the changes in Macbeth, Lady Macbeth and their relationship in more detail, picking up on what the characters are saying and doing in order to bring about their transformation. To do this in detail, a reread of both Act II, Scene ii and Act III, Scene ii may be in order. Ask students to check over the inferences they made on the redacted resource once you have looked back over both scenes, ticking the ones that are correct and deleting the ones that are not.

### Quotation explosion
Having considered how the relationship between the Macbeths has changed, ask students to consider one of Macbeth's most famous lines in this scene: 'O, full of scorpions is my mind, dear wife'.

✎ ....................................................................

'O, full of scorpions is my mind, dear wife'

*Who says the line/whom or what is it about?*
*Explain what the line means*
*Explain what the line suggests*

....................................................................

## Connotation circles

Another way of exploring language in detail is through the use of 'connotation circles'. There are lots of variations of this resource. It has also been referred to as 'rainbow word analysis' and is a technique introduced to me by Caroline Spalding (@MrsSpalding on Twitter). This is where students take one word from a quotation and explore its connotations in detail to help extend their thinking. For example, one may take the word 'scorpions' from the quotation and place it in the first circle. They would then consider a connotation of the word 'scorpions' and place it in the second circle. Let us imagine a student says 'poison' for that first connotation. For the third circle, they would find connotations of 'poison' and so on and so forth. In practice, this might look something like Resource 11.7.

## RESOURCE 11.7

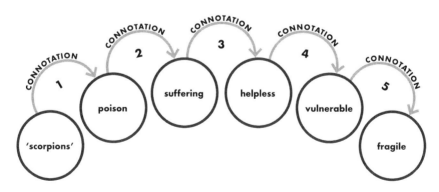

↑ PLACE QUOTATION HERE!

After completing this activity, I then give my students a general question to help them 'join up' their ideas. For example, once students have filled in the connotation circles above, I may set them the question: 'What is Macbeth's state of mind in this scene?' It is a question specifically designed for students to use the quotation we have been discussing. This method will need explicit modelling. Ideas could be joined up like this:

> *Macbeth is a tortured man in this scene and cannot stop thinking dark thoughts. He exclaims 'O, full of scorpions is my mind, dear wife'. The image of scorpions implies Macbeth believes his mind to have been **poisoned**, perhaps because of the constant violence he is committing. He cannot put an end to his mental **suffering** which leaves him **helpless** and **vulnerable**, even though he feels he should be strong and powerful in his position as king. Perhaps Shakespeare makes Macbeth so **fragile** at this point to warn his audience about the damage ambition can cause because he sees it as a negative trait in people.*

Notice how the ideas above have also brought in elements of the authorial intent work explored earlier. Once students have progressed through the text a certain amount, exploration of authorial intent should definitely be encouraged whenever the opportunity arises.

Finish by drawing students' attention back to the Big Question to discuss before progressing on to Act III, Scene iii.

## Banquo's murder

Act III, Scene iii is short and can be read very quickly. There are some important elements, however, that you may want to pose to students as questions to think about:

1. Why does Macbeth send a third murderer to accompany the other two?
2. Fleance carries a torch when he enters. Why is this symbolic?
3. Why is it important that Fleance escapes?
4. How has Macbeth, by sending a third murderer, caused the plan to fail?
5. Why do you think Shakespeare includes the murder scene instead of having it take place offstage like Duncan's?
6. What will be the repercussions of this event moving forward?

Once students have finished reading the scene, they should update their light and dark trackers, considering where light and dark have been mentioned across what they have read of Act III so far. They may include examples such as Macbeth's 'Come, seeling night' command and Fleance's torch going out once Banquo is killed.

## Suggested 'Extra Challenge' activities

- Discuss the estrangement of Macbeth and Lady Macbeth in the beginning of Act III.
- 'In a society in which fatherhood formed a vital cornerstone of male identity and was the bedrock of male power, Macbeth's sterility, his inability to produce a son and heir, fundamentally undermines his authority and emasculates him.'[30] To what extent is this sense of emasculation the driving force behind Macbeth's plans?
- Using the evidence presented in the play, who, in your opinion, is the third murderer?

## Key vocabulary:

Malice, emasculation

---

30. Neil Bowen et al., *The Art of Drama Volume 2: Macbeth GCSE & Beyond*, (Peripeteia Press, 2019), p. 122.

# CHAPTER 12
## Act III, Scene iv

*Why does Banquo's ghost appear to Macbeth?*

## What?

### Scene analysis: Act III, Scene iv

The banquet scene truly is a turning point for Macbeth as he realises that he is no longer able to control the world in the way he thought he could. In asking for Banquo and Fleance to be murdered, and failing in this with only Banquo 'safe in a ditch', Macbeth's grip on his kingdom is weakened. Fleance has escaped and therefore a perceived threat will now hang over Macbeth, who is fearful of retribution, and thus Banquo's final prophecy coming true. Macbeth's knowledge of this, however, is still to come.

#### 'YOU KNOW YOUR OWN DEGREES, SIT DOWN'

The banquet itself is something of a power play by Macbeth. He wishes to secure and reaffirm his role as monarch by holding a formal banquet, likely in celebration of his coronation. There is order in a banquet such as this with regard to etiquette, so arguably Macbeth also uses this occasion to try to restore order and sense to a reign which is already at risk of careening wildly out of control. There is a distinct irony in Macbeth holding an event representing harmony and friendship, but it is clear he is putting on a performance, a 'player' playing a role (as he realises later in Act V, Scene v), in order to assuage his own concerns about his rule.[1]

A strong hierarchy would have been present at banquets such as this, and Shakespeare alludes to this in Macbeth's opening words: 'You know your own

---

1.  Ed. Sandra Clark and Pamela Mason, *The Arden Shakespeare: Macbeth*, (London: Bloomsbury, 2015), p. 217.

degrees, sit down.'[2] He expects those in attendance to sit in their proper place according to their importance and rank. As we know, this obsession with hierarchy is a contributing factor to Macbeth's downfall, and Shakespeare's emphasis on it here reminds the audience of the fact that his rule as king, even as it begins, is precarious. Macbeth's obsession with people knowing, and conforming to, their place in society is, again, ironic, given that Shakespeare has consistently explored, throughout the play, the fact that Macbeth has acted out of his place in the Great Chain of Being in order to subvert nature and take the crown for himself.

Macbeth's preoccupation with his 'performance' continues as he reminds the assembled lords of the roles he and his wife will play. Macbeth will 'play the humble host', and he explains that for the time being his wife will 'keep her state.' It is important to note Shakespeare's use of the word 'play'. Perhaps he is hinting at the fact that Macbeth knows, at heart, that he is assuming a role beyond his natural place and order. It also suggests that Macbeth's grasp on his position is precarious: he does not truly feel like the King, and is instead playing a part. Macbeth's mingling, too ('Ourself will mingle with society') is perhaps indicative of the fact that Macbeth is new to this role and could be uncertain of his true purpose at the banquet – rather than taking his seat, he is instead set to 'mingle' with men who may not be of appropriate ranking. However, this could also suggest that Macbeth is attempting to win over as many of the assembled lords as he possibly can in order to reaffirm his position and, in his mind perhaps, reduce the chance of his losing the crown through an uprising.

Macbeth's suggestion that Lady Macbeth will remain seated until he 'require[s] her welcome' indicates the fact that he has truly taken charge in the relationship now. Of course, he has acted out on his own several times in recent scenes, most notably to call for the murder of Banquo and Fleance, but here he is taking a very public stance of dominance. Shakespeare emphasises this when Lady Macbeth requests that he 'pronounce it for me, sir' to tell the lords that she welcomes them to the banquet. She is assuming such a submissive role at this point in the scene that she is even unable to welcome them herself, despite her very public greeting of King Duncan, his sons and court in Act I, Scene vi. This is possibly because she believes that, in assuming her prescribed gender role and allowing Macbeth to take the lead, the assembled lords will be more likely to accept their authenticity as king and queen and realise Macbeth is a valid ruler.

---

2.    Enyclopedia.com, ' Medieval banquets', https://www.encyclopedia.com/food/encyclopedias-almanacs-transcripts-and-maps/medieval-banquets.

**'IS HE DISPATCHED?'**

Directly after Lady Macbeth explains how welcome everyone is ('For my heart speaks, they are welcome'), the murderer appears. This is a direct juxtaposition: Lady Macbeth declares that everyone is welcome, precisely at the moment that the person Macbeth undoubtedly does not wish to see at the banquet makes an appearance.

Contemporary societal expectations would place a guest of honour – in this case the King – at either the head of the table or halfway down one side.[3] However, at this banquet 'both sides are even', and Macbeth chooses instead to sit 'i'th' midst'. Perhaps there is a deliberate choice on his part, here, not to sit in the place of honour in order to further ingratiate himself with his guests. However, it also suggests that Macbeth has no 'proper' place at this table, as he secured the crown through duplicitous means.

Having told the lords that they will be 'large in mirth', Macbeth notices the murderer, moves towards him and declares: 'There's blood upon thy face.' The tension of the scene truly begins to build: the appearance of the murderer is directly at odds with the atmosphere Macbeth is attempting to create at the banquet. Here, Shakespeare draws again upon the recurring motif of blood being associated with, and representative of, guilt. Whilst the blood is on the face of the murderer, it was under Macbeth's direct instruction that he acted to murder Banquo. If the guests see the blood, there would immediately be implications of Macbeth's dealings with this man and his own part in the crime that has been committed.

Unlike the aftermath of the murder of King Duncan, where Macbeth felt incredible levels of guilt at the sight of the blood, the suggestion here is that Macbeth remains largely unmoved by the sight. His immediate focus is less on the blood and significantly more on whether the murderer has achieved Macbeth's aim. In fact, he has grown so cold to the sight of blood that he comments the blood is better on the murderer's face than remaining in Banquo's body: a direct contrast to his reaction to seeing Duncan's blood.

Upon learning that his friend has been murdered, Macbeth declares the murderer 'the best o'th' cut-throats', Shakespeare again emphasising Macbeth's descent into an unfeeling, uncaring tyrant. His blood lust does not end with Banquo, of course, and upon learning that Banquo is dead Macbeth immediately asks after the fate of Fleance. Macbeth is adamant that if the murderer was able to kill both Banquo and his son, suggested as being a mere child, he would be unparalleled – 'nonpareil' – a clear indicator that Macbeth's brutality and ruthlessness have truly taken over.

3.    Danièle Cybulskie, 'Let's Eat! Banquets in the Middle Ages', *Medievalists.net*, https://www.medievalists.net/2014/05/lets-eat-banquets-middle-ages/.

### 'I AM CABINED, CRIBBED, CONFINED'

All has not gone to plan, though, as Macbeth is soon to learn. Despite the murderer's best efforts, he is forced to confess that 'Fleance is 'scaped', and it is at this point that Macbeth's demeanour shifts rapidly. Gone is his stability – 'Whole as the marble, founded as the rock'. Instead, his relief is immediately replaced with an intense feeling of claustrophobia: he is 'cabined, cribbed, confined'. This hard, guttural, plosive alliteration emphasises the overwhelming, harsh emotions Macbeth feels in this moment. The repetitive and restrictive sounds also add to the sense of claustrophobia Macbeth feels: his language is restricted, reflecting how he feels as his freedom to reign slips away from him. The plosives also imply a sense of aggression on Macbeth's part – an invocation of a 'fight or flight' response given the unexpected twist in the plan he had hoped would go so well. Whilst he had thought his kingship – and lineage – would be safe with the death of Banquo and Fleance, the survival of Fleance calls into question once more whether he has committed the ultimate crime of regicide for himself and his own children or whether he holds 'a barren sceptre in [his] gripe' on behalf of 'Banquo's issue'.

Despite the fact that 'Fleance is scaped', it is difficult not to notice the brutality with which Banquo's murder has been carried out. He has 'twenty trenched gashes on his head, / The least a death to nature.' Any of these deep wounds would have been enough to kill Banquo: the nature of the barbaric injuries inflicted upon him emphasise the cruelty of which Macbeth is capable. There is a level of uncontrolled, senseless savagery here that echoes many of Macbeth's actions elsewhere in the play.

### 'THERE THE GROWN SERPENT LIES'

Evoking the audience's understanding of the serpentine imagery used thus far, Macbeth becomes preoccupied with the fact that Fleance has escaped and survived and could cause a threat to the crown at any time: 'There the grown serpent lies; the worm that's fled / Hath nature that in time will venom breed'. Where before Macbeth was encouraged to act like a serpent by Lady Macbeth, with all the connotations of evil and duplicity, here he attributes the same characteristics to Banquo, who has, to all intents and purposes, been a good and noble character. This emphasises Macbeth's hypocrisy: his Machiavellian scheming has left him blind to the truth. Whilst he believes Banquo is the evil one who deserved to die – or whilst, perhaps, he is trying to convince himself of this fact – the audience is very aware that it is Macbeth himself who has acted in the most snake-like manner.

Banquo is the 'grown serpent', Fleance the 'worm'. Macbeth's fears are voiced here: he believes that Fleance has the potential to perhaps become king, or father kings as the witches told Banquo in his prophecies. Rather than describe the potential lineage in any other, moderate way, Macbeth chooses the word 'venom' to represent 'Banquo's issue'. This emphasises Macbeth's apparent feelings towards Banquo and his children: their existence is poisonous to his own reign.

Whilst Macbeth acknowledges that Fleance's claim to the throne is potentially distant, as he has 'no teeth for th' present',[4] it does not preclude Macbeth from being fearful of future repercussions. Not satisfied to have had Banquo murdered, therefore, Macbeth declares to the murderer that 'tomorrow / We'll hear ourselves again.' This is presumably so that Macbeth is able to plan a further attempt on Fleance's life.

### 'ENTER THE GHOST OF BANQUO'

There is some debate about the ghost of Banquo's entrances and exits in this scene. In different editions of the folio his entrance is often moved later in the scene to coincide with Macbeth invoking Banquo's spirit with the line 'were the graced person of our Banquo present'. Other editions place his entrance immediately following Lennox's invitation for Macbeth to 'sit'. The Arden Shakespeare places his entrance immediately preceding Macbeth's toast to the assembled lords. There is a delicious irony in this: as Macbeth welcomes the lords to the table, he is also welcoming the one key lord who is missing.[5]

There is also an argument for Banquo's ghost to make its first entrance before Macbeth's toast. Macbeth declares his wife 'sweet remembrancer' – in other words, he thanks her for reminding him of the societal requirements by which he must abide. However, 'remembrancer' can also refer to 'a royal official of the Exchequer tasked with recording and collecting debts due to the Crown; hence also, figuratively "Death".'[6] In this sense, there is an irony as Banquo's ghost appears, perhaps to recover the debt owed by Macbeth. Ultimately, as we know, Macbeth pays for his crimes of murder with his own life. The catalyst for the hastening of Macbeth's downfall certainly coincides with this scene, and in that sense Banquo's ghost is, in a way, the 'remembrancer'. Not only that, but if, figuratively, 'remembrancer' also meant 'death', there is an interesting duality. Banquo's ghost represents that of a dead man, but, by the same token, could also represent the idea that the ghost's appearance hastens Macbeth's downfall as his behaviour worries the collected lords.

4.  Miguel A. Bernard, 'The Five Tragedies in Macbeth', *Shakespeare Quarterly*, Vol. 13, No. 1 (Winter 1962), pp. 49–61, https://www.jstor.org/stable/2866894.

5.  Ed. Sandra Clark and Pamela Mason, *The Arden Shakespeare: Macbeth*, (London, Bloomsbury, 2015), p. 220.

6.  Etymonline.com, 'remembrancer', https://www.etymonline.com/search?q=remembrancer.

Macbeth's next line, in which he declares that he hopes Banquo's absence is rather because of 'unkindness / Than pity for mischance', seems to suggest that, despite Macbeth's fears for Fleance, he is still keen to keep up the appearance that he is innocent of all knowledge of Banquo's absence. Indeed, Shakespeare demonstrates how cold Macbeth has become in that he declares that he hopes Banquo is not there because he is rude rather than because anything bad has happened to him. Much like he persuaded the murderers that Banquo was at fault for their poor lives, so too he hopes to convince the lords that Banquo is not the man they remember.

This appears to work, for Ross declares that 'His absence, sir, / Lays blame upon his promise.' In other words, Ross believes that Banquo has broken his promise to attend the banquet and therefore Macbeth (and the others present) should no longer pay any attention to his absence. As Lennox has already done, Ross reaffirms the lords' desire for Macbeth to sit down. Whilst there is no concrete stage direction to indicate at what point Banquo's ghost takes its seat, it is clear that Macbeth is so preoccupied by his own thoughts of Fleance, or Banquo's ghost looks so solid to Macbeth, that he does not acknowledge the ghost's presence for several more lines.

## 'WHICH OF YOU HAVE DONE THIS?'

Once Macbeth does see Banquo's ghost, his first thought is to ask: 'Which of you have done this?' It could be perceived here that Macbeth is asking which of the collected men has played such a cruel, practical joke on him. However, his following line, 'Thou canst not say I did it: never shake / Thy gory locks at me', implies that he could be accusing one of the men of murdering Banquo. It is like a knee-jerk reaction: in assuming that everyone can see Banquo, bloodied and sitting in Macbeth's seat, Macbeth immediately begins to point fingers, just as he did following the murder of King Duncan.

Another interpretation of this line, and one often arrived at by students, is that Macbeth is reacting to Banquo's ghost shaking its head. This open denial is symptomatic of Macbeth's approach to guilt at this point in the play. He felt incredibly guilty for the murder of Duncan, believing that he would never be able to metaphorically wash his hands clean. However, by paying others to murder Banquo, Macbeth feels morally able to deny any responsibility for his death even though, in appearing to him as a ghost, Banquo is blaming Macbeth for his murder.

Banquo's ghost – regardless of whether or not a director chooses to physically embody it on stage – clearly shakes its head at Macbeth. This could be at the lies Macbeth has chosen to tell about Banquo, for the fact that he has claimed no responsibility for Banquo's untimely demise, or, indeed, that he has let others think ill of Banquo for his non-attendance at the banquet. It could be at the decision Macbeth made to have Banquo killed. Macbeth has betrayed Banquo and his trust for his own ill-gotten gains. It could also be, however, because Banquo is now in a position whereby he understands the lengths Macbeth has gone to: he now has confirmation of Macbeth's 'foul' role in the murder of Duncan and the guards and in Banquo's own murder.

### 'GENTLEMEN, RISE; HIS HIGHNESS IS NOT WELL'

Macbeth's response to seeing the ghost is clearly so troubling and visceral to the lords that Ross asks those assembled to rise from their seats in acknowledgement of the fact that Macbeth is 'unwell'. They can see and recognise his state of mind here. Then, Lady Macbeth steps to the fore once again to try to 'stage manage' the situation she is in and account for Macbeth's behaviour. In attempting to maintain a sense of normalcy and allow the banquet to continue, she downplays Macbeth's state of mind, declaring that he 'is often thus' and that these fits of madness have been a feature of his character since childhood. In doing so, she perhaps hopes to assuage the fears of the lords as to whether Macbeth is fit to rule. If he has always had similar experiences, it might not mean that he is unable to continue being king, which might not be the case were these behaviours a new occurrence.

Lady Macbeth's aside at the end of her short speech, however, indicates to the audience her true fears for her husband. She again calls into question his masculinity, asking of him 'Are you a man?' In doing so, she is suggesting that his emotional state and less logical approach to what he purportedly sees marks him out as less of a man. Her grasp on rational speech and thought, once more, in her mind at least, is attributable to her more masculine qualities. She again begins to dominate the scene here, as she has elsewhere, taking control of an otherwise quite uncontrolled situation.

Where Macbeth has responded before that he 'does all that may become a man', here his response is more strident and definite. Having looked at the ghost of Banquo, he is adamant that the thing that marks him out as a man is his ability to 'look on that / Which might appal the devil.' In this instance he has already *done* the thing that he believes makes him a man, and therefore this is a clear turning point in their relationship: in this argument, he is attempting to take back control, whereas before he allowed Lady Macbeth to dominate discussions. Whether inadvertently or not, Macbeth is also drawing comparisons between himself and the devil, something the audience is able to ratify with the long list of crimes he has committed. He is quite appalled by what he has seen, as the devil would be, too, as far as Macbeth is concerned.

## LADY MACBETH'S REACTION

Lady Macbeth's approach, next, is one which pours scorn on Macbeth's behaviour and is evocative of her treatment of her husband following the murder of Duncan, in which she chastised him for what she perceived to be unmasculine behaviour. She is overwhelmed with chagrin: his behaviour initially, though it frightens her later, is embarrassing her in front of the lords and threatens to reveal their crimes. Shakespeare even has Lady Macbeth compare Macbeth's fears now to the same fears he felt after killing the King: fears she felt were unfounded. In Act II, Scene ii, Lady Macbeth tells her husband that "'tis the eye of childhood / That fears a painted devil.' Here, she describes his behaviour as 'the very painting of [his] fear' – she believes that the appearance of Banquo's ghost is the same as the 'air-drawn dagger' which she also references. The visions he is having, she believes, are *because* he is scared and are not *causing* him to be scared. She does not believe either the ghost or the dagger are real.

Lady Macbeth continues to be very dismissive of Macbeth's feelings, a stark contrast with her own breakdown to come in Act V. She tells him that his behaviours now are 'imposters to true fear' – she believes him to be childish and overly sensitive. Not only this, but she again draws comparison between Macbeth's experience and the role of women as the weaker sex: she tells him that his stories of ghosts and floating daggers 'would well become / A woman's story at a winter's fire, / Authorised by her grandam.' She is suggesting that the experiences Macbeth is reporting would be better suited to a woman telling a spooky story she had been told by her grandmother. There is nothing to really fear. Alternatively, she could be suggesting that his experiences are more like a fairytale: interesting, engaging, possibly moralistic, but not true or real.

Macbeth's attention, though, is still held by the ghost, which Shakespeare has left on stage throughout Lady Macbeth's diatribe. Whilst the audience's attention may well have been on Lady Macbeth's attempt, albeit ferociously, to reason with and distract her husband, the audience has also watched on as Macbeth's attention has remained firmly focused on Banquo's ghost. This is representative of the widening gulf between Macbeth and his wife: where before he had listened to her, now she is unable to reach him.

## 'IF CHARNEL-HOUSES AND OUR GRAVES MUST SEND / THOSE WE BURY BACK, OUR MONUMENTS / SHALL BE THE MAWS OF KITES'

Shakespeare next explores Macbeth's disbelief and perhaps anger at the fact that, despite having Banquo murdered, the ghost will not leave Macbeth at peace to continue his reign. 'If charnel-houses and our graves must send / Those we bury back,' he says, 'our monuments / Shall be the maws of kites.' 'Charnel-houses' are vaults in which the bones of the dead are stored, and Macbeth is pouring scorn on the fact that these places – both charnel-houses and graves – are unable to hold on to the dead, instead sending them back, in this case to haunt Macbeth. His fear, therefore, is that if graves do not hold the dead, then the final resting place of the dead (and therefore the 'monuments' which celebrate them) will be the 'maws' – the eating apparatus of birds (mouth, gullet and stomach).[7] In other words, the bones will be picked clean by carrion birds such as kites. If the dead rise from their graves in such a way, Macbeth wonders what the point is in burying them at all.

Macbeth does not seem to be fully reflecting on the fate of Banquo, though. As we know already, Banquo has been denied a proper burial: his body lies in a 'ditch'. In all likelihood, it is a 'burial' in the maws of kites that will befall him. Could Macbeth, therefore, be reflecting on what he fears will happen to him? He already fears being denied passage to heaven – he has feared this from his first thoughts to murder the King. Could he now be concerned that he will be denied proper burial, his body left to be eaten by carrion birds? He knows his crimes will, most likely, not afford him the royal treatment of being interred at Colmekill, but he fears that his final resting place may be one more wild and savage. This is evocative, again, of the concept that 'Bloody instructions… being taught, return / To plague th'inventor.' He has left Banquo's body to nature, and the same will happen to him. Macbeth has subverted the natural order and, as a result, he will be destroyed by nature.

### 'QUITE UNMANNED IN FOLLY'

Whilst Macbeth has been predisposed in focusing on the ghost, Lady Macbeth's attack on his masculinity has continued unabated, describing him as 'Quite unmanned in folly.' In her eyes, his silly behaviour has rendered him weakened and timid: he has none of the manly courage that she expects him to have. Whilst Macbeth is adamant that he has seen the ghost of Banquo ('If I stand here, I saw him'), she is still disbelieving: 'Fie, for shame.' This, again, is an ironic response on her part, given that the next time the audience will see her, she will be sleepwalking and having visions of her own. This scene marks her last moments of fortitude before her inevitable breakdown.

Macbeth reflects on times gone by, in which bloodshed was more commonplace. The 'humane statute' – in other words, laws which were humane and compassionate – 'purged the gentle weal'. There is a deep-rooted irony, here. A 'gentle weal' is a civilised state, but Macbeth claims it has become so because of a purge. His belief is that, historically, it has been bloodshed that has led to harmony and peace. This

---

7.    Shakespeare Navigators, 'Birds', https://shakespeare-navigators.com/macbeth/Birds.html.

is not entirely inaccurate: across Europe, kings were murdered and replaced with relative frequency.[8] However, for each emerging ruler, the peace was an uneasy one and many were deposed themselves, their crowns seized by others. Indeed, in James I of England's own familial line, James I, II and III of Scotland were all murdered, either in battle or, in the case of James I of Scotland, in his bed by a group of conspirators. The peace Macbeth hopes to have conjured through his murderous rampage is at best uneasy, as the events of the play have shown.

### 'THE TIMES HAVE BEEN, THAT WHEN THE BRAINS WERE OUT THE MAN WOULD DIE, AND THERE AN END'

In a line sometimes now played for comedy in this moment of high tension verging on melodrama, Macbeth remains incredulous that the murder of Banquo has not resulted in him being entirely removed from Macbeth's life as he had planned. Macbeth believed 'The times have been, / That when the brains were out, the man would die, / And there an end.' However he is now faced with Banquo's ghost: 'But now they rise again / With twenty mortal murders on their crowns, / And push us from our stools.' Not only is the ghost sitting in Macbeth's own seat at the banquet, but Macbeth also voices his fears that, if Banquo's ghost is here (and especially because Fleance escaped his murder), he is still able to take over Macbeth's place and succession plan. His worst fear appears to have been validated.

Macbeth's incredulity and disbelief extends to the entire situation unfolding in front of him. Regardless of how huge the decision might have been to have Banquo murdered, the appearance of his ghost has left Macbeth feeling that 'This is more strange / Than such a murder is.'

Whilst Macbeth's focus has once again been on the ghost, he has been distracted from the banquet and from the assembled lords, even now the ghost has seemingly departed. Lady Macbeth's reference to her husband as her 'worthy Lord' is at odds with the way she has addressed him elsewhere in the scene: it is clear that this is a public statement aimed to draw Macbeth back to the banquet and remind the collected men that she still considers him 'worthy' to be king. Her focus is still entirely on their public presentation of themselves rather than truly on the experiences and health of her husband.

Her actions work though, albeit temporarily, and Macbeth is able to rejoin the banquet in his honour. He is able to call for a (large!) glass of wine, and begins to give a toast to the assembled party, including a mention of Banquo when he asks

---

8.  Manuel Eisner, 'KILLING KINGS: Patterns of Regicide in Europe, ad 600–1800', *The British Journal of Criminology*, Vol. 51, No. 3, Violence in Evolutionary and Historical Perspective (May 2011), pp. 556–577, https://www.jstor.org/stable/23640326.

the men to drink 'to our dear friend Banquo, whom we miss'. Macbeth describes that he 'thirsts' for Banquo – he longs that he was here, at least publicly. However, this could also be Shakespeare demonstrating Macbeth's hidden guilt and regret for calling for the murder of his best friend. As we know, whilst Macbeth hoped this would put an end to his fears for his crown, Fleance's escape and Banquo's ghost have entirely prevented this from happening. Now, he regrets his actions and wishes Banquo could genuinely join the party.

### 'THY BONES ARE MARROWLESS'

The ghost reappears. Shakespeare uses the phrases 'bones are marrowless' and 'blood is cold' to emphasise Macbeth's interpretation of the ghost and the fact he is coming to terms with the impact of his actions: his friend and confidant is dead.

Lady Macbeth's focus is once again on trying to normalise Macbeth's behaviour and assure the lords that he remains fit to be a king. She tells them that his behaviour is a 'thing of custom' – a regular behaviour of his that should be ignored, given that the worst impact of it is that 'it spoils the pleasure of the time.'

Meanwhile Macbeth's focus is now on proving himself and his masculinity to the ghost – whether or not it actually exists. 'What man dare, I dare' is reminiscent of his comment 'I dare do all that may become a man, / Who dares do more, is none' from Act I, Scene vii. It is clear that Lady Macbeth's comments on Macbeth's masculinity have affected him, even though he is not listening to her at this moment. Even when faced with the ghost, he feels the need to assert himself not just as a person but, specifically, as a man. It is almost as if everything he has done since his masculinity was first called into question has been an action to assert his dominance.

### 'THE RUGGED RUSSIAN BEAR, THE ARMED RHINOCEROS, OR THE HYRCAN TIGER'

His fighting stance is revisited here, and the audience is reminded of Macbeth's previous occupation as a fierce fighter and revered soldier. Macbeth would rather fight 'the rugged Russian bear, / The armed rhinoceros, or the Hyrcan tiger'. He would rather fight anything corporeal than be faced for a second with Banquo's ghost. He would even, he confirms, wish Banquo alive again, and allow Banquo to 'dare [him] to the desert with [his] sword.' In other words, he would allow Banquo to fight him, unimpeded. None of these things would scare Macbeth, he claims – but the thing that makes him 'tremble' is the ghost in front of him. Macbeth knows that he is still physically strong, but he is terrified now of anything he cannot face and fight directly, such as the ghost. The line where he states he would allow Banquo to 'dare [him] to the desert with [his] sword' is telling, and is possibly indicative of the fact that Macbeth regrets his actions.

The final tool in his arsenal is to command Banquo's ghost to leave: 'Hence, horrible shadow, / Unreal mockery, hence.' Despite trying to exert his masculinity, it is only once the ghost departs for the final time that Macbeth declares he is 'a man again.' In doing so, arguably Macbeth sees his fear as a feminine attribute and one not befitting a man. Perhaps he has internalised Lady Macbeth's – and society's – expectations on his gender.

Macbeth still wishes to proceed with the banquet, imploring the guests to 'sit still.' However, even Lady Macbeth's efforts have not been enough to persuade the lords that everything is fine with Macbeth. His 'admired disorder' has 'displaced the mirth', and Lady Macbeth realises she can no longer hide the truth. What she can do, however, is attempt to mitigate the impact of his behaviour, and his talking about having seen a ghost is not part of her plan.

### 'AT ONCE, GOODNIGHT'

When Macbeth declares to the assembly that he defies the men to 'keep the natural ruby of [their] cheeks / When [his] is blanched with fear', Ross begins to question what it is Macbeth claims to have seen. The lords are growing suspicious of Macbeth and concerned about him, neither of which Lady Macbeth has any interest in promoting. She instead implores them to leave: 'At once, goodnight.' Where at the start of the scene Macbeth had invited the men to sit because they 'know their order', Lady Macbeth has dispensed with formalities in order to be rid of the guests all the faster, asking them to 'Stand not upon the order of your going' – to leave in their order of importance and place in the hierarchy – 'But go at once.' Much to her relief, the lords do leave, but it is clear that they are deeply concerned about the King. Lennox hopes for 'better health' for Macbeth, though this could be read as either genuine concern and wishes for the King to recover or, alternatively, more arch, ironic and sneering, perhaps sharing others' viewpoint that Macbeth should no longer be king.

### 'IT WILL HAVE BLOOD THEY SAY: BLOOD WILL HAVE BLOOD'

Macbeth's fear of 'bloody instructions' in Act I, Scene vii appears to have rapidly moved towards fruition, and this is exemplified through his famous next line: 'It will have blood they say: blood will have blood'. Now that he has been seen to behave so erratically in front of others, and now that his murderous plan has not gone right, he finally recognises that he will never get away with his sins. There is a biblical allusion here, with Shakespeare referencing Genesis 9:6: 'Whoso sheddeth man's blood, by man shall his blood be shed.'[9] He has

---

9. Shakespeare Online, 'Biblical Imagery in Macbeth', http://www.shakespeare-online. com/plays/macbeth/bibimagery.html.

shed blood – soldiers' blood, the blood of the King, the blood of the King's men, Banquo's blood… and this can now only be punished in one way: the shedding of his own blood at the hand of others.

### 'MAGGOT-PIE AND CHOUGHS AND ROOKS BROUGHT FORTH / THE SECRET'ST MAN OF BLOOD'

Shakespeare then returns to imagery around birds, in this instance 'maggot-pies' (magpies) and choughs (members of the crow family). Both these birds are steeped in superstition, with belief about them being focused on their role in making predictions. Both birds were also believed to bring bad omens.[10]

Both can be taught to speak a few words, and Macbeth reflects on the fact that murderers ('secret'st man of blood') will always be found out – sometimes in strange ways – for example, from being exposed by birds. Macbeth knows he cannot control these birds, just as he realises he cannot control nature, despite his efforts throughout the play. In referring to these birds, Macbeth acknowledges that it is now an inevitability that his crimes will be discovered. His next set of actions can only delay what he knows is coming for him.

Macbeth's question 'What is the night?' and his wife's reply that it is 'Almost at odds with morning' implies the coming dawn. Just as the Macbeths had spent the earlier parts of the play calling for darkness to hide their acts, they are representative of darkness and evil itself. Shakespeare has used light throughout the play to symbolise good and just characters. Now, however, the night is 'Almost at odds with morning'. The coming of the morning implies that the two opposing forces of good and evil will soon come into direct conflict, foreshadowing the events of the following Acts.

Macbeth's murderous rampage, however, is not yet over. He questions his wife as to why she thinks Macduff did not attend the banquet. In an act of paranoia (though, as the audience will soon discover, not unfounded, as Macduff travels to England to raise an army), Macbeth tells his wife that he has spies in the castles of all his lords, including Macduff's. The implication here is that he will be able to discover any motives behind Macduff's non-appearance – though, as the audience has known for some time, Macduff is already deeply suspicious of Macbeth's role in the murder of King Duncan. As the audience will discover in Act III, Scene vi, Macduff's absence was also, in part, from fear: his 'broad words' suggest that whilst Macduff has been outspoken in his criticism of Macbeth, he does not wish to come face to face with his foe, knowing how dangerous he truly can be.

---

10.   Mike Jeffries, 'In defence of magpies: the bird world's bad boy is simply misunderstood', Northumbria University, https://www.northumbria.ac.uk/about-us/news-events/news/2015/09/in-defence-of-magpies-the-bird-worlds-bad-boy-is-simply-misunderstood-1/.

## 'I AM BENT TO KNOW BY THE WORST MEANS, THE WORST'

In a further change of subject, as Macbeth frantically flits from thought to thought, he declares that he will visit, for a second time, the 'weïrd sisters'. He wants answers – is 'bent to know' – though very aware that the news they have for him is likely to not be positive. He wishes to 'know, / By the worst means, the worst; for [his] own good'. It is possible Macbeth is referencing two proverbial expressions here.[11] The first, 'to know the worst is good', suggests that Macbeth will feel more settled and satisfied if he knows what fate will befall him. The second, 'it is good to fear the worst', suggests that he almost wishes for a reverse *Schadenfreude*: he wants to feel something: in this case, terror about what might be coming for him. Regardless of which proverb Shakespeare is alluding to, he is clear that Macbeth desires to know the truth by 'the worst means'. Macbeth seems to recognise and understand, for the first, true time, the implications of visiting the witches: he now knows that no good can come from them, and seems to acknowledge the hugely negative impact they have had on his life.

## 'I AM IN BLOOD / STEPPED IN SO FAR'

Macbeth returns, again, to the imagery of blood, declaring that at this point: 'I am in blood / Stepped in so far, that should I wade no more, / Returning were as tedious as go o'er.' Macbeth appears to acknowledge here the level of his brutality and the sheer volume of blood spilled as a result. He sees no reason to stop now – he has killed so many people that there is no turning back: he could forge ahead, shedding more blood, and be no worse off. What difference would it make, ultimately, to his fate? This seems to be reaffirmed in Macbeth's next comment: 'Strange things I have in my head, that will to hand'. He still has murderous intent that he wishes to act on. He clearly feels no remorse at this point, but instead is resigned to his plans to continue to murder. In this image of Macbeth having 'stepped' in blood there is perhaps also a reference to Seneca's *Agamemnon*, in which we find the line 'per scelera semper sceleribus tutum est iter': 'the safe way through crime, is by further crimes.'[12]

Lady Macbeth has no real recourse to respond to this, but Shakespeare does allow us a hint that Macbeth's earlier fears have come to pass. When Macbeth declared that he would 'sleep no more' following the murder of King Duncan, Lady Macbeth told him not to 'think / So brainsickly of things.'

11. Ed. Sandra Clark and Pamela Mason, *The Arden Shakespeare: Macbeth*, (London, Bloomsbury, 2015), p. 227.

12. Seneca, 'Four Tragedies and Octavia translated with an introduction by E.F. Watling' (London: Penguin, 1966).

However, it is clear now that Macbeth has struggled to sleep since the start of his murderous rampage, and Lady Macbeth tells him: 'You lack the season of all natures, sleep.'

## Ghosts

Ghosts are prevalent in many of Shakespeare's plays. From Old Hamlet in *Hamlet*, the King's victims in *Richard III*, the spectre of the eponymous hero in *Julius Caesar* and Banquo's ghost in *Macbeth*, they hold important and telling roles in the various plots in which they appear (and disappear).

The presentation of ghosts in theatre can be traced back to Ancient Greece, and to Senecan traditions. The plays of Seneca had a strong influence on lots of Elizabethan dramas (and, in particular, revenge tragedies), with playwrights attracted by the melodrama and strong, moral impetus of his work.[13] In Senecan tragedy, ghosts were often used to threaten, in some way, the safety of the living: often Senecan ghosts are used as an inciting force in a play, drawing characters on to commit dangerous acts. The ghost of Old Hamlet in *Hamlet* is probably the most Senecan of Shakespeare's ghosts, comparable as he is to the ghost of Thyestes in *Agamemnon*, who rises at the play's opening in order to incite his son, Aegisthus, to enact revenge against his brother, Atreus, who has wronged him.[14]

The ghost of Banquo also draws on Senecan tradition: whilst it does not actively threaten the safety of the living directly, Macbeth's reaction to it means that he puts himself in a precarious position. The gathered lords see his terrified reaction, which arouses suspicion. It is the appearance of the ghost that spurs Macbeth on to revisit the witches and hear his final set of prophecies, in turn causing the death of Macduff's family, Macduff's revenge and ultimately Macbeth's own murder. The ghost is, absolutely, an inciting force in the Senecan sense, driving the plot on.

Shakespeare's ghosts have a huge impact on the characters with whom they interact and, especially in the case of *Macbeth*, the ghost drives on the plot and speeds Macbeth's mental descent and ultimate downfall. This active role for ghosts in Shakespeare's plays is what sets him apart from his peers. This can be largely attributed to contemporary understanding of, and belief in, ghosts. Elizabethan tragedy drew heavily on the work of Seneca, yet Shakespeare's ghosts often break from Senecan convention. Banquo's ghost is a good example

13. E.M. Spearing, *The Elizabethan Translations of Seneca's Tragedies*, (Cambridge: W. Hefper & Sons, 1912), Shakespeare Online, 2 Aug. 2011, http://www.shakespeare-online.com/plays/hamlet/senecadrama.html.

14. Ibid.

of this in that, whilst it is clearly influenced by Senecan tradition, it is also rooted in Elizabethan understanding and belief.

There were arguably some 'religious uncertainties'[15] with regard to the existence of ghosts in Elizabethan England. Following years of the country formally switching from Catholicism to Protestantism, and back, and back *again*, Shakespeare's England was a Protestant one. However, there were many families with more complex relationships to religion than this. It is in this context that we must frame our understanding of Shakespeare's ghosts.

In Catholicism, thinking around the fate of souls after the death of the body centres around the ideas of heaven, hell and Purgatory. The teaching is that '[t]hose who die in God's grace and friendship and are perfectly purified live for ever with Christ'.[16] This state is called heaven, and 'is the ultimate end and fulfilment of the deepest human longings, the state of supreme, definitive happiness.'[17] At the other extreme is hell, the 'state of definitive self-exclusion from communion with God and the blessed'[18] which results from dying in mortal sin 'without repenting and accepting God's merciful love [and] remaining separated from [God] for ever by [one's] own free choice.'[19] 'Purgatory' is the name given to the 'final purification'[20] of those 'who die in God's grace and friendship, but still imperfectly purified... so [they may] achieve the holiness necessary to enter the joy of heaven.'[21] Given that in the past many would have understood ghosts as the souls of those still in the state of Purgatory, there is perhaps some explanation here for the appearance of Banquo's ghost: untold sins on Earth may have resulted in his reappearance as his soul fought for a place in heaven.

Protestantism, on the other hand, is generally clear in its belief that Purgatory does not exist and, following the Reformation, there was a move away from belief in ghosts as souls awaiting a place in heaven, which may have arisen from the idea of Purgatory. In a Jacobean, Protestant England, the belief was that ghosts were apparitions, sent from hell, to seduce people into committing crimes. Indeed, in *Daemonologie* James I suggests that ghosts were not 'the

15. John Mullan, 'Ghosts in Shakespeare', British Library, (2016), https://www.bl.uk/shakespeare/articles/ghosts-in-shakespeare.

16. *Cathechism of the Catholic Church*, (London: Catholic Truth Society, 2016), 1023.

17. Ibid., 1024.

18. Ibid., 1033.

19. Ibid.

20. Ibid., 1031.

21. Ibid., 1030.

spirits of dead men, but manifestations of the devil.'[22] This reading of ghosts could seem compelling when examined through the lens of Shakespeare's desire to ingratiate himself with the King. It would have appealed to James I's religious beliefs and thereby positioned Shakespeare as a Protestant, shaking off the associations his family had with Catholicism as explored in Chapter 4.[23]

However, in *Macbeth* our titular character needs no persuading to commit terrible crimes. By now he has, in a few short days, committed regicide, killed the King's guards and now ordered the murder of Banquo (ostensibly his best friend). This understanding of ghosts does not seem applicable to Banquo's appearance in Act III, Scene iv.

However, a third interpretation of the belief in ghosts in Elizabethan and Jacobean society does provide a compelling explanation for Shakespeare's inclusion of Banquo's ghost, and for the purpose of the apparition. Ghosts were, in essence, believed to be unthreatening – a sidestep from the threat perceived in Catholic and Protestant discourse. Many believed that the purpose of the appearance of ghosts was to haunt sinners, pushing them towards repentance for their crimes.[24] It is here, then, that we see the most likely reason for Shakespeare to have used the ghost of Banquo: his appearance is intended to encourage Macbeth to atone for his sins. However, the ghost's appearance means that Macbeth is driven further from rational behaviour, believing that he has been found out.

Whilst Banquo does not himself enact divine justice on Macbeth, it is his appearance that, almost more than anything else, drives forward and accelerates Macbeth's downfall. In the ghost's appearance, Macbeth sees two things: 'The Shakespearean ghost is at once the embodiment of remorseful presentiment and the instrument of divine justice.'[25] He sees his future: a bloody death at the hands of others, and punishment by God.

---

22. F.W. Moorman, 'Shakespeare's Ghosts', *The Modern Language Review*, Vol. 1, No. 3 (April 1906), pp. 192–201, https://www.jstor.org/stable/3713608.

23. In discussing topics such as ghosts, Purgatory, heaven and hell, it is worth acknowledging that there can be a difference between the official teaching/doctrine/ statements of belief of religious denominations and how those teachings/doctrines/ statements of belief were/are commonly interpreted and manifested in everyday culture at a particular time. These paragraphs therefore present some interpretations that may have emerged from religious beliefs of the time, and are not intended as definitive accounts of Catholic or Protestant theology.

24. Hamlet Dramaturgy, 'Did Elizabethans believe in ghosts?', https://delshakeshamlet. weebly.com/ghosts-in-elizabethan-england.html.

25. F.W. Moorman, 'Shakespeare's Ghosts', *The Modern Language Review*, Vol. 1, No. 3 (April 1906), pp. 192–201, https://www.jstor.org/stable/3713608.

## Act III, Scene iv at a glance

## RESOURCE 12.1

This is the first time Macbeth's guilt has been demonstrated in public. It is a departure from his previous behaviour, and an indicator that his guilt is, by now, entirely overwhelming.

The vision of Banquo, covered in blood, is vivid, magnifying for the audience Macbeth's inner torment and guilt at his actions.

His emotional state and less logical approach to what he purportedly sees marks him out as less of a man.

He is quite appalled by what he has seen as the devil would be, too, as far as Macbeth is concerned.

Vaults in which the bones of the dead are stored.

The bones will be picked clean by carrion birds such as kites. If the dead rise from their graves in such a way, Macbeth wonders what the point is in burying them at all.

---

**MACBETH**
Thou canst not say I did it: never shake
Thy gory locks at me.

**ROSS**
Gentlemen, rise; his highness is not well.

**LADY MACBETH**
Sit, worthy friends; my lord is often thus,
And hath been from his youth. Pray you, keep seat,
The fit is momentary; upon a thought
He will again be well. If much you note him
You shall offend him, and extend his passion.
Feed, and regard him not. [to Macbeth] Are you
a man?

**MACBETH**
Ay, and a bold one, that dare look on that
Which might appal the devil.

**LADY MACBETH**
O, proper stuff.
This is the very painting of your fear:
This is the air-drawn dagger which you said
Led you to Duncan. O, these flaws and starts,
Impostors to true fear, would well become
A woman's story at a winter's fire,
Authorized by her grandam. Shame itself.
Why do you make such faces? When all's done
You look but on a stool.

**MACBETH**
Prithee, see there. Behold, look, lo,
how say you?
[to Ghost] Why, what care I? If thou canst nod,
speak too.
If charnel-houses and our graves must send
Those that we bury back, our monuments
Shall be the maws of kites.

---

Vivid. Magnifies for the audience Macbeth's inner torment and guilt at his actions.

She perhaps hopes to assuage the fears of the lords as to whether Macbeth is fit to rule. If he has always had similar experiences, it might not mean that he is unable to continue being king, unlike if these behaviours were a new occurrence.

She believes that the appearance of Banquo's ghost is the same as the 'air-drawn dagger' which she also references. The visions he is having, she believes, are because he is scared and are not causing him to be scared. She does not believe either the ghost or the dagger are real.

The experiences Macbeth is reporting would be better suited to a woman telling a spooky story she had been told by her grandmother. There is nothing to really fear.

## How?

## Retrieval

This retrieval activity links prior knowledge to this lesson's Big Question, and allows students not only to consider what they know but also to consider their own views of the importance of different pieces of information. Resource 12.2 focuses on key quotations that demonstrate something about the nature of the relationship between Macbeth and Banquo. Students should first rank order the quotations: which quotation tells them the most about the relationship between the two? Which quotation tells them the least? Students should also consider *what* each quotation shows them about their friendship, and *why* they have ranked it where they have. By foregrounding knowledge about Macbeth and Banquo here, students have been reminded of their broader understanding in advance of answering the Big Questions later on.

## RESOURCE 12.2

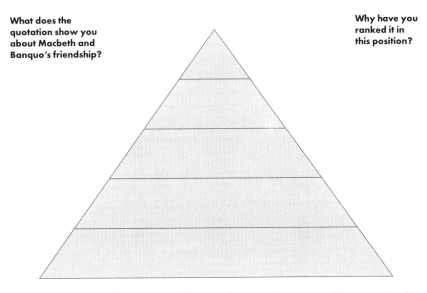

**What does the quotation show you about Macbeth and Banquo's friendship?**

**Why have you ranked it in this position?**

'So they doubly redoubled strokes upon the foe.'    'Your children shall be kings.' 'You shall be King.'    'Noble Banquo, that hast no less deserved, nor must be known / No less to have done so.'    'I have observed / The air is delicate.'    'I dreamt last night of the three weïrd sisters...' 'I think not of them'.

### Pre-reading activity

Once students have revisited their knowledge, encourage students to make a prediction: given their relationship, will Macbeth be able to accept what he has done and move on from this once he knows that Banquo has been murdered? This could be a powerful, discussion-based activity, and the predictions students make will stand them in good stead as they approach the scene itself.

### Reading the scene

Breaking with the tradition of this book, for this lesson I recommend holding off on sharing the Big Question ('Why does Banquo's ghost appear to Macbeth?') until the students have had the opportunity to see this happen for themselves.

It is one of those beautiful, tense moments in the play and so much of the joy of it is in discovering what happens, together.

Because of the sheer magnitude of events in this scene, and the fact that the important twists and turns link specifically to certain lines and moments, the questions you might like to ask are here presented in a table so that you can really help students understand these pertinent moments:

| Line/moment | What do students need to know? |
|---|---|
| 19: 'Then comes my fit again: I had else been perfect'. | What is Macbeth's reaction to the news that Banquo is dead and Fleance has escaped? |
| 28: 'There the grown serpent lies; the worm that's fled / Hath nature that in time will venom breed'. | Who is Macbeth referring to? What does this show us about how Macbeth is feeling? |
| 30: 'My royal lord, / You do not give the cheer'. | Why does Lady Macbeth refer to him as 'my royal lord'? What does she mean by 'the cheer'? Why is this an important part of proceedings? Macbeth is distracted. What perilous position might this put him in? |
| 38: 'Were the graced person of our Banquo present, / Who may I rather challenge for unkindness / Than pity for mischance.' | What is Macbeth doing here? Why? What does it show us about how callous Macbeth really is at this point? |
| 47: '[N]ever shake / Thy gory locks at me.' | What does this suggest about the appearance of the ghost of Banquo? |
| 50: '[M]y lord is often thus, / And hath been from his youth.' | What is Lady Macbeth doing here? Why? Is she telling the truth? Why not? |
| 98: 'Approach thou like the rugged Russian bear... Hence, horrible shadow, / Unreal mockery, hence.' | What is Macbeth saying he would rather face than Banquo's ghost? What does this suggest about the level of fear he feels? |
| 120: 'It will have blood they say: blood will have blood'. | What does this mean? What else does it remind us of? ('Bloody instructions which, being taught...') |
| 130: 'I will tomorrow, / And betimes I will, to the weïrd sisters.' | Where is Macbeth going tomorrow? Why? |

## Checking understanding

Having read the scene for understanding, and to appreciate the sense of drama Shakespeare has created, it is worth taking a moment to check students' broader understanding. You might, therefore, use some comprehension questions such as those which follow:

1. What does the murderer have on his face when he arrives back at Macbeth's castle?

2. Why do you think Macbeth compares Banquo and Fleance to snakes?
3. How many injuries does Banquo sustain to his head? What does this show the audience about the nature of his murder?
4. Where does Banquo's ghost sit? Why is this significant? Think about the witches and their prophecies!
5. What does Banquo's ghost look like? What can we infer about it from how Macbeth describes its appearance and actions?
6. What does Macbeth say the sight of Banquo's ghost would do to the devil? What might this suggest about how the vision has affected Macbeth?
7. How does Lady Macbeth try to cover up Macbeth's behaviour? Why?
8. What does Macbeth say he would rather face than Banquo's ghost? What does this suggest?
9. Where does Macbeth say he is going tomorrow? Why?
10. Summarise what happens in this scene in no more than four sentences.

The final question, asking students to write a summary of the scene, is a really effective way to assess that students have understood key moments and the chronology of them. Depending on your class, it is often worth 'crowdsourcing' a summary collaboratively before moving on with the lesson so that all students have a high quality, accurate summary of the scene.

With this knowledge secured, students can now be given the 'Big Question': 'Why does Banquo's ghost appear to Macbeth?' It is with this in mind that the lesson proceeds.

Once it is clear that students have a functioning understanding of the scene, one can then move on to looking in more detail at Shakespeare's craft. In the first instance, this can be done through tracking the emotions of three key characters throughout the scene to see how Shakespeare develops the drama and tension in Act III, Scene iv.

## Emotion wheel

For this, I suggest a return to the 'Emotion Wheel' that was first used in Chapter 3. The emotion wheel allows for students to give clear responses and think carefully about the specific emotions Shakespeare evokes for each of his characters.

At the start of the scene, for example, Macbeth is, broadly speaking, feeling fear. He wants to know what has happened to Banquo and Fleance and is desperate to re-emphasise his position as king with the lords of Scotland. We can then move out from the middle of the circle. Which of the second-level emotions is Macbeth feeling? One could argue that at the start of the scene he is probably 'scared'. Finally, students can then select a third-level emotion. Arguably, this is possibly 'frightened' – though 'helpless' could also be applicable specifically to his feelings around Banquo and Fleance. Until the murderers return, the fates of Banquo and Fleance are out of his hands. We can see, though, that Macbeth's emotions develop as the scene goes on, and this is where the emotion wheel really comes into its own. At varying times in the scene, he feels hysterical, panicked, frustrated, sorrowful… and students benefit hugely from being specific like this. It means they can track the changes in a character's emotions and feelings, even if, in the broadest terms, a character's emotions develop in one specific range.

I would recommend that students at first focus on one particular character – either Macbeth, Lady Macbeth or the collected lords. They could then use a grid like the one below, and a copy of the emotion wheel itself, to track a character's emotions. Ideally, a student would choose between three and six key moments to identify and consider. An example, for Lady Macbeth, is below.

## RESOURCE 12.3

| Line | Emotion | Analysis – why do they feel this way? |
|---|---|---|
| 30: 'My royal Lord, / You do not give the cheer'. | Perplexed | She knows how important this banquet is – and there is an inference that Macbeth, too, knows how important the banquet is. Therefore, it is confusing for her as to why he is so distracted. She doesn't know about the plan to murder Banquo, so doesn't know why he is stepping out to speak to anyone else. |
| | | |
| | | |
| | | |

## Quotation explosion

Quotation explosions are not unique to this lesson, though regardless of the activity being a repeat, it is still a useful way to approach language analysis. The ability to take an independent lead when looking at quotations such as these is a good way for one to gauge the level of understanding a student has, and the scaffolding supports independence.

## RESOURCE 12.4

| | |
|---|---|
| Macbeth is describing the ghost. He is feeling... | The alliterative 'b' sounds (plosive alliteration) give the effect of... |

**'Thy bones are marrowless, thy blood is cold.'**

| | |
|---|---|
| What two words create a contrast here? What image does this contrast create of Banquo's ghost? | Blood is associated with murder and violence, which shows that Macbeth cannot stop thinking about... |

---

| | |
|---|---|
| Macbeth uses the imperative 'never shake' here. This suggests... | The adjective 'gory' tells the audience that Banquo's hair is... This implies that his murder was... |

**'Thou canst not say I did it: Never shake thy gory locks at me.'**

| | |
|---|---|
| Banquo's ghost is shaking its head at Macbeth because... Banquo's ghost is shaking its head at Macbeth but... Banquo's ghost is shaking its head at Macbeth so... | 'Thou canst not say I did it' suggests that Macbeth... |

---

| | |
|---|---|
| What is Macbeth's state of mind here? | How do you think a contemporary audience would react to seeing Banquo's ghost? Why? |

**'Ay, and a bold one, that dare look on that / Which might appal the devil.'**

| | |
|---|---|
| Connotations of the devil include... The fact that Banquo's ghost would appal the devil suggests that what Macbeth is seeing is... | Macbeth describes himself as a 'bold man' because... |

Once students have completed their analysis of these quotations, they could summarise verbally to a partner, or as part of a wider discussion, how Macbeth is feeling and what his reactions have been to the appearance of his best friend's ghost. Direct student responses to focus particularly on Shakespeare's choice of language.

## Knowledge snapshot

Analysing language of course forms a key part of students' knowledge, but the use of a 'knowledge snapshot', such as the one in Resource 12.5, can emphasise the key information they must know in order to be successful.

## RESOURCE 12.5²⁶

Macbeth has a banquet to reaffirm his position as king. He seems obsessed with hierarchy – 'You know your own degrees, sit down.'

Fleance has escaped. Macbeth uses a metaphor here to explain that he fears what Fleance will do in the future, 'There the grown serpent lies; the worm that's fled / Hath nature that in time will venom breed, / No teeth for th' present.'

Lady Macbeth tries to explain away Macbeth's behaviour: 'my lord is often thus, / And hath been from his youth.'

Macbeth claims he is a man because he is looking at something (Banquo's ghost) that would even scare the Devil: 'Ay, and a bold one, that dare look on that / Which might appal the devil.'

The lords leave and are clearly very concerned about Macbeth's state of mind: 'Good night; and better health / Attend his majesty!'

Macbeth discovers Banquo is dead and the wounds he suffered were brutal: 'safe in a ditch he bides, / With twenty trenched gashes on his head, / The least a death to nature.'

Banquo's ghost appears – Macbeth tries to dissociate himself from the murder, as he didn't personally carry it out. 'Thou canst not say I did it: never shake / Thy gory locks at me.'

Macbeth explores the idea that burying someone doesn't mean they are gone – like Banquo's ghost. He also suggests that if bodies don't stay in their graves they will be eaten by birds – perhaps the fate that will befall him. 'If charnel-houses and our graves must send / Those that we bury back, our monuments / Shall be the maws of kites.'

Macbeth recognises he is scared whilst the lords look on – he asks them to: 'keep the natural ruby of your cheeks, / When mine is blanched with fear.'

Macbeth declares he would rather fight any number of dangerous animals than be faced with Banquo's ghost, demonstrating his fear. 'Approach thou like the rugged Russian bear... / Take any shape but that...'

Lady Macbeth tries to draw Macbeth back from his madness, reaffirming his position and his expected behaviour. 'My worthy lord, / Your noble friends do lack you.'

Reminding the audience of Macbeth's fears that 'Bloody instructions' will 'return / To plague th'inventor', he says that: 'It will have blood they say: blood will have blood.' By this he means that he finally realises his actions will come back to haunt him.

Macbeth's later actions are explained here – he realises that there is no recourse for his actions so he may as well continue to behave in a tyrannical manner: 'I am in blood / Stepped in so far, that should I wade no more, Returning were as tedious as go o'er.'

Macbeth decides he wants to know for once and for all what fate has in store for him, and he decides that he will go 'to the weïrd sisters' to find out more.

Lady Macbeth believes her husband is so unwell because he lacks 'the season of all natures, sleep.' This echoes Macbeth's earlier fears that he 'does murder sleep'.

---

26. Blood by Alex Muravev, Ghost by Olga Dorofeeva, crown design by ProSymbols, Snake by Alice Noir, Bird by Alena Artemova, all from the Noun Project.

In this lesson, though, I will be using the knowledge snapshot resource in order to help students answer the 'Big Question'. The knowledge snapshot, whilst focused on Macbeth, is consistently underpinned by the appearance, disappearance and reappearance of Banquo's ghost. Each slip and recovery in Macbeth's stability directly correlates to Banquo's ghost. Being able to spot this is therefore key to students being able to answer the Big Question successfully. Once students have had the opportunity to look carefully at the knowledge snapshot, and perhaps engaged with them using some of the methods explained below, students should put the snapshot away. Using a blank copy, they should try to recreate the snapshot. Whilst this does not test what they will remember in the long term, it does indicate to the teacher the areas that are likely to need revisiting. It also helps confirm for both the teacher and the student what they now know that they did not know previously.

There are lots of ways these revision snapshots can then be used to aid students' understanding and, of course, revision. For example, they could:

- work in pairs, with one student holding the snapshot, quizzing their peer on the content.
- transform the snapshots into flashcards.
- reduce the information down.
- expand the information using their knowledge of the rest of the play.

### Answering the Big Question

In the final part of the lesson, students should answer the Big Question, ensuring they write in as much detail as they can. Upon reading the answers, one can then plan for future knowledge retrieval practice.

### Suggested 'Extra Challenge' activities

- 'The Shakespearean ghost is at once the embodiment of remorseful presentiment and the instrument of divine justice.'[27] How is this reflected in Banquo's ghost?

---

27.  F.W. Moorman, 'Shakespeare's Ghosts', *The Modern Language Review*, Vol. 1, No. 3 (April 1906), pp. 192–201, https://www.jstor.org/stable/3713608.

- In Proverbs 28:13 it is written: 'He that covereth his sins shall not prosper, but whoso confesseth and forsaketh them shall have mercy.'[28] How is this alluded to in *Macbeth*?
- Guilt. Discuss.

## Key vocabulary:

Corporeal, peripeteia

---

28. *The Holy Bible Containing the Old and New Testaments*, Authorised King James Version,www.kingjamesbibleonline.org, Proverbs 28:13.

# CHAPTER 13
## Act III, Scenes v and vi

*Who is Hecate?*
*What are the perceptions of Macbeth amongst the Scottish nobility?*

### What?

Act III, Scene v is the topic of much debate amongst Shakespearean scholars. The scene serves as a brief interlude to the main action and somewhat of a prologue to Act IV, Scene i, where Macbeth actively seeks out the witches in order to learn more of what fate has in store for him. In it, Hecate, the goddess of witchcraft, makes a fleeting appearance, causing many critics of Shakespeare to argue exactly what her purpose is.

The uncertainties over her function render her, on the surface, somewhat unimportant to the story. Indeed, most productions of *Macbeth* cut the scene entirely. The removal of Hecate's character does not affect the plot in any way, something which cannot be said for almost any other moment in the play. Perhaps this is why many believe her scenes were not written by Shakespeare himself. There are, however, some aspects of Hecate that I think are worth exploring in greater detail.

### Hecate in mythology

Historically, the ways in which Hecate has been presented, discussed and analysed have changed a multitude of times, but put simply, she is a goddess in ancient Greek religion and mythology. Because of this, she is often given the title of 'leader of the witches' amongst those who study *Macbeth* in schools, yet there is more to say about her than this.

Arguably, Hecate's famous and most notable appearance in literature comes from Hesiod's *Theogony*, composed between 730 and 700 BC, meaning the genealogy of a group or system of gods. Hecate is portrayed as a 'direct force in human life' in which the goddess has 'personal involvement in affairs of state, wars and games, in all of which she has the power to aid and advance her favourites.'[1] This is particularly pertinent given how she is used in *Macbeth*: 'from the political assembly to the farmer's stable, Hecate is seen as a vital factor in the success of human endeavour.'[2]

What is particularly noteworthy is Hecate's positive portrayal in Hesiod's *Theogony*, a far cry from the Hecate of Shakespeare's *Macbeth*. In being a 'direct force in human life', Hecate is often seen to *help* people rather than act as a force against them:

> *Whom she will she greatly aids and advances: she sits by worshipful kings in judgement, and in the assembly whom she will is distinguished among the people. And when men arm themselves for the battle that destroys men, then the goddess is at hand to give victory and grant glory readily to whom she will. Good is she also when men contend at the games, for there too the goddess is with them and profits them: and he who by might and strength gets the victory wins the rich prize easily with joy, and brings glory to his parents. And she is good to stand by horsemen, whom she will.*[3]

Hesiod seems to imply that Hecate picks and chooses those who earn her favour and the ease at which she bestows good fortune upon those she holds in high esteem. However, if she can help people as easily as Hesiod describes, she can hinder, too. In a rare moment of negativity, Hesiod, in describing fishermen and herdsmen says:

> *And to those whose business is in the grey discomfortable sea, and who pray to Hecate and the loud-crashing Earth-Shaker, easily the glorious goddess gives great catch, and easily she takes it away as soon as seen, if so she will.*[4]

The idea of taking something away shows how Hecate can make someone's fortune but destroy it just as easily, a threat which looms over her scene in *Macbeth*. Although Hesiod's Hecate shares similarities with the Hecate of

---

1.  Patricia A. Marquardt, 'A Portrait of Hecate', *The American Journal of Philology*, Vol. 102, No. 3 (1981), pp. 243–260, www.jstor.org/stable/294128.

2.  Ibid.

3.  Hesiod, *Theogony*, (Project Gutenberg Ebook), https://www.gutenberg.org/files/348/348-h/348-h.htm.

4.  Ibid.

Shakespeare's play, the two are, in essence, different characters, and are two interpretations rooted in mythology and disparate in their purpose.

In including Hecate in *Macbeth*, a hierarchy has been created amongst the witches. Even supernatural forces abide by the strict order that dominates the world of Shakespeare's play, and the 'weïrd sisters' must conform to a chain of command where Hecate is seemingly positioned in the upper echelons. Yet in associating Hecate so closely with the witches, the implications are that she must have connections with magic, darkness and the spiritual realm, and that is before one even considers the chthonic (relating to or inhabiting the underworld) links that could be made. None of these really have a place in Hesiod's poem, which makes one wonder how *Macbeth*'s Hecate came to fruition.

The Hecate we associate with *Macbeth* is one of evil. Appearing with the witches cements her status as a figure of the supernatural, one who is clearly in charge of the 'weïrd sisters' and presented as the goddess of the moon and witchcraft.

Hesiod's *Theogony*, however, does not refer to Hecate's chthonic links that we, as an audience of Shakespeare's play, would expect her to have. This is what makes Hecate so confusing when we look at her through a historical lens. As *The Oxford Classical Dictionary* states, 'because her functions overlap with those of other divinities, she lacks individuating features.'[5]

Hecate received 'both public and private cult' and 'sacrifices to her were as anomalous as the goddess herself.'[6] Pillars depicting Hecate, known as 'Hecataea' were placed at crossroads and in doorways, and later representations adopted a trimorphic version of her, with three bodies standing back to back, observing all directions of paths coming together. Crossroads represent an uncertain direction of travel. Perhaps one of the reasons Hecate has come to be associated with crossroads is because of her assistance in helping Demeter search for her daughter, Persephone, who was abducted by Hades and taken to the underworld.[7] Hecate is often depicted in this search as holding two torches, lighting the uncertain path ahead.

Hecate's lack of 'individuating features'[8] means she is also identified with other divine figures such as Enodia, who was a Thessalian road goddess, and Artemis, the Olympian goddess of the moon. Perhaps the most important link,

---

5.   Ed. Simon Hornblower and Antony Spawforth, *The Oxford Classical Dictionary: Fourth Edition*, (Oxford: Oxford University Press, 2012), p. 650.

6.   Ibid., p. 651.

7.   Judy Hall, *The Hades Moon: Pluto in Aspect to the Moon*, (Maine: Samuel Weiser, Inc., 1998), p. 46.

8.   Ed. Simon Hornblower and Antony Spawforth, *The Oxford Classical Dictionary: Fourth Edition*, (Oxford: Oxford University Press, 2012), p. 650.

however, stems from her associations with Ereschigal, the Babylonian goddess of the underworld. It is this connection to an afterlife which helps us recognise the Hecate we encounter in *Macbeth*. *The Oxford Classical Dictionary* labels her as someone who lacks a mythology of her own, though 'her nocturnal apparitions, packs of barking hell-hounds, and hosts of ghost-like revenants occupied a special place in the Greek religious imagination.'[9] As such, she is clearly a figure of magic and the supernatural, so much so that 'sorceresses of all periods and every provenance… invoke her name as one who makes powerful spells more potent.'[10]

An example of this in literature can be found in Euripides' *Medea*, where 'the famous sorceress [invokes] Hecate as her mistress and helper in the performing of magic.'[11] This, of course, sounds more like the Hecate in *Macbeth*: sinister and mighty, a figure to be feared because of her associations with powerful sorcery beyond the realms of human understanding.

## The question of authorship

Act III, Scene v has been subject to much speculation; it is said Shakespeare did not write it at all.[12] It is not difficult to see how one might arrive at such a conclusion. The scene appears to be somewhat of an anomaly, for it can be excised with no repercussions and does not drive the plot forward. It is extremely short and oddly placed, and Hecate's scolding of the witches is written in a way which does not reflect Shakespeare's style.

Although the scene is based around the schemes and ploys of the witches, their function is questionable. The sense of foreboding that lingered through Act I, Scene i and Act I, Scene iii is lost; the 'weïrd sisters' no longer possess the eeriness of their past appearances, and although all are said to participate in the action, only the First Witch speaks to Hecate, the others silent. They are no longer the threatening figures they first appeared to be, but rather the threatened, put in their place by Hecate, who admonishes them for meddling in Macbeth's affairs without her. Even the way Hecate speaks is different; her lines are written in iambic octosyllabic couplets rather than the trochaic tetrameter

9.   Ed. Simon Hornblower and Antony Spawforth, *The Oxford Classical Dictionary: Fourth Edition*, (Oxford: Oxford University Press, 2012), p. 651.

10.  Ibid.

11.  Ed. Pierre Brunel, Companion to Literary Myths, *Heroes and Archetypes*, (New York: Routledge, 2016), p. 130.

12.  Gary Taylor, 'Empirical Middleton: "Macbeth", Adaptation, and Microauthorship', *Shakespeare Quarterly*, Vol. 65, No. 3 (2014), pp. 239–272, www.jstor.org/stable/24778582.

established as the convention of supernatural characters in Act I, Scene i.[13] Hecate is not mentioned by the witches in any shape or form, and Macbeth only speaks of her name in passing when deep in thought about the evil which infests the world.

Of course, this is just one side of the argument. Other Shakespearean scholars agree that Hecate's scene *does* hold a certain credence, because by appearing before Act IV, Scene i, where Macbeth is given his second set of prophecies, the action 'balances the play's opening scene',[14] in that both show the witches preparing for correspondence with Macbeth. The verse forms, as well, have been argued to be intentionally different. Hecate, after all, 'is a goddess from a machine and as such has a different verse from the Weïrd Sisters',[15] as do gods and goddesses in other Shakespeare plays who are given alternative forms of verse to distinguish themselves from other characters.

The scene is commonly attributed to Thomas Middleton, most likely due to the remarkable similarities it shares with one of his plays, *The Witch*. Two songs briefly mentioned in stage directions in *Macbeth*, 'Come away, come away' and 'Black spirits', make full appearances in Middleton's play. Their cursory mention in Act III, Scene v and Act IV, Scene i respectively have led some to believe the songs were later inserted for the printing of the First Folio, an idea further strengthened by the idea that 'Come away, come away' is incredibly isolated. There is no reference to it in the action surrounding it, although 'Black Spirits' is introduced somewhat by the preceding dialogue.[16]

The debate is ongoing, and this book certainly does not contain the answer of who authored Hecate's dialogue. What one can be sure of, though, is that Act III, Scene v continues to be included in *Macbeth* as part of the play, and so is worthy of study and further exploration.

## Scene analysis: Act III, Scene v

Seeing as Hecate is associated with crossroads, her appearance at this point is timely, for Macbeth stands at a crossroads himself. He has already resolved to go and see the witches again in order to shed light on an uncertain future, and it is clear he has a decision to make: attempt to escape the cycle of bloodshed he has found himself in or be consumed by it forever. This decision, however, is extremely important, for it is arguably the last crossroads he will encounter in

13.  Ed. J.H. Walter, *The Player's Shakespeare: Macbeth*, (Oxford: Heinemann, 1962), p. 213.

14.  John Russell Brown, *Focus on Macbeth*, (Abingdon: Routledge, 2005), p. 57.

15.  Ed. Sandra Clark and Pamela Mason, *The Arden Shakespeare: Macbeth*, (London: Bloomsbury, 2015), p. 330.

16.  Ibid., p. 329.

the play, and whatever path he takes will leave him a success or a failure. Hecate's appearance also echoes previous crossroads Macbeth has found himself at, the most significant being whether he should betray Duncan in order to seize the crown or wait and see if truth will manifest itself from the prophecies without intervention. Whether or not this interpretation stems from Hecate's appearance is irrelevant: *Macbeth* is not just a tale of ambition but a story about choice. The choices we make in life are ones that determine who we are. Macbeth, of course, will leave a bloody legacy tainted with death and destruction.

Hecate, when she first appears, is 'angerly', and she launches into a tirade at the witches regarding the way their 'trade and traffic with Macbeth' has impacted the choices he has made. Her reprimand demonstrates how there is an ordered hierarchy in the supernatural world. The witches, although powerful, are still subservient, and answer to higher powers that until now have remained inconspicuous.

It seems the witches do not at first understand what they have done. They have to ask Hecate why she looks so angry, prompting their leader to ask rhetorically, 'Have I not reason, beldams as you are, / Saucy and over-bold?' In fact, Hecate's diatribe opens with *three* rhetorical questions, an indication of her disbelief at the witches' actions and how they did not seek permission from their 'mistress of… charms'. She feels undermined by the actions of her subjects and must put them in their place if she is to avoid something similar happening again.

Describing herself as the 'close contriver of all harms' is significant for two reasons. Firstly, audiences learn she is the one who brings about harm to others, the one who secretly arranges their downfall, echoing Macbeth's description of 'black Hecate' earlier in the play. Secondly, it reveals just how far Macbeth has fallen, how 'un-Christian' he has become, for he mirrors Hecate's behaviour exactly. He is a 'close contriver' himself, subtly planning to ruin those who threaten him. The writer of this scene, whoever it may be, has closely aligned Macbeth with the witches; whereas at the beginning of the play it could be argued he is presented as a victim of their schemes, he has now adopted their ways to the extent that he is becoming evil incarnate.

Yet Hecate dislikes Macbeth and the way he presents himself, saying the witches have wasted their energies on a 'wayward son, / Spiteful and wrathful, who, as others do, / Loves for his own ends'. Macbeth's appalling and ugly attributes are only strengthened by what the witches have said to him. They have been feeding his arrogance, self-gain and greed, and amends must be made.

To do this, Hecate issues the witches with orders, reasserting her command and power over them. Her links to mythology are referred to when she tells them to meet her once more 'at the pit of Acheron' the next morning. Acheron is the name of one of the seven rivers of Hades which leads straight to the underworld and serves as the 'river of woe'.[17] Hecate foresees that Macbeth will meet them there 'to know his destiny'; the symbolism here is undeniable. In leading Macbeth to the 'pit of Acheron', he will allegorically enter hell itself in order to find out what his future holds. Having lamented offering his 'eternal jewel' (his soul) to 'the common enemy of man' (the Devil), in Act III, Scene i, it seems no action is too extreme any more in order to discover his destiny. Furthermore, Acheron as the 'river of woe' foreshadows Macbeth's fate, for his visit to the witches at this place will, in the long term, only cause him further pain and suffering.

Hecate instructs the witches to bring all their charms and spells with them, resolving the night will be spent planning something fatal. Together, they will guide Macbeth to his end, described by Hecate as 'great business'. The writer of this scene uses Hecate to repeat Lady Macbeth's earlier words, establishing a connection between them. In Act I, Scene v, Lady Macbeth tells her husband to put 'this night's great business into [her] despatch'; she is, of course, talking about the murder of Duncan. It seems acts of evil will always be described as 'great', perhaps to highlight the sheer enormity of what is occurring and the power of supernatural forces at work.

As the scene moves towards its end, Hecate observes a 'vaporous drop' which is hanging 'upon the corner of the moon', a reference, perhaps, to her role as goddess of the moon. In actual fact, the 'drop' is most likely referring to a foam which the moon was said to elicit from herbs.[18] She expresses her intentions to use the drop to 'raise such artificial sprites' which she will present to Macbeth in order to begin the process of overthrowing him. Referring to the moon gives Hecate's spell a celestial quality, and with heavenly agents dominating the higher ranks of the Great Chain of Being, we are given an indication of the power it will take to raise such apparitions.

Hecate is trying to trick Macbeth with these apparitions. She believes they will foster a sense of security within him, causing him to believe he is safe from anything with harmful intentions. Once again, appearances can be deceiving. The reality of Hecate's creations is much more sinister. In causing him to believe he is protected, Hecate, through the apparitions, will cause Macbeth's hubris to establish itself and dictate any future decisions he has to make, leading him blindly to his downfall. He will 'spurn fate, scorn death, and bear / His hopes 'bove wisdom, grace and fear'. In essence, the witches are washing their hands

---

17.  Mike Dixon-Kennedy, *Encyclopaedia of Greco-Roman Mythology*, (California: ABC-CLIO, 1998), p. 144.

18.  T.F. Thiselton-Dyer, *Folk-lore of Shakespeare*, (Glasgow: Good Press Publishing, 2019).

of Macbeth, assembling the conditions needed for him to instigate his downfall himself rather than striking at him directly. He is not as in control of himself as he would like to believe.

Hecate concludes with a disturbing truth: 'you all know, security / Is mortals' chiefest enemy.' 'Security' is an adversary of humanity because it lulls one into a false sense of protection. While Macbeth has always believed any threat toward him to be external, he has failed to recognise that his greatest threat is himself. That which would bring about his downfall, his ambition, is inherent within him, and because he has mostly succeeded in getting what he wants, his confidence continues to build. He cannot see what he has become, and that is the biggest threat of all.

As Hecate hears music, she withdraws to her 'little spirit' and the First Witch says 'Come, let's make haste, she'll soon be back again', suggesting they are afraid of her or dislike her. One thing is clear, however. This scene shows how major events in the play are planned and carefully created by the writer in order for the characters to achieve their dark and evil goals. Everyone and everything is manipulated, whether they know it or not, leaving audiences to consider whether authenticity exists in this bleak world of Shakespeare's.

## Scene analysis: Act III, Scene vi

Like so many of *Macbeth*'s later scenes, Act III, Scene vi mirrors earlier action in the play. It is a commentary, like Act II, Scene iv, where audiences are invited to hear the opinions of those characters who have not participated in the main action of the plot. Again, this scene involves just two characters: Lennox and a lord who is similar in his anonymity to the old man whom Ross meets in Act II, Scene iv. Like the audience, Lennox is a witness to major events in the play. His first appearance is in Act I, Scene ii, where he listens to the Captain's report on Macbeth's prowess in battle. He is also present when Duncan bestows the title of Prince of Cumberland upon Malcolm and accompanies Macduff to Macbeth's castle in Act II, Scene iii. As such, he is a suitable character to be able to comment on the state of affairs in Scotland, although his allegiance is hard to place because of the obscure way he expresses himself. His language is extremely ambiguous.

### 'THE GRACIOUS DUNCAN WAS PITIED OF MACBETH'

Lennox chooses his words carefully, delivering an ironic speech which strengthens the ambiguity of his role. This speech can often be confusing, for audiences learn just as much about Lennox's allegiances based on what he does *not* say as they do from what he does say. In relaying information about 'things… strangely borne', we begin to understand the deep irony which pervades this scene. By referring to the former king's murder, Lennox observes 'The gracious Duncan / Was pitied of Macbeth', suggesting Macbeth presented himself as sorry for the King, but only after he killed him: 'marry, he was dead.' Note how Duncan is referred to as 'gracious', the same way he is described by Macbeth in Act III, Scene i, a moment of truth perhaps, amid the verbal irony dominating Lennox's words.

Further irony can be found in Lennox's recounting of Banquo's actions who 'walked too late', an ambiguous reference either to the time of day in which he was journeying, or to his death. Lennox, in a half-spoken thought, sarcastically invites the lord to believe Fleance was the one who killed Banquo; his words, 'if't please you', toy with the idea that many are living in ignorance because they blindly accept Fleance's escape and see failure to make his whereabouts known as evidence of his guilt. '[M]en must not walk too late,' he says. Lennox's sarcastic warning may be deemed a genuine attempt to help others avoid a similar fate, although his ambiguity shows that he does not believe Banquo died purely because of the time of day in which he was journeying; Macbeth *must* have had something to do with it. Perhaps he is relaying Macbeth's own words in a moment not witnessed by the audience, for these are clearly Macbeth's versions of events, and Lennox is surreptitiously ridiculing them. He must speak in closed terms to ensure his safety; Macbeth's tyrannical grip continues to suffocate Scotland, and to speak out so openly against the king is to risk one's life.

Lennox's incredulity continues when he asks 'Who cannot want the thought how monstrous / It was for Malcolm and for Donalbain / To kill their gracious father?' In early modern English, two negatives help to intensify the meaning of what is being said instead of cancelling each other out.[19] Therefore, 'want' means lack, and A.R. Braunmuller notes that 'technically "cannot" should be read "can" but the negative element in "want" elicits denial ("cannot") which becomes intensification.'[20] In other words, Lennox's line could be translated as: 'Who can fail to think that' it was monstrous of Malcolm and Donalbain to kill their father?[21]

The prospect of Malcolm and Donalbain killing their father, according to Lennox, grieves Macbeth further. In sarcastically suggesting that it was noble and wise for Macbeth to kill Duncan's servants in a 'pious rage', Lennox is drawing

19. Ed. Sandra Clark and Pamela Mason, *The Arden Shakespeare: Macbeth*, (London: Bloomsbury, 2015), p. 231.

20. Ed. A.R. Braunmuller, *The New Cambridge Shakespeare: Macbeth*, (Cambridge: Cambridge University Press, 2008), p. 203.

21. Ed. Sandra Clark and Pamela Mason, *The Arden Shakespeare: Macbeth*, (London: Bloomsbury, 2015), p. 231.

attention to the fact that everything has suspiciously fallen into place for the King. 'Pious' would imply Macbeth is loyal and dutiful, yet through his use of irony, Lennox shows he has not been loyal at all; conveniently, the only two people who could have attested to what truly happened have been silenced. In an ambiguous sense, Lennox's use of 'pious' could imply Macbeth's rage was justified. In a way, he is right. Macbeth *had* to kill the servants if he was to succeed in his endeavour. Lennox, cleverly, has understood Macbeth's perspective, and uses it, not to agree with Macbeth, but to highlight just how disloyal he has become.

Lennox does, however, entertain the idea that Macbeth killed Duncan's servants because it would 'have angered any heart alive / To hear the men deny't.' This is a striking example of the 'double-talk' which characterises the scene.[22] Braunmuller argues it is needed, a necessity borne out of the distrust felt by many living under Macbeth's tyrannical rule. Lennox's remark has two meanings. Firstly, he is arguing that he believes Macbeth would be 'angered by the grooms' allegedly false denials', and secondly, and perhaps more subtly, he acknowledges the 'dead Duncan (who is not a 'heart alive') cannot confirm the grooms' innocence',[23] which is suspicious but beneficial for Macbeth.

### 'HAD HE DUNCAN'S SONS UNDER HIS KEY'

In a final moment of irony, Lennox divulges his belief that if Malcolm and Donalbain were in Macbeth's custody they would learn the punishment for committing parricide, as would Fleance. These lines, like the rest of his speech, are fraught with double meanings and half-said truths; he hopes Macbeth will not have the former king's sons under lock and key ('As, an't please heaven, he shall not'). This could have two interpretations, one being that the statement would align Lennox with Macbeth. Lennox could be suggesting he hopes for their sake that Malcolm and Donalbain do not fall into Macbeth's clutches; if they are caught, Macbeth would deliver swift justice and would be right to do so. This interpretation, of course, would satisfy any of the King's spies who would happen to be listening. However, another reason, the *truthful* reason, as to why Lennox wishes Malcolm and Donalbain freedom from Macbeth's imprisonment would be because they serve as a beacon of hope for Scotland. If Macbeth kills them, the rightful heir will no longer be alive to take back his throne, leaving the usurper victorious.

With the threat of Macbeth's victory looming, Lennox turns his attention to Macduff, who, it is revealed, has spoken outwardly against the king and 'failed…

---

22. Ed. A.R. Braunmuller, *The New Cambridge Shakespeare: Macbeth*, (Cambridge: Cambridge University Press, 2008), p. 203.

23. Ibid.

the tyrant's feast', his words alluding to the command Macbeth gave Banquo before his murder, a command Banquo honours through his ghostly appearance. More significant is Lennox's use of the word 'tyrant', the first time this label has been assigned to Macbeth in the play, though certainly not the last.

The lord, in reply, also refers to Macbeth as a 'tyrant', aligning himself with Lennox's views. He says Malcolm has fled to the English court, where he 'is received of the most pious Edward', referring of course to Edward the Confessor, known for his strictly devout religious beliefs. Notice how both Macbeth and Edward have been referred to as possessing 'pious' qualities. Edward is deserving of this label, but it only heightens the irony of Lennox's former words, for Macbeth is as far from 'pious' as one could get, which shows just how far he has fallen.

Macduff, according to the lord, has also travelled to England to 'pray the holy king' (Edward) helps him 'to wake' the Earls of Northumberland 'and warlike Siward'. In doing so, they can march together against Macbeth in the hope 'we may again / Give to our tables meat, sleep to our nights, / Free from our feasts and banquets bloody knives'. Whilst referring to Edward as a 'holy king' could be a way of taunting Macbeth's descent into despair, it is most likely alluding to Edward's rightful place as monarch; he has, as the Divine Right of Kings dictates, been chosen by God, for God's purpose, showing how Macbeth is an imposter. Whilst Macbeth remains king, the threat of hunger, sleepless nights and 'bloody knives' at 'feasts and banquets' will linger, the mention of 'banquets' thick with the memories of Macbeth's frantic episode in reaction to Banquo's ghost.

It is Macduff's hope that the people of Scotland will one day be able to pay 'faithful homage' to their king and receive the honours they long for in return. The lord's choice of language here is equally as revealing as Lennox's at the beginning of the scene, for it implies Macbeth's subjects are not, at the present time, authentically loyal to him. They fawn over Macbeth because, like all who live under the oppression of tyranny, they are terrified of him. Ironically, they are exhibiting just the kind of behaviour Macbeth and Lady Macbeth have shown throughout the entire play. His subjects have made their 'faces vizards to [their] hearts' in an attempt to survive and conceal their true feelings.

### 'THIS REPORT / HATH SO EXASPERATE THEIR KING'

The lord goes on to reveal that 'this report / Hath so exasperate their king, that he / Prepares for some attempt of war.' It is necessary to be careful when dealing with these lines, for they can change the meaning of the situation depending on how they are read. Perhaps the most obvious interpretation of the lord's summation is that news of Malcolm and Macduff's actions has reached Macbeth, and his subsequent animosity has led him to prepare for a declaration of war. This is supported by Lennox's ensuing question – 'Sent he to Macduff?' – a query as to whether Macbeth called the Thane of Fife back to the Scottish court when he heard the Thane had fled to England.

However, the report could be referring to Malcolm's report to Edward of the events occurring in Scotland, and it is the king of England who is instigating threats of war. If this is the case, it would certainly show that Macbeth, through his actions, has backed himself into a corner that no amount of rhetoric can fix. Some editions of the play change 'their king' to 'the king' to clarify that the lord is speaking of Macbeth.[24] It would be easy for audiences to infer that Malcolm and Macduff see Edward as their true king whilst Scotland remains under the rule of a usurper. Either way, representatives of Scotland and England are cooperating with one another, establishing a firm connection which mirrors the personal union of these sovereign states under King James I's reign in the time Shakespeare was writing.[25]

Macduff, we learn, has refused Macbeth's orders to return to Scotland, behaviour which stuns the lord. Lennox, in response, wishes for a 'holy angel' to fly to the 'court of England' to summon Macduff back in order to help his 'suffering country, / Under a hand accursed.'

Act III, Scene vi serves two purposes: to reveal the perspective of the Scottish nobility on Macbeth's reign, and to establish Macduff as a credible threat to the King. Throughout the play runs imagery of infection and disease, usually associated with mentality. Here, though, Macbeth himself is seen as infecting Scotland, ruining it, destroying it. The noble's perspective is clear: Macbeth must be removed if Scotland is to heal.

---

24. Ed. Sandra Clark and Pamela Mason, *The Arden Shakespeare: Macbeth*, (London: Bloomsbury, 2015), p. 233.

25. Alan Stewart, *The Cradle King: A Life of James VI and I*, (Eastbourne: Pimlico, 2004), p. 209.

## Hecate at a glance

## RESOURCE 13.1

Hecate is scolding the witches for meddling in Macbeth's affairs without her. In ancient Greek mythology, Hecate was believed to be a direct force in human life. Hecate may be feeling the witches are challenging her authority or undermining her by toying with Macbeth without her permission.

As Hecate describes herself as a 'mistress' to the witches' 'charms', audiences understand that even the supernatural world must conform to a hierarchy and a sense of order, of which Hecate is in the upper echelons.

Hecate disapproves of Macbeth's self-centred attitude. His appalling and ugly attributes are strengthened by what the witches have said to him.

Hecate says she will spend the rest of the night planning something fatal. She refers to their plans for Macbeth as 'great business', echoing Lady Macbeth's description of their plans to murder Duncan.

Hecate's trickery is evident here, and what appears to be is not always the case. The apparitions she conjures will foster a sense of security within Macbeth, and his hubris will be fully realised. This, of course, will propel him towards his tragic end.

Hecate is a 'close contriver of... harms'. Here, we see how Macbeth has mirrored her behaviour. He has also planned in secret to bring harm to others. Aligning his behaviour with this supernatural being shows just how far he has fallen.

Hecate was said to have the power to aid her favourites and bolster their fortune. Here, it is clear Hecate does not favour Macbeth, foreshadowing a dark fate which will befall him.

Acheron is the name of one of the rivers of Hades, leading straight to the underworld. It serves as the 'river of woe'. Hecate says Macbeth will meet the witches there in the morning. She does not speak of a literal hell here, but by Macbeth's being led to the pit of Acheron', he will symbolically enter hell itself to learn more of his destiny. The fact Acheron is the 'river of woe' foreshadows Macbeth's future, which will not be kind to him.

**HECATE**
Have I not reason, beldams as you are,
Saucy and over-bold? How did you dare
To trade and traffic with Macbeth
In riddles and affairs of death;
And I, the mistress of your charms,
The close contriver of all harms,
Was never called to bear my part
Or show the glory of our art?
And, which is worse, all you have done
Hath been but for a wayward son,
Spiteful and wrathful, who, as others do,
Loves for his own ends, not for you.
But make amends now; get you gone,
And at the pit of Acheron
Meet me i'th' morning; thither he
Will come, to know his destiny.
Your vessels and your spells provide,
Your charms, and every thing beside.
I am for th'air; this night I'll spend
Unto a dismal and a fatal end.
Great business must be wrought ere noon.
Upon the corner of the moon
There hangs a vaporous drop profound,
I'll catch it ere it come to ground;
And that, distilled by magic sleights,
Shall raise such artificial sprites
As by the strength of their illusion,
Shall draw him on to his confusion.
He shall spurn fate, scorn death, and bear
His hopes 'bove wisdom, grace and fear;
And you all know, security
Is mortals' chiefest enemy.

Macbeth has always believed any threat toward him to be external. He has failed to recognise that his greatest threat is himself. That which would bring about his downfall, his ambition, is inherent within him and because he has mostly succeeded in getting what he wants, his confidence continues to build.

## How?

There are two Big Questions to be addressed in this lesson; both pertain to two very different scenes, structurally and tonally. Therefore, depending on lesson time, it may be easier to split the process described here into two lessons.

## PART ONE:

### Retrieval

A particular favourite retrieval activity of mine is 'spot the error' or 'find and fix'. This is where the teacher provides the class with a set of statements which are incorrect. Students must identify the error, explain why it is wrong and fix it. All statements need to be fixed. There are no catches, no tricks, just a concerted effort to address the errors they see. Work together as a class and model what is expected of students before setting them off independently.

## RESOURCE 13.2

*The Macbeths call upon darkness to hide their crimes from the prying eyes of others, but also from themselves. They know what they are doing is wrong and yet still decide to proceed. However, darkness enables them to feign ignorance and deny all involvement if they need to. Darkness is a symbol of moral corruption. By shrouding themselves in it, they are destroying any goodness they had left within them.*

| EXPLAIN WHY THE FOLLOWING STATEMENTS ARE INCORRECT. | | |
|---|---|---|
| The Porter's sole purpose in the play is to provide comic relief after the intensity of Duncan's murder in the previous scene. | The Macbeths call upon darkness so that people cannot recognise them when they commit their crimes. | Macbeth decides to revisit the three witches because he is not content with the way his prophecies have played out. |
| The violent weather on the night of Duncan's murder reflects God's anger and/or sorrow at how Macbeth has corrupted the Divine Right of Kings. | **FIX THE ERRORS** | Macbeth hallucinates a dagger because he is sick and feverish. |
| Violence and bloodshed are loathed at the beginning of the play, which is why Macbeth is conflicted as to whether he should kill Duncan or not. | Hands are symbolic of violent actions in the play. They are never used to commit good deeds. | Lady Macbeth maintains her power over her husband through her duplicity, even when he becomes king. |

*Violence and bloodshed are celebrated at the beginning of the play. Macbeth's violent actions in response to Norway's invasion of Scotland are committed out of honour for his king. This is also where Macbeth's inner conflict stems from. He knows he should continue to be loyal to Duncan but is spurred on by his ambition to kill him.*

## Pre-reading activities

Introduce the first of this lesson's Big Questions:

*Who is Hecate?*

Students have yet to come across Hecate, although her character has been mentioned twice by Macbeth already. Ask students to look back at these moments and get them to consider what we can learn about her from the way she is referred to.

## RESOURCE 13.3

**Act II, Scene i**
Now o'er the one half-world
Nature seems dead, and wicked dreams abuse
The curtained sleep; Witchcraft celebrates
Pale Hecate's offerings, and withered Murder,
Alarumed by his sentinel, the wolf,
Whose howl's his watch, thus with his stealthy pace

**Act III, Scene ii**
There's comfort yet: they are assailable.
Then be thou jocund; ere the bat hath flown
His cloistered flight, ere to black Hecate's summons
The shard-borne beetle, with his drowsy hums,
Hath rung night's yawning peal, there shall be done
A deed of dreadful note.

Although students are not dealing with much text here, I still think the extracts in Resource 13.3 are too long for the type of inferences I want students to make. To fix this, I ask my students to strip Macbeth's speech to single words. First of all, they should locate where Macbeth says Hecate's name. I then ask them to choose just three words from the passage which are associated with her and get them to write them down in an ordered list, including the name. With both extracts, this may look something like this:

> *Witchcraft – pale – Hecate's – offerings*
> *black – Hecate's – summons – beetle*

Just like the scene crunching method explored in Chapter 1, there may be some variation on this, but that is okay. The purpose of this is to narrow the focus to single words.

Once students have found their words, create a class version for the purpose of discussion. Before homing in on a particular word or phrase, I will often ask students what they generally notice and what these words tell us about Hecate. Common things classes pick up on range from connections between 'witchcraft', 'black' and 'beetle' to comments on the dualism of 'pale' and 'black'. 'Summons' is often linked to the idea of a command or order, with some suggesting Hecate is a powerful figure, whilst 'offerings' usually bring about ideas of sacrifice, honour and ceremony. The purpose of this is not to create a completely accurate character profile of Hecate, but to make predictions, as a pre-reading strategy, as to what she could be like.

## Non-fiction guided reading

Next is an activity students first came across in Chapter 8, the guided reading strategy, originally created by Simon Beale (@SPBeale on Twitter), which will be used a little differently this time. In Chapter 8, I adapted the method slightly to help students decode Shakespeare's language. Here, however, it will be used as Beale originally intended.

Provide students with a copy of the 'Hecate in mythology' essay from the 'What?' section of this chapter. Read this out loud to the class, pausing after each paragraph, allowing students the time to highlight a maximum of two sentences in each. The sentences they choose should be ones which strengthen their understanding of who Hecate is and her purpose in the play. I always impose a two-sentence maximum rule with this activity, as we all know what happens when students are let loose with highlighters!

Once the entire essay has been read and sentences highlighted, ask students to go back and give each paragraph a title in the left-hand margin. In the right-hand margin, students should summarise the content of the paragraph in two to three bullet points. Upon completion, instruct the class to summarise the entire essay as a small paragraph to strengthen and clarify their knowledge of what it contains. The activity will look something like Resource 13.4.

## RESOURCE 13.4

| Section title | Hecate in mythology | Section summary |
|---|---|---|
| | There is no single interpretation of Hecate. Historically, the ways in which she has been presented, discussed and analysed have changed a multitude of times, but put simply, she is a goddess in ancient Greek religion and mythology. Because of this, she is often given the title as 'leader of the witches' amongst those who study *Macbeth* in schools, yet there is more to say as to why her character might have been included in the play. | |
| *Ancient Greek goddess* | | *No single interpretation of Hecate.*<br><br>*Often described as leader of the witches* |
| *Hecate's role in human endeavour* | Arguably, Hecate's famous and most notable appearance in literature comes from Hesiod's *Theogony*, meaning the genealogy of a group or system of gods. In her study of this poem, Patricia A. Marquadt discusses how Hecate is portrayed as a 'direct force in human life' in which the goddess has 'personal involvement in affairs of state, wars and games, in all of which she has the power to aid and advance her favourites.' This is particularly pertinent given how she is used in *Macbeth*. Marquadt goes on to say, 'From the political assembly to the farmer's stable, Hecate is seen as a vital factor in the success of human endeavour.' | *Appeared in Hesiod's Theogony.*<br><br>*She was a direct force in human life.*<br><br>*She had the power to aid and advance her favourites.* |

At this point, I always ask a selection of students for their titles and some bullet points as well, just to verbally summarise ideas. Ensure you refer the class back to the words discussed in the earlier task too, checking whether inferences were correct and discussing whether the new information they have gained from the essay can be applied to vocabulary from Macbeth's speech describing Hecate.

## Strategies for struggling readers

Read Hecate's scene through once and discuss initial meaning. Ask students to think about how the Hecate of ancient Greek mythology mirrors the Hecate of Macbeth. If students are struggling, they could always complete the following activity, something I have found works particularly well in helping those who find Shakespeare's language incredibly challenging.

This method, first introduced to me by Emma Illiffe, can be applied to any area of the play, but works best with shorter extracts, a soliloquy or brief conversation. Asking students to complete this process for entire scenes will likely see them run into problems.

Provide students with a blank copy of Hecate's diatribe and provide them with the following instructions:

1. Read through the text independently and place a ? at the end of each line you do not understand. It does not matter if there is a ? at the end of every line.
2. Read the lines that have a ? next to them and circle one word which stands out for you. There are no right answers here. The word you circle may be one you understand or can say a lot about, or it may be the one piece of vocabulary which stops you from understanding the line.
3. Use the glossary I have provided you with to check your understanding of unfamiliar words.
4. Now break the text up into six parts as detailed below:
   **Part 1** – 'Have I not reason, beldams as you are'
               to 'In riddles and affairs of death'.
   **Part 2** – 'And I, the mistress of your charms'
               to 'Or show the glory of our art?'
   **Part 3** – 'And, which is worse, all you have done'
               to 'Will come, to know his destiny.'
   **Part 4** – 'Your vessels and your spells provide'
               to 'Great business must be wrought ere noon.'
   **Part 5** – 'Upon the corner of the moon'
               to 'Shall draw him on to his confusion.'
   **Part 6** – 'He shall spurn fate, scorn death, and bear'
               to the end.

5. Using your circled words and the glossary, focus on each section at a time and see if you can work out what Hecate is saying in each.
6. Find a partner and compare your ideas. Fill in any missing gaps you may have.
7. Now go through the speech again. Cross out any question marks next to lines you now understand. If there is still a question mark left, do not worry!

Go through each individual section as a class to break down Hecate's argument. Once meaning has been established for a line or section, reread it to help consolidate understanding. As per the instructions above, a glossary of words will be needed. Resource 13.5 demonstrates what I would expect a glossary for Hecate's speech to look like.[26]

## RESOURCE 13.5

### Glossary of words

**beldam**
A spiteful and bitter old woman

**Acheron**
The 'river of woe' in ancient Greek mythology believed to lead to the underworld

**contriver**
Someone who plans and schemes in secret

**sleights**
Tricks

**wayward**
Difficult to control or predict because of difficult behaviour

**spurn**
To reject

I am usually wary of providing students with a glossary when teaching Shakespeare, and if I do, I do so sparingly. I do not advocate for using a glossary and then moving on to the next activity without having explicitly taught the vocabulary in it. It is vital these words which students struggle with are taught, for they will not remember them long term if they are not.

## Answering the Big Question

Having looked at Hecate's speech and drawing on their knowledge from the 'Hecate in mythology' essay, ask students to respond to the Big Question.

---

26. Icons by Adrien Coquet, Gan Khoon Lay, Landan Lloyd, Vectors Point, Dong Ik Seo and Art Shop on The Noun Project.

**PART TWO:**

Introduce the lesson's 'Big Question':

*What are the perceptions of Macbeth amongst the Scottish nobility?*

## Recognising tyranny

As discussed in the 'What?' section, this is the first scene where Macbeth is labelled a 'tyrant'. It is important students get to grips with the concept of tyranny if they are to understand the political and social ramifications of Macbeth's further actions. This presents itself as an excellent opportunity to help students see how Shakespeare's stories are just as relevant today as when he was writing, for tyranny and authoritarianism are styles of leadership we have all come to recognise, whether we have experienced it first hand or through the media. With this in mind, I always start a lesson on Act III, Scene vi by showing my class Resource 13.6.[27]

## RESOURCE 13.6

Some of the pictures may need explaining, but gauge student understanding with the following questions:

1. Who are these people?
2. What do they have in common?

Through the ensuing discussion, try to tease out the idea that these are all people who have ruled through fear. Some students may use the word 'tyrant' in their description of these figures, but if not, introduce it as a way of referring

27. From left to right: Adolf Hitler (Bundesarchiv, Bild 183-H1216-0500-002/CC-BY-SA, licensed under the Creative Commons Attribution-Share Alike 3.0 Germany licence), Kim Jong-un (public domain), Benito Mussolini (public domain), Joseph Stalin (public domain).

to the people in the photos. This will allow your class to explore tyranny and how viable they think it is as a form of leadership. Whether you ask students to produce a written response or discuss with their partner, group or the class, useful questions that could be asked include:

1. Can tyrannical rule ever be seen as effective?
2. How could tyrannical rule be seen as ineffective?
3. How do you think people living under these tyrants would view them during their rule?
4. How do you think citizens who have outlived these tyrants view them looking back?
5. What legacy have these tyrants left?

## Niccolò Machiavelli's *The Prince*

Follow up this activity by introducing students to extracts from Niccolò Machiavelli's *The Prince*, a sixteenth century 'handbook' on how to maintain power. The ideas contained within it are frightful, controversial and shocking, yet as a stimulus for discussion it is an important text, particularly in one's study of *Macbeth*. I begin by showing my class the following quotation:

> *Is it better to be loved rather than feared, or vice versa? The answer is that **one would prefer to be both** but, since they don't go together easily, **if you have to choose**, it's much **safer to be feared** than loved.*[28]

There is so much to pick out here, but as with all quotation explosions, begin by asking the class what Machiavelli's observation means and then what it suggests. I then draw attention to the parts in bold, but give no other direction so I can see what my students say about them independently. We often discuss why a ruler would see benefit in being loved *and* feared, as well as the element of choice one has in how they rule. *Macbeth*, as I have said before, is a play about choices, causing us to consider whom we will choose to be and why. I also ask my class to consider the veracity of such a statement: do they think it is honest and truthful? Is it accurate? Is it safer to be feared than loved? We also consider omissions in Machiavelli's short statement. Are fear and love the only two qualities a ruler can have? Here, I introduce a second quotation to discuss:

---

28. Niccolò Machiavelli, *The Prince*, (London: Penguin Classics, 2011), p. 66.

*If a ruler wants to survive, he'll have to learn to stop being good.*[29]

The responses these quotations elicit are extremely interesting. After all, power is a fascinating notion to explore, and students will often apply their own historical knowledge to their answers when drawing on real world examples to back up a point.

## Silent debate

A silent debate is where students write their thoughts down in response to a question rather than verbally sharing them. I will often have five to six pieces of sugar paper on tables or on the walls around the classroom with a question on each. Students walk around the room and write a detailed response to the question on the paper before moving on to answer a new one. I encourage students to respond to comments already shared and to go back to questions they have already answered to see if they can argue back against any responses made to their original comment. It is a way of ensuring all students engage with the questions posed. Once the time for answering questions is over, I will group students, assign them to one of the questions and ask them to summarise people's thoughts before sharing verbally as a way of concluding the task. I always find statements, followed by 'to what extent do you agree?' work best for silent debate tasks. In this task, one could use a statement from *The Prince*. For example:

'If a ruler wants to survive, he'll have to learn to stop being good.' To what extent do you agree?

## Vocabulary

At this point, I would ask students to begin thinking about how these ideas link to Macbeth's character, querying how he has demonstrated similar qualities to the examples of real tyrants and the behaviour advocated for by Machiavelli in *The Prince*. Students are more likely to have heard the term 'tyrant' than 'Machiavellian', but both are examples of vocabulary students need to know in order to understand *Macbeth*. As such, the following resource uses 'Machiavellian' as the example, but could just as easily be adjusted for the term 'tyrant' as well. Ask students to complete the 'Thinking Hard' exercises in Resource 13.7 to help increase their understanding of the term.

---

29. Niccolò Machiavelli, *The Prince*, (London: Penguin Classics, 2011), p. 66.

## RESOURCE 13.7

| Vocabulary Check |
|---|
| **Revise the key vocabulary by completing the tasks.** |
| **Machiavellian (adjective)** cunning and scheming, especially in politics. |

| TASK ONE: READ IT | TASK TWO: TRANSFORM IT |
|---|---|
| Read about the etymology (where a word originates from) of 'Machiavellian'. | Transform the adjective 'Machiavellian' into an image to help you remember it. |
| *1570s, from Niccolò Machiavelli, a Florentine statesman and author of The Prince, a work which advised rulers to maintain power immorally.* | |

| TASK THREE: DEBATE IT |
|---|
| 'Machiavellian behaviour is the best way of getting what one wants.' To what extent do you agree? Answer in full sentences. |
| |

| TASK FOUR: USE IT | TASK FIVE: LINK IT |
|---|---|
| Can you use the following words in a sentence? *Machiavelli, Machiavellian* | Explain in full sentences how the adjective 'Machiavellian' links to *Macbeth*. Discuss characters and events in your explanation. |

The study of tyranny and Machiavellianism will put students in a strong position going into a reading of Act III, Scene vi, where Lennox's ironic and ambiguous retelling of events can often be confusing. It is important students understand that Lennox's use of equivocal language is necessary, serving as protection against the prying eyes of spies whose allegiance has been bought by Macbeth. Questions to ask when completing a first read could include:

1. According to Lennox, what are Macbeth's feelings about Duncan, Malcolm and Donalbain?
2. What have Fleance, Malcolm and Donalbain done which makes people believe they are guilty of parricide?
3. Where has Macduff gone and for what purpose?

To explore the scene in more detail and discuss the ambiguity of Lennox's words, a further two readings could take place. One reading, for example, could be completed with the mindset that Lennox is completely loyal to Macbeth. A second reading, for comparative purposes, would be completed with the mindset that Lennox is *against* Macbeth, scared of telling the outright, explicit truth for fear of discovery and punishment. Ask students why Lennox has to be careful with the language he uses. See if they can identify the moment where both characters trust one another enough to honestly share their views on Macbeth as a man blinded by his own ambition.

Activities students could complete on this scene include the following:

1. Summarise the conversation between Lennox and the lord in no more than fifty words.
2. Explain why Lennox uses so many rhetorical questions and what this suggests about his views on Macbeth.
3. Identify three examples of where Lennox and the lord allude to their dislike of Macbeth. Explain your choices.
4. Look back at Act II, Scene iv. Explain how its purpose is similar to that of Act III, Scene vi.

As always, refer back to the Big Question to conclude the lesson and take feedback from students to assess whether they can answer it.

## Suggested 'Extra Challenge' activities

- '*Macbeth* is a play about choice.' Discuss.
- 'Of all rulers, a man new to power simply cannot avoid a reputation for cruelty since a newly conquered state is a very dangerous place. Virgil put these words in Queen Dido's mouth: "The difficult situation and the newness of my kingdom/Force me to do these things, and guard my borders everywhere."'[30] How far do you agree that Macbeth has no choice *but* to act cruelly in order to maintain his grip on the crown?
- How would our understanding of the witches be different if Hecate did not appear?

## Key vocabulary:

Chthonic, hubris

---

30. Niccolò Machiavelli, *The Prince*, (London: Penguin Classics, 2011), p 65.

# ACT FOUR

# CHAPTER 14
## Act IV, Scene i

*What do the apparitions tell Macbeth?*

## What?

### Scene analysis: Act IV, Scene i

Act IV, Scene i brings with it, for the second time in the play, a clandestine meeting between Macbeth and the three weïrd sisters. This time, however, Macbeth believes that the meeting is on his own terms: he has told his wife he will revisit them because he is desperate to know what is coming next for him. Once more, Macbeth aims to achieve one thing – control over his life – but instead receives something very different. In this case, Macbeth is foolishly buoyed by what he hears, rather than being, as he ought to be, scared of what they say.

The scene opens with the witches, again appearing in the middle of a thunderstorm, who clearly are aware that Macbeth will soon join them. They add ingredients to a cauldron, according to a recipe they all know by heart. In many respects the setting of this scene acts as a contrast to the royal banquet in Act III, Scene iv as they prepare the meal – or potion – that will show Macbeth the apparitions. We are reminded, through this, that the witches are not able to deliver the comfort or salvation Macbeth is seemingly looking for. Their preoccupation is with evil, and we are reminded, though Macbeth has forgotten, that the three weïrd sisters are not to be trusted.

Not for the first time in the play, Shakespeare leans heavily on recognisable tropes, emphasising the disturbing behaviour and other-worldly nature of the witches. They acknowledge that the time is ready to prepare for Macbeth's arrival because of the signals they have been given by animals: the 'brinded cat' and the 'hedge-pig'. The third witch, however, knows it is time because of the cry of a 'harpier', which is perhaps her familiar – we did not learn of her familiar in Act I, Scene i. This could be a reference to the harpy, a mythical creature from Greek and Latin mythology which had a woman's head and body and the wings and ferociously sharp claws of a bird of prey.[1] Whilst 'harpy' can also be an insult used to refer to an unpleasant woman, if we consider that Shakespeare is making an allusion to Greek and Latin mythology, he is perhaps further reminding the audience that the witches are able to transcend the natural world in their abilities and actions.

The witches move round a 'cauldron', and whilst today this is a symbol strongly associated with witchcraft, at the time it would have been a more commonplace cooking vessel in many households.[2] Throughout the opening of this scene, there is a continued combination of the regular and the supernatural, beginning with the cauldron. Some of the ingredients, whilst odd to use in cooking, are at least familiar to an audience. Others are more unknown and seem more exotic. Yet others have clearly been obtained by more barbaric means. This is perhaps suggestive of the fine line between normalcy and witchcraft: a warning that witchcraft surrounds the audience and that they must be on their guard against it.

### 'FIRE BURN AND CAULDRON BUBBLE'

The first ingredient to be added to the pot is a toad. Whilst this is what we might imagine as a typical ingredient for a witch's potion, there is more significance in Shakespeare's inclusion of the toad here. In 1591 a witchcraft pamphlet was published: *Newes From Scotland*. The pamphlet reported on the North Berwick witch trials in Scotland, and the confessions given by a range of 'witches' for their actions against James I. One of these women, Agnes Sampson, admitted to having collected poison from a black toad in order to place it on clothing owned by the King and subsequently kill him. So affected was he by this apparent plot, and given that she was one of the women accused of attempting to shipwreck him on his return from Denmark with his new wife, James I included the story of Agnes Sampson in *Daemonologie*.[3]

Once the poisonous toad has been added to the pot, the audience hears the now infamous refrain for the first time:

> *Double, double, toil and trouble;*
> *Fire burn, and cauldron bubble.*

---

1.  Jenny March, *Dictionary of Classical Mythology*, (Oxford: Oxbow Books, 2014), p. 214.

2.  Diane Purkiss, *The Witch in History: Early modern and twentieth-century representations*, (London: Routledge, 2005), p. 212.

3.  King James I, *Daemonologie*, http://www.gutenberg.org/files/25929/25929-pdf.pdf.

These lines, of course, have a major significance in the play, and the fact that Shakespeare has the witches repeat them not only emphasises to the audience the spell-like way in which they speak, but arguably that these words also form part of their prophetic language. Macbeth has a variety of problems in his life. His troubles, too, are doubled, just as the witches suggest here: Macbeth's actions and reign have often been 'doubled': his behaviour is duplicitous – he 'looks like the innocent flower' but behaves as if he is 'the serpent under't'. His mistakes with Duncan's murder mean that two murderers end up visiting the chamber, carrying with them two daggers. The two guards are killed. There are two scapegoats, Malcolm and Donalbain, who flee in two directions. The murders of Banquo and Fleance are intended to be a double murder, though, of course, Fleance escapes. Macbeth, in Act V, will face two armies: the Scots and the English. These moments of 'two-ness' are often to the disadvantage of Macbeth; contributing factors in his progressive downfall.[4]

### 'FILLET OF A FENNY SNAKE'

The next list of ingredients from the witches, including 'fenny snake', 'eye of newt' and 'howlet's wing', are all examples once again of nature being used in a deeply unnatural way. It is a further dismantling of the Great Chain of Being: these animals all belong in their own positions in nature, and here their roles are being subverted, being used for supernatural ends and becoming unnatural as a result. These animals are used in a similar way to Macbeth himself. He has been removed from his position in the Great Chain of Being by the witches, manipulated and used for the witches' own entertainment. It is almost as if Shakespeare is warning the audience how easily things that are part of nature can be manipulated and distorted for one's own gain: the audience must guard against a similar fate.

### 'SCALE OF DRAGON, TOOTH OF WOLF'

The third list of ingredients, however, beginning with 'scale of dragon', initially takes a step away from reality and, instead, the third witch calls upon mythical beings and creatures to be added to the pot. The inclusion of these mythical ingredients further demonstrates that the witches are able to transcend nature.

The inclusion of the '[w]itch's mummy' is particularly interesting, and is worth some specific consideration. This is, indeed, the use of powdered, mummified remains. The process of mummification was one with which the Elizabethans were familiar, with it being common practice to place a

---

4.    Marian Gleason, 'As We Three Meet Again', *The English Journal*, Vol. 56, No. 7 (October 1967), pp. 1005–1006, https://www.jstor.org/stable/812642.

mummified cat in the walls of fifteenth and sixteenth century homes with the belief that this would deter mice.[5] The 'mummy' here, though, is likely to be human remains. Mummified flesh had been used as a type of medicine since the start of the reign of Elizabeth I to treat conditions such as gout. The ingredients included 'an arthritic powder composed of scrapings of an unburied human skull, herbs, white wine.'[6] James I, however, was against the use of 'corpse medicine' as it was known in all forms, and even when he was diagnosed with gout, the doctors changed the recipe to include the skull of an ox because 'the king hates eating human bodies.'[7]

The Witchcraft Act of 1604 made it an offence to use human bodies for witchcraft. The Act stated that:

> *If any person… take up any dead man, woman, or child, out of his, her, or their grave, or any other place where the dead body resteth… in any manner of Witchcraft, Sorcery, Charme, or Inchantment… [they] shall suffer paines of death as a Felon.*[8]

This is therefore another indicator to a contemporary audience of the fear they should hold for the witches and the horrifying crimes they have committed. The witches, who acted as a catalyst for Macbeth's murder of the King, are shown once more – to the watching James I – to be heretical and capable of leading men into dire circumstances. Shakespeare reminds a contemporary audience here, once again, that no good can come of dealing with witchcraft, just as the audience sees with regard to Macbeth's encroaching demise.

James I's preoccupation with witchcraft's use of mummified human flesh did not just extend to the 1604 Witchcraft Act, but also appears in *Daemonologie*. Here, the use of mummified remains moves from following the medicinal beliefs of doctors during Elizabeth's reign and instead becomes specifically related to evil: the Devil, writes King James, 'causeth [witches] to joynt dead corpses, and to make powders thereof.'[9] Shakespeare is also alluding here to the fact that the witches do not act of their own accord; nor have they been

5.  Desmond Morris, *Fantastic Cats: A Feast of Famed and Fabled Felines*, (St. Albans: Little Books Ltd, 2007), p. 36.

6.  Richard Sugg, *Mummies, Cannibals and Vampires: The History of Corpse Medicine from the Renaissance to the Victorians,* (London: Routledge, 2011), p. 50.

7.  Ibid.

8.  The Statutes Project, '1604: 1 James 1 c.12: An Act against Witchcraft', http://statutes.org.uk/site/the-statutes/seventeenth-century/1604-1-james-1-c-12-an-act-against-witchcraft/.

9.  King James I, *Daemonologie*, http://www.gutenberg.org/files/25929/25929-pdf.pdf.

guided by Hecate. Instead, by using the 'mummy' he is demonstrating the close relationship between the witches and the Devil himself.

The 'hemlock', a poisonous plant, was 'digged i'th' dark', emphasising the link between the witches and the metaphorical and literal darkness of the play and the witches' actions. Hemlock, alongside similarly poisonous plants such as mandrake, monkshood and belladonna, were again stereotypical ingredients for witches' potions. It perhaps indicates, when it is fed to Macbeth, that he is metaphorically poisoned in a number of ways. Though he largely chooses to ignore the information he is given, the witches' final prophecies doom him, finally, to his ultimate downfall. Not only this, but the knowledge Macbeth gains is poisonous in itself: having heard the prophecy from them that he must 'Beware Macduff; / Beware the Thane of Fife', he chooses to have everyone dwelling in his castle murdered. This spurs Malcolm on to return to Scotland with an English army and depose the tyrant, and drives Macduff to commit his final act of the play: a technical regicide, to avenge the deaths of his family.

### 'MAKE THE GRUEL THICK AND SLAB'

This speech also brings with it a series of 'ingredients' that are often very difficult to understand and explain today. The witches call for the inclusion in their potion of 'liver of blaspheming Jew', 'Nose of Turk', 'Tartar's lips' and 'finger of birth strangled babe'. All four, writes Lois Leveen, are 'cast as dangerously magical outsiders because they don't fit with normative Christian identity.'[10] Contemporary belief dictated that, because these groups of people were not baptised, they were not protected by a Christian God against evil.

This moment in the speech moves the witches on in their ability to enact evil. We have heard of some of the heinous things they have done, but it is Macbeth whom we see 'metamorphose from the human to the monstrous.'[11] However, Act IV, Scene i, and in particular the fact that these ingredients are parts of humans, shifts the audience's understanding of the witches further towards the evil and brutality of which they are capable.

If we take each 'ingredient' in turn, there is much modern questioning of Shakespeare's 'moral obtuseness in connection with the religious and racial prejudices of his time.'[12] For a long time in England, Jewish people had been

---

10. Lois Leveen, 'A Historical Look at Jews in the Works of Shakespeare,' https://www.jewishbookcouncil.org/pb-daily/shakespeare-shmakespeare-jews-and-the-bard.

11. Madhubrata, 'Liver of Blaspheming Jew: Visions of the Other in Shakespeare's Macbeth', https://medium.com/@bengali_beat/liver-of-blaspheming-jew-visions-of-the-other-in-shakespeares-macbeth-44273ba4f455.

12. Martin D. Yaffe, 'Reviewed Work: *Shakespeare and the Jews* by James Shapiro', *AJS Review*, Vol. 23, No. 2 (1998), pp. 235–244, https://www.jstor.org/stable/1486908.

subject to an appalling legacy of treatment, arguably from as far back as 1290, when they were expelled from England by Edward II.[13] They were not readmitted until the reign of Cromwell, and even then it was not until the 'Jew Bill' in 1753 that naturalised Jewish people could become English citizens.[14] James Shapiro explores the possibility that the preoccupation with Jewish people as being 'other' than the English citizens of the time is partially ascribable to 'not merely decorating the recently formed social bond connecting all Englishmen, but helping to cement it.'[15] The 'otherness' of Jewish people with specific regard to *Macbeth* is focused upon the fact that they are 'denied the divinity of Christ' because of the fact they are not protected by baptism.[16]

The 'Nose of Turk' and 'Tartar's lips' demonstrate contemporary fear not only of those who are religiously 'different' but also of those who are of different races or nationalities and therefore considered as 'other'. For a modern audience, this is often seen as grotesque, and not just because of the fact that the witches are using their 'nose' and 'lips'. Students are often surprised by the cultural insensitivity of this: the fact that these people who have become mere 'ingredients' in the witches' potion have been persecuted – not just in this moment of the play but in wider Elizabethan and Jacobean society, as well as during the time periods stretching far before, and far after, this moment of the play.

The same is true for the 'finger of birth strangled babe'. This baby, born to a prostitute ('drab') has been killed at birth and therefore will not have been baptised. It is also considered 'other'. The baby represents absolute innocence, and its death is perhaps an indicator of the elimination of innocence in the form of the murder of Macduff's children in Act IV, Scene ii. It is also evocative of the fact that Lady Macbeth, whose actions and behaviour are often closely associated with the witches, has said that she would 'dash the brains out' of her own child.

### 'AND NOW ABOUT THE CAULDRON SING'

As with Act III, Scene v, it is very likely that Hecate's appearance was inserted before the publication of the First Folio and is often therefore not considered to

13. British Library, 'Expulsion of Jews from England, 1290', https://www.bl.uk/learning/timeline/item103483.html.

14. Avinoam Yuval-Naeh, 'The 1753 Jewish Naturalization Bill and the Polemic over Credit', (Published online by Cambridge University Press: 29 June 2018), https://doi.org/10.1017/jbr.2018.82.

15. Martin D. Yaffe, 'Reviewed Work: *Shakespeare and the Jews* by James Shapiro', *AJS Review*, Vol. 23, No. 2 (1998), pp. 235–244, https://www.jstor.org/stable/1486908.

16. Sandra Clark and Pamela Mason, *The Arden Shakespeare: Macbeth*, (London: Bloomsbury, 2015), p. 236.

have been the work of Shakespeare. There is some belief that these lines, like Act III, Scene v, were written by Thomas Middleton when he revived the play.[17]

However, if we for a moment ignore the incongruities of this passage, it seems here that the witches' actions have redeemed them in the light of Hecate's earlier anger towards them: 'O, well done. I commend your pains,' she says. However, the fact that 'everyone shall share i'th' gains' might also suggest that their efforts in retrieving the various ingredients and making this potion have not just been for their own benefit but also for the benefit of Hecate and the three other witches she seems to have arrived alongside. Perhaps their efforts have been more of a punishment for acting without permission – victory for their hard work will not be theirs to claim.

### 'BY THE PRICKING OF MY THUMBS, SOMETHING WICKED THIS WAY COMES'

Macbeth's arrival is heralded with the lines 'By the pricking of my thumbs, / Something wicked this way comes.' The fact that it is a witch who feels the sensation that represented a superstition associated with approaching evil and a sense of foreboding is demonstrative of the fact that Macbeth has been truly debased by his crimes.[18] The witches' ability to foresee Macbeth's arrival is nothing new.

Macbeth has also, because of his appalling actions in destroying the will of nature, lost his humanity: his arrival is not heralded using his name ('Macbeth doth come'), but instead he is called 'Something' – not his name, or the man or warrior that he had previously been. The metaphorical door is open to him ('Open locks, / Whoever knocks'), and his final meeting with the witches begins. Could Macbeth's 'knocking' here in order to find out his fate echo Macduff's knocking on the castle gates earlier in the play? Macduff brings Macbeth's destiny to his door, but so too do the witches' apparitions.

### 'HOW NOW, YOU SECRET, BLACK AND MIDNIGHT HAGS?'

The Macbeth who arrives, however, is different from the one who arrived in Act I, Scene iii. Gone is his curiosity: he now has a hunger – almost to the point of greed – for information about what is coming for him next. He is desperate in his search for answers and for closure on his circumstances, even if he does still consider them part of the wider semantic field of darkness, describing them as 'secret, black and midnight hags'.

---

17. British Library, 'First edition of Middleton's *The Witch*', https://www.bl.uk/collection-items/first-edition-of-middletons-the-witch.

18. Sandra Clark and Pamela Mason, *The Arden Shakespeare: Macbeth*, (London: Bloomsbury, 2015), p. 237.

Macbeth once more relies on the imperative verbs he used in his previous interaction, imploring them to 'answer [him]'. Shakespeare's suggestion, perhaps, is that Macbeth continues to feel he is able to challenge and overpower the witches despite them holding the knowledge he so desperately craves – and he wishes to have that knowledge at the ruin of the rest of the world.

Macbeth's acceptance of devastation ('untie the winds and let them fight / Against the churches') in return for the answers to his questions extends to accepting 'castles [toppling] on their warders' heads'. However, there is a sense of bitter, proleptic irony here as the destruction Macbeth is willing to entertain, 'Even till destruction sicken', in order to hear his fate is, in itself, the very destruction that will eventually befall him. His castle will be stormed and his own crown removed. Subconsciously, in visiting the witches and through this speech, Macbeth foreshadows his own downfall and ultimate demise.

Macbeth here believes he can reason his way to an answer: he invites the destruction if it means he can gain the knowledge he so desperately craves. He relies upon reason and logic to gain access to powerful information, pleading with them to: 'answer [him] / To what [he] asks [them].' The witches, however, represent more of the Ancient Greek idea of the Fates. In Greek mythology, their role was to ensure that the fate of a person was allowed to play out, unimpeded. Their role was also to determine 'human destinies, and in particular... his allotment of misery and suffering.'[19] Because the witches know his fate, they are able to 'play' with him: regardless of whether they tell him or not, or how the news is delivered, they know that his fate is inevitable. Therefore, when they ask him if he would rather 'hear it from [their] mouths, / Or from [their] masters?' they know the outcome will be exactly the same. Macbeth calls for the 'masters' – he wants to see a physical manifestation of the Fates and therefore his future: he wants the hard evidence of what will befall him.

## THE APPARITIONS

Not for the first time, Macbeth in Act IV, Scene i is faced with apparitions, though these are of an altogether different kind from those that have gone before – namely the dagger pointing him to Duncan's bedchamber and the ghost of Banquo, returned from the dead to haunt him. Here, the apparitions are unequivocally conjured by the witches to further prophesise for Macbeth his future. Despite this, there are still similarities between these visions. All of them point the 'way' for Macbeth to an action in his future. The dagger points him to his murder of the King. Banquo's ghost points him back to the witches

---

19. Encyclopedia Britannica, 'Fate', https://www.britannica.com/topic/Fate-Greek-and-Roman-mythology.

and, finally, the apparitions in this scene point Macbeth towards the murder of Macduff's family and, ultimately, his demise.

Arguably, the dagger and Banquo's ghost could have been – and indeed Macbeth argues for them having been – images produced by his 'heat-oppressed brain'. However, the apparitions of Act IV, Scene i are clearly conjured by the witches themselves. This calls into question the previous apparitions, making it seem more likely that these, too, could well have been the work of the witches.

The first apparition, 'an armed head', could represent one of several things. It is often considered to be Macbeth's own head, foreshadowing his own death and decapitation at the hands of Macduff. The audience knows that Macbeth has been a warrior, and so the armour worn by the head correlates with this interpretation, especially when one considers that Macbeth declares in Act V, Scene v that he will 'die with harness on [his] back.' John Upton argues that 'the armed head represents symbolically Macbeth's head cut off and brought to Malcolm by Macduff.'[20] However this interpretation is, as A.W. Crawford argues, 'entirely conjectural'.[21] When we consider Upton's thoughts in relation to the second and third apparitions, it is apparent that we could well arrive at a different conclusion. It is, however, our understanding of the second and third apparitions which influences our final interpretation of this first one.

The second and third apparitions are demonstrative of something to fear in Macbeth's future. Therefore, it would stand to reason that the first apparition should also represent something Macbeth fears: 'It was Macbeth's ambition, as we shall see later, not only to gain the crown for himself, but also to pass it on to his descendants. His fears, then, were not more for his life than for his crown.'[22]

If the second and third apparitions are analogous with this fear, it stands to reason that the first apparition must also be linked to this. The person who causes Macbeth to lose his crown is, of course, Macduff, who defeats him in battle and executes him. Therefore, this 'armed head' most likely represents Macduff himself, coming to threaten Macbeth's crown.[23]

This correlates with the words the first apparition has to share with Macbeth: 'Beware Macduff, / Beware the Thane of Fife' and also with Macbeth's response to it, in which he tells the witches that the apparition has 'harped [his] fear'. In other words, it has expressed the precise fear Macbeth has – in this case, about Macduff's lack of loyalty to him.

---

20.  John Upton, *Critical Observations on Shakespeare*, (London: G. Hawkins, 1748), p. 53.

21.  A.W. Crawford, 'The Apparitions in Macbeth', *Modern Language Notes*, Vol. 39, No. 6 (June 1924), pp. 345–350, https://www.jstor.org/stable/2914653.

22.  Ibid.

23.  Ibid.

In appearance, the second apparition of the 'bloody child' resonates in a number of ways. It evokes the audience's memory of the attempted murder of Fleance. It will shortly suggest the brutal slaughter of Macduff's son. It perhaps can even be associated with Lady Macbeth's statement in Act I, Scene vii when she stated that she would have 'dashed the brains out' of her own child. However, the most compelling interpretation of this apparition, again when we consider the words it speaks ('none of woman born / Shall harm Macbeth'), is that it represents Macduff, as a child who was 'from his mother's womb / Untimely ripped.' This is certainly borne out in Holinshed's *Chronicles*. Macbeth is told by the witches that 'he should never be slaine with man borne of anie woman.'[24] In Act V, Macduff reveals himself as the root of this apparition, and thus the conclusion that this bloody child represents Macduff can be drawn.

It is at this point that Macbeth makes a fatal mistake. Despite being told that he must 'beware Macduff', this second apparition's message – that 'none of woman born / Shall harm Macbeth' – fills him with an unwarranted sense of bravery and machismo: 'Then live, Macduff: what need I fear of thee?' We know that Macbeth's hamartia is his unchecked ambition, but secondary to this, it could be argued, is his inability to see the truth that is in front of him. Perhaps these two aspects of his character are intertwined: he cannot, or will not, see the truth because he is so distracted and obsessed by his ambition for a successful reign that he is metaphorically blind to the reality of his situation. Macbeth ultimately decides, though, to murder Macduff as an insurance against the second apparition's promises, declaring 'thou shalt not live'.

The third apparition, 'a child crowned, with a tree in his hand', further facilitates the explanation that these apparitions are representative of Macbeth's deepest fears. Malcolm is the direct fulfilment of this prophecy when he later commands the troops to hew down the branches of trees in Birnam Wood and hold them in front of them. Macbeth's misplaced confidence is apparent here again, as he immediately chooses to decide that no one 'can impress the forest, bid the tree / Unfix his earth-bound root'.

Despite the level of information and new warnings given to Macbeth by the three witches via the apparitions, it is telling of Macbeth's level of panic and paranoia at this point that his curiosity is not sated by what he has heard. The prophecies from the apparitions so far have focused on those who pose the biggest immediate threat to his crown: Macduff and Malcolm. However, it quickly becomes clear that thoughts of the future of Banquo's children and

---

24. Raphael Holinshed, *Chronicles of England, Scotland and Ireland*, (London: J. Johnson et. al., 1808), https://www.troup.org/userfiles/929/My%20Files/ELA/HS%20 ELA/12th%20ELA/Unit%202/Holinshed%20and%20Macbeth.pdf?id=11638.

their own claim to the crown have been plaguing Macbeth since Act III, Scene iv, and there is one more thing he craves to know: whether Banquo's prophecy will come true and his descendants will hold the crown of Scotland.

The fourth and final apparition the witches offer Macbeth comes as a direct response to his final question: 'Shall Banquo's issue ever reign in this kingdom?' He is warned and almost teased by the witches – 'Seek to know no more' – but his curiosity is not to be abated, and with some considerable irony Macbeth threatens to 'curse' the witches themselves: an indication that, despite everything that has gone before, Macbeth still feels that he is in a position of authority against these dark and supernatural beings.

The vision is heralded by '[h]autboys'. Hautboys were a predecessor of the modern oboe: a double-reeded wind instrument. The sound of an oboe is often described as being quite mournful, and indeed the Arden Shakespeare draws comparison between the use of hautboys here and the use of the same instrument in *Antony and Cleopatra*. In that play, at the moment at which Antony is abandoned by the god Hercules, hautboys play below the stage to signify the underworld and the ominous atmosphere of the moment.[25] In *Macbeth* hautboys are again used to create an ominous tone, and it is no different here in Act IV, Scene i as the fact that Macbeth's reign is doomed finally becomes apparent to him.

### 'EIGHT GHOSTLY KINGS'

This fourth apparition is the only one for which no evidence exists in Holinshed's *Chronicles*, and is therefore apparently of Shakespeare's own invention.[26] The eight ghostly kings followed by the Ghost of Banquo secure for Macbeth that his worst fears will be realised: he really does hold in his hand a 'barren sceptre' and wears on his head a 'fruitless crown'. All his crimes, including his original act of regicide, have been for nothing, because whilst he has the crown for himself now, this is where his lineage stops. Its appearance brings to the audience a new understanding of the depth and extent of Macbeth's ambition for his family to hold the crown for years to come: 'All four apparitions… by prophesying symbolically the loss of Macbeth's crown and the defeat of his ambition to found a line of kings, develop very dramatically the true tragic nature of Macbeth's great passion.'[27]

---

25. Sandra Clark and Pamela Mason, *The Arden Shakespeare: Macbeth*, (London: Bloomsbury, 2015), p. 243.

26. A.W. Crawford, 'The Apparitions in Macbeth, Part II', *Modern Language Notes*, Vol. 39, No. 7 (November 1924), pp. 383–388, https://www.jstor.org/stable/pdf/2914760.

27. Ibid.

There is perhaps a further significance in the inclusion of this fourth apparition. In Holinshed's *Chronicles*, Banquo is painted as Macbeth's accomplice for his various plots and crimes, including the murder of King Duncan. Holinshed portrays Banquo as a catalyst in Macbeth's decision to kill the King, telling him that he 'hast obteined those things which the two former sisters prophesied, there remaineth onelie for thée to purchase'.[28] Macbeth is also reported as having shared with Banquo all of his plans in the run-up to the regicide: he explained 'his purposed intent with his trustie friends, amongst whome Banquho was the chiefest,'[29] before killing the King.

Shakespeare's presentation of Banquo, however, is at odds with these reports. He is a foil to Macbeth, standing for the moral good and in the literal light whilst Macbeth occupies darkness and represents a range of evil sins.

Whilst this departure from the historical text adds an additional element of tension and dramatic conflict to the play, it is possible that Shakespeare made these changes particularly to court favour from James I. The historic figure of Banquo was believed, at the time, to be an ancestor of James I himself. King James accepted 'the lineage as true history rather than legend or myth',[30] and indeed a genealogy prepared by a sixteenth century historian suggested a lineage beginning with Banquo, moving through a succession of eight kings and ending with King James VI of Scotland.[31]

### 'TWO-FOLD BALLS AND TREBLE SCEPTRES CARRY'

This is further supported by Macbeth's comment that the 'glass' shows him more kings, some of whom 'twofold balls and treble sceptres carry.' It was tradition in the coronation of Scottish kings that, as part of the ceremony, they would be given a gold orb and a sceptre representing the Scottish nation. English kings and queens in the equivalent coronation ceremony would be given a golden orb and two sceptres, representing the crown of England and the claim to the throne of France.[32] King James was crowned twice, first in Scotland and then, 36 years later, in England, as he formally united the crowns of the nations for the first time.[33]

28. Raphael Holinshed, *Chronicles of England, Scotland and Ireland*, (London: J. Johnson et. al., 1808), https://www.troup.org/userfiles/929/My%20Files/ELA/HS%20 ELA/12th%20ELA/Unit%202/Holinshed%20and%20Macbeth.pdf?id=11638.

29. Ibid.

30. Faith Nostbakken, *Understanding Macbeth: A Student Casebook to Issues, Sources, and Historical Documents*, (London: Greenwood Press, 1997), p. 28.

31. Ibid.

32. Shakespeare Navigators, 'Note to Macbeth, Act 4, Scene 1, line 121', https://shakespeare-navigators.com/macbeth/Macbeth_Note_4_1_121.html.

33. Kenneth Muir, *Shakespeare Survey 32: The Middle Comedies*, (Cambridge: Cambridge University Press, 2002), p. 245.

Shakespeare's inclusion of the last of the eight ghostly kings holding a 'glass' is interesting, too. There are two generally held interpretations of this, the first of which supports Shakespeare's repurposing of Banquo's character. The 'glass' could be a mirror, reflecting James I's image back to himself and thereby solidifying his position as the descendant of Banquo – he himself being the 'many more' Macbeth refers to. It ties the apparition back to the witches, too, who do have the skill of prophecy, reminding both Macbeth and the audience of the supernatural soliciting that brought about many of the events of the play.

The apparition ends with Banquo, who walks behind the last of the eight kings with his hair 'blood-boltered' (matted with blood). This gruesome image not only reminds Macbeth of the terrible crime he committed against his closest friend but also that his murder did not stop Macbeth's greatest fear coming true. Banquo's ghost 'smiles upon [Macbeth] / And points at them for his.' The ghost almost mocks Macbeth as he reaffirms that these ghostly kings are his own lineage.

### MACBETH'S NEXT PLAN

Macbeth, dumbfounded by what he has seen, is mute as the witches perform a dance and vanish, but Lennox immediately arrives. He has, of course, come to tell Macbeth that there is word that Macduff has fled to England, and therefore to Malcolm who is in self-imposed exile there. This seemingly contradicts the conversation Lennox has with a lord in the previous scene, where it is implied that Macduff's whereabouts are already known to Macbeth. There are some temporal inconsistencies regarding the timeline here that remain unexplained.

What is clear, however, is that in the moments Macbeth spent with the witches, the world has already moved on and he seems to be almost exhausted by the pace his crimes must take: 'The flighty purpose never is o'ertook / Unless the deed go with it.' A decision is brewing for Macbeth here – he decides that if he is to succeed he must act immediately and not dwell on actions or their consequences. His first, burgeoning thoughts on a topic must now lead to immediate action if he is to prosper – the 'firstlings of [his] heart shall be / The firstlings of [his] hand.'

These are the actions of a panicked man who, despite what he has heard from the witches, remains steadfastly determined to continue his reign and fulfil his ambitions. His immediate decision now, then, having heard that Macduff has fled to England, is a kneejerk one: his idea is to 'give to th'edge o'th' sword / His wife, his babes and all unfortunate souls'. He will talk about it no further in case his 'purpose cool[s]', and it is this close of the scene that leads to arguably the most heartbreaking moment of the play, with the senseless murder of Macduff's innocent wife and children.

## The role of children in *Macbeth*

We would usually associate a child as symbolic of innocence and purity, and whilst there are elements of this in Shakespeare's play, the role of children is far more nuanced and ambiguous. For Banquo, children promise opportunity, a future of ascension and holy eminence. For Macduff, children offer family and the intimate bond shared by kin. For Macbeth, however, children represent something very different. In the absence of progeny, children act as a reminder of what he does not have: an heir to whom to pass on his crown. Other people's children, then, represent a threat; they linger on the periphery of the action and threaten to take what Macbeth sees as rightfully his.

The witches are the first to allude to Macbeth as remaining childless. In Act I, Scene iii they overtly proclaim Banquo 'shalt get kings' although Banquo himself will not be crowned; perhaps this is what renders him 'Not so happy, yet much happier'. He will not be consumed by the obsessive and compulsive behaviour exhibited by Macbeth, because he has not been promised royalty, yet he will be 'father to a line of kings', which ultimately demonstrates from the beginning that there are far more precious things to gain than the crown: the establishment of descendancy. Audiences understand very quickly that Macbeth desires power above all, and whilst being king will give him that, he ironically remains powerless because he has no heir, highlighting the instability of the line of succession and Macbeth's vulnerable rule over Scotland.

Children's status as something to be feared does not fully come to fruition until Macbeth is crowned king. Indeed, in Act I the role of children is associated with obedience and innocence; upon receiving praise from Duncan for his bravery in Scotland's fight against Norway, Macbeth metaphorically adopts the role of the child, replying 'Your highness' part / Is to receive our duties; and our duties / Are to your throne and state, children and servants'. In referring to himself as a child of Duncan's 'throne and state', he acknowledges his role is to obediently carry out what is required of him whilst Duncan, in return, will care for his people like a father cares for his offspring.

This idea of obedience and innocence is further explored in Macbeth as a child-like figure. Lady Macbeth, for example, tends to adopt the role of Macbeth's mother more than his wife at certain points throughout the play, and Macbeth obediently follows her commands, despite minor attempts on his part to seize control of the situation. It could be argued that even the witches act as mother figures for the child within Macbeth that needs affirmation and validation. Although they do not necessarily instruct him in the way Lady Macbeth does, he still seeks them out like a child seeking out a mother for the one thing all children need: help.

Even Lady Macbeth sees children as allegorical of innocence. When chiding Macbeth for his lack of courage in seeing through their murderous plans, she openly admits she would have 'dashed the brains out' of a child suckling at her breast 'while it was smiling in [her] face' had she promised to do so. It is a gruesome image framed by the symbolic innocence she threatens to destroy; Lady Macbeth understands purity cannot exist if one is to get what they want, and so, to her, a necessary sacrifice must be made.

This moment provides an interesting turning point for how children are represented. If in Act I children are reminiscent of innocence, this scene also shows how, for the Macbeths, children will come to symbolise loss. There is a strong possibility that Lady Macbeth was a mother before the action of the play begins, yet this is the only moment where she alludes to maternal duties. The child, whoever they were, is no more. As a result, children signify absence: absence of parental responsibility and absence of lineage. This loss of something physical transmutes for Macbeth into loss of power. If he cannot father another child, he will not have a successor of his own flesh and blood, a situation which emasculates him, especially when compared to Banquo.

This lack of succession is what haunts Macbeth, and it only intensifies when he is finally crowned king. He denounces and decries the 'unlineal hand' which threatens to wrench his power from him, thinking perhaps of the relative 'ease' in which *his* 'unlineal hand' took power from Duncan. Macbeth in this situation is a child, stealing from his father, his king. Macbeth's crown will remain 'fruitless', his line of succession barren, a fact which eats away at him and causes an onslaught of violence unleashed on his command. 'For Banquo's issue have I filed my mind,' he says. Children are the source of the anguish raging within him; they must be eliminated.

This, however, presents Macbeth with a dilemma, for it is at this point that audiences realise that children embody the very words the witches spoke at the beginning of the play: 'Fair is foul, and foul is fair.' Children are 'foul' to Macbeth because of the threat they pose, yet 'fair' in the sense that Macbeth needs them in order to establish a royal line that will secure power in his family for generations to come. It is an interesting paradox highlighting how Macbeth must overcome his fear if he is to get what he wants. Fear in the play, however, is an extremely powerful force, one which dictates Macbeth's actions and leads him to further bloodshed.

Macbeth's willingness to commit infanticide is beyond horrendous, but his solution to obliterating the threat posed by Fleance, and later Macduff and his children, is not entirely new. In fact, it roots itself in the New Testament, with Macbeth's killing of children analogous to Herod's 'Massacre of the Innocents' as described in Matthew 2:16–18. The passage details how Herod, fearful of the Christ-child prophesied as the 'King of the Jews', ordered the execution of all male children aged two and under in the regions around Bethlehem. Both Macbeth and Herod justify the slaughter of innocent children 'in a vain and futile attempt to preserve kingships threatened by prophecies.'[34] One may wonder, then, why Shakespeare has made this connection. Herod's legacy is one tainted by cruelty; a similar legacy awaits Macbeth.

With Malcolm and Donalbain in England and Ireland respectively, Macbeth cannot get to them. Fleance also escapes his attempted murder, and so Macbeth is rendered somewhat impotent in his actions. His only passage of recourse is to chide and denounce them linguistically by suggesting that Malcolm and Donalbain are guilty of their father's murder. Their act of fleeing, as revealed by Lennox in Act III, Scene vi, is suggestive of the fact that Macbeth has turned to the next best thing he can do, that is, to try to destroy their lineage and any right to the throne they had left through a war of words. They are children, they are threatening, but he cannot get to them, and this frustrates him beyond measure as he cannot clearly put an end to the threat they pose.

Perhaps the most striking image of a child is that of the second apparition, summoned by the witches in Act IV, Scene i. The 'bloody child' appears to Macbeth, and whilst its words clarify for an audience that it likely represents Macduff, its appearance alone is a physical manifestation of Macbeth's fears: a nightmarish and twisted image of lost innocence, called upon to deliberately frighten him. It could be argued that by fusing the images of blood and children together, Shakespeare is cleverly foreshadowing the infanticide which will occur at the hands of this tyrant. Important to note is the fact that both Macbeth and Lady Macbeth have spent the play calling upon darkness, not just so that others cannot see their evil deeds, but so that they themselves cannot see them either, in the vain attempt they may feign innocence and remain ignorant of their terrible actions. By being forced to look upon an image of a 'bloody child', Macbeth has failed and can now see the consequences of the violence he advocates in order to secure his position on the throne.

Perhaps of greater significance is the fact that here Macbeth is presented with a manifestation of Lady Macbeth's earlier words to him: 'I would, while it was smiling in my face, / Have... dashed the brains out'. Arguably, the image of the 'bloody child' alludes to this moment. Notably, both instances cause Macbeth to commit violence.

Ultimately, though, children come to represent hope in the play. Although order is restored when Malcolm is proclaimed king during the closing lines of *Macbeth*, it must be remembered that Fleance is still out there, the key to making Banquo's prophecy a reality, the only prophecy we do not see fulfilled in the play. If Banquo's progeny are anything like him, we know they will be

---

34. Chris R Hassel, '"No Boasting like a Fool?" Macbeth and Herod', *Studies in Philology*, Vol. 98, No. 2 (2001), pp. 205–224, www.jstor.org/stable/4174697.

kingly. Children in the play are seen as threatening and are wiped out as a result, but in Fleance, the sole surviving child character in *Macbeth*, a brighter future is finally seen as a realistic possibility.

## The fourth apparition at a glance

## RESOURCE 14.1

Represents Macbeth's 'fruitless crown' and 'barren sceptre' – Banquo's lineage has taken the throne.

Refers to the fact they are all wearing crowns.

Representative of the crown of Scotland (one orb and sceptre) and the crown of England/claim to crown of France (one orb and two sceptres). Represents James I bringing the crowns together.

Hair matted with blood reminds Macbeth that his brutal murder of Banquo was for nothing.

Either a mirror to reflect the image of King James I (as Banquo's believed descendent) or a glass to be used for predicting the future.

> *A show of eight kings, the last with a glass in his hand; and BANQUO*
>
> **MACBETH**
> Thou art too like the spirit of Banquo; down:
> Thy crown does sear mine eyeballs. And thy hair,
> Thou other gold-bound brow, is like the first.
> A third is like the former. Filthy hags,
> Why do you show me this? – A fourth?
> Start, eyes!
> What, will the line stretch out to th' crack of doom?
> Another yet? A seventh? I'll see no more;
> And yet the eighth appears, who bears a glass
> Which shows me many more; and some I see
> That twofold balls and treble sceptres carry.
> Horrible sight. Now, I see 'tis true;
> For the blood-boltered Banquo smiles upon me
> And points at them for his.

Another reference to not wanting to see – the truth almost blinds him.

List of numbers emphasises Macbeth's incredulity in the number of kings stretching out into the future that belong to Banquo.

Reference to judgement day – Macbeth fears this lineage will continue until the end of the world, when his crimes are likely to see him sent to hell.

Almost mocking – despite Macbeth's best efforts Banquo's prophecy will come true.

## How?

## Retrieval

Sometimes, basic retrieval starters are the best. 'Five a day' questions are incredibly popular as a quick, easy, high impact way of getting students to recall knowledge: Usually, I like to mix up the questions I ask to include all the GCSE texts, but here are five you could use that focus solely on *Macbeth*:

1. According to Duncan, what will shine 'like stars... on all deservers'?
2. Who are the people who the Porter allows into 'hell' and what do they represent?
3. Why is Banquo teaching Fleance to sword fight at the start of Act II, Scene i?
4. Who is Macbeth referring to when he says that 'the grown serpent lies; the worm that's fled / Hath nature that in time will venom breed'?
5. How does Macbeth convince the murderers to kill Banquo?

## Pre-reading activities

Students' understanding of this scene hangs on their understanding of the word 'apparition'. Introduce the Big Question to the class and then explicitly teach the word, its etymology and connotations. It is important not to just introduce the word and tell students what it means: the students need to work with the word in order to truly understand it. You could use one of the vocabulary models in this book to help deliver this.

## Reading the scene

When reading the scene, it is advisable not to read straight through because, in order to understand the second part of the scene, it is important students have a good grasp of the first. Read from the opening of the scene to 'By the pricking of my thumbs, / Something wicked this way comes.' The following questions may help whilst you are reading:

1. What are the witches doing?
2. What do they put in their potion?

## Considering the witches' potion

As we know, the witches know Macbeth is coming and are preparing for his visit by creating a hell-broth from multitudinous ingredients, and the ingredients themselves help us understand more about the witches' intentions. There are, of course, many ingredients which *could* be commented on, but there are some specific components which warrant closer inspection.

Invite students to complete the following activities.

The ingredients that include parts of humans need further, sensitive exploration. Students need to understand the context of these ingredients, but also that they are demonstrative of Shakespeare positioning the witches as opposing God and Christianity. This topic is complex and needs careful exploration to ensure that students consider cultural and religious sensitivities. Therefore, we have not included the human elements in Resource 14.2, but would encourage discussion before or after the activity to help teach students about contextual awareness.

With this in mind, provide students with the following list and instruct them to categorise the ingredients however they choose to do so:

| Dog | Dragon | Tiger | Snake |
|---|---|---|---|
| Wolf | Toad | Howlet | Baby |
| Frog | Goat | Mummy | Lizard |

They must be able to justify the categories they have chosen. I would suggest there are two categories that make particular sense:

| Nature | Fantasy |
|--------|---------|
| Dog | Wolf |
| Frog | Dragon |
| Goat | Mummy |
| Toad | |
| Tiger | |
| Howlet | |
| Snake | |
| Lizard | |

Then, it is important for students to have the opportunity to explore why these ingredients, within their categories, have been used. Nature and fantasy are quite straightforward – the imagery of nature being used in an unnatural way extends Shakespeare's exploration of the destruction and subversion of natural order. The fantasy ingredients tie the supernatural activities of the witches to fictional and – to a contemporary audience – scary creatures and beliefs.

It would be interesting for students to select perhaps one or two ingredients from each category at this point and consider the specific connotations of that ingredient. You could feed in some of the knowledge from the 'What' section of this chapter to expand students' understanding, as demonstrated in Resource 14.2.

## RESOURCE 14.2

### Further pre-reading activities

Before reading the prophecies, you could show the class three images which are representative of the first three apparitions. In pairs, they could discuss these images, making suggestions as to whom or what they might represent. By temporarily separating out the apparitions from their words, students are able to consider the symbolism of what is *seen* on stage before moving on to analyse what is *said*.

## RESOURCE 14.3[35]

The witches show Macbeth three apparitions (visions). Who or what do you think they represent?

'An armed head'          'A bloody child'          'A child, crowned, with a tree in his hand.'

It is important that students are aware following this activity that there are multiple accepted interpretations of these visions, some of which play into Macbeth's own desires and others which paint a perhaps slightly truer image of what is to come next. At this point, without knowledge of the complete text, they may consider during the class discussion some of the following ideas:

| Apparition | Who or what could it be/represent? |
|---|---|
| An armed head | *Macbeth as a warrior. Macduff who has gone to raise an army in England.* |
| A bloody child | *The child Lady Macbeth referred to when she said she would 'dash the brains out'. What Macbeth wishes had happened to Fleance.* |
| A child, crowned, with a tree in his hand | *Malcolm, the child of Scotland, becoming king. Fleance becoming king. The tree could represent 'new shoots' of a new lineage (not Macbeth's).* |

## Reading the scene

At this point, read the remainder of the scene. These questions might help:

1. What does Macbeth seek to know?
2. What do the first three apparitions tell Macbeth?
3. What does the final apparition tell Macbeth?
4. How does Macbeth react to the apparitions?
5. What news has Ross come to deliver?

---

35. Blood by Alex Muravev, Tree Branches by Vectors Market, Child by Musmellow from The Noun Project, Crown and Helmet from Flat Icon.

## Macbeth's language

As we know, in this scene Macbeth's tone is different: he is no longer a curious receiver of information, but has, instead, specifically sought the witches out so that he can hear his fate. Therefore, the lesson continues with a consideration of Macbeth's use of language towards the witches.

The resources for this can look quite simple and straightforward – even just a slide (as demonstrated in Resource 14.4) used to prompt discussion between the students.

## RESOURCE 14.4

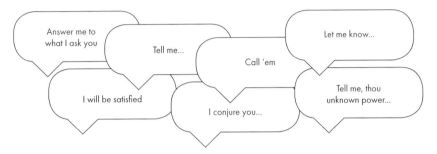

Answer me to what I ask you

Tell me...

Let me know...

Call 'em

I will be satisfied

I conjure you...

Tell me, thou unknown power...

The way Macbeth speaks to the witches in this scene has changed.
What types of words does he use?
What does this reveal about his character and how he feels at this point?
**A helping hand:** Think about how this meeting has come about – what did Macbeth say at the end of Act III?

Of course, the key to unlocking Macbeth's perspective here is in Shakespeare's use of imperative verbs, with Macbeth commanding the witches to do as he asks. By giving students some time to discuss these words and phrases, particularly when they consider their knowledge of his motives for this visit, they are likely to come to the conclusion that Macbeth is desperate for answers in order to soothe his troubled mind. His demands show us that he feels there is a changing relationship between himself and the witches.

These ideas can be summarised in writing or, alternatively, as part of an oracy task: the prompts lend themselves to both approaches.

## Macbeth's apparitions

Having read the remainder of the scene, it will be possible for students to complete a grid like the one below to capture their knowledge and, thus, help them to answer the Big Question later in the lesson. It draws from the work students did as part of their further pre-reading activities. The grid should capture what the apparitions are, what they say, what our interpretation of each is and how Macbeth understands what he has heard. One row has been completed to illustrate the activity.

## RESOURCE 14.5

| Apparition | What it says | What it means | What Macbeth thinks |
|---|---|---|---|
| An armed head | 'Beware Macduff. Beware the Thane of Fife.' | | |
| A bloody child | 'None of woman born / Shall harm Macbeth.' | No one who was born from a woman can hurt him. | He is safe, because everyone is born from a woman. He therefore stops being scared of Macduff. |
| A child, crowned, with a tree in his hand | 'Macbeth shall never vanquished be until Great Birnam wood to high Dunsinane Hill Shall come against him.' | | |

### The final apparition

Despite the fact that Macbeth feels generally reassured by his prophecies, his final request to hear specifically about the descendants of Banquo is crucial to students' understanding of his desperation to secure his position.

Read the final apparition to the point at which the witches vanish. The imagery here will take some unpicking, but through class discussion students should arrive at the key points, guided by the teacher:

- The procession of kings represents the descendants of Banquo (they all look like him, and he follows the procession).
- The final king holds a glass – either some kind of device for prophecy or else a mirror (James I may have been in the audience, and sees himself reflected).
- At the time, it was believed that James I was a descendant of Banquo. Shakespeare was attempting to gain favour with the King and thus wants to represent Banquo and his long, successful lineage, leading to James I himself.

Add a fourth line to the previous table to capture the students' knowledge of this final apparition.

### Answering the Big Question

By this point in the lesson, students will have the knowledge they need to be able to answer the Big Question. Students should use their notes and resources from the lesson to write a detailed answer: What do the apparitions tell Macbeth?

## Suggested 'Extra Challenge' activities

- 'Double, double, toil and trouble': Why do you think Shakespeare pays so much attention to numbers in *Macbeth*?
- In the play, Banquo is repurposed from his historical counterpart. Does Shakespeare do this to flatter King James I or to tell a good story? Discuss.
- How do children embody the idea of 'Fair is foul, and foul is fair'?

## Key vocabulary:
Divination, providence

# CHAPTER 15
## Act IV, Scene ii

*Who is Lady Macduff and what
happens to her and her son?*

## What?

### Scene analysis: Act IV, Scene ii

Act IV, Scene ii, which sees the horrendous murder of Lady Macduff and her children, is further evidence of just how far Macbeth will go in the name of self-preservation. Audiences are invited back into a domesticated setting: the first time we see such a place since Duncan's arrival at the Macbeths' castle. This home, however, is built on foundations of trust, honesty and the love of a family rather than self-gain, malice and manipulation, although these qualities will have breached the walls of the Macduffs' castle by the scene's climax.

Macbeth is fully tyrannical by this point in the play, and this scene goes some way to quashing the argument that he does not have free will over his actions. Having received his second set of prophecies in the last scene, Macbeth chooses to issue the order to murder Lady Macduff and her children. The witches have not driven his actions here; in fact, if one is to take their words at face value, the only person he needs to fear is Macduff; the prophecy 'for none of woman born / Shall harm Macbeth' would seemingly absolve Lady Macduff from any wrongdoing. Nor has Macbeth any need to fear Macduff's children, yet he actively chooses to have them slaughtered, perhaps to punish Macduff. It is his decision and his alone. There is no place for innocence and kindness in this cruel Scotland ruled by a paranoid tyrant.

Perhaps this is why the peaceful nature of home life is often emphasised in stagings of *Macbeth*. Some productions 'build up the domestic aspect of the scene, with Lady Macduff doing needlework or rocking a cradle [and] servants tending to the children'[1] in order to add weight to the flagrant brutality and shocking violence which will shatter the routines of everyday existence.

## 'OUR FEARS DO MAKE US TRAITORS'

The scene opens with Lady Macduff questioning Ross as to why her husband has journeyed to England. She speaks in an accusatory manner, ready to blame her husband for something which has caused him to run, yet Ross responds, saying she must have patience, a quality she cannot see in Macduff, saying, 'His flight was madness. When our actions do not, / Our fears do make us traitors.' She fully recognises that actions speak louder than words. Macbeth's intricately spun rhetoric means the action of fleeing gives an impression of guilt; Macduff, in leaving Scotland, has precariously opened himself up to accusations of criminality and his wife admonishes him for it.

It is most likely she feels extremely vulnerable in Macduff's absence. After all, he has left her and their 'babes' in a place he himself has deemed unsafe, and now she is left to fend for herself. Whilst one may question Macduff's motives, it is probable he does not even comprehend that Macbeth could sink to such levels of depravity. The thought that his children will become victims of infanticide may not have crossed his mind because infanticide is an action so evil that no one would ever consider it. Macbeth, however, is beyond all reasoning and, as such, the stage is set for slaughter. Although Lady Macduff and an unnamed 'son' are the only immediate relatives of Macduff to appear, her use of the plural 'babes' suggests they have more than one child. 'Son' therefore encompasses all their children; their butchery and the ensuing carnage is left to our imagination.

Lady Macduff comes to the conclusion that they are unloved by Macduff. She argues, first and foremost, that he is a soldier above all; she claims 'He loves us not' and 'He wants the natural touch.' With this line, Shakespeare establishes the first in a long list of parallels between the Macduffs and the Macbeths. Here, we are offered insight into Lady Macduff's view of her husband; she believes he lacks basic human feelings, neglecting his paternal duties and role as a husband in his leaving them. This alludes to Lady Macbeth's own view of her husband, first voiced in Act I, Scene v, where she exclaims he is 'too full o'th' milk of human kindness'. Both wives have mistaken their husbands' actions for traits they do not possess: Macbeth is far from kind and Macduff *does* love his family, a point proved when we witness his grief upon hearing news of his wife's and children's demise. In this case, what Lady Macduff cannot see is that her husband's actions are made purely because he *has* that 'natural touch'; he has left Scotland in the

---

1.    Ed. Alexander Leggatt, *William Shakespeare's Macbeth: A Sourcebook*, (London: Routledge, 2006), p. 171.

hope he will return to make it safer. As a side note, perhaps Macduff is perceived to lack 'the natural touch' by his wife because of his 'unnatural' birth.

In voicing their opinions on their husbands, both Lady Macbeth and Lady Macduff reveal their idealised forms of masculinity. For Lady Macbeth, machismo is demonstrative of violence, bravery and the ability to shun kindness, much like the Macbeth presented to audiences in the Captain's report during Act I, Scene ii. In comparison, Lady Macduff perceives masculinity as a compassionate attribute, evident in a man who loves his family and embraces his duties as husband and father.

## 'THE MOST DIMINUTIVE OF BIRDS WILL FIGHT'

In continuing to lament Macduff's absence, Lady Macduff says that even a 'poor wren, / The most diminutive of birds, will fight, / Her young ones in her nest, against the owl.' Further parallels exist here if we see the birds as allegorical of Lady Macbeth and Lady Macduff, these analogies now drawing attention to their maternal instincts (or lack thereof). Where Lady Macbeth admits she would be prepared to kill her child if she had promised to do so, Lady Macduff is willing to protect her children no matter the cost. In saying this, Lady Macduff conforms to the stereotypical role of the traditional wife and mother, fulfilling her parental obligations of nurturer and protector. She remains apolitical, more interested in her family than in her hierarchical position and the political intrigue enveloping Scotland.

Perhaps the birds Shakespeare chooses to include in this metaphor are symbolic of the Macduffs' and the Macbeths' respective personalities. The 'wren', small and vulnerable, matches Lady Macduff's defenceless position, whilst it can be no coincidence that the 'owl', like Macbeth and Lady Macbeth, stalks the night in search of its prey.

Ross urges Lady Macduff to control herself and to be patient; he defends Macduff from his wife's diatribe. Macduff, according to Ross, is 'noble, wise [and] judicious', qualities Macbeth could only hope to possess. Through his nobility and wisdom, Macduff is well aware of the political turmoil engulfing Scotland, referred to by Ross as '[t]he fits o'th' season', his language deliberately vague to ward off any suspicion that he may be talking ill of his new king's rule. He cannot 'speak much further' because 'cruel are the times when we are traitors / And do not know ourselves'. This phrase may allude to the proverbial 'know thyself' which, if true, shows how Macbeth has become a stranger to himself; he has lost sight of who he used to be.[2]

---

2.   Ed. A.R. Braunmuller, *The New Cambridge Shakespeare: Macbeth*, (Cambridge: Cambridge University Press, 2011), p. 236.

This loss of identity contributes, in a way, to the uncertainties gripping Scotland; Ross says they are living in times 'when we hold rumour / From what we fear, yet know not what we fear'. Rumours and whisperings are afoot, creating fright amongst those who are not even sure what they are afraid of. He compares these fears to the idea of floating upon a 'wild and violent sea'; fear pushes one in all directions with little chance of escape. Shakespeare's use of a sea analogy is not only metaphorical of the fact Macbeth has become uncontrollable and unpredictable, but also alludes to the abilities of witches and their summoning of storms. Maybe it reveals the supernatural as the source of this fear, plunging Scotland into a period of turbulence which threatens to tear it apart.

### 'FATHERED HE IS, AND YET HE'S FATHERLESS'

Lady Macduff continues to lament the situation, exclaiming, 'Fathered he is, and yet he's fatherless', a paradoxical remark which ironically bears similarities to Macduff himself. His son is 'fathered' in the sense he can call Macduff his father, but 'fatherless' in the sense Macduff is gone and his son is left vulnerable with the rest of the family. This mirrors the prophecy given to Macbeth regarding Macduff who had a mother but remains 'motherless', as he was from his 'mother's womb / Untimely ripped,' resulting in her death. Paternity, like with Banquo, is presented as being quite significant here. Macbeth is once more emasculated as audiences are reminded of another male figure who has fulfilled his role as a man and fathered children bearing the family name.

Ross's exit is tinged with sadness: he 'is overcome with sorrow at their plight [and] can offer no comfort or reassurance',[3] and so has no choice but to leave. Consolation and solace have no place in Macbeth's world any more. Ross has seen at first hand the cruelty and brutality of which Macbeth is capable; he knows the Macduffs' fate is inescapable and thus can only offer them a blessing – there is no more he can do to save them.

The main crux of Act IV, Scene ii is the relationship between Lady Macduff and her son, where, somewhat darkly, she plays a humorous game with him and teases that his father is dead, perhaps deducing that his likely fate for his flight is reminiscent of that of a traitor. What follows is an exchange which reveals Macduff's son to be a quick-witted child, almost precocious in his confidence. He is arguably 'self contained, his own person, not an utterly dependent infant unable to speak for himself, feed himself to fend for himself. He is an upstart, outdoing his mother in wit, courage and logic.'[4] Macduff's son 'upstages'

---

3.  Ann Blake, 'Children and Suffering in Shakespeare's Plays', *The Yearbook of English Studies*, Vol. 23 (1993), pp. 293–304, www.jstor.org/stable/3507985.

4.  Sid Ray, *Mother Queens and Princely Sons*, (Palgrave Macmillan: New York, 2012), p. 101.

his mother during performances of this scene, and 'not only has an intense dramatic presence but agency as a surrogate for the absent father.'[5]

### 'HOW WILL YOU LIVE?'

Lady Macduff, in saying 'Sirrah, your father's dead', asks her son, 'How will you live?', once again echoing her belief that a husband and father's role is to protect his family. He replies simply, 'As birds do, mother', saying 'With what I get, I mean; and so do they.' Through the boy's words, Shakespeare may be alluding to Matthew 6:26 which states that Jesus said: 'Behold the fowls of the air: for they sow not, neither do they reap, nor gather into barns; yet your heavenly Father feedeth them.'[6] This biblical current running through his words unwittingly draws further parallels between the Macduffs and the Macbeths. Whilst the Macbeths have shunned God and his holiness by inviting the supernatural into their lives, the Macduffs embrace his presence. At the core of these words is a trust in God's protection, a comparison to birds who trust they will somehow be fed. In short, he expresses hope; there is always a path out of darkness.

Shakespeare's use of ornithological imagery continues when Lady Macduff responds to her son by calling him a 'poor bird', claiming he would 'never fear the net nor lime, / the pitfall nor the gin.' Although she is gently jesting, her words are not without menace; by listing a series of traps designed to catch birds, Shakespeare reminds audiences that just because one hides oneself from the political machinations of an authoritarian government, one is not guaranteed safety and security. 'Lime', for example, is a substance which was often spread across branches to hold birds in place when they landed on it.[7] Whilst the son believes he is free as a bird, unlikely to be trapped or ensnared, Lady Macduff seems to be at least somewhat aware of the darkness spreading through Scotland and the pitfalls which await those oblivious to such darkness.

Young Macduff, in a sense, is ignorant to some things, but demonstrates a surprising astuteness to others. For all his quick wit and comical, sharp replies, he cannot possibly comprehend the violence which will soon befall his family. Indeed, he questions why he should worry about these traps, saying 'Poor birds they are not set for.' Who would target a bird of little worth when there is something greater to catch? Unfortunately, he has not and never will realise that

---

5.  Sid Ray, *Mother Queens and Princely Sons*, (Palgrave Macmillan: New York, 2012), p. 101.

6.  *The Holy Bible Containing the Old and New Testaments*, Authorised King James Version, www.kingjamesbibleonline.org, Matthew 6:26.

7.  James A Bateman, *Animal Traps and Trapping*, (Machynlleth: Coch-y-Bonddu Books, 2003), p. 129.

the greater catch is his father, and the family a necessary sacrifice (in Macbeth's eyes) to ensure the preservation of tyrannical rule.

On the other hand, he is perceptive with his word play and demonstrates he has some knowledge of good and bad. One may wonder *how* he is quick-thinking and alert; Young Macduff is often portrayed as being around seven to ten years old, meaning his replies to his mother are far beyond his years. Macduff's son, according to critic Hardin Craig (quoted by Alice N. Benston), 'exemplifies Shakespeare's handling of children. They are, [Craig] says, precocious grownups, and he further warns us that "[t]here was no knowledge of child psychology in Shakespeare's time"'.[8] This precociousness is certainly evident in the way Young Macduff cleverly alters his mother's use of 'poor bird'. Lady Macduff clearly describes her son as 'poor' to mean regrettable or unfortunate rather than suggesting he is low quality.

Indeed, his quick wit is further evident when he expresses his belief that his father is not dead, asking '[H]ow will you do for a husband?' Lady Macduff replies 'I can buy me twenty at any market', for the son to observe 'you'll buy 'em to sell again.' Young Macduff cheekily suggests Lady Macduff will only buy twenty husbands if she is to resell or deceive them, for if marriage is solely just a form of trade, then loyalty between husband and wife is non-existent.

### 'WHAT IS A TRAITOR?'

The conversation between the two ends with a verbal dissection on what makes someone a traitor and an honest man. A traitor, according to Lady Macduff, is someone who 'swears and lies' and they 'must be hanged [by] the honest men' as punishment for doing so. While it is easy to take this conversation at face value, something more complex is taking place. An interesting idea put forward by @GCSE_Macbeth is that if Lady Macduff's definition of a traitor is correct, Macbeth is a traitor, and the audience would see him as such. However, Macbeth is now king, and under his authoritarian rule, the definition of a traitorous man surely has to change, much like that of an honest man.[9] Anyone who speaks out against Macbeth's regime is branded a traitor, yet in a sense, this must mean they are honest, for they do not stand for the fear and terror Macbeth has brought upon Scotland. They are loyal to their country and cannot stand to see it buckle under the sheer force of tyranny. The same, then, can be said for honesty. If one is honest to Macbeth, one is loyal to him, yet being so

8.    Alice N. Benston, 'Freud Reading Shakespeare Reading Freud: The Case of Macduff', *Style*, Vol. 23, No. 2 (1989), pp. 261–279, www.jstor.org/stable/42945790.

9.    @GCSE_Macbeth, 28 February 2020, https://twitter.com/GCSE_Macbeth/status/968239342249545728.

helps Macbeth strengthen his devastating grip on Scotland. To align oneself with Macbeth is to be a traitor.

When Lady Macduff says 'the honest men' hang the traitors, she is right, but not necessarily in the positive way one might interpret this line on first reading. Under Macbeth's administration, Macduff is a traitor who will be executed by an honest man, meaning one loyal to the King. It could be argued, then, that Young Macduff unwittingly vindicates his father from his mother's diatribe by saying the 'liars and swearers are fools, for there are liars and swearers enow to beat the honest men, and hang up them.' There is no way Young Macduff could know, but his father, 'the liar' under Macbeth's rule, has gone to do just that; by travelling to England he is hoping to 'beat the honest men' and restore proper order to Scotland.

Young Macduff concludes that his father must be alive because his mother does not weep for her lost husband. He seems to understand the reason behind Lady Macduff's ire and subsequent 'game', perhaps enjoying the wordplay between them. The presentation of 'Young Macduff' is an interesting one. After all, he could easily have been used by Shakespeare to serve the pathos of the scene.[10] Macbeth's willingness to commit infanticide is horrific, and by making Macduff's son the typical weak and feeble child, Shakespeare could have used the child's vulnerabilities to consolidate a portrait of Macbeth as a monster. However, he does not. Macduff's son's 'prattle is not altogether innocent. He may not know the meaning of the word "traitor" but he knows that snares are set for rich birds, not poor ones, that there are more liars and swearers in the world than honest men, that if a marriage is a market no loyalty is involved, and that his mother is lying to him.'[11]

The pace of the scene quickens at this moment when a messenger enters, warning Lady Macduff of approaching danger; interestingly, the messenger acknowledges Lady Macduff's status and reputation, and in his description of himself as a 'homely man', audiences understand he is not like other Shakespearean messengers, 'a functionary whose role it is to carry news.'[12] By stressing his simplicity and ordinariness, we understand this messenger is acting of his own accord; he has warned Lady Macduff as a simple act of kindness and does not mean to frighten her, but must tell her the truth if the family is to survive.

His words, of course, incite dread: Lady Macduff asks where she should run, citing the fact she has done nothing wrong and therefore has no reason to flee. It is a futile comment, one made in a brief moment of panic which may stem

10. Ed. Alexander Leggatt, *William Shakespeare's Macbeth: A Sourcebook*, (London: Routledge, 2006), p. 171.

11. Ibid.

12. Ibid., p. 174.

from Ross's earlier words, 'we are traitors'; no one in Macbeth's world is exempt from suspicion and, as such, Lady Macduff feels she has to feign innocence for something she has not done in an attempt to save her life. Even then, she quickly realises her protestations are useless and asks herself 'Why... do I put that womanly defence, / To say I have done no harm?' Acknowledging that to do evil is often commended and to do good is foolish, Lady Macduff allows herself a brief moment of bravery. Indeed, '"womanly defense" should be "manly defense."' Her defense – that only those who have done wrong need fear danger – is perfect logic, ideal logic: the kind of logic that reasonable men, rather than emotional women supposedly use.'[13] Of course, in Macbeth's 'perverted' world, logic is not recognised.[14]

In her momentary appearance on stage, Lady Macduff does not demonstrate the kind of power audiences have witnessed from Lady Macbeth, and while it could be argued that Lady Macduff seems 'to embody [a] kind of female power in her forceful denunciation of her husband's "unnatural departure", ... she is physically defenceless without him'.[15] She 'exists only to disappear'.[16]

#### 'TO DO HARM IS OFTEN LAUDABLE'

Shakespeare's thread of duality that runs through the play is evident once more. Lady Macduff knows that 'to do harm / Is often laudable', mirroring the witches' chant of 'Fair is foul, and foul is fair'. From the beginning, we have been told that 'foul' things in Macbeth's world are good, and this mantra of sorts has come to fruition, especially here. Macbeth is lost. It is his decision to kill the Macduffs and no one else's.

Marie Syrkin notes, however, how 'a new era in classroom Shakespearean criticism [saw students begin] to suggest that the technique of terror was both "motivated" and merciful since it discouraged the population from attempting futile uprisings.'[17] It is a reading where Macbeth is fully realised as a tyrant, perhaps influenced by similar figures in modern history, although it seems to

13. William T. Liston, '"Male and Female Created He Them": Sex and Gender in 'Macbeth'', *College Literature*, Vol. 16, No. 3 (1989), pp. 232–239, www.jstor.org/stable/25111824.

14. Ibid.

15. Nicolas Tredell, *Shakespeare: Macbeth: A reader's guide to essential criticism*, (Hampshire: Palgrave Macmillan, 2006), p. 141.

16. Janet Adelman, *Suffocating Mothers: Fantasies of Maternal Origin in Shakespeare's Plays, 'Hamlet' to 'The Tempest'*, (New York: Routledge, 1992), p. 131.

17. Marie Syrkin, 'Youth and Lady Macduff', *Bulletin of the American Association of University Professors (1915-1955)*, Vol. 40, No. 2, 1954, pp. 317–323, www.jstor.org/stable/40221016.

dismiss the idea that his actions only spur Macduff to strike with vengeance; one should not underestimate how far a man will go for his family.

The first murderer enters, asking 'Where is your husband?' Lady Macduff defends her husband, replying outspokenly, 'I hope in no place so unsanctified / Where such as thou mayst find him.' She finally defends her husband and once again aligns her family with God by voicing her hopes that he will never be discovered in such unholy places frequented by the type of men who confront her now. Although Lady Macduff has spent most of this scene engaging in banterous quips with her son regarding his father, she has spent her life investing 'all of her intellectual powers into the achievements of her husband and children'. She is, in a sense, 'the epitome of motherhood'[18] and now channels her candid opinions to safeguard those she loves instead of criticising them.

Even her son attempts to defend his father's honour. In labelling Macduff a 'traitor', the murderers spark a response in Young Macduff where audiences 'see the real man in the child, the little boy ready to become a man on the pressure of the moment to protect his mother'.[19] In a sense, he literalises the image of the wren fighting off the owl, protecting its territory from invasion. Perhaps it is here where Young Macduff's purpose is fully realised. Macbeth's victims are difficult to relate to; after all, we will never understand what it is like to be a king or even a thane of great nobility. Whilst previous deaths hold gravitas because of the victims' societal status, there is still a distancing between the audience and Shakespeare's characters which renders their death as nothing but a fictionalised murder. Lady Macduff and her son's demise are different because their familial love is something we can all relate to; although all characters are constructs, the gentle banter between mother and son revealing their obvious closeness seems like a clear attempt by Shakespeare to convey how ordinary people are affected by tyrannical regimes attempting to maintain authority. Innocent families, who hold no stake in political echelons, will always suffer because of the actions of others.

### 'WHAT, YOU EGG!'

Young Macduff, hearing his father branded as a 'traitor', shouts back, 'Thou liest, thou shag-haired villain.' The murderer, in reply, says, 'What, you egg!' This line, which often provokes much hilarity in students, is more distressing than often credited. On a basic level, 'egg' can be read as a contemptuous term

---

18.   Marion A. Davis, 'A Brief Look at Feminism in Shakespeare's Macbeth', *Inquiries Journal* (2009), http://www.inquiriesjournal.com/articles/1691/a-brief-look-at-feminism-in-shakespeares-macbeth.

19.   Arlin J. Hiken, 'Shakespeare's Use of Children', *Educational Theatre Journal*, Vol. 15, No. 3 (1963), pp. 241–248, www.jstor.org/stable/3204782.

for a baby;[20] Young Macduff is the child of a traitor and so, from the murderer's perspective, he must logically be a traitor too. It can be no coincidence that Shakespeare uses the term 'egg' in a scene full of avian imagery. In reality, an egg has not left the nest, has not yet hatched, and is easy to steal or break, much like Young Macduff's own situation; he has not left the home and is too young to really defend himself. The murderer is not only scorning him, but also mocking the fact that Young Macduff feels he is a match for the murderers; he can and *will* easily be crushed.

More interpretations can be read from this line if one looks at an egg as an isolated symbol pertaining to bird imagery and the fact that mother and child cannot survive without the other. Just as Young Macduff has alluded to the idea that God will provide for them, the boy – metaphorically – is an egg, relying on his mother to protect him because he has not grown enough to be able to leave the nest, his home. At this moment, however, the two are separated through death. The boy is murdered and his mother has no purpose. She attempts to fly from the nest but fails; she is killed along with the rest of her children in a bloodbath which mirrors the 'Massacre of the Innocents' as detailed in the New Testament. The murderer, of course, does not have this in mind when he calls Young Macduff an 'egg', but the links to birds and the symbolic significance of the Macduffs' home as a nest is accentuated and therefore deserving of further exploration.

Even as he is being murdered, Young Macduff is concerned with his mother's safety, instructing her: 'Run away'. He does not call for the maternal protection of a mother that another child would perhaps call for, and uses his death as something of a distraction to help her escape, becoming the man Lady Macduff says her husband should have been. He is now the protector, tragically forced to give up his life to help the others survive.

Audiences never see Lady Macduff's death, perhaps because Shakespeare wants to foreground the scene with Young Macduff's murder. The act of infanticide must be clearly presented to accentuate Macbeth's fall from humanity. Of course, audiences only realise Lady Macduff is killed at this point on a second viewing of the play, for her fate is not revealed until Act IV, Scene iii.

The purpose of the scene is clear and sets up events which will quickly propel the play to its bloody end. The play, Alice N. Benston says, quoting L.C. Knight, '"is a succession of violent acts—culminating in the murder of Macduff's babes", [rendering] Macbeth the most debased of tyrants, and we thus are prepared to accept Macduff's eventual killing of Macbeth as the act of avenging innocence.'[21]

20.   Ed. John Seeley, *Heinemann Shakespeare: Macbeth*, (Harlow: Heinemann, 2010) p. 148.

21.   Alice N. Benston, 'Freud Reading Shakespeare Reading Freud: The Case of Macduff', *Style*, Vol. 23, No. 2 (1989), pp. 261–279, www.jstor.org/stable/42945790.

## The persecution of Macduff in *Holinshed's Chronicles*

The tragedy of Act IV, Scene ii is really elevated when we take into account *Holinshed's Chronicles*, which offers slightly more detail as to what happens to Lady Macduff and her children under Macbeth's subjugation of her husband. Holinshed tragically details how the murder of this family is made all the more easy by the fact those in the castle freely open the doors to Macbeth's men because they, by their very nature, are not mistrusting or suspicious, something they pay for with their lives:

> *Immediatlie then, being aduertised whereabout Makduffe went, he came hastily with a great power into Fife, and foorthwith besieged the castell where Makduffe dwelled, trusting to haue found him therein. They that kept the house, without anie resistance opened the gates, and suffered him to enter, mistrusting none euill. But neuerthelesse Makbeth most cruellie caused the wife and children of Makduffe, with all other whom he found in that castell, to be slaine.*[22]

There are echoes of this trust in Shakespeare's play. Lady Macduff observes how 'to do harm / Is often laudable', meaning trust, as a positive, hopeful characteristic is unfavourable in the aggressive and vicious world Macbeth presides over. As we can see from what has been derived from Holinshed, trust is a 'fair' quality resulting in a 'foul' outcome.

---

22. Raphael Holinshed, *Chronicles of England, Scotland and Ireland*, (London: J. Johnson et. al., 1808), https://www.troup.org/userfiles/929/My%20Files/ELA/HS%20 ELA/12th%20ELA/Unit%202/Holinshed%20and%20Macbeth.pdf?id=11638.

## Lady Macduff at a glance

# RESOURCE 15.1

This is the first look at a domestic setting that audiences have received since the arrival of Duncan to Macbeth's castle. Many performances often emphasise the domestic aspect of this scene, perhaps alluding to the Macduffs' innocence which in turn makes their murder all the more striking.

Patience is obviously a quality to be admired. Ross urges it and Lady Macduff criticises her husband for not having it.

Whereas masculinity has always been associated with violence, Lady Macduff sees a man's role as honouring his duty to his wife and children. First and foremost, Macduff is a soldier who will fight for his country, yet Lady Macduff wishes him to be kinder, while kindness is a trait Lady Macbeth fears in her own husband. 'Unnatural touch' could also be a subtle nod towards Macduff's unnatural birth.

Ross alludes to the idea of losing sight of oneself. This is a common theme which runs through the play. Macbeth, in murdering the Macduff family, has completely distanced himself from the loyal solider he once was. He no longer possesses the humanity or loyalty which could control his violent behaviour.

**LADY MACDUFF**
What had he done, to make him fly the land?

**ROSS**
You must have patience, madam.

**LADY MACDUFF**
He had none;
His flight was madness. When our actions do not,
Our fears do make us traitors.

**ROSS**
You know not
Whether it was his wisdom or his fear.

**LADY MACDUFF**
Wisdom? To leave his wife, to leave his babes,
His mansion and his titles in a place
From whence himself does fly? He loves us not;
He wants the natural touch. For the poor wren,
The most diminutive of birds, will fight,
Her young ones in her nest, against the owl.
All is the fear and nothing is the love;
As little is the wisdom, where the flight
So runs against all reason.

**ROSS**
My dearest coz,
I pray you, school yourself. But for your husband,
He is noble, wise, judicious, and best knows
The fits o'th' season. I dare not speak much further;
But cruel are the times, when we are traitors
And do not know ourselves; when we hold rumour
From what we fear, yet know not what we fear,
But float upon a wild and violent sea
Each way and move. I take my leave of you;
Shall not be long but I'll be here again.
Things at the worst will cease, or else climb upward
To what they were before. My pretty cousin,
Blessing upon you.

**LADY MACDUFF**
Fathered he is, and yet he's fatherless.

**ROSS**
I am so much a fool, should I stay longer,
It would be my disgrace and your discomfort.
I take my leave at once.

Actions speak louder than words. The act of fleeing has become synonymous with guilt. Malcolm and Donalbain fled after the murder of Duncan, leaving Macbeth free to pin the murder on them. Fleance too ran when his father was killed, suggesting he had something to do with it. Lady Macduff sees her husband's actions as an invitation to accuse him of criminality.

Bird imagery dominates this scene. The conflict between the wren and the owl as described by Lady Macduff foreshadows the events which are about to occur in the Macduff household. The owl, a creature associated with the supernatural, symbolises Macbeth's evil which will invade the household. The wren, 'poor' and defenceless, is reminiscent of Lady Macduff's current situation. She must fend for the lives of her and her children in Macduff's absence.

Young Macduff is 'fathered' in the sense he can call Macduff his father but 'fatherless' in the sense Macduff is gone and his son left vulnerable with the rest of the family. This mirrors the prophecy given to Macbeth regarding Macduff, who has been 'mothered' as a child but remains 'motherless', as he was from his 'mother's womb / Untimely ripped'.

# How?

## Retrieval and pre-reading strategies

Start by introducing the lesson's Big Question.

*Who is Lady Macduff and what happens to her and her son?*

By now, students should know the Macduffs have been created as alternative characters to the Macbeths, embodying loyalty, faith and virtue, everything Shakespeare's eponymous tragic hero shuns. As a retrieval task *and* pre-reading strategy, place Lady Macbeth centre stage of this next activity and ask students to recall what they know about her. Resource 15.2 shows how this could be done and also contains a range of prompts students could use to help them consider the knowledge they should recall.

## RESOURCE 15.2

**Who is Lady Macbeth?**
Consider everything you know about Lady Macbeth and make notes around her silhouette that answer the question above. Use the prompts to help you think about different points if you get stuck.

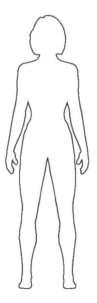

**Lady Macbeth alone:**
*Calls upon the supernatural to aid her in her pursuit of the crown.
Asks for darkness to hide her evil to maintain a shroud of secrecy.*

*Secretly fears her husband is too kind to go through with the plans she has in store.*

**Prompts:**
1. Lady Macbeth's dual self (her internal thoughts vs her external behaviour).
2. Lady Macbeth's relationship with her husband.
3. Lady Macbeth's calls for darkness.
4. Lady Macbeth's affinity with the supernatural.
5. Lady Macbeth as an 'Eve' figure.

**Lady Macbeth and Macbeth:**
*Influences her husband by challenging his masculinity.*

*Is not necessarily supportive of Macbeth. She criticises what she perceives as weaknesses instead of championing him and his opinions.*

**Lady Macbeth and others:**
*Acts the dutiful wife and loyal servant, particularly to Duncan.*

*Seems to conform to the stereotypical role of women because that's what people expect of her. (eg. Faints after Duncan's murder to feign innocence)*

Take feedback, but ensure students have a solid understanding of Lady Macbeth, for this will help with the inferences they are about to make to help paint a picture of Lady Macduff. Any missing gaps in knowledge should be added so each student has a complete picture of Lady Macbeth as a character. Ask students to consider what the opposite of their previous points would be. For example, if they stated Lady Macbeth was an 'Eve figure' who ignores God's word and brings about the downfall of man, the opposite would be a woman who accepts God, who lives by his word and in doing so does not initiate the downfall of others. It is important to stress that this mirror image of Lady Macbeth is not necessarily who Lady Macduff is. She is not an exact opposite and it would be unfair to label her as such. However, this does give students something to consider as they read the scene, and they can return to this character outline to judge how neatly Lady Macduff fits into it once they have understood what is going on.

I particularly like teasing out inferences from students, adding evidence bit by bit to help challenge the way they think. To help do this, provide students with the following quotations:

| 'He loves us not' | 'Wisdom? To leave his wife, to leave his babes, His mansion and his titles in a place From whence himself does fly?' | 'His flight was madness' |
| --- | --- | --- |

Ask students to consider these questions:

1. What could Lady Macduff be talking about?
2. How do you think Lady Macduff is feeling?
3. How do these quotations support the character you created of an alternative Lady Macbeth?
4. How do these quotations challenge the character you created of an alternative Lady Macbeth?

Use the responses to these questions as a stimulus for discussion. Students should have enough evidence across these three quotations and the third-party reports of Macduff's whereabouts in Act IV, Scene i to begin to piece together what is happening. Some students may even pick up on similarities between Lady Macduff and Lady Macbeth: both women are critical of their husbands, questioning their actions and their motive for behaving the way they do. If one wishes to tease these inferences out further, one could add another three quotations and ask students if they consolidate their previous ideas or oppose them.

## Reading the scene

Questions one could ask to check basic understanding when reading the scene include:

1. What does Lady Macduff think of her husband's travels to England?
2. What does Lady Macduff think a parent's most important duty should be?
3. What does Ross think of Macduff?
4. What does Lady Macduff tell her son about his father?
5. How does the son say he will live?
6. How do birds live?
7. What does Lady Macduff say about 'traitors' and 'honest men'?
8. Is Macduff really dead?
9. What does the messenger who enters say to Lady Macduff?
10. What happens to Lady Macduff and her son?

## Ornithological imagery

One aspect of this scene that students need to consider is the ornithological imagery. There are many ways this could be approached. In an attempt to avoid convoluting something which has the potential to be tricky, I have often provided my students with a blank copy of the scene and asked them to highlight all the references to birds they can find. This is so they can easily visualise just how prominently birds are spoken about through the scene and gives them a reason as to why they are about to complete the next activity.

Begin by asking students what they associate with different kinds of birds. They may want to consider what birds have in common as well as their differences. What may seem like a 'filler' activity is in fact vital in helping students understand Shakespeare's intentions. There is no point telling our classes that birds are used as a metaphor for different characters' circumstances without assisting them in finding out why. Answers may include those indicated in Resource 15.3.

## RESOURCE 15.3

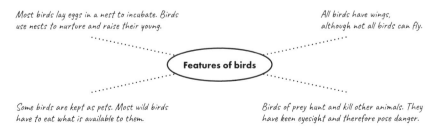

Most birds lay eggs in a nest to incubate. Birds use nests to nurture and raise their young.

All birds have wings, although not all birds can fly.

**Features of birds**

Some birds are kept as pets. Most wild birds have to eat what is available to them.

Birds of prey hunt and kill other animals. They have keen eyesight and therefore pose danger.

Next, ask students to consider what type of bird they would associate with Lady Macbeth, Lady Macduff and Young Macduff. Ask them to explain why. I suppose this is a little like a 'thunk', an unusual, unexpected question which makes one stop and think. There is not necessarily a right answer, but the answer *must* be thought through. It is likely students will opt for a vicious bird or one associated with death for Lady Macbeth, and something small and calmer for the Macduffs. At this point, students could find quotations from the text to help them explain their choices. This in turn, will help them appreciate the concept of metaphor.

This idea, of course, can be explored further, through Lady Macduff's following line:

> '... the poor wren,
> The most diminutive of birds, will fight,
> Her young ones in her nest, against the owl.'

Complete a quotation explosion on this line and ask students how it foreshadows the Macduffs' fate – either as a written response or verbally. Their explanations will reveal whether they have understood Shakespeare's method of using bird imagery to mirror what is happening to the human characters. Now that students know the mention of birds could be metaphorical and microcosmic of the Macduffs, read the scene again, asking them to stop whenever they encounter an avian reference which they highlighted earlier on. Make sure you refer back to this quotation once you have finished an analytical reading of the scene with the class so students can see how this image manifests itself in both Lady Macduff and Young Macduff, who both stand up to those who would seek to end their life.

## Quotation drills

There are two references which I believe probably warrant further investigation and closer analysis. The first involves Lady Macduff asking her son how he will live without a father. He replies that he will live 'As birds do, mother' before clarifying, 'With what I get, I mean; and so do they.' I believe this to be an important moment because of its biblical allusions; it aligns the Macduffs with God, allowing students to see how they are positioned as foils for the Macbeths. The following resource, similar to a quotation drill, allows students to see how Young Macduff's reply echoes Jesus' words from Matthew 6:26.

Introduce students to this verse and ask them to complete the quotation drill (Resource 15.4) and discuss. The focus of this task is not necessarily to analyse language, but to help students understand that the Macduffs trust in God, a trust ultimately misplaced, as they will find out when their home is invaded by the murderers sent by Macbeth. It works as a resource because it breaks down how to consider the meaning behind a quotation into bite-sized chunks, sequencing the process of understanding.

## RESOURCE 15.4

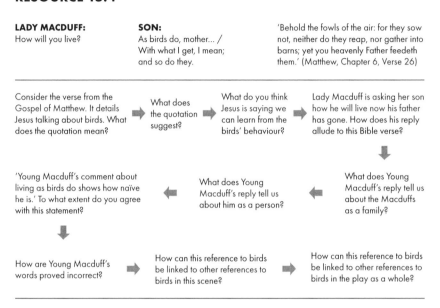

| **LADY MACDUFF:** | **SON:** | |
|---|---|---|
| How will you live? | As birds do, mother... / With what I get, I mean; and so do they. | 'Behold the fowls of the air: for they sow not, neither do they reap, nor gather into barns; yet you heavenly Father feedeth them.' (Matthew, Chapter 6, Verse 26) |

The second reference involves Lady Macduff calling her son a 'poor bird'; she laments his lack of caution, comparing him to birds that are unaware of traps. Again, take time to consider Young Macduff's carefree attitude here; although he is knowledgeable and witty, he is also wrong. He will be targeted and become yet another victim of Macbeth's bloodthirsty attitude.

### 'What, you egg!'

This line always invokes laughter, perhaps because students cannot see past its apparent absurdity. Because it sounds funny, students always seem to remember it, something of which I think we can all take advantage. I always ensure I explicitly teach the line's significance, acknowledging that, yes, it does come across as a little odd, but it also has more of a devastating interpretation as well.

Begin by explaining how 'egg' is used as a hateful term for 'offspring', but then ask students to consider what an egg could mean in a more symbolic sense.

Ask students to think about how Young Macduff literalises the image of an egg in the nest, and how he is vulnerable to attack because he is not the fully grown 'bird' and able to defend himself. By learning about the egg as a metaphor, students can begin to appreciate just how crazed Macbeth has become in enacting his desire to rid this child of his life.

## Lady Macbeth and Lady Macduff: Power matrix

Apart from the three witches, Lady Macbeth and Lady Macduff are the only female voices in the play, and so parallels between the two should be made.

In the past, I have been guilty of confusing this comparison by diving into the characters' more subtle attributes before checking that students have a basic understanding of where they stand in relation to one another. Ultimately, the characters in the play are navigating a world of good and evil, where one's strengths and weaknesses dictate who survives, who wins and who loses. The Macbeths have committed terrible atrocities up to this point, and audiences would be forgiven for thinking that there is no hope left in Shakespeare's bleak and dismal portrayal of Scotland. Yet I have always believed that Shakespeare has Lady Macduff and her son appear at this point specifically to remind us that good, virtuousness and morality still exist, if only as a faint flicker.

To highlight the comparison between the two, a simple matrix is effective and allows students to visualise the difference between those characters who would seek to maintain dignity and those who actively set out to destroy it. This is a resource I first came across in the Heinemann edition of the text.[23]

Begin by asking students to plot where they would place Lady Macbeth and Lady Macduff on the character matrix, a question which could be discussed before everyone commits their answer to paper. This is shown in Resource 15.5. Once students have placed the characters on the matrix, ask them to complete the following tasks:

1. Add a quotation from the play to support your choice.
2. Explain as annotations on the matrix how this quotation supports your choice.
3. Discuss Shakespeare's purpose in making these two characters different. What is he criticising, revealing, exposing, warning us about or advocating?

---

23. Ed. John Seeley, *Heinemann Shakespeare: Macbeth*, (Harlow: Heinemann, 2010), p. 168.

## RESOURCE 15.5

**Lady Macbeth**
*'Look like the innocent flower, / But be the serpent under't.'*

*This shows Lady Macbeth is strong and wicked because she is willing to lie her way into getting what she wants. This quotation epitomises the idea of dual self (being one thing but pretending to be another). She is strong because she is instructing her husband, using his masculinity to manipulate him into behaving the way she needs him to. Shakespeare is criticising those who pretend to be loyal and warning us that power gained through illicit means in ephemeral.*

**Strong**

**Wicked** ━━━━━━━━━━━━┿━━━━━━━━━━━━ **Good**

**Weak**

**Lady Macduff**
*'Why then, alas, / Do I put up that womanly defence, / To say I have done no harm?'*

*Could be placed in 'strong' and 'good' because she comes to defend her husband after questioning her 'womanly defence'. Ultimately though, she is no match for the power of Macbeth or his bloodthirsty rampage and becomes another of his victims. Although she embraces her maternal role of protector of her children and supporter of her husband (in her last moments) she is physically weak. She embraces God but it is not enough to protect her. Shakespeare is revealing the human cost of tyranny, exposing how those who seek power will do anything to get it.*

One could follow this up by asking students to plot Macduff's character on the matrix, based on his appearance in Act II and what his wife has said about him. Similarly, one could include Macduff's son on the matrix, or any other character worth comparing to Lady Macduff. I also like the idea of changing the label on each axis and asking students to rearrange the characters in response. By doing this, students can begin to appreciate how characters are multi-layered and complex. Other labels could include:

Rational vs Irrational
Suspicious vs Trusting
Loyal vs Disloyal
Responsible vs Irresponsible

Honest vs Dishonest
Ambitious vs Unambitious
Forgiving vs Unforgiving
Authentic vs Inauthentic

This activity is always a great one for helping students visualise ideas about discourse around the writer's message, and should help with the final activity which, like previous lessons in this book, asks students to respond to the Big Question having completed their study of the scene.

## Suggested 'Extra Challenge' activities

- Lady Macduff 'exists only to disappear.'[24] To what extent do you agree with this statement?
- Hardin Craig, in his critical reading of this scene, argues 'there was no knowledge of child psychology in Shakespeare's time.' How is this evident in the way Shakespeare writes Young Macduff's dialogue?[25]
- An honest man, under a tyrannical regime, would be a traitor. Explain how the role reversal of traitors and honest men is alluded to in this scene.

## Key vocabulary:

Traitor, ornithology

24. Janet Adelman, *Suffocating Mothers: Fantasies of Maternal Origin in Shakespeare's Plays, 'Hamlet' to 'The Tempest'*, (New York: Routledge, 1992), p. 131.

25. Alice N. Benston, 'Freud Reading Shakespeare Reading Freud: The Case of Macduff', *Style*, Vol. 23, No. 2 (1989), pp. 261–279, www.jstor.org/stable/42945790.

# CHAPTER 16
## Act IV, Scene iii

*What is the relationship like between Malcolm and Macduff?*
*What qualities make a good king?*

## What?

### Scene analysis: Act IV, Scene iii

#### 'NEW WIDOWS HOWL, NEW ORPHANS CRY'

After the murder of Macduff's family, the action switches to an unnamed place in England. With Macduff by his side, Malcolm laments the state of their country, which suffers under Macbeth's iron fist. Of course, Macduff does not know his family's fate at this point; by the end of this scene his world will truly have collapsed, spurring him on further to strike back at the disease which has ravaged Scotland: Macbeth. Shakespeare is positioning Macduff as Macbeth's nemesis by having him say to Malcolm that they should 'Hold fast the mortal sword, and like good men / Bestride our downfall birthdom.' Macduff believes it is his duty to defend his homeland, whereas Macbeth shuns all sense of duty in the name of self-preservation and gain. In doing so, 'New widows howl [and] new orphans cry', their sounds a call to arms for Macduff, tempered only by Malcolm's somewhat defeatist attitude. Macduff's words paint the image of a man standing over the body of a fallen ally with the purpose of defending them. Scotland is vulnerable and fragile and has no choice but to succumb to Macbeth's brutal actions, yet Macduff is ready to stand between his country and the man who has presided over its collapse in order to help his fallen 'comrade'.

Macduff's intentions, however, arouse suspicion within Malcolm. Malcolm wonders why Macduff has come to bring him back to Scotland, perhaps suspecting an ulterior motive. Malcolm has been hurt before by the duplicitous nature of other characters. Whilst Macduff is seeking Malcolm's help in removing Macbeth, Malcolm is disbelieving of this at first because of his previous experiences.

Malcolm speaks formally to Macduff; conversing, they do not seem like two people who share a common foe, which is strange, seeing as their experiences are broadly similar. After all, both have felt the need to flee their country, yet Malcolm, whom one might think would be ready to exact revenge on the man who killed his father, is far more cautious, dismissing Macduff's notion that the sword is the answer, and using this conversation to suss Macduff's intentions out instead. Clearly, he has learned that 'Fair is foul, and foul is fair': appearance is not reality.

Malcolm is naturally sceptical. He uses Macbeth as an example of this scepticism that has led to suspicion when he remembers the start of Macbeth's reign: 'This tyrant, whose sole name blisters our tongues, / Was once thought honest'. The very mention of Macbeth's name is so horrendous that it hurts anyone who utters it; blisters, of course, are associated with infection and pain. What is most sinister about Malcolm's response to Macduff is his observation that 'He hath not touched you yet.' Macduff is yet to experience the true extent of Macbeth's power, and Malcolm acknowledges that this is not a question of *if* this will happen but *when*. What makes this all the more heartbreaking is that Macduff unknowingly *has* been 'touched' by this devastating power, and audiences are just waiting for him to find out.

Malcolm surmises that Macduff could be traitorous; he fears Macduff has travelled to England to win his favour before offering him up to Macbeth in order to prove his allegiance. In voicing his concerns, Malcolm compares his situation to that of a 'weak, poor, innocent lamb' sacrificed 'T'appease an angry god.' In comparing himself to a lamb, Malcolm's words contain holy allusions. In Christian tradition, a lamb symbolises innocence,[1] something which Malcolm feels he still has to protest in relation to the murder of his father. Additionally, lambs are often associated with the phrase 'like a lamb to the slaughter' (based on Jeremiah 11:19). If Malcolm returns to Scotland with Macduff, he perhaps fears that he, too, will be offered up like the symbolic lamb, murdered just as his father was before him.

### 'I AM NOT TREACHEROUS'

Macduff replies, 'I am not treacherous', insisting on his innocence in an attempt to convince Malcolm to join his cause. It is a short, brief statement and one which needs no elaboration. It is quite obvious that Macduff embodies loyalty

---

1. University of Michigan, 'Lamb', *Dictionary of Symbolism*, http://umich. edu/~umfandsf/symbolismproject/symbolism.html/L/lamb.html.

to the state, even if Malcolm refuses to see it. Unfortunately, it is this loyalty in part which will lead to the deaths of his family. Malcolm, ever cautious in his reply, states 'But Macbeth is [treacherous]. / A good and virtuous nature may recoil / In an imperial charge.' He highlights, in a simple sentence, how power can corrode one's sense of morality and virtue, even if one is aware of this possibility of corruption. It is almost impossible to guard against.

Alternatively, Malcolm could be reflecting upon Macbeth's own degeneration through his words, recalling 'Holinshed's praise for the historical Macbeth's first ten years on the throne'.[2] Regardless of how one reads Malcolm's words, it is clear that a further victim of erroneously used power is trust. Malcolm professes that trust is close to non-existent under Macbeth's regime. He has brought this distrust with him to England. He highlights just how difficult it is to differentiate between good and bad, saying 'Angels are bright still, though the brightest fell', a reference to Satan, the fallen angel, the 'Light-Bringer,' also known as Lucifer.[3] This is an interesting observation, seeing as the Macbeths have endeavoured throughout the play to seem good but have rapidly fallen from grace. Not only this, but the audience would be aware that they have spent the play trying to extinguish light that threatens to expose their evil.

Perhaps this disintegration of trust is what causes Macduff to proclaim, 'I have lost my hopes.' This is where the roles Shakespeare wants these characters to play in this scene become clear:

> *Macduff is clearly genuinely and sincerely concerned about the state of the nation. He's also genuinely committed to the manly and soldierly way of doing things. He's determined to express himself through his sword.*[4]

As such, he cannot understand Malcolm's moderate response to his call to arms. Macduff has a 'comparative lack of intelligence'[5] compared to Malcolm, which manifests itself here. Macduff believes the solution to Scotland's woes

2.  Ed. A.R. Braunmuller, *The New Cambridge Shakespeare: Macbeth*, (Cambridge: Cambridge University Press, 2008), p. 240–241.

3.  Richard Leviton, *The Imagination of Pentecost*, (New York: Anthroposophic Press, 1994), p. 325.

4.  Andrew Gibson, 'Malcolm, Macduff and the structure of *Macbeth*', *Critical Essays on Macbeth*, ed. Linda Cookson and Brian Loughrey, (Glasgow: Longman Group UK Limited, 1988), p. 94.

5.  Ibid.

lies with the sword. As a king, Malcolm would be expected to scrutinise, to question, to listen and consider, not just to respond to things with violence because he can. He is acting as a king would. How one is raised, then, conditions how one responds: Malcolm with thoughtfulness and Macduff with force.

Malcolm aims to investigate Macduff's motive for his actions, asking 'Why in that rawness left you wife and child – / Those precious motives, those strong knots of love – / Without leave-taking?' Perhaps Malcolm believes Macduff is able to leave his family in Scotland because they require no protection, especially if Macduff has aligned himself with Macbeth. Malcolm reiterates he is only questioning Macduff to look after his own safety.

### 'BLEED, BLEED, POOR COUNTRY'

Malcolm's reluctance to trust Macduff causes Macduff to cry out 'Bleed, bleed, poor country. / Great tyranny, lay thou thy basis sure, / For goodness dare not check thee.' 'Goodness' here could mean the qualities of virtue and righteousness in general; tyranny and evil have become so powerful that anything else is unable to thrive. It could, however, mean Malcolm himself, for Macduff has clearly travelled to England believing Malcolm to be a moral man. Macduff is intent on securing his support in fighting back against Macbeth. One cannot blame him for lamenting the lacklustre, cautious response Malcolm offers in return. The fact Macduff is instructing the country to 'bleed' implies there is nothing left for it to do but wither and die. Scotland is now doomed, for no one is willing to shield it from those who would do it harm.

No one that is, apart from Macduff, whose honour has clearly been hurt by Malcolm's suspicions and subsequent interrogation of him. Macduff states he would not give into temptation and become the villain Malcolm believes him to be, even if everything Macbeth has was offered. He knows his role is not to lead Scotland but to fight, protecting and honouring his country. Malcolm's doubts have offended him.

From this moment on, Malcolm really decides to test Macduff's loyalty. Malcolm agrees Scotland is suffering, claiming that 'It weeps, it bleeds, and each new day a gash / Is added to her wounds.' This may allude to Christ's suffering before his crucifixion,[6] an interpretation which would make sense when one considers the Captain's words in Act I, Scene ii when he claimed Macbeth and Banquo's actions were suitably violent to 'memorize another Golgotha'. Golgotha is characterised as a 'dry, dusty [place] without vegetation except some

---

6.   Ed. A.R. Braunmuller, *The New Cambridge Shakespeare: Macbeth*, (Cambridge: Cambridge University Press, 2008), pp. 241–242.

scrubby hyssop.'[7] Malcolm, then, is acknowledging Scotland as a place which has become as infamous as the site of Christ's crucifixion. The barren imagery used to describe Golgotha could, in a way, be applied to Macbeth's Scotland too. Nothing is allowed to thrive under his kingship, his reign has become synonymous with death, and he is ensuring, whether intentionally or not, that his Scotland is just as memorable.

What happens next is extremely surprising, for he states that he, as king, would be worse than Macbeth: '...my poor country / Shall have more vices than it had before, / More suffer, and more sundry ways than ever, / By him that shall succeed.' It is an unprecedented admission and one which audiences do not expect. Shakespeare has clearly been using this scene to help audiences consider how the play will end, steering Malcolm's character to the forefront of the action so we recognise him as Scotland's redeemer, despite bearing witness to his reserved response to Macduff's pleas. This moment, however, threatens to derail Malcolm as a figure of redemption, and audiences are suddenly faced with the prospect of a worse successor than Macbeth. But all is not as it seems.

If we are to agree that Macduff has a 'lack of intelligence'[8] compared to Malcolm, it should come as no surprise that Macduff cannot see through Malcolm's words for what they are: lies. As Malcolm begins to paint a portrait of what Scotland would be like under his kingship, audiences would be forgiven for thinking he would be a worse tyrant than Macbeth. Of course, this is not the case. This odd little game is Malcolm's way of testing Macduff's loyalty to Scotland and is a clever inversion of 'Fair is foul, and foul is fair.' Throughout the play, Shakespeare has only evidenced the first half of the witches' mantra, that things seeming 'fair' will often turn out 'foul'. In Malcolm's character, though, audiences are presented with something 'foul' which will, thankfully, turn out to be 'fair'. The vices Malcolm begins to list are nothing but a ruse to help him work out where Macduff's loyalties lie: '[Malcolm is] setting out to determine how far Macduff would be prepared to compromise on his morality as king in order to install him on the throne in place of Macbeth.'[9]

---

7. Lew Wallace, *Ben Hur: A Tale of the Christ*, (London: Pan Books, 1959), p. 303.

8. Andrew Gibson, 'Malcolm, Macduff and the structure of *Macbeth*', *Critical Essays on Macbeth*, ed. Linda Cookson and Brian Loughrey, (Glasgow: Longman Group UK Limited, 1988), p. 94.

9. Neil Bowen et. al., *The Art of Drama Volume 2: Macbeth GCSE & Beyond*, (Bristol, Peripeteia Press, 2019), p. 107.

## MALCOLM AS A FIGURE OF TYRANNY

For now, though, Macduff remains confused as Malcolm persists with his trickery: 'Malcolm speaks with apparent relish of the dreadful things he will do when he becomes king, or rather, as he forecasts, tyrant.'[10] He claims that when his vices are 'opened, black Macbeth / Will seem as pure as snow, and the poor state / Esteem him as a lamb, being compared / With my confineless harms.' Using 'black' to describe Macbeth's character is significant. Most references to 'black' in the play are associated with the supernatural and evil, whether it be Macbeth's 'black and deep desires', 'black Hecate' or the 'secret, black and midnight hags'. Malcolm has unwittingly (surely unwittingly, because he has no way of knowing about Macbeth's communion with the witches) aligned Macbeth with the supernatural and still maintains he would be a worse king than the current tyrant Scotland suffers under.

Macduff refuses to believe Malcolm's claims, replying: 'Not in the legions / Of horrid hell can come a devil more damned / In evils to top Macbeth.'

Malcolm acknowledges Macbeth as a man with many vices, listing tyrannical qualities but not necessarily *Macbeth's* tyrannical qualities. For example, whilst it is generally agreed that Macbeth shows avarice through his pursuit of power as well as deceit and malice, his 'luxurious' (meaning lecherous) behaviour is less certain. Arguably, 'the association of the tyrant with excessive sexual desire was a commonplace of Renaissance political thought, but we have never witnessed or even heard about Macbeth engaged in any specifically lecherous acts.'[11] Malcolm's description of Macbeth is categorised as 'propagandistic exaggeration',[12] which is more than plausible considering Malcolm is attempting to explore who Macduff considers a suitable successor to Macbeth's throne. In over exaggerating Macbeth's evil qualities and then saying he would be even worse, Malcolm can see what Macduff is willing to accept and what he is not. Macbeth as a lecherous character is not, one supposes, within the realms of impossibility; such is the depth of his sin that accusing him of another becomes too easy.

Malcolm seems to enjoy creating verbal portraits of sinners and tyrants. In attempting to convince Macduff of his own sins, Malcolm draws attention to his own lechery, his 'voluptuousness'. He claims his lust, which endangers, 'wives... daughters / ... matrons and... maids', is insatiable, an example he uses to highlight how desire is stronger than both internal and external restraint. Macbeth, he concludes, would be the better king.

---

10. R.S. White, *Ambivalent Macbeth*, (Sydney: Sydney University Press, 2018), p. 78.

11. Christoph Clausen, *Macbeth Multiplied: Negotiating Historical and Medial Differences Between Shakespeare and Verdi*, (New York: Rodopi, 2005), p. 218.

12. Ibid., p. 219.

Perhaps this is why critics turn to Act IV, Scene iii when questioning how Shakespeare defines 'tyrant' and 'king'. Macduff believes 'boundless intemperance' to be a kind of tyranny, one which has caused the 'fall of many kings', but a forgivable quality nonetheless, especially when compared to Macbeth. After all, 'boundless intemperance' for power is surely more damaging than 'boundless intemperance' for women. It should not, Macduff argues, prevent Malcolm from taking the crown.

In response, Malcolm continues to add detail to his portrait of himself as a tyrant, testing Macduff's limits, seeing what the Thane will accept and what he will not. He claims to possess 'stanchless avarice' and details:

> *That, were I king,*
> *I should cut off the nobles for their lands,*
> *Desire his jewels and this other's house,*
> *And my more-having would be as a sauce*
> *To make me hunger more.'*

Macduff acknowledges that greed has become the downfall of many kings. Indeed, greed as a sinful quality is far more applicable to Macbeth than lechery and has, in part, initiated the downfall Macbeth is experiencing (whether he knows it or not). Macbeth's greed, of course, manifests itself in his quest for more power; he is never content to settle for what he has. Perhaps this is why Macduff is willing to accept Malcolm's supposed greed; Malcolm speaks of his avarice in monetary and materialistic terms, whereas power is more of an abstract quality which cannot necessarily always be measured by what one owns. Whilst it is true money can buy power to a certain extent, Macbeth places greater emphasis on his position as king as being his true wealth.

### 'THIS AVARICE STICKS DEEPER... THAN SUMMER SEEMING LUST'

Macduff responds: 'This avarice / Sticks deeper.../ Than summer-seeming lust'. Macduff associates lust with summer in that it is hot but short-lived.[13] His words echo Macbeth's from Act III, Scene i: 'Our fears in Banquo / Stick deep'. Like Macbeth's fears, Macduff is saying greed roots itself deep in those who suffer from it; avarice is not a quality one can shun with ease. Pertinently, Shakespeare alludes to Macbeth's fears and reminds us of Banquo through 'stick deep' because it is Macbeth's greed that drives him to fear his friend; Macbeth's greed is partly to blame for Banquo's death because, not content with just having the

---

13. Ed. Sandra Clark and Pamela Mason, *The Arden Shakespeare: Macbeth*, (London: Bloomsbury, 2015), p. 259.

crown for himself, he is determined to safeguard his royal title against those who pose a threat.

This echo would certainly lend itself to an alternative reading of Macduff's following words. In saying avarice 'hath been / The sword of our slain kings' he is arguing that greed has led to the downfall of many kings, a fact which will certainly prove true for Macbeth. Yet in an ironic sense, the same is true for Banquo, who will be father to a line of kings. Avarice causes his downfall too, although it is not his own greed which drives him to his grave. It is Macbeth's greed for a royal lineage that kills Banquo.

### MACDUFF MISUNDERSTOOD?

Macduff listens and responds saying 'All these are portable, / With other graces weighed.' He is saying he can accept Malcolm's lechery and avarice. They are forgivable and still a better alternative to Macbeth's regime. Scotland will see him provided with women and resources if he agrees to challenge Macbeth for the crown. Audiences are, however, presented with something of a moral quandary here; Macduff is positioned by Shakespeare as Macbeth's foil, and so one may be forgiven for interpreting his character as being that of a noble thane whose follies are non-existent, but this is not entirely the case. So willing is he to accept (or ignore?) Malcolm's self-professed vices that his own integrity can be called into question:

> *Macduff... displays a curious worldliness in his interview with Malcolm. Of course he finally passes the test which Malcolm offers, he is finally revolted by Malcolm's self-portrait of vice; yet how much, how very much of vice will Macduff accept in a sovereign before his stomach turns.*[14]

Where does one draw the line? The answer to *that* comes in Malcolm's next speech; upon hearing Macduff believes him to possess 'other graces', he replies 'But I have none.' This is where audiences learn what Shakespeare perceives to be a good king; if *Macbeth* really is an example of pro-royalist propaganda, this speech would certainly please King James I. Malcolm lists 'king-becoming graces' as '...justice, verity, temperance, stableness, / Bounty, perseverance, mercy, lowliness, / Devotion, patience, courage, fortitude'. He distances himself from all of these, saying 'Nay, had I power, I should / Pour the sweet milk of concord into hell', 'concord' meaning 'harmony' and a brief throwback to Lady

---

14. Robert Ornstein, *The Moral Vision of Jacobean Tragedy,* (Madison: University of Wisconsin Press, 1960), p. 233.

Macbeth's fears in Act I, Scene v that her husband is 'too full 'o'th' milk of human kindness' to be able to go through with Duncan's murder. Arguably, it could be this moment which affects Macduff the most.

### 'POUR THE SWEET MILK OF CONCORD INTO HELL'

'Milk' has appeared three times in the play before Malcolm refers to it: the aforementioned fear of Lady Macbeth's, 'take my milk for gall' in Act I, Scene v and 'the babe that milks me' in Act I, Scene vii. Each reference to milk is uttered by Lady Macbeth, and 'in every case the image has amounted to a perversion of nature'.[15] The same could be said in Act IV, Scene iii: 'the equation is made through the image [of milk] that peace is a feminine function and concern.'[16] The fact Malcolm would actively 'pour' this 'sweet milk… into hell' shows there would be no hope of peace under his regime.

Macduff can only respond with 'O Scotland, Scotland', perhaps lamenting his failure to find the hope he so desperately sought by travelling to England. He faces the increasingly realistic prospect that Scotland is beyond saving and, in a frustrated tirade directed at Malcolm, says Malcolm is not 'fit to govern' and not fit to live either. It is this tirade which helps Macduff pass Malcolm's test, and although his own integrity has been called into question somewhat, audiences sense Macduff's desperation and understand his willingness to lay Malcolm's vices of lechery and avarice aside if it means it is the right thing for Scotland. Hope is a very dangerous thing to lose, and Macduff has been holding on to it for as long as he can, only now accepting defeat.

His loss of hope makes him unabashedly forward; he has no qualms about calling Malcolm a disgrace to his family, comparing him to Duncan, the 'sainted king', and his mother who devoted her life to prayer. Macduff cannot recognise these qualities in Malcolm. As such, with no one else to turn to, Macduff prepares to banish himself from Scotland forever. Apart from his family, who he still believes to be alive at this point, there is nothing left for him there.

Finally, Malcolm reveals the truth and 'foul' turns 'fair' as he explains who he really is and why he had to create a tyrannical portrait of himself instead of being his honest, moral self. His doubts in Macduff are removed; realising Macduff has not aligned himself with Macbeth despite his protestations of sinfulness, Malcolm knows Macduff is true to his word. Arguably, whilst Malcolm is certainly cleverer than Macduff, this 'game is unnecessary from the

---

15.  William T. Liston, '"Male and Female Created He Them": Sex and Gender in 'Macbeth'", *College Literature*, Vol. 16, No. 3, 1989, pp. 232–239, www.jstor.org/stable/25111824.

16.  Ibid.

start', for Macduff 'is quite obviously no Machiavel.'[17] Malcolm, it seems, has become so distrusting that he must do whatever he needs to do in order to feel safe, even when it is deemed unnecessary. His brother's words still ring clearly in his ears: 'Where we are, / There's daggers in men's smiles'.

An alternative reading of the scene up until this moment is a little more sinister. Malcolm's ability to 'act', whilst framed as a protective measure, in actual fact shows just how manipulative he can be, a trait one would usually associate with Macbeth. Macduff's 'blind idealism'[18] is something which could easily be used against him. Both Malcolm and Banquo, then, possess qualities that threaten to make them tread a path similar to Macbeth's. Everyone has dark qualities within them, yet it is how we control these qualities which interests Shakespeare:

> *The uneasy implication is that subjects in a kingdom cannot actually know in advance whether they are getting a saint or a tyrant, an Edward [the Confessor, the king of England, known for his piety and who Malcolm will speak more of later in the scene] or a Macbeth, until it is too late.*[19]

Audiences are left to wonder what type of king Malcolm will truly be, 'but the issue is certainly raised and left unresolved.'[20]

### 'CHILD OF INTEGRITY'

Malcolm tries to placate Macduff by calling him a 'child of integrity'; 'Macduff's honesty is metaphorically joined with the new generations that will defeat Macbeth.'[21] He explains how Macbeth has tried to 'win' Malcolm back into his favour through all kinds of trickery and deceit; Malcolm cannot believe people too quickly or it could mean his death. This is a quality of Macbeth's often overlooked; his belief in what he is told is unwaning, and although he initially questions the original set of prophecies he is given, it does not take him long to deduce that the witches are telling the truth and his ascension to

17. Andrew Gibson, 'Malcolm, Macduff and the structure of *Macbeth*', *Critical Essays on Macbeth*, ed. Linda Cookson and Brian Loughrey, (Glasgow: Longman Group UK Limited, 1988), p. 95.

18. Neil Bowen et al., *The Art of Drama Volume 2: Macbeth GCSE & Beyond*, (Bristol, Peripeteia Press, 2019), p. 148.

19. R.S. White, *Ambivalent Macbeth*, (Sydney: Sydney University Press, 2018), p. 81.

20. Ibid.

21. Ed. A.R. Braunmuller, *The New Cambridge Shakespeare: Macbeth*, (Cambridge: Cambridge University Press, 2008), p. 244–245.

kingship is not beyond the realms of impossibility. Indeed, in Act IV, Scene i, he takes at face value the idea that 'none of woman born / Shall harm' him, and in doing so believes himself to be invincible, building upon his hubristic and narcissistic traits to unimaginable levels. Malcolm has to be different if he is to avoid becoming another Macbeth, and so the fact that he would be cautiously sceptical makes sense. Macduff has had to build Malcolm's trust, and as a result Malcolm now puts himself into Macduff's hands and allows himself to be guided by him.

Having denounced his artificial evil, Malcolm begins constructing a more moral, trustworthy image of himself. He is not lecherous; he is a virgin. He is not avaricious; instead, he places little importance on material things, even what he owns himself. He says he has never spoken a false word before this moment; he is quite the honest man. Such are the qualities of a good king. It seems, however, that Malcolm is not the fully formed monarch we see later in Edward the Confessor who has harboured this Scottish refugee. He speaks as a man of his status should, yet his words are somewhat inflated – high sounding but meaningless. For example:

> *It's surprising to find that, only twelve lines after referring to Macbeth as 'devilish', Malcolm is telling Macduff that he wouldn't betray 'The devil to his fellow' himself... This little contradiction is striking. It seems devised to show how little Malcolm thinks about what he says, how little brain there is in his bombast.*[22]

Perhaps this is done to separate Malcolm from Edward the Confessor. Malcolm is a good man, but is yet to reach Edward's level of piety.

As Malcolm's speech progresses, he informs Macduff that Old Siward is on his way with 'ten thousand warlike men', prepared to fight against Macbeth. This is what Macduff has sought all along, and yet all he can do is remain silent, dumbfounded by this sudden change in Malcolm's character.

Macduff's confusion ('Such welcome and unwelcome things at once / 'Tis hard to reconcile) is cut short by the appearance of a doctor, therefore leaving his response to Malcolm's duality unresolved.

---

22. Andrew Gibson, 'Malcolm, Macduff and the structure of *Macbeth*', *Critical Essays on Macbeth*, ed. Linda Cookson and Brian Loughrey, (Glasgow: Longman Group UK Limited, 1988), p. 96.

## EDWARD THE CONFESSOR

Malcolm asks the doctor whether Edward will be joining them and is informed that 'wretched souls' have sought their king in hope of a cure to their 'malady', an illness no medicine can put an end to. This 'malady' is likely 'scrofula', a disease that causes glandular swellings, recognised today as a form of tuberculosis.[23] Malcolm describes scrofula as 'the Evil', cured, it seems, by the 'royal touch'. A monarch healing their subjects through a simple touch was first ascribed to Edward the Confessor and was later practised by King James, perhaps explaining why this brief interlude in the scene takes place:[24]

> *There is a definite New Testament feeling about the whole passage, and Edward's shadowy miracle-working presence, never directly visible, carries the connotation of the Savior at his holy work amongst men. Edward in the play is grace itself, not quite incarnate; he presides over Malcolm as the witches preside over Macbeth. The good king's power is spoken of entirely in terms of sanctity.*[25]

Audiences are never invited to witness this miracle first hand, perhaps because it is such a holy act. This secrecy creates a shroud of mystery around goodness and the form it takes. Edward, like all good things, remains elusive throughout the play, but audiences are reminded of his presence here and, with it, the presence of virtue, morality and righteousness.

In Edward, the 'king-becoming graces' listed by Malcolm are made real, meaning a comparison between the King of England and the King of Scotland is now inevitable: 'at one moral extreme stands the witches and damnation; at the other stands Edward the Confessor and the highest potency of human grace.'[26] Furthermore, Edward's 'curative power' runs parallel to Macbeth's destruction and a series of oppositions follow suit:

---

23. Richard C. McCoy, "'The Grace of Grace' and Double-talk in Macbeth', *Shakespeare Survey: Volume 57, Macbeth and its Afterlife*, ed. Peter Holland, (Cambridge: Cambridge University Press, 2004), p. 30.

24. James F. Turrell, 'The Ritual of Royal Healing in Early Modern England: Scrofula, Liturgy, and Politics', *Anglican and Episcopal History*, Vol. 68, No. 1 (March 1999), pp. 3–36, https://www.jstor.org/stable/42611999.

25. B.L. Reid, '"Macbeth" and the Play of Absolutes', *The Sewanee Review*, Vol. 73, No. 1 (1965), pp. 19–46, www.jstor.org/stable/27541080.

26. Ibid.

*Edward has a gift of prophecy; Macbeth is the victim of prophecies.*
*Edward can pass the gift to his successors; Macbeth will have no*
*successors. More powerful that Duncan, Edward represents an*
*ideal of kingship. He remains off stage, suggesting that such ideas*
*are at a remove from the reality the characters have to live in.*[27]

## 'ALAS, POOR COUNTRY'

At this point, Ross enters, having left Scotland to bring news of Macduff's wife and children. Macduff recognises him almost immediately, but Malcolm does not, seeing only that Ross is 'my countryman', but unaware of his identity, cleverly mirroring the beginning of the scene where he establishes that he does not really know Macduff, even though they are both Scots. Macduff identifies him as 'My ever gentle cousin', causing Malcolm to respond, 'I know him now... betimes remove / The means that make us strangers', suggesting Ross enters wearing something that identifies him as a Scot but conceals his true identity until he is told to remove it.

Ross paints a bleak picture of Scotland, saying the country is 'Almost afraid to know itself', a theme that becomes more prominent as the play moves towards its climax. The idea of losing touch with oneself is explored in the previous scene; in Act IV, Scene ii, he says to Lady Macduff 'cruel are the times, when we are traitors / And do not know ourselves.' To be 'afraid to know itself' suggests Scotland has become unrecognisable, so steeped is it in bloodshed and villainy. However, whereas Macbeth has lost sight of who he is through the choices he has made, Scotland has been forced to become a stranger to itself through the wounds tyranny has inflicted upon it.

As a result of this tyranny, Scotland cannot 'Be called our mother, but our grave.' It is no longer the nurturing place it was or a place of protection, but a place where death reigns, 'Where sighs, and groans, and shrieks that rend the air, / Are made, not marked'. This is a devastating image. Ross's claim that sounds of pain and death are heard but not remarked on demonstrates just how fearful Macbeth has made his people. Silence ensures their survival.

Shakespeare's ideas around sound in this scene, in a way, hark back to the very beginning of the play. These 'groans' and 'shrieks' are the 'hurly-burly' of Macbeth's Scotland, denoting the tumultuous battle between tyranny and innocence. It is not, as audiences can tell, a battle being won by innocence; indeed, people have stopped asking for whom the 'deadman's knell' tolls, for there are far too many deaths to count. The image of a 'knell' here is cleverly

---

27. Ed. Alexander Leggatt, *William Shakespeare's Macbeth: A Sourcebook*, (London: Routledge, 2006), p. 176.

placed, for it reminds us of the knell that summons Duncan 'to heaven, or to hell', a moment just before Macbeth commits his first crime. It reminds the audience of a moment when he still had the opportunity to choose good over evil and thus maintain himself as a figure of loyalty and honour rather than deception and duality.

Macduff, as one would expect, asks after his wife and children. Ross says they are 'well', delaying the news of their murder, perhaps because he is daunted by the sheer enormity of the news he must deliver. Again, Macduff's decision in leaving his wife and children in Scotland must be called into question. In asking Ross, 'The tyrant has not battered at their peace?', Macduff fully acknowledges an attack taking advantage of their vulnerability in his absence is extremely likely. Ross replies that 'they were well at peace, when I did leave 'em.' His ambiguity is all too evident; Macduff, of course, believes Ross's words to mean his family are safe, untouched by the evil spreading through Scotland. Ross, in saying Macduff's family are 'at peace' is not technically lying; they are at peace in death.

Instead, Ross opts to tell them news of good men coming together to fight against Macbeth. He believes Malcolm's presence would inspire many others to fight, leading Malcolm to say he will return. 'Gracious England', meaning Edward, has sent Malcolm 'good Siward and ten thousand men; / An older and a better soldier none / That Christendom gives out.'

### 'YOUR CASTLE IS SURPRISED'

It is here that Ross decides to deliver the news about Macduff's wife and children in an exchange which, arguably, is one of the most devastating moments in the play: Macduff's 'wife and babes' have been 'savagely slaughtered'.

Macduff cannot possibly comprehend what he is hearing. Macduff's role here must be considered; Shakespeare has, after setting Macduff up to be so, finally allowed the character to fully adopt his position as Macbeth's double. The news Macduff has just heard will result in his vow to kill the King, just as Macbeth, after expressing initial doubts, vowed to kill Duncan. Macduff, if he decides to go through with killing Macbeth, will commit regicide; Macbeth's death may be more of a symbolic purging of evil, but it is still regicide, and Macduff will be guilty of the very same sin that causes Macbeth's downward spiral. It could be suggested that 'strange as it may seem, Macbeth has hacked Macduff into a suitable double of himself. By the end of the play, both soldiers will be bereft of wife and children, fueled by a fury unmatched by anyone else in the play, and abiding the moment when each can destroy the other.'[28]

---

28. Marina Favila, '"Mortal Thoughts" and Magical Thinking in "Macbeth"', *Modern Philology*, Vol. 99, No. 1, 2001, pp. 1–25, www.jstor.org/stable/439153.

Interestingly, it is Malcolm who is the first to respond, suggesting Macduff has been stunned into silence, caught in the grip of grief and only jostled out of his confused stupor when Malcolm instructs him to 'Give sorrow words.' Macduff can only respond with a question – 'My children too?' – shocked at this unexpected bombshell which has brought his world crashing down. Ross has to repeat himself several times; Macduff persists with his questions, perhaps hoping, in some small way, that Ross is lying and the situation is not as dire as he has been led to believe. After all, having just been fooled by Malcolm, one would forgive Macduff for hoping that this 'foul' thing will have a 'fair' outcome.

## MACDUFF AND MASCULINITY

What follows is an interesting examination by Shakespeare as to what constitutes masculinity. From the beginning of the play, audiences are given the impression that masculinity is inextricably linked with violence and the ability to purge oneself of emotion. Lady Macbeth's plea to spirits to 'Make thick my blood, / Stop up th'access and passage to remorse' and 'take my milk for gall', as well as reports of Macbeth's prowess on the battlefield, perpetuate this stereotype that masculinity, violence and negative emotion go hand in hand. Indeed, this is certainly Malcolm's view; he instructs Macduff to 'be comforted' in the vengeance they will wreak upon Macbeth. It is a cold response, one which does not consider the emotion Macduff experiences towards his wife and children. Revenge should be had as a way of venting the hatred one feels.[29]

Malcolm's suggestions of 'Give sorrow words' and 'Be comforted. / Let's make medicines of our great revenge / To cure this deadly grief' imply there is a conventional way of expressing one's sorrow as a man, one to which Macduff is expected to conform. Macduff evades this anticipated behaviour, responding by saying: 'He has no children.' On an initial reading, one could deduce Macduff is referring to Macbeth himself. He has no children and so he has found it easy to take away the children of others, oblivious to familial bonds of love. Alternatively, Macduff could be noting that there is no way of getting his own back in an equal manner; Macbeth has no children for him to kill in order for Macbeth to feel the pain Macduff feels now.

Others, however, have read this line as being directed towards Malcolm; Macduff could be scolding him for the ease with which he suggests a violent

---

29. Ed. Sandra Clark and Pamela Mason, *The Arden Shakespeare: Macbeth*, (London: Bloomsbury, 2015), p. 268.

response instead of offering him the sympathy he needs to be shown.[30] Either way, it could be argued that this comment alludes to the great fear that has permeated through the play: that of an absent lineage. After all, Malcolm will undoubtedly suffer the same anxieties as Macbeth. He may succeed in overthrowing Macbeth; he may take his crown; but like this tyrant, he has no children to whom he can pass on his royal status. This would certainly be a familiar anxiety, not only in royal circles but in public circles too. Perhaps the most striking example of this was the worry England felt throughout Queen Elizabeth I's reign as to who would succeed her.[31]

### 'ALL MY PRETTY CHICKENS'

Macduff, however, cares little for the challenges that may face the new king. At this point, he cannot comprehend the thought of retaliation. His 'pretty chickens' (continuing with the avian imagery from the previous scene) have been killed by the 'hell-kite', perhaps the most fearsome bird of prey mentioned in the play, and a metaphor for Macbeth. His reference to his children as 'chickens' has a pathetic, hopeless quality to it. This man, this loyal soldier who lives and dies by the sword, has been reduced to a quivering wreck. It is a quiet moment, a moment of truth and honesty without pretence amidst the turmoil and chaos of the action and perhaps one of the only examples of grieving we see in the play. Here, audiences are allowed a glimpse into the human cost of death and the grief which follows.

Malcolm's response is simple: 'Dispute it like a man.' He still expects Macduff's grief and anger to manifest itself in the form of violence. Macduff, however, says 'I shall do so, / But I must also feel it as a man.' The difference between Malcolm's 'like a man' and Macduff's 'as a man' is monumental. Macduff embodies the idea that masculinity is far more than violence. He knows what he must do in that moment to cope with what he has heard; he does not and will not live up to an ideal set out by anyone else and, in doing so, acknowledges that to be powerful does not mean that one must be lacking in feeling, but that one can be compassionate. He fundamentally disagrees with Macbeth and Lady Macbeth's view of gender. Sensitivity is not unbecoming of a man, and Shakespeare rejects the narrow definition set forth until this point that masculinity means to be insensitive, violent and uncompassionate. Macduff must experience his loss and weep non-manly

---

30. Ed. Sandra Clark and Pamela Mason, *The Arden Shakespeare: Macbeth*, (London: Bloomsbury, 2015), p. 268.

31. Paul E.J. Hammer. 'Elizabeth's Unsettling Succession', *Huntington Library Quarterly*, Vol. 78, No. 3, 2015, pp. 553–561, www.jstor.org/stable/10.1525/hlq.2015.78.3.553.

tears, for 'only a fully human warrior can confront and conquer the "fiend" that Macbeth has become.'[32] This is a far cry from Macbeth, who believes 'manhood is not a constant, fixed quality but one which must continually be proved by manly deeds.'[33]

Macduff blames himself, noting 'they were all struck for thee.' Malcolm, once again, tries to elicit a vengeful response from Macduff, saying 'be this the whetstone of your sword. Let grief / convert to anger; blunt not the heart, enrage it.' This time, he succeeds. Macduff considers the idea of continuing to weep, but ultimately dismisses this as a possibility, saying 'Bring thou this fiend of Scotland and myself; / Within my sword's length set him. If he scape, / Heaven forgive him too.' Up until this point, Macduff has been a victim of the false notions of the role of men to protect their families and provide for them; this is certainly a view held by Lady Macduff. She expects Macduff, as her husband, to be there to protect his family. Macduff must have suffered through this dichotomy: does he stay and fulfil his wife's beliefs in him as the family protector and do nothing, not act against Macbeth and demonstrate his manliness in this impotent (as far as he is concerned) way, or does he go and play an effective part in the 'real' world of men? In choosing to do what is expected of him, he has lost everything precious. He is feeling this loss 'as a man', but now must 'dispute it like a man', not necessarily just to avenge his family, but to stop others suffering a similar fate.

Malcolm commends his change of heart, saying 'This time goes manly.' Macduff is now conforming to the expectations set upon him. Malcolm claims their armies are ready and preparations are afoot. 'Macbeth,' he says, 'Is ripe for shaking'. This autumnal image, suggesting Macbeth is ready to fall from the throne, holds wider symbolic implications. Autumn is the season of change, something both Malcolm and Macduff wish to bring about by marching on Macbeth's Scotland. It is the season of preservation, where animals hibernate in preparation for the winter; Macduff and Malcolm must act quickly if they have any hope of preserving what little is left of the Scotland they know. There is a real sense of an ending here. As Act IV draws to a close, Malcolm utters the words: 'The night is long that never finds the day.' The threat of yet more bloodshed and further violence lingers in the air, yet, this time, it is tinged with a sense of hope – small, but present nonetheless.

---

32. Carolyn Asp, '"Be bloody, bold and resolute": Tragic Action and Sexual Stereotyping in *Macbeth*', *Macbeth: Critical Essays*, ed. S. Schoenbaum, (Abingdon: Routledge, 2015), p. 379.

33. Ibid.

## Basilikon Doron and the qualities of kingship

Act IV, Scene iii of *Macbeth* scrutinises what it means to be a good king. Shakespeare, through the character of Malcolm, voices his opinions as to what qualities a king should possess. The scene establishes the idea that masculinity, in and of itself, is not enough to make someone a good king, let alone a good man. It would be easy to assume what makes a good king; *being* that person, however, is something different altogether. The ideas Shakespeare presents here may root themselves (alongside Holinshed's *Chronicles*) in a text penned by James I himself: the *Basilikon Doron*, meaning 'The King's Gift' when translated from the Greek.[34] Written in the form of a letter to his son Henry, Duke of Rothesay, the text serves as a 'rule book' of kingship, a treatise on government.

The *Basilikon Doron* is split into three parts, each containing a set of what one may call 'guidelines' on how to be an efficient monarch. The first part describes a king's duty towards God, how one must trust in God yet also fear God. One must strive to be a good Christian. The second focuses more on the responsibilities of a good king. James discusses how one should aim to rule with justice as opposed to becoming a tyrant. The third and final part concerns a monarch's behaviour 'in matters to be judged on the basis of expediency rather than on moral grounds.'[35] It is not 'a book on absolute kingship.'[36] Instead, the *Basilikon Doron* 'is far more concerned with its practical aspects.'[37] It is a 'didactic work on behaviour and morality – a demonstration of James's suitability as a godly king, interspersed with concrete advice on the government of Scotland.'[38]

Whilst there is not enough time to go into detail here regarding everything James says about kingship and the advice he imparts, the *Basilikon Doron*:

> *Contains traditional advice on moral kingship, such as appointing wise counsellors and discreet and learned judges,*

34. British Library, 'Printed edition of King James VI and I's *Basilikon Doron* or "The King's Gift", 1603', https://www.bl.uk/collection-items/printed-edition-of-king-james-vi-and-is-basilikon-doron-or-the-kings-gift-1603.

35. Lily B. Campbell, 'Political Ideas in Macbeth IV. iii', *Shakespeare Quarterly*, Vol. 2, No. 4, 1951, pp. 281–286, www.jstor.org/stable/2866240.

36. Jenny Wormald, 'James VI & I, Basilikon Doron and the trew law of free monarchies', *The Mental World of Jacobean Court*, ed. Linda Levy Peck, (Cambridge: Cambridge University Press, 1991), p. 52.

37. Astrid Stilma, *A King Translated: The writings of King James VI and I and their interpretation in the low countries, 1593–1603*, (New York: Routledge, 2016), p. 143.

38. Ibid.

> *travelling the realm to impart justice personally, impartiality to*
> *rich and poor, and especially the condemnation of flattery as the*
> *main cause of the corruption of [a] king.*[39]

From this alone, we can see how Macbeth's own kingship completely disregards James's own principles. Whilst Macbeth's early actions in the play may be subtle in their secretive nature, they soon develop into loud, grandiose, violent enterprises; his rule is anything but discreet. Macbeth does not 'impart justice personally'. In fact, he imparts *in*justice and even then he does not do that himself; instead, he sends murderers to do his bidding in an attempt to feign innocence. Even flattery, in a sense, has lent a hand in his own corruption in that he flatters himself; his hubris has deluded him into thinking he is untouchable and, as such, it has lured him into a false sense of security. In essence, Macbeth embodies the very opposite of what is set out by James I in the *Basilikon Doron*.

Arguably, some elements in the *Basilikon Doron* read 'almost as though *Macbeth* had been written with it in mind',[40] drawing on James's advice to Prince Henry as evidence:

> *For the part of making, and executing of Lawes, consider*
> *first the trew difference betwixt a lawfulll good King, and an*
> *vsurping Tyran, and yee shall the more easily vunderstnad your*
> *duetie herein.*[41]

Certainly, Malcolm's listing of 'king-becoming graces' bears huge similarity to the 'princely virtues James I sets out in his words about the 'science of rule'.[42] When speaking to Macduff about the kingly qualities he supposedly lacks, Malcolm lists virtues including 'justice, verity, temperance, stableness, / Bounty, perseverance, mercy, lowliness, / Devotion, patience, courage [and] fortitude'. Malcolm's words echo James I's own. James I 'advises his son to make temperance queen of all [the four cardinal virtues] and to use temperance even in justice which is "the greatest vertue that properly belongeth to a Kings

---

39. Astrid Stilma, *A King Translated: The writings of King James VI and I and their interpretation in the low countries, 1593–1603*, (New York: Routledge, 2016), p. 143.

40. Christoph Clausen, *Macbeth Multiplied: Negotiating Historical and Medial Difference Between Shakespeare and Verdi*, (New York: Rodopi, 2005), p. 194.

41. Ibid.

42. Debra Charlton, *Holistic Shakespeare: An Experiential Learning Approach*, (Bristol: Intellect, 2012), p. 54.

office.'"[43] James lists the qualities he deems to reflect moral excellence: 'as I saye of iustice sa saye I of clemencie, magnanimitie, liberalitie, constancie, humilitie, and all other princelie uertues.'[44] Here, then, we see Malcolm's speech and James I's views hand in hand:

> *Justice and temperance and devotion are common to the two lists. James's clemency becomes mercy in Malcolm's list; humility becomes lowliness; liberality becomes bounty; constancy is equated with stableness; and magnanimity as James explains it is the equivalent of patience, consisting of not being vindictive, 'empyring over your owne passion,' triumphing in forgiveness but using wrath when justice demands.*[45]

## Malcolm in *Holinshed's Chronicles*

Shakespeare follows *Holinshed's Chronicles* extremely carefully in Act IV, Scene iii, particularly the first part of the scene. Holinshed describes how Malcolm stated:

> *I am trulie verie sorie for the miserie chanced to my countrie of Scotland, but though I haue neuer so great affection to reliue the same, yet by reason of certeine incurable vices, which reigne in me, I am nothing méet thereto. First, such immoderate lust and voluptuous sensualitie (the abhominable founteine of all vices) followeth me, that if I were made king of Scots, I should séeke to defloure maids and matrones, in such wise that mine intemperancie should be more importable vnto you, than the bloudie tyrannie of Makbeth now is.*[46]

This is just the first of many similarities. Beat for beat, in the first part of Act IV, Scene iii, Malcolm's testing of Macduff plays out in exactly the

---

43. Lily B.Campbell, 'Political Ideas in Macbeth IV. iii', *Shakespeare Quarterly*, Vol. 2, No. 4 (1951), pp. 281–286, www.jstor.org/stable/2866240.

44. Ed. James Craigie, *The Basilicon Doron of King James VI*, (Edinburgh: William Blackwood and Sons Ltd, 1944), p. 140, https://deriv.nls.uk/dcn23/1072/2751/107227516.23.pdf.

45. Lily B. Campbell, 'Political Ideas in Macbeth IV. iii', *Shakespeare Quarterly*, Vol. 2, No. 4 (1951), pp. 281–286, www.jstor.org/stable/2866240.

46. Raphael Holinshed, *Chronicles of England, Scotland and Ireland*, https://www.troup.org/userfiles/929/My%20Files/ELA/HS%20ELA/12th%20ELA/Unit%202/Holinshed%20and%20Macbeth.pdf?id=11638.

same way as Holinshed describes in *Chronicles*. One could argue, then, that there is no 'Shakespeare's Malcolm'. The vices he claims to have are identical to those in *Chronicles*, whilst his good qualities are taken, largely, from the *Basilikon Doron*. They are referenced in Holinshed too. Malcolm is, in part, an amalgamation of both sources, meaning Shakespeare has had little input in the creation of this character. Even if Shakespeare did not consider the *Basilikon Doron* and only drew on Holinshed for Malcolm, we can still see how Malcolm is not his own.

It would seem Shakespeare has to be careful with Malcolm. After all, he is the man who should be sitting on the throne and therefore symbolises a return to order and the end of anarchy. It is not for Shakespeare to decide what sort of man the king should be, just that Divine Right states he is the rightful successor. His role, in a dramatic sense, is to be present for when he is needed at the play's climax. Shakespeare can take more liberties with Holinshed's presentation of Macduff than he can with Malcolm. Perhaps this is why Macduff is chosen as the person to kill Macbeth; it is important Malcolm does not start his reign with a morally questionable action. If Malcolm were the one to kill Macbeth, he would be committing regicide to gain the crown, the exact same crime as that committed by Macbeth.

Having said that, by drawing on elements from both *Chronicles* and the *Basilikon Doron*, Shakespeare has created something of a manipulative figure in Malcolm. Malcolm's 'vices', taken from Holinshed, are almost hyperbolic in the way he describes them to Macduff (compared to the kingly virtues that the characters spend little time discussing). He plays the part of the casual misogynist well, pretending to revel in his description of lechery and enjoyment of his avarice and greed. Yet in a sudden U-turn, Malcolm's good self, the self he claims is his true self, taken from the *Basilikon Doron*, is accentuated; audiences would be forgiven for finding it hard to trust Malcolm entirely. In this case, then, Shakespeare *has* had a hand in creating Malcolm. Through his easy adoption of a dual self, there is a slight, ominous threat that he could become the man Macbeth is, but in the *Basilikon Doron*, James I acknowledges tyranny as something kings must avoid by asking Henry to consider the true difference between a 'lawful, good king and a usurping tyrant', and so these qualities can be hinted at in Malcolm without fear of repercussion.

## Kingship at a glance

## RESOURCE 16.1

Malcolm lists tyrannical qualities but not necessarily *Macbeth's* tyrannical qualities. Malcolm will soon claim to possess similar qualities. Macduff does not realise Malcolm is testing him. Little does Macduff know that he has more in common with Malcolm than first thought. Both, after all, have had loved ones killed because of Macbeth's thirst for power.

Malcolm does contain some deceitful qualities. He is able to lie easily to Macduff as to who he really is. He is creating a dual self, much like Macbeth has done and, as such, we are left wondering whether he is entirely trustworthy. These suspicions are left open by the scene's end.

Malcolm seems to speak with casual misogyny here. He revels in his description of lechery. This is not a sin which can be attributed to Macbeth, but Malcolm's aim is to see just how far Macduff would be willing to cast aside his own morality in order to remove Macbeth from the throne.

**MALCOLM**
I grant him bloody,
Luxurious, avaricious, false, deceitful,
Sudden, malicious, smacking of every sin
That has a name. But there's no bottom, none,
In my voluptuousness. Your wives, your daughters,
Your matrons and your maids could not fill up
The cistern of my lust; and my desire
All continent impediments would o'erbear
That did oppose my will. Better Macbeth
Than such an one to reign.

Renaissance political thought often associated tyranny with sexual desire, perhaps explaining why Malcolm claims to possess lecherous traits.

Malcolm considers his supposed lack of restraint through his discussion of lechery. This, then, is where the links to Macbeth make themselves known. Macbeth is not lecherous as Malcolm describes, but his lack of restraint is one of the first steps he has taken on the road to destruction.

---

These 'graces' are the complete opposite of what Macbeth embodies. In fact, throughout the play, audiences have seen how he actively shuns these characteristics. Macbeth is more interested in preservation of his own power than actual kingship.

The qualities one would deem a king to have are influenced by Holinshed's *Chronicles* and the *Basilikon Doron* by James I.

From the *Basilikon Doron*, we know that temperance is a quality advocated for by James I. Malcolm realises a king must have temperance, which is precisely why he says he does not have it here.

**MALCOLM**
But I have none. The king-becoming graces,
As justice, verity, temperance, stableness,
Bounty, perseverance, mercy, lowliness,
Devotion, patience, courage, fortitude,
I have no relish of them, but abound
In the division of each several crime,
Acting it many ways. Nay, had I power, I should
Pour the sweet milk of concord into hell,
Uproar the universal peace, confound
All unity on earth.

'Milk' in the play is often associated with peace, yet every time it is mentioned, it is followed by an unpeaceful, dark image, suggesting peace cannot exist.

It is ironic that Malcolm says he would 'confound all unity', as it is his role in the play to re-establish unity. He knows he is the rightful king and it is his divine right to sit on the throne. By the play's end, he will start to bring unity to Scotland once more. In creating a dual self to deceive Macduff, he says and does the complete opposite of what he will actually do.

## How?

In all the years I have taught *Macbeth*, I have found Act IV, Scene iii the hardest to teach. It is a wonderful scene, but an intimidating one, and I think it is this which forces many teachers to ignore it altogether. If we do this, however, we are denying our classes something very special. Act IV, Scene iii offers so much, including an alternative look at masculinity (so students can appreciate that violence is not the only thing Shakespeare suggests a man is capable of), the qualities of kingship scrutinised (so students can begin to deliberate on what makes a good leader and whether leading is easy), and a look at the emotional cost of so much death, seen through the eyes of a father mourning the loss of his entire family (so students can see that, for all its bloodshed, *Macbeth* is a very human play). There is too much here to just pass over. In fact, I would argue that Act IV, Scene iii has the power to change our reading of the play entirely; this is not just a play about violence and ambition any more. It is a play about oppression, insurgency, rebellion and the cost of fighting back for one's freedom, no matter how futile the cause may seem. Whilst it has a reputation for being dull and dry, Act IV, Scene iii is so much more.

This 'How?' section is a little different from the others, in that whilst it details how one could approach the scene, it also includes elements of self-reflection regarding the mistakes I have made in the past when trying to teach it.

The first mistake I have made is to try to teach the scene in a single lesson. I have often tried to rush through events, hoping students will pick up on everything they need to know so that we can move on to Act V, Scene i. In the process, I have offered half-hearted explanations as to what is happening. It does not work. There are too many ideas to consider and understand in one lesson. Secondly, I have also been guilty of abridging the scene. Again, it does not work. Whilst it may speed up the process of 'getting through' a scene, it dilutes the challenge, and I am a firm believer of upping expectations rather than lowering them. As a result, the ideas described below have been split into two parts, although they may take longer than two lessons to complete.

## Part One:

### Retrieval

As the end of the play approaches, what knowledge you might deem important to retrieve really depends on how your class is progressing. As such, it is difficult to recommend a precise task to complete at this stage. However, because of the complexities of this scene, I have always found it useful to focus students' attention back on ideas of masculinity and kingship; these two themes often dictate my approach to retrieval at the beginning of this particular lesson. Resource 16.2 is effective in helping students do this.

This task uses icons, but this is not an example of dual coding, as the images are not being used to help explain and teach the concepts they visualise. In fact, students have never come across these icons before in this scheme. The images presented should act as a simple prompt to get students thinking about the themes I want them to consider. It may even be that one uses a piece of artwork to ask students to consider instead.

As a class, discuss what each image could represent, asking students to explain their ideas and choices. Once the class has established what each icon means (as revealed in the example), ask them to make notes on the following two things:

1. What each concept means
2. How the concept has been explored by Shakespeare in the play so far.

## RESOURCE 16.2

King seen as God's spokesperson on earth and placed near God on the Great Chain of Being. Duncan is seen as an ineffective king at the beginning of the play, but the universe is still thrown into disarray when Macbeth kills him.

Masculinity is seen as a desired trait. It is closely associated with violence at the beginning of the play, something which is celebrated. Lady Macbeth seeks to shun her femininity in order to possess the strength needed to go through with her murderous plans.

Kingship

Masculinity

Dictatorship

Free Will v Predestination

Duplicity

'King' by AFY Studios, 'Strong' by Priyanka, 'Dictator' by Luis Prado, 'Manipulation' by auttapol and 'Duplicity' by Y from The Noun Project.

## The Big Questions and pre-reading activities

Introduce the lesson's Big Questions:

> *What is the relationship like between Malcolm and Macduff?*
> *What qualities make a good king?*

This pre-reading activity is designed to help students consider the ideas explored in Act IV, Scene iii before they encounter them.

Provide students with a copy of the cards in Resource 16.3. Ask them to discuss the scenario and questions on one or all of the cards, depending on how you would like to manage the discussion. These resources help students build a picture of what they are about to encounter; they can apply the scenarios – set out here in a non-threatening manner – to the scene itself, once they eventually begin reading.

## RESOURCE 16.3

| | | |
|---|---|---|
| *In Act IV, Scene iii, Macduff arrives in England, having left his family in Scotland to try to rally support for his cause to oust Macbeth from his position of king. He is not aware of his family's murder.*<br><br>Considering he is away from his family, how do you think Macduff will act in this scene? Why do you think he will act in this way? In your response consider how parent and child relationships have been presented in the play so far. | *In Act IV, Scene iii, Macduff, seeing Malcolm as the rightful king, hopes Duncan's son will join the cause in ousting Macbeth from the throne.*<br><br>What do you think Malcolm's response to Macduff's call to arms will be? Why do you think he will respond in this way? In your response consider what might persuade/dissuade Malcolm from joining Macduff. | *In Act IV, Scene iii, Macduff meets with Malcolm and they discuss the qualities they believe a King should possess.*<br><br>What do you think they will say about kingship? Will their views on what makes a good king be similar or different? What has brought you to your opinion? In your response consider what both of these men have experienced under Duncan's kingship compared to Macbeth's kingship. |

Ask students to share their ideas as a class. It is always interesting to compare what they say. Discuss the similarities and differences that emerge from the scenarios and together you can build a picture of what Act IV, Scene iii might look like. This may be a good opportunity for students to explore their own opinions as to the qualities a good king should embody. This will allow them to review their answers to the scenario tasks. Have they really considered what the characters will say about kingship or have they just applied their own opinion to a character without consideration of the character's context? Students must acknowledge the difference between the two and, most importantly, understand why a character would hold such a view, as this will help them see the characters as constructs. Draw any inferences and opinions together verbally or as a written response.

## Reading the scene

Firstly, it is important to note the entire scene will not be read all at once. This is a very deliberate decision; Act IV, Scene iii is very much a scene of two halves, the first focusing solely on Malcolm's deception and Macduff's test of character, the second revolving around Macduff's grief and the news of his family's death. With this in mind, the first reading activity will only focus on Malcolm and Macduff, ending at the doctor's entrance.

I think the best way to approach a reading of Act IV, Scene iii is to chunk it. How teachers decide to chunk the scene is really up to them. Some classes will crave more text at a time, while others may appreciate stops at regular intervals to consolidate their understanding. I usually split the scene into seven chunks, reading one before stopping, questioning and ensuring everyone is keeping up to speed.

After every chunk, and once I have asked my clarifying questions, which the class should answer verbally, I will ask students to write down in three sentences or fewer what has happened within that section of the scene. One may deride this as being a pointless exercise, but it helps me to gauge who has understood the meaning of the scene and who has not before I even read what a student has written. Quite often in my teaching, I stand back and watch. One can gain a lot from doing this; in this instance, those who understand will start writing immediately and those who do not, will not. That is not to say that those who are writing have completely understood; after all, they may be writing the wrong thing entirely, but this at least gives me a starting point in selecting whom I need to go and intervene with, picking up on misunderstandings and misconceptions on a one-to-one level. If several people are struggling, I can pick these up at class level once more. Try standing back and watching after setting a task instead of diving straight in. You may be surprised at what you see!

Depending on the needs of the class, I will often pick on students to verbally summarise what has happened in the scene so far after every two chunks. This, I have found, helps to begin piecing the chunks together. One of the risks of this 'stop/start' approach is that students have forgotten what has happened at the beginning of the scene because it is lengthy and the time one spends on it is extended because of the time taken to ensure understanding. Here are the questions I have asked in past lessons:

**Chunk 1:**

*Read from the beginning to 'T'appease an angry god.'*
1. How is Malcolm feeling here?
2. What, according to Macduff, is happening each new day in Scotland?
3. Does Malcolm believe everything Macduff is telling him?
4. What does Malcolm worry Macduff is there to do?

**Challenge**: Malcolm alludes to himself as a lamb. What are the religious connotations of this?

*Now summarise what is happening in this section in no more than three sentences.*

**Chunk 2:**

*Read from 'I am not treacherous' to 'Whatever I shall think.'*
1. What does Macduff mean when he says he is not 'treacherous'?
2. What does Malcolm say can cause someone's 'good... nature' to change?
3. Why does Malcolm ask for Macduff's 'pardon'?
4. What does Malcolm ask Macduff about his wife and child and what reason does he give for asking?

**Challenge**: Are Malcolm's suspicions justified?

*Now summarise what is happening in this section in no more than three sentences.*

At this point, I will ask one or two students to verbalise everything that has happened from the beginning of the scene to this point. This, I have found, helps refresh students' memory and helps link these isolated chunks together.

**Chunk 3:**

*Read from 'Bleed, bleed, poor country' to 'With my confineless harms.'*
1. What, according to Macduff, will allow tyranny to succeed?
2. What does Macduff say he could be offered and he still wouldn't be a tyrant?
3. What does Malcolm say is happening to Scotland under Macbeth's leadership?
4. What has England offered Malcolm?
5. What does Malcolm say Scotland will be like under his own kingship?

**Challenge**: Do you believe what Malcolm says?

*Now summarise what is happening in this section in no more than three sentences.*

**Chunk 4:**

*Read from 'Not in the legions' to 'Finding it so inclined.'*
1. What qualities does Malcolm say Macbeth possesses?
2. What does Malcolm say is one of his worst qualities and who would be unsafe because of it?
3. What is 'boundless intemperance' and what does Macduff say about this?
4. Who will be readily available for Malcolm if he so desires?

**Challenge**: How has Macbeth demonstrated 'boundless intemperance'?

*Now summarise what is happening in this section in no more than three sentences.*

At this point, I will ask one or two more students to verbalise everything that has happened from the beginning of the scene to this point in order to link these chunks together. Allow other students to help should they need to.

**Chunk 5:**

*Read from 'With this there grows' to 'All unity on earth.'*
1. What does Malcolm claim he will do to the nobles and why?
2. What does Macduff say Scotland has in response?
3. What are the qualities a good king should possess according to Malcolm?
4. What does Malcolm wish to do to peace and unity on earth?

**Challenge**: What is milk symbolic of in the play and how is it treated by the characters?

*Now summarise what is happening in this section in no more than three sentences.*

**Chunk 6:**

*Read from 'O Scotland, Scotland' to 'Thy hope ends here.'*
1. Macduff says Malcolm is not fit to do two things. What are they?
2. Macduff wonders if Scotland will ever see what again?
3. What does Macduff say about Malcolm's father?
4. What does Macduff say about Malcolm's mother?

**Challenge**: So far, Macduff has accepted Malcolm's treatment of women and his greed. Why does he break and tell Malcolm he is not fit to live here?

*Now summarise what is happening in this section in no more than three sentences.*

Once again, ask one or two students to summarise verbally what has happened from the beginning of the scene to this point. Here, you may want to ask some questions that delve into the scene a little more, such as 'Is Malcolm who you expected him to be?'

| **Chunk 7:** | |
|---|---|
| *Read from 'Macduff, this noble passion' to the Doctor's entrance.* | Now students are beginning to get to grips with what happens in the scene, complete a reread from the beginning of Act IV, Scene iii, focusing on the following: |
| 1. How does Malcolm describe Macduff here? | |
| 2. What does Malcolm reveal in this speech? | |
| 3. What does Malcolm say he has never done? | 1. Consolidating the plot |
| 4. Why has Malcolm tricked Macduff? | 2. Comparison between Malcolm and Macbeth |
| **Challenge**: Malcolm has easily deceived Macduff. Why could this be dangerous? | 3. Presentation of Macduff |
| *Now summarise what is happening in this section in no more than three sentences.* | |

## Rereading

In no way am I suggesting students will miraculously understand everything this scene has to offer on a first read. This is just one approach, a 'way in', with later tasks clarifying elements and opening the door to wider exploration. One thing I would encourage is a reread without stopping and starting once you reach the doctor's entrance. It is all too appealing to move on, particularly if students are finding something challenging, but persevere and go over the first part of the scene once more; it will help students pick up on new ideas and points missed the first time round. Students will encounter unfamiliar vocabulary in this scene. Choose the vocabulary you think needs more explicit teaching and go through this before a second read.

## The text in isolation

At this point, students should revisit their inferences to see if what they said was right. One of the main points of the scene is the exploration of what makes a good king. Once students have understood the idea that Malcolm is deceiving Macduff as a way of protecting himself, they could look closely at *how* he is doing it: he is painting a picture of himself as worse than Macbeth. In doing so, he lists the qualities he believes Macbeth to possess and so, in theory, he must be saying that he himself possesses these traits too. He presents himself as a tyrant and does not believe himself to possess the qualities of a king. This resource, partly inspired by Chris Curtis's 'declutter'[47] ideas, allows students to consider these qualities in isolation; they are the characteristics that drive the play, that consume Shakespeare's characters, that destroy them and, in terms of kingship, that restore order as well.

---

47. Chris Curtis, *How to Teach English*, (Carmarthen: Independent Thinking Press, 2019), p. 84.

## RESOURCE 16.4

| | |
|---|---|
| I grant him bloody, luxurious avaricious false deceitful sudden malicious voluptuousness  | king-becoming graces justice verity temperance stableness bounty perseverance mercy lowliness devotion patience courage fortitude  |

Complete the following activities as annotations around the tyrannical and kingly qualities above:

1. Define each of these terms.
2. Is any character made up solely of these tyrannical behaviours? If so, who? How do they demonstrate these behaviours?
3. Could any of these tyrannical behaviours be beneficial to kingship? Why would they be beneficial?
4. Which characters have demonstrated at least three of the kingly qualities? How have they demonstrated them?
5. Which characters have demonstrated elements of both tyrannical behaviours and kingly qualities? How?
6. Is Malcolm's list of qualities a king should possess realistic? Can anyone possess all of these things? Consider events that have occurred in the play already in your response.

*Icons by AFY Studios and Landan Lloyd from The Noun Project

Ask students to focus on the tyrannical behaviours first. Students need to work out what they are and what they mean. Having done that, they can begin to consider the dangers of possessing such qualities and how they can consume one's character and dictate one's actions. I often ask my class to do this verbally before committing their ideas to paper. The questions provided can be used as a prompt or ignored altogether, depending on how successfully students have engaged with the text. I do, however, advocate strongly for this isolated approach. Stripping everything else away so only single words or short phrases are being considered allows students to hone in on and explore what makes someone a tyrant and who is at risk of becoming one. The same can be said for the kingly qualities spoken by Malcolm. Looking at these qualities side by side, students can begin to consider what makes a good king, and it would certainly make an interesting conversation when discussing whether some vices are beneficial to kingship.

I also like getting students to consider who has embodied these values so far and whether this tells us anything about good versus evil. Is it as clear-cut as we are often led to believe?

## Studying the character of Malcolm

The activities listed above are certainly what I would call the 'non-negotiables', although they only begin to scratch the surface of what students can learn from this scene. It may be necessary, for example, to compare one of Malcolm's speeches to Macduff's to really look at the text at sentence and word level using the 'find it/highlight it/annotate it' technique explored in earlier chapters. These methods will certainly help students pick up on some of the finer details of Shakespeare's text, such as the biblical allusions covered in the 'What?' section of the chapter.

To finish the first lesson on Act IV, Scene iii, I think it is extremely important to consider who Malcolm really is. When I have taught this scene before, I have directed students to think about how he is the antithesis of Macbeth, probably because it is easier to treat him in this way. After all, he does reject the tyrannical vices he claims to possess early on in the scene, which must mean he is the perfect character. On reflection, I think this does Malcolm an injustice. He is a complex individual and needs to be treated as such. Resource 16.5 has been designed to help students think about Malcolm's character.

## RESOURCE 16.5

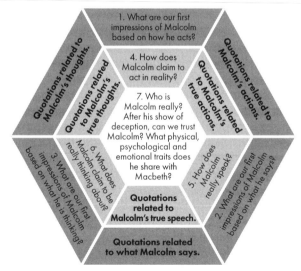

I decided to present this resource as a hexagon to really get across the idea of Malcolm as a layered character. This, of course, could be applied to any character in the play, but I am presenting it here for the first time as a way of helping students understand the idea that Malcolm is not the perfect alternative to Macbeth he is often made out to be. Students should start from the outside layer and work their way around the hexagon in a clockwise direction to track our first impressions of Malcolm and who Malcolm says he really is before deciding whether he is as trustworthy as he claims to be.

Take feedback and discuss before asking students to respond to the lesson's Big Questions.

## Part Two:

### Retrieval
To help students understand the complexities of Act IV, Scene iii, retrieval should be based around knowledge learnt in the last lesson. Have students write down everything they can remember about the plot of the scene, the relationship between Malcolm and Macduff and Malcolm's character.

### Reading the scene
Read the rest of the scene. I have split it as follows:

| Chunk 1: | Chunk 2: |
|---|---|
| *Read from the doctor's entrance to 'That speak him full of grace.'* | *Read from Ross's entrance to 'O, relation too nice, and yet too true.'* |
| 1. What does the doctor say the King, Edward the Confessor, is doing? | 1. Thinking back to the previous scene, where has Ross been? |
| 2. What is the disease Edward is supposedly able to cure? | 2. What has Scotland become, according to Ross? |
| 3. What evidence are we given that Edward is a deeply religious man? | 3. Where else would noise of pain have filled the air in Scotland? |
| 4. How does Edward differ from Macbeth? | **Challenge**: Consider Ross's reference to a 'knell'. Where else has a knell been mentioned and how has its meaning changed here? |
| **Challenge**: Does Malcolm embody Edward's qualities? | |
| *Now summarise what is happening in this section in no more than three sentences.* | *Now summarise what is happening in this section in no more than three sentences.* |

At this point, I will ask one or two more students to verbalise everything that has happened from the beginning of the scene to this point in order to link these chunks together. Allow other students to help should they need to.

| Chunk 3: | Chunk 4: |
|---|---|
| *Read from 'What's the newest grief?' to 'To doff their dire distresses.'* | *Read from 'Be't their comfort' to 'To cure this deadly grief.'* |
| 1. What does Ross say about Macduff's wife and family? | 1. How is England supporting Malcolm and Macduff's cause? |
| 2. Why do you think he does this? | 2. What does Ross say he has? What does he mean? |
| 3. What, according to Ross, are 'worthy fellows' doing in Scotland? | 3. What is Ross worried will happen when he delivers his bad news to Macduff? |
| 4. What will Malcolm's presence in Scotland do, according to Ross? | 4. What news does Ross deliver to Macduff and how does Macduff take the news? |
| **Challenge**: Why is truth hidden in the play? | **Challenge**: How does Malcolm conform to the traditional expectations of masculinity here? |
| *Now summarise what is happening in this section in no more than three sentences.* | *Now summarise what is happening in this section in no more than three sentences.* |

Once again, ask one or two students to summarise verbally what has happened from the beginning of the scene to this point. Here, you may want to ask some questions that delve into the scene a little more, such as 'What differences are beginning to emerge between Malcolm and Macduff here?'

| Chunk 7: | Chunk 8: |
|---|---|
| *Read from 'He has no children' to 'Heaven rest them now.'* | *Read from 'Be this the whetstone of your sword' to the end of the scene.* |
| 1. Who do you think Malcolm is referring to when he says 'He has no children'? Macbeth or Malcolm? Why? | 1. What does Malcolm continue to press Macduff to do? What does Macduff say he could do in response to the news his wife and children are killed? |
| 2. Why does Macduff ask so many questions in this part? | 2. What does he decide to do instead? |
| 3. What does Malcolm tell Macduff to do and what does this mean? | 3. How does the scene end? |
| 4. What does Macduff mean when he says he should 'feel it as a man'? | **Challenge**: What does Act IV, Scene iii add to the play? |
| **Challenge**: How is Macduff acting against typical masculine stereotypes here? | *Now summarise what is happening in this section in no more than three sentences.* |
| *Now summarise what is happening in this section in no more than three sentences.* | |

This process *will* take time, and although this is a precious commodity to us teachers, I would stress that it is necessary to slow down when teaching a particularly challenging text. Reading and understanding is not a lesson wasted.

There are lots of activities that could be completed here. For example, one could compare Macbeth to Edward the Confessor through scrutiny of Malcolm's description of both characters. One could even consider Ross's description of Scotland in further detail for a true understanding of what Scotland is like under Macbeth's reign. What I would like to focus on here, however, is Shakespeare's presentation of gender, particularly his transgressive representation of masculinity through the character of Macduff.

## Transgressive gender representations

Malcolm embodies what it is to be stereotypically masculine; his immediate reaction upon hearing news of Macduff's family's demise is to strike back with violence. Macduff, however, says he must 'feel' the loss as a man, suggesting he needs time to mourn instead of shunning his emotions. This sets up the next task nicely for students to consider the traditional representation of masculinity in relation to Macduff's perception of it. An easy way to do this is by using a method first introduced to me by Kat Howard. Howard explains how students should look at presentation of characters physically, emotionally and psychologically,[48] and this is exactly what Resource 16.6 asks the class to do:[49]

---

48. Kat Howard, *Stop Talking About Wellbeing*, (Woodbridge: John Catt Educational Ltd., 2020), p. 178.

49. 'Man' by lipi and 'Plus' by Three Six Five from the Noun Project.

## RESOURCE 16.6

| **Physically?** | **Emotionallly?** | **Macduff physically?** | **Macduff emotionally?** |
|---|---|---|---|
| Stereotypically, men are presented as being very strong. With this strength usually comes violence. | Men are usually less likely to share their emotions with others. The men throughout the play suppress their emotions unless they are in a private space or alone. | Although Shakespeare does not give us a clue as to Macduff's physical appearance here, I do not think he would appear to be strong and imposing at this point. I believe he would be... | Macduff refuses to conform to the way in which society expects him to react. He reveals his emotions and freely expresses his love for his family. |

| **Traditional view of masculinity** | **VS** | **Transgressive gender roles** |
|---|---|---|
| **Psychologically?** | | **Macduff psychologically?** |
| **Who embodies these stereotypes in the play?** | | **Why is Shakespeare's presentation of masculinity in Act IV, Scene iii so powerful?** |

The resource allows students to consider typical masculine stereotypes. Once students have finished, they should consider where in the play these stereotypes have been seen. They will, most likely, think of Macbeth in Act I, Scene ii, whose masculinity and violent actions are celebrated because they are associated with loyalty, at least to begin with. They may also find themselves discussing Lady Macbeth's perceived masculinity, or, at the very least, lack of femininity. Others may consider the idea of securing an heir as indicative of masculinity.

On the flip side, however, is Macduff, who refuses to conform to the traditional expectation of his gender. Students should explore how he challenges prescribed gender roles, and once they have completed the activity, ask them the following question: 'Why is Shakespeare's presentation of masculinity so powerful?'

I do not think there is a 'right' answer to this question, but it is always interesting to see what students have to say. For me, Shakespeare's presentation of masculinity is powerful because it shows, to an extent, how ahead of his time he was; breaking down the image of men as suppressors of their emotions because of societal expectations is still something we are fighting today. This question, however, allows students to tackle the non-tender masculinity that can pervade so many of our classrooms.

## Exploring literary criticism

Before the lesson ends, it may be pertinent to explore some literary criticism. One piece I find particularly interesting is a point made by Marina Favila. She says:

> *Macbeth has hacked Macduff into a suitable double of himself.*[50]

Present students with this quotation and ask them how Macduff is now a 'suitable double' of Macbeth. In essence, students are exploring the similarities between the two characters (and the task can even be framed as such if students are struggling to access what is required of them), but I like the idea of linking tasks to critical commentaries to instil the view that we can all be consumers of literary criticism, regardless of age or ability, and make valid contributions to those same discussions. Take feedback before revealing the rest of Favila's comments to compare responses:

> *By the end of the play, both soldiers will be bereft of wife and children, fueled by a fury unmatched by anyone else in the play, and abiding the moment when each can destroy the other.*[51]

To finish, ask students to revisit their responses to the Big Questions and see if they can add anything extra based on what was read in this lesson. Ensure students consider authorial intent in their answers.

## Suggested 'Extra Challenge' activities

- How far could one describe Malcolm's description of Macbeth as 'propagandistic exaggeration'?[52]
- 'Malcolm's character proves there is a tyrant lying dormant in all of us.' Discuss.
- Explore gender roles in *Macbeth*, with particular focus on Macduff as a transgressive, masculine figure.

## Key vocabulary:

Transgressive masculinity, virtue, misogyny

---

50. Marina Favila, "'Mortal Thoughts" and Magical Thinking in "Macbeth"', *Modern Philology*, Vol. 99, No. 1, 2001, pp. 1–25, www.jstor.org/stable/439153.

51. Ibid.

52. Christoph Clausen, *Macbeth Multiplied: Negotiating Historical and Medial Difference Between Shakespeare and Verdi*, (New York: Rodopi, 2005), p. 219.

# ACT FIVE

# CHAPTER 17
## Act V, Scene i

*What becomes of Lady Macbeth?*

## What?

### Scene analysis: Act V, Scene i

Lady Macbeth has been missing from the stage for some time, having last been seen at the banquet in Act III, Scene iv. Despite having been such a catalyst for Macbeth's motivation in the early scenes, his prior decisions to act out without her continues, leaving her behind.

This forgotten and marginalised Lady Macbeth marks a radical departure from the woman who had called upon evil spirits to fill her with strength, drive and determination. Instead, she is destroyed by the guilt of what they have done. She can no longer hide her part in the horrors they have committed together, and her conscience finally overwhelms her in this scene. Whilst she did not actively murder the King, she was a key catalyst in Macbeth's ultimate decision to do so. She has played a part in regicide and thus cannot prosper. The punishment for her crimes comes in the form of her breakdown, paranoia and ultimate death by suicide.

#### LADY MACBETH'S LETTER

Before Lady Macbeth arrives on stage, her behaviours and actions are described by her gentlewoman to the doctor. There are echoes here of Act I Scene ii, when the Captain explained Macbeth's behaviour on the battlefield to the King. Whilst we do not initially see her actions for ourselves, we are invited by Shakespeare to hear about what others perceive of her. The gentlewoman's use of an extensive list alerts the audience not only to the variety of her nocturnal activities but also to the fact that, if the gentlewoman is able to list her actions so confidently, this must have been going on for some time before this point.

It is clear that a repeated action of Lady Macbeth's is the writing of letters. She has been doing so since Macbeth 'went into the field', and this harks back to Act I, Scene v, where the two had been exchanging letters, which was how she first learned of his initial meeting with the witches. Now, she 'take[s] forth paper, fold[s] it, / write[s] upon't, read[s] it, / afterwards seal[s] it, and again / return[s] to bed'. That this scene comes so soon after Macbeth's final meeting with the weïrd sisters in Act IV, Scene i cannot be accidental: there is a poetic symmetry in the structure of the play. Her first appearance begins with a letter promising her success. Her final appearance begins with her frantically writing a letter, perhaps reliving earlier moments, but also demonstrating how far she has fallen from grace in the ensuing scenes. Lady Macbeth moves from the woman driven by ambition on receipt of the first letter to a troubled, sleepwalking woman destroyed by her actions in her final engagement with letter writing.

There is also symmetry to the play when we consider what Lady Macbeth is preoccupied with during this scene. Much of her speech here recalls the murder of King Duncan and its aftermath. The ramifications of the Macbeths' actions are about to come to fruition, with the English forces massing outside the castle, ready to retrieve the crown and give it to its rightful heir, Malcolm.

### 'SHE HAS LIGHT BY HER CONTINUALLY'

When Lady Macbeth does arrive on stage, she does so with a 'taper'. Her behaviour with the taper is almost childlike. To protect her from the 'thick night', she carries a light to save her from her biggest fear: the dark. This candle is literally a light, but also metaphorically represents her potential desire for absolution for her crimes. If hell and the Devil are represented by darkness, then heaven and God are represented by light, and in carrying the light she perhaps seeks a renewed relationship with God. However, it is significant that the candle described is, specifically, a 'taper'. As the smallest type of candle, Shakespeare uses it to demonstrate how overwhelming the darkness truly is. Where once she invited darkness into her life, the taper is now the only protection she has to 'safeguard against the powers of darkness.'[1] The only light remaining in her life is miniscule, symbolic of the battle for salvation she is losing against the encroaching darkness.

The Doctor notices that she 'rubs her hands.' This is a key motif in the scene, and another compulsion of her somnambulism – her gentlewoman has watched her rub her hands like this for 'a quarter of an hour.' Her action, of course,

---

1.   John Mullan, 'Conjuring darkness in *Macbeth*', https://www.bl.uk/shakespeare/ articles/conjuring-darkness-in-macbeth.

is one of handwashing. Washing of the flesh is emblematic of the purging of sin in Christianity. The act of baptism is to purge the person of sin, and the frantic washing of her hands suggests that Lady Macbeth is now also asking for absolution. As it says in James 4:8: 'Cleanse your hands, ye sinners; and purify your hearts'.[2]

## 'OUT, DAMNED SPOT'

The very fact that Lady Macbeth only has a 'spot' of blood on her hands does nothing to lessen her somnambulistic panic: she cannot remove it from her hand, symptomatic of the level of guilt she carries with her. It is also, potentially, representative of the fact that there have been small actions made by both her and Macbeth which have, slowly, chipped away at the confidence others have in them. Suspicions in them arose almost immediately after the murder of Duncan, spurred on by seemingly small actions, just like the spot of blood Lady Macbeth sees now on her hands. It is almost, though not quite, an example of synecdoche: the spot of blood represents the many crimes the pair have committed in pursuit of their hamartia.

It could come from any of their crimes. However, it is the appearance of blood on her hands that she clearly relives through her somnambulism; it is the dialogue largely from Act I and II which she speaks, and these link the spot of blood almost irrevocably to the murder of King Duncan. When we consider Lady Macbeth again in relation to her original sin (doubling again for the biblical Eve), the act of tempting her husband to commit regicide has led directly to her downfall here, much like Eve's ejection by God from the Garden of Eden after she ate fruit from the Tree of Knowledge and encouraged Adam to do the same.

Her next lines confirm for the audience – and for the watching doctor and gentlewoman – that Lady Macbeth is, in her somnambulistic state, reliving the night of King Duncan's murder. Her remark of 'one; two' alludes to the ringing bell that she rang to invite Macbeth to kill the King. She speaks in fragments, haunting memories of her actions coming back to her in short bursts, and her relentless questions go entirely unanswered. She veers from questioning once more Macbeth's masculinity ('a soldier, and afeared?') to conjuring images of darkness ('Hell is murky.').

If we take these two images in turn, we can understand the rapidly oscillating frame of mind that has plagued Lady Macbeth throughout the play. Outwardly to her husband she has attempted to play the strong, authoritative leader,

---

2.   *The Holy Bible Containing the Old and New Testaments*, Authorised King James Version, www.kingjamesbibleonline.org, James 4:8.

steering Macbeth to what she believes is glory. She reflects this role here, asking him not only if he is 'a soldier, and afeared' but also chiding him for those very anxieties: 'What need we fear? Who knows it when none can call our power to account?' Lady Macbeth, it could be argued, is hoping that their royal power is enough to hide (or explain?) their actions. As King and Queen, they do not need to justify their behaviour to anyone, except, perhaps, God.

Her reminiscence about darkness demonstrates not just that she calls for the darkness as she did in Act I, but instead knows, intimately, what it is to be enshrouded in that darkness. Her decisions – and those of her husband – have been rooted in darkness and in hell, the place she now fears her actions will take her. This moment is almost 'a proleptic glimpse of the hell to which she would be confined.'[3]

## 'WHO WOULD HAVE THOUGHT THE OLD MAN TO HAVE HAD SO MUCH BLOOD IN HIM?'

Shakespeare also has Lady Macbeth contemplate not just the blood on her hands but also the aftermath of King Duncan's murder. One of her fragmented thoughts marks her surprise: 'Yet who would have thought the old man to have had so much blood in him?' It was believed that the supply of blood would dry up in old age, so her surprise at the amount of blood present after his murder quite possibly conveys that he had, at the time of his death, a great deal of life and therefore reign ahead of him.[4] This amplifies the idea that the actions of the Macbeths cut his reign short, that his death was artificial and therefore that the punishment for the Macbeths must befit the heinous crime they have committed.

Lady Macbeth moves on from her preoccupation with the literal blood on her hands to consider the metaphorical blood she is responsible for spilling. Despite not actively committing any of the murders in the play herself, it was her influence on Macbeth that led, indirectly, to every murder that has happened to date. If she had not convinced her husband to murder Duncan, arguably, none of the other murders would have taken place. This includes the recent murder of the only other named female character – Lady Macduff. Lady Macbeth reflects: 'The Thane of Fife had a wife. Where is she now?' The destruction of the only other named woman has clearly had a marked impact on Lady Macbeth. Perhaps, given that Lady Macduff would originally have been

---

3.  S. Viswanathan, 'Sleep and Death: The Twins in Shakespeare', *Comparative Drama*, Vol. 13, No. 1 (Spring 1979), pp. 49–64, https://www.jstor.org/stable/41152816.

4.  Morriss Henry Partee, *Childhood in Shakespeare's Plays*, (Oxford: Peter Lang, 2006), p. 81.

in a similar position to herself, married, as she was, to a thane, Lady Macbeth finally recognises the perilous position her own life is now in.

### 'ALL THE PERFUMES OF ARABIA WILL NOT SWEETEN THIS LITTLE HAND'

The handwashing and preoccupation with the blood on her hands continues throughout the scene; her behaviour is now entirely at odds with her beliefs in Act II, Scene ii, where she told her husband that 'a little water clears us of this deed.' Shakespeare, now, demonstrates how it is not just the sight of the blood that alarms her, but the fact that she is now equally disturbed by the olfactory elements of the sight, stating that '[a]ll the perfumes of Arabia will not sweeten this little hand.' This echoes Macbeth's concern that his hands could not even be washed clean by 'great Neptune's ocean', and in both cases is symbolic of their overwhelming sense of guilt. It is a hyperbolic analysis of her situation.

Notice how Lady Macbeth speaks in prose in this scene: 'it is almost as if the verse line, already strained by the events of the play, cannot cope with her fractured memories.'[5] It is notable, then, that the line 'The Thane of Fife had a wife, where is she now?' has a sense of rhythm and rhyme about it. It is not, though, laid out as verse would be. It is unlikely, given his prowess and skill in writing, to be an error on Shakespeare's part. More likely, perhaps, is the fact that 'Shakespeare frequently inserts bits of verse... in the mouths of his mentally perturbed characters.'[6] This fusion of verse and prose indicates the turmoil Lady Macbeth feels at this point – she is unwell, and her confused style of speech reflects this. The fact that she has to ask about something Macbeth has done symbolises that Macbeth has 'drift[ed] away from her; her overwrought nervous system helps him no more.'[7] She is expendable, and expended, a fact made all the more evident when she says that 'there's knocking at the gate... To bed, to bed, to bed.' This sound, a throwback to Macduff's arrival at the Macbeths' castle, is a haunting echo of her own fate catching up with her, just like Macduff symbolises Macbeth's fate catching up with him.

The Doctor and Gentlewoman, meanwhile, have heard everything she has said and seen everything she has done. Given that Lady Macbeth has given all of herself to become Queen but has destroyed herself in the process, the

---

5.   Emma Smith, *Macbeth Language & Writing*, (London: Bloomsbury, 2013), p. 102.

6.   George R. Stewart, Jr., 'A note on the sleepwalking scene', *Modern Language Notes*, Vol. 42, No. 4 (April 1927), pp. 235–237, https://www.jstor.org/stable/2914260.

7.   Montagu Griffin, 'Some Notes on "Macbeth". II', *The Irish Monthly*, Vol. 26, No. 298 (April 1898), pp. 169–179, https://www.jstor.org/stable/20499264.

Gentlewoman sums up the opinion arguably held by the entire audience, giving a voice to the moral lesson they have learned and understood: 'I would not have such a heart in my bosom for the dignity of the whole body.' In other words, not even being Queen would be a big enough reward for this onlooker to commit the crimes Lady Macbeth has, and to feel and behave as Lady Macbeth does now. The Gentlewoman almost wraps up Shakespeare's point about knowing one's place in the Great Chain of Being: if one dares to step out of one's own place in society, then this is one's fate.

Such is the severity of Lady Macbeth's perceived madness through her somnambulism that the Doctor does not consider himself adequately qualified to treat her, telling the Gentlewoman that '[t]his disease is beyond my practice'. However, he also comments that he has known similar patients who 'have walked in their sleep, who have died holily in their beds.' Despite the Gentlewoman being certain that Lady Macbeth is guilty, the Doctor appears to want to give her the benefit of the doubt. Is this because of her gender, and the assumption that, because she is a woman, she is unlikely to have been capable of committing the crimes she is talking about? Or is he perhaps, being in Macbeth's employ, keen to downplay her role on the basis that she is the Queen and he is in a subordinating position?

He also recognises, commensurate with contemporary understanding of mental health, that her condition is related to her 'infected mind' and is therefore not attributable to her physical health. Her 'unnatural deeds' have indeed bred 'unnatural troubles' as far as the Doctor is concerned.

### 'MORE NEEDS SHE THE DIVINE'

The Doctor comments: 'More needs she the divine than the physician. God, God forgive us all.' There is a real sense that he is suggesting she is in need of some form of purging by a priest; her actions have infected her mind and cannot, therefore, be cured by a doctor. In addition to this, his horror is not just for the condition of Lady Macbeth but is also:

> *Compounded when he realises that her infected psyche, resulting from the sin of regicide, has far-reaching implications for Scotland 'abroad.' The entire nation is not only infected with disease but also implicated in her sin.*[8]

---

8.   Bryan Adams Hampton, 'Purgation, Exorcism, and the Civilizing Process in Macbeth', *Studies in English Literature, 1500–1900*, Vol. 51, No. 2, Tudor and Stuart Drama (SPRING 2011), pp. 327–347, https://www.jstor.org/stable/23028078.

Shakespeare's suggestion of Scotland's sin is an interesting one. In *The Trew Law of Free Monarchies*, King James I writes:

> *A wicked king is sent by God for a curse to his people, and a plague for their sinnes: but that it is lawfull to them to shake off that curse at their owne hand... that I deny.*[9]

In other words, it was not for the people of Scotland to remove Macbeth from the throne, despite his position as a tyrant. They have 'deserved their tyrant king and fiendish queen.'[10] It must be an outside force who removes Macbeth so that the new king is established as the true and just king. Macduff's actions of regicide, coupled with the support of the English army, remove Malcolm from sin and mean that his reign will be able to cure the ills of Scotland. The Doctor is not to know this; hence his call for God to 'forgive us all.'

The only advice the Doctor really has for the Gentlewoman is to keep Lady Macbeth from 'the means of all annoyance' – in other words, anything with which Lady Macbeth might be able to harm herself. In this phrase, he acknowledges not only how little he is able to do to help her, but also the dire straits of her current condition.

His parting words, that he 'think[s], but dare not speak', correlates with contemporary understanding of kingship. Macbeth at this point is the absolute ruler of Scotland and thus any move to criticise the rule or actions of the King or his wife amounts to treason. Having now heard the depths the King and Queen would plumb to secure their reign, the Doctor, quite rightfully, fears the retribution he might face at Macbeth's hands if he were to speak up. This is the sway Macbeth still has over Scotland at this point, adding fuel to the fire of Macduff's desire to see him deposed and for Malcolm, the rightful heir, to take the throne instead.

## The history of sleepwalking

The understanding of somnambulism – sleepwalking – was very much in its infancy. Indeed, it was not really researched or written about until the 19th century.[11] However Shakespeare, in *Macbeth*, wrote a prototypical

9.  *The Political Works of James I*, King James I, (New Jersey: The Lawbook Exchange Ltd., 2002), p. 67.

10. Bryan Adams Hampton, 'Purgation, Exorcism, and the Civilizing Process in Macbeth', *Studies in English Literature, 1500–1900*, Vol. 51, No. 2, Tudor and Stuart Drama (SPRING 2011), pp. 327–347, https://www.jstor.org/stable/23028078.

11. Clete Kushinda, *The Encyclopedia of Sleep*, (London: Elsevier Inc., 2013), p. 155.

example of pathological somnambulism in Act V, Scene i. In this specific type of sleepwalking, the subject speaks and behaves as they would when awake, with eyes open, in a regular and formulaic way, with no recollection of having been sleepwalking once awake.[12] The scene is littered with Lady Macbeth's subconscious paranoia and guilt about the events in which she has become embroiled. Indeed, so accurate is Shakespeare's portrayal of this condition that the scene was quoted in 1881 in a paper detailing the science of somnambulism.[13]

The primary understanding of sleepwalking, from the middle ages to the start of research in earnest in the 19th century, was that those who sleepwalked 'were classed with sorcerers and those supposed to be possessed by the devil.'[14] This adds another dimension to the scene. Perhaps it is not just Lady Macbeth's guilt that has caused her to sleepwalk, but instead her potential links with the witches. She called on 'spirits that tend on mortal thoughts' and arguably the resolution of her storyline is symbolic of these ties with evil that she made earlier in the play; those spirits are feeding off her mind and, as a mere mortal, she cannot cope with their intrusion.

During the scene, Lady Macbeth relives, intensely, her crimes and duplicitous behaviour. Helkiah Crooke, James I's court doctor, described sleepwalking thus:

> *Wee answere first, that the imagination in sleepe is stronger then when wee are awake, as appeareth in those that walke and talke in their sleep. Againe, in sleep the senses are not so drowned in sencelesnesse but that they are rowzed vp by a violent obiect, and therefore such awake if they be violently stirred: and for the most part such nightly pollutions doe awaken those who are troubled with them.[15]*

This is a surprisingly familiar explanation of sleepwalking when we consider it in the context of Act V, Scene i.

---

12. Syed M.S. Ahmed, MD, 'Sleepwalking', *Medscape*, https://emedicine.medscape.com/article/1188854-overview.

13. M. Regnard, 'Sleep and Somnambulism. II', *Science*, Vol. 2, No. 50 (11 June 1881), pp. 270–274, https://www.jstor.org/stable/2900510.

14. Ibid.

15. Helkiah Crook, *Mikrokosmographia OF THE EXCELLENCIE OF MAN. Together with the Profite, Necessitie, Antiquitie, & Method of ANATOMY*, https://quod.lib.umich.edu/e/eebo/A19628.0001.001/1:7.10.7?rgn=div3;view=fulltext.

## The motif of hands in Act III, IV and V

Here, we see Lady Macbeth washing her hands, a repeat of her actions in Act II, Scene ii, just after Duncan's murder. Once more, then, it is pertinent to discuss the development of the motif of hands and what they come to represent under Macbeth's tyrannical reign. The ideas expressed here are influenced by the work of Matt Lynch.[16]

Whilst initially hands are symbols of loyalty and devotion, they are soon associated with betrayal and foul intentions. *Macbeth*, in essence, is a play about the choices we make. Macbeth and Lady Macbeth actively choose to break bonds of loyalty to their king and, as such, turn to deceit and duplicity in order to carry out their will. In Act III, we begin to see the consequences of the actions committed by their hand; the reality of kingship, it seems, is far different from their perceived idea.

This is most strikingly explored in Act III, Scene i, where Macbeth voices his concerns regarding the threat posed by Banquo. Macbeth muses on the fact that his crown will be taken away from him, 'wrenched with an unlineal hand', ensuring no son of his can succeed him. Macbeth, then, is afraid of the very thing he himself is guilty of; it was *his* 'unlineal hand' that wrested the crown from Duncan only a short time ago. Having completed the action himself, he is well aware of others capable of doing the same, especially those who have been prophesied to do so. This fear drives him to action; once again, his hands break the bonds already established before the play has begun, although, interestingly, there is a subtle difference in the way action is carried out. Whereas before, Macbeth killed Duncan himself, here his hand is stayed by his position as king. He must hire murderers to kill Banquo for him for fear of discovery.

In an ironic way, this is what Macbeth has always wanted. He has always believed in his ability to segregate thought and action having called upon darkness to do so. Now, however, he is in a powerful enough position to instruct others to translate his thoughts into action for him (albeit secretly). This, in a sense, lulls him into a false sense of security, for surely one cannot feel guilty if they have not carried out the act with their own hands themselves. Of course, he is wrong. Macbeth is haunted by the ghost of Banquo, confronted by the very image of what he has done, even if his physical hands have not done the deed themselves.

If Banquo's ghost, in Act III, shows audiences how much destruction hands can cause, Act IV demonstrates their ability to heal. Macbeth's hands, the bringers of destruction, are completely at odds with those of Edward the Confessor's; his piety and divine right enable him to cure those suffering from

---

16. Originally shared as part of the LitDrive (@LitdriveUK) CPD sessions.

'the King's Evil', scrofula, a form of tuberculosis, purely by touching those who suffer from it.

The image of Edward healing the sick alludes to Christ's ability to do the same, further emphasising that Macbeth, a man who claimed his kingship through violent means, is only capable of committing further violence. He is not, like Edward, God's spokesperson on Earth, but defies God in the name of self-preservation. Ultimately, it is Malcolm who has Edward's healing touch, for it is he who will restore order and 'heal' Scotland (as Edward heals his people) from its sickness: Macbeth. As a result, hands are representative of honesty and truth here; Shakespeare is showing his audiences what *could* be rather than what is.

In Act V, audiences witness Lady Macbeth incessantly scrubbing her hands, trying to rid herself of a spot of blood she believes to be staining her skin. Lady Macbeth, distressed, is unable to purge herself of the guilt consuming her because of how her hands have translated her thoughts into action. Notice how she describes her hand as 'little'; she projects her mental vulnerabilities onto her physical self. She feels weak and so is incapable of seeing her hands as the destructive forces they are. Instead, she sees them as fragile and close to breaking.

One could argue, then, that hands are part of a wider cycle of thought. Hands translate our thoughts to action, but those actions are translated, in a sense, back into our thoughts. Macbeth and Lady Macbeth's actions torment them, yet they originally perceived their thoughts to be a good idea. The actions of their hands now plague their minds and drive them further towards their own destruction.

Our hands realise our choices, making them not only dangerous to others but dangerous to ourselves, a thought voiced by Malcolm in the closing lines of the play: '...this dead butcher, and his fiend-like queen, / Who, as 'tis thought, by self and violent hands / Took off her life'.

Hands, overall, are an extension of our thoughts. They have the ability to wreak havoc, but also to heal and to restore order.

## Act V, Scene i at a glance

## RESOURCE 17.1

Suggests she can no longer command things to carry out her will, as she did with Macbeth.

Also suggests that her mind has disintegrated so far that she no longer has the power of thought to remove the threat of fictional blood.

Clearly weighs very heavily on her mind.

Reminiscent of the bell ringing to summon Macbeth to commit regicide – this was her input on the murder.

Repeated imperative – the blood does not go at the first attempt.

'Fie' suggests how disgusted she is with Macbeth.

Recalls, in this fragment, how angry she was with Macbeth for being scared – an emotion she now clearly embodies.

**LADY MACBETH**
Out, damned spot: out, I say. One; two. Why then, 'tis time to do't. Hell is murky. Fie, my lord, fie, a soldier, and afeard? What need we fear. Who knows it, when none can call our power to account? Yet who would have thought the old man to have had so much blood in him?

This reminds the audience of her call for darkness, but also the fact she now knows, intimately, what it is to be enshrouded by that darkness.

This is exactly what is happening now, elsewhere – and her fear of being found out and held to account has driven her to madness.

Referring to King Duncan. A drying up of blood was associated with old age; this emphasises her realisation of how long he still had in his reign.

Olfactory imagery – not just visually disgusting but affecting her in every way.

Suggestive of longevity of the smell and therefore how much it affects her.

Hyperbolic!

Evocative of Macbeth's fear that 'all Neptune's oceans' would not clean his hands of blood.

**LADY MACBETH**
Here's the smell of the blood still. All the perfumes of Arabia will not sweeten this little hand. Oh, oh, oh.

'Sweeten' is opposite to everything she has called for so far – including to be filled with 'gall'.

There is something decadent in this image – an echo of her ambition and desire for the best in life.

Metaphorically marked by the crimes they have committed.

Indicative of her realisation that her call for darkness, etc. was misplaced – perhaps beyond the bounds of her gender (in terms of contemporary views on this).

## How?

This lesson focuses specifically on what happens in Act V, Scene i, allowing students to answer the Big Question: 'What becomes of Lady Macbeth?' However, there is a need to revisit this lesson's Big Question after reading and studying Macbeth's own downfall, looking at the events after the sleepwalking scene which end with Lady Macbeth's apparent death by suicide in Act V, Scene v. Students therefore answer the Big Question in two phases – firstly, what she has become compared to the woman she was at the start of the play and, secondly, what the final outcome of her story is.

## Retrieval

Aside from one solitary scream, Act V, Scene i marks the last moment the audience sees or hears from Lady Macbeth, and this affords us the opportunity to be more synoptic in our approach to retrieval practice at the start of this lesson. As we know, Lady Macbeth's lines in this scene are largely echoes of previous lines and moments from elsewhere in the play.

For this lesson's retrieval practice, give students an amalgamated version of all Lady Macbeth's lines in this scene (Resource 17.2). For each line, students should use the bullet pointed prompts to consider Shakespeare's choices. Many of these lines are facsimiles of lines she has previously said, and so whilst this is a new scene, theoretically much of her language will be familiar to students.

## RESOURCE 17.2

> Yet here's a spot.
> Out, damned spot: out, I say. One; two. Why,
> then, 'tis time to do't. Hell is murky. Fie, my
> lord, fie, a soldier, and afeard? What need we
> fear? Who knows it, when none can call our power to
> account? Yet who would have thought the old man
> to have had so much blood in him?
> The Thane of Fife had a wife. Where is she now?
> What, will these hands ne'er be clean? No more
> o'that, my lord, no more o'that: you mar all with
> this starting.
> Here's the smell of the blood still. All the
> perfumes of Arabia will not sweeten this little
> hand. Oh, oh, oh.
> Wash your hands, put on your nightgown, look not so
> pale. I tell you yet again, Banquo's buried; he
> cannot come out on's grave.
> To bed, to bed: there's knocking at the gate.
> Come, come, come, come, give me your hand. What's
> done cannot be undone. To bed, to bed, to bed.

- Have we heard her say this somewhere before? Where?
- Are there any lines that are not familiar/she has not said before?
- If there are unfamiliar lines, what might she be referring to?
- What or who do these lines remind us of?

Students should label each line accordingly, demonstrating their broader understanding and knowledge of Lady Macbeth's character. For example, the annotations around 'Here's the smell of blood still...' may look something like this:

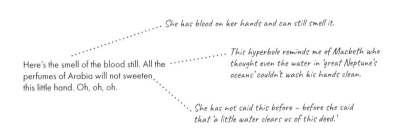

She has blood on her hands and can still smell it.

Here's the smell of the blood still. All the perfumes of Arabia will not sweeten this little hand. Oh, oh, oh.

This hyperbole reminds me of Macbeth who thought even the water in 'great Neptune's oceans' couldn't wash his hands clean.

She has not said this before – before she said that 'a little water clears us of this deed.'

Once students have done this independently, it is a good idea to go through this as a class. This means that you are able to identify where there might be broader knowledge gaps that need reteaching and overlearning, but also helps tease out more complicated ideas, such as the one in the example about comparing both Macbeth's and Lady Macbeth's use of hyperbole.

## Reading the scene

A pre-prepared list of questions to ascertain students' understanding of the scene may be useful, such as the ones below:

1. What does the Gentlewoman say Lady Macbeth has been doing? How long has this been happening?
2. What action does the Doctor observe Lady Macbeth doing?
3. Who is Lady Macbeth talking about when she says 'a soldier, and afeared'?
4. What does Lady Macbeth say about Duncan?
5. What does Lady Macbeth say about Lady Macduff?
6. How does the Gentlewoman react to what she has heard?
7. How does the Doctor react to what he has heard? What does he decide to do?
8. What does Lady Macbeth say about Banquo?
9. What moment is Lady Macbeth recalling when she says 'there's knocking at the gate'?

## Because/but/so

The next important step is for students to understand *why* Shakespeare has Lady Macbeth repeat so many of her previous lines. This could be done through class discussion, but also lends itself nicely to a *because, but, so* task. It is useful here to get students thinking really deeply about Shakespeare's authorial intent.

- Shakespeare has Lady Macbeth repeat her previous words because...
- Shakespeare has Lady Macbeth repeat her previous words but...
- Shakespeare has Lady Macbeth repeat her previous words so...

The 'but' in particular here allows students to demonstrate their understanding of the ways in which Lady Macbeth has changed since the start of the play.

## Revisiting the light and dark tracker

This scene holds an important addition students can make to the light and dark trackers they have worked on elsewhere during their study of the play. Lady Macbeth's taper, her sole defence against the encroaching darkness, is rich with interpretation. Before moving on, students should therefore add this to their tracker. In doing so, they will better understand Lady Macbeth's current situation and have a richer answer to give for the Big Question. More importantly, they will enhance their ability to understand how the symbolism of light and dark has not only developed but completely turned on its head for Lady Macbeth across the entire play.

## Then and now

The next activity takes into account students' understanding of the scene and their broad knowledge of the whole text and also brings into play the considerations made during the retrieval practice at the start of the lesson.

It will be very clear to students at this point that Lady Macbeth has changed from the woman they first saw at the start of the play. They should, using all the powerful knowledge they now have to draw from, create two mini mind maps. What was Lady Macbeth like then? What is she like now?

Next, for each word or phrase on their mind map, students should endeavour to recall or find a brief quotation that demonstrates their understanding. You can see an example of this in Resource 17.3.

## RESOURCE 17.3

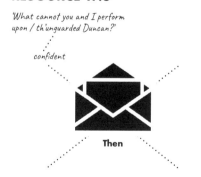

'What cannot you and I perform upon / th'unguarded Duncan?'

confident

**Then**

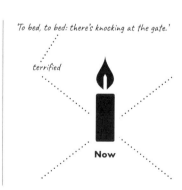

'To bed, to bed: there's knocking at the gate.'

terrified

**Now**

'Letter' by creative outlet and 'Candle' by glenn dane from the Noun Project

410

One thing students might notice – and it is important that they do – is that part of the reason this scene is so shocking is because there was seemingly no warning that this would be the likely outcome for Lady Macbeth. When one considers the contextual knowledge of this – that her assumption of a more masculine role and her part in a heinous regicide would lead to her inevitable downfall – her demise becomes more readily understandable, but nonetheless shocking for a modern, or indeed contemporary, audience.

## Oracy

One would hope that students, throughout the play, understand the complexity of Shakespeare's characters. Therefore, an oracy task such as this can prompt some fiery, passionately explained opinions, and helps students to use their knowledge of the play at large to explain their position.

There are two questions you might like to pose to your students – although my advice would be to look at one, and then the other. Students could be given time to discuss the question in small groups, using the work they have done throughout the lesson. They should seek to provide evidence for the choices they make.

1. Is Lady Macbeth still a villain?
2. Lady Macbeth is not the villain of the piece. She is ambitious, but ambition is not a bad thing. To what extent do you agree?

The second question allows for a potentially deeper consideration of her character, but also offers the opportunity for students to weigh up her character against others. Is she evil, for example, when compared to Macbeth or the witches?

## Answering the Big Question

To conclude, students should be invited to answer, in detail, the Big Question, drawing on their knowledge of Lady Macbeth's downfall so far. They could also include, if you so wished, a prediction as to what will happen to her next. Do they predict only one logical conclusion to her story?

## Extending symbolic knowledge

Lady Macbeth's symbolic handwashing in this scene makes it a logical place to revisit the motif of hands across Acts III, IV and V. To do this, you could use Resource 17.4, which gives students three quotations, which are prompts that allow them to think about what hands represent:

## RESOURCE 17.4

**Consider the quotations** and **make notes** as to what hands represent in Acts III, IV and V of *Macbeth*. **How** does their meaning and significance change as the play progresses? **Why** does their meaning change?

'Upon my head they placed a fruitless crown / And put a barren sceptre in my gripe, / Thence to be wrenched with an unlineal hand'.

Act III: Macbeth is voicing his concerns about Banquo's lineage.

'Such sanctity hath heaven given his hand, / They presently amend.'

Act IV: A doctor speaks of how Edward the Confessor heals the sick.

'Will these hands ne'er be clean?'

Act V: Lady Macbeth is wondering if she will ever be free of the 'blood' on her hands.

## Suggested 'Extra Challenge' activities

- 'Lady Macbeth. The fourth witch?' Discuss.
- 'When all is said and done, Lady Macbeth's sole purpose, like that of Lady Macduff, is to disappear.' To what extent do you agree?
- 'Macbeth does murder sleep.' To what extent is this a self-fulfilling prophecy for Lady Macbeth?

## Key vocabulary:
Somnambulism

# CHAPTER 18
## Act V, Scenes ii–viii

*What becomes of Macbeth?*

## What?

### A note on the structure of Act V

When one considers modern cinema, there are many similarities between the remainder of *Macbeth* and the structure of the climax of action films. Considering almost any blockbuster, a trope heavily relied upon by directors is the idea of short shots, showing the two sides of an army, gang, alien races or superheroes and villains. Leaning heavily on dramatic irony to drive the audience's engagement with these pivotal moments, we see time after time each side in turn planning their next move and hearing, without their own knowledge of the situation, the opposition's plans to overrun their enemy.

Whilst this is potentially a slightly reductive view of what Shakespeare achieves in Act V of *Macbeth*, I think the concept can be a useful one to help students understand the foundation of the structure of these scenes. The writing 'cuts' back and forth from Macbeth in his castle and the massing army outside the walls, as the tension ramps up and up the more Macbeth realises his fate is sealed and his reign is certainly doomed.

### Scene analysis: Act V, Scene ii

The start of these quick, tension-building scenes begins outside the castle walls as a number of Scottish lords wait with soldiers for Malcolm, Siward and Macduff to arrive with the English forces.

Menteith and Caithness have not, until this point, been mentioned by name by Shakespeare. The audience has heard briefly from Angus in Act I, Scene iii, and from Lennox slightly more regularly than this, but these are largely new and unknown characters. Even if these men had been Macbeth's lords, attending the banquet in Act III, Scene iv, it is clear from their actions here that their alignment has shifted, radically: they, too, now want to see an end to Macbeth's tyrannical reign.

Despite the fact that in a few short scenes Macduff will himself commit regicide in order to avenge his innocent family and help return the rightful king, Malcolm, to the throne, he is described by Menteith as 'good Macduff'. This supports the difficult decision Macduff will make when faced with Macbeth in Act V, Scene viii: his decision is a moral one, and he has the support of his fellow Scotsmen.

### 'REVENGES BURN'

Menteith acknowledges that Macduff has 'revenges burn' in him, and Menteith's suggestion here is that the revenge Malcolm and Macduff wish to enact is felt strongly enough that it could 'Excite the mortified man.' In other words, they feel so strongly about deposing the tyrannical king that their energy could bring dead men back to life. There is, perhaps, a metaphorical meaning to this line too. In removing Macbeth, they are able to put Malcolm back on the throne. He is the legitimate heir and continues Duncan's bloodline. Despite the fact that they are not, literally, able to bring Duncan back to life, in placing his son on the throne it at least brings the descendants of the murdered king back to their rightful position. In a sense, the 'mortified man', King Duncan, regains the throne through his family.

Shakespeare next gives us the first taste of dramatic irony in this scene. The men discuss meeting with the English army at Birnam Wood – the place, we know, is instrumental in the apparitions' prophecies for Macbeth. Despite the fact that the army is made up of 'unrough youths' (in other words, first-time soldiers who are therefore inexperienced), the audience already begins to get the sense that luck is not on Macbeth's side.

It becomes clear through Caithness's and Angus's lines that it is not just Lady Macbeth who is thought to be mad, by this point. It appears to be the case that most people consider that Macbeth is, too. Others, who dislike him less than perhaps Caithness and the assembled men, think that his behaviour can be attributed to 'valiant fury'. Given Macbeth's dark and relentless crimes throughout the play, there are still those who are almost apologising, and finding explanations, for his wild and irrational behaviour. This could, of course, link back to characters such as the Doctor, who steps gently and tenderly in order to not be accused of treason.

### 'HE CANNOT BUCKLE HIS DISTEMPERED CAUSE'

Shakespeare conjures further imagery of clothing to explore Macbeth's precarious position. From his wearing of 'borrowed robes', he is now no longer able to 'buckle his distempered cause / Within the belt of rule.' In other words, the metaphorical waist of his anger has now grown so large that he can no longer keep it under control. This metaphor also brings together the idea of clothing ('belt') and illness ('distempered').[1]

Angus's attention, interestingly, is on the metaphorical blood Macbeth has on his hands. His 'secret murders sticking on his hands' shows Angus's belief that Macbeth is no longer able to hide from the heinous crimes he has committed. Just because the literal blood has been washed clean, his responsibility for his actions has not been, something Lady Macbeth, of course, has already discovered.

Angus is also clear that Macbeth has been abandoned by those who once respected him. He acknowledges that there are still soldiers fighting for Macbeth, but they do so not out of love or respect for him, but because they are commanded to do so. In Shakespeare's words, they 'move only in command, / Nothing in love.'

He also evokes the imagery of clothing once more, as he explores the idea that Macbeth must no longer feel like a king. He explains that his 'title hang[s] / Loose about him, like a giant's robe'. His 'borrowed robes' now swamp him; he is not fit to wear the crown. Not only that, but Angus also compares Macbeth to a 'dwarfish thief', emphasising their position that Macbeth has stolen the crown and is not entitled to continue his role as king.[2]

These images help Shakespeare to justify the actions of Macduff and the army in the coming scenes. Regardless of Macbeth's actions, his death is still, technically, regicide – and just as was the case for Macbeth when he murdered King Duncan, the crime is generally entirely unjustifiable. If Shakespeare wanted to secure his point that regicide is an unforgivable crime, he had to ensure that the reasons for deposing Macbeth gave a suitable excuse for those actions.

Caithness goes on to describe that their forthcoming actions are justified insofar as Malcolm is 'the medicine of the sickly weal', who will be the man able to heal Scotland and therefore must be elevated to the throne as soon as possible.

## Scene analysis: Act V, Scene iii

Macbeth has been missing from the stage for some time. He was last seen in Act IV, Scene i, when he met the weïrd sisters for the final time, and the only action we know for certain he has taken since that point is the murder of all those in Macduff's castle. There were indications in Act IV, Scene i that Macbeth knew his grip on the crown was becoming less strong.

---

1.  R. Chris Hassel, Jr., '"No Boasting like a Fool?" Macbeth and Herod', *Studies in Philology*, Vol. 98, No. 2 (Spring 2001), pp. 205–224, https://www.jstor.org/stable/4174697.

2.  Ibid.

Here, Shakespeare presents Macbeth pacing, frantically, and trying desperately to hold on to his interpretation of the witches' final set of prophecies. He repeats their words and his own belief of their significance, telling possibly the assembly, but more likely trying to reassure himself, that 'till Birnam Wood remove to Dunsinane, / [he] cannot taint with fear.'

Macbeth also attempts to play down the threat of his enemies, using the diminutive 'boy' to describe Malcolm, and holding Malcolm up to the second of the apparitions' prophecies: that 'none of woman born / Shall harm Macbeth.' He believes – or is trying to believe – that he is beyond 'all mortal consequence'. His opening speech ends with a vow to himself that he will never 'sag with doubt, nor shake with fear.' To the audience, though, and undoubtedly the assembled servants, his frantic speech with no pause for others to interject gives a very different explanation of Macbeth's state of mind.

### 'GOOSE-LOOK'

The first indication Macbeth truly gets of the scale of his situation comes when his servant returns with a 'goose-look'. Again, Shakespeare turns to ornithological imagery in order to explore the feelings of his characters. Proverbially, geese were associated with giddiness – Shakespeare even joins the two together in *Henry IV Part 1* in the line 'go, ye giddy goose' – and so Macbeth's description of the servant suggests that the servant himself is dizzy, faint or weak as a result of what he has seen. Geese are also white, which, when combined with Shakespeare's description of the servant as 'cream-faced', 'lily-livered' and having 'linen cheeks', and Macbeth's calling him 'whey-face', is suggestive of the servant's shock. Macbeth learns here the magnitude of the battle ahead: there are, says the servant, ten thousand approaching soldiers.

Macbeth is still determined to forge on, telling the servant to 'Go prick thy face and over-red thy fear, / Thou lily-livered boy.' In telling the boy to artificially make his cheeks red by pricking them so they would be covered in blood, Macbeth might be indicating his own, inner fear. Is his behaviour bluster and bravado, too? Shakespeare's use of 'lily-livered' here is notable. As well as meaning the servant is pale, the liver was associated with bravery and courage in Elizabethan and Jacobean England.[3] Indeed, the liver's association with courage is far reaching, from Galenic medicine to ancient Chinese medicine:

> *The organ containing or producing such a bitter essence [bile] was a primary influence upon character and temperament,*

---

3. Sherman M. Mellinkoff, 'Some Meanings of the Liver', *Gastroenterology*, Vol. 76, pp. 636–638 (1979), https://www.gastrojournal.org/article/S0016-5085(79)80235-8/pdf.

*that its excess produced anger and its absence cowardice and its*
*proper amount courage or an even temper?*[4]

Next, Macbeth calls upon Seyton. He calls his name three times in the course of the next eleven lines before Seyton finally appears, perhaps symptomatic of Macbeth's loosening grip on power. Even his own staff do not bend to his will; Macbeth is increasingly isolated from others and lacks the authority he once had. Aside from this, though, these eleven lines are vital in understanding Macbeth's true knowledge of his position.

### 'TILL FROM MY BONES MY FLESH BE HACKED'

He tells Seyton that he has 'lived long enough', not because he is old but because he has lost everything in his life worth living for. He lists these to the absent Seyton: 'honour, love, obedience, troops of friends, / I must not look to have'. He seems to pity himself and his own position, realising, perhaps for the first time (at least out loud) that the crimes he has committed have not given him the things he really needed to live a happy life.

Macbeth, however, is still not willing to give up. When Seyton confirms that the servant's reports are true, and there are ten thousand soldiers massing outside the castle, Macbeth vows to fight until the end, and until 'from [his] bones [his] flesh be hacked.' He urges the moment to come, asking for his armour even though it is not yet needed. This is an early echo of his later words, when he tells Seyton that at least he'll 'die with harness on [his] back.' He calls, too, for Seyton to organise to 'Hang those that talk of fear.' Macbeth, despite his frantic terror, still leans on his tyrannical power to destroy those who are still around him but will not support him. He rules through fear and punishes fear – this oxymoron is an indicator of the now deep-rooted issues in his reign.

### 'THEREIN THE PATIENT MUST MINISTER TO HIMSELF'

Attention moves, then, to Lady Macbeth. The Doctor confirms she is 'sick' – not with regard to her physical health but in terms of the 'thick-coming fancies' that plague her sleep. Macbeth, as many would have done in a contemporary setting, entirely misses the severity of the situation and underplays the Doctor's limited resources in treating her condition. He tells him, simply, to 'cure her of that'. Macbeth lists the things he believes the Doctor should do, as the Doctor looks on, in quiet contemplation. The Doctor's position is perilous: he knows that he cannot reveal that Lady Macbeth's somnambulistic tendencies mean he

---

4.   Sherman M. Mellinkoff, 'Some Meanings of the Liver', *Gastroenterology*, Vol. 76, pp. 636–638 (1979), https://www.gastrojournal.org/article/S0016-5085(79)80235-8/pdf.

is aware of the Macbeths' various crimes and that he is at risk of being murdered himself for that knowledge. Instead, he takes a non-partisan position: 'Therein the patient / Must minister to himself.' Shakespeare's deliberate choice of a male pronoun, here, is fascinating. Whilst Macbeth asks about his wife's condition, the Doctor subtly acknowledges that Macbeth, too, is clearly increasingly unwell.[5]

Macbeth's next speech is quite frenetic, fractured and fragmented. He calls out a list of instructions and demands – perhaps to Seyton, perhaps to the attendants who have been present since the start of the scene with nothing to do. He vacillates wildly – having asked for his armour to be put on, he now asks for someone to 'Pull't off' again. He then looks to medicine again – despite having just announced 'Throw physic to the dogs, I'll none of it' – to provide a treatment which would purge the English army from his castle. He will look to anything to buy him time.

Despite his clear hysteria, Macbeth repeats again, before leaving the stage, that he 'will not be afraid of death and bane, / Till Birnam forest come to Dunsinane.' It is as if he is trying to convince himself of the security of his position, despite the volume of evidence to the contrary. The Doctor is left alone on the stage at this point, voicing the feelings, one imagines, that many of those still aligned with the despotic leader would share: he is going to leave Dunsinane, and says that nothing – no amount of money or bribery – could or would ever bring him back again.

## Scene analysis: Act V, Scene iv

This scene contains one, hugely vital moment that marks impending doom for Macbeth. Though the audience has known for some time that Macbeth's reign is marching towards its final battle, Macbeth himself to date has not openly admitted his own fear. Having held on, at the end of Act V, Scene iii, to the fact that he does not believe he can be defeated until Birnam Wood moves to Dunsinane, Malcolm's next instruction will entirely floor the tyrannical leader. He tells the collected men to instruct the army to 'hew… down a bough and bear't before' them.

There is compelling evidence that this action would have been recognisable to a contemporary audience through the practice of the Maying procession. This was an annual celebration of 'the triumph of new life over the sere and yellow leaf of winter'[6] and is the foundation for modern May Day celebrations.

5. Michael Bristol, 'Macbeth the Philosopher: Rethinking Context', *New Literary History*, Vol. 42, No. 4, Context? (Autumn 2011), pp. 641–662.

6. John Holloway, *The Story of the Night: Studies in Shakespeare's Major Tragedies*, (Abingdon: Routledge, 2005), p. 66.

Malcolm is the 'new life' being celebrated in this case, rather than the coming of spring. It is apparent that we can draw an even closer parallel with this practice when we look at Macbeth's words in Act V, Scene iii, where he says that his 'way of life / Is fallen into the sere, the yellow leaf'. Macbeth knows that his mechanism of reigning through terror is over and the new way of being a king is on the cards. The youth of the boughs and the allusion to Maying secure this: a new king approaches; a child, carrying before him a branch.

Meanwhile, word returns from a reconnaissance mission: Macbeth is ready to wait it out whilst the army camps at the foot of the castle. The fact that Malcolm hears this about Macbeth suggests, perhaps, that the tyrannical king has not been the only person with spies. The news has perhaps come from one of the numerous people who, in appearance, are still on Macbeth's side: the only ones left are those whose 'hearts are absent too.' Many others have 'given him the revolt' already: his numbers are dwindling, his allies few.

## Scene analysis: Act V, Scene v

The scene begins with Macbeth, back on stage and in a defiant mood, relishing in the apparent strength of the castle and bragging about the seeming confidence of his men. This is symptomatic of the delusions under which Macbeth labours: where he sees strength, there is really weakness. It could, of course, be the case that Macbeth is trying to convince himself, as much as anyone, of what he *dreams* will be true. He talks of his men meeting their opponents 'beard to beard'. There is an indication, then, that Macbeth equates beards with strength and masculinity. At the start of the play, he said he would 'do all that may become a man', and his final act of masculinity will be to go down, fighting.

### 'IT IS THE CRY OF WOMEN'

His preparations are quickly disrupted by the stage direction 'A cry within of women.' This cry of 'women' is at odds with the masculine posturing Macbeth has relied upon so far in Act V, a reminder that Lady Macbeth – or whoever 'cries' offstage – demonstrates the emotional vulnerability Macbeth is doing his best to suppress in himself. It is an outward display of the frustration and increasing instability Macbeth suffers from.

This 'cry of women' does lead Macbeth, for a moment, to reflect on how he has changed. He says that he has 'almost forgot the taste of fears.' It has been some time since he has felt scared, or worried. He declares that there would have been a time that his 'sense would have cooled / To hear a night-shriek'. This juxtaposes his feelings on the night of King Duncan's murder, where 'every noise' appalled him. Now, he claims to be more resilient; even the scream of a woman is not enough to shake his 'fell purpose'. He seems buoyed by this lack of humanity. There is a hint that he realises he has hardened past the point of recovery, and is now unable to feel. He declares that 'direness… / Cannot once start me' because of the number of horrors he has thought of, seen and committed since the opening of the play.

The final act of Lady Macbeth is revealed to Macbeth, and his frantic preparations are, at least temporarily, cut short by Seyton's announcement: 'The Queen, my lord, is dead.'

## Macbeth's final soliloquy

Macbeth's final soliloquy, where he reflects on the death of his wife, is thought to take influence from the Senecan play *Agamemnon* and, in particular, the translation by John Studley, published in the few decades before Shakespeare was writing.[7] The first chorus explores the fundamental futility of people's endeavours in life: 'From hygh and proud degre dryues down in dust to lye'[8] epitomises this: no one can escape decay and death, and this speech and the death of Lady Macbeth help Macbeth to realise that this is where he, too, is rapidly heading.

On the evening of Banquo's murder, Macbeth described that 'Good things of the day begin to droop and drowse'. This demonstrates 'the tragedy of the twilight and the setting-in of thick darkness upon a human soul.'[9] Unequivocally, this same thought can be applied to Macbeth's final soliloquy: there is a real sense, one could argue, of pathos here. Macbeth's realisation is that everything he has done in the course of the play has been entirely futile, because the end is coming for him, as it does for everyone, and his heinous crimes have not, and cannot, change that. Shakespeare has provoked in his audience a sense of almost aching pity.

### 'SHE SHOULD HAVE DIED HEREAFTER'

The opening line of Macbeth's speech, 'she should have died hereafter', is such a defining moment for his character. Macbeth has become nihilistic in his outlook. He knows the end for him is coming, and so the 'hereafter', in this reading, is perhaps a suggestion that, sooner or later, she would indeed have died. It is almost inconsequential that this was the moment of her death. His behaviour is

---

7. Sandra Clark and Pamela Mason, *The Arden Shakespeare: Macbeth*, (London: Bloomsbury, 2015), p. 287.

8. Seneca, *Agamemnon*, translated by John Studley, https://quod.lib.umich.edu/e/eebo/A11910.0001.001/1:7.1?rgn=div2;view=fulltext.

9. Edward Dowden, *Shakespeare: A Critical Study of His Mind and Art*, (London: Henry S. King and Co., 1875), p. 186.

cruel and callous and he does not care what happens to others. She would have died anyway, so what difference does it make to him that she has died now?

Perhaps it is the case, with Macbeth about to go into battle, that he believes Lady Macbeth should have died at a later point when she could have been properly mourned: she will not be remembered or laid to rest in the way, arguably, Macbeth would have liked because of the present circumstances in which he finds himself. This is suggestive of a more tender relationship between the two. Despite not having been seen together on stage since the fateful banquet, and despite the fact that Macbeth has stopped referring to his wife in his decision-making, there is an indication of a more loving relationship – one in which Macbeth genuinely cares for, and is absolutely broken by, her death.

There is also the interpretation, given Macbeth's increasing understanding that he will soon die himself, that Lady Macbeth ought to have waited for him. They entered this part of their lives together with her compelling him to commit regicide. Perhaps he thinks it is only right for them to depart in the same way?

The final generally held view of this line is that Macbeth does not believe it was her time to die. She should have died long into the future – when the time was right. He says 'There would have been a time for such a word.' This could be indicative of several things. Firstly, it could suggest that Macbeth wishes that their reign had been longer and more successful, so that their deaths came much later. Secondly, it could indicate that he wishes they had never made the decisions they did. Had he been satisfied with his lot in life, and not so driven by his hamartia, there could have been every chance their present situation would have been far, far different.

Lastly, it could be argued that Macbeth still relies upon his wife more than the audience has been led to believe in recent scenes. Her death might be considered untimely because, without him knowing she would be there to support him, he may feel the battle is now undoubtedly his to lose. She has been his strength, his 'mother figure' and, without her, he knows he will not win.

### 'TOMORROW, AND TOMORROW, AND TOMORROW'

The concept of Macbeth as the tragic hero is further explored in the line 'tomorrow, and tomorrow, and tomorrow, / Creeps in this petty pace from day to day, / To the last syllable of recorded time'. The repetition of 'tomorrow' demonstrates Macbeth's understanding of the futility of his life as he crawls towards his inescapable fate. Following the death of Lady Macbeth, he envisions his days as filled with inescapable drudgery, his life an almost intolerable burden on him. This is not the future he had pictured for himself. This journey alone will be a difficult one, and the audience is aware of Macbeth's concern at the yawning chasm of time ahead of him.

The concept of the 'last syllable of recorded time' may be a biblical allusion to the Book of Revelation, and the idea Macbeth has pondered elsewhere about the Day of Judgement. In Revelation 20:12, it states that Christ will judge all souls:

> *And I saw the dead, small and great, stand before God; and the books were opened: and another book was opened, which is the book of life: and the dead were judged out of those things which were written in the books, according to their works.*[10]

In other words, Macbeth thinks that he may be doomed to this drawn out suffering until the very last record of time and the moment of his judgement.

There is further biblical allusion next, as Macbeth says that all his 'yesterdays have lighted fools / The way to dusty death.'[11] This continues the nihilistic view that everything he has done was foolish: all he has done only propels him closer to his inevitable death. Additionally, the phrase 'dusty death' is evocative of the 'Order for the Burial of the Dead' in the *Book of Common Prayer*, which reads: 'we therefore commit his body to the ground; earth to earth, ashes to ashes, dust to dust; in sure and certain hope of the Resurrection to eternal life.'[12] Macbeth, then, remains preoccupied with whether he stands any hope of being accepted by his God. This has never *not* been important to Macbeth. If it had been, he would not have felt the need to ask to be hidden from God's eyes, but the closer he comes to death, it seems, the more the topic of his salvation troubles him.

Shakespeare has also made reference to the Book of Genesis through his aligning of Macbeth and Lady Macbeth with the roles of Adam and Eve. The concept of 'dusty death' also appears in Genesis 3:19: '…dust thou art, and unto dust thou shalt return.' This further emphasises Macbeth's belief in the futility of his life: he does not see or appreciate the things he has done or accomplished, but instead realises that his endeavours have been for nothing.

### 'OUT, OUT, BRIEF CANDLE'

Here, there is a 'restoration of light.'[13] Macbeth has, in this soliloquy, 'a brilliant flash of tragic vision in which [he] perceives, in all of its ramifications, the

---

10. *The Holy Bible Containing the Old and New Testaments*, Authorised King James Version, www.kingjamesbibleonline.org, Revelation 20:12.

11. Sandra Clark and Pamela Mason, *The Arden Shakespeare: Macbeth*, (London: Bloomsbury, 2015), p. 288.

12. *Book of Common Prayer*, (Oxford: Oxford University Press), pp. 395–396.

13. Barbara L. Parker, '"Macbeth": The Great Illusion', *The Sewanee Review*, Vol. 78, No. 3 (Summer 1970), pp. 476–487, https://www.jstor.org/stable/27541839, p. 486.

nature of the delusion he has harboured.'[14] This imagery is carried through to his consideration of Lady Macbeth's life as having been a 'brief candle': his future is suddenly illuminated to him, and it is full of nothing more than emptiness and death.

Macbeth compares his wife's life to a 'brief candle'. There is arguably something deeply moving about this line. A candle itself is not particularly poetic, yet its personification (its burn is not 'short', it is 'brief') adds so much more sentiment to the object. Candles throw out light, indicative of Lady Macbeth's role as the guiding light in Macbeth's life. Lady Macbeth herself was last seen with a taper, trying to hold on to the thing that gave her comfort a little longer. Perhaps the same is true for Macbeth.

### 'LIFE'S BUT A WALKING SHADOW, A POOR PLAYER'

In describing life as 'a poor player,/ That struts and frets his hour upon the stage, / And then is heard no more', Shakespeare presents the concept that Macbeth has always performed a role in society. At the play's opening this was as the Thane of Glamis, but his role has almost careened out of control as the play has progressed. The idea of man being a 'poor player' is evocative of the imagery of costuming in 'borrowed robes'. In using this image, Shakespeare perhaps suggests that life is intrinsically performative in nature. If this is the case, it stands to reason that life is also in some way scripted, bringing back into focus the role of fate and predestination in the play. Arguably, Macbeth's frustrations come from the fact that whilst he felt he could steer himself to greatness, his latter realisation is perhaps that this was never the case. He is just a 'player' with no real sway over his own life. His actions have been nothing but a 'hollow charade of autonomy.'[15]

In addition, the line demonstrates how Macbeth recognises the limitations of his influence: soon, he will be 'heard no more.' Throughout the play, Macbeth has sought glory: his biggest ambition, to be king, has been fulfilled and there was, at least momentarily, the feeling that he had been successful. However, he knows from his prophecies that there is no future to his reign: he holds in his hand a 'barren sceptre'. His realisation that his crimes have been for nothing makes him question whether any of it was worth it in the first place. He has denounced a place in heaven, has sinned against God and has blood on his hands.

---

14. Barbara L. Parker, '"Macbeth": The Great Illusion', *The Sewanee Review*, Vol. 78, No. 3 (Summer 1970), pp. 476–487, https://www.jstor.org/stable/27541839.

15. Bryan Lowrance, '"Modern Ecstacy": "Macbeth" and the meaning of the political', *ELH*, Vol. 79, No. 4 (Winter 2012), pp. 823–849, https://www.jstor.org/stable/23356185.

### 'IT IS A TALE TOLD BY AN IDIOT'

This concept of futility is carried through to the next line, where Macbeth decries that life is 'a tale / Told by an idiot, full of sound and fury / Signifying nothing.' It is the logical conclusion to Macbeth's nihilistic outlook: his hamartia has come full circle, and here is his moment of realisation that his ambition will be what ultimately destroys him. In this line, Macbeth 'is expressing a sentiment which comes to all men at those odd moments at which they are crushed by failure or disappointed by success and thus forced to pause and reflect.'[16]

It can be argued that these lines reach to the very heart of the play. The core of what Shakespeare writes is not about witchcraft or the supernatural. It is not even about kings, or kingly behaviour. He instead addresses 'the fundamental problem of human action and agency – whether individuals are freely able to decisively seize the moment... or whether it is, in fact, negated by forces beyond its ken and control.'[17]

Throughout this soliloquy, Shakespeare explores a duality. It is a different one from the dichotomous characterisation of Macbeth and Lady Macbeth, but there is a definite paradox between the life Macbeth dreamed of living and the one he is currently experiencing. Macbeth wanted to defy the Great Chain of Being in order to create his own future, yet in having done so prevents himself from accessing the happy future he envisions because of his crimes. Regardless of what he has done, what he aimed to do or how he did it, he cannot outrun his own mortality and his realisation of this is hugely significant in our understanding of Shakespeare's purpose in this scene. In this soliloquy, 'the greatest irony of all is that phenomenon accompanying the moment of truth – that phenomenon wherein Macbeth, in suddenly comprehending the limitations imposed by mortality, transcends that mortality.'[18] He has a clarity of vision now that he has had at no other point in the play: he confronts 'the inevitability of his own doom.'[19] This, 'together with the absolute and transcendent clarity of his vision, belongs only to greatness and gods.'[20]

### 'THE WOOD BEGAN TO MOVE'

Macbeth's reverie is fractured, however, by the return of the Messenger. His announcement is another crushing blow for Macbeth, who learns that 'Birnam...

---

16. Thomas Callaghan, 'What I look for in poetry', *The Irish Monthly*, Vol. 70, No. 831 (September 1942), pp. 351–353, https://www.jstor.org/stable/20515043.

17. Ibid.

18. Barbara L. Parker, '"Macbeth": The Great Illusion', *The Sewanee Review*, Vol. 78, No. 3 (Summer 1970), pp. 476–487, https://www.jstor.org/stable/27541839, p. 487.

19. Ibid.

20. Ibid.

began to move.' The third apparition's prophecy has been fulfilled and Macbeth's initial reaction is one of intense anger: 'If thou speak'st false, / Upon the next tree shalt thou hang alive'. It is a true demonstration of the fight or flight reflex: Macbeth lashes out against those around him in his terror at his realisation.

His frustration with the Messenger soon moves on to consideration of the words of the witches themselves, and his error in assuming the meaning of their words when they were actually speaking much more equivocally. 'He has recognised the amphibology in the witches' riddles... and he will soon come to know that "none of woman born" was not the impossible and inhuman reference he took it for.'[21] He has begun to 'doubt th'equivocation of the fiend, / That lies like truth'. The thing that has been particularly challenging for Macbeth was the ease with which he has fallen for the elements of their speech which *sounded* as if they might be true.

Macbeth's decision is to fight until the bitter end, despite the fact that he ''gin[s] to be aweary of the sun, / And wish[es] th'estate o'th' world were now undone.' His sole remaining impulse is to 'destroy for the sake of destruction... with no hyperbolical or metaphorical intention.'[22]

### Scene analysis: Act V, Scene vi

Malcolm's address to the collected men throws into sharp contrast how these characters regard one another compared to Macbeth. He describes Siward and Macduff as 'worthy' and Young Siward as 'noble', with Siward describing Macbeth as a 'tyrant'.

The moment of Macbeth's demise is so nearly upon him, and what is striking in this scene is the determination with which the men approach the battle. Their words echo those of Macbeth when they consider the trumpets that will herald the start of the battle – the 'clamorous harbingers of blood and death.' Imagery surrounding blood has been so often associated with the actions Macbeth plans to do to others: here, it describes his own end.

### Scene analysis: Act V, Scene vii

At the opening of the scene, Macbeth decries that 'They have tied me to a stake; I cannot fly, / But bear-like I must fight the course.' This gives a sense of the claustrophobia Macbeth feels, trapped in his castle and surrounded by enemy

21.  Steven Mullaney, 'Lying Like Truth: Riddle, Representation and Treason in Renaissance England', *ELH*, Vol. 47, No. 1 (Spring 1980), pp. 32–47, https://www.jstor.org/stable/2872437.

22.  William Blissett, 'The Secret'st Man of Blood. A Study of Dramatic Irony in Macbeth', *Shakespeare Quarterly*, Vol. 10, No. 3 (Summer 1959), pp. 397–408, https://www.jstor.org/stable/2866862.

soldiers. His position is also one of futility. Macbeth has no real recourse here; he will meet his end whilst tied to his metaphorical 'post'.

Macbeth attempts to keep hold of the witches prophecies, however, and this is an interesting dichotomy between his knowledge that he will soon die and his continued grasp of his belief that 'none of woman born' can harm him. He acknowledges he either has someone who fits this category to be fearful of, or no one to be fearful of at all. This again is interesting and shows a shift in Macbeth's mentality towards his situation.

The moment of the battle is upon Macbeth as Young Siward arrives. This is the first time we have met this character, though we have heard him alluded to by his father before. Young Siward's hatred of Macbeth is apparent in the following line, when he asks Macbeth his name and realises he is faced with the tyrant himself: 'The devil himself could not pronounce a title / More hateful to mine ear.' This is the precise opposite of what Macbeth hoped he would be. Where he perhaps had dreams of being lauded and celebrated, much like his predecessor, his actions have led to people considering him in the same league as the Devil himself. However, Macbeth embraces this, declaring that his name could not be more hateful 'nor more fearful.' The two men fight, and Young Siward is brutally killed.

Young Siward's death is only the third presented on stage, with Banquo's and Young Macduff's deaths before his. It is the first murder we have seen Macbeth actually perform, though. Whilst the audience will remember that Macbeth has been described as a fierce warrior in Act I, Scene ii, this is the first time they have seen it for themselves. It is not as impressive now as it sounded then. The audience sees a man acting out of desperation, in a futile bid to retain his position. There is an almost pathetic quality to it.

As Young Siward dies, Macduff arrives on stage and the moment of Macbeth's final confrontation falls upon him, though Macbeth does not yet recognise this to be the case.

Macduff confirms that it is 'his wife and children's ghosts' which haunt him and encourage him to kill Macbeth. He is determined to be the one to kill the tyrannical king; he is determined for Macbeth to be the only death committed by his sword. His vision of killing Macbeth is almost compulsive.

The scene continues apace with Macduff departing to find Macbeth and being replaced by Malcolm and Siward. Siward announces that Macbeth's castle was 'gently rendered.' In other words, there has been little fight put up by anyone in the castle. This is suggestive of the fact that those Macbeth believed to stand with him have fled or been easily defeated. Some of those who had been loyal to Macbeth 'on both sides do fight', and Siward declares that 'little is to do' before Macduff will have the opportunity to kill Macbeth.

## Scene analysis: Act V, Scene viii

Macbeth knows that the moment of his death is upon him. His question, 'Why should I play the Roman fool and die / On mine own sword?' demonstrates to the audience that Macbeth has indeed acknowledged that his time is almost up. He considers dying by suicide only briefly; he fears that he would be a 'fool' to do so: 'His spiritual destruction must be reflected in an ignominious physical destruction,'[23] and that is what will shortly befall him.

Macduff breaks this reverie, his rage overflowing as he says: 'Turn, hell-hound, turn.' 'Hell-hounds' are mythical creatures with roots reaching back to Ancient Greece,[24] and are generally believed to be creatures which guard the entrance to hell or the underworld. From the fourteenth century, the word was also used to describe a 'wicked person, agent of Hell'[25] and it is likely *this* interpretation Shakespeare leans on here.

Macbeth warns Macduff away, telling him that his 'soul is too much charged / With blood of thine already.' This is an 'apparently compassionate, apparently moral warning.'[26] Perhaps, though, Macbeth is not actually concerned for Macduff. He may be instead exhibiting for the first time, almost at the moment of his death, 'an intolerable guilt.'[27] Even if that *is* the case, it is not enough to absolve him of his considerable sin. Macduff declares him to be 'thou bloodier villain'. There is no recourse for Macbeth now, though he still holds on to the second apparition's prophecy: he claims to 'bear a charmed life, which must not yield / To one of woman born.'

The most significant moment of dramatic irony in *Macbeth* is held in the next line, as Macduff declares he 'was from his mother's womb / Untimely ripped.' Macbeth, in this moment, realises that he has grossly misinterpreted the witches' words. Macduff was not of 'woman born'. Instead, he was 'of woman ripped – delivered from the confines of his mother's womb by being ripped out rather than by being given birth to.'[28]

23. Irving Ribner, 'Macbeth: The Pattern of Idea and Action', *Shakespeare Quarterly*, Vol. 10, No. 2 (Spring 1959), pp. 147–159, https://www.jstor.org/stable/2866920.

24. Encyclopedia Britannica, 'Hellhound', https://www.britannica.com/topic/hellhound.

25. Etymonline.com, 'Hellhound', https://www.etymonline.com/word/hellhound.

26. Howard C. Cole, 'Reviewed Work: Shakespeare's Tragic Practice by Bertrand Evans', *The Journal of English and Germanic Philology*, Vol. 80, No. 2 (April 1981), pp. 244–247 https://www.jstor.org/stable/27708801.

27. Ibid.

28. Nicholas Wolterstorff, 'Was Macduff of Woman Born? The Ontology of Characters', *Notre Dame English Journal*, Vol. 12, No. 2, Belief and Imagination: Religious Traditions in Literature (April 1980), pp. 123–139, https://www.jstor.org/stable/40062404.

Macduff's birth was undoubtedly a violent one; his mother would most likely have died either before his birth or immediately following it. The first written record of a woman surviving a caesarean section was recorded in 1500. However, the written record was not made until 82 years after the event, and its veracity is therefore called into considerable question.[29] His coming actions echo this violence.

Macbeth realises that 'these juggling fiends no more believed / That palter with us in a double sense'. Whilst it is undoubtedly the case that to some extent it was Macbeth's desire to read into the prophecies what he wished to hear, here he realises that he has been lied to: 'each crisis or defeat in the outer world [is] matched by a further step in the spiritual awakening of the doomed protagonist.'[30]

Upon his realisation that the witches told the truth and *here* is the man he must fear, Macbeth declares: 'I'll not fight with thee.' Macduff tells him to yield, telling him that as punishment, he'll be 'Painted upon a pole, and underwrit, / "Here you may see the tyrant".' This public exhibition seems disgusting and unthinkable to Macbeth, who will not 'yield to kiss the ground before young Malcolm's feet' and instead vows, despite the fact that he now knows his fate, that he 'will try the last' and fight until his final moment.

It is here that Macbeth meets the end that has been inevitable since the opening moments of the play. He and Macduff fight, and Macbeth is slain.

## Macbeth and mental health

In Jacobean society, the discussion of mental health was in its infancy, to the extent that, despite innumerable deaths by suicide depicted in Shakespearean plays, there was no word for death by suicide until long after Shakespeare's death. Instead, death by suicide was referred to as 'self-murder', was considered a mortal sin by the church, and was illegal, with survivors of attempted suicide often prosecuted for their crime.[31]

Indeed, such was the stigma of death by suicide in contemporary society that, often, families tried to cover up this as a cause of death in records, including offering bribes for coroners not to examine the death too closely. To be listed as a 'murderer' on one's death certificate would bring shame on one's family.

29. US National Library of Medicine, 'Cesarean Section – A Brief History', https://www.nlm.nih.gov/exhibition/cesarean/preface.html.

30. Charlotte Spivack, 'The Elizabethan Theatre: Circle and Centre', *The Centennial Review*, Vol. 13, No. 4 (Fall 1969), pp. 424–443, https://www.jstor.org/stable/23737722.

31. Harry Lesser, 'Suicide and Self-Murder', *Philosophy*, Vol. 55, No. 212 (April 1980), pp. 255–257.

Not only was the stigma difficult for families to deal with, but, additionally, the knowledge that a person had died by suicide would often preclude a family from seeking a Christian burial.

Indeed, this is a situation Shakespeare explores himself in *Hamlet*, with the gravediggers, following Ophelia's death by suicide, discussing whether she is permitted to have a Christian burial. In this short exchange, we see a clear summary of contemporary thought on the subject of suicide.[32]

> **First Clown**
> *Is she to be buried in Christian burial that*
> *wilfully seeks her own salvation?*
> **Second Clown**
> *I tell thee she is: and therefore make her grave*
> *straight: the crowner hath sat on her, and finds it*
> *Christian burial.*
> **First Clown**
> *How can that be, unless she drowned herself in her*
> *own defence?*
> **Second Clown**
> *Why, 'tis found so.*
> **First Clown**
> *It must be 'se offendendo;' it cannot be else. For*
> *here lies the point: if I drown myself wittingly,*
> *it argues an act: and an act hath three branches: it*
> *is, to act, to do, to perform: argal, she drowned*
> *herself wittingly.*
> **Second Clown**
> *Nay, but hear you, goodman delver,—*
> **First Clown**
> *Give me leave. Here lies the water; good: here*
> *stands the man; good; if the man go to this water,*
> *and drown himself, it is, will he, nill he, he*
> *goes,—mark you that; but if the water come to him*
> *and drown him, he drowns not himself: argal, he*
> *that is not guilty of his own death shortens not his own life.*
> **Second Clown**
> *But is this law?*

---

32. Michael MacDonald, 'Ophelia's Maimèd Rites', *Shakespeare Quarterly*, Vol. 37, No. 3 (Autumn 1986), pp. 309–317, https://www.jstor.org/stable/2870101.

**First Clown**
*Ay, marry, is't; crowner's quest law.*
**Second Clown**
*Will you ha' the truth on't? If this had not been
a gentlewoman, she should have been buried out o'
Christian burial.*

Lady Macbeth's apparent death by suicide, therefore, would have likely been met, in reality, with a similar level of stigma.

By the late 16th century, there were advances being made in the study of mental illnesses and, whilst society's acceptance and understanding was still in early development, doctors endeavoured to understand more about it. Often, doctors drew on the work of Galen, a Greek physician, whose 'Four Humours' theory explored the idea that physical and mental health was reliant upon a balance of four so-called 'humours' in the human body – blood, yellow bile, black bile and phlegm. Galen's understanding was that ill health – whether in terms of physical health or mental health – was caused by a loss of balance of these fluids.

In addition to this, however, doctors in Shakespeare's England thought that, largely, 'madness' was caused by unrequited love. Alongside this, 'mischance or trauma, overwork or excessive intellectual stimulation, shock or religious torment'[33] were also commonly believed to be catalysts for mental ill-health. For Macbeth, a number of these are true – even if some are very much self-inflicted.

Some critics attribute Macbeth's declining mental health to his progressive sinking into sin. However, contemporary beliefs would have recognised that the first of Macbeth's sins – regicide – is nonpareil: he has committed the ultimate sin at this point, and further crimes will not deepen the level of sin he carries. His difficulties with his mental health cannot, therefore, be attributed to the sins he commits.

Macbeth veers between confidence, anger and deep-rooted paranoia, with numerous conditions in between. It was believed, in relation to mental health, that the Four Humours could exist in two states: balanced (and therefore the person would, too, be 'balanced') and unbalanced. This would lead to a 'constantly shifting mercurial temperament',[34] which seems to explain Macbeth's own frame of mind.

---

33. Will Tosh, 'Shakespeare and Madness', (British Library), https://www.bl.uk/shakespeare/articles/shakespeare-and-madness.

34. John W. Draper, 'Macbeth, "Infirme of Purpose"', *Bulletin of the History of Medicine*, Vol. 10, No. 1 (June 1941), pp. 16–26, https://www.jstor.org/stable/44440637.

Those who had these 'shifting mercurial temperaments'[35] were commonly believed to be more likely to listen to, and be influenced by, others – and so we see with Macbeth from the opening of the play as he is influenced by the witches, and then his wife, to commit horrendous crimes. He takes little persuasion ultimately, despite his own misgivings, and this plays into contemporary belief about mental ill health.

However, there is more at play than a misbalance in the Galenic Four Humours in contemporary understanding of mental health, and therefore more to play in Shakespeare's presentation of Macbeth. Arguably, in addition to the Four Humours, understanding of mental health also navigated 'folklore, faculty psychology... and narratives of the occult.'[36] There is a focus on 'the border between the interior or exterior, the native and the alien, sanity and sickness.'[37] To what extent is Macbeth's ultimate downfall to blame on his own internal, integral decisions and wellbeing, and to what extent can it be blamed on external factors?

Jacobeans had complex ideas about the purpose of imagination based on theories and thoughts from centuries before. Dreams, visions and hallucinations were believed to be generated by the mind's image-making faculty, and disorders relating to imagination, and specifically people who were particularly melancholic, were commonly believed to be so due to an imbalance in black bile. This belief was taken from Aristotle, who believed that 'confused and monstrous visions tended to appear in the dreams of the melancholic... [and] produced outlandish delusions.'[38]

For *Macbeth*, then, an audience could interpret that Shakespeare includes aspects such as Macbeth's hallucinations to highlight the mental torment his protagonist is under. Whether this torment is due to his guilt or due to his mental ill health, or, indeed, to a cyclical combination of the two, remains open to interpretation.

---

35. John W. Draper, 'Macbeth, "Infirme of Purpose"', *Bulletin of the History of Medicine*, Vol. 10, No. 1 (June 1941), pp. 16–26, https://www.jstor.org/stable/44440637.

36. Suparna Roychoudhury, 'Melancholy, Ecstasy, Phantasma: The Pathologies of *Macbeth*', *Modern Philology*, Vol. 111, No. 2 (November 2013), pp. 205–230, https://www.jstor.org/stable/10.1086/673309.

37. Ibid.

38. Ibid.

## 'Tomorrow, and tomorrow, and tomorrow' at a glance

### RESOURCE 18.1

Repetition shows the futility of his life as he crawls towards his inescapable fate.

Macbeth thinks that he may be doomed to this drawn out suffering until the very last record of time and the moment of his judgement.

He envisions his days as filled with inescapable drudgery, his life an almost intolerable burden on him.

All he has done only propels him closer to his inevitable death.

Macbeth has always performed a role in society. Is his life intrinsically performative in nature?

> Tomorrow, and tomorrow, and tomorrow,
> Creeps in this petty pace from day to day,
> To the last syllable of recorded time;
> And all our yesterdays have lighted fools
> The way to dusty death. Out, out, brief candle,
> Life's but a walking shadow, a poor player,
> That struts and frets his hour upon the stage,
> And then is heard no more. It is a tale
> Told by an idiot, full of sound and fury
> Signifying nothing.

His future is suddenly illuminated to him, and it is full of nothing more than emptiness and death.

He is just a 'player' with no real sway over his own life.

This is his moment of realisation that his ambition will be what ultimately destroys him. Everything he has done has been for nothing.

## How?

### Retrieval

When used carefully, multiple choice questions can tell us a great deal about our students' thought processes and understanding. It is worth noting that multiple choice questions are quick to answer but not always quick to set up. This is because there is certain advice, worth following, to get the most out of this method of retrieval.[39] The most important of these, I believe, is the inclusion of 'plausible distractors'. These are intended 'to serve as distractors, which should be selected by students who did not achieve the learning outcome but ignored by students who did achieve the learning outcome',[40] and are particularly effective when based on prior misconceptions made by students in that class.

It is difficult, without knowing your specific class and their context, to give you a definitive list of questions for this retrieval task. However, my advice would be to focus on the character of Macduff, the latest set of Macbeth's prophecies and the discussions between Macduff and Malcolm in Act IV,

---

39. Steve Wheeler, 'Writing multiple choice questions – a handy guide', (The University of Manchester), http://www.elearning.fse.manchester.ac.uk/blog/2018/01/23/writing-multiple-choice-questions-handy-guide/.

40. Cynthia J. Brame, 'Writing Good Multiple Choice Test Questions', (Vanderbilt University, 2013), https://cft.vanderbilt.edu/guides-sub-pages/writing-good-multiple-choice-test-questions/.

Scene iii as the foundation of these questions. For example, you could include a question like the one below:

1. Which of the following options was promised to Macbeth by the apparitions?

   a. That he should be worried about/'Beware' Siward
   b. That he could only be killed by someone not 'born of woman'
   c. That he won't be defeated until the river comes to his castle
   d. That Banquo's sons will not be king

## Pre-reading activities

The students, by this point, have a clear understanding that the play is only going in one direction. Remind them, or tease out using questioning, what they know so far about the inevitability of Macbeth's fate.

Then, students should make some predictions using these three questions to prompt their ideas, bearing in mind the Big Question: 'What becomes of Macbeth?', which you could introduce here.

- Will Macduff be successful in removing Macbeth from the throne?
- All of Macbeth's prophecies so far have come true. Will the current set of prophecies come true? How?
- What will be the final outcome of these scenes for Macbeth? How about Lady Macbeth?

Students could write these predictions down first before discussing as a class. It is interesting and pertinent to see what similarities and differences students can identify between their predictions. This may give them a sense of what the most likely outcome is, based on what they know so far, and gives them a basis of ideas as they read the subsequent scenes.

## Reading the scenes

The scenes from this point onwards are short and sharp, and I think it is useful sometimes to couch this in the terms of the quick-paced, fast cuts used in films at the moment of highest tension. This helps them visualise the pace of the Act but also helps them to track the rising tension.

Here are some questions which could be used during or after reading each scene. Accompanying these questions, I would ask students to write a very short summary of the scenes (aiming for between 20 and 30 words). They could do this after each scene or every few scenes.

## Act V, Scene ii

- Who is leading the English troops?
- Who is Malcolm's uncle?
- Where does Angus say they will meet the troops?
- What does Caithness say is happening inside the castle?
- Why does Angus compare Macbeth's clothes to being like a 'giant's robes / Upon a dwarfish thief'?

## Act V, Scene iii

- How is Macbeth feeling at the start of this scene?
- How does Macbeth react when he discovers there are ten thousand troops outside?
- What does Macbeth decide to do next in response to the threat of these soldiers?
- What news does the Doctor bring Macbeth about his wife?
- How does Macbeth react to this news?
- Why does Macbeth continue to act in a hubristic manner?

## Act V, Scene iv

- Where does this scene take place?
- What does Malcolm instruct each soldier to do?
- Why does he instruct the soldiers to do this?

## Act V, Scene v

- What are Macbeth's plans for the English army?
- What happens to Lady Macbeth?
- How does Macbeth react to this?
- What does Macbeth say about life, and what life is like?
- Why do you think Macbeth feels this way?
- What news does the Messenger deliver to Macbeth?

## Act V, Scene vi

- Who does Malcolm instruct to lead the first battle?
- Who will lead the second wave?

## Act V, Scene vii

- Why does Macbeth refuse to give Young Siward his name at first?
- What happens to Young Siward?

## Act V, Scene viii

- How does Macduff refer to Macbeth?
- What does Macduff reveal about himself?
- What happens to Macbeth?

### Guided analysis: Macbeth's soliloquy in Act V, Scene v

Macbeth's soliloquy tells the audience so much about Macbeth's frame of mind now. I would usually, at this point, use some guided analysis to help students consider Shakespeare's craft in this speech. You can see an example of this in Resource 18.2.

### RESOURCE 18.2

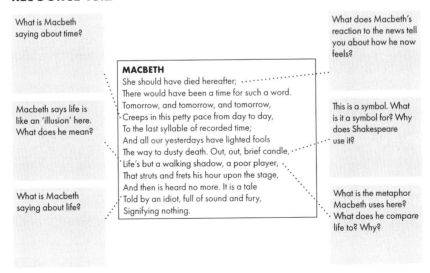

What is Macbeth saying about time?

What does Macbeth's reaction to the news tell you about how he now feels?

Macbeth says life is like an 'illusion' here. What does he mean?

This is a symbol. What is it a symbol for? Why does Shakespeare use it?

What is Macbeth saying about life?

What is the metaphor Macbeth uses here? What does he compare life to? Why?

**MACBETH**
She should have died hereafter;
There would have been a time for such a word.
Tomorrow, and tomorrow, and tomorrow,
Creeps in this petty pace from day to day,
To the last syllable of recorded time;
And all our yesterdays have lighted fools
The way to dusty death. Out, out, brief candle,
Life's but a walking shadow, a poor player,
That struts and frets his hour upon the stage,
And then is heard no more. It is a tale
Told by an idiot, full of sound and fury,
Signifying nothing.

## Then and now

In their GCSE exam, students will need to be able to draw on their knowledge of the whole play. Whilst this has been a skill practised throughout these resources, this activity specifically asks students to compare two moments in the play. The Macbeth we see now is a radical departure from the Macbeth the audience first heard about in Act I, Scene ii.

Using Resource 18.3, ask students to explore how Macbeth's character has changed over time.

## RESOURCE 18.3

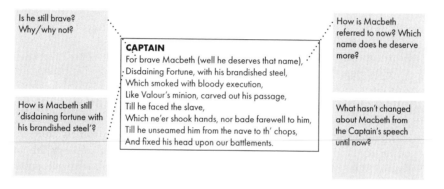

Is he still brave? Why/why not?

How is Macbeth referred to now? Which name does he deserve more?

**CAPTAIN**
For brave Macbeth (well he deserves that name),
Disdaining Fortune, with his brandished steel,
Which smoked with bloody execution,
Like Valour's minion, carved out his passage,
Till he faced the slave,
Which ne'er shook hands, nor bade farewell to him,
Till he unseamed him from the nave to th' chops,
And fixed his head upon our battlements.

How is Macbeth still 'disdaining fortune with his brandished steel'?

What hasn't changed about Macbeth from the Captain's speech until now?

## 'Hell-hound' or 'brave Macbeth'?

The conclusion of *Macbeth* can be quite divisive. For a contemporary audience, the play is structured so that Macbeth receives the punishment befitting his crimes. For a modern audience, looking through the lens of the twenty-first century, there could be another consideration, though. His behaviour and decisions have been manipulated by his wife and the witches, as well as his own innate ambition. Macbeth is a more complex character, and there is evidence to support calling him a 'hell-hound' or 'brave Macbeth' – or, indeed, both.

In this activity, students will create a Venn diagram to explore the duality of Macbeth's character. Start by giving them a blank template. Students should fill each section with examples of what makes him a 'hell-hound', what makes him 'brave', and any events from the play which are more morally ambiguous. They should then find quotations that demonstrate these moments or events in the play, or offer further, detailed explanation. A partially completed example is included in Resource 18.4.

## RESOURCE 18.4

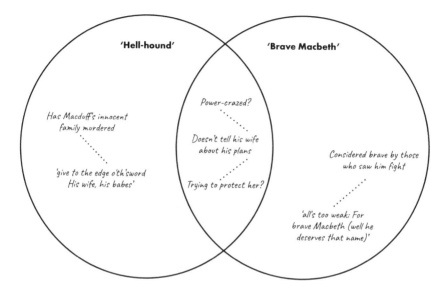

'Hell-hound'

'Brave Macbeth'

Has Macduff's innocent
family murdered

'give to the edge o'th'sword
His wife, his babes'

Power-crazed?

Doesn't tell his wife
about his plans

Trying to protect her?

Considered brave by those
who saw him fight

'all's too weak: For
brave Macbeth (well he
deserves that name)'

## Conscience alley

Throughout the play, Macbeth has been plagued by his conscience. He has tried, time and time again, to reject his feelings of guilt and welcome metaphorical darkness into his life. His has been quite the journey. This activity helps students explore that journey, considering Macbeth's character development throughout the play.

The resource for this activity is based on the idea used in drama lessons of the 'conscience alley'. In it, an actor walks down an alleyway formed by their peers who try to compel the character to make the 'right' decision by presenting them with evidence of the many facets of the character. This activity takes that concept and instead transfers it to the written word – though this would also work well as an oracy activity if this worked best with your students.

Starting at the bottom of the sheet, students should list on the 'walls' of the alley the choices Macbeth faces and, where relevant, what he subsequently chooses to do. They will see, as they complete this activity, that his brutality grows in almost equal measure with his paranoia. They will also see that his crimes do not abate; if anything, they continue apace. A partially completed resource might look something like this:

## RESOURCE 18.5[41]

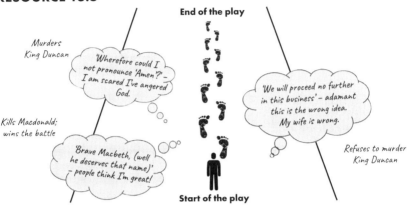

If it helps, consider Macbeth's first few choices as a class to get students going. Once they have completed this, they should imagine Macbeth moving through the 'alleyway'. What does he think at each point? They could use quotations here, or their own knowledge.

### Answering the 'Big Question'

The activities throughout this lesson have been built to allow students to answer the 'Big Question'. It becomes less a quick 'question' and more of an extended piece of writing, allowing students a moment of reflection to explore their thoughts, feelings and reactions.

### Suggested 'Extra Challenge' activities

- Bryan Lowrance argues that Macbeth's '...actions have been nothing but a 'hollow charade of autonomy.'[42] To what extent do you agree?
- Nihilism in *Macbeth*. Discuss.
- What is the significance of time in *Macbeth*?

### Key vocabulary:

Nihilism, futile

---

41. Standing by Jake Dunham from the Noun Project and footprints by Jaime Serra from the Noun Project.

42. Bryan Lowrance, '"Modern Ecstacy": "Macbeth" and the meaning of the political', *ELH*, Vol. 79, No. 4 (Winter 2012), pp. 823–849, https://www.jstor.org/stable/23356185.

# CHAPTER 19
## Act V, Scene ix

*How does the play end?*

## What?

### Scene analysis: Act V, Scene ix

The First Folio does not indicate a new scene here, although 'editors since Pope'[1] have had one, perhaps because there are no actors on stage at this point and the audience needs 'some conventional encouragement to imagine a change of place from where Macbeth and Macduff fight to wherever Malcolm and his company are' when they are greeted by Macduff with Macbeth's head.[2]

#### A CELEBRATION OF VIOLENCE

It makes logical sense for this revision to be made, for Act V, Scene ix, arguably, is a mirror image of the beginning of the play. Macduff, as we come to realise, kills Macbeth by beheading him, a fitting end for a traitor and one which alludes to Macbeth's killing of Macdonald in Act I, Scene ii. Violence is celebrated once more. Although it has come to represent betrayal and distrust, ironically, it is only violence which can heal Scotland. Would it be too far to say that violence is associated with order then? It is not necessarily violence which has thrown the Great Chain of Being into disarray but the act; violence is present regardless of whether things are ordered or disordered. Indeed, Macduff is treated as a hero, but in committing violence, he is guilty of the same crime as that committed by Macbeth: regicide.

The scene, however, begins with Malcolm entering, stating, 'I would the friends we miss were safe arrived.' It is clear the battle has been long and hard,

---

1.  A.R. Braunmuller, *The New Cambridge Shakespeare: Macbeth*, (Cambridge: Cambridge University Press, 2008), p. 252.

2.  Ibid.

although Siward confirms that although some have been lost, their numbers remain strong. He has, however, lost his son, and Ross reveals the news.

### 'YOUR SON, MY LORD, HAS PAID A SOLDIER'S DEBT'

Yet again, another exploration of masculinity comes to our attention. Ross, in telling Siward of his son's death, says he paid the price of being a soldier. In paying this price, he has become a man. Masculinity, then, is once more inextricably linked with violence, further emphasised by the fact that Siward clarifies whether his son's wounds were on his front or back. 'Aye, on the front,' Ross replies, sealing Young Siward's status as a man. He did not flee as would be denoted by wounds on his back. Instead, he faced his enemy, and this knowledge acts somewhat as a balm for Siward's grief. In fact, he remains rather emotionless and definitely does not 'feel it as a man' like Macduff in Act IV, Scene iii. He simply states, 'Why, then, God's soldier be he. / Had I as many sons as I have hairs, / I would not wish them to a fairer death,' implying he would wish this fate upon other sons if he had them. It is an odd sentiment: it seems, in this harsh world, that honour and duty are two things that can only be achieved through violent means. Indeed, even Ross seems eager to suppress Siward's emotions for him: 'Your cause of sorrow / Must not be measured by his worth, for then / It hath no end.'

A small, compelling moment here belongs to Malcolm, who believes Young Siward is 'worth more sorrow'. To walk along the path of grief is important, something Malcolm has perhaps learnt by witnessing Macduff embracing his emotions rather than shunning them. Mourning is not reminiscent of femininity, but a necessity, although Siward, along with most of the other male characters, is still to learn this, believing his son to be 'worth no more'.

### 'HAIL KING, FOR SO THOU ART'

It is Macduff's entrance that heralds the arrival of something more ominous. When Macduff enters, he says to Malcolm, 'Hail King, for so thou art,' brandishing Macbeth's head like a trophy. The word 'hail' is particularly pertinent, especially seeing as it is used a total of three times, perhaps an allusion to the three witches who use it as a form of greeting in Act I, Scene iii. One only has to consider its previous uses to see that it is not the 'fair' commendation it initially seems to be. In Act III, Macbeth says '[the witches] hailed [Banquo] father to a line of kings.' In Act I, Lady Macbeth addresses her husband as 'Great Glamis, Worthy Cawdor, / Greater than both, by the all-hail hereafter' and Macbeth even recounts the witches' words in the letter he sends to his wife. 'Hail', then, is inextricably linked with the witches, and so the fact that Macduff uses it here is somewhat worrying. Malcolm is hailed as Macbeth was; the witches are still very much present even if they are physically absent. There may be joy at the return to order but, as Neil Bowen observes, 'The witches win. They are never held to account for their actions. They remain powerful, ungoverned and at large.'[3]

Suspicion, then must fall on Malcolm. His earlier deception has gone unscrutinised and unchecked; because of interruption by the Doctor, we never get to see Macduff holding him to account, and our concerns are left hanging. Here, then, audiences could be forgiven for being sceptical of his final speech, especially now, seeing as he has, arguably, been positioned by Shakespeare as a man connected through language to the witches.

If this is the case, Malcolm's final speech can be read in two ways. His words could be truthful. Macbeth's reign, tainted by bloodshed, is over. Malcolm's final words could be heard in a celebratory sense: this truly is a happy ending and Scotland can begin her process of healing. However, perhaps Shakespeare cannot resist one last allusion to 'Fair is foul, and foul is fair'. He may not be as authentic as one may wish to believe, particularly when one keeps his inauthentic episode in mind; if this is the case, his words are vacant of meaning. Audiences are not sure if they can trust exactly what he is saying, and although Malcolm states his immediate intentions as king, in reality, we are left wondering exactly what kind of king he will actually be.

One may be surprised that Shakespeare even gives the final lines of the play to Malcolm. Millicent Bell, in her study of Elizabethan theatre, cites George Lyman Kittredge's observation that 'the dramatic character of highest rank customarily spoke the speech bringing an Elizabethan play to a close.'[4]

He speaks of a new chapter in Scotland's history, making 'thanes and kinsmen / ... earls, the first that ever Scotland / In such an honour named', his reward echoing his father's words in Act I, Scene iv: 'signs of nobleness, like stars, shall shine / On all deservers.' He expresses his hope to purge Scotland of those who showed loyalty to Macbeth whilst bringing home 'exiled friends abroad' who fled the 'dead butcher, and his fiend-like queen'. It is a striking image of savagery. Not only has Macbeth butchered his enemies and people he deems to be a threat, but Scotland too. The country needs time to repair and heal itself, helped by the 'grace of grace': God. And so Malcolm ends the play with the final two couplets:

---

3.  Neil Bowen, et. al., *The Art of Drama Volume 2: Macbeth GCSE & Beyond*, (Bristol, Peripeteia Press, 2019), p. 117.

4.  Millicent Bell, *Shakespeare's Tragic Skepticism*, (New Haven: Yale University Press, 2002) p. 74.

'*So thanks to all at once, and to each one,*
*Whom we invite to see us crowned at Scone.*'

The characters exit, the play ends and Malcolm stands ready to take the throne. Really, though, our thoughts are still with Macbeth, the 'dead butcher', an overly complex character summed up in two simplistic, blunt words. They do not seem enough to convey exactly what Macbeth, and indeed Lady Macbeth, are guilty of. Perhaps B.L. Reid sums up Malcolm's label of Macbeth best when saying,

> *Malcolm spoke better in the fourth act, when he said, 'A good and virtuous nature may recoil / In an imperial charge'; and reminded Macduff that 'Angels are bright still, though the brightest fell.' One recalls, as Shakespeare obviously recalled, the fallen Lucifer. Macbeth falls to dark, but he falls from light. He and his lady show us the angel and the devil that live in the soul of man.*[5]

## The end at a glance

## RESOURCE 19.1

Malcolm delivers this final speech, being the character of highest rank who has survived the events of the play.

A striking image of savagery, but perhaps too simplistic to convey the extent of Macbeth's crimes.

After Malcolm's deception in Act IV, Scene iii, can we really trust what he is saying here?

**MALCOLM**
We shall not spend a large expense of time
Before we reckon with your several loves
And make us even with you. My thanes and kinsmen,
Henceforth be earls, the first that ever Scotland
In such an honour named. What's more to do,
Which would be planted newly with the time,
As calling home our exiled friends abroad,
That fled the snares of watchful tyranny,
Producing forth the cruel ministers
Of this dead butcher, and his fiend-like queen,
Who, as 'tis thought, by self and violent hands
Took off her life – this, and what needful else
That calls upon us, by the grace of grace,
We will perform in measure, time and place.
So thanks to all at once, and to each one,
Whom we invite to see us crowned at Scone.

This is perhaps a throwback to Duncan's line in Act I, Scene iv when he says 'signs of nobleness, like stars, shall shine / On all deservers.'

Those that have run away from Scotland will be called back home.

Many who have been, or are still, loyal to Macbeth will be found and brought to justice.

Malcolm claims he will be guided by God to heal Scotland.

5.  B.L. Reid, '"Macbeth" and the Play of Absolutes,' *The Sewanee Review*, Vol. 73, No. 1, 1965, pp. 19–46, www.jstor.org/stable/27541080.

## How?

This final 'How?' section is a little different; it does not start with a retrieval practice activity. That is because once the final scene has been read, students can complete a series of activities that are designed to look at the play holistically, requiring them to retrieve. These activities are not sequenced into a lesson itself, but you may wish to complete them once the class has finished studying Malcolm's final speech. These activities will allow you to prepare for more conceptual responses, tracking ideas throughout the play. As such, there are also no 'Extra Challenge' activities in this chapter.

## Reading the scene

Read through this short scene, which covers Macbeth's death and Malcolm's final speech. Use the following questions to help ascertain student understanding:

1. What does Ross say has happened to Young Siward?
2. What is Siward's reaction to the death of his son?
3. What does Malcolm say he will do for Young Siward?
4. How has Macduff killed Macbeth?
5. How does Macduff address Malcolm?
6. Who does Malcolm wish to bring back to Scotland?
7. How are Macbeth and Lady Macbeth referred to by Malcolm?
8. Where will Malcolm be crowned?

## Find it, highlight it, annotate it

There are so many things students could explore here, including Siward's stereotypical view of masculinity and Macduff's act of regicide. However, the main crux of the scene revolves around Malcolm's final speech, and that is what is focused on here. Give students a blank copy of the scene and ask them to complete the following 'find it, highlight it, annotate it' task. A variation of this was first used to analyse the Captain's speech in Act I, Scene ii, where we were first introduced to Macbeth. It seems only right to use it again here to consider Malcolm's final words.

Ask students to number the lines for the entire speech, beginning like so:

1. We shall not spend a large expense of time
2. Before we reckon with your several loves
3. And make us even with you. My thanes and kinsmen

This will ensure the line numbers match up with the following activity, guiding students with their analysis. Present students with these questions and ask them to add their answers as annotations:

1. Line 1 – Highlight 'We' – How is Malcolm's new status as king evident through the language he is using?
2. Line 3 – Highlight 'My thanes and kinsmen' – What is the effect of the word 'my'? What does this tell us about Malcolm?
3. Line 7 – Highlight this line – What does the word 'exiled' imply about the circumstances in which Malcolm's countrymen left Scotland?
4. Line 8 – Highlight 'snares of watchful tyranny' – What is a snare and how can one link it to the concept of tyranny?
5. Line 10 – Highlight 'dead butcher, and his fiend-like queen' – Why does Malcolm refer to Macbeth as a 'butcher'? What are the connotations of this word? How is Lady Macbeth presented through the term 'fiend-like'?
6. Line 11 – Highlight 'self and violent hands' – Having tracked the motif of hands through the play, what do they come to represent in these closing moments?
7. Line 13 – Highlight 'the grace of grace' – Explain what this means and discuss how Malcolm's rule could be different from Macbeth's.
8. Line 16 – Highlight this line – How has order been restored to Scotland?

### Silent debate

After feedback, this could then be followed up with a silent debate activity, asking students what they think is in store for Scotland's future, using evidence from the play to help back up their ideas. It is a way of ensuring everyone contributes. For instructions on how to run a silent debate, see Chapter 13. Silent debate questions could include:

- Using evidence from the play, what do you think is in store for Scotland's future?
- Why has Shakespeare written *Macbeth*?
- What is Shakespeare trying to teach us? What is the most important thing he wants us to learn?

These questions are a stimulus for further discussion around authorial intent and act as a fitting end to the study of the play. After sharing responses, students could pick one to write about, or, indeed, could write a response to the final Big Question.

### Exploring the play holistically

I have always found there is a tendency to jump straight into exam practice once classes have finished a text; I have certainly been guilty of this in the past. However, we have to be careful about doing this too quickly. Completing an initial read and study of a text does not necessarily mean a unit is done and dusted. We must not deny our students the opportunity to reconsider a text holistically. Now, I will often ask students to go back and revisit certain areas of the text where more can be taught once everyone has an understanding of the entire play. As with all texts, there are things students will not pick up on a first reading because they simply do not have the knowledge to do so.

This holistic approach may take the form of rereading scenes and picking up on elements of foreshadowing. One may even want to consider revisiting entire soliloquies at sentence or word level. For example, students will be able to get far more out of Macbeth's reference to Hecate in his soliloquy in Act II, Scene i having learnt more about her in Act III, Scene v. Sometimes, I make these connections as I go along, but sometimes it is appropriate to wait until the end. Here, I explain two effective methods to get students looking at the play holistically, although there are a wealth of activities students could complete to do this.

### *Macbeth* and 'The Human Condition'

An effective activity to help draw together ideas is to look at a text in relation to the human condition. Here, I will explain the process in relation to *Macbeth*, but this works for any text. The idea for looking at the human condition was first introduced to me by Lance Hanson (@LHanson1711 on Twitter), who shared a blog post about his study of it in relation to *The Strange Case of Dr. Jekyll and Mr. Hyde*.[6] The prospect intrigued me, and so I planned the following activity for *Macbeth*.

Start by asking students what they think is meant by the 'human condition'. To help them, I have always encouraged students to consider the definition of each word separately before putting them together and thinking about what the term could mean. Take feedback before showing students the following definition:

> 'The **characteristics**, *key **events**, and* **situations** *which* **compose**
> *the* **essentials** *of human* **existence**, *such as* **birth**, **growth**,
> **emotionality**, **aspiration**, **conflict**, *and* **mortality**.'[7]

I like this definition because of the way it breaks down the 'human condition' into the 'essentials of... existence', offering students six lenses through which

---

6. Lance Hanson, 'Because – but – so: thinking about Jekyll, Hyde and the human condition', *Mr Hanson's English*, https://mrhansonsenglish.wordpress.com/2019/02/06/because-but-so-thinking-about-jekyll-hyde-and-the-human-condition.

7. Your Dictionary, 'human-condition', https://www.yourdictionary.com/human-condition.

to explore *Macbeth*. Establish as a class what each of these six components of the 'human condition' means before giving out Resource 19.2, designed to help students make connections:

## RESOURCE 19.2

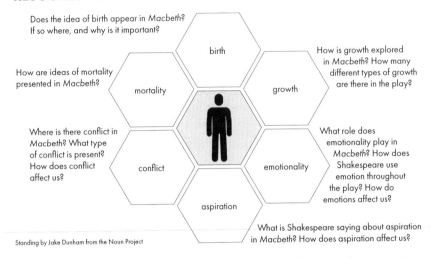

Does the idea of birth appear in *Macbeth*? If so where, and why is it important?

How is growth explored in *Macbeth*? How many different types of growth are there in the play?

How are ideas of mortality presented in *Macbeth*?

birth

growth

mortality

What role does emotionality play in *Macbeth*? How does Shakespeare use emotion throughout the play? How do emotions affect us?

Where is there conflict in *Macbeth*? What type of conflict is present? How does conflict affect us?

conflict

emotionality

aspiration

What is Shakespeare saying about aspiration in *Macbeth*? How does aspiration affect us?

Standing by Jake Dunham from the Noun Project

How you set up the task is up to you, but students should make annotations around each of the questions, drawing together ideas that may seem disparate on first reading but in fact can be connected upon review of the text. Whether this is completed as part of a wider group or individually, ensure everyone has the opportunity to focus their thoughts further by offering a series of concluding questions that could be completed verbally or as part of a written answer:

1. If you had to pick one aspect of the 'human condition' that Shakespeare focuses on the most, which one would you pick and why?
2. Why do you think Shakespeare uses a character like Macbeth to comment on the 'human condition'? Why not Macduff, Malcolm or even Lady Macbeth?
3. Which aspect of the human condition is Shakespeare most critical of?
4. Which aspect of the 'human condition' does Shakespeare champion?

This is only one way of exploring the human condition; there is lots one could do to look even more closely at the brief ideas introduced here. This, however, is certainly a start in helping students consider the idea that writers are commentators on society, using their characters and plot to say what they need to say.

## Thinking and linking grid

This is an idea I originally came across in Kate Jones's *Love to Teach*. Although the example Jones shared in her book is for a history lesson, I believe it works well for English too.[8] A 'Thinking and Linking' grid is used to help students make connections in the knowledge they have learned.

## RESOURCE 19.3

|  | 1 | 2 | 3 | 4 | 5 | 6 |
|---|---|---|---|---|---|---|
| **1** | Macduff | Guilt | Infanticide | Power | Murder | Tyranny |
| **2** | The supernatural | Light | Prophecy | Visions and hallucinations | Hamartia | Animal imagery |
| **3** | Lennox | Equivocation | Witches | Macbeth | Morality | Lady Macbeth |
| **4** | Hubris | Masculinity | Kingship | Appearance vs reality | Violence | Children |
| **5** | Sleep | Banquo | Loyalty | Hands | King Duncan | Time |
| **6** | Blood | Regicide | Lady Macduff | Ambition | The Porter | Darkness |

| Links made | | |
|---|---|---|
| Box 1 | Box 2 | Link between the two |
|  |  |  |
|  |  |  |
|  |  |  |

---

8.  Kate Jones, *Retrieval Practice: Research and resources for every classroom*, (Woodbridge: John Catt Educational Ltd., 2019) p. 138.

Students should work in pairs for this activity. Rolling the dice will give them their first coordinate, which will give them their first word. For example, a coordinate of 3,4 will give students the word 'Macbeth'. They should write 'Macbeth' in 'Box 1' and discuss what they know about the character. Students should then roll for a second time for their second word. A coordinate of 5,4 would give students the word 'Hands'. Students should add it to the second box, discuss and then write down the links that can be made between the two.

This is a fantastic way of getting students to start making connections between pockets of knowledge, considering ideas that could be linked.

## Key vocabulary:

Irony, restoration

# WHY?

# Why?

Thematically, there are several pedagogical practices on which the foundations of this book have been built, and to conclude, we will explore the particular areas of pedagogy we are passionate about and which have had the most profound impact on our teaching and our students. Here, we will explain to you our thoughts that underpin *why* we have approached the lessons found in this book in the way we have. Presented here are a series of short introductions to the cognitive science, research and ideas that have informed our practice. Learning does not happen accidentally: it is something planned for and carefully nurtured. We all have our own approaches to teaching and learning.

This is *our* 'why'.

## Big Questions & Ebbinghaus's Forgetting Curve

Regular retrieval of knowledge is key, as we know, in helping our students achieve exam success. However, retrieving information once, or even twice, does not mean that this knowledge is held securely by our students. It sometimes happens, when students can recall information at the end of a lesson, that it feels like our job is done. However, Ebbinghaus's Forgetting Curve hypothesises that there is a marked decline in memory retention over time if information is not regularly revisited and recalled.[1] In various studies, it has been observed that learners forget at least half of their newly gained knowledge and memory within days unless they consciously review the material learned. This concept of transient memory – the idea that memory is lost over time – is one of the seven key types of memory failure, and one we can do much to address in the classroom.[2]

---

1.  E.O. Finkenbinder, 'The Curve of Forgetting', *The American Journal of Psychology*, Vol. 24, No. 1, (Illinois: Illinois University Press, 1913), pp. 8–32, jstor.org/stable/1413271.

2.  Daniel L. Schacter, 'The Seven Sins of Memory: Insights from Psychology and Cognitive Neuroscience', *American Psychologist*, Vol. 54, No. 3, pp. 182–203, (Washington: American Psychological Association, 1999), https://scholar.harvard.edu/files/schacterlab/files/schacter_american_psychologist_1999.pdf.

Whilst Ebbinghaus's results are complex, and also take into account uncontrollable factors such as stress and levels of sleep, in his study one thing is clear: repetition based on active recall of knowledge – especially spaced repetition – is key in committing concepts, knowledge and ideas to the long-term memory. It is this, combined with high quality initial teaching, that allows our students to recall key information, and routine revisiting of the Big Questions helps with this.

Students will use Big Questions in every lesson to categorise their learning; the activities they complete and knowledge they gain help them to answer it. By reviewing the Big Question at the end of each lesson, students will begin to recall and organise their knowledge in relation to the topic. By regularly reviewing the Big Questions overall, students are ensuring that the knowledge they need is at their fingertips.

In this book, you will see that we have taken opportunities to revisit Big Questions. However, it is also the case that, in future schemes of learning, there are huge benefits in including review of the material learned – and the Big Questions used – from *this* scheme of learning. The more regularly we ask students to call upon, and retrieve, key information, the more they increase the likelihood of having this information committed to their long-term memory. Whilst this can be done in a more explicit way, conceptual interleaving can also be a successful way to allow students the opportunity to recall specific information in relation to their current topic of study. For example, if we were studying the corrupting influence of power in Shelley's 'Ozymandias' from the AQA Power and Conflict poetry cluster, there are opportunities to exploit this with regard to *Macbeth*, too: how have other writers students have studied presented this corruption?

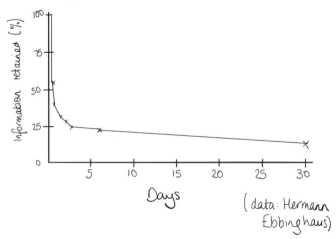

As you can see in the above figure, Ebbinghaus found not only that information learned can be forgotten very quickly – with a noticeable decline in memory even twenty minutes after learning – but that if information and memory are not revisited within a day, as much as 75% of the original knowledge is lost.[3]

However, by planning clear opportunities for students to revisit this knowledge regularly, they have the opportunity to commit this information to their long-term memory. Each time the information is reviewed, Ebbinghaus found, less of it is forgotten.

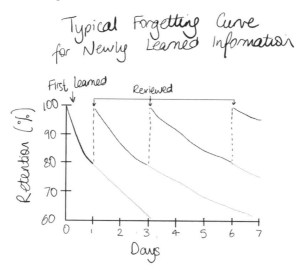

By revisiting the Big Questions, we are encouraging overlearning of material and, each time they do this, students will remember increasing amounts of the reviewed information.

## The importance of reading

The importance of reading can never be overstated. It underpins everything we do as teachers and everything our students will do in the classroom. If a student cannot read effectively, they will fall behind and widen the gap between their peers and themselves to disproportionate levels. No study is needed to tell us that. For effective learning to take place, students must have the knowledge they need to be able to read.

---

3.  Theatlas.com, 'Hermann Ebbinghaus' self-measured forgetting curve', (2018), https://theatlas.com/charts/H16nE-jvM.

Statistical analysis of reading levels is quite alarming. Research from the National Literacy Trust 'estimates that 5.1 million adults in England are functionally illiterate, meaning that they have a reading age of 11 or below.'[4] An adult with this reading age will be able to understand 'only the most straightforward, short texts on familiar topics.'[5] This becomes even more alarming considering that 'in the later years of secondary school, pupils are reading at least three years below their chronological age',[6] meaning it is increasingly difficult for many to access the GCSE exam papers. For some of us, just reading these statistics will conjure the names of students who will not be able to access the paper. When we step back and consider this, it is not only worrying but truly devastating, for these are the students who are at a disadvantage before they even enter the exam hall.

These facts should act as a call to arms to every teacher, not just those who teach English. Reading strategies are not just English strategies. Students are required to read in every subject, and so we should all take responsibility for helping them become confident and independent. We have a moral duty to help our students access the texts they may initially shun because they deem them inaccessible. It is not always the case that they do not *want* to read something, it is that they *cannot* read it. And if 5.1 million adults in England are 'functionally illiterate', there will be some parents who desperately want to help their children but lack the capability to do so. If our students are not receiving help at home or in school with their reading, their progress will stagnate. It is up to us, then, to close the reading gap and to teach our students to read at every opportunity.

Research completed by the Education Endowment Foundation (EEF) dives into this issue further. Their 'Reading Comprehension Strategies' paper is a useful starting point, where it states that 'on average, reading comprehension approaches deliver an additional six months' progress.'[7] These approaches

---

4.  Anita Singh, 'Millions of British adults are functionally illiterate but problem is ignored, Dame Gail Rebuck warns', The *Telegraph*, (2019), https:// www.telegraph. co.uk/news/ 2019/01/05/millions-british-adults-functionally-illiterate-problem-ignored/.

5.  Ibid.

6.  Grant Hill, 'Study uncovers literacy challenge among teenagers due to lack of reading focus in secondary school', https://www.dundee.ac.uk/news/2018/study-uncovers-literacy-challenge-among-teenagers-due-to-lack-of-reading-focus-in-secondary-school.php.

7.  Education Endowment Foundation, 'Reading Comprehension Strategies', Education Endowment Foundation, (2020), https://educationendowmentfoundation. org.uk/pdf/generate/?u=https:// educationendowmentfoundation.org.uk/pdf/ toolkit/?id=160&t=Teaching%20and%20Learning%20Toolkit&e=160&s=.

can include 'inferring meaning from context summarising or identifying key points; using graphic or semantic organisers; developing questioning strategies; and [students] monitoring their own comprehension and identifying difficulties themselves.'[8]

This research continues further in their 'Improving Literacy in Secondary Schools' report. The EEF summarise their findings in seven key recommendations to help raise literacy levels. They are:

1. 'Prioritise "disciplinary literacy" across the curriculum;
2. Provide targeted vocabulary instruction in every subject;
3. Develop students' ability to read complex, academic texts;
4. Break down complex writing tasks;
5. Combine writing instruction with reading in every subject;
6. Provide opportunities for structured talk;
7. Provide high quality literacy interventions for struggling students.'[9]

*Ready to Teach: Macbeth* has been deliberately written with the majority of these points in mind. We are well aware that these strategies have been designed to help students decode informational texts, yet we believe they hold weight when dealing with tricky fictional texts too. Also, non-fiction texts can be used to aid the study of Shakespeare. The British Library, for example, offers a wide range of free subject-specific articles that are incredibly useful in pushing and challenging students with their reading material. The Globe Theatre also offers fact files about a range of plays, stagecraft and context – resources we have found particularly useful for students with a lower reading age.

## Literacy beyond the school gates

Whilst these are strategies we can use in school, we must consider facts about literacy that lie beyond the school gates. Whilst it is true that parents who are functionally illiterate may find it too difficult to assist their children with their schoolwork, there is strong evidence to suggest that for the poorest readers and most illiterate – in terms not only of reading and writing but

---

8.  Education Endowment Foundation, 'Reading Comprehension Strategies', Education Endowment Foundation, (2020), https://educationendowmentfoundation. org.uk/pdf/generate/?u=https:// educationendowmentfoundation.org.uk/pdf/ toolkit/?id=160&t=Teaching%20and%20Learning%20Toolkit&e=160&s=.

9.  Education Endowment Foundation, 'Improving Literacy in Secondary Schools: Guidance Report', Education Endowment Foundation, (2019), https:// educationendowmentfoundation.org.uk/public /files/Publications/Literacy/EEF_ KS3_KS4_LITERACY_GUIDANCE.pdf.

also of speech and discourse – there are genuine limitations on their health and even their lifespan.

The National Literacy Trust published an evidence review[10] in 2018 which built on the 'Literacy Changes Lives' report of 2008. Both studies are unequivocal: there is a direct relationship between literacy and life chances, including both physical and mental health as well as economic wellbeing, the likelihood of a person engaging in civic society, including through voting and enfranchisement, their family life and relationships, and even their relationships with crime.

The example given in the 2018 study takes a boy, born in Stockton, who has a life expectancy of 26 years lower than a boy born in North Oxford. This disparity is not exclusive to males, either, with a girl born in Queensgate, Burnley, expected to live almost 21 years less than a girl born in Wealdon. Stockton and Queensgate both have some of the highest challenges with regard to literacy in the country. North Oxford and Wealdon both have some of the fewest.

Of course, while the relationship between literacy and life expectancy is very complex, this study does not appear to have shown up a tangential cause and effect correlation. The two are closely linked. There are numerous factors which contribute to a lower life expectancy, but many of these socioeconomic factors are directly related to low literacy levels.

People with low literacy levels earn, on average, 12% less than those with good literacy. Low incomes, globally, are associated with higher mortality and lower life expectancies – the World Health Organisation found that children born into families with low incomes are expected to live, on average, 17 years less than those born into families with high incomes.[11]

Those with low literacy levels also have a harder time accessing materials around health and wellbeing. Low 'health literacy', as it is known, means that a person cannot make sense of, or use, everyday health information such as leaflets you might find in a doctors' surgery or national health campaigns that promote healthy lifestyle choices. A person with low literacy skills may also struggle to articulate effectively what symptoms or problems they have, leading to medical professionals being potentially less able to accurately identify health complaints.

10. Lisa Gilbert, Anne Teravainen, Christina Clark and Sophia Shaw, 'Literacy and Life Expectancy: An evidence review exploring the link between literacy and life expectancy in England through health and socioeconomic factors', National Literacy Trust, (2018), https://cdn.literacytrust.org.uk/media/documents/National_Literacy_ Trust_-_Literacy_and_ life_expectancy_report.pdf.

11. Statista Research Department, 'Average life expectancy at birth worldwide in 1990 and 2013, by income group (in years)', Statista, (2018), https://www.statista.com/ statistics/280024 /average-life-expectancy-at-birth-worldwide-by-income-group/.

An inability to access this kind of information, or to articulate symptoms of illness accurately, is associated with a 75% greater risk of dying earlier.[12]

The data from education, nationally, indicates a worrying trend in the numbers of young people leaving our schools without adequate literacy skills. The National Literacy Trust states in their paper that 36% of all students fail to leave school with good passes in English and maths at GCSE. This rises to a staggering 60% of disadvantaged young people.[13]

We could go on. There are so many reasons why greater literacy levels contribute to greater life chances for our students. The National Literacy Trust paper is an alarming read, but one we fully recommend to you. The literacy crisis is a national one, not one which is confined to particular areas of the country. In a joint study with Experian, the National Literacy Trust found that 86% of constituencies in England contained *at least* one ward with significant vulnerabilities with regards to literacy.[14] The best thing is, we have the incredibly lucky position as teachers to be able to do something about this, and to reverse these issues for our students.

Time pressures us. We are always in a constant rush to get things done, to tick things off the list and say it is finished so we can move on to the next task in need of completion. As teachers, we feel that pressure on a daily basis; it is a pressure which never relents, never subsides. We are always in a hurry to get to the next slide on the PowerPoint, because the further along we are in a lesson or a scheme of work, the more progress we feel has been made. This is an illusion. Learning to read, to *truly* read, to see the subtleties and suggestions in a text, takes time. With that in mind, reassure yourself with the knowledge that it is okay if it takes an entire lesson to read and understand a scene, an article, a letter or any other form of text. A lesson spent reading is not a lesson wasted, and although it is in our nature as teachers to 'dot the *i*s and cross the *t*s' whilst keeping one eye on the clock, slow down. Ensure you are giving students time to think, to access, to learn how to do the things we want them to do. If a student has an understanding, a *true* understanding of a text, or at the very least a set

12. Education Endowment Foundation, 'Improving Literacy in Secondary Schools: Guidance Report', Education Endowment Foundation, (2019), https://educationendowmentfoundation.org.uk/public /files/Publications/Literacy/EEF_KS3_KS4_LITERACY_GUIDANCE.pdf.

13. Ibid.

14. Lisa Gilbert, Anne Teravainen, Christina Clark and Sophia Shaw, 'Literacy and life expectancy: An evidence review exploring the link between literacy and life expectancy in England through health and socioeconomic factors', (2018), https://cdn.literacytrust.org.uk/media/documents/National_Literacy_Trust_-_Literacy_and_life_expectancy_report.pdf.

of strategies they can use to independently make sense of that text, then that is when they will discover the joy of reading and the opportunities it brings.

## Reading aloud, and reading fluency

We believe that a crucial part of literacy is the ability to read aloud fluently. Fluently does not just mean being able to read quickly or with accuracy, either. Fluency is about reading accurately, smoothly *and* with expression, without struggling to decode words as one reads. It is reading that sounds fluid, like speech. Fluency is vital, because it bridges the gap between recognising and reading the words and true comprehension of what has been read.

As teachers, we often model fluent reading and are particularly good at exemplifying prosody. Prosody not only relates to the patterns of stress and intonation in a language, but also (and importantly when studying Shakespeare), to poetry. Prosody is absolutely key in making sense of complex texts, and good prosody can aid immeasurably in comprehension. In a paper by Schwanenflugel, the author commented that:

> *Prosodic reading, or reading with expression, is widely considered to be one of the hallmarks of the achievement of reading fluency. When a child is reading prosodically, oral reading sounds much like speech with appropriate phrasing, pause structures, stress, rise and fall patterns, and general expressiveness.*[15]

Teaching these skills can be complex, but there are a number of ways we can help our students find fluency in their reading. It is wonderful when students volunteer to read aloud, and where they are already fluent readers with good prosody this is a joy to listen to. Valid, also, of course, is the teacher reading aloud and using *their* skills of prosody to help students make sense of the scene. Better even than this, however, is helping students who may not yet be fluent readers to not only engage with a particular section of the text, but also to learn skills to understand the remainder of the play, too.

Choral reading, or echoes, can be incredibly powerful in helping students shape their prosody when reading Shakespeare. How often do you help a student overcome a difficult word in a text when they are reading aloud, only to hear them repeat the word with the same intonation, pacing and stress as you? This can be harnessed in the teaching of fluency and prosody in particular.

---

15. Paula J. Schwanenflugel, 'Becoming a Fluent Reader: Reading Skill and Prosodic Features in the Oral Reading of Young Readers', *J Educ Psychol.*, (2004), Vol. 96, No. 1, pp. 119–129, https://www.ncbi.nlm.nih.gov/pmc/articles/PMC2748352/.

Take Macbeth's 'Is this a dagger?' soliloquy. One way to explore this, and enhance students' fluency, is in repeated reading. For example, a student may read the speech aloud. Then, with a special focus on the prosody of one's speech, a teacher might read it again. Finally, choral or echoed reading can be helpful. Either the class can read the whole speech aloud, mimicking the teacher's prosody, or otherwise it could be read in a 'call and response' style, with the teacher reading small segments – perhaps a phrase or two – before the students collectively read the same segment back, mirroring the style in which the teacher reads it. The same could even be done for individual words to aid students with their pronunciation. This call and response strategy is something Modern Foreign Language (MFL) teachers are wonderful at doing. We truly believe we, as English teachers, can learn a lot about vocabulary instruction and language acquisition from our MFL colleagues, and strongly suggest you seek out the opportunity to observe these colleagues in action if you have not already done so. This type of instruction can also be effective when reading is modelled and the thoughts of the teacher are articulated aloud: 'Now I've come to a semi-colon. What am I doing here? Why?'

Of course, teaching reading fluency can be much more complex than this, as it should be, and for students with significant challenges with fluency it is often the case that more bespoke or individualised intervention is required. However, this approach can help improve the fluency and prosody of all students.

Beyond this, it is always vital that we remember that Shakespeare's plays were intended for performance, not to stagnate on a page. The more we can bring his words to life for our students the better, and reading aloud with good fluency and prosody helps this immeasurably. So does performance, and we often use opportunities for performance in aiding students' reading fluency. Shakespearean soliloquies are great for some short performances, perhaps with students working in pairs, with one as a director focusing on the actor's delivery of the lines. This kind of opportunity should not be overlooked, even if it takes time, because the skills the students learn as a result will carry them in good stead with further study and other texts.

## Cognitive Load Theory

Cognitive load is something we must consider when teaching Shakespeare. We are asking our students to read and engage with language which is unfamiliar whilst encouraging them to work out what it means, not just on a literal level but on a symbolic and metaphorical level too. It is very demanding and, as such, it is our duty as teachers to decrease the threat of cognitive overload.

Research proves that our brains can only process so much new information at a time. If we overload our students with too much information at once, the process of learning will become ineffective and anything students *do* learn will promptly be forgotten. The simple fact is, we can only teach new knowledge and skills effectively if we strip everything back by focusing on the most important elements. Remember: less is more. 'Information overload erodes the quality of work.'[16]

Dominic Shibli and Rachel West summarise three different forms of cognitive load:

> **'Intrinsic cognitive load:** *the inherent difficulty of the material itself, which can be influenced by prior knowledge of the topic*
> **Extraneous cognitive load:** *the load generated by the way the material is presented and which does not aid learning*
> **Germane cognitive load:** *the elements that aid information processing and contribute to the development of "schemas".*'[17]

The idea behind 'find it, highlight it, annotate it' roots itself in the principles behind reducing cognitive overload. This area of cognition concerns itself with the challenge of the material we present to students with each new task. As the language Shakespeare uses can provide a challenge to the modern reader (adding to students' intrinsic cognitive load), students are more likely to experience increased difficulties with comprehending and analysing simultaneously. A solution may be to break down subject content into clear, manageable chunks, teaching sub-tasks individually before linking them together and exploring them holistically. This approach reduces extraneous cognitive load, ensuring students are not overwhelmed by the acquisition of new knowledge.[18]

If you are struggling to distinguish the knowledge students will need from the knowledge they will not need, we find the following two questions really help when looking at each scene:

1. Do students really need to know this knowledge?
2. Is it going to make a vital difference to their understanding of the entire play?

---

16. Ruth C. Clark, Frank Nguyen and John Sweller, *Efficiency in Learning: Evidence-Based Guidelines to Manage Cognitive Load*, (San Francisco: Pfeiffer, 2006), p. 7.

17. Dominic Shibli and Rachel West, Cognitive Load Theory and its application in the classroom, (2018), https://impact.chartered.college/article/shibli-cognitive-load-theory-classroom/.

18. Ibid.

If the answer is yes, incorporate it into planning so students are able to secure this knowledge. If the answer is no, then read it and ensure students know what is going on. 'Find it, highlight it, annotate it' allows students to focus on and learn the most important parts and learn them well without the threat of cognitive overload.

Put simply: teach less, but teach it better.

## Quotations

Often when we ask students to consider quotations, we encourage them almost immediately to jump in to analysing the words in front of them. They become conditioned to do this, looking for language techniques or specific word classes. Of course, the ability to analyse language is a lynchpin in students' ability to perform well in an examination, but what it really means to *read*, as an adult, lies far beyond this limited, analytical scope.

Lia Martin's quotation explosion method allows teachers to take a step backwards from this preoccupation with analysis, and to look instead at the broader significance of Shakespeare's words, taking cognitive load into account at the same time. When reading out in the 'real' world, decoding and inference play significant roles in a reader's understanding of a text. It is only once these are secured pieces of knowledge that a reader might come to appreciate the craft of the writing. Therefore, whilst the quotation explosion method might appear to be quite simple, we are teaching students to understand and appreciate any text they encounter.

The first stage – encouraging students to answer the question 'Who says the line/whom or what is it about?' is very much concerned with decoding the line and understanding the context in which it is spoken. It is focused on comprehension, and nothing more than this. This starting point – comprehension – has two key functions in the lesson. The first is that encouraging students to verbalise their understanding moves them from being 'passive' readers to 'active readers'. In doing this we are encouraging students to activate and connect with their prior knowledge.

Secondly, this focus on comprehension gives more students a high rate of success with the reading they are doing. This is vital if we are to continue to break down any misconceptions students might have about the perceived difficulty of Shakespeare. Barak Rosenshine's *Principles of Instruction* explores the concept of the necessity for a high rate of success: as much as 80%. This success rate 'shows that students are learning the material, and it also shows that the students are challenged.'[19] Similarly, though, Rosenshine also stresses

---

19. Barak Rosenshine, *Principles of Instruction*, https://www.aft.org/sites/default/files/periodicals/Rosenshine.pdf.

the importance of ensuring that students know, remember and use the correct knowledge. If students are unsure at this stage of the activity as to who is talking and whom or what they are talking about, they will not be able to access the later inference or analysis questions: 'when we learn new material, we construct a gist of this material in our long-term memory. However, many students make errors in the process of constructing this mental summary.'[20] By starting with comprehension, we ensure our students capture and practise the correct knowledge.

The next two stages, then, are to encourage students to look at what they can infer from a quotation. The second prompt question is: 'What does this line mean?' The answer to this tends towards a slightly expanded comment linked to comprehension (for example, a student might explain the literal meaning of the line, 'translating it' into modern English).

The final question calls for an inference to be made: 'Explain what this line suggests.' This call for inference is not a leap: students have already experienced success in their comprehension of the scene, and this task just builds on their existing knowledge, not only of the quotation at hand, but also of the wider play. Anne Kispal of NFER suggests that 'pupils are most receptive to explicit teaching of inference skills in their early secondary years',[21] and so whilst a robust key stage 3 curriculum will have helped students develop these skills, activities like these help bring inference back to the fore before allowing students to dive in deeper and explore more complex analysis.

## Authorial intent and analytical verbs

As teachers, we appreciate texts have been written because the author has something to say – a message they wish to present to readers. Texts are conscious constructs and exist because people have been compelled to write because of societal and personal influences and experiences. Plot, character and theme are a product of one's view of the world, a fact that students must understand when writing about them. Too often, students write about texts as if they really happened. Yes, certain plots may be based on historical events or characters or real people, but the way circumstances play out and how characters act are a manifestation of an author's imagination. Students must understand this if they are to be able to think critically.

---

20. Barak Rosenshine, *Principles of Instruction*, https://www.aft.org/sites/default/files/periodicals/Rosenshine.pdf.

21. Anne Kispal, 'Effective Teaching of Inference Skills for Reading: Literature Review', (2008), https://www.nfer.ac.uk/publications/edr01/edr01.pdf.

Thinking critically, however, does not mean that students must analyse every single word or phrase in a text. If we teach our students that everything in a text has a hidden, deeper meaning, we are actually doing them a disservice. Part of being a critical thinker is to select and choose which parts of a text are worthy of further analysis. In order to consider authorial intent properly, students need to be comfortable with the decisions they make about which elements of the text they have selected to analyse.

Analytical verbs help with this, as they are a way of directly instructing students to consider an author's intentions. The ones we often use include: criticise, warn, challenge, expose, celebrate, reveal and advocate. We always find that introducing these verbs for students to use in their analysis part way through a scheme of work is more effective than doing so right at the beginning. If students were asked to consider intent in Act I, Scene i of *Macbeth*, for example, they may be able to answer, but would not have the depth of knowledge required to do justice to the task. However, by the halfway point, students will know this is a tale revealing the consequences of ambition and obsession and a warning about the guilt which can consume us all. Even if students have not thought about intent explicitly, they will know enough by now to create thoughtful, developed answers.

An example of an analytical verb task, first introduced to us by Lia Martin, is as follows:

Shakespeare **may have** included this scene in the play:

- to expose
- to criticise
- to advocate for
- to challenge

The task requires students to know the part of the text they are studying well in order to manipulate their knowledge and complete the sentences four different ways. Introducing this type of task with a more generic sentence opener is an effective way of easing in those students who may find this deeper level of analysis challenging. However, as students become more adept at understanding authorial intent, the sentence starters can be a little more specific.

They can even be used to help students consider a writer's deliberate language choices as seen in the example here.

Shakespeare **could be** using the word 'scorpions':

* to expose
* to criticise
* to echo

As students practise this method more, they will eventually be in a position where they are able to begin these types of sentences without any direct input from their teacher. It goes without saying that authorial intent needs to be explored beyond just one sentence, but this is certainly a 'way in', one which takes little effort to prepare.

Let us also draw your attention to the wording of these sentence starters. Consider the parts we have placed in bold. This is what is known as tentative language, meaning 'hesitant' or 'cautious', and is something we need to instil in our students as a conventional form of literary criticism. The claims we make in our discussions around authorial intent, most often, cannot be substantiated. The writers we study in our classrooms are often deceased, meaning they are not around to ask whether our inferences are correct. This means we need to teach our students to avoid writing in statements when making their predictions.

Indeed, it is almost irrelevant whether or not the author is around to answer our questions about our inferences. Whilst the 'death of the author' theory of Roland Barthes is quite complex, we often find an introduction to it can help clarify *why* using tentative language is useful here. We cannot hope to know what the author intended, but, fundamentally, this does not matter: once a book has left the writer and gone out into the world, the interpretations are ours for the taking. We project onto what we read our own experiences, understanding and beliefs about the world around us. There is no definitive understanding of the text to be found because there *cannot* be.

# Conclusion

Ben Jonson referred to Shakespeare as 'not of an age but for all time.'[1] In the introduction of this book, we said 'Shakespeare's stories have survived because they are still relevant over 450 years later.' We argued that 'time is relative in relation to the human condition [and] what makes us human never changes.' Yet this is not the only reason why Shakespeare endures.

His plays live on because, for all the truths he dramatises, he poses just as many questions for us to consider. *Macbeth* is littered with unanswered questions by the play's conclusion. Humans, by their very nature, are curious beings. We always have to find the answer, always need to solve the peculiar, the puzzling, the inexplicable. We crave to find order in disorder. Maybe this is why Shakespeare's texts are still pored over today.

Yet perhaps, through the multitude of interpretations Shakespeare's plays elicit, we have to face the fact that a right answer is not always waiting to be found. Shakespeare's writing will forever remain enigmatic and we will always be intrigued. It is as powerful and visceral as it is because Shakespeare's characters still exist today, in us, in people we know. We can still recognise and empathise with them. Humans innately feel ambition, guilt and excitement, and whilst no one can entirely stand in the shoes of Macbeth and his wife, their human nature is something which resonates with us, powerfully. As modern readers, we bring to Shakespeare our own feelings, experiences and beliefs. Alan Bennett says it best:

> *The best moments in reading are when you come across something – a thought, a feeling, a way of looking at things – which you had thought special and particular to you. Now here*

---

1.  Ben Jonson, 'To the Memory of My Beloved the Author, Mr. William Shakespeare', https://www.poetryfoundation.org/poems/44466/to-the-memory-of-my-beloved-the-author-mr-william-shakespeare.

*it is, set down by someone else, a person you have never met, someone even who is long dead. And it is as if a hand has come out and taken yours.*[2]

There is so much one could say about *Macbeth*, so much more we could have written in this book. We hope *Ready to Teach: Macbeth* has, at the very least, given you some ideas to help you guide students to think, to consider, and to question their own place in society.

---

2.    Alan Bennett, *The History Boys*, (London: Faber & Faber, 2004), p. 56.

# Index